By the same author

David Caute

UNDER THE SKIN

The Death of White Rhodesia

NORTHWESTERN UNIVERSITY PRESS

EVANSTON   1983

To Judith Acton

Contents

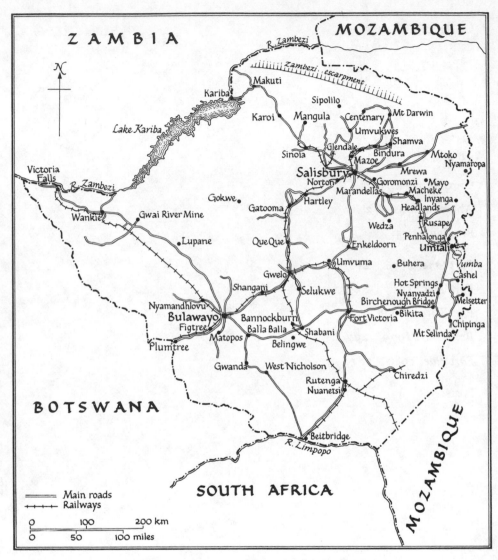

Map 1. Rhodesia: Main Road and Rail Links

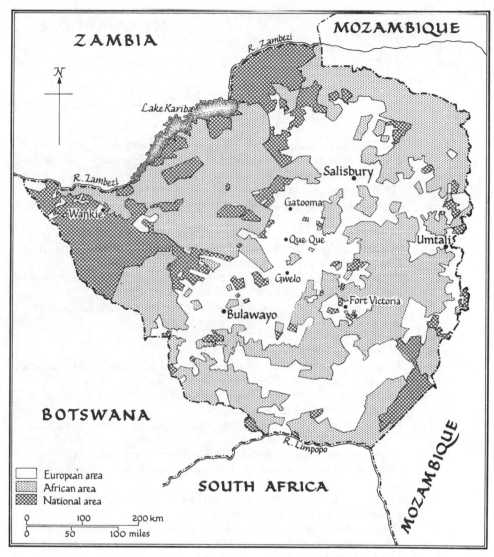

Map 2. European and African Land Areas in Rhodesia

Chronology

1890   Cecil Rhodes's British South Africa Company dispatches the Pioneer Column into Mashonaland, where the whites establish control. Dr Jameson is appointed 'Administrator' by Rhodes.

1893   White settlers invade Matabeleland, defeat the Ndebele impis and rout their monarch Lobengula. Massive expropriation of Ndebele lands and cattle by the whites.

1895   Mashonaland and Matabeleland are united under the name of Rhodesia.

1896   Ndebele uprising. Whites in outlying districts are murdered. The rising spreads to Mashonaland. Whites crush Ndebeles, then Shonas.

1923   Britain terminates BSAC rule and annexes Southern Rhodesia as a British colony, establishing a locally elected white Government.

1930   Land Apportionment Act codifies the division of Southern Rhodesia into white and black areas.

1953   Federation of Rhodesia and Nyasaland established.

1955–60 Period of mounting black-nationalist agitation.

1961   Hopes of a constitutional agreement are dashed. Whitehead introduces emergency legislation to deal with nationalist agitation.

1962   Nkomo's Zapu is banned. The Rhodesian Front is founded and defeats Whitehead in the general election.

1963   Sithole, Mugabe and others break away from Nkomo to form Zanu. Faction-fighting continues.

1964   Smith becomes leader of the RF. A white referendum votes 10–1 in favour of Independence for Rhodesia. Nationalist leaders are detained without trial.

1965   On 11 November Smith announces the Unilateral Declaration of Independence (UDI) from Britain. State of Emergency declared.

1970   Rhodesia becomes a Republic, with a new constitution reserving fifty out of sixty-six seats to whites and protecting racial zoning of land through the Land Tenure Act.

1971   Smith agrees a new constitution wih Sir Alec Douglas-Home. The ANC is formed to coordinate resistance, led by Muzorewa.

1972   The Pearce Commission reports that the settlement terms are unacceptable to Africans. In December the new guerrilla war begins in the north-east. Three years of heavy recruitment follow but the war remains at a comparatively low level with few white casualties until 1976.

1975   Mozambique gains its Independence from Portugal. The new Frelimo government actively supports Zanla. Mugabe reaches Mozambique.

1976	Escalation of the war. Casualty figures rise sharply. Mozambique closes the border. Under South African pressure Smith meets Kissinger and accepts majority rule. Britain convenes the Geneva Conference, which ends in failure. Nkomo and Mugabe form the Patriotic Front.
1977	The Carter administration (Andrew Young) and the British insist that no settlement is viable without the PF's participation. A right-wing revolt within the RF leads to the creation of the RAP, which Smith duly crushes at the August election. Smith rejects the Anglo-American constitutional proposals and begins 'internal' talks with Muzorewa and Sithole.
1978	The war inside Rhodesia escalates. On 3 March Smith signs the Salisbury Agreement with Muzorewa, Sithole and Chirau. A multiracial Transitional Government is set up. Rhodesians launch more cross-border raids. Smith visits the USA. Britain fails in its efforts to convene an all-party conference.
1979	The internal election is boycotted by the PF. Rhodesians claim 64 per cent turn-out among the African electorate. Muzorewa wins and becomes Prime Minister of 'Zimbabwe Rhodesia'. Thatcher wins British election but refuses to grant immediate recognition. Lusaka Commonwealth Conference: Britain convenes an all-party conference in London. Agreement is reached. Britain assumes direct rule in December and Lord Soames arrives as Governor.
1980	Zanla and Zipra guerrillas assemble in APs. Mugabe rejects Nkomo's offer to run on a joint PF ticket. Mugabe's Zanu-PF wins fifty-seven out of eighty black seats. 18 April: Zimbabwe achieves Independence.

Abbreviations

ANC	African National Council
AP	Assembly point
ARnI	Association of Rhodesian Industries
BSAC	British South Africa Company
BSAP	British South Africa Police
CFMF	Cease Fire Monitoring Force
CIIR	Catholic Institute for International Relations
Comops	Combined Operations Headquarters
DA	District Assistant (black)
DC	District Commissioner (white)
IDA	International Defence & Aid
JOC	Joint Operations Command
JPC	Justice and Peace Commission
NUF	National Unifying Force
OAU	Organization of African Unity
Patu	Police Anti-Terrorist Unit
PF	Patriotic Front
PSA	Public Services Association
PsyAc	Psychological Action Unit
PV	Protected Village
RAP	Rhodesian Action Party
RAR	Rhodesian African Rifles
RBC	Rhodesian Broadcasting Corporation
RF	Rhodesian Front
RIO	Rhodesian Information Office (USA)
RLI	Rhodesian Light Infantry
RNFU	Rhodesian National Farmers' Union
RP	Rendezvous point
SAS	Special Air Service
SB	Special Branch (police)
TTL	Tribal trust land
UANC	United African National Council
UDI	Unilateral Declaration of Independence
UNFP	United National Federal Party
Zanla	Zimbabwe African National Liberation Army
Zanu	Zimbabwe African National Union (from 1978 Sithole also called his internal faction within Rhodesia by this name)
Zanu-PF	Zimbabwe African National Union Patriotic Front (*see* Zanu *above*). The name adopted by Robert Mugabe's party in January 1980
Zapu	Zimbabwe African People's Union
Zipa	Zimbabwe People's Army
Zipra	Zimbabwe People's Revolutionary Army
Zupo	Zimbabwe United People's Organization

Note. Exchange rate: In 1978–9 the Rhodesian dollar was officially worth about £0·70 or US$1·25.

Prologue

I peeled out of the armed convoy at the village of Chitomba. The driver of the rearguard machine-gun truck flashed his headlamps, a warning perhaps, or wishing me luck, one white man to another. Heading west into the tribal trust land along a single strip of tarmac, I passed a road sign advising motorists 'not to proceed beyond this point after 3 p.m.'. It was the first week of May 1979, in the seventh year of the Rhodesian war.

The vast, silent terrain offered no intimation of a war so brutal that the International Red Cross had rebuked both sides for their callousness. The utilities continued to function, the main roads were kept in good repair with neatly trimmed verges by gangs of labourers wearing bright yellow overalls; at country bus-stops knots of Africans squatting beside their baggage observed one's rapid passage without visible hostility.

Yet the approach of a kopje, the rocky outgrowths scattered across the Rhodesian countryside, induced a brief inner dialogue between fear – they form perfect vantage points for an ambush – and fatalism. And where thickets of bush pressed close to the roadside there was a noticeable quickening of the pulse. 'Always go slowly,' an old African teacher had advised me. 'The "boys" don't like whites who travel fast. If they wave you down, stop.' But they didn't wave you down; in reality the first sign of a guerrilla ambush was the sparkle of incoming tracer bullets; the normal instinct was to put the foot hard down and keep going.

Shortly after 5 o'clock, an hour before dusk, I reached my destination, St Anselme's School at Mangwende, south of Bulawayo in Matabeleland. John Bhebe, the school Principal, offered me a bed in the guest-room. A year ago, at the time of my previous visit, Bhebe had been visibly shaken by the arrival in the area of guerrillas belonging to Robert Mugabe's Zanla. After crossing the Mozambique border in the south-east, they had tracked through the southern provinces, keeping mainly to the tribal trust lands, steering clear of army patrols, taking cover at the approach of helicopters. Having levied twenty Rhodesian dollars from each black teacher, and having set wives and daughters to work cooking a meal, the 'boys', the vakhomana, had summoned all 450 pupils to the school chapel and harangued them about the nationalist struggle. But their attitude was friendly and, as Bhebe put it, 'correct'. They brought messages of greeting from former pupils of St Anselme's who had joined their ranks, assured Bhebe that it was Zanla policy to keep 'honest' schools open, and then vanished into the night with a warning to him that, on pain of his life, he must not report the incident to the security forces until 8.30 the next morning.

He did as he was told. In the morning the army arrived in four trucks and embarked on a half-hearted and ineffective 'sweep' of the area. The white officer in charge summoned the pupils back to the school chapel and treated them to an hour of admonition and counter-propaganda. 'Do you want Russian Communism here?' They, a captive audience for the second time in twelve hours, yielded to the white officer no intimation of their real feelings, offering only the maddeningly neutral gaze adopted by frontier peoples frequently visited by the thundering cavalry of rival kings. Yet these young boys and girls, however firm their ties to the kraals from which they sprang, and to which they would return during the holidays, were no dull illiterates; the white officer knew himself to be wrestling with the ingrained antipathy of an élite destined – some of them – to enter British or American universities. He knew also that it was from among these neutral, passive expressions that the guerrilla cadres constantly replenished themselves.

I asked Bhebe whether he supported the Patriotic Front. At this he withdrew into himself. 'We teachers never discuss that, it's too dangerous. Many of my pupils become mujibas (guerrilla scouts) in their villages. One could be denounced. Besides, both Zanla and Joshua Nkomo's Zipra operate in this area. The two armies of the Patriotic Front are not on good terms.'

Since that first visitation early in 1978, St Anselme's has experienced several (Bhebe would not say how many) incursions from guerrillas needing food, clothes, money and liquor. Sometimes a mujiba was sent with a shopping list. Had the 'boys' ever spent the night in the school dormitories? 'Never,' Bhebe said quickly. He lit a Kingsgate cigarette. 'As a matter of fact,' he went on, gazing out of his office window towards the physics laboratory (built with church funds from West Germany), 'it did happen, once. Perhaps twice.' I smiled and he laughed as many Africans do, an irrepressible gurgle rolling up from the throat and culminating in a high cry: 'Aaee!'

'When was the last time?'

'Two nights ago. Tonight they will send a mujiba to inquire about you.' He read my thoughts. 'They know everything that happens in the area, they have eyes and ears everywhere. Already they will have noted the registration number of your car, the fact that you are alone, and that you carry no weapon. I'm very happy that you don't carry a gun,' John Bhebe added, 'very happy.'

'Any chance of my meeting the "boys"?'

The Principal's eyes moved back into neutral.

John's brother Joseph teaches history at St Anselme's. I walked up the dusty path to his house where maize and beans were growing in the garden and chickens scuttling in and out of the kitchen. He took two bottles of Coke out of the refrigerator while his wife hovered shyly in the background. Joseph had only recently emerged from three years' political detention without trial in Wha Wha prison.

'A terrible place, overcrowded huts with tin roofs, sweltering in summer, freezing in winter, filthy food brought in wheelbarrows, pig's lard with hairs sticking out of it, cooked by common criminals, unwashed plates, no table or chair. The only exercise I had for three years was walking round a small yard, everyone knocking into everyone else. I'm a thin man, but I lost twenty pounds and acquired a permanent rash across my body. I tried to study, but the only reading stool was the overnight communal latrine bucket turned upside down – there was always a rush for it, even fights sometimes . . .'

Joseph had been released during the partial amnesty which followed the signing of the internal settlement on 3 March 1978. 'I hear you want to meet the "boys",' he chuckled grimly, twisting his fingers into knots. 'Perhaps you'd like to meet the ones who killed my father. John didn't tell you about our father? For many years he worked as a government District Assistant under the orders of the white District Commissioner in Kazi. He was responsible for the arrests of many young people who had helped the "boys". Two of them were executed, hanged, last year in Salisbury gaol. My father was much hated in our district. Even his friends were afraid to confide in him.'

Later I called on Ellen Dziwinga, sister to John and Joseph Bhebe. Small, alert and bursting with administrative bustle, she manages the village store at Mangwende on behalf of a wealthy African businessman. Ellen spoke of her father's death without inhibition. 'He deserved to die. He clung to his bad ways. We tried hard to warn him but he was proud and stubborn. He hit me so hard over the ear that I couldn't hear for three days. One night the Zipra "boys" came to our house and dragged him from his bed. They killed him with axes and iron bars, then they warned us to leave him there, lying in the open. "Let the government come and bury him," they said. "Let Smith come from Salisbury and bury him."'

I had seen enough photographs of Rhodesian corpses to imagine how the old man had looked – head and stomach gashed open, brains and intestines spilling out in coils, flies colonizing the wounds.

'So you want to meet the "boys",' she said with a broad, almost sardonic smile. 'And what shall we tell them about you? They don't like white journalists, you know.'

I knew that Ellen was in frequent contact with the guerrillas at night. During the day the army would call at the store and pay cash; after dark the 'boys' would come, paying nothing and keeping their tempers on short fuses. Ellen detested the regime, the security forces: whether they owed nominal allegiance to Smith or to Bishop Abel Muzorewa made no difference to a woman who had been so badly beaten by soldiers in her own home that she miscarried and almost lost her life. This incident followed a series of guerrilla attacks on a nearby mine compound inhabited by white artisans and their families. The security forces retaliated by a savage, punitive sweep of the district, arresting many Africans and beating others; Ellen was one of those accused – quite falsely, she insisted – of complicity in the attacks.

'I screamed,' she recalled, 'but no one dared to come and help me – it's the excuse the soldiers are waiting for, to shoot people for leaving their houses after the curfew.'

She was lucky: on average about one hundred black Zimbabweans died violently in any period of seventy-two hours.

On the following day I was summoned to Joseph's house, where I met for the first time Samuel Mpisa, a retired head teacher and a greatly respected figure in the district. John and Ellen were also present. I had the feeling from the outset that Samuel Mpisa had been sent by the guerrillas to weigh me up.

Yet Samuel – and here one touches on the central paradox of rural Rhodesia – was soon grumbling about the behaviour of the 'boys'. 'One day they knocked on my door. It was 6.30 in the morning. "Why haven't you closed your school?" they demanded. I said, "Why should I close my school, we have only small children here, don't you want them to learn to read and write?" They said, "Old man, you're closing it now. Send your pupils home."'

'Zanla or Zipra?'

'Zipra forces. Zipra close all the schools, we don't know why.'

'This was the same group that killed our father,' Ellen said.

'Surely Zanla also close many schools?' I objected.

'Some,' Samuel said. 'But not always. The Zanla "boys" come to me and ask my advice about this teacher and that headmaster. Is it true that he invited the District Assistant to his house? Is it true that he has been feeding the soldiers? Is it true that he makes the pupils pay for their Bibles? Is it true that he has a police escort when he takes the school fees to the bank?' Samuel shook his head and sighed. 'I'm getting too old for this.' Everyone in the room laughed. 'Too old! Do you know what happened here during the week of the voting? The "boys" came to our village and ordered us all to leave our houses because they were sure the soldiers would herd us to the mobile voting station. For a whole week we had to sleep in the bush, under the stars, like wild beasts. I can tell you, that week felt like a month – I'm covered in bites!' He tilted his bald head back and rocked with laughter.

'And did the soldiers show up?' I asked.

'Oh, certainly! A white officer arrived with a truck and a loudspeaker: "You must exercise your democratic rights!" he bellowed.'

The conversation now turned to Zanla's regular village meetings, or 'pungwes', which often lasted half the night and were accompanied by nationalist songs, harangues and invocations of the 'chimurenga', the ninety-year-old war of liberation – meetings designed both to radicalize the peasantry and to demonstrate Zanla's physical control of the countryside.

'I am a Christian,' Samuel said. 'Many of the "boys" come from mission schools. But as soon as they go into the bush it all seems to fall away from them. They talk of Mwari, the Shona god, and they make appeals to Chaminuka, the most famous of the spirit-mediums who have brought divine guidance to the people. The "boys" even kill local witch-doctors on the grounds that they are spoiling their magic. They say they're not against God, but this Jesus, they'd shoot him if they could. They invoke Mudzimu – a pagan spirit.'

'Do the guerrillas discuss economic issues?'

'Land,' Joseph put in. 'People ask the "boys": when you come to power, shall we still be confined to these rocky patches of soil where nothing grows well and no water flows? The "boys" tell them, no, the big white estates will be divided up, you shall have the fertile land.' Joseph was kneading his hands with passionate intensity. I could see why the regime had locked him away in Wha Wha.

Ellen spoke up, infected by her brother's fervour: 'The "boys" say to the people, "Do you really believe these lies that Smith is handing over power, don't you know that Muzorewa is the arms of Smith, Chirau the legs of Smith and Sithole the ears of Smith?"'

Tentatively I asked about Zanla's relationship, on the ground, to Zipra. Mugabe's Zanu and its guerrilla army, Zanla, were drawn mainly from the sub-tribes of the Shona people, who comprise 80 per cent of the population of Zimbabwe. Although the political cadres of Nkomo's Zapu included many notable Shonas, the military wing, Zipra, derived its strength almost exclusively from Ndebeles and Kalangas, who feared political and cultural domination by the Shona majority.

When I posed the question an uneasy silence followed.

'The regime puts out all sorts of propaganda,' Joseph muttered. But Samuel was too old for dissembling.

'Listen,' he said, 'we all know the truth – the Zanla "boys" never speak well of Zipra. They use a word, "machuwachuwa", which describes the way the Ndebeles walk along . . . like this: chug-chug-chug. "Pasi ne machuwachu-wa!" they say.'

'And they call Nkomo a rich capitalist working hand in glove with Smith,' Ellen agreed. 'They even blame him for the air attacks on his own people in Zambia. They say that Nkomo has assassinated many of his followers and that Zipra is not really fighting the war. "Pasi ne vanematumbu!" they say.'

'Meaning?'

'Down with big stomachs!'

I drove Ellen back to her store. 'The old people, like Samuel and my brother John, don't like these Zanla "pungwes",' she explained. 'They are very dangerous. Sometimes they are held in the middle of the village, quite close to a road, and the "boys" dance to gramophone records and get very drunk on gin or brandy. It makes the village people an easy target for the security forces. There has been too little discipline among the "boys" recently. A year ago there was more fighting and less drinking. And there is one other thing you should know. All of us support the "boys", they are our only hope, but recently their behaviour with the girls has been very bad. They order the parents to bring their best blankets and then they take their daughters . . . sometimes when it rains they turn people out of their houses and take the girls inside . . . This upsets the old people very much. It's against all our customs.'

'What do the girls feel about it?'

'They keep their feelings to themselves. No one dares say anything. But the "boys" lead a hard life. Many of them get killed. It's a pity they listen to so many false rumours, people whisper in their ears, you know, "That man is a sell-out, and that one over there, he has a secret police radio in his house." The "boys" kill these people and afterwards they say sorry, they were misin-formed, then they go off and kill the ones who misinformed them. We are all very short of food now, there was very little rain this year. But when the "boys" come everyone must provide a chicken and they won't eat the legs or wings or the insides of the chicken, only relish. One man was beaten to death because he threw a chicken liver into the pot. He was only joking.'

We drove in silence for a few minutes and then, as her store came in sight, she said: 'If you really want to meet the "boys", they are willing to see you tomorrow. These are the Zipra "boys" who killed my father. Last week they also killed a white farmer and the army has been out looking for them. I think you will be perfectly safe unless there is a contact with the security forces. That would be very dangerous for you.'

'Where do I meet them?' I was aware that my voice sounded a bit thin.

'You will be taken to the place.'

I was picked up next day at an agreed rendezvous. Presently, we left the main road and headed into the tribal trust land across a maze of dirt tracks. Very little was said, although one of my companions, noticing a ribbon of pale skin round my wrist, remarked with a smile: 'So you forgot to bring your watch?' All I carried was an empty notebook and twenty Rhodesian dollars. A large slice of me wanted to be back in England.

The car eventually stopped outside a house made of brick. After a brief exchange we were led inside. The house, which seemed to consist of two rooms, was dark and stiflingly hot. A fragmentary conversation in Sindebele passed me by.

At least twenty minutes passed before the driver of our car announced: 'The "boys" have arrived.' A moment later two young men walked through the door carrying AK47 rifles and Kalashnikov sub-machine-guns. The shorter of the two wore a woollen beret, the other a khaki bush hat. Both were shod in gleaming white Bata tennis shoes, their trousers tied at the ankles with white shoe-laces. From the waist to the neck their sweating bodies were coiled by bandoliers of ammunition and stick grenades – my first impression was of the sheer weight of armament they were carrying.

I hesitated to offer them my hand, but these two Zipra guerrillas insisted on a triple handshake: 'It brings luck,' said the one in the beret – indeed it was he who was to do most of the talking. He looked very young, with a smooth, gentle face, quick-moving eyes and a pale brown skin. He sat opposite me with his AK47 and its notorious shark's fin magazine straddling his knees.

'So what will you write about us, then?' His stare was intense but not necessarily hostile.

As he told his own story, this young guerrilla came from an impoverished kraal in northern Matabeleland. He had been forced to leave school after Grade 7 (the last year of primary education), found no work, and soon crossed with two companions into Botswana, where they made their way on foot to the refugee camp at Francistown. Having declared their support for Nkomo, they were airlifted to Zambia, where they received their first military instruction.

'Where were you trained?'

'In Russia,' he said. 'Soviet Union.' I asked him where in Russia but failed to extract any convincing details – the suspicion dawned that Russia was the glamorous, important place to have been, a mark of selection, particularly since Nkomo himself had begun to appear in the uniform of a Soviet marshal. Were his instructors Russians? Yes, Russians. Did they speak good English? Not very. Was that a problem? No, not really – everything was very good in Russia. Was it cold there? Sometimes, but they had warm clothes and blankets. Did the trainees learn about Communism? 'No Communism.'

Later he was sent to a camp in Tanzania. How had his section infiltrated Rhodesia? 'We crossed the Zambezi near Kariba, at night.' Having tracked along the Zambezi Valley into Botswana, they had finally re-entered Rhodesia in the south-west, near Plumtree. That was five years ago. 'Impossible now,' he volunteered. Why? 'The Botswana government won't let us in carrying arms. They fear reprisals by the Rhodesian regime.' A bad situation, then? 'Yes, very bad,' he agreed.

He leant forward. 'I want to tell you something. In Tanzania we had very bad shootings with the Zanla people. They massacred many of our fighters. President Nyerere is not with us, he is an agent of Smith.' (Joshua Nkomo's relationship with Julius Nyerere was notoriously bad.)

How had he obtained the new Bata tennis shoes? He laughed for the first time. 'We stopped a big truck on the road to Kezi. It was full of shoes! Hundreds of thousands of shoes! We had information. The fascist regime is giving us a hard time getting leather boots. In the bush you need strong boots.'

'That's a problem for you?'

'Yes, big problem.'

What about the black driver of the truck they had ambushed?

'We gave him a warning for his boss: we want two hundred dollars a week or this road is closed to your trucks.' He smiled gently.

'You killed a white farmer, Ericson, last week, and set fire to his barns?'

He stiffened. Had an unintended aggression crept into my voice; or was it because of hot pursuit by the army following the murder? Or simply because I was white?

'Yes. This man Ericson ignored our warnings to take his wife and children and leave Zimbabwe.'

Was it Zipra policy to kill all white farmers?

'No. We are not racists. This Ericson was a very bad farmer.'

In what way?

'He supported the regime. Police Reserve.'

But had he paid exceptionally low wages or maltreated his labour force?

The young guerrilla nodded. 'Yes, of course.'

How much had he paid his farm workers?

The guerrilla shrugged, his answers becoming increasingly indistinct and obscure. I offered him a Kingsgate cigarette. Politely he pocketed the whole packet. 'We prefer Madisons,' he grinned. Then he glanced at my left arm.

'You have no watch, then?'

I told him it was broken.

He nodded. 'You thought we would take your watch, eh?'

I said no, it was broken. I was quite keen to change the subject. It seemed time to give him the $(R)20 I carried.

Why was it Zipra policy to close all the schools?

'They are government schools. The school fees go to the fascist regime. That's the only reason they keep these schools, to buy helicopters and napalm with the money. Also, another thing: they don't teach liberation in the schools, they don't teach armed struggle, they teach compromise with the system.'

But didn't it worry him, for the future of Zimbabwe, that so many children were now out of school?

This provoked his first display of real anger, a sudden coiling of his body. 'Did I ever get a school? Why should they sit in school while we are fighting, you tell me? When Zimbabwe is liberated everyone will be in school, everyone. I tell you that. You write that.' I nodded but he gestured angrily towards my open notebook. 'You write that now.' I wrote in my notebook the word 'schools' and asked him – smoother topic – how and when Zimbabwe would be liberated.

'We will march in and take Salisbury. Now I ask you a question. Who will be the real boss, who will command the fascist army, Muzorewa or General Walls – you tell me.' I said General Walls (which was indeed the case). He nodded thoughtfully. 'And how long do you think Muzorewa will last, eh?'

I should have remembered that in this part of the world predictions always mirror preferences. If you wish to discover how a man will vote you ask him who will win.

'The Bishop could hold out for two or three years,' I said carelessly. The AK47, abruptly, was no longer inert across his knees but an active agent of his hands.

'You mean you support Muzorewa!' he shouted.

When I reminded him that Muzorewa enjoyed powerful backers, notably South Africa, he cooled down a bit and nodded sombrely. 'Our struggle may be a long one,' he said quietly. But when I asked him how his comrades had reacted to the 64 per cent turn-out at the election, he began instantly to spark again: 'You believe the fascist regime's propaganda? These figures are all lies. These elections are irrelevant. The soldiers forced the people to vote. We did not try to stop them because we knew the people would suffer.' (In fact, I suspect that the main reason I was granted this interview was the severe blow dealt to guerrilla morale by their failure to disrupt the elections.)

How many men were there in his section?

'Thirty-eight.'

Who made the decisions?

'We all make decisions, democratic process.'

But they received orders, presumably?

'Yes, from Zambia, sometimes by messenger, sometimes by radio.'

Did his section have a political commissar?

'Excuse me?'

I repeated the question but he looked blank. Did Zipra talk to the people about socialism and land reform? He shook his head – this surprised me. I pointed out that Zanla promised the people that the big white farms would be divided up. He shrugged contemptuously.

'All that will be decided when we are in power. The Zanla forces are not politically educated. They don't operate like soldiers. We are soldiers in Zipra. We don't hold these big "pungwes", too dangerous for the people.'

Had there been armed clashes between the two wings of the PF?

'We don't make trouble unless they do. We send them messages not to come into our area, among our people. But they come. Some of them are looking for trouble.'

Did he support the unity of the Patriotic Front?

'Yes, yes.' Mechanical reply to mechanical question.

Who would be President of a free Zimbabwe?

'Joshua Nkomo is the leader of all our people.'

What about Robert Mugabe?

He laughed. 'This man doesn't control his own army, did you know that?'

When they punished people they believed were sell-outs, did they ever discover they had made a mistake? He understood the question only when I had twice repeated it.

'Always we make careful inquiries. We do not listen to false reports.'

How many people had he himself killed?

He thought about this. 'I can't say that. These are collective decisions.'

Had he ever made contact with his own family since the day he crossed the border, seven years ago?

'No, never, too dangerous for them. They don't know whether I am alive or dead.'

How many of his comrades had been killed by the security forces?

'Not many. The soldiers are scared of us. In the day they go to the villages and make a big noise and beat the people, but at night they stay at home, very scared. I tell you, we have killed many soldiers, white soldiers too, but the fascist regime tells lies about it.'

It was almost dark now and I could no longer see his features clearly, only the burning tip of his cigarette as it moved restlessly in and out of his lips. A third guerrilla appeared in the doorway – time to leave. I asked whether I could spend the night with them, a request which generated an animated discussion in Sindebele and soon concluded in a polite refusal. 'Not possible.' I thought: thank God. We all walked out of the hut. The whole village had congregated silently round our car; beyond them, set apart, stood a group of about ten armed guerrillas.

One could feel that the villagers were happy: a white man from England had come to meet the 'boys', had been accepted by the 'boys', and had learned the truth. The guerrilla whom I had interviewed accorded me the ritual triple handshake – hands, thumbs, hands. It struck me, then, how very small he was.

'What will you tell your children?' he asked.

Part One: 1976

1. a fair question

Alex Maddocks, company director, resident of Borrowdale, a suburb of Salisbury:

'OK, David, you ask me what Rhodesia means to me and I'd like to answer that; it's a fair question but I can't promise you the same Rhodesia you'll hear denounced by the United Nations, by the OAU, and by certain intellectuals and journalists – no offence to you, David – who come here for ten days and then write down nothing but lies about this country. I was born and raised in this country, so that's the first thing Rhodesia means to me, it's my country – and no one is going to come in here and tell me where to go, no ways.

'I don't know if you have travelled around this country, David, but to my mind this is a super country, the best on earth, it has everything, sunshine, good soil and the finest people you could find anywhere; in my opinion our black Rhodesians are the finest in Africa, they're fine people and I'm proud of them. If certain people would only get off our backs and let us get on with the job of building up this wonderful country then I believe we could make this thing work, I do believe that, David, I wouldn't stay here if I didn't.

'So what does Rhodesia mean to me? It means standards, it means law and order, and it means civilization as we know it. It means well-repaired roads, telephones that work, it means sanitation, hygiene and medicine second to none in Africa. It means a country where each race, each people, can remain faithful to its own identity, its own language, in mutual respect – and I do mean that, David, the black Rhodesian is a man I respect.

'Rhodesia means a land of opportunity and free enterprise, a country where a farmer can make a living if he puts his back into his work and keeps pace with modern techniques. David, the Rhodesian doesn't lie down under sanctions, he doesn't trot around the world with his begging bowl; the Rhodesian believes that God helps those who help themselves; the way that people have risen to the challenge in Rhodesia is a story that I, personally, would like to read about one day. Maybe you'll write it, David. No, honestly, you should.

'Rhodesia means to my mind banks run by men who won't scoop the till; a civil service based on merit, a police force uncorrupted by bribery and nepotism. It means due process of law before impartial judges uninfluenced by intimidation and superstition. It means accurate statistics, honest tax collectors, clean streets, a spirit of civil discipline. Rhodesia is a country where your wife and daughter are safe on the streets and that's no mean achievement; it's a country where if your car breaks down black people will stop to give you a hand – now where else will you find that in Africa?

'David, Rhodesians can't ignore what's happened to the north. In Zambia you get robbed at gunpoint in your own home but don't bother to call the police, all their bicycles have been stolen. There were 74,000 whites living in Zambia at the time of Independence. Within four years 41 per cent of them had gapped it. In Mozambique the economy lies in ruins. In Uganda, Caligula reigns; in Tanzania they are herding villagers into collective farms in the name of socialism and believe me you won't hear a word about it at the United Nations, whereas even in the West our Rhodesian protected villages are called concentration camps. In Kenya corruption starts at the top. In Nigeria and Ghana it's one military coup after another. Where in black Africa does the civilian not step into the road to let the soldier pass? You tell me, David, you have more opportunity to see these things than I do.

'David, I want you to proceed to Harare or Highfield right now and just drive around, get out of your car and take a walk, chat to a few people, then you come back and tell me whether you ever felt scared, whether anyone gave you the evil eye, whether you saw any adult person without shoes or proper clothes. Go to Harare Hospital, David, and ask some of our black doctors: which country in Africa has the lowest infant mortality? You don't have to take my word for it, David, you go and ask them. And you go into any hotel and ask for a beer and I guarantee your black waiter will be a polite waiter, no cheeky stuff at all; if you show that man respect, he'll show you respect, which is the way it is in Rhodesia.'

2. a short history

A short history of the White Tribe in Rhodesia:

In 1890, the Pioneer Column reached the site of the city later called Salisbury.
By 1900, the 11,032 whites were reckoned to constitute 2·2 per cent of the population.
By 1921, the 33,620 whites constituted 3·8 per cent.
By 1941, the 68,954 whites constituted 4·7 per cent.

By 1951, the 135,596 whites achieved a peak percentage of 6·3.

In 1961, the white population had reached 223,000.

Then came five years of instability, of nationalist unrest, urban violence and political strife culminating in the Rhodesian Front's Unilateral Declaration of Independence (1965). As a consequence the white population declined by 25,000.

But as soon as the Smith regime displayed its will and its capability to withstand world condemnation and economic sanctions, whites once again responded to the lure of a 'land of opportunity': between 1967 and 1973 the white population of Rhodesia increased by 39,000. Like the Jewish Agency in Israel, the Salisbury regime openly campaigned for immigrants of the right stock. But now the guerrilla war began to bite. Net immigration was rapidly transformed into net emigration. In 1976 the net loss of whites was 7,072; in 1977, 10,908; in 1978, 13,709; in 1979, 11,817; and in 1980 it was estimated at 10,833, although the Zimbabwean government no longer provided a racial breakdown of immigrants or emigrants.

Thus between 1 January 1976 and Zimbabwean Independence in April 1980 about 48,196 whites left Rhodesia and did not return – a net loss of about 20 per cent.

3. men without knees

No black chief, neither the Ndebele king Lobengula nor the Mashona paramounts over whom he (spuriously) claimed suzerainty, ever made a genuine grant of land to Cecil Rhodes's British South Africa Company. The Pioneer Column which trekked up into Mashonaland in 1890, guns bristling, embodied that imperial urge, that boundless appetite for gain, conquest and expansion of which Rhodes had become the symbol. 'You have the proud satisfaction of knowing that you are civilising a new part of the world,' he told the Pioneers.

The Company allowed adventurers and settlers a free and rapacious hand. Having pegged out 'their' land without reference to the natives, whites defended their 'rights' by forming vigilante posses, by staging punitive expeditions, and by commissioning themselves as policemen of convenience. Kraals were fired on, burnt to the ground. When a white trader, Bennet, believed himself to have been robbed by men from the kraal of a certain headman, Ngomo, the result was a bombardment in which twenty-one natives were killed and forty-seven head of cattle taken in reprisal.

Although the white settlers did not formally enslave the natives they did insist that local headmen provide them with labour. When this was refused and resisted, the Company's police forces were called in to impose the requisition and flog the insolent, 'idle' blacks: fifty lashes was a fair punishment for a recalcitrant headman, plus six goats and three head of cattle. In 1894 the journalist H. C. Thompson noted: 'It is not pleasant the way in which the Mashona avoid coming into contact with the settlers, and to recollect that when we first went up to Mashonaland they welcomed us gladly.' Confronted by this sudden catastrophe, by rape and pillage, forced labour and the sjambok, the natives learned to flee from their kraals and hide in caves at the approach of whites.

Under the forced-labour system a native would be made to work for a month before he got paid. It was a common trick among whites to maltreat what they called the 'boys' as the end of the working month approached, in order to induce flight and thus avoid payment. Neither Rhodes, his appointed Administrator, Dr L. S. Jameson, nor the vacillating British government was prepared to intervene effectively to provide the natives with protection against buccaneering exploitation and frontier vandalism.

White settlers lost no time in accusing natives of 'trespassing' on land they had occupied for generations. The Company granted the land to the settlers but it had absolutely no right, other than that of naked conquest and seizure, to do so.

Then they started taxing the natives: the hut-tax at the rate of 10 shillings per hut per year. Local European farmers and traders were appointed collectors with power to gather the tax in the form of money, labour on the roads or livestock. Those who resisted were described as 'cheeky niggers' who needed to be taught a lesson. The whites taught the natives one much-needed lesson after another until the natives rose up and split their heads open with axes.

In his famous book, *Revolt in Southern Rhodesia*, Professor Terence Ranger recalls the style of Chief Native Commissioner Brabant, described by one contemporary as 'a rough diamond' and by another as 'a rough and ready illiterate young man with an aptitude to learn to speak primitive African languages. He was a great believer in corporal punishment and was as brave as a lion, a good rider and rifle shot, intensely loyal to the BSA Company, quite honest, and with an unquenchable thirst for kaffir beer.' To bring African chiefs who refused to pay tax to their senses, Brabant was prepared to burn, shoot and destroy everything in sight, take his pick of the native cattle, and demand 500 men to work in the mines. Young Brabant was much esteemed by Rhodes and Dr Jameson.

Almost the first step taken by the white invader is to flash the gold or silver in his pocket and thus recruit black porters, herdsmen, guides and auxiliary policemen. Not only does he bring armed blacks from the Cape (the 'Cape Boys') to help keep order among the Shonas and Ndebeles, he also recruits locally, calling these levies 'friendlies' or 'loyal' – whereas in fact they are essentially *dis*-loyal, traitors in the most elementary sense to their own kith and kin, and to their own liberties. (Thus the Third Reich termed collaborators in occupied Europe 'loyal'; the Resistance movements favoured a different semantic code.) Blacks were lured into the police by money, uniforms, handcuffs, and by the intoxication of a power previously unheard of. The 'chamboko' (sjambok) epitomized the new authority; each man in uniform had to be addressed as 'mwana we nkosi', son of the Native Commissioner. Fathers, headmen, village councillors were abused in front of their own people. Native Commissioner Campbell, known as 'Vuta' (Full of Airs) by the VaShawasha people, ruled Salisbury and Goromonzi; during the rebellion of 1896 Campbell was a prime target but managed to escape by the skin of his teeth.

When the 'vasina mabvi', the white men 'without knees', first arrived, the Shona entertained no fear of them. Lawrence Vambe recalls in his book, *An Ill-Fated People*: 'My father, who was a very young man at the time, said that these people, with their long, animal-like hair and beards, wild eyes, uniforms, hats and shoes, as well as horses, ox-wagons and other accoutrements, were like a circus. For several weeks, all the Shona society round Harare would be irresistibly drawn to gape and often split their sides in wonder and amusement. Most extraordinary and ridiculous were the Pioneers' habits of living, such as military formations, drilling to the bark of their commanders, bugle-sounding and the hoisting and unhoisting of their flag. These strange antics, never seen before, were greeted by the Shona as signs of incomprehensible eccentricity, and conclusive evidence that the people "without knees" were deranged.'

Lawrence Vambe, born and bred amongst the VaShawasha in the Goromonzi area east of Salisbury, grew up in a village 'belonging to' the Jesuit mission at Chishawasha, where the all-powerful Fathers, unseen and unheard of before 1890, now tolled a bell loudly every day to summon the 'faithful' and did not shrink from expelling families or individuals whose behaviour offended Christian principles. Afrikaner policemen appeared on the scene, enforcing the dog-tax and calling the VaShawasha 'skellums, kaffirs, bastards, bobojaans', which means baboon. Vambe heard members of his tribe addressing their dead ancestors: 'For reasons we have never been able to understand you permitted this ngozi (curse, catastrophe) to fall upon us.'

In 1893 the Ndebele monarchy was crushed by force. The motivation was plunder, the vast pastures and herds of the Ndebele. Virtually all Ndebele land and the majority of their cattle passed into the hands of white 'Pioneers' and adventurers within three years. Speculators made fortunes. Whites of British and Afrikaner stock hurried up from the Cape Colony and the Transvaal in search of rich pickings. The process of pegging out lots, of sale and re-sale, baffled and outraged the Ndebele. White men of varied origin and race became in a day their landlords, their overlords, with power to dispossess and drive forth. Jameson surrounded himself by young English aristocrats and adventurers described by Lord Grey as filled 'with the jolly reckless spirit of adventure, which aimed at making a million in half an hour and then clearing home to Piccadilly'.

Ranger quotes a contemporary report which nicely illustrates man's capacity for glossing his own motives and actions. Soon after the capture of Bulawayo from Lobengula in 1893 news was brought to Fort Victoria that the Mashonas were crossing over into Matabeleland and 'stealing' the King's cattle. 'The King's cattle were looked upon as loot and if this thieving continued it would mean so much less for members of the column.' Thus looting is not thieving, but some nobler law of war – if undertaken by oneself. Yet everyone white was helping himself to Ndebele cattle including enterprising South Africans who hurried north and then drove the Ndebele's oxen back south. By 1895 only 74,500 cattle out of 200,000–300,000 were left in the hands of the Ndebele; of these the Chief Native Commissioner was prepared to allow the natives to keep 40,390.

Any white who bought a ranch in Matabeleland during the next eighty-odd years merely came late to the game of pillage. But is not all property theft, as Proudhon claimed? Is not all economic and political power originally rooted in conquest, in *force majeure*? Had not the Ndebeles themselves invaded the area round Bulawayo, cruelly subjected the tribes living there, made themselves masters by brute force?

The objection is not without validity. But what is the reach of this narrative? Not, surely, to prove that white Rhodesians, whether Pioneers or followers of Ian Smith, are uniquely rapacious, exploitative and imperialistic. Our subject is, in fact, a collective state of mind; more particularly the extraordinary mental manoeuvres by which pillage is termed responsible government, repression becomes law and order, usurpation is called authority, violence is lauded as restraint; the peculiar indignation, the outrage, the sense of ingratitude, experienced by the conquerors when the dispossessed natives attempt to recover by force what was taken so recently from them by force. Our subject is the myths, evasions, legends, reifications and strategies of false consciousness; the bones, nerves and flesh of an ideology.

4. five times a night

Headlamps rake the bush. An owl stares amazed and outraged at the onrushing columns of light, then flaps huffily off the narrow country road. Bob Pennington's perimeter fence is floodlit and his dogs start barking and snarling behind the wire at the approach of vehicles through the night. Pennington unlocks the gate, clasping his FN rifle in his left hand, and pacifies the rearing dogs with a few words whispered in strict confidence.

Security fencing is now a highly competitive business. A firm called Fencing Services preceded their flying visit to Pennington's tobacco-farm at Rusape with a batch of promotional literature, including a pull-out wire fence which folded up like a three-dimensional children's book: 'Is your home a soft target? Why take a chance? Airborne quotation teams are available. Phone now on Salisbury 47154 and clear your airstrip.' A rival firm, The Fencers, P.O. Box A97, Avondale, declare competitively: 'We're all over the place — when and where you need us.' But they didn't get to Bob Pennington and his $(R)1,000 in time.

The man pours himself a stiff drink; his wife Trish is already on her third, a bit bleary-eyed, sunk in cushions, listening to Rusape Control going through the routine call-signs on the Agric-Alert. Trish isn't cooking dinner tonight because the cookboy Matthew is cooking dinner; she is heavily into drugs and 'wants out' of Rusape. She stares at the Agric-Alert talking machine on the wall.

'Kilo 2, checking you out. Over.' (Silence.)
'Kilo 4, checking you, over.'
(Female voice) 'Reading you fives, out.'
'Will those who haven't checked in now do so, please.' (Silence, crackle. . . .)
'Kilo 6, I wonder if you can tell me whether Kilo 48, Mr Holt, and Kilo 56, Mr Van Hanagem, are away from their farms.'
'They may have checked their sets with the DC, over.'
'They're both on leave, that's why I wondered.'

Pennington refills his glass and switches on the television. He now employs three full-time black security guards, at $(R)80 per month; they wear balaclava helmets in a vain effort to conceal their identities and prevent reprisals against their families in the neighbouring Chiduku TTL. In vain, because sooner or later they'll go wenching and the 'boys', the vakhomana, will learn their identities by a time-honoured transmission belt.

Pennington has already reserved space in a Salisbury storehouse for his coming tobacco crop. With the 'terrs' burning one barn after another, it would be madness to attempt to store the cured leaf here on the farm, despite the Salisbury storage fee of a dollar per bale. Pennington will pick and sell his bottom leaves first, hoping for a price of 50–60 cents a kilo, but he fears the worst: sanctions, too much rain, and a high nicotine content at a time when the world demands low-tar cigarettes. Sanctions can be broken, but at a price – the grim commissions demanded, and extracted, by a succession of anonymous middlemen leave the Rhodesian farmer with only two-thirds of the price obtained by Malawian tobacco producers. The British inspectorate, meanwhile, applies the screws with methodical cruelty, catching up on illicit Rhodesian leaf by checking samples of the stems and waste on which the tobacco companies claim excise-duty relief.

A journalist from a British newspaper comes down to Rusape to talk to Bob Pennington. The farmer momentarily recoils when a tape recorder is produced, then shrugs:

'What the hell, this is a free country, isn't it? You realize *they* started the killing here? They're all cowards, those fellows – mind you, a few of the section leaders coming in from Mozambique now are quite switched on . . . Listen, I'll tell you who's running those gooks. It's the communists. And why? Because we in this country have the best race relations in the world. You go and tell your readers that. It's because if you go into the reserve there, into the Chiduku, and you stop any black you meet and ask him whether Bob Pennington's a good man, I guarantee that black will say: "Yes, he's a good man." The majority of your Afs are completely loyal to Rhodesia and that doesn't suit the Kremlin one bit.'

His wife Trish stirs in her drugged lethargy. Her glazed eyes are fixed on the reporter from London.

'We are all going on to a better world,' she says. 'For me, the sooner the better. I've had this place up to here.' Vaguely she lifts her hand to nose level. Bob Pennington coughs, digs into the pockets of his khaki shorts and lights another Madison. But she rambles on, nostalgic, about the old days when you could picnic anywhere, or ride on horseback cross-country, camping and fishing up at Inyanga, boating on Lake Kariba, the annual trip to Beira with its exotic Portuguese-African smells and its 'Continental' food. Landlocked, she dreams of great expanses of ocean, of a blue horizon stretching away to Mauritius, the Seychelles, waiters in white jackets, sea-food curries . . . castanets, romance. . . .

'My sister and her husband tried Australia last year,' she mumbles. 'They couldn't get work so they came back.' Her eyes close.

Bob Pennington throws the stub of a cigarette towards the fireplace. 'Listen, we're prepared to believe in this country so long as the white man gets a fair deal. I mean, none of us is going to hang around if we're discriminated against because we're white.' He sighs, pours two fresh beers. 'I'm going to tell you something, strictly between you and me – what is it you fellows say, "off the record"?'

The journalist composes himself attentively. He's not at all sure that Rhodesia is really his kind of subject.

'I was out on patrol duty, police reserve. A Patu stick had reported a contact inside the reserve and we'd put up this road block. Then this old Morris Minor comes bumping towards us in a cloud of dust. I saw this black fellow behind the wheel. The gooks had revved two farms within forty-eight hours so I told this chap to step out of his car pretty smartly and open up the boot. He didn't move. "It's not locked," he said and I could feel the blood rushing to my head, know what I mean? So I said: "Boy, you step out of that car smartly and open the boot . . ." Then he sort of smiled, though I wouldn't call it a humorous smile, he got out of the car quite slowly and he opened the boot. I told him to open up his suitcase and show me his pass, his situpa. He showed me a passport, a British passport. I said, "Boy, where's your situpa?" Do you know what he said? He said, "British subjects don't carry situpas." Educated voice. The smile was kind of fixed to his face and I thought: this is what we're up against, this kind of kaffir. Inside his suitcase there was a book, kind of a heavy paperback, called *Dynamics of Colonial Expansion*. I said to him, "Is this a banned book?" He just stared at me as if I were a baboon, you get these chaps who go to study in London, maybe they've picked up a few O-levels at some mission school . . .'

Bob Pennington lights another cigarette and takes a deep breath. 'I shouldn't be telling you this story, I'm not at all happy about that tape recorder of yours, anyway this character had got right under my skin so I said to him, "How many English girls have you had, boy?"'

Pennington breaks off. Suddenly his appetite for this story has evaporated. 'Anyway . . . You think I'm a racist, don't you? And maybe I am, though I'll judge any man on his merits. But I wouldn't have that nig eating at my dinner table.'

The following morning Bob Pennington takes the reporter on a tour of the 1,000-hectare farm, starting with the primary school which costs him about $(R)500 a year: 'And people say we don't care!' When the two white men enter the tin-roofed shack, everyone rises and the silence is absolute. Mr Mukono, an extraordinarily emaciated man, ragged at the cuffs, patched at the elbows and knees, stands almost to attention while the rows of saucer-wide eyes turn towards the door. Pennington starts talking loudly about Mukono as if Mukono were a tree or a horse or a Bushman without English:

'I pay him thirty dollars a month plus hut and he complains that the younger teachers are getting more. I chose this fellow myself because otherwise the Department of Education might send me some London-educated "red" who'd start stirring the kids here.'

Inside the shack it is swelteringly hot: the harassed Mukono is attempting to cope simultaneously with the kids of all ages from grade 1 to 6.

'Carry on,' Pennington nods cursorily to Mukono.

The teacher turns back to his children. 'Put-your-finger-under-your-chin,' he says slowly, in English. 'What-are-you-doing?'

'I-am-putt-eeng-my-feeng-er-un-der-my-cheen,' they chorus shyly, hesitantly, many of them continually swivelling their saucer eyes towards the white presence, the baas power, at the door. Mr Mukono's shoes are coming apart at the soles.

'Touch-your-nose. What-are-you-doing?'

'I-am-touch-eeng-my-nose.'

Later, on the way back to the homestead for lunch, the journalist asks Pennington about his own children.

'Tom's 14, a boarder at Umtali Boys' High School. Taller than I am, shooting up like a beanstalk, captain of the rugby team. Scored the winning try against St George's last weekend. You see the flayed bark on those gum-trees there? That was Tom practising with my FN. The girl, Jenny, she's at school in Salisbury.'

When they go in for lunch they find Mrs Pennington lying unconscious on the living-room floor. Matthew, the cookboy, who is bending over her, gestures helplessly towards an empty gin bottle.

After lunch the reporter sleeps. Although he has not slept on a Rhodesian farm before he feels no fear because daylight filters through the shutters and the warm air is replete with reassuring farm sounds.

In the next block Pennington lies dozing with an FN rifle at his side and two loaded pistols within reach.

The dogs begin to bark and howl when the guests arrive for dinner – local farmers and their wives, they stack their guns in the corner of the drawing-room. One lady loses no time in explaining that she bought her sten gun from the District Commissioner for $(R)90 but that a magazine of thirty rounds costs $(R)3 and the Salisbury gunsmiths are now charging extortionate prices, 'But that's your Jew everywhere, isn't it?'

Another woman says bluntly, 'I can't stand British journalists.'

'And what's your opinion of our country?' asks her husband.

'The more I know about it, the less I know about it,' the reporter says. It's a practised answer; the farmers and their wives soften noticeably.

'Very few outsiders take the trouble to understand Rhodesia,' Pennington says. 'They just pick up the Moscow line. Mind you, we've made our share of mistakes round here.' The middle-aged men immediately concur, but taking care not to fall out among themselves by defining the mistakes. The woman with the sten gun dissents: what mistakes? She grabs the reporter's wrist:

'The African male does his exhausted wife five times a night every night, then the rest of the world tells us we've got to educate all these thousands of little piccaninns.'

The females concur, ritually. The males, as if recognizing the tenors' cue, come forth with their parallel lament, the heart of their matter:

'Your kaffir farmer, your average tribesman, overstocks his grazing land with cattle, counts his riches by the size of his herd, and exhausts his land. And the world holds us to blame.'

Over the T-bone steaks a fifteen-stone rancher called Lambert or Lannart (the reporter isn't sure) launches a volley of what he calls 'K-factors'.

– 'I suppose you know their word for "give me"? You don't? It's "nigamina". Could this be the origin of the word "nigger"?'

– 'How do you tell the true socialists in Zambia? They're the ones in the Mercedes-Benz!'

– 'Mind you, don't forget that everyone has equal access to medical care. There isn't any!'

– 'Socialism is nothing equally distributed!'

(It takes about twenty years for an idea, or a bad joke, to travel from Europe down to the 20th parallel and into rancher Lambert's cranium.)

The lady with the sten gun announces that she and her husband are contemplating a move to Malawi. Whereas Zambia symbolizes all the vices of black Africa – inefficiency, corruption, tribalism, posturing, terrorism – good old Hastings Banda (once vilified and imprisoned in Rhodesia) has provided the white man with an opportunity to exercise his skills, gather fruit, export 75 per cent of it, and get out while the going is good.

'Most of your farm managers in Malawi are Rhodesians,' she concludes.

'Doc Banda keeps his population down by restricting the import of measles vaccine,' her husband says. 'We should try that.'

Though it's midnight by the time the reporter retires to bed he does not sleep. Presently he hears sounds in the night, shuffling along the veranda, whispers in the garden. He has no gun and the window doesn't lock. The reporter tiptoes, trembling, to the lavatory, where he bolts the door and feels like a trapped rat. After half an hour of this he grows bored and unbolts the lavatory door.

5. 'chimurenga': revenge is sweet

Any image of Shona life as idyllic and arcadian, as a Rousseau-esque model of cooperative farming and peaceful craftsmanship, would be wide of the mark. Terence Ranger quotes a report from Captain Lendy in 1892 showing that the paramount chiefs of the Salisbury district were at each other's throats and constantly complaining of raids and counter-raids the one against the other: Chief Chishawasha against Kunzwi-Nyandoro, Chief Marondera against Chiduku, Chief Mbelewa against Makoni. The astonishing achievement of the whites was to unite a fundamentally divided and warring Shona people in coordinated rebellion within six years of their arrival.

The risings of 1896 took most whites entirely by surprise. Then, as during the subsequent eighty years, white settlers and all but a few administrators shrouded and shielded themselves in ignorance of the native mind – largely by inventing the notion of the 'native mind' or 'your native' as a species apart, incapable of normal European reactions to being beaten, bullied, robbed and requisitioned by foreign conquerors; and partly by insisting that the natives' grievances were 'imaginary', the product of whispers and rumours, of magicians, witch-doctors and spirit mediums with a vested interest in stirring disaffection.

Armed revolt, treachery, the cowed, quiescent 'nigger' suddenly flashing his panga, his axe, on the trusting white skull; the barbarous savage surfacing in the heart of his own pagan darkness – this nightmare of fact and fiction was not new to Rhodesia. Indeed, the Ndebele and Shona rebellions of 1896–7 began with an abrupt, coordinated, vicious blood-letting – tom-toms, spirit-mediums, magical cults, mutilations, the whole palaver – not matched by the guerrilla war of the 1970s.

In 1896 almost every white Rhodesian – whether administrator, Native Commissioner or settler – was taken by surprise. Marshall Hole, the Resident Magistrate of Salisbury, remarked of the Shonas: 'With true kaffir deceit they have beguiled us into the idea that they were content with our administration . . . but at a given signal they have cast aside all pretence. . . .' Lord Grey concluded that the Shona 'have the habits of a whipped cur and not infrequently bite through terror the hand outstretched to help them'.

In the last week of March 1896 no fewer than 122 white males, five white females, and three white children were killed in Matabeleland, almost all of them living in outlying country districts. When the Shona rebellion broke out in June, 120 whites living in remote areas perished in the space of a few days. Within months the uprising, the 'chimurenga', had accounted for 372 white settlers, with a further 129 wounded – almost 10 per cent of the total.

The ferocity of the white reaction in 1896 matched the fury of the rising. W. A. Jarvis, adventurer and former Tory MP, wrote from Gwelo on 29 March 1896: 'There are about 5,500 niggers in this district and our plan of campaign will probably be to proceed against this lot and wipe them out, then move on towards Bulawayo wiping out every nigger and every kraal we can find . . . after these cold-blooded murders you may be sure that there will be no quarter and everything black will have to die, for our men's blood is fairly up.' It was Jarvis's opinion – an opinion increasingly prevalent among the later generation of white Rhodesians as the war of the 1970s mounted in ferocity – that 'the beastly missionaries have a lot to do with it, teaching the nigger that he is as good as the white man. It won't do. The nigger has got to be treated as a nigger all the world over.'

Lawrence Vambe was a great-grandson of Chief Mashonganyika, who was hanged after the rebellion of 1896, but not before the rebels had made mincemeat of twenty-five African policemen, 'imbga dza vasungate, white men's dogs', and British troops rushed in from Beira had scorched the earth, dynamited the guerrillas' caves, and destroyed their houses and food stocks. Vambe's grandfather Gukwe was a rebel leader from whom the police failed to extract a confession even though they crushed the palm of his right hand with hammer blows. The hand had to be amputated from the wrist, whereupon gangrene set in; the arm was cut off from the elbow, then from the shoulder joint; then Gukwe died.

The conqueror sees himself as a man – or race – which is 'slow to anger'. But when his comrades are murdered, shot down 'in cold blood', reluctantly he takes up his rifle with a strong and terrible rage rising inside his belly. Then look out! On 22 June 1897 *The Nugget* published some lines of doggerel called 'The Rhodesian' which, had the taper of the antiquarian spirit burned more strongly, might well have been carried in every troopie's knapsack eighty years later (see Ranger, op. cit., pp. 131–2):

> Tho' he's not been trained to fightin', 'tis a game he takes delight in,
> And he's proved himself a rough and ruly chap,
> For he'll trail the rebel nigger till he grasp his woolly wig,
> And he'll scale the top-most kopje for a scrap . . .

> . . . .

> While he pots his man he'll hum 'there goes another for my chum',
> But a thousand blacks won't bring the white lives back;
> So he thinks 'Revenge is sweet' as he just grips his saddle seat,

And his horse bounds forward on the rebels' track.
Oh, he glories in the pig-skin as he holes another nig-skin . . .

. . . .

Let the folk in Exeter Hall and such-like other Grundies bawl,
And rave and shout and cry that he's inhuman . . .

. . . .

The black fiends never cared so why should one of them be spared?
First raise up the dead; *then* ask our hearts to melt.

6. the beginning of the end

For the armed uprising of the 1970s – the second 'chimurenga' – white
Rhodesians were forewarned and well prepared. The famous civic peace, the
unique harmony between the races, in which whites took such pride, was first
disturbed in 1960 when eighteen blacks were killed by police in the course of
demonstrations or riots. The Law and Order (Maintenance) Act was rushed
on to the statute book. Yet it was not for a further sixteen years that the black
nationalists were able to mount an effective war of insurgency. Such was the
mastery enjoyed by the security forces from the Limpopo to the Zambezi that
during the first ten years after Smith's Unilateral Declaration of Independence
in 1965 only sixteen white civilians were murdered. Between 1967 and 1972
not a single white person died as a result of guerrilla action. In 1972–3
military expenditure still accounted for only 8½ per cent of the national
budget, despite the wars of insurgency holding down 150,000 troops in
Portuguese Africa.

Divided, dispersed, imprisoned, exiled, penetrated by police informers and
closely monitored by the Special Branch, the nationalist parties were unable
to mount any campaign or incursion impressive enough to dent the whites'
confident assumption of total and enduring superiority.

Even when Zanla launched a new offensive in December 1972 and the
attacks spread from Centenary and Mount Darwin to Karoi and Shamva,
there was no great sense of alarm. Despite modern weapons and expert
instruction the guerrillas found it harder to kill white farmers in the 1970s
than did their ancestors in 1896. The Ndebele elder Mhlope later recorded
how in 1896 he and his comrades accounted for three unsuspecting whites in
a single day: one they killed in his store with a blow of an axe; another they
killed in the maize fields with a knobkerrie and an axe; and the third they

dispatched by similar means in his hut. All three victims were taken completely by surprise. But the whites of the 1970s were on their guard; heavily armed
and defended by fences, radio alarm systems and mobile patrols, they
provided difficult targets. And there is evidence to suggest that, in any case,
Zanla concentrated during the early 1970s on establishing itself in the tribal
trust lands, on securing its popular, peasant base. Nevertheless killings did
occur:

1973: Mrs I. Kleynhans, Centenary, 24 January; Mr L. M. Jellicoe, Centen-
ary, 4 February; Mr D. M. Stacey, Karoi, 9 March; Mr D. J. Vincent,
Centenary, 3 April; Mr T. V. Forbes, Mount Darwin, 23 April; Mr B.
Couve, Shamva, 6 June.

1974: Mr N. Wills, Shamva, 14 February; Mr E. Fletcher and Mrs B. Fletcher,
Centenary, 17 February; Mr P. Rouse, Centenary, 18 February; Mr V.
Stockil-Gill, Marandellas, 27 October.

1975: Mr C. A. S. Young, 29 April; Mr P. J. D. Knight, Doma, 17 May; Mr A.
V. Howe, Umvukwes, 24 June; Mr P. Snyders, Vumba, 9 October.

Although 1974 and 1975 were years of heavy recruitment by both Zanla
and Zipra, attacks on whites other than farmers were extremely rare before
1976; land surveyors, road contractors, farm-equipment salesmen and those
in similar occupations were more obviously at risk in the north-east. Two
white road contractors were ambushed and killed in the Binga area on 11
April 1975.

*The beginning of the end of white Rhodesia dates from the early months of
1976*. In the course of that year at least thirty members of white farming
families were murdered. In 1977 the farmers came under even heavier attack,
losing at the minimum reckoning a further fifty-two. During 1978 the figure
more than doubled to no less than 117. Over seventy members of farming
families were killed in the course of 1979.

By the early months of 1976 the war was penetrating the southern
provinces. Alarm bells sounded throughout white Rhodesia and South Africa
after four South African tourists travelling on two motor cycles from Fort
Victoria to Beitbridge came upon guerrillas robbing three cars on 18 April.
Janos Sziliagyi, Julius Mojzes, Gavin Adcock and Vonda Hope-Davies were
all killed when the guerrillas opened fire on them. The same guerrillas also
blasted three diesel locomotives and a string of wagons on to their sides on the
line to South Africa. The main road was closed while a massive sweep was
launched and when the road was reopened at the beginning of May motorists
were urged to travel from Fort Victoria by escorted convoy. Two months
later, on 9 July, the convoy system was extended to the road from Beitbridge
to Bulawayo.

The long lines of civilian cars, theoretically spaced at fifty-metre intervals, would proceed at 80–100 k.p.h., depending on the mood of the police driver in the front escort truck. The two grey police pick-ups, at the front and rear of the convoy, carried powerful two-way radios and heavy machine-guns. The machine-gunners wore space-age helmets and stood behind their weapons throughout the journey, supported by a waist harness and a rope behind the knees. In civilian life these police reservists might run a hardware store or an electrical business in Salisbury or Bulawayo.

The first recorded attack on an escorted convoy took place on 17 August between Fort Victoria and Chiredzi. Two white women were injured. There was now a growing uneasiness about all forms of travel, except by air.

The pattern of killings during 1976 involved almost the entire country, from Karoi and Lupane in the north-west to Chipinga and Melsetter in the south-east, from Plumtree, Filabusi and the Matopos in the south-west to Mtoko, Bindura and Centenary in the north-east.

On 21 April Helgard Muller, 25, a farmer, was wounded in the shoulder while driving to inspect a cattle dip near Nuanetsi.

On 22 May Jacob van Vuuren, 45, and his 14-year-old son were killed during an attack on their farmhouse in the area south of Matopos.

At the beginning of June, two engineering contract technicians working on a protected village in the north-east, John Downham and Daniel Jordaan, were killed while in their tent.

On 6 June there occurred at Chipinga one of the most horrifying tragedies of the entire war. Leaving their farm on a Whitsun holiday outing, a family hit a mine near the Skyline Road junction. Killed were Mrs Elizabeth Botha and her two daughters by a previous marriage, Marianne Habig, 14, and Louber-lie Habig, 8 (spelt Harbing in press reports). Injured were Mr Louis Botha's daughter Yvonne, who later died of her injuries, and a friend, 16-year-old Shirley Wicksteed, who had to have both legs amputated. This young woman's cheerful stoicism became during the next few years a symbol of courage and fortitude for all victims of landmines.

The funeral service took place at the Dutch Reformed Church in Chipinga and was conducted in both English and Afrikaans. Three hundred people attended.

A week later guerrillas killed Frank Pitcher, 47, father of three, near his Bindura farm.

A few days after General Walls opened the new barracks for the Rhodesian African Rifles at Balla Balla, on 7 July, an attack took place on a store close to the barracks. The farmer owner, Leonard Ashby, 55, was killed and his wife wounded.

At about the same time guerrillas killed Edward Court, 48, who worked on the Mukorsi River ranch south of Fort Victoria. His death brought the total of white civilians murdered since December 1972 to thirty-two.

On 13 July Mrs Daphne Adams was driving with her husband some fifty kilometres south of Fort Victoria on the Beitbridge road when they were confronted by (she estimated) thirty to forty men wearing dark camouflage fatigues. Mrs Adams managed to stop, turn and speed away under a hail of fire, with bullets hitting the petrol tank. Seeing other cars approaching the ambush point from the opposite direction, she frantically flashed her lights, sounded the horn, waved, but to no avail. At least three cars ran into the ambush. René Trenet Helena du Plessis, a child of 8, was killed. Henry Carmichael, driving another car, tried to turn round but was wounded by guerrilla fire, after which he was dragged from his car and bayoneted. Seriously injured, he was later picked up by a passing motorist after the guerrillas had withdrawn. In a third car Reginald Randall, aged 11, was injured by gunfire while travelling with his father.

On 26 July there were two murders. Llewellin Davies, 64, a rancher, was shot dead as he sat at dinner with his wife at their home near Lupane. On the same day Jochgan Botha, 75, a timber-company employee, was found dead of gunshot wounds in the smashed cab of his vehicle. Botha had been travelling through a TTL some sixty kilometres from Victoria Falls. About five weeks later, police shot dead in Luveve township, Bulawayo, a man who, they said, had been responsible for the killing not only of Botha but also of Jacob van Vuuren and his son in May. A white police detective was killed in the course of the arrest.

Two elderly farmers' widows were killed in rapid succession. On 7 September Mrs Lorna May McFedden, 66 years old and bedridden, was murdered on her farm, Cold Ridge A, near Plumtree. Two days later it was the turn of 64-year-old Mrs Kathleen Backe-Hansen, killed in an African colliery village near Wankie. Having shot her, guerrillas set fire to her store.

On 19 September Mrs Wayanne Palmer, an Australian-born farmer's wife, was killed and her husband Rodney Palmer, 38, severely injured when they were ambushed in the Mrewa/Mtoko area.

Petrus Naude, 42, a tobacco-farmer from the Somabula area, was killed on 17 October during an ambush which wounded two of his labourers and led to the destruction of four vehicles.

In June 1896, at the onset of the Shona rising, a triangle of territory, half-way between Salisbury and Umtali, had become a place of terror: from Macheke to Mayo (at the apex of the triangle), then down to Headlands and, further south, Rusape, the whites had been compelled to evacuate their farms.

Until the early months of 1976 the guerrilla war scarcely penetrated the triangle, but in August of that year the police post at Mayo was hit by a rocket and an African constable killed. A few weeks later, on 16 September, a 61-year-old farmer, Theophilius Greyvensteyn, was shot dead outside his farmhouse, which was then set ablaze.

The belt of European farming land round Mayo lay trapped between tribal trust lands that gave Zanla guerrillas both a base and a retreat: Mangwende to the west, Weya to the south, Tanda to the east. Sandbags were now piled against bedroom walls. In the early sixties there had been fifty-six white families living in the area, which boasted two rugby teams; by early 1977 the district was dotted with empty farms. Nicholas Swanepoel's farm was hit at two in the morning. Having cut through the security fence, guerrillas opened fire a few yards from the homestead. Swanepoel rolled out of bed, grabbed a rifle and returned fire, while his wife Lydia shoved 5-year-old Nicola under the bed in the next bedroom, then seized a gun herself and started firing. Swanepoel called frantically, 'We are under attack, we are under attack', into his Agric-Alert radio alarm, but no help came and the guerrillas pressed their attack for a further forty-five minutes. The Swanepoels decided to quit and move to Salisbury.

On 26 January 1977, Gert Myburgh and his wife Loekie, who had farmed in Mayo for twenty years, were paying a late afternoon visit to relatives on a nearby farm. Approaching it, they were confronted by a dozen guerrillas who stepped in front of the car and opened fire. Myburgh leapt out, loosed off a full magazine, then took a ·303 shot-gun from the rear seat and fired one round from it before he was hit in the chest. He staggered back into the car and his wife managed to drive away through a hail of bullets, but Myburgh died on the way to hospital.

7. how do you know?

Sensing the crisis, the regime clamped down on the free flow of information. The D-notice regulations – another institution inherited from the home country – of 26 April established a National Security Committee empowered to prohibit the publication of information. Armed with powers of search and seizure, the Committee was not required to explain its decisions. D-notices were not subject to judicial appeal. A newspaper served with a D-notice was forbidden to tell its readers that it had been served with a D-notice.

A familiar tactic. When, twelve years earlier, the *Rhodesia Herald* had responded to censorship by leaving the censored columns blank, the regime had played a higher card by stationing its censors *sur le champ* to check each page as it went to press. The press was cowed, then broken. John Parker, Chairman of the Guild of Rhodesian Journalists, had his phone tapped, was shadowed by the Special Branch, arraigned under the Official Secrets Act, and imprisoned for refusing to divulge a source. Acquitted on appeal, he was then deported. Smith's Government had already closed down the *Daily News*, a paper owned by the Thomson organization and sympathetic – mainly for commercial reasons – to Joshua Nkomo's banned party, Zapu.

In 1972 the radical Catholic paper *Moto* was banned. Its successor, *Mambo*, was also banned. *Kristo*, next in line from the Mambo Press at Gwelo, was forbidden to print anything of a political complexion.

Albert Plangger, Director of the Mambo Press, is a small Swiss Bethlehem Father who looks a bit like Herbert Morrison. Twice convicted in court of subversion, he suffers what he calls 'intermittent' Special Branch surveillance. His fire-eating predecessor as director of the Mambo Press, Father Michael Traber, had printed an editorial in *Moto* denouncing the RF's 1969 constitution, thus incurring a prison sentence of six months with hard labour, conditionally suspended. *Moto* had also infuriated the Censors by printing a cartoon showing a white hand gripping a clutch of writhing African bodies from which both sweat and blood were dripping. Caption: 'The proposed constitution will ensure that government will be retained in responsible hands.' It was typical of Traber, a witty, chain-smoking, passionate radical, and it was equally typical of the regime to deport him. There were emotional scenes at the airport, with black friends and white (including Bishop Donal Lamont) singing 'Ishe Komborera Afrika'.

The repression continued. In November 1972 Plangger was given a suspended prison sentence for printing in *Moto* an article by Bishop Lamont in which the Irish Carmelite wrote: 'Dogs and guns and internment and restriction are all that the Rhodesian Front Government has to keep it in power.' When the case came before the High Court, Justice Hector Macdonald detected in the article at least seven 'subversive' statements likely to excite disaffection against the Government or constitution.

Truth was no defence. In February 1973 Peter Niesewand, who worked for the BBC and several newspapers, including the *Guardian*, was thrown into prison in reprisal for having reported that Rhodesian troops were operating inside Mozambique in pursuit of guerrillas who threatened the supply routes to Beira and Lourenço Marques. Initially detained without charge or trial, Niesewand came across the names of forty-two African detainees chalked on a board in Gwelo prison. Although himself a well-informed reporter, he had never heard of a single one of them – publication of their names was forbidden. Niesewand was allowed newspapers in prison but only after they had been doctored to remove any reference to his own case. Finally brought to trial, Niesewand argued that his report had been accurate and that in any case it did not tell the 'terrorists' anything they did not already know.

'How do you know? Have you contact with terrorist organizations?' shouted Brendan Treacy, Director of Public Prosecutions (and later Attorney-General).

8. hot pursuit

It was during 1976 that white Rhodesians were shaken from their complacency. In over three years the guerrillas had managed to kill only eighty-four members of the security forces, at a cost of 734 of their own men. By 11 November, however, when the Liberty bell tolled twelve times to herald the twelfth year of unilaterally declared Independence, 171 members of the security forces and 1,965 guerrillas had died; even more disturbing, fifty-four white civilians had been murdered. Having closed the Mozambique border in March 1976, seizing Rhodesian rolling-stock and cutting the artery by which Rhodesia exported 40 per cent of her goods, President Samora Machel delivered increasingly bellicose speeches while mortar bombs rained down on Rhodesian border posts. Five white servicemen from Umtali were killed in the course of a single mortar attack.

Smith and his Defence Minister, P. K. van der Byl, came under increasing criticism for what most whites angrily regarded as a 'no win' strategy; guerrilla ambushes against cars travelling along the main roads intensified the desire to hit back in 'hot pursuit'. On 9 August, the Rhodesians, capitalizing on months of planning and the interrogation of prisoners, and greatly inspired by Israel's spectacular Entebbe raid which had occurred only a month earlier, crossed the Mozambique border at Penhalonga and staged a devastating assault on Nyadzonia camp fifty kilometres to the north. Seventy-two men were involved. Wearing Frelimo uniforms, singing Frelimo songs and completely hoodwinking the guards at Nyadzonia, the attackers (who included white troops with blackened faces) were able to stage a holocaust, killing an estimated 1,200 people. Teurai Ropa Nhongo, at that time a 19-year-old commander at Nyadzonia and later (Zimbabwe's first woman Minister, claims that a Zanla commander called Nyati played a treacherous role and led the disguised Rhodesian troops to the camp on a day of annual Zanu celebration. While insisting that no one at the camp was armed, Mrs

Nhongo does refer to military and political training there, to cadres and platoons.

Salisbury claimed that 300 terrorists had been killed and described the camp as a strictly military one. A Dutch TV crew which was granted access to Nyadzonia (or 'Nhazonian' as some papers called it) on 14 August reckoned at least 1,000 had been killed and 1,500 injured. The UN High Commission for Refugees then announced that Nyadzonia was strictly one of its refugee camps. An official reported: 'Visit to camp was desolating. Ten mass graves were covered by bulldozers . . . dried up blood stains on the ground, stench from graves, thousands of bullet shells. . . . Counted dead so far 675 but more likely have died in surrounding bush. . . . Wounded 295 in Chimoio and 204 in temporary camp. In addition 176 serious cases in Beira hospital. . . .' On 25 August the UN High Commissioner issued a statement: 'It escapes my understanding as to what those responsible for it thought they were accomplishing through such an atrocity.'

The Rhodesians weren't having any of this. They produced 'documents', including a list of male Zimbabweans undergoing military training at Nyadzonia with their 'chimurenga' names. In fact Nyadzonia was neither exclusively a military nor a refugee camp. Operating under Zipa military control, it contained about 3,000 Africans mainly drawn from the eastern district of Rhodesia, approximately one-third of whom were undergoing military training. The disastrous consequences of failing to separate women, children and old people from military trainees were again to be tragically demonstrated more than a year later, in November 1977, when the Rhodesians struck at Chimoio. Even allowing for the administrative difficulties of transporting non-military refugees further into the interior of Mozambique, the Zimbabweans were too slow to forgo the comforts of organic community life; too reluctant to live without women; too long in realizing that by walking across the border they did not acquire immunity from attack and persecution.

Immediate retaliation followed. On 10 August Umtali became the first Rhodesian city to suffer bombardment. Mortar bombs rained down on the Greenside and Darlington suburbs, hitting half-a-dozen houses but killing no one. The Cecil Hotel became an evacuation centre. It was enough to kindle a pseudo 'spirit of the Blitz'. Two hundred girls from the (white) Girls' High School in green skirts and white blouses, plus seventy from the Boys' High wearing straw boaters, marched along Main Street bearing placards saying 'We will not be moved', 'Umtali can take it' and 'Rhodesia is super'. Singing heartily, they were preceded by a military Land-Rover bearing a heavy machine-gun and the Headmistress of the Girls' High School.

Rhodesian manhood was not found wanting. A new generation of heroes arose worthy in spirit and deed of the legendary figures of 1893 and 1896: Allan Wilson, Major Forbes, the Mazoe patrol. But the new war of counter-insurgency was not directed against 'savages' or 'niggers': the new enemy was 'external terrorism'. As Lt-Gen. Peter Walls, Victor Ludorum at Plumtree School and now Commander of the Army, announced: 'We will not be pushed around or surrender to any Marxist-inspired land-grab. We are going to fight. We are no wishy-washy colonialists with no stake here.'

Between May 1976 and February 1977 Sgt John McKelvie was involved in fourteen 'contacts' in each of which he displayed 'leadership, initiative and gallantry', accounting for a total of sixty 'terrorists'. Most spectacular was his performance on 9 November 1976 when he and seven men were dropped by helicopter into a terrorist-dominated area. Although the chopper was grounded and despite lack of air support, McKelvie and his men killed eighteen terrorists in the space of three hours. Silver Cross of Rhodesia for Sgt McKelvie.

Silver Cross, too, for Lt Michael Stobart-Vallaro who showed 'a complete disregard for his personal safety' during a contact on 28 April, leading his men forward through heavy small-arms and mortar fire. Later, on 6 March 1977, accompanied only by a tracker and two soldiers, he pursued a large force of terrorists and then, though wounded by bullets and shrapnel, personally dispatched three terrorists at close quarters – five to ten yards.

Close-quarters heroism brought Lt Graham Schrag the Bronze Cross. Leading his platoon in a two-phase, set-piece attack on 31 October, he took an enemy base camp under heavy fire, then charged into a river bed alone and killed two terrorists at a range of 'less than ten yards'.

On the morning of 16 December Lt Graham Murdoch discovered that his 'stop group' had unwittingly penetrated an enemy base camp during the night. Although wounded during the ensuing contact, Murdoch remained in full command, 'killed five terrorists' and directed three air strikes before leading a successful assault on the enemy position. Bronze Cross.

Why young Rhodesian warriors were held to have achieved such peaks of bravery against a foe notorious for his cowardice, for directing his attacks against old women and babies, for shamelessly 'gapping' it at the first sign of resistance, must remain a puzzle. How would the white commandos have fared against an enemy enjoying total dominance of the sky, exclusive possession of the deadly air strike; an enemy able to ferry out its wounded by helicopter rather than drag bleeding shattered limbs through hundreds of miles of bush?

Any Rhodesian could tell you that the Charlie Tangos (communist terror-ists) attacked only crèches and the geriatric wards of hospitals. But WO 2

Malcolm Forbes's citation for bravery refers to a heavy terrorist attack on his base camp and the deaths of four men in his unit. We learn that Cpl Noel Ross-Johnson's army base camp was attacked on four out of six nights in February 1977 (the corporal proved his valour by repeatedly climbing a 30-m radio mast to direct retaliatory fire, despite acute danger from recoil-less rifle and small-arms fire).

Among the greatest of Rhodesia's modern heroes was Maj. Patrick Armstrong, who held the crucial position of Commanding Officer, Support Commando, 1 Rhodesian Light Infantry from June 1975 to May 1977. In the course of some forty contacts about 250 terrorists were killed: even when wounded on 9 November while airborne in his command helicopter, he continued to direct the operation 'with outstanding ability in the elimination of twenty-four terrorists'. Not only was Armstrong made an Officer of the Legion of Merit, in September 1979 he received the supreme accolade when he was appointed Commanding Officer of the Selous Scouts.

9. kith and kin

'RLI Support Commando.' These are the words carved, beneath a rampant eagle, on the gravestone of Richard Cecil.

'The grass is so thick that a man a few feet away is quite invisible and most Rhodesian Army casualties are taken at this range,' wrote Cecil in a dispatch from the Mount Darwin area, published in *The Times* on 15 June 1976. Seven months later a further battle report from Cecil appeared in the *Daily Telegraph*:

'The fighting is often a series of duels. I remembered how the soldier had died the day before. A guerrilla had jumped out of the long grass two yards in front of him and cut him down with a burst of automatic fire.'

Fourteen months later Cecil himself was to die in identical circumstances.

Richard Cecil was an unusual reporter in several respects. Totally committed to the cause of 'Rhodesia' (the single word was preferred to 'white Rhodesia'), he frequently carried a gun and was prepared to use it. The second son of the Marquess of Salisbury, the unreconstructed champion of old-fashioned Tory imperialism, of 'kith and kin', he was descended from Queen Elizabeth I's great Minister, William Cecil (Lord Burleigh). In the centre of Salisbury stands Cecil Square; it was here that the Pioneer Column halted on 12 September 1890 and named the site of the future capital after Richard Cecil's great-great-grandfather, Lord Salisbury, the British Prime Minister of the day.

Inspired by Winston Churchill's youthful embrace of both the pen and the sword, Richard Cecil also sought a career in the House of Commons. Sent down from Oxford after one year, he had been commissioned into the Grenadier Guards, served in the Middle East and done three tours of duty in Ulster, where, in 1973, he was mentioned in dispatches. After leaving the army (frustrated, it is said, by the restraints imposed upon its counter-terrorist tactics), he gravitated naturally to Rhodesia, where his family owned property on a large scale (there are suburbs of Salisbury named after the English country homes of the Cecils – Hatfield and Cranborne, for example). Even so, it initially took six months to convince a suspicious military bureaucracy that he should be the first British journalist permitted to witness hand-to-hand fighting at the front. A helpful factor was his friendship with P. K. van der Byl, the Minister of Defence, a rampant, pseudo-Anglicized social snob from the Cape who later described Cecil as possessing 'everything that made Britain great and built the British Empire'. Tall, rangy and strong, Cecil was a capable pilot, an ace parachutist and, by all accounts, an affable fellow.

His reports were spectacular and well written. On 26 February 1977 the *Telegraph* carried this:

'My "stick" was next in. We prepared to sprint down the landing apron as the first helicopter returned from the contact area. . . . Only Cpl Hennie Du Toit, commanding the "stick", had headphones to listen to the briefing from the contact area. The only order he gave his men was to jab his finger towards a narrow strip of bush between some maize fields as we swooped down to land. Everyone knew what he meant. . . . A huge explosion and a black hole appears in the ground to my right. Cpl Du Toit is thrown backwards and at the same time the bush in front of us erupts as unseen automatic weapons open up on us.'

At this juncture a young officer called in an air strike (favourite resort of the white knights when dealing with stubborn black pawns). The rockets from the diving aircraft 'passed low over our heads before crashing into their targets'. But the pawns displayed tenacity: 'Chinese stick grenades started exploding just in front of us,' wrote Cecil, 'showering the crouching troops with mud and debris. . . . Now the light was fading and I edged out of cover to try and get film of the enemy.' Spotted by a guerrilla machine-gunner some thirty yards away, Cecil recoiled as bullets splattered into the mud directly in front of where he lay. By the next morning the action was completed, with a haul of six dead 'terrs' for three wounded Rhodesians.

On 14 October, the *Telegraph* ran a report sent by Cecil from the Operation Repulse theatre in the south-east. It began: 'We dropped from 500 feet. The helicopter had gone in first and the fire-fight had already started. . . .

Inside the aircraft (a Dakota), 20-odd paratroopers stood shoulder to shoulder. . . . Canary yellow flashes on their black helmets proclaimed "Support Commando, Rhodesian Light Infantry". Most of them were wearing shorts and teeshirts, and their legs and arms were smeared with stripes of camouflage cream. . . . A despatcher teased one of the paras: "Your 13th jumpy? You'd better give me that watch, now." When the green light came on over the door 15 men hurtled out in eight seconds as the despatchers screamed "Go, go, go!"'

The hill below was now criss-crossed with tracer bullets. A mere seven seconds after jumping – 150 metres being a dangerously low altitude from which to parachute – Cecil missed a nasty-looking stump and 'rolled comfortably on some soft dirt on the edge of an African kraal'. The battle continued for six hours as the sun turned the surrounding rocks to furnace heat. Cecil celebrated the resourceful audacity of these 'Rhodesian boy-veterans' whose 'fitness and quick wits' time and again turned almost certain death into miraculous escape. When the action finished twelve guerrillas were dead. But there was no respite for the tired paras. Thirty more guerrillas had been sighted. Within an hour they were airborne again and heading for a new jump.

The paradox of Richard Cecil's reporting was that it implicitly undermined the myths it was intended to foster: although heroism is possible against a cowering foe (when flushing him from a cave for example), it's hard to accumulate medals when taking on panic-stricken zombies who 'gap' it at the first sign of trouble.

In the autumn of 1978 Thames Television's *TV Eye* screened a film about the Rhodesian security forces by Nick Downie and Richard Cecil – a passionate tribute to the warriors holding barbarism at bay. Though spectacular at a technical level (parachute drops, hand-to-hand fighting, guerrillas not merely dead but writhing in their last spasms), Downie's film, which he himself narrated, displayed the same ambiguity towards violence that characterized the run of cheap Rhodesian war novels. On the one hand the viewer was invited to vomit at the sight of the molten corpses of villagers burnt alive in their huts by terrorists of the Patriotic Front; on the other hand the viewer was required to empathize with the ruthless killer instincts of the white knights and to exult in the blood and gore, the ripped flesh of dead 'terrs' as they are dragged by their heels to the helicopters or hung like meat for the benefit of villagers.

Downie and Cecil revelled in the daring and panache of Rhodesian counter-insurgency – the parachute drops from 150 metres, the spectacular free falls from 6,000 metres by the SAS over Mozambique. Depicted as worthy, dependable, were the black troops of the Rhodesian African Rifles, whose supportive role was cited in support of Rhodesia's 'non-racial' image – this mythology reaches back to the nineteenth-century cult of the 'loyal' or 'friendly' native askari. By contrast the guerrilla, careless with his weapon, amateurish in his habit of carrying an operational diary, is granted no relationship with the rural population other than one of terror.

Richard Cecil is shown in the film helping to lift a mortally wounded black machine-gunner shot through the head by a guerrilla. But Cecil did not live to see the completion of the film. On 20 April he was on the most dangerous of locations, moving with a line of ten soldiers towards a suspected guerrilla camp in the Mtoko TTL when a lone insurgent suddenly rose from the long grass only seven metres away and opened fire. Hit in the legs, chest and stomach, Richard Cecil died a few moments later, the first journalist to be killed in the Rhodesian war. He was 30 years old.

Four days later his body was flown to Britain and on 27 April more than 500 people attended his funeral service in the thirteenth-century parish church of Cranborne, in Dorset. This was home territory: in 1603 the Manor and Lordship of Cranborne had been granted by James I to Sir Robert Cecil, later Viscount Cranborne and Earl of Salisbury. The present Marquess of Salisbury, Richard Cecil's father, is patron of the church.

Richard Valentine Cecil was buried close to the tower at the west end of the church in a small group of Cecil graves. Two buglers from the Grenadier Guards sounded the last post. The engraving on the stone also bears allegiance to a second regiment: beneath a rampant eagle are carved the words 'RLI Support Commando'.

10. head down and chin up

It's Sunday, around three in the afternoon, time for RBC's version of the BBC's long-running radio request programme, *Family Favourites*. In a tone of unflagging pertness the female announcer relays messages of love and comfort to our men in the bush. 'Love from mum and the two little ones . . . take great care and god bless from Nigel, Niddy, Albert, Lynette . . . super to have had you home, can't wait till the next time, from Lynn and Sharon . . . praying for your safe return, love Donna . . . all these messages for Junior Commandant Peter Donaldson. Head down and chin up, Peter, and keep out of range of those mortar attacks!'

Courage, *esprit de corps*, in the face of private anguish: on 18 May 1976 the death in action had been reported of Captain Leon Pitch, 35, a territorial, father of three and son of Alderman Ivor Pitch, a former Mayor of Salisbury and a staunch supporter of the RF. His mother, Mrs Chummy Pitch, opened the Goodies for Troopies Centre the year after her son's death, starting off with $(R)840 collected during a golf tournament and subsequently depending mainly on goods handed in, gratis, to the depot on Stanley Avenue. Christmas parcels sent to 2,000 servicemen in the bush included condensed milk, radios, cigarettes, biltong (dried meat), razor-blades, games, balaclavas and mittens. 'We can never thank these boys enough for what they are doing,' said Mrs Pitch with a big smile for the front page.

'The sight of soldiers always stirs the female heart,' wrote a woman in the *Shangani District Digest*. 'This is an emotion as old as history. But when the local recce. stick – rugged, hairy, weary, hungry – pitches up at the farm back/front door (most farms have back/front doors) I get positively weepy. It's one of the nicest sights in the world. Besides wanting to burst into tears of pure pleasure and patriotism, I also wish (a) that I'd cooked roast or T-bones with chip-potatoes instead of stupid macaroni cheese, (b) that I'd had time to put on my best dress and lipstick, (c) that I'd remembered to put the beer on ice, and (d) that I could write poetry. Recce. sticks always make me want to burst into verse.'

(And more in this vein. . . .)

The white Rhodesian female also sublimates her energies in physical exercise. She tends to be a very sporting girl: the ethic of competitive sport is drilled into her at Mount Pleasant, Roosevelt, Oriel, Arundel, Queen Elizabeth, Girls' High, Umtali Girls', Mabelreign, Chaplin, Chisipite and Evelin. Swimming at the Les Brown Pool, dressage at the Oakley Equestrian Club, show-jumping at the Oldenby Livery Stables or the Ascot Equestrian Club, horse trials at Lark Hill, tennis, squash, diving, hockey – she does it.

On Sunday morning the top women's hockey teams gather at the Old Hararians ground. The first match begins early, to beat the heat of the day, which becomes oppressive by eleven and insufferable by noon. The teams turn out in traditional English gear, flared skirts and long socks (but with black servants to do the washing and ironing). Old Georgians, in an all-white strip, tackle Postals (yellow shirts, green skirts), watched by a scattering of spectators who have brought their own fold-up chairs. The game is fast, intense and no one argues with the ref.

The second match of the morning is played in a temperature of twenty-five degrees centigrade and the girls soon turn beetroot pink. Salisbury Sports Club (red and white) are challenged by Police (all yellow), the players are fleet and agile, whack! wham! against the goalie's pads. Flick, twist, turn, down the wing, cross, shoot!

Some of these girls will be selected for the national hockey squad. Others will make the B team, the Flame Lilies.

Afterwards, a bath, drinks, a cigarette, an afternoon with the kids and then, maybe, whatever man is not away in the bush. 'How do you expect me to survive on my own for six months?' Exercise is not enough.

11. if I've told him once

It was a hard life, of course: the Pioneer men and women were for the most part extraordinarily tough people, willing and able to cope with malaria, sleeping-sickness, tsetse fly, flood and drought, elementary sanitation, lions in the bush (no joke in the early days), and ox-wagons which moved forward at three kilometres an hour along 'roads' that had to be hacked out of the scrubland. The Pioneers lived in huts and rondavels built out of pole and dagga; their nights were plagued by fat mosquitoes, they ate and drank from kipper tins and old cans, there were no doctors, no dentists. Natives not always friendly.

Even between the two world wars life remained hard. Lawrence Vambe recalls the footsore white vagabonds searching for gold in the Goromonzi area, the local traders and shopkeepers who eked a living by learning the local African language and customs and by selling penny buns or sweets. There was Mr Pondo, Mr One Pound, who travelled on an old rusty bike with a wicker basket, leather bag and two haversacks, one at his back and the other over his chest. Whatever Mr Pondo offered for sale, his starting price was invariably one pound sterling. Other poor whites worked on the roads and railways with pick and shovel for five shillings a day, living under flattened tar drums and lining up for rations at the local magistrate's office.

No one who reads Doris Lessing's remarkable novel *The Grass is Singing* will forget the grinding poverty of Richard and Mary Turner, their desperate farm at Ngesi, the tiny house with its tin roof and terrible heat, the inevitable failure of Dick's farming schemes and calculations, hard though he toils. Yet this manifest, grinding poverty is *relative*: the Turners depend on hired labour, and if a poor white labourer earns five shillings a day the Turners' houseboy gets only one-tenth as much, fifteen shillings a month. And Mary Turner, even though she was brought up in an exposed village backed by a file of bunchy gum-trees with a square of dust that was always swirling and settling as the ox-wagons passed through, even though she grew up in a place where most faces were black, nevertheless regards all blacks with distaste and a deep, hysterical fear. The greater the poverty she experiences as a farmer's wife, the greater her hostility towards the blacks – lazy liars and cheats. Not until her husband falls ill can she ever bring herself to go out to the fields and confront the black labour force: soon she is screaming at them, cutting their pay for being late, whipping one of them in the face. Inside the tin shack (where she sleeps for three hours every hot afternoon out of sheer boredom) she loses one houseboy after another: 'If I've told him once, I've told him fifty times!' she yells.

Whatever Karl Marx may have said about employers and workers, about 'surplus value' and exploitation, he did not concern himself with the intimate psychology of the relationship. When labour (or labour power) is bought and sold for a wage the two contracting parties invariably experience difficulty in perceiving the other's humanity, the totality of the other's needs and fears, because each views the other through the narrow prism of I Want. What Lessing's Mrs Turner wants is a polite, clean, healthy, energetic, efficient, patient, dependable domestic machine on two legs who understands English, needs little sleep, little food, has no children to feed, and does not 'smell' even though he is happy to sleep in a hole in the ground.

When she doesn't get one her only resource is rage, a fury compounded by a glimmering suspicion that if she learned the houseboy's language (or 'lingo' – can that maddening monkey chatter she hears among the black women be dignified with the name of 'language'?) then she would do a lot better. But she can't, or won't, because she is trapped in the cultural web of domination: if she ever steps over on to her houseboy's terrain, enters the mysterious, threatening corridors of his humanity, he will merely laugh at her commands, rape her instantly, then cut her throat. Or so she senses. She suffers from a collective hysteria: the respect of the native, like the respect of a powerful dog, would vanish at the first sign of 'weakness'.

The post-war British immigrant was in flight from austerity, red tape, rationing, bleak winters, fuel shortages, the whole package described as 'socialism'; from higher income tax, nationalization, the health service; from smog, the cold war and national service. A number of RAF men who came out to train at Thornhill as pilots saw a 'land of opportunity' and developed a yearning for sunshine, wide open spaces, sport, hunting, non-unionized labour and cheap domestic servants. In colonial Africa the humble white man became a Boss; the African was obliged to call him just that, 'Baas'.

A land of 'opportunity' is invariably a land of opportunists, of mobile, itinerant people who are willing to 'have a go', to 'try their luck'. Some will sweat doggedly to build a farm out of barren bush, others will move in and out of Salisbury like gadflies, sharp and shifty city slickers, confidence men, grafters. The officer class moving on from India or Kenya settled in and

55

around Umtali. No fewer than 125,000 Europeans arrived in Rhodesia between 1945 and 1951, while 53,000 quit. Less than one-third of Rhodesia's whites had been born there. But they lost no time in calling themselves 'Rhodesians' and referring to 'everything we have built up here' (for which 'your native' was notoriously, congenitally, ungrateful).

The immigrants created suburbs of neat hedges and flowering shrubs. Few houses occupied more than one storey, land was so plentiful. In 1951 the average European household employed two black domestic servants. In certain respects the Rhodesian way of life was more American than British: competitive, conformist, mobile, rather ostentatious; virtually every family owned a car, a situation it would take Britain a further twenty years to achieve. As in America there was urban sprawl, home ownership was the norm, public transport was almost non-existent. Whereas in Britain social classes 4 and 5 accounted for just under 30 per cent of men in employment, among white Rhodesians the figure was 3 per cent. So white Rhodesians were a cut above the average in skill and initiative; quite a deep cut. When they entered a shop they got immediate service, while African customers stood aside for them; in Post Offices they were served at separate counters. It was only 'sensible' that Africans should be legally debarred from drinking anything but kaffir beer.

For whites living in the suburbs life became increasingly soft in the Federation era, the 1950s. Wages and salaries were about 50 per cent higher than in England. By 1963 one out of every five families in Salisbury had installed its own swimming-pool. Barbecues, fold-up tables, easy chairs, sunshades and iced drinks – this was patio life in the evening, at the weekend. Servants were paid £4 a month. Yet the myth of the Pioneer people died hard and Salisbury schoolboys wore wideawake hats thought suitable for life in the veld at the turn of the century.

Racist jokes about Dr Banda of Malawi (later reincarnated as a hero of responsible moderation) abounded. Nationalist political activity in the townships was derided, belittled, its intimidatory aspects (real enough) vastly exaggerated: the average housewife delighted in reporting that her 'boy' carried the cards of both political parties to avoid getting beaten up. Pay the blacks more? They'd just spend it on beer.

Almost every letter to the press stressed (a) that Rhodesia is a beautiful country, and (b) that many Rhodesians fought for Britain during the second world war – a fact as irrelevant for dispossessed, disfranchised blacks as the Holocaust in Europe is for dispossessed Palestinian refugees. But this is the perennial problem: the white colonist penetrates distant lands bursting with his own story, a drama utterly obscure to his victims.

John Parker saw a 'Land of Opportunity' poster in the window of Rhodesia House in the Strand. In March 1953 Parker set sail for Cape Town with his wife and two small children, taking a carry-cot and less than £100. They were heading for Rhodesia, where you could buy a packet of fifty cigarettes for only two shillings and ninepence.

In the white suburbs of Bulawayo people lived in bungalows set in 1,500 square metres of garden – the Parkers were overwhelmed by those gardens, by the orange, yellow and purple bougainvillaeas, by the violent scarlet of the tulip-trees, by the wonderful displays of jacaranda, by the flame-trees at the roadside. Stakes cut from mulberry-trees sprouted and bore fruit the following year. The Parkers' modest little garden provided a paradise of oranges, grapefruit, avocado pears, potatoes the year round, while beans, peas and carrots flourished in the chicken compost, as did cucumbers and tomatoes.

The Parkers joined the master race. Membership was obligatory. In Bulawayo's buses a partition separated the upholstered 'European' seats from the cramped wooden seats set aside for blacks. (In Salisbury a municipal by-law was passed making it an offence for an African not to step off the sidewalk to let a European pass.) The Parkers' servant lived in a 'kia', a small room of unplastered brick: one addressed the cookboy and the gardenboy in 'kitchen kaffir' or 'fanagalo', a word derived from 'fanaga-lo', meaning 'like this this'. Thus one would say (or snap) 'make these beds fanagalo' with an accompanying gesture to indicate whether the beds should be made or stripped for laundry. The flow of command in kitchen kaffir, as recalled by John Parker in his book *Rhodesia: Little White Island*, sounded something like this:

'Fanagalo carpets checka outside and bomba them, fanagalo beds jusnow, fanagalo vegetables mush and puttem onna stove, gahli, gahli mind.'

The white Rhodesian inhabited a world within a world. His children attended (at virtually no cost to the parents) racially exclusive schools. Only on farms did small white children play with small black children; but such intercourse stopped with adolescence. Social clubs, sports clubs, cinemas, swimming-pools – these were all built by whites (using black labour) for the exclusive use of whites, and whites alone.

The white man and his 'missus' or 'meddem' knew that all the rules and regulations were necessary and sensible. Your African had to carry a certificate of registration which allotted him to an African rural area under the Land Apportionment Act, even if he had been born in a town. (This corresponds to the South African 'Bantustan' system today.) Thus the African entered an urban area not by right, not as a free man, but on sufferance, bound by a labour contract: to enter Highfield or Harare, for example, the

African had to produce a Current Visiting Pass or a Town Pass to Seek Work. If he got a job then he had to carry a Certificate of Service or a Certificate of Self-Employment. A woman could not live with her man in a township unless she possessed a Certificate of Recognition of an Approved Wife. This whole system of supervision and surveillance was somewhat liberalized in the early 1960s, but extensive documentation was still required.

To obtain all these pieces of paper, Best Beloved, your African had to wait in a queue. To wait and wait and wait. To stand in a line, sleep in a line, silently, patiently, humbly, uncomplainingly, day and night. And when his moment finally came, he must remove his hat, shuffle his feet and meekly address the bored, arrogant, red-faced, sun-sore white man through an often officious black interpreter intent on proving his worth and his loyalty to the white man by treating other blacks like shit. The District Commissioner would say to the official interpreter: 'Inodeyiko pano?', meaning 'What does *it* want here?' The DC had to be addressed as 'Nkosi', or 'lord', and an assistant DC as 'Nkosana' or 'junior lord'.

Go away, you haven't got the right document to obtain a document. Go away and get it. Walk, walk. Then come back and stand in the line all over again.

12. a blocked windpipe – Operation Overlord

The Catholic Commission for Justice and Peace became the thorn in the flesh. Set up by the Bishops' Conference in an attempt to acquaint white Catholics with the Church's modern teaching about social and racial justice, the JPC soon became, under the chairmanship of the outspoken, abrasive Bishop of Umtali, Donal Lamont, a point of witness for the cruelties suffered by rural Rhodesia. Complaints were heard from the tribespeople of Chiweshe who had suffered communal fines and the confiscation of their cattle – one of the main punitive tactics used to crush Shona dissidence in the 1890s.

In April 1975 Father Dieter Scholz, a German Jesuit serving as the JPC's deputy chairman, left Salisbury for London, carrying dossiers on atrocities committed by the security forces. Although Scholz discovered on arrival that the vital manuscript had been removed from his suitcase by the Rhodesian CID, a month later *The Man in the Middle* was published, bringing to public attention for the first time the appalling conditions prevailing in the protected villages and the brutal methods employed by the security forces in the war zones.

Simultaneously the JPC's lawyers were preparing private legal actions against the ineffable Minister of Law and Order, Desmond Lardner-Burke – a man with the flushed complexion and silver-smooth hair of a saloon-bar bigot – two of which related to the demonstrable appetite of a Mount Darwin policeman called Kruger for torturing kaffirs, coons and munts under interrogation. To kill these legal actions and their as yet unborn offspring stone dead, the Government rushed through its notorious Compensation and Indemnity Act. As President John Wrathall explained to the House of Assembly, 'It is unfortunately inevitable that anti-terrorist activity by the security forces sometimes causes injury and loss to civilians. It is wrong that bona fide actions done in the national interest should lead to litigation against those alleged to be responsible.' On 2 July, van der Byl told the House that villages found harbouring guerrillas 'will be bombed and destroyed in any manner which the commander on the spot considers desirable'.

On 22 July 1976 African and European soldiers surrounded a house at Mtize Chikata Kraal, Mtoko. They set up an office in one of the huts and proceeded to question people, one by one, including a boy, Athanasio Mutikiti; after quite some time another boy came running to Athanasio's father to ask him if his son ever had fits – in any case Athanasio had just died. The soldiers allowed the father inside the hut where Athanasio lay stripped naked and soaking wet; the soldiers explained that they had wanted to keep him cool; the body was removed to Bindura Hospital; the father was told that his son had died from a blocked windpipe 'when the fit began'.

All quite clear: the soldiers had brought about the death of Athanasio Mutikiti. To achieve any form of redress his father would not merely have to prove this (how could he?), he would also have to prove that the soldiers had acted in bad faith, *mala fide*, and how could he do that, how could he know more about the true intentions of white soldiers than they did themselves? Besides, nothing would bring back his son.

Parading kids before corpses, or corpses before kids, was common practice. It happened in 1976 at Chikore mission school, 230 kilometres south of Umtali, when on three occasions pupils were shown bodies which the security forces had brought to the school and dumped in the parking lot – genitals exposed, fingers cut off from the knuckles, horrifying. Not surprisingly, 140 of the school's 380 pupils responded to this treatment by walking across the border into Mozambique in July 1976, whereupon the Government closed the school and expelled five teachers, including John and Joy Lowe, who had worked at the mission for eighteen years and whose sixteen-year-old daughter was the only white pupil at the school.

As of December 1976 International Defence and Aid could name 1,839 'political prisoners' in Rhodesia. Some had been convicted of an offence –

usually 'terrorism or aiding and abetting terrorists' – in a court of law. Others were detained without trial: this had been the fate of most of the leaders of the nationalist movement, including Mugabe, Nkomo and Sithole, as well as the future President of Zimbabwe, the Reverend Canaan Banana.

A man might be detained in a variety of circumstances. Some had already served sentences after being convicted of politically related offences: no sooner were they released than they were detained indefinitely without trial. Yet another category had actually been acquitted in court, whereupon the police, impatient with such unrewarding concessions to due process, promptly detained them. Publication of the names of detainees was not permitted; they became non-persons.

The relatives of these non-persons wrote for help to Christian Care and the International Defence and Aid Fund. From Mount Darwin, a former prisoner, now released but living under restriction, wrote in March 1977: 'I am here to tell you my life history in my home land Zimbabwe. I am a sickling man but out of that I tried to fight for my country. But the country I got is prison. I did nothing wrong . . . I have been in that prison for 8½ years. From there I was sent to Wha Wha Detention Camp. Now I have been . . . detained at my home . . . How am I going to plough my field? . . . Please I beg for your help in any way.'

Many of these African petitioners invested a touching faith in a highly formalized style of writing, no doubt the help of local scribes was enlisted: 'I am here kindly pleading or entreating your good offices . . . I do not doubt that you will attend to this matter promptly as it is the mission of your Organisation, dear Sir, to assist those in desperate need. . . . I strongly appreciate to hear such a positive acceptance of assisting me on behalf of my families and the furthering up of my children. . . . I am a lady of 9 years old. I wish to apply for the financial assistance and aid. My father and mother died. I am with grandfather and grandmother. My grandfather is at . . . prison. Our home was burnt by soldiers. . . . We are in the Cage (protected village) where we cannot do anything to help ourself.'

Unable to drive the guerrillas from among the people, the regime decided to remove the people from the guerrillas. This operation, which was undertaken by the Ministry of Internal Affairs (red berets) supported by the army and police, was directed locally by the eight Provincial and sixty District Commissioners. They duly uprooted half a million people from their villages and fields, tore them from their ancestral moorings, and herded them at gunpoint into 'protected villages' (PVs).

It was this operation, rather than the lack of the vote, which proved to the native that he was a second-class man, without civil rights, without property rights, without the right of appeal, entirely subject to the command, or whim, of white masters. The PVs proved conclusively to the peasants that the guerrillas, the vakhomana, the 'boys', deserved their allegiance.

There were precedents: such villages had been established with some success during the Malayan counter-insurgency operation in the 1950s; later the Portuguese set up *aldeamentos* in Mozambique to combat Frelimo; the United States had developed similar strategies in Vietnam. In Rhodesia the first PVs were installed in the north-east: by the end of 1974, 70,000 people had been herded into thirty-six 'keeps', of which twenty-one were sited in the Chiweshe TTL, six in Madziwa, the rest in the Zambezi Valley. As the war escalated the programme spread down the eastern border to the south-east. By the middle of 1978 some 580,000 people, or about 11·5 per cent of the entire peasant population of the reserves, were living in some 200 PVs.

In April 1974, 255 Africans, including forty-seven women and 187 children, had been evicted from Musiwa village in the guerrilla-saturated Madziwa TTL, south of Mount Darwin, and transported hundreds of miles to a PV near Beitbridge. Their cattle were sold, their crops and huts destroyed. Indeed, they themselves were moved like cattle as a punishment for helping and harbouring guerrillas. Operation Overlord involved removing the entire population of Chiweshe from their villages, fields, stores, schools and churches, tearing them up by the roots and then dumping them down on alien, barren ground without shelter or poles to build huts. Spokesmen for the Salvation Army and other agencies of relief appealed urgently for blankets and warm clothing: children in particular were at risk.

When Coenraad Brand, a young sociologist at the University of Rhodesia, addressed the ninth World Congress of Sociology at Uppsala, Sweden, in August 1978, he argued, very persuasively, that the 'keep' was essentially a variant of an old white strategy in southern Africa, a strategy exemplified in the mine compounds with their military discipline, fines and floggings, as well as their more subtle methods of manipulating the labour force: company-store credit, the control of beer brewing, of prostitution and dagga (marijuana) supplies. Brand wrote: 'The Keep Commander has his counterpart in the Compound Manager. The headman and chief in the keep have their counterparts in the "boss boy" or "old hand" of the labour compound and the Advisory Board of the township.'

The inmates of the keeps were issued with numbered identity bracelets. The old man sits outside his hut, half blind with trachoma, the inner surface of the lids marked by granular excrescences. The schoolteacher interprets for him: 'They give us this bangle, they just want to know, if you haven't got this bangle, they can say that you are a terrorist, you see, if you've got this bangle

61

they can say you are a man who lives in this keep. Actually, if you have forgotten this thing, at your home, you can say you have lost your life because they can shoot you so they don't even ask.'

Even women and girls must carry passes. It has never been part of their experience to carry any form of documentation – that is a male prerogative – and so they lose the passes. Then they are punished. When relief agencies like the Red Cross arrive with food supplies, the women queue up and ululate, wailing and hooting, to show their relief and gratitude. In Madziwa TTL long queues formed outside the camp gates during the half-hour before the 6 p.m. curfew. The women and girls were required to shake the bottoms of their tunics and blouses as well as the hems of their skirts, before showing their identity papers and a matching bracelet. Boys were expected to jump with legs wide apart and arms extended, emitting a shout – a whole population ritually humiliated and forced to prove its 'innocence'.

Imagine a village in the middle of the African bush composed of 'stands', each fifteen metres square, shoulder to shoulder, surrounded by a high fence whose entire length is illuminated at night by outward-facing floodlights. Imagine propaganda from the African service of the Rhodesian Broadcasting Corporation being relayed from dawn until after dark along the keep's public-address system. No one can enter or leave without showing a pass. So rigorously is the movement of people and food controlled that a person who travelled 140 kilometres from Salisbury through tribal trust lands to a PV had his identity checked forty-one times. Summary searches of huts may take place at any time of day or night.

Few white Rhodesians protested. The supposedly liberal *Illustrated Life Rhodesia* published a favourable report of the PVs established in the Honde Valley: 'Until a ceasefire is secured, military priorities will inevitably mean that civilians will suffer restrictions on their freedom, not least for their own protection. . . . The only way to meet [guerrilla] strategy is by isolating the tribespeople – forcibly if necessary – from any chance of contact with the guerrillas.' (11 May 1978.) The magazine's reporter confidently concluded that the PV programme had won the Honde Valley, a fertile area of tea plantations north of Umtali, back from the terrorists. 'Today Rhodesian officials, civil and military, display it to the world as proof that counter-insurgency wars can be won.'

The native joins the Guard Force – a uniform and $(R)60 a month – and becomes a Collaborator. Examine photographs (if too young to recall the reality) of French *milice* giving the Hitler salute in occupied France. The native-in-uniform is elevated to a position of power over his brethren; he is the white man's surrogate and the European deliberately short-loans him a touch of his own authoritative magic. The District Assistant covets the wives and daughters of the villagers and he draws aside those he wants. He also takes radios, sums of money. . . .

At Shopo PV in Mazoe district the DA shot dead two brothers, mere kids, because one of them had carelessly leant against a bench on which a gun was resting. The white District Commissioner later offered $(R)100 for each child 'to offset funeral expenses and any inconvenience caused to the parents', the funds having been obtained from the Terrorist Victims' Relief Fund (which was capable of spending four times as much on sending a white war widow and her children for a fortnight's recuperative holiday in Durban).

Bhebe Saul, 23, leader of a section of five DAs on night patrol, arrived at a PV near Mtoko, demanded beer, drank several bottles, then started shooting indiscriminately, killing two women and a man. Another DA, Charles Muza, accused of rape, admitted previous convictions before joining the Guard Force. These cases came to court; most did not.

13. not in a thousand years

All roads from Salisbury led eventually to Pretoria. On 3 March Samora Machel, revolutionary President of Mozambique and veteran Frelimo guerrilla commander, had closed his border with Rhodesia, banned all communication by land or air, confiscated all Rhodesian assets – and effectively cut off the outlet of 40 per cent of Rhodesia's exports. All roads from Salisbury now led *directly* to Pretoria. If you imagine Rhodesia as a human head on the map – it more closely resembles a teapot – then the short stretch of border with South Africa (Kipling's great, grey-green greasy Limpopo) is the neck and South Africa's sombre, rheumy-eyed Afrikaner Prime Minister, Vorster, had his fist wrapped round Rhodesia's jugular.

But why should he wish to squeeze his little white ally to the north? The Portuguese empire had crumbled, black regimes professing Marxist ideology had taken power in Angola and Mozambique, guerrilla movements were gathering momentum in Rhodesia and Namibia, and the United States seemed paralysed in the face of the growing Soviet-Cuban presence. Surely Vorster would wish to bolster the white minority regime in Rhodesia, not merely out of sentiment but, more shrewdly, to maintain a buffer zone to the north and prevent South Africa's own guerrillas – the ANC army dedicated to liberating 'Azania' from apartheid, Bantustans, pass laws and minority rule – from establishing bases there?

However, the world is a complicated place, as Kipling's Elephant Child discovered when he reached the Limpopo and met the crocodile. In the white mansion called Libertas, perched high on the hills overlooking Pretoria, it became increasingly apparent to Johannes Balthazar Vorster that Ian Smith's white minority regime, recognized as it was by not a single country in the world (including Vorster's), cursed by illegality and condemned by the United Nations, was a mixed blessing. It raised tension in the area, radicalized the kaffirs, offered a pretext for Red Cubans to play Che Guevara in or around Mr Vorster's back yard, and gave the blacks of Soweto one more pretext for behaving badly (the famous township outside Johannesburg duly exploded in June: riots, strikes, arson, police repression, hundreds of dead and injured – all of it giving apartheid a bad name).

The Smith regime, then, had outlived its usefulness from Pretoria's point of view. For the past two-years Vorster had been wheeling and dealing with the black states, most notably with Kenneth Kaunda's Zambia, in the hope of achieving a settlement in Rhodesia: a gradual, orderly transition to some form of stable, 'moderate', pro-Western and preferably cosmetic black rule which would permit white enterprise and expertise to thrive north of the Limpopo and, simultaneously, join in a constellation of 'moderate' black states extending up to Zaire, all of them linked to South Africa by commercial ties, loans, credits, expertise – the benevolent paternalism for which your Boer is world-famous.

But it was hard going. The wrong blacks constantly threatened to subvert Vorster's great trek towards continental stability – blacks belonging to Zapu and Zanu, blacks operating from base camps in Tete and Gaza in Mozambique, blacks who made trips to Moscow (as Nkomo did) or Peking (as Mugabe did) or Havana (as they both did). Faced with rampant black nationalism, Johannes Balthazar Vorster preferred Ian Smith, leader of 270,000 white Rhodesians, even though Smith had in July 1976 categorically rejected the three principal recommendations of the Quenet Commission of Inquiry into Racial Discrimination, a timid body set up by the Rhodesian Government itself. No, he would not make agricultural land hitherto reserved for Europeans accessible to all races; no, there would be no common electoral roll; no, there would be no declaration of rights.

The right wing of the Rhodesian Front, pinning its faith in a policy of 'provincialization', hoped to imitate the South African Bantustans, or homelands, by putting the Rhodesian tribal trust lands nominally under the control of elected black assemblies, while retaining absolute white domination of the towns, the European farming areas, finance, defence and foreign affairs. Thus, the ostrich. By contrast the 'meritocrats' gathered round David Smith preferred to protect white power by a snail's-pace assimilation of the more conservative black élites, in the hope that Rhodesia would emerge in some distant future as a cross between Kenya and Malawi – and Rhodesia.

Vorster closed his fist round the jugular. Bannockburn – Rutenga – Beitbridge – and across the Limpopo into South Africa (Messina): down this single artery flowed the bulk of Rhodesia's exports and imports. Vorster squeezed, the goods began to pile up. The South Africans had been paying half of Rhodesia's defence budget (which had not yet reached its 1978 level of $(R)1 million a day, but was on the way there). Abruptly the money stopped. Weapons, ammunition, spare parts, they too dried up. On 26 August Pretoria withdrew all of its military personnel, including fifty helicopter pilots and technicians, plus twenty-six of the forty helicopters on loan to Rhodesia. South Africa was Rhodesia's Heart Machine; symptoms of cardiac arrest soon followed. By 20 August rail congestion had created inside South Africa a pile-up of Rhodesian goods worth £50 million; 16,000 tonnes of citrus fruits had to be buried by Hippo Valley Estates because they could not be exported; leaders of business and industry urgently petitioned Smith to act rapidly.

On 18 September Smith flew to Pretoria haunted by the shocking words of South Africa's Foreign Minister, Hilgard Muller: 'A solution to the Rhodesian issue on the basis of majority rule with adequate protection for minority rights is acceptable to the South African Government.' Smith took with him Commander of the Army Walls, Commissioner of Police Allum, Chief Justice Beadle and three senior Ministers. The American Secretary of State, Henry Kissinger was in town. Trailing badly behind Governor Jimmy Carter on the run-in to the Presidential election, Kissinger's master, President Gerald Ford, needed black votes, liberal votes: in short, he needed Smith's head.

Having held exhaustive discussions with Vorster, Kissinger informed Smith he was into a no-win war and supported the contention with an impressive array of statistics, logistics and geopolitical calculations. The Russians would raise their commitment to the guerrillas, but the United States would simply write off Rhodesia. There was, however, a way out; a five-point package deal. Dr Kissinger handed Smith a piece of paper. Smith began to read it. The room was silent.

Smith looked up: 'You want me to sign my own suicide note,' he said. The room stayed silent. Kissinger maintained the grave, considerate demeanour of one attending a wake – soon Rhodesia's newspapers would depict him with a swollen face, peering through hooded eyes, speaking guttural Jewish German; 'A villain', as Denis Hills put it, 'in an old Pabst film.'

Point 1: black majority rule within two years. Two years! Smith had said, famously, 'Not in a thousand years.'

He read on down the list: a conference with black nationalist leaders to organize an interim government; the interim government to consist of a Council of State, half white, half black, charged with drawing up the future majority-rule constitution, and a Council of Ministers containing a black majority under a black Prime Minister. That was all bad news.

Rhodesia's oil supplies were now down to 19·6 days and ticking away. Smith haggled a bit. How about substituting 'responsible majority rule' for 'black majority rule'? Dr Kissinger should have said no. Instead he suggested, simply, 'majority rule'. Then Smith demanded that whites should occupy three key portfolios in the interim Council of Ministers: Defence, Law and Order, Finance. Kissinger shrugged: it sounded reasonable but he would have to consult the front-line Presidents; knowing that the Zimbabwean guerrillas were dependent on the front-line states for base camps, supplies and munitions, he wrongly assumed that the Presidents could 'deliver' the fractious and bitterly divided nationalist leaders. Of these, Kissinger actually spoke to only one, Nkomo.

Ian Smith broadcast to the nation (and to the world) at 8 p.m. on 24 September 1976. He stressed the benefits that Kissinger had offered: an end to the war (though Smith didn't believe the 'terrorists' would oblige), an end to sanctions, international recognition, free access to the world's markets, and a large trust fund (in reality a vague proposition rather than a firm commitment) to soften the blow, to guarantee pension rights, investments, property.

'But I would be dishonest if I did not state quite clearly that the solutions do not represent what in our view would be the best solutions for Rhodesia's problems.' Yet there was no alternative. Take heart. As Churchill had said, 'Now is not the end; it is not even the beginning of the end, but it is, perhaps, the end of the beginning.'

14. Geneva: separate tables

Thirteen days before Smith's fateful meeting with Kissinger, the front-line Presidents had summoned Zimbabwe's exiled nationalist leaders to Dar es Salaam and commanded them to settle their differences. This, as usual, they failed to do. Ndabaningi Sithole and Robert Mugabe both claimed to be the authentic leader of the Zimbabwe African National Union (Zanu) and both claimed the allegiance of the guerrillas based in Mozambique. Joshua Nkomo remained uncontested leader of the Zimbabwe African People's Union (Zapu), but his Zipra guerrillas were on terms of turmoil with Mugabe's.

Then there was Bishop Abel Muzorewa, the only one of the four leaders never to have suffered imprisonment (Sithole, Nkomo and Mugabe had been detained without trial for a decade of their lives); Muzorewa reckoned himself miserably treated by his exclusion from the guerrilla camps which the front-line Presidents had put under the eighteen-man Military Command Council of Zipa, the 'Zimbabwe People's Army', which currently threatened to disown all the old-guard nationalist leaders, while utterly rejecting the Kissinger plan and promising to hot up the war.

As the Elephant Child discovered, around and about the Limpopo you have to be at least a 100-year-old Bi-Coloured-Python-Rock-Snake to know the score. On 1 October Nkomo and Muzorewa were brought together for half an hour in Gaborone after much sparring. 'I am not going to follow him about like a cat mewing,' Muzorewa told reporters. Two days later the Bishop finally returned home to Salisbury and was greeted with unprecedented displays of enthusiasm by 100,000 people – by chants of 'Zi!', by clenched-fist salutes, by cries of 'Heavy!' and 'Chimurenga!', and by placards calling for war not negotiation. Puffed up with popularity, the tiny Bishop now scorned all overtures by Nkomo, who angrily flew off to Dar es Salaam to sign up with the cool and clinical Mugabe.

On 9 October the two leaders issued a joint statement announcing the formation of the Patriotic Front, claiming the allegiance of Zipa, and setting radical preconditions for attending the forthcoming Geneva Conference which had been convened by the British Foreign Secretary, Anthony Crosland: the immediate release of all political prisoners; the abolition of protected villages; and free political activity inside Rhodesia.

The *Daily Telegraph*'s A. J. McIlroy flew from Lusaka to Dar on the plane carrying Muzorewa, Sithole and Mugabe on the first leg of their journey to Geneva. He noted that the three leaders staged rival simultaneous press conferences in the airport, boarded the plane with their delegations at five-minute intervals, and kept themselves well apart inside it. At Geneva the six delegations sat in a square at separate tables, the British facing the Rhodesians, the two wings of the PF facing Muzorewa and Sithole.

Geneva was at that time Europe's second most expensive city. The British were prepared to pay £50 (US$83) per day per head for only nine members of each nationalist delegation. This parsimony was not well taken, since Geneva represented to the nationalist factions a rallying of the clans, a display of strength and patronage, and a reward for fidelity. The Intercontinental Hotel, moreover, charged a minimum of £35 per day.

The Rhodesians alone were not short of money. Leading Ministers of the Rhodesian Front Government, Smith, van der Byl, Hilary Squires and Mark Partridge, took up residence in the Hotel du Rhône where a team of Ministry of Information officials headed by Enoch Gloster established a slickly efficient press-room offering free drinks, reports on the poor economic performance of the black states, and evidence of guerrilla atrocities.

The first formal meeting of the Conference was scheduled for 28 October, but only Smith's delegation turned up. 'My opponents seem to have appealed against the light,' said Smith, affably employing a cricket metaphor. When the delegates did at last take their places in the UN's European headquarters, amidst murals of muscular figures wrestling with life's difficulties, the atmosphere was electric with animosity. As the Conference Chairman, Ivor Richard, noted, ex-prisoners do not love their gaoler. And the war had intensified.

On 7 October Anthony Crosland had described everything as negotiable. Smith, however, stuck rigidly to his dug-out: Kissinger's five points or nothing. For their part the black nationalists virtually ignored Kissinger's proposals as irrelevant; the first four weeks of the conference were consumed in mutual insults and wrangles about the date of Independence for black Zimbabwe.

'I don't want to be unkind but there were some odd-looking creatures there,' Smith remarked, referring to the Zanla guerrilla commander Josiah Tongogara, recently released from a Zambian gaol, who appeared in a denim suit and a deceptively relaxed manner. Tongogara, Mugabe and Rex Nhongo, among others, occupied the Intercontinental Hotel, where the corridors swarmed with security guards and scores of reporters magnetized by the nightmarish purity of Mugabe's Marxist invective: 'But in Zimbabwe', he warned, 'none of the white exploiters will be allowed to keep an acre of their land.' Mugabe held court, received journalists in batches, expounded and employed boxing metaphors; his aide, Eddison Zvobgo, referred to the conference as 'a load of crap'.

Smith responded sourly. 'There is a lot of acting going on in Geneva and the mass communications media seem to have fallen for it.' Mugabe, he said acidly, was 'riding round on cloud nine with a camouflage terrorist uniform. I don't think he's heard a shot fired in anger in his life. . . .' Unlike Muzorewa and Nkomo, Mugabe had never engaged in direct negotiations with the White Chief and Smith realized that he never would. Not only had Smith stolen ten years of Mugabe's life – detention without trial – but when his only child died Mugabe had been refused parole to attend the funeral. P. K. van der Byl called Mugabe 'a bloodthirsty Marxist puppet'.

Smith flew home to Salisbury, leaving his delegation in the charge of his swinishly suave Foreign Minister, van der Byl. Asked why Salisbury did not publish the names of those it hanged, he drawled, 'Why should we? I am not certain that we don't . . . Anyway, it's academic, because they are normally dead after it.' Born in Cape Town of a wealthy South African family, 'PK' (as he was widely known in Rhodesia) had taken a law degree from Cambridge, studied at Harvard and been commissioned into the 7th Queen's Own Hussars, serving in the Middle East, Italy and Austria. A leading representative of the Rhodesian tobacco industry with a passion for huntin', shootin' and fishin', he became an RF MP in 1962 and a Minister six years later. Famous for his pseudo-aristo, ultra-British drawl, van der Byl had as Defence Minister recently been responsible for the raid on Nyadzonia in the course of which 1,200 Zimbabweans were slaughtered.

The Rhodesians had regained their confidence. Vorster had relaxed his suffocating grip. The railway was functioning again. Appalled by the radicalism of the nationalist demands, the South African Premier stated on 31 October that a just and viable settlement could be achieved only within Kissinger's five points. Smith became more arrogant, commenting on 5 November that Kissinger had not referred to 'black majority rule', only to majority rule; the future constitution would have to be based on a restricted franchise. Nkomo got hold of a resumé of a speech delivered to an RF audience in Rhodesia by Smith's aide Ted Sutton-Price, which stressed the advantages that Rhodesia would enjoy if the war had to be resumed after two years of international recognition and unrestricted trade on the world market.

Of Rhodesia's 2,964 kilometres of border, only the 222 kilometres bordering South Africa were now safe against infiltration. During the last three months of 1976 an unprecedented influx of guerrillas, estimated at about 2,000, took place, partly inspired by the Geneva Conference (though it was not clear whether the Zipa commanders aimed to increase Mugabe's bargaining power or to demonstrate contempt for the conference, or both).

On 31 October, three days after the Geneva Conference formally opened, the Rhodesians struck at camps in Tete and Gaza, destroying quantities of arms and ammunition. In November they hit Frelimo's barracks at Mavne in Gaza province, using jet fighters and armoured cars. (The jets had a habit of performing victory rolls over Umtali.) Once again resorting to subterfuge and Israeli-style panache, the Rhodesians raided deep into Mapai, using four armoured cars and seven Berliet trucks flying Frelimo flags and carrying Mozambique number-plates. Heavy damage was inflicted on the Mozambique rail system. During the seven weeks of the Geneva Conference the Rhodesians also intensified their counter-insurgency operations inside Rhodesia, killing a claimed 321 'terrorists' (compared with 304 in the whole of 1975).

15. not much of an actor

11 November, 1976: the élite of the Rhodesian Establishment gather, 750 strong with their wives, on the vast floor of the sanctions-busting tobacco-auction sale-room. The occasion is the annual Independence Ball, tickets $(R)24 per couple, organized by the Lions' Club of Rhodesia. Proceeds to 'those less fortunate than ourselves'. At midnight Smith peals the Liberty bell – a gift from the extreme American right – twelve times to herald the start of the twelfth year since his Unilateral Declaration of Independence on 11 November 1965. He raises his glass of Rhodesian 'champagne': 'To Rhodesia,' he says drily (he prides himself on 'not being much of an actor'). The band plays antiquated rock and a few waltzes, foxtrots, quicksteps; the only blacks present are waiters. Smith's son-in-law leads the company in singing 'Rhodesians Never Die':

> We'll preserve this little nation
> For our children's children too,
> Once you're a Rhodesian
> No other land will do.
> We will stand tall in the sunshine
> With the truth upon our side,
> And if we have to go alone
> We will go alone with pride.
> But we're all Rhodesians
> And will fight through thick and thin,
> We'll keep our land a free land
> Stop the enemies coming in.
> We'll keep them north of the Zambezi
> Till the river's running dry,
> And this land will prosper
> For Rhodesians never Die.

Mr and Mrs Francis Mee, of Inyanga, farmers in their seventies, were killed by guerrillas on 26 October.

On 11 November Hugh Myerson, from the West Nicholson area, became the fifty-fifth white civilian victim. Four days later Arthur Ross Cumming was shot by guerrillas at Matetsi, nineteen kilometres south of Victoria Falls, when he went to lock the back door of his farmhouse. Further tragedy was later to overtake other members of the Cumming family.

16. the Christian conscience

The missionary must offer his potential converts many things – beads, rolls of Lancashire cloth, medicine, an alphabet, education – in order to persuade them to embrace, finally, One Thing. In the opinion of most white Rhodesians modern European missionaries offered one inducement too many in their quest for African hearts, minds and souls – support for black nationalism and majority rule. In refusing eight Bethlehem Fathers admission to Rhodesia, Smith told Bishop Haene that in the Catholic diocese of Gwelo the Bethlehem Fathers were stirring the Africans against the Government.

Stirring was one thing: more than a score of missionaries had been deported for it, Protestants and Catholics. But with the escalation of the guerrilla war a new, more dangerous crime surfaced like a shark's fin. The first missionary to be charged with failing to report the presence of terrorists was Dr Luisa Guidotti, a 44-year-old Italian doctor who had worked at All Souls mission hospital, Mtoko, since 1969. In June 1976 she treated a young African wounded in the arm, although aware of a recent clash between troops and guerrillas in the area. Accused of 'assisting terrorists', she was held in prison for two weeks until the charge was withdrawn. Greatly loved locally, Dr Guidotti continued her work until tragedy befell her three years later, on 5 July 1979, when she was shot dead in her car after failing to stop at a security-forces check-point. She had slowed, then turned off down a side-road and tried to accelerate away – one can only guess what was in her mind.

Sister Vianney, an Irishwoman, was working at the remote Avila mission twenty-four kilometres from the Mozambique border when four guerrillas turned up and demanded medicines. Two months later it happened again. Sister Vianney consulted Bishop Lamont, who counselled her to keep silent. The security forces nevertheless got wind of it and arrested two black priests working at Avila. A white soldier pressed his gun to Father Patrick Mutume's ear: 'You black bastard, speak up, one dead missionary is better than a hundred dead terrs.'

Both priests were sentenced to four years' imprisonment (later suspended on appeal).

Meanwhile in Gwelo diocese, the heartland of the rural church, a group of ten guerrillas arrived at the remote Berenjena mission in the Chibi TTL and insisted on addressing the assembled staff of 350 pupils. After 45-year-old Father Paul Egli had given a short address and said the Lord's prayer, the guerrillas danced and sang before taking off with requisitioned food supplies. Egli, a Swiss who had worked in Rhodesia for seventeen years, later pleaded in court that the guerrillas had threatened him with death if he reported their presence. The priest spent a year in gaol and was then deported suffering, according to Catholic sources, from a severe depression.

Donal Lamont was the most outspoken Catholic critic of white supremacy in Rhodesia: small, irate, Irish, a box of fireworks. The regime finally got the Bishop of Umtali on a 'failure to report terrorists' charge, stripped him of his citizenship, and deported him. Though none would say so in public, quite a few members of the Catholic hierarchy breathed a sigh of relief; almost the entire white population of Rhodesia, including the 30,000 European Catholics in the diocese of Umtali, rejoiced – indeed many felt that hanging was too good for him. Bishop Lamont was not one of nature's conciliators.

Born in 1917 in County Antrim, he had studied for the priesthood in Rome from 1933 to 1939 – the heyday of Mussolini's unchallenged supremacy. Direct experience of Fascism, of the absolute supremacy of the temporal power over its citizens, of blind, fawning leader-worship, left a lasting impression on the young Irish priest. In later years he readily associated the 'Good old Smithy' belched forth by beer-swilling Rhodesians with the regimented 'Heil Hitler' of Aryan fanaticism.

In 1957 Pius XII constituted the diocese of Umtali and appointed Donal Lamont as its first bishop. He was only 40. His innate sense of justice quickly became apparent to a wider audience in his inaugural sermon: '. . . we must do something about land hunger among the African people. Go into the Reserves and see what they have to live on, and you will understand what I mean.' When he looked out of the window of his residence some 350 metres from the Mozambique border, he could see chain-gangs at work in the diocese of Bishop Dom Sebastião de Rezende. As a rural priest, Lamont had been shocked to discover that in some of Rhodesia's suburban churches Africans were not admitted to the main body of the building but had to worship from the sacristy; he had no hesitation in describing Rhodesia as 'parochial, morally primitive and racist. . . .' In *Peace Through Justice*, issued at Whitsun 1961 by the Catholic Bishops, Lamont's influence was nowhere more clearly seen than in this uncompromisingly provocative passage:

'Though many fail to see it, or refuse through sheer selfishness to acknowledge it, the doctrine of racial superiority as taught and practised by many in this country, differs little in essence from that of the Nazis. . . .' History was forever on the tip of the angry leprechaun's tongue.

The colonial oppression of one people by another was close to home – likewise the anticipation of martyrdom, of a public funeral, of the magic embrace of words and gunpowder. He liked to refer to the 'Irish war of independence' and the creation of the Irish Free State. But he was no Marxist, no Camillo Torres. Liberation theology was not for him. For years he did not contest the Rhodesian Church's repeated condemnation of political violence, nor its Cold War references to 'godless world powers' that 'insidiously foment disorder' among the masses who feel despised and exploited.

Indeed the Church establishment itself was of necessity a colonial enterprise. For what had provided the Church with its lands, its immunities, its ultimate protection, if not the *force majeure* of the Pioneer Column, backed up by the ruthless repression of the Shona and Ndebele rebellions? As late as March 1977, 329 Catholic priests in Rhodesia were non-African while only fifty-one were black. Among male missionaries the corresponding disproportion was 133–20; only among the more numerous Sisters were the races almost evenly balanced (564 non-Africans to 435 Africans). English Jesuits, German Jesuits, Swiss Bethlehem Fathers, German Mariannhill Fathers, Spanish Burgos Fathers, Irish Franciscans and Irish Carmelites – they were all busily engaged in weaning the native population from the religious core of its own culture. Working in competition with the various Protestant denominations, the Catholic Church claimed 76,000 blacks in 1950 and over half a million in the mid-seventies.

Lamont's Church is an instrument of colonial penetration: the God and Saviour of which he brought news were as African as St Patrick. All the more dangerous, then, when the leader of a morally influential establishment institution starts preaching sedition. As President of the Catholic Bishops' Conference from 1970 to 1972, Lamont had led the opposition to the 1969 constitution and to the new Land Tenure Act, foundation-stone of the RF's apartheid system. He had also waded into battle on the question of church schools. The regime had decreed that black pupils could be admitted to private schools for white children on condition they did not exceed 6 per cent of the enrolment. In practice the RF merely provided the Church with an alibi for its own racial conservatism. Of 5,558 pupils in the Catholic independent schools, only 246 were African. Lamont wanted to close church schools rather than bow to the Government.

The Chichester Society, a body of conservative lay Catholics, formally requested Pope Paul VI to remove the Bishop of Umtali.

Volatile, emotional and quick-tempered, Lamont was one of those rebel autocrats whose self-righteousness tends to anaesthetize self-awareness. A Bethlehem Father working in the diocese of Gwelo recalls how three Irish Carmelites from Lamont's diocese had 'fled' and flung themselves on the mercy of the Bishop of Gwelo, begging him to give them refuge. But Lamont stood on his dignity and would not countenance their transfer, with the result that the three refugees had to leave the country. Lamont would also turn up at conferences of the Catholic Bishops with a prepared text which anyone could dare to amend only at the risk of an explosion.

His style was inflammatory, apparently devoid of pity, understanding, compassion. He made little attempt to discuss his views with the whites in his diocese, regarding them less as God's misguided children than as objects for collective scorn. In his speech from the dock he referred to 'the wrath of all Rhodesian white racists, with their telephone calls in the middle of the night to disturb my sleep, these brave people, their threats in the street, their unspeakably filthy letters and their drawings of abuse. Such is the penalty for presuming to suggest that morality has any place in public life.' One Catholic woman, not untypical, cursed Lamont as a hypocrite, a coward, a victim of the sin of pride. 'He thinks he's bigger than God. He sucked up to the blacks in the hope of becoming the first cardinal here.'

On 27 August 1976 Lamont was summoned to appear in court to answer two counts of failing to report the presence of terrorists, and two counts of inciting others to commit the same offence. The Bishops came out with a statement rallying behind him and blaming the predicament of the rural priest on racially discriminatory laws. Sixty people crowded into Umtali court-house on 22 September, including Archbishop Chapaika and Bishops Prieto, Haene and Karlen. Appearing as defence witnesses, the two Anglican Bishops, Burrough and Mercer, stressed the insoluble dilemma confronting missionaries working in the war zones. Lamont pleaded guilty to what was, of course, a capital offence, and read an unsworn statement. On 1 October the Regional Magistrate, W. R. Henning, and his two assessors handed down a sentence of ten years' hard labour.

The following February the case came before the Court of Appeals, which eventually reduced the sentence to four years, three of them suspended. Lamont was here confronted by a formidable and equally partisan protagonist, Chief Justice Hector N. Macdonald, who paraded his own political views in court and stoutly defended the whites' treatment of blacks during the past eighty-seven years in his twenty-five-page Judgment. The Chief Justice was a raging bigot and a hanging judge: neat moustache, prim mouth, glasses with a double bridge. Born in Bulawayo of a Scots father and an English mother, he had followed an orthodox career: after Plumtree school he went to Gray's Inn, served as a Captain in the western desert of North Africa and in Sicily, became a QC, a Judge of the Rhodesian High Court, a Judge of Appeal, Judge President of the Appellate Division in 1970, and Chief Justice in 1977. 'Everyone of us, without exception, was against UDI,' he declared, but since the British had failed to provide an alternative government there had been none to uphold. 'On balance,' Macdonald added, 'I am satisfied that the Rhodesian Government was more sinned against than sinning.'

Bishop Lamont had instructed all missionary staff within his diocese not to report visits by guerrillas and to give out medicines to both the guerrillas and the security forces. He seemed torn between an image of the guerrilla as hero and the standard portrait of the debased, anti-Christian, Communist-indoctrinated fanatic. But the seal of silence was broken at Avila mission after a priest and two nuns had been summoned out into the night by the vakhomana and so frightened that they fled the next day. Reaching Inyanga, the African priest reported the matter to the authorities.

'According to the priest [at Avila mission], he and the Sister were lectured on the glories of Communism and the evils of capitalism as represented by the Kennedys, the Rockefellers and the Catholic Church. The visitors ordered the priest to reduce the school fees and the charges made at the mission clinic. They then threatened that the mission would be destroyed and other vengeance taken if other requests for watches, radios, cameras, etc. were not granted.'

Well, then, was the Government not justified in hunting down such evil bandits? And was it not morally entitled to the assistance of all decent citizens? At this point in his testimony, Lamont switched gear into neutral:

'... to inquire into the political and religious beliefs of the needy person before giving aid, is quite contrary to the Christian conscience ... when the guerrillas, heavily armed, come to lonely outposts where there is neither the protection of weapons and ammunition nor even the comfort and relative protection of a telephone, what can anyone do but obey their demands under threats ... ?'

Two quite separate thoughts coexist uneasily here; under pressure Lamont's intellect had fragmented; a structure of thought had collapsed into a series of discrete justifications, each of equal weight:

'Government propaganda has ... given gruesome details of the mutilation alleged to have been carried out by terrorists on those who have dared to inform on them. What does the State demand of this young nun ... who has dedicated herself for life ... to the service of the underprivileged, the hungry? ... Is the missionary-informer not responsible for the death of any young man or woman who, in defence of his own fundamental rights, takes up arms for what he believes is a just cause?'

Again the Bishop has engaged in a mid-course correction. The Government depicts the guerrillas as terrorist fiends and the rural missionaries are therefore entitled (perhaps?) to believe the worst of them. But a moment later political violence is justified (contrary to the pastoral letters issued by

Lamont and his colleagues) and the terrorists become noble freedom fighters.

Chief Justice Macdonald was singularly unimpressed. Since in his view it was abundantly clear that the terrorists belonged to a 'Communist' organization, how could it be a Christian's duty to bring them comfort and support? He nailed Lamont for evading the question of whether the guerrillas were in fact guilty of atrocities, and whether they were in reality Communists.

Macdonald's written Judgment was a collage of cherished white-Rhodesian myths. The only period of oppression in the modern history of Rhodesia, insisted the judge, had occurred during the era of Matabele domination from 1840 to 1893; indeed, the white Pioneers 'had ended the despotic reign of Lobengula, who had kept the whole of this country in thrall . . .'. The African owed to the European, claimed the Chief Justice, law and order (but whose law, whose order?), skills, expertise – a rate of 'progress' more rapid than that in any other African country.

It was a dialogue of the deaf. Lamont was 60 years old and deeply shaken when he was deported on 23 March 1977. He withdrew to Ireland; according to one sympathetic witness, he stuttered and broke down when the room was empty and there were no young priests to show off to. He knew that almost the entire Church, including its liberal wing, had been glad to see the back of him.

Epilogue: In June 1979 the Muzorewa Government allowed Lamont to return for three weeks to perform the consecration of the Auxiliary Bishop of Umtali, Mgr Patrick Mutume, in Sakubva stadium. The press was prohibited from publishing any information about Lamont's activities or his statements, other than strictly religious ones. On 8 August 1980 Lamont returned in triumph as a full citizen of Zimbabwe and was accorded a royal welcome at the airport. Chief Justice Macdonald, meanwhile, had gapped it to South Africa.

17. death of a bishop

Adolph Schmitt, the Roman Catholic Bishop of Bulawayo, was interviewed in Germany during the Geneva Conference. 'The white Rhodesians claim to be Christians,' remarked the 71-year-old Mariannhill Father, 'but only seldom do they act in a Christian way. They have frittered away the goodwill of the black population without any hope now of reconciliation. The African majority is today convinced that no other choice remains open to them but violence.'

A few weeks later, on 5 December, with the Geneva Conference still deadlocked, the Bishop fell victim to the violence he described. On a lonely road near Lupane, in northern Matabeleland, Schmitt was murdered together with Father Possenti Weggartner and Sister Maria van der Berg. They, with the fourth member of their party, Sister Ermenfried Knauer, were driving from their home mission station to Regina Mundi to visit a sick friend in St Luke's when a lone man wearing a balaclava and camouflage uniform held the car up with a machine-gun and demanded money. They told him they had none and offered to take him back to the mission. Twice shouting the slogan 'Missionaries are enemies of the people!', the bandit then riddled Bishop Schmitt with bullets, cut down Father Weggartner a metre away, and killed Sister Maria, whose body, dressed in a white habit, was found sprawled across the Bishop's. Sister Ermenfried, who escaped with a wound in her left leg as she scrambled for cover under the car, reported that the killer had been unable to look his victims in the eye as he pulled the trigger.

Father Weggartner had known Nkomo well and had indeed taught his daughters at Regina Mundi; Nkomo's wife was a respected leader of the Catholic community in the parish. Not only the Patriotic Front but also Bishop Muzorewa blamed the murders on the regime's notorious counter-insurgency unit, the Selous Scouts. Later, in a Bulawayo township, the police arrested a certain Albert Ncube, who had attended a Catholic primary school and been confirmed by Bishop Schmitt; in a confession statement, almost certainly genuine, Ncube admitted to this and other killings as well. By a strange quirk of fate, however, this prize villain escaped from Victoria Falls while 'making indications' to the police on 9 January 1977, and swam across the Zambezi into Zambia. The white Detective Inspector at fault got it in the neck from his superiors.

The propaganda value of the murders to the white supremacists was considerable. Within a day the 'Catholic laity of Bulawayo', self-styled, promptly blamed 'those people who have advocated and supported terrorism in Rhodesia'. It seems that Sister Ermenfried was willing to travel to Geneva to bear witness, despite her injuries, and to testify that the killer had been a guerrilla, but she was not granted permission by her superiors; the *Rhodesia Herald* was full of offers by businessmen to pay her fare and suggestions that the good nun was being muzzled by a Church intent on appeasing Communism.

Two days earlier, on 3 December, a Swiss-born Bethlehem Father had apparently been abducted from his car and spirited into the void. Father George Joerger, of the Bandolphi mission, had served as a missionary in Rhodesia for twenty years. Father Joerger was known to have delivered at least one sermon against the theft of cattle from farms, including those owned by Europeans. Equally unacceptable to the vakhomana would have been his habit of giving lifts in his car to all and sundry including – and perhaps notably – members of the security forces.

On New Year's Eve, 1976, Father Thomas McCloughlin, Rector of the St Charles Catholic Seminary at Melsetter, was returning with two African nuns and the mission cook from a shopping expedition to Umtali when his car was ambushed on the main road. Father McCloughlin was wounded and the cook injured. When one of the black nuns bravely stepped out of the car and shouted to the assailants that they were shooting at a missionary, the firing promptly stopped.

18. why do Californian fruit-growers prefer Mexicans?

If you will attempt to kill a white farmer, burn down his homestead and his barns, then will you not also take the lesser step of bringing his enterprise to a halt, a close, by depriving him of native labour? And what will you do if his labour force ignore all warnings and threats?

The Geneva Conference was still in progress on 20 December when a Zanla platoon entered the compound of a tea estate in the Honde Valley at 8.30 in the evening, rounded up all the men, women and children they could find, and marched them away. Arriving outside the tea factory, they separated the men from the women and children, forced them to lie on the ground, then opened fire, slaughtering twenty-seven men, of whom nine came from Mozambique, eight from Malawi and ten from Rhodesia. When the news reached Geneva there was uproar.

Journalists are flown to the scene of the massacre. The bodies sprawl on the ground, ragged bullet holes in the dungarees. Some are almost naked, some lie pathetically with their wrists tied by strips of cloth. One wears sandals: half his face is blasted away and his entrails have spilt out of a hole the size of a small football in his right flank. He probably had five children, who watched him die. Is this liberation?

The plantation manager, 55-year-old Peter Gresham, had during the previous year given two anonymous interviews to overseas journalists. Born and educated in Britain, he had lived in Rhodesia for twenty-nine years, sixteen of them in the Honde Valley. 'I was brought up to believe in Queen and country,' he told reporter Ian Jack. 'This crumbled when Britain exposed its double standards and gave independence to two members of the Federation but not to us.' The condition of Britain appalled him, even the royal family wasn't what it had been. 'And please don't give us all that stuff about one man, one vote. I'm far too old and cynical for that . . . no, this is all about trade, you want to buy oil from Nigeria.' Seated beneath a portrait of Churchill, Gresham opened a bottle of Rhodesian red and complained that life now was just 'hassles', what with the terrorist 'stonks' (mortar attacks), 'eggs' (landmines) and the 'freddies' (Frelimo) making trouble over the border.

Losing twenty-seven workers had been nasty, but a 4,000-hectare estate employing 1,600 Afs and thirteen white families could cope. Now Gresham and three white army reservists were distributing to the work-force crude line drawings depicting demonically grinning killers bending over bleeding bodies: 'See the mad dog Communist terrorists shooting old men and young girls with their Communist AK guns.'

The situation deteriorated rapidly throughout the eastern border areas. When guerrillas launched a 45-mm rocket, mortar and machine gun attack on Chris Talbot's tobacco and banana plantation in the Burma Valley, all but one of the fifty-nine workers fled. Unable to hire replacements, Talbot was forced to abandon his farm. On Good Friday, 1977, seven black labourers on a tea plantation in the Honde Valley were killed after a brutal beating. Political commissars in the area had repeatedly warned workers to quit.

So effective was Zanla intimidation that Aberfoyle Plantations began advertising 'free houses in guarded villages' and wages $(R)10 a week above the norm. Not that the normal wage offered by Rhodesian tea plantations was anything but crudely exploitative: 60 cents a day for men, 50 cents for women, 40 cents for child workers, and a bonus of $(R)2 for every 100 kilos picked. When asked why they advertised for Malawians, Aberfoyle replied candidly: 'Why do Californian fruit-growers prefer Mexicans?'

According to the Rhodesian National Farmers' Union, the 'real value' to a black farm worker of average payments in cash and kind amounted to $(R)37–$(R)40 a month: this calculation included the wage, free food, primary schooling and medicine. Nevertheless in June 1976 there were 236,669 Africans working in the European agricultural sector for cash wages of less than $(R)30 a month, most of them for half that amount, even though the Poverty Datum Line for a rural family of six was estimated at over $(R)40 a month. Whites working in agriculture earned on average 23·6 times as much as blacks – this was the true indicator of the exploitation suffered by the black work-force.

Traditionally the farmer provided the black labourer with a mealie sack which was supposed to serve both as a food carrier and as an overcoat in winter. 'Bamba lapa!' – Catch there! – he shouted as he poured the ration of mealie meal, round beans and monkey nuts into the bag. The wage was paid in arrears every five weeks or thirty working days. As Nathan Shamuyarira has recalled, the blacks, while respectfully addressing the white farmer as Ishe (in Shona) or Nkosi (in Sindebele), referred to him by less flattering titles in the privacy of the labourers' compound: 'Mukanda butsu' – the one who throws the boot; or 'Chamboko' – the one who uses the sjambok freely.

From its very inception in 1890, the Rhodesian state had been a settler state. Crossing the Limpopo with his black servant, his horse and his rifle, the white settler, whether British or Afrikaner by origin, carved himself out a property, seeking as much land as he could ride across in a day, his title-deed acquired from the local agent of Rhodes's Charter Company. By 1899, 6·4 million hectares (the figure is worth a moment's reflection) of Mashonaland and Matabeleland had been seized and declared private property by Europeans.

In time the legal segregation of farming land into areas exclusively owned by whites and tribal trust lands reserved for black peasant farmers was codified. The whites, of course, took possession of the most fertile areas, whereas only 13 per cent of the TTLs fell into this category – in the main the reserves suffer from lighter-textured soils (prey to erosion), high temperatures and low rainfalls.

By the Land Apportionment Act of 1931 some 6,000 European farmers (including foreign-owned giants like Anglo-American, Liebigs, Lonrho and Halletts Corporation) were granted exclusive custody of almost half the country's available agricultural land. Evictions continued. Between 1936 and 1959, 113,000 Africans were forced to quit areas reserved for Europeans.

The Tangwena people had lived in the Inyanga area for at least eight generations. In 1905 their ancestral land was sold, unknown to them, to a private company by the British South Africa Company – who had in effect seized all of Mashonaland in 1890. In 1930 their area was legally designated 'European land'. Acting under pressure from the first RF Government, the Gaeresi Ranch Company tried to evict the Tangwena in 1963. Even though the Government lost the legal battle in the courts in 1968, it burnt and bulldozed their homes and impounded their cattle, finally scattering them into the bush and providing Zanu with the kind of support that intimidation could never achieve.

By 1979 there were 1·6 million hectares of unused land in the commercial farming areas while land famine prevailed in the reserves, where 675,000 black peasant farmers and their 3 million dependants were crowded into 17·6 million exhausted hectares. The Commercial Farmers' Union freely conceded that 25 per cent of white-owned land was available for government-financed resettlement projects – at a price.

In 1900 there were only 710,000 blacks in Rhodesia; by 1970 there were 5·5 million, and by 1980 7·5 million. The TTLs were fast becoming dustbowls. The veld (pasture) was denuded. In fact the reserves could properly sustain only 275,000 peasant cultivators, not the 675,000 now attempting to eke a livelihood out of the soil.

The white farmers blamed the bad farming habits of the Africans. But the population explosion among the Africans placed intolerable pressures on the reserves, most particularly in Mtoko, Buhera, Enkeldoorn and south of Fort Victoria. In the Selukwe European farming area (where Ian Smith farmed), each inhabitant occupied 24·2 hectares; in the neighbouring Selukwe TTL, each inhabitant occupied 2·3 hectares. In Victoria the corresponding figures were 21·4 for the European land and 2·2 for the TTLs. Whereas the European farmer allocated 20 to 25 hectares to each head of cattle, the tribal farmer could find only 4 hectares per beast.

Part Two: 1977

1. starting again

By the end of November it was clear that the Geneva Conference was doomed. Following President Ford's defeat by Jimmy Carter, Henry Kissinger was now a 'lame duck' Secretary of State and could not intervene effectively, even had he been so inclined. The Zimbabweans remained bitterly divided. Ivor Richard, portly and professionally sanguine, 'adjourned' the Geneva Conference on 14 December. It never resumed. Nkomo reached his stronghold, Bulawayo, on 18 December and was promptly forbidden to make political statements or hold meetings. Nkomo departed: it would be three years before he could return.

Nkomo's popularity was now minimal outside Matabeleland; the younger generation of Shonas, secondary-school children and students, despised and distrusted him – his protracted negotiations with Ian Smith, which had broken down in March, had done him no good. Mugabe remained a remote, mysterious figure: following his release from ten years' detention in December 1974, he had spent only four months inside Rhodesia before crossing into Mozambique (he was not destined to set foot on Rhodesian soil again until 27 January 1980).

From Milton Buildings, Salisbury, the unity of the Patriotic Front did not appear impressive or intimidating. Nkomo's Zipra, the military wing of Zapu, most of them young Ndebeles, had been chased out of the camps in Mozambique in the course of 1976. Henceforward they would operate exclusively from Zambia. Smith doubted whether Mugabe's Zanu exercised genuine control over the guerrillas in Mozambique – the young turks of the Zipa Command Council apparently recognized no authority other than themselves. Salisbury's Military Intelligence was slow to appreciate that President Machel had engineered the arrest of twenty-five leading Zipa radicals in mid-January 1977, thus effectively restoring party control and forging a tight unity between Mugabe's Zanu and the new military force, Zanla, commanded by General Josiah Tongogara.

Yet the Patriotic Front remained a fragile coalition of convenience.

Mugabe called for military unity to precede political unification, whereas Nkomo, whose strengths were in reverse order, naturally reversed the priorities. It was deadlock.

Smith embarked on a long struggle of attrition, coaxing his white constituents into acceptance of certain reforms – or retreats – as the necessary price of retaining real power, 'responsible government', the privileged status which was the linchpin of white Rhodesia. Smith had already identified his next target: Muzorewa. The Bishop, who had been 'in exile' until shortly before the Geneva Conference, had gained kudos in Mashonaland – many of the militants convicted in the courts of sabotage and violence at this time were supporters of Muzorewa's ANC. If the Bishop was now excluded, by a concerted decision of the front-line Presidents, from the guerrilla camps in Zambia, Mozambique and Tanzania, then his only route to power (or 'power') was the internal one – courtesy of Ian Smith. The Prime Minister would make his move in his own good time.

Smith once again believed that time was on his side, though he no longer spoke in terms of millennia. Vorster had done another U-turn. Petrol and ammunition supplies flowed again. South African combat police returned to the 'Operation Repulse' area in the south of Rhodesia, their liaison officers quite visible in and around Fort Victoria. The training of Rhodesian jet pilots in the Transvaal was stepped up. Young South Africans with a taste for bush warfare and culling kaffirs were permitted to discharge their national-service obligations in the Rhodesian security forces. Vorster and his new Foreign Minister, R. F. Botha, now favoured an 'internal' solution which would exclude the PF, the armed guerrillas, entirely.

In the fools' paradise, standing room only.

Ivor Richard, the porky son of a Welsh coalminer, formerly a Labour MP and now British representative at the UN, embarked on a grand tour of Rhodesia soon after the Geneva Conference stalled. In the north-east, tobacco farmers warned him they would rather raze their farms to the ground than surrender them to terrorists. Richard listened, looking like a bullfrog and chewing Cuban cigars. Anti-British feeling ran high, a strong sense of fratricidal betrayal sharpened by the mild contempt in which the metropolitans held the colonials and the colonials' answering rage at the diabolical alliance of Eton and Karl Marx – the British pin-stripe, public-school establishment cynically serving a Labour Government. To get a sense of this enmity, the reader should recall the Joe McCarthy era in America, the small-town, redneck backlash against the New Deal, the secret Commies, the posh, Ivy League 'traitors' like Hiss and Acheson, and the labor unions.

Smith flatly rejected the package proposal that Richard brought him: a transitional government headed by a British Commissioner with a Council of Ministers containing equal numbers from each of the five delegations represented at Geneva. Smith said no and the two men parted company acrimoniously.

In mid-January 1977 the Rhodesian Front caucus decided to amend the Land Tenure Act, cornerstone since 1969 of Rhodesia's version of apartheid. White farming areas would henceforward be open to all races, the 6 per cent quota on non-white pupils at white private schools would be lifted, and blacks would be able to buy homes in specially designated multiracial areas of towns. But urban racial segregation would otherwise remain in force.

Despite Ian Smith's personal prestige, revolt broke out in the ranks. Harold Coleman, deputy Chairman, accused the Government of departing from RF principles. Twelve members of the RF parliamentary caucus broke away. Since the amendment of the Land Tenure Act required a two-thirds majority to become law, the vote was a cliff-hanger: needing 44 votes, the Government got precisely 44 – thirty-eight loyal RF members plus six of the sixteen African MPs. Had he not obtained his majority Smith would merely have dissolved the House and called for elections, which he eventually did in any case.

It was a difficult moment for the RF. As usual Smith rallied the clan: in mid-April a one-day conference of the party gave him a free hand to negotiate a settlement, voting overwhelmingly in favour by 422 to 25. At the end of the month the twelve rebel MPs were publicly expelled from the RF. On 2 July Chairman Des Frost resigned, describing Smith as 'tired and negative'. Smith replied: 'Clearly the man is completely two-faced. . . .' Within days the Rhodesian Action Party was formed.

2. a refugee from the welfare state

Richard Cartwright is an MP of the Rhodesian Front. Born in Manchester, Cartwright served during the war in the Royal Artillery in France, the Far East and India; you can be sure he wears the regimental tie and his Lancashire accent remains as thick as pea soup. He describes himself as a refugee from the welfare state. After the war he set up a transport business in North Staffs but in 1948 Labour Party policy got to him in the shape of a registered letter for compulsory purchase of his business. 'More than 50 per cent of our income came from long-distance haulage. No appeal was allowed.' His MP, the left-wing fellow-traveller Harold Davies, was, of course, no help. 'Churchill called him Nenni goat.'

Cartwright hung on for three years, becoming manager of his own fleet of lorries for British Road Services. After the final instalment of his £2,000 compensation came through in November 1951 he said goodbye to the UK.

'I'd been to the cinema and seen a travel film of the Leopard Rock Hotel and of a tobacco-farm in Rhodesia. I had friends in Durban who had a relative living in Umtali, so I wrote to him then flew out here. On the plane I met a Gurkha officer. We stopped over at Nairobi. Lots of Indians, you know, dustbins . . . it looked like India. When I got here I stayed at the old Grand Hotel and heard people singing "The Mountains of Mourne". I felt, my God, I'm home. Everything was so English, you know.' Cartwright found a job with a Salisbury bus company, went back to the UK, resigned, and came out for good in May 1952. He arranged for London double-deckers to be shipped out and drove one of them from Durban to Salisbury.

In 1956 he started his own transport business. As for the RF, he was a founder-member: 'Our purpose was to keep Rhodesia as it was. To avert the chaos of a quick handover. Everyone realized the country would eventually go over to the African. That's where we've differed from South Africa.'

He recalls the Congo, Angola, Mozambique, all 'fallen'.

'After Smith's meeting with Kissinger we discussed the situation in the caucus. The twelve who broke away to form the RAP were in full agreement at the time that we had to accept. But they have these Bantustan ideas. Their rebellion had been brewing for a long time.'

Cartwright's constituency is white working class, artisans, fitters, turners. 'They'll stick it out, don't worry,' he says. 'Rhodesians don't run away. Of course . . . a lot of them have gone already. The types to leave, they're the ones who've gone. The ones who have stayed, they'll stay . . . provided they have confidence. There's a lot of feeling about getting the African to do his share. The whites go into the army while the blacks go to university, that can't be right.'

Cartwright has been a police reservist for years. 'We've always had to fight clean. If you get African fighting African they won't be so scrupulous, believe me.'

A census survey taken at a time when the total white population was estimated at 228,296 showed that 92,934 had been born in Rhodesia, 52,468 in the UK, 49,586 in South Africa. These figures tell their story: the majority of 'Rhodesians' had not been born in Rhodesia, still less were they descendants of the Pioneers; when they spoke of 'everything we have built up here' that first-person plural depended on a self-serving osmosis.

Most white Rhodesians were not pioneering farmers hacking down the bush and bringing the barren, arid veld to life. They were townsmen before they left Britain or South Africa and townsmen they remained after their arrival in Rhodesia. In 1977 it was estimated that 215,000 out of 263,000 whites lived in towns. Of these, 124,000 occupied the sprawling suburbs of Salisbury while 59,000 lived in Bulawayo.

In 1968 only 8,351 whites worked in agriculture and forestry, whereas 31,275 worked in 'services', 21,290 in trade, hotels and restaurants, 7,587 in manufacturing industry, 10,627 in transport and communications, 6,680 in finance, insurance and real estate, and 3,353 in mining.

When the exodus began in 1976 the first to leave were engineers, draughtsmen, technicians, mechanics, electricians, construction workers – indeed the construction industry lost one-quarter of its skilled manpower over a period of three years. In the course of 1978 over 150 accountants left Rhodesia. Military conscription was clearly the decisive factor, with its attendant risks of death or injury. African majority rule, even in its 'moderate' version, was viewed as the thin end of a wedge which would eventually erode 'standards', 'law and order' and white cultural hegemony.

3. the head prefect – if Churchill were alive today

Smith was the first Rhodesian Prime Minister to have been born in Southern Rhodesia. When he took office in 1964 he had visited Britain only four times, briefly. With a long, prominent nose, a skin graft on the upper part of his right cheek and a marginally closed right eye – the injuries caused by crashing his Hurricane in North Africa during the war – he was regarded in the Commonwealth Office as a raw colonial of sour disposition, but recognized as inspiring adulatory devotion among white Rhodesians by his intransigent resistance to British and world pressure.

His father, Jock Smith, had come out from Lanarkshire in Scotland at the age of 18, two years before the turn of the century, and gradually prospered in Selukwe as farmer and rancher. He bred horses, rode them in races, won cups, judged cattle at shows, presided over football clubs, did good works. Ian Smith's mother, who came from Cumberland, was of the same active breed. Sport was the great passion: at Chaplin School, Gwelo, Ian Smith became head prefect, captain of rugby, captain of tennis, captain of cricket. He also learned to read and write, but the act of writing always involved a deliberate shooting of cuffs and preliminary circling of the pen hand. He developed a pedantic yet inaccurate language of his own – he would say 'the factual situation' when he meant 'the actual situation'.

The Union Jack flew over the public buildings in Selukwe and both his parents in their time were awarded the MBE, an Empire medal. At the outbreak of war in Europe, it was an instinctive response to interrupt his course at Rhodes University, Grahamstown, and volunteer for the Royal Air Force. His Hurricane crashed in October 1943, gravely injuring him; later, in June 1944, his Spitfire was shot down over the Po Valley and he baled out. For five months he was protected by pro-Ally Italians until he and his three companions finally walked through the German lines, above the snow line, into Southern France. He admired Winston Churchill above all others.

'If Churchill were alive today,' he said, 'I believe he'd probably emigrate to Rhodesia – because I believe that all those admirable qualities and character-istics of the British we believed in, loved and preached to our children, no longer exist in Britain.' The same viewpoint was expressed by Harold Soref, a leading light in a right-wing Tory ginger group, the Monday Club: 'Rhodesia represents Britain in its halcyon days: patriotic, self-reliant, self-supporting, with law and order and a healthy society. Rhodesia is as Britain was at its best.' Possibly Smith was unaware that the disparagement of effete Britain in the name of the bold, manly, adventurous values of the imperial frontier had been a habit since Kipling's time. 'England is a stuffy little place, mentally, morally and physically,' Kipling had written to Cecil Rhodes.

Yet Smith knew how to appeal to British nostalgia, as when he informed readers of the *Daily Telegraph* that the actions of the Rhodesian security forces 'are in the very best traditions of the British Army and the Royal Air Force, which is not surprising for in moving among them one hears just about every accent and dialect from Land's End to John o'Groat's, not to mention the Emerald Isle'. Smith always claimed 'terrific support' from the British people – their love of cricket and rugby provided the last cement of the extended Anglo-Celtic family.

That Smith genuinely felt that Britain had let Rhodesia down in the Macmillan–Butler, 'wind of change' era cannot be doubted. Smith had not fought in Churchill's war, and Churchill had not led that war, to promote black majority rule or any kind of black mischief. Churchill believed in the British Empire and the British were white people who treated the King's loyal black subjects as well as they deserved or better. The Smith family had carved out a thriving property in the middle of Africa, but if they handed the country over to a black rabble then everything would go to pot – corruption, killer gangs, preventable diseases – and the Smiths would have to abandon everything.

Lean, upright, decent, balanced, rarely raises his voice in anger; Smith is a plain man, no trimmings, fond of simple food, but not really religious, despite his father's Presbyterianism and an early immersion in the Protestant ethic. Smith described himself as a man whose great passion is farming; farming was a 'beautiful' thing and he would have pursued it had his natural selfishness not constantly been transcended by the call of patriotic duty. Yet Smith became not only ruthless in dispatching rivals (his predecessor Winston Field, William Harper, Lord Graham), he also clung to power tenaciously, then to semi-power (the short-lived Zimbabwe Rhodesia era), and ended up still leading the RF in an Assembly dominated by black nationalists whose first act was to haul down the statue of Cecil Rhodes on Jameson Avenue.

'I am not', Smith says, 'an emotional sort of person, an actor, an orator. . . . If I can't convince people by logic and sound common sense, then I would rather not convince them.' Yet the cult of Ian Smith, the mass adulation, was not purely spontaneous, it was also master-minded by a South African neo-fascist, Ivor Benson, whom Smith recruited as a PR man – hence the shop-windows full of plaster busts and ugly effigies, the Smith ashtrays, the dishcloths portraying the Prime Minister and his Spitfire, the copper plaques of Ian Smith produced by the thousand. And just in case 'logic and sound common sense' didn't convince everyone, Smith, defender of Western civilization, which he occasionally defined as 'fair play', muzzled his critics by means of censorship and detention without trial. 'We have struck a blow for the preservation of justice, civilization and Christianity,' he declared on his UDI broadcast, 'and in the spirit of this belief we have this day assumed our sovereign independence.'

His complete mastery of his own white constituency cannot be doubted. In the first election it ever fought, under the leadership of Winston Field, the RF won thirty-five out of fifty seats. But in May 1965 Smith led his party to a clean sweep, fifty out of fifty; between then and the time of writing not a single RF candidate has ever been defeated. Such ascendancy was maintained by pandering to prejudice and putting the clock back wherever possible. Thus where Edgar Whitehead's Government had abolished separate queues at post offices and banks, allowed Africans to enter cinemas and hotels, opened a door to multiracial sport and permitted private schools to enrol black pupils – modest enough reforms, one might think – Smith empowered municipalities to segregate parks, sports grounds and toilets while restricting multiracial sport and the admission of black pupils to private schools.

Whereas Whitehead's 1961 constitution at least pointed in the direction of majority rule, however timidly and problematically, Ian Smith emerged from the *Fearless* talks in October 1968 with the assurance that 'there will be no majority rule in my lifetime – or in my children's'. Eight years later, in March 1976, when his talks with Nkomo finally broke down, he said: 'But I don't believe in majority rule, black majority rule, ever in Rhodesia, not in a thousand years.'

Yet he cultivated an alibi against the charge of being a racist. According to Smith, it was not the colour of a person's skin which morally determined whether he was entitled to vote, it was his income-tax assessment: 'This is surely a reasonable yardstick for assessing worth and contribution to the common weal.' Presumably, then, white adults who paid little or no tax would be disfranchised? Not at all. White housewives could vote because *the white race as a whole* paid more than its share of income tax.

What Smith did was to empty racism not only of its pseudo-intellectual content, but also of its buccaneering romanticism. His attitude towards Africans was empty of hatred; he bullied them, but politely; he hectored and lectured them, but not at the level of personal abuse. Because he could always ban them, detain them, lock them up, which he often did, he felt unthreatened by them at a personal level: they were opponents but within the wider contours of history and geography. His white detractors, on the other hand, liberals, Foreign Office smarties, metropolitans, generated in him a deep, smouldering bitterness.

'I have tried,' he said, 'to avoid letting bitterness dominate my thinking. But I never believed in one man, one vote in any country, including the UK.'

4. massacre at Musami

Dr Corrie van den Bosch lived at Glenroe Farm, Mrewa. A neighbour, Mrs Geraldine Melrose, had brought her three children over for afternoon tea. It turned out to be an unhappy tea party. Two Africans armed with a rifle and a machine-gun walked through the french windows while four more waited outside. The leader, dressed in a broad-brimmed slouch hat with a leopard's-skin headband, kept grinning and saying he intended to kill them all. Ordering Dr van den Bosch into the bedroom and grabbing the guns she and her husband kept at their bedside, he forced her to open the safe in the farm office. He then smashed his rifle butt into her face and kicked the side of her head when she fell, causing internal bleeding. Mrs Melrose was able to grab her three children, jump into her car and reverse away at speed. They shot at her but missed.

The lands reserved for Europeans in the southern Low Veld contain vast ranches. On the B–J–B ranch, at Nuanetsi, for example, 34-year-old Norman Bristow kept 5,000 head of cattle on 35,000 hectares. On Sunday, 9 January 1977, Bristow, his wife Lena and their children Derek, 14, Paul, 9, and Mandy, 3, were roused in the early hours by automatic fire, mortar shells and rockets. They were well prepared for such an eventuality. A police reservist posted on the ranch as a 'bright-light' was already returning fire from a bunker as the Bristow family made a dash for the sand-bagged dug-out in the garden, where husband and wife returned fire for ninety minutes while Derek reloaded the rifles. The two smaller children remained calm. Mrs Bristow shot one of the attackers, about a dozen of whom were involved. Eventually they took off.

The abduction of Ivan Cecil Taylor (men recover their middle names when misfortune befalls them) took place on 3 February, only 300 metres from the Mozambique border. A 30-year-old field assistant employed on the Jersey Tea Estate, Taylor was seized at 9.30 in the morning near a divisional office. His wife Hilary, mother of two small children, received a letter from him posted on 8 March from the Chipinga area. It was accompanied by a note from Zanu stating that Taylor was held prisoner in Mozambique.

On the same day, 3 February, Alexander Hamilton, 59, was visiting Kye Mine, north of Mtoko, to pay the employees when guerrillas marched him and ten workers away; the Africans were later released.

The Jesuit mission of St Paul at Musami consists of a cluster of tin-roofed buildings erected on a slight rise in a tract of rocky scrub land in the Mangwende TTL, east of Salisbury. The mission's school caters for 100 students and the hospital contains 100 beds. It was here, on 7 February 1977, that a gang of about twelve Africans, some wearing camouflage uniforms, murdered two priests, a lay brother and four nuns.

The victims had been watching a British detective series on television when the gang arrived at 10 in the evening. Sister Anna Victoria Ereggael, aged 75, was sitting on her bed reading when a 'guerrilla' walked in and told her to follow him. Her arthritis – and perhaps fear – caused her to stumble to the floor; the man took her watch before impatiently leaving her and striding to the common-room, where he found Sister Epiphany Bertha Schneider, another elderly German-born nun. It was Sister Anna's arthritis, or her stumble, that saved her life. She was left behind, forgotten.

The eight other white missionaries of St Paul's were lined up in the night on a narrow road. According to the sole survivor among them, Father Dunstan Myerscough, one of the 'guerrillas' said: 'We want our country.' There was, he added, some argument among them as to who should do the killing. One stepped forward then withdrew; eventually three volunteered and the rest ran off. The three then opened sustained, murderous fire on the pathetic knot of missionaries. The police later claimed to have collected 111 spent cartridges from a machine-gun and assault rifles.

Father Myerscough was not even hit; the person next to him took the bullets as they fell to the ground and Myerscough lay still until the killers had departed into the night. Around him sprawled the bodies of his colleagues: the Rev. Martin Thomas, 45, and the Rev. Christopher Sheppard-Smith, 34, both English Jesuits from Heythrop College in Oxfordshire; Brother John Conway, from Wales; and four Dominican nuns. Of these one, Sister Joseph Paulina Wilkinson, was English, the others being German-born – Sister Magdalene Christa Lavanbossky, 42, Sister Ceslaus Anna Stiegler, 59, and Sister Epiphany Bertha Schneider, 73, already mentioned as having been abducted from the common-room.

The evidence of the survivor, Dunstan Myerscough, was considered suspect by liberals within the Church. Educated in South Africa, he knew no Shona and had a reputation for extreme conservatism; indeed his verdict was made a meal of by the Rhodesian propaganda services. The massacre, declared the priest, was 'obviously the result of Russian indoctrination. In my opinion, if you want proof the Communists are behind this, come to this mission. The terrorists must have been got at to have such brutality in them.' The BSAP had no quarrel with this line of inquiry. Testifying at the inquest, Chief Inspector David Perkins, a ballistics expert, claimed that the police had recovered an AK rifle bearing the number 3036, of North Korean manufacture, which had been proven under microscopic examination to have been one of the weapons used.

Some six weeks later, in mid-March, an attack took place on a farmstead near Shamva in which a white woman and a girl were killed. Eleven-year-old Sharon McRoberts had lost both her parents in a car accident when she was 3 and was now living with her grandparents on the Shamva farm. On 11 March 1977 she and her granny, Mrs Muriel Hastings, were eating their supper at 7.30 in the evening when guerrillas broke in, having obtained a key to an unused back gate in the security fence. They shot Sharon as she tried to run to her room, then killed Mrs Hastings in the dining-room. Mr Hastings, who had gone outside to await the return of a tractor, drew his pistol, ran into the house, killed one attacker, wounded another and put the remainder to flight.

But the family tragedy did not end with two dead. An hour later, while giving details to the police, Mr Hastings suffered a fatal heart attack. Later Mrs Norma Sim, Sharon's great-aunt, died in Salisbury of a heart attack when told of what had happened. According to the police, the guerrilla shot dead by Mr Hastings had the name of Mombi Macheni and was carrying a notebook containing an account written in Shona of the killing of seven Musami missionaries. The telling passage in the notebook was said to read as follows: 'On Sunday the day of 6/2/77 we went to Musami at St Paul's mission. We reached there at 9.15 and we had a storming raid. We shot four Europeans who were priests. Sisters were five, and altogether there were nine, eight dead. We took a watch only. No comrades were injured in the action. On the same day we went to Mazvidva and killed informers, kraalhead and the other one.' The account was signed 'No Talks Mabhena'. Beside his name was the number 3036. Detective Inspector Peter Begg informed the press that this terrorist Mabhena had been killed by troops on 13 March in the Mangwende TTL, where St Paul's mission is situated.

On 16 May, Robert Mugabe, speaking in Maputo, blamed 'Smith's killer squad' both for the murder of Bishop Adolph Schmitt and his companions early in December and for the Musami killings two months later; it was all part of a 'well-orchestrated' campaign to 'smear the freedom fighters'. Both Mugabe and Nkomo continued to deny the PF's involvement in the Musami massacre. The Justice and Peace Commission, despite the most detailed investigations, was never able to arrive at a firm conclusion.

5. visitors

Michael Pocock was Principal of St Mary Magdalene School, which he himself had founded in a remote, isolated spot at the end of a dirt track in the Inyanga mountains. Thirteen armed guerrillas put in an appearance on 2 February 1977, demanding that he lose no time in assembling the staff and pupils. After an hour of speeches Pocock and his African staff were invited to make a contribution to the cause: an offer too good to refuse. Thereafter Pocock made periodic deductions from staff salaries besides providing the guerrillas with food, clothes, beer and watches. On 27 February the same group of vakhomana arrived at Mount Mellery mission, to the north of St Mary Magdalene School; Father Laurence Lynch, a Carmelite from County Cork, offered them food and soft drinks, though well aware of what had befallen his Bishop, Donal Lamont. Three of the guerrillas attended Mass. Later, on the evening of 6 March, the 'boys' repaired to the priest's house, where they drank beer and gin in a friendly fashion.

Pocock and Lynch were duly betrayed and arrested. Indicted before Umtali Regional Court (like Donal Lamont before them) they were given suspended prison sentences under the Law and Order (Maintenance) Act, then deported.

6. eaten by a crocodile

Leo Ossowski gets up at 5 in the morning, slots his tanned limbs into khaki shorts and his head into a soft blue hat, kicks his motorbike into life at first light and begins his daily three-hour, pre-breakfast prowl of his 1,300-hectare tobacco-farm which lies 100 kilometres north-east of Salisbury at Mtoko. It's rough going on the back of his motorbike, skirting the anthills, looking out for the pythons he boasts of. 'Only the most dedicated farmers survive,' he says. 'Only the most vigilant.' Unlocking a steel safe containing two automatic shot-guns, an FN rifle and a revolver, he fondles each weapon with pride. But he refuses to carry a gun with him while touring the farm.

Stocky, alert and rather handsome, he speaks perfect English with a noticeable Polish accent. He addresses his black workers in pidgin Chilapalapa, sucks on his pipe, chuckles, reminisces, throws out a couple of East European political jokes, then bursts into laughter as he recalls the mad doctor who used to tell old ladies that the secret of health was to 'piss regularly'. The doctor finally went berserk, bit his own nurse and fled – leaving the whole area without a single qualified physician.

'What's the difference between England and Poland?' he asks me, then waits, blue eyes twinkling, busy with his pipe.

'What, then?'

'In Poland there are no Communists.'

He glances impatiently at his watch: the tractor-and-trailer is running late and this is the height of the tobacco-picking season. He shrugs: 'Every day my labour team receives a work assignment. Sometimes they work fast, sometimes slowly. It's up to them.' He pays $(R)12 a month plus free food. His wife Emma drives to the butchery where she buys fine cuts of beef for the house and grey, scrawny lumps for the farm labourers.

Leo motions towards a gnarled foreman of great years. 'He's a rare fellow that. From Malawi. Been with me for eighteen years. His wife was eaten by a crocodile.'

Born into an anti-Communist landowning family, Leo Ossowski had left Poland after the Communists confiscated his father's estate and the family had been forced to sell off most of its inheritance to keep pace with penal taxation. Reaching France after a spectacular series of border crossings, he took a train to Paris, where he had relatives, and became a student. One day he saw a newspaper advertisement soliciting settlers for Rhodesia. The British Consul granted him a visa but the French police were furious when they found out about it: if he wanted to live in an African colony, fine, but why choose a British one?

'I'm a refugee, I've seen it all before so I'm philosophical. I can move again, if I must.'

He patrols and prowls his farm, probing for kaffir laxity, laziness, in-efficiency, for good tobacco leaves left to rot on the ground – in short, for what whites call the 'K-factor'.

'You know something? If they have a car, they'll charge their own people extortionate amounts for a lift, they'll pack in ten or twelve. But when one of my sons wants a lift into Mtoko, the blacks with cars never ask for money.'

Emma Ossowski, Leo's wife, could probably trace her ancestry back to the Domesday Book but does not bother: 'When my boys were younger they ran wild with the African boys from the compound. And when they strayed too far or stayed out too late, the older African children would lead them back by the hand to the house. Then you get to the age when it stops; they go their separate ways.' (At some stage Christopher Robin must have stopped playing with Winnie the Pooh and Piglet.) 'Imagine *Gone with the Wind* before the American Civil War and you have a picture of our farm before all this started. . . . Always carefree, smiling faces. . . . Particular favourites with my children were the abandoned lambs which they would bring up as pets. . . . The African children would come up and say "hello hello hello". Mine would say "hello hello hello" back and they'd come and play. . . . In a child's world there is no black or white. . . . Now it's horrible. Men with guns and burnt-out huts and all the Africans looking so frightened.'

The tobacco leaf is piled high on Leo Ossowski's trailer. The women work with babies strapped to their backs and avert their gaze if stared at. The leaves are picked into metal clips, carried to the curing ovens, fastened on to racks, then passed through a heat of 55 degrees centigrade for twenty-four hours. Leo sniffs and probes for the giveaway sweet smell of leaf rot. Late at night he wakes up the old, ragged Rip Van Winkle whose job it is to keep the boiler fuelled and stoked. 'A rare fellow, that,' Leo says. 'He's not afraid of the dark. Most of them are scared of the dark. They see spirits or lights in the sky.'

The dried leaves are sorted, re-sorted, pressed into crates. Leo fingers the tobacco lovingly: if he sells an acre's crop for $(R)700, then about $(R)500 of that will be pure profit. Between 1970 and 1977 $(R)138 million passed from the state to the white farmers by way of subsidies and assistance; of that about $(R) 91 million was spent on bolstering the tobacco-farmers against the impact of sanctions. But sanctions remain a problem. 'We have to achieve a political settlement,' he says, lighting his pipe. 'But when, eh? In time for this year's auction sales? Is that possible?'

The sale and export of Rhodesian tobacco is swathed in secrecy and no national output figures are published. What Leo cannot know is that the volume of tobacco sales will fall during 1977 by 24 per cent. Leo will of course attend his moment of truth in one of Salisbury's gigantic auction warehouses. Striding in a pack from bale to bale, dealers will finger the leaf and make bids to a selling agent representing the farmer but appointed by the auctioneers. The buyers never reveal whom they represent, bidding on behalf of 'Number 2' or 'Number 5'. Their first bid is not irrevocable; sometimes their assistants will finger the leaf disparagingly as a prelude to a diminished offer. For the farmer it's agonizing.

Every precaution is taken to conceal the Rhodesian origin of the leaf. There is a constant fear of a small coin, or even a cigarette-end, getting caught up in the leaf to reveal the country of origin. It's the middlemen who take the risk, and the middlemen are numerous because it is by constant resale that Rhodesian tobacco exports are disguised and dispatched to the world's nicotine addicts.

At the end of the day Leo leaves the auction room with a cheque: all his children attend private schools and he needs money. In his best year he harvested a record 890 kg per hectare. With 50 hectares under tobacco he is expecting a total revenue from the crop of $(R)120,000. Against this figure his wage bill looks modest: seventy workers at $(R)20 a month (including the value of their free rations) comes to $(R)16,800 a year. Add the black foreman at $(R)1,440 a year, and you begin to see what Marx meant by surplus value. In addition Leo has the profits from his maize crop, his soya beans, his eighty Herefords. Of course this colonialism is not without its benevolent trimmings: school-books for the 120 children who live on his farm may cost him $(R)500 a year (the Government pays the salaries of the three teachers in residence). But, invited to erect a second school building at his own expense, Leo refused: 'When we have peace and my farm is secure I will build.'

Emma is a bit shy about the low wages; her ear, as Leo complains, has been tenderized by priests. Every morning she emerges from her kitchen to minister to the line of people waiting patiently outside the door: this one needs a small loan, this mother wants eye drops for her baby, this boy has a swollen gland in his groin, this one a septic foot. She says: 'They come to depend on one, like children.' We give one such invalid a lift back to the farm from the local clinic. In the back of the car is a heavy box laden with provisions. It seems wrong to let the invalid carry it to the kitchen but I'm also subconsciously probing for a reaction as I reach to lift the box myself. The reaction is sharp, unanimous and perhaps close to hysteria: 'Let him carry it! They can play you up, they limp past your window then walk on quite naturally!'

They.

Though Leo is a Catholic he believes missionaries who harbour or comfort terrorists should be punished. Dead against Donal Lamont. Emma has a much softer view on both counts. She'd have the Irish Bish to dinner, gladly; Leo would probably vanish on police reserve duty, to make a point – or play loudly his favourite new 45 r.p.m. release, 'From Bulawayo to Mkumbura', savagely sung, or belted out, by a squad of RLI troops to the tune of 'It's a Long Way to Tipperary'.

He takes a boyish delight in weapons, particularly the bizarre steel angularities and protrusions of the latest anti-terrorist vehicles: 'Zoom! You press a button and bullets spray from the side of your car! They make a noise! The terrs run away! They're cowards. Zoom!' He recalls his spells of duty in the police reserve: 'You're in an open truck, a sitting target. But if you look alert, they'll think twice. That's the problem with the Coloured soldiers, they slouch in the truck, they don't look alert. So they get hit.' He stoutly defends the protected villages as a long-term solution for tribal agriculture. 'Much easier to rotate the grazing of cattle; it discourages the bad habit of chewing up one area. And you get more social contact in the PVs.'

'You mean rape of the women by the Guard Force?'

He revolves the cheese platter, offers me a slice of Rhodesian 'Stilton' and refills my glass. There are certainly tensions in the family, but Leo is tight-lipped on the subject whereas Emma talks freely of the dilemmas confronting boys in the 18–23 age group – the collision of patriotism and parental love, the abrupt departure of young men on the eve of their call-up, the study courses abroad from which they don't return, the comments of neighbours, the constant worry about passports, the manoeuvring to obtain foreign currency allowances from Exchange Control.

Emma is lonely now. She wants to leave. It's just possible that she believes the war her husband and sons are waging is not a just war.

7. the farmer and his state

The state lent money to whites to buy and develop agricultural land; it did not lend money to blacks for the same purpose. In 1976–7 the Agricultural Finance Corporation, a para-statal board operating under the Ministry of Agriculture, handed out $(R)135 million in credits to 6,000 white farmers; but only $(R)13 million (one-tenth) to the 8,500 black Purchase Area farmers.

If white farmers suffered losses (cattle, machinery, buildings, stocks) as a result of the war, then the state awarded them 90 per cent compensation. Not bad! Black farmers received no compensation. White farmers were benefiting from 100 per cent initial tax allowances on farm improvements, purchase of machinery, African housing, motor vehicles and tractors. Such were the exploitable allowances and loopholes available to farmers that in 1976 60 per cent of European farmers were paying no income tax. A further 13 per cent declared taxable incomes of less than $(R)6,000 a year, and only 5 per cent owned up to earning more than $(R)30,000 per annum.

In addition the Government introduced various 'wear-and-tear' allowances. On the first water dam built the farmer received a 100-per-cent tax allowance; on the second dam, the same amount but aggregated over three years.

Even so, 4 million hectares (or 40,000 square kilometres) of white farming land stood vacant or chronically under-used. The Ministry of Agriculture and Comops thereupon launched a new joint scheme to provide farmers with grants for armed guards, fencing, and armoured vehicles.

8. Owen and Young

Then came young David Owen. Welsh, but born in Devon, a Cambridge graduate and a Doctor of Medicine, Owen was only 38 years old when James Callaghan appointed him Foreign Secretary in February 1977 on the death of Anthony Crosland. Firmly on the right of the Labour Party, a social democrat devoted to the Common Market, Nato and the Navy, Owen presented himself as a thrusting young man in a hurry – good-looking, arrogant, priding himself on his quick mastery of detail and capable of being bloody rude to his civil servants.

Under fire for 'appeasing' the Patriotic Front or for 'condoning' terrorism, he entertained a romantic view of his besieged condition: 'It's on these occasions when . . . people will discover whether their leaders are able to take the flak, if you like, take the strain of public life, take the long view. You must be judged and will be judged by history.'

In the meantime Owen was judged by white Rhodesians. After an initial meeting with Ian Smith in Cape Town on 13 April 1977 Owen paid a quick visit to Salisbury, bringing with his entourage sufficient jerrycans of petrol to avoid using the fuel which had broken sanctions. While rejecting the PF's claim to be the sole authentic representative of the people of Zimbabwe, Owen made it clear that he would not ask the PF to abandon the armed struggle until Smith had stepped down and provided genuine guarantees of majority rule. On Rhodesian TV he described the guerrillas as 'essentially men of good will driven to take up arms'. Rhodesians dubbed him 'Doctor Death'.

In February it became clear that with the election of Jimmy Carter, United States policy towards Rhodesia – and towards southern Africa in general – had taken a turn distinctly unfavourable to Salisbury and Pretoria. Despite his grey personality and conventional Yale-and-Wall Street background, Secretary of State Cyrus Vance made clear the new Administration's progressive posture on 15 February when he ruled out any purely 'internal' solution to the Rhodesian problem and urged – successfully, as it turned out – repeal of the Byrd Amendment which permitted the USA to import Rhodesian chrome in clear violation of Article 25 of the UN Charter.

The Africa desk of the State Department now came under the sway of radicals eager to commit their country to the support of liberation movements rather than military juntas and multinationals. (Within limits – let's not exaggerate.) Richard Moose became Assistant Secretary of State and senior State Department official concerned with Rhodesia, while the post of policy-planning director went to W. Anthony Lake, 39, author of The 'Tar Baby' Option, a critical study of the consequences of recent American support for white-minority regimes in Africa.

The key animating figure of the new team, however, was neither a career diplomat nor a conventional politician; he was 'Andy', otherwise known as Andrew Young. Appointed US Ambassador to the United Nations by a grateful Jimmy Carter – whose electoral debt to him was considerable – Young brought to his job not only the idealism of Martin Luther King's civil-rights campaigns but also an easy, relaxed, informal personal style and a sharp appetite for pursuing personal diplomacy on the continent of Africa.

Owen and Young hit it off – a young and dynamic team committed to a solution in Rhodesia which embraced the Patriotic Front, the guerrillas. America's duty, said Young, was 'to unwrite some real neglect and outright wrongdoing on the part of much of the West'. The best way to thwart Marxism was not to engage in duels and confrontations round the world but to demonstrate that a flexible, progressive capitalism would genuinely serve the aspirations of black nationalism and the African people. Young could spellbind an audience of civil servants in Washington with wit which was both unconventional and facile: 'At the junction of Jomo Kenyatta Avenue and Uhuru Avenue in Nairobi I saw a sign. It read: "Kentucky Fried Chicken".'

The black American Andrew Young soon joined David Owen in white Rhodesia's pantheon of infamy. Both men were convinced that there could be no viable solution to the conflict without the consent of the Patriotic Front. And they said so.

9. out of order

Four helicopters and a spotter plane appeared over Kandenga school in Buhera tribal trust land. At 12.30 p.m. one of them opened fire. According to a Justice and Peace Commission investigation, Jackson Tachiona Maisiri, a teacher, was hiding under a desk when shot dead by soldiers searching the classrooms for terrorists. Teacher Muchina was injured while hiding near the latrine when a helicopter circling overhead dropped grenades and fired through the roof. Three children were killed and eight admitted to hospital. The Ministry of Defence later claimed that 'it was equally if not more likely that terrorists shot them'. Even the sycophantic *Herald* was moved to regret that the authorities had attempted to hush up 'this tragic event'.

Describing a similar atrocity, an African MP, Mr Elijah Nyandoro, blamed 'this House [of Assembly] which had passed abominable laws'. He was promptly ruled out of order by the Speaker, Col. George Hartley, on revealing grounds: 'The honourable Member is well aware that to reflect upon the statutes passed in this House is out of order.'

Salisbury admitted having killed more black civilians in the course of 1977 than the guerrillas had: 780 as against 485. The deaths inflicted by the security forces were justified by the invention of spuriously exact categories of banned behaviour and by the attachment of statistics of bogus precision to each category. Thus, for example, during the first six months of 1977 the black civilians killed were said to have included fifty-eight 'curfew breakers', fifty-three 'running with or assisting terrorists', ninety-nine 'terrorist re-cruits', thirteen 'failing to halt', seven 'crossing to Mozambique', and fifty-four 'caught in crossfire'.

'If villagers harbour terrorists, and terrorists are found running about in the villages, naturally they will be bombed and destroyed in any manner which the commander on the spot considers desirable in the suitable prosecution of a successful campaign' (P. K. van der Byl in the House of Assembly, 2 July 1976).

Attempting to justify a small massacre at Dabwa kraal in the Ndanga TTL which took place on 3 May 1977, Supt Jim Carse of Chiredzi CID said: (a) 'They [the villagers] know they have got to attend these meetings, otherwise the terrorists may come back and kill them'; (b) 'I think the locals knew they had done wrong by allowing the terrorists to come into the area and call a meeting.' But how can one reconcile (a) with (b)? The security forces entered the kraal area, saw a meeting in progress, and the shooting took place (at this juncture in the official version it is invariably the terrorists who *open* fire while the security forces merely *return* it). The firing lasted seven minutes.

People panicked, fled, fell. The toll: thirty-five Africans dead, including sixteen women and twelve children, thirty-one wounded. Yet only one terrorist was reported killed and none of the fifteen soldiers, suggesting that the latter were in no great danger and fired indiscriminately. The *Rhodesia Herald* commented: 'After all, when bullets and people start to fly on a dark night who can say who is friend or foe, let alone civilian?'

The mood was vindictive. Of 254 members of the security forces killed since December 1972, fully 92 per cent had died during 1976 alone. Security-force casualties mounted – 94 were killed during the first five months of the year, temporarily reducing the famous 'kill ratio' from the 10:1 which General Walls found satisfactory to 6:1. In January Kalashnikov rifle fire had brought down a Canberra bomber over Mozambique, killing its crew of three: Flt Lt Ian Donaldson, 46, Sub-Lt David Hawkes, 21, and Capt. Robert Warraker, 36, an officer of the Selous Scouts who had been awarded the Silver Cross after spearheading several cross-border raids. P. K. van der Byl introduced a note of apocalypse:

'Inevitably and unavoidably the land will suffer. Indescribable chaos and irreparable destruction will follow but, come what may, we will uphold the ideals for which these men fought.'

10. the worst time

The young soldier stands alone at the side of the road, wearing the green beret of the RLI. By habit he has set himself apart from the knots of Africans who are also waiting for a lift at Christmas Pass; in this part of the world white drivers stop for whites, black drivers for blacks. He is blond, tubby and bronzed, an Afrikaner by origin, a boilermaker by profession, apprenticed at the Trojan Nickel Mine, Bindura, but now working in the Low Veld at Mashaba Mine. He plays prop in the Mashaba pack. Two blacks carry the tools of his trade and they're really lazy, these munts, unless you get on top of them. Otherwise they'll do nothing. They have their own cocktail bars, nicer than ours, he reckons, which is just fine so long as they stay there: just so long as they don't try and get into our social clubs.

Reserve duty with 2 RLI since 1974, a very aggressive bunch, always beating up other people or each other. 'I'm not the aggressive type.' Had to hitch a lift because those bastards in Umtali wouldn't give him more than six petrol coupons. At the end of the road is a three-day break with a bird in Salisbury, there aren't many you get for free nowadays, they're always asking where you've been and all that rubbish. He sits with his FN upright between his sturdy thighs, Africans are just savages, primitives, how he hates these kaffir buses belching black diesel smoke, you can't get past them on the road.

After twenty-one days in the bush you really begin to smell, that tinned food's monotonous, mind you some of these gooks are switched on, there was this Coloured Zanla commander in the Melsetter area, Brigadier Henriques, one time he had us pinned down and he called down the hill, 'That's your last tin of bully beef, corporal.' But it wasn't and later Henriques was found full of holes in a clinic. What you really fear are the rockets which will go through steel plate this thick, luckily they usually miss, it's the same with the mortars though sometimes they get switched on and before you know what's up three or four of your buddies are dead.

The worst time he was in this Mercedes 4/5, they cost $(R)22,000 or so he heard, we call them bookies, you know, wide-axled, I remember saying 'This driver isn't earning his breakfast he's going too fast for mine detection' and sure enough one went off, I just remember us rising up, no noise at all, at least I didn't hear anything, and I thought Christ we're going to turn turtle and everything fell on top of me there was mud and oil everywhere and I thought if this is an ambush I've had it because I'll never get this FN to work now. My gun. One chap was shaking with shock, couldn't stop drinking water, he was supposed to be getting through on the radio, the police radios are bigger and better than the portable ones the RLI carry. We had to stay with that vehicle all night.

I mean, you go into a village after one of your mates has been killed and you feel just bad and they say they've never seen or heard of a terrorist and you beat the hell out of them, the other side kill and mutilate them, I mean we wanted to know why we couldn't do that. You look in the reserves, they're just savages, terrible farming.

With your cross-border raids you can bring in air support, we'd come in and find piles of bodies, they'd rebuild the camp and we'd take it out a second time, just everything flattened. The RAR are not the same as the RLI, your black soldier is not the same and now we have to have all this extra drill just to keep the blacks in line, mind you the blacks in the Selous Scouts are the finest, they dress up as gooks, one group stayed with Zanla for a week until they'd removed all the firing-pins of their rifles and then they brought them in just like that, incredible. The real trouble is to find those gooks, their bushcraft is super, once you make contact you wipe them out no problem.

11. we are the lions of the bush

Alec is frugally sipping a Lion lager in a downtown bar in the company of an American mercenary captain of the Special Air Service, C Squadron. Alec says he works in the Parks Department as a game ranger and is also a Lieutenant in the Selous Scouts. He says he has spent a lot of his life telling lies – 'I've got to be honest with you about that' – but now he is telling the truth.

So what about his life as a Selous Scout? Alec is very earnest in his response, reflective even: 'I've killed a lot of blacks not because it's a race question but because they're Communist terrs. I've lost five flankers in the last year, including my best friend last February.' Alec talks about spoor, which he calls 'sign', about aerial spoor (tall grass lying down) and ground spoor. As for Zipra, 'Some of them are brilliant. One chap was a phenomenon. My ambition was to get him and talk to him. It took five days. The SoB pulled every trick in the book. He was a Shona operating in the north-west. Sometimes you read their letters which are mainly in English, it takes you back, I mean he really believes what he's doing, he believes in his freedom, you feel respect for him even though Uhuru's crap.'

Founded in 1974, upstarts in a hurry to describe themselves as legendary, the Selous Scouts were named after Frederick Courtney Selous, hunter, guide and Africanist, who joined Rhodes's payroll and guided the Pioneer Column to Salisbury. (Selous is held to be the model for Rider Haggard's Allan Quatermain in *King Solomon's Mines*.) Anxious to promote the myth that the whites were rescuing the whole of Mashonaland from incessant sub-jugation and plundering by Lobengula's Ndebele impis, Rhodes is said to have bribed Selous not to publish articles describing the real relationship of the Shonas and the Ndebele.

The Selous Scouts were the most celebrated and the most notorious military unit in Rhodesia: intrepid heroes, strong as lions, silent as cats – or vicious racist murderers, slayers of missionaries, masquerading in pseudo-gangs. Their commander, Maj. Ron Reid-Daly, a veteran of the British Special Air Service who had fought in Malaya, was a smallish man with a bulbous nose who relished publicity and invited the world's press to inspect the mysteries of bushcraft and super-survival at Wafa Wafa on the shores of Lake Kariba. It was wonderful copy and the reporters wrote it all down – the first full meal allowed to trainees came after fifteen days and consisted of maggot-ridden rotten meat, boiled baboon in fact. The standard bush diet included baboon brains, snakes, and the eyes and brains of the kudu, a large antelope, eaten raw. If thirsty, slit the kudu's stomach and you'll drain off a gallon of green fluid, half-digested grass.

The Selous Scouts' emblem was a fierce bird of prey and they wore brown berets (when not disguised as Zanla, Zipra or baboons). While the Scouts in their clandestine capacity bypassed the conventional military command structure, reporting directly to Special Branch 2, the Prime Minister's private intelligence unit, the 'Selousies' served mainly as adjuncts to more conventional units like the Fireforce of the RLI.

Finally, their numbers swelled to 2,000 and they became a unit much like any other.

To the World Council of Churches the Selous Scouts meant Dirty Tricks, Deep Throat and worse – army deserters testified to the World Council about white mercenaries disguised as blacks who trapped innocent villagers into believing they were freedom fighters before killing everyone in sight. In *Zimbabwe News*, meanwhile, Zanu published the confessions of a captured Selousie, Wonderful Mukoyi, an extravagant farrago of white super-devilry. It was no coincidence that Zanu accused the Selousies of precisely the same atrocities for which the guerrillas were held responsible by Salisbury, most notably cutting off the fingers and lips of a man or woman and then forcing the spouse to eat them. The pot was constantly calling the kettle black.

Citations: WO2 Charles Ernest Krause, Selous Scouts, for 'courage and aggressive leadership of a high order ... personal example, tenacity and ability to withstand extreme hardship ...'. Acting Cpl Boniface Mzinda, Selous Scouts, for 'aggression, determination and leadership ... an example to all his comrades'. Rhodesia's most decorated soldier, Sgt Head Waranda, lost a leg in a landmine explosion, then won a further combat medal while wearing a wooden leg. To perpetuate the mystique, citations for Selous Scouts were always brief and abstract – 'continuous courage of a high order' – whereas the brave deeds of other regiments were described in detail. No one must learn what the Scouts really did.

In June 1978 Capt. Christoph Schulenberg of the Scouts, who had once owned a bar in Pretoria, became the only holder of Rhodesia's Grand Cross of Valour. So precious would a glimpse of this superhero's face have been to the enemy that photographers at the ceremony were permitted only a rear view – a very broad back indeed. The Selousies sang their funeral march, 'We are the Selousies, the lions of the bush . . .', and their standard was on public view for the first time, more than three metres tall: at the top an osprey stretched out its wings, below it were two bull horns with a zebra skin, the horns bound in elephant hide. From their tips hung wildebeest tails on silver chains (to ward off evil spirits). The motto, Pamwe Chete, Forward Together.

12. ze smell of zem

There were, of course, no 'mercenaries' serving with the Rhodesian armed forces. All foreign conscripts were placed on exactly the same three-year terms of service as the Rhodesian regulars. OK? Maj. Nick Lamprecht, Rhodesia's main recruiting officer, nevertheless established a chain of agents round the world. The bait was £500 a month. Twenty men flew in from Ringway Airport, Manchester. At the Great Northern Hotel, King's Cross, a Hertfordshire insurance agent who had founded the World Deed a Day movement handed out Rhodesian military recruiting material to unemployed men who had answered a newspaper ad. In Texas, embittered veterans of Vietnam distributed Lamprecht's pamphlets – for a fee. In West Germany Capt. Edgar Teilan attempted to circumvent the law by advertising for 'safari guides' with military experience. About 1,300 replies flooded in from safari guides with military experience, many of them no doubt greatly attached to the memory of the Great Safari Guide himself. But Herr Teilan went to prison.

Maj. Lamprecht's sweeping net was not fitted with a humane filter. When the ashes of L/Cpl Matthew Lamb were flown home from Salisbury to Windsor, Ontario, in November 1976, it transpired that Lamb had been declared criminally insane in 1967 after shooting two people at a bus-stop in Canada. Peter Binion of Melbourne had more luck. Returning to Australia after service with the RLI which earned him the Bronze Cross for Valour, he explained: 'I came here for the principle of the thing.'

From Portuguese Angola and Mozambique they also came – and died. Lamb's death was followed shortly by a requiem Mass in the Catholic Cathedral, Salisbury, for Tpr Duarte da Costa.

But none of these soldiers, of course, was a mercenary.

The French mercenaries were stationed at Hurricane HQ, Bindura. Smart and dapper, with neat haircuts and hard, smiling faces deeply tanned, they appeared regularly in the bars and discos of Salisbury accompanied by female camp-followers. Some were ex-paras who had messed about in Ordre Nouveau and other rightist outfits which regarded Algeria as one betrayal and Vietnam as another – killers forever seeking revenge for what had happened somewhere else. By the time they reached Rhodesia these fellows had been all over: Zaire, Angola, the attempted invasion of Benin in West Africa. Many of their 'officers' were self-appointed. Specialists in rifle-butting black tribespeople in the mouth and stomach, when they hit genuine guerrilla formations during their sweeps of the Mozambique border they frequently broke and gapped it.

The 'mercenary' became a demonological figure in Zanla–Zipra myth-ology. Thus: 'Three female patriots from St Michael's mission, Mhondoro, reported to Comrade Tonderai Nyika . . . that African school girls are raped by enemy troops/mercenaries, most of whom suffer from chronic venereal diseases. . . . The mercenaries tell their victims that they fought against the people of Vietnam, Mozambique and Angola . . . some are Malawians, American Negroes, British, Red Indians and Israelites.' (Chimurenga war communiqué No. 19, Sept.–Oct. 1978.)

But evidently not invisible: 'The people's militia in Chikukwa area, Muta-mabara, arrested a lone drunk French mercenary. Questioned by the vigilant locals about the whereabouts of his fellow terrorists, the mercenary could not give a clear answer. He was detained.'

Mme Vaillant is very small of stature; the shot-gun she insists on carrying is larger than she is. Of all the weapons I have seen in Rhodesia, hers is the least practical; after each shot fired the barrel has to be broken and a new cartridge inserted in the breech. Studying her out of the corner of my eye as I drive down the Arcturus Road towards Goromonzi, I can see no way that she could ever get this blunderbuss out of the window, let alone take aim. But she might easily blow a hole in the roof of the car. Mme Vaillant is in high spirits because we are invited to lunch at a farm which has been attacked five times in six months. Her husband had been killed by a landmine.

Long grass closes round us on each side of the narrowing road: two large rocks loom ahead of us, bearing no resemblance to sentinels. To my horror Mme Vaillant now cocks her shot-gun. Incoherently I voice my doubts, anxieties.

'Eet ees the noise,' she explains. 'Zees gooks run away from noise.'

The cheery widow now supports herself and her children by teaching French at the University and the Institute of Foreign Languages. The black students, she explains, are never as good as the white ones; half-blacks are better students than all-blacks; quarter-blacks better than half-blacks; and so on.

'Zay love to talk and to hear zemselves and to argue use-less points. And I cannot tolerate ze smell of zem! Zumtimes I geeve zum black stu-*dents* a leeft in my car and I tell you I can hardly bear ze smell of zem!'

'You don't like blacks then?'

'Of course I like zem! Vun vood not leeve in Afrique all vun's life eef vun deed not like ze people!' She gestures eloquently. 'Vee could not leeve in Europe,' Mme Vaillant adds.

'Why?'

'Vy? Because of ze univers-*el* surrender to Communism.'

Evidently M. Vaillant had worked as a farm manager in Tunisia while that country remained a French colony. But after Independence, 'Ve voz chased out.' Then they tried French Guinea where 'Ze povertee voz tereeble'. Chased out again. Moving, retreating, south, the Vaillants worked as farmers or farm managers in the French Congo, then Zaire, then in Katanga. 'In Zaire eet voz tereeble, you ver nut'eeng, could not carry a goen eeven. . . .' The police were in the habit of making extortionate demands; Africans, she reminds me, are inherently incapable of governing themselves. The huge shot-gun wobbles on her lap; her hands are motored by her thoughts.

And what, I ask Mme Vaillant, fully anticipating her answer, of de Gaulle? A traitor! No need to hand over Algeria! The Arabs were beaten and in any case did not want full Independence! As for Ian Smith, a great man, honest and decent: 'Rhodesia ees a vunderfull country, ze best een Afrique!' But a bloody one for this tiny, cheerful woman: not only had her husband lost his life, but her daughter's fiancé, a bilingual Mauritian serving as interpreter to the French mercenaries in Rhodesia, had also been killed. Mme Vaillant had developed a low opinion of those French mercenaries: 'Zay ver ambushed and zay deed not fight back! Zay gapped eet!'

13. Sithole burns his boats

The Rev. Ndabaningi Sithole, former President of Zanu but now thoroughly repudiated by the OAU and front-line states, decided to burn his boats and return to Rhodesia. On 9 July 1977 he put through a call from Blantyre to the *Rhodesia Herald*: 'I am opposed to terrorism,' he announced, only hours after his last plea to the OAU for arms and money had been rejected. The following day he reached Salisbury and began to cash in on disaffected elements of the Bishop's party. It was a squalid operation. A fleet of Mercedes cars materialized; the men surrounding Sithole wore the smartest business suits and the darkest glasses. On Sunday, 28 August, he was heard in respectful silence by an audience of white farmers north of Salisbury. 'Don't get too frightened and run away,' he told them. Some of them did leave early but only to play golf.

14. fifty out of fifty

On 18 July Smith announced that an election would be held on 31 August. The British press treated the fissure within the ranks of the RF as a profound crisis, quite possibly heralding the political disintegration of white Rhodesia. Smith bluntly told his TV audience that those who believed there was any hope of continuing with 'those ideals and policies we believed in ten years ago' were not only 'completely out of touch with the world they lived in' but were on a 'suicide course'.

The new right-wing Rhodesian Action Party faced a formidable task. Under Smith's leadership the RF had won every seat at three successive general elections and at all intervening by-elections.

John Wright, a 33-year-old farmer, and one of the twelve MPs who had defected to form the RAP, campaigned in the Melsetter constituency on the eastern border, addressing white farmers and their families, denying the inevitability of black majority rule and calling for an unlimited war against the terrorists. The reaction was emotionally sympathetic yet sceptical. An elderly widow living alone on a remote farm, protected only by her dogs and her late husband's revolver, arrived at one RAP meeting damning James Callaghan as a Communist and expressing horror at the prospect of an all-black government (it would 'want everything'). She would nevertheless stick by Smith.

Only eight people turned up to hear yet another RF defector, 52-year-old Rodney Simmonds, a wartime Royal Air Force pilot born in Marandellas, address an RAP meeting at the Enterprise Country Club, thirty-nine kilometres north-east of Salisbury. Possessing a degree in economics and anthropology, and having worked for twenty-five years in Native Affairs, 'Sjambok' Simmonds – as he had been widely known following a dramatic altercation with an African – laid claim to understanding the 'African psyche'. Meanwhile Des Frost, former Chairman of the RF and a leading party strategist since UDI, warned a meeting: 'I don't believe we will be in this country as free people within a year if the RF comes to power again.' But only twenty-seven people were listening. The air was raw with fratricidal fury. It wasn't a penny on the income tax that was at stake here, nor segregated swimming-pools, it was staying or leaving – survival. Periodicals of the lunatic right like *Property and Finance* or *Rhodesia and the World* fulminated against betrayal, creeping integration in the army, and the blasphemy of handing over to 'the undeserving black majority' all that the whites had achieved.

But Smith was careful to blur the contours of what the future held in prospect. 'I know enough of the blacks of Rhodesia to hope that they will oppose a system of one man, one vote. . . .'

The challenge to the RF from white liberals was even less of a threat to Smith's supremacy. The liberal Rhodesia Party had displayed a fastidious disdain for the crude racism of the RF, but faced with any prospect of imminent black majority rule it recoiled.

In 1977 liberals created a new pressure group, the National Unifying Force, whose greatest asset was its president, Allan Savory. His Action Man credentials as an all-Rhodesian tracker were exemplary; he alone of the liberals possessed genuine charisma. Born in Bulawayo in 1935, he served the colonial administration in Northern Rhodesia, specialized in counter-insurgency, then formed, trained and commanded the Tracker Combat Unit, forerunner of Patu and the Selous Scouts. Holder of three medals, he had served in Parliament for over six years as a Rhodesian Fronter. But the logic of black nationalism finally reached him: and once it had got to him he faced it unflinchingly, with an unbending realism his followers found hard to stomach. In 1974 he had been disowned by the Rhodesia Party, of which he was a founder-member, for urging Smith to negotiate with the detained nationalist leaders; yet before the year was out Smith was doing precisely that.

Savory worked as an agricultural consultant, specializing in high-density cattle-farming. He made money, travelled widely in his own plane. When the NUF was founded in 1977 he was elected its first president. 'I know your fears,' he told an election meeting. 'I'm a Rhodesian like you. I'm a Rhodesian right-winger. A conservative. I have the same fears. I have two ranches. My home is here. Everything is here.' But there was no alternative to genuine majority rule. 'If I were a black,' Savory said, 'I'd be a terrorist too.'

The election was a white-out. As usual Smith swept the board. The RAP contested forty-seven out of fifty white seats and did not win one of them. The dynamic dentist, Dr Colin Barlow, standing for the RAP in the same Avondale constituency for which he had been elected in 1974 with 1,397 votes, limped away with only 217.

15. a very cunning scheme

Owen and Young set out for Africa with the new British proposals during the last week of August. Although Owen was normally the first to speak into the banks of microphones at each port of call, Young's presence symbolized America's support for the Labour Government's approach. Flying from Lusaka, where they met the front-line Presidents, to Pretoria, where they talked to Vorster and 'Pik' Botha, the terrible twins reached Salisbury the day after Smith won yet another landslide election victory.

The plan presented in Her Majesty's Government's White Paper,

Rhodesia: Proposals for a Settlement, was bound to feed and fatten the worm of hatred in Smith's belly. He and his 'illegal' regime were utterly to be swept aside — he must sign himself over into oblivion. A British Resident Commissioner would be appointed and the Union Jack would fly again over Government House. On top of that a UN force (as white as a box of Smarties) would help keep the peace while Rhodesia's precious security forces were merged, synthesized and emasculated by the British Resident Commissioner. The emergent stew, the so-called Zimbabwe National Army, would contain strong elements of the two guerrilla forces, Zanla and Zipra.

No way! For virtually every white Rhodesian, from the RAP to the NUF, this was the acid test. OK, your black politicians could feast in Meikles Hotel, lord it in Parliament, and crash their Mercedes to their heart's content, so long as the guns remained in good, responsible white hands. Otherwise — Congo Mozambique Angola rape looting horror murder flight. Not even the granite-jawed soldier-intellectual, Field Marshal Sir Michael Carver, whom young Owen wheeled out of retirement and presented as his potential Resident Commissioner, could allay the fears of white Rhodesians.

Life without the British South Africa Police was unimaginable.

The BSAP derives its name from the fact that it was once the private police force of Rhodes's British South Africa Company (which took possession of Mashonaland in 1890 on the pretext of a royal 'charter'). The BSAP was, of course, the finest in the world. Advertisements would appear in *The Times*: 'For the sons of gentlemen who can ride and shoot and are fond of an open-air-life. Join the BSAP.'

It was a matter of standards. All white recruits entered the BSAP as Patrol Officers — on parade they flaunted jodhpurs and high boots — whereas black recruits must enter with the rank of Constable. Police Commissioner Allum explained in 1976 why he had rejected all applications by black policemen for promotion to the rank of Patrol Officer, regardless of their years of service: (a) disapproval by European members of the Force; (b) non-acceptance by the European public; (c) disapproval by African members of the Force; (d) non-acceptance by the African public.

Allum did in fact have plans to promote a few old sweats to the rank of Patrol Officer but he had no intention of admitting to the Force any of your clever kaffirs or arrogant black graduates. That could only alienate the European policemen with the inevitable result that the BSAP would cease to be 'a truly multiracial Force'.

Ian Smith's attitudes had not been softened by his clean sweep in the election. The Owen–Young approach not only abolished Ian Smith in the most humiliating way, it threatened the whole strategy agreed between

Salisbury and Pretoria. Smith called the plan 'crazy', 'insane' and 'a very cunning scheme to get the PF into power'. He also claimed to have found Owen's tone of voice suggestive of a desire for revenge and retribution.

Between Smith and the British there was no love lost. Deputy Under-Secretary of State John Graham, a Foreign Office diplomat and Owen's principal trouble-shooter in Africa, described Smith's handshake as 'cold and wet' and the man himself as leading his people to civil war and disaster. (On the other hand, Graham got on well with Smith's Cabinet Secretary and *éminence grise*, Jack Gaylard.) Graham took out to Rhodesia a memory of how two Guards regiments had laid down their colours and picked them up again as part of a new, amalgamated regiment. So why could not the RLI and other Rhodesian outfits do likewise, eh? Perfectly reasonable. This bland British appetite for parallelism maddened the Rhodesians. How could you compare merging with a sister Guards regiment to amalgamating with Zanla and Zipra? – bloodthirsty, fanatical, Communist-indoctrinated baby-butchers.

16. blacklist

It was not only the 50,000 holders of the green Rhodesian passport who were barred from entering Britain and other countries by United Nations Sanctions (No. 2) Order 1968. In Salisbury a fifteen-page 'stop list' of proscribed Rhodesians circulated among the political and business élite: it included those who actively supported the regime and those who were known by London to be engaged in sanctions-busting.

In 1968 the Foreign Office set up a committee to review individual cases and re-examine cases on appeal; by 1978 the committee had examined about 700. Chaired by Sir William Murrie and composed of Lt-Gen. Sir William Oliver, Sir Frederick Pedler and Sir John Newey, this committee permitted appellants no legal representation, prided itself on its fairness and impartiality, and remained immune from judicial review. A good school and a second-class degree in Literae Humaniores were regarded in Whitehall as a suitable substitute for what Americans call 'due process'.

Admittedly Rhodesians whose offence was political were informed of the reason for their exclusion from Britain. This ban applied to members of the Government, RF MPs and Senators, senior officials of the Reserve Bank, of the RBC, of Air Rhodesia, and of the economic advisory committee. But those suspected of sanctions-busting were not provided with chapter and verse – the British didn't want them to know what the British knew.

Yet there were loopholes when convenience dictated. Ken Flower and Derrick Robinson, the regime's top intelligence and security officials, came and went at will. A Rhodesian Ministry of Information official could enter Britain on holiday, read or hear a report from a Salisbury-based correspondent, then get the journalist in question into deep trouble on his return to Rhodesia: Peter Niesewand of the BBC and the *Guardian* was among the victims. Rhodesian Special Branch ofıcers encountered no difficulties when entering Britain on holiday: tokenism was substituted for a genuine attempt to make the rebellion painful for the rebels.

17. where English is spoken

Eric Sinclair is a fitness fanatic who plays polo and used to run a farm in the White Highlands of Kenya. Now a Salisbury estate agent, he wears checked shirts with tropical cavalry twill and is followed around by a couple of large dogs whom he periodically kicks in a practised manner much appreciated by large dogs as a sign of true mastery and affection. His children have fair hair and fair skins; his wife Sally is English too and awfully nice.

The Sinclairs live in the outer suburb of Glen Lorne, where the houses are luxuriantly spaced in expansive gardens and the Chinamora TTL is close enough to offer a hint of danger, a whiff of Africa. Eric expresses contempt for Ian Smith but fervently believes that Britain is duty-bound to recognize the kind of internal settlement that Smith will negotiate. 'We should have done a deal with the Afs ten years ago. Now look at the mess.'

Recently Eric paid his first visit to Kenya since they sold up their farm in the late sixties. 'Pretty hopeless,' is his verdict. 'Fewer than one per cent of the white farms remain. Bribery and corruption have become a way of life. No day passes without a bank robbery or payroll snatch. Your main roads are breaking up and traffic obeys no rules. Half the creameries have closed down: the stud books, breed societies and milk-recording schemes are all defunct. East Coast fever is decimating the cattle because they use under-strength dip. Cholera is country-wide, at its worst near the Tanzanian border. Elephant and zebra are disappearing. The indigenous forests are being destroyed. If you care, it's heartbreaking. Of course, there's an alternative view.'

'What?'

'That it's simply black Africa.'

The Patriotic Front is not something Eric could live with. The very thought of it makes Sally Sinclair shudder and dispatches her mind in the direction of what she calls 'the spread of Communism' in Britain. As an example of this virus she cites the case of a 'great friend and a really nice man, too' who owns a firm in Liverpool which has to run at a loss can you believe it because if he laid off part of his work-force he would be confronted with a walk-out in another factory just incredible.

Eric Sinclair shrugs at the story. 'Hopeless,' he says. He is not, he wishes to make it clear, a racist of any stripe, but he can quote 'blacks I respect' who advise him that 'coons' aren't yet ready for senior posts in industry and commerce. 'Put the educated blacks in the civil service. They can't do more harm than the present bunch . . . overpaid parasites.'

Talk round the swimming-pool is boisterous, hearty, loud. Those trapped in the laager by exchange-control regulations plan foreign holidays, real or imaginary: boating in the Med, skiing in Italy, a camping tour of Crete.

'I'm not a racist,' Eric Sinclair wishes to emphasize. 'No, I'll tell you where you'll find your true racist – the white artisan class here, the railwaymen, the electrician who comes to your house with two coons to carry his tools – a peasant who suddenly finds himself a king.'

Sally nods supportively. 'You wouldn't believe the way the Asians treat the blacks,' she says.

'They brought Indian coolies here to build the railways because they understood time and could clock in,' Eric explicates. 'They should have been sent home afterwards but they were allowed to stay. In the course of time they grew rich, avaricious and rapacious.'

Eric is none of these things. But about one thing he's adamant: Britain is not for him because 'frankly, paying 83 per cent income tax doesn't appeal.' So where will they go if, as Sally insists, black Communism is on the way?

'Somewhere', she is determined, 'where English is spoken. I don't want to be a foreigner.'

Eric's polo takes him not only up the Mazoe Road to Thorn Park ground but round the country – though transporting horses is no longer feasible in many 'operational areas'. Quite a few polo-players are Grey's Scouts and Eric describes with some scorn – he loathes Afrikaners – how South Africans raised 75,000 rand to buy one hundred horses for the Grey's.

'That oaf Rowan Cronje went down to Pietermaritzburg for the handing-over ceremony. Said the horses would be fighting Marxism. The stupid Boers sent up – can you believe it – one hundred Persil-white nags. Terrs could hardly believe their luck; in Matabeleland they could see the Grey's coming from ten miles away. The poor sods tried rubbing brown boot polish all over the horses but it wore off too quickly, damn it, you have to wash a sweating horse down. Then they experimented with dyes. Several beasts came out crimson, others resembled zebras . . . all rather like a *Just So* story that went wrong.'

Eric Sinclair's Sandhurst laugh echoes across Glen Lorne towards the Chinamora TTL.

18. the bars to the cage

Alex Maddocks is on the road by 7 every morning, sweeping down the long Enterprise Road with the vanguard of the rush hour. Lighting the first of the forty Madisons he will smoke in the course of the day, he flicks the car radio:

'Rhobank! The Bank that keeps pace with today's people presents the Winners, people who made it all the way to the top!'

'The Beverly Building Society presents the Shona language clinic. . . . Now, Ishmael, can you tell us how we should say in Shona "this white cloth"?'

Ishmael obliges. End of spot. Tomorrow Ishmael will teach us to say 'this black cloth'.

Maddocks parks his car behind Meikles Hotel and walks briskly across Cecil Square, dressed in a safari suit with very short shorts. He passes the flagstaff, scene of the annual Pioneer Day ceremony when the Union Jack flies again and the BSAP band sound reveille. Excellent for business, 12 September being spring time with the jacarandas in full bloom. All such atavistic ceremonies are good for business if you own a nostalgia shop near Cecil Square – Independence Day, Battle of Britain day, Arnhem day. . . .

Maddocks unlocks the shop, withdraws the iron grilles from the windows. He sells replicas of just about everything, including little bronze figurines of Baden-Powell, heroic defender of Mafeking: they go like hot cakes when 6,000 attend the annual Scout and Girl Guides' parade at the National Sports Centre. Last year his own youngest daughter narrowly missed getting the Rhodesian Award for Fortitude and Endurance, which went to a certain Gillian Cowen of 20th Salisbury (Oriel) Company.

Joshua the security guard turns up with his helmet.

'Morning, Baas.'

At 9.15 a white craftsman comes by appointment bearing a bronze steam engine which he offers exclusively to Maddocks, provided Maddocks will take ten replicas, the ploy being that 550 members of the Rhodesian Society are scheduled to put on Victorian or Edwardian costume and travel from Salisbury to Marandellas on board a train drawn by a Class 15A Garrett Locomotive – let the terrs attack if they dare! Mike Kimberley, Chairman of the Society, is planning to make the trip dressed in a pith helmet and jodhpurs. . . .

Maddocks haggles with the craftsman. A deal is struck over a slug of brandy.

Oh England, olde England, only here, in this teapot-shaped enclave of southern Africa, are you true to yourself.

So, at least, Maddocks has discovered: a five-shilling stamp bearing Churchill's bust, with the Queen's head and Parliament in the background, overprinted with the words 'Rhodesia' and 'Independence 11 November 1965', is currently fetching $(R)250. But the price reflects more than the passions of philatelists; stamps are a way of getting money out of Rhodesia.

So too are medals, Maddocks can't get hold of enough of them to meet demand. Even the mundane BSAP Long Service, Good Conduct and General Service medals fetch nice prices; as for a Bronze Cross or a Legion of Merit, the sky's the limit. Flags; a book called *The Valiant Years*; watercolour reproductions of Thomas Baines's Victoria Falls sketches painted during the time he spent with Livingstone; drawings of the current terrorist war showing a young father on crutches, legless, with his tiny son holding fast to one of the crutches; Nazi medals, Iron Crosses, SS daggers, Rhodesia is Super T-shirts, I'll Zap a Gook T-shirts. . . . Hand-carved furniture, jewellery, coins, regimental insignia, clocks, leopard-skins, silverware, Sandawana emeralds from Belingwe. (Many smuggled these emeralds out yet could not sell them abroad.)

Alex Maddocks does also provide additional services for his customers. He would backdate a sales invoice for anyone he knew.

During 1976 Foreign Exchange Control regulations have been brutally tightened. Departing families can now take only $(R)1,600 out of the country in cash, plus a further $(R)400 per person, plus clothes and household goods purchased more than six months prior to leaving Rhodesia.

The holiday allowance is set at $(R)320 (later $(R)370) per person per annum: two years' allowance can be accumulated and spent in arrears.

Every adult white Rhodesian knows these figures by heart. They are the bars to the cage.

Maddocks does not invariably go straight home. A drink in Meikles may suit his mood. Or a drink plus girl in the Ambassador. If he wants to impress an overseas client he'll take him to the stately Jameson. Otherwise he may drive down to Annabelle's massage parlour on Rotten Row. Annabelle caters for 'today's men' in a bungalow with a corrugated tin roof half concealed by a wilderness of garden. Specializing as she does in pelvic massage, Annabelle has 'the utmost faith in Rhodesia' and offers a 10 per cent discount to all members of the security forces. 'I'm a normal girl,' she tells Alex and everyone else. 'Just because I've been a stripper people brand me. It isn't fair.' Annabelle charges seven dollars for thirty minutes. 'I'm writing a book,' she adds.

Emeralds are sold very discreetly in the Maddocks shop near Cecil Square. And Alex knows many people, people who come, people who go; he can arrange for emeralds – legally restricted for export only – to be set in finger rings (in which he does trade) and taken out of the country on the hands of bona fide visitors, tourists, women members of foreign television teams. A certain amount of trust is required, of course, but almost all risks are worth taking when you're desperate to get your money out of Rhodesia. Alex's knowledge of the foreign press corps in Salisbury is certainly very useful. He can arrange for a reporter to spend the weekend on a white farm in a 'hot' area, in return for which a financial transaction takes place: the farmer hands the reporter (say) $(R)200 in bank notes and the reporter gives the farmer a sterling cheque payable in the UK. Instead of the official exchange rate of $(R)1·45 to £1 obtainable in the Standard Bank, a foreign journalist can pick up $(R)2 or even $(R)2·50 to the £1 on a war-battered farm in Mtoko or Headlands.

On such occasions Alex Maddocks might take an indirect commission in cash; or in kind; or in patronage; or in alleviation of his military reserve commitment (where the client is in a position to help). Alex can arrange things. His South African subsidiary company buys a wide range of goods – the catalogue calls them 'Memorabilia' – from his Rhodesian company at extremely modest prices: which means that extremely modest sums of money are remitted from South Africa to Rhodesia. It is at the re-export stage, when Alex's South African company sells the product in West Germany and the United States, homelands of the great White Supremacy collections, that the real profit is made – a profit lodged in rand in a Barclays Bank account in Durban.

But in one area Maddocks got caught out badly and no amount of wheeling, dealing or petitioning has brought him a reprieve. Though he had anticipated UDI in 1965 he had failed to foresee its full consequences: all his assets in the UK, including a deposit account, have been frozen for more than a decade, though the Bank of England allows him to draw £20 a day while visiting Britain. One helpful Bank official suggested that he could achieve the release of his blockaded funds by assigning them to educational, relief or indeed missionary enterprises in Rhodesia.

But Alex Maddocks is not a religious man.

19. at home

The Maddocks family occupy a large house in the suburb of Borrowdale, not far from the famous racecourse. The purchase took place through Eric Sinclair's estate agency, which described it thus:

'BORROWDALE: $45,000, impressive Moorish style residence on 2 acres with magnificent gdn. with pool, watercourse, fish pond, etc. Ent. hall, 2 lounges, sep. d.r., study, 3 brms, 2 bathrms, sep. toilet on gnd floor, large covered veranda, balcony off 2 brms, garage, fitted carpet in lounge.'

Mrs Sheila Maddocks and her lovely, 18-year-old daughter Sharon buy their clothes at Borrowdale Fayre or at the Tub Bathroom boutique. Both mother and daughter carry the groomed, lacquered, sun-kissed appearance characteristic of Rhodesian women. Sharon, currently working for the BSAP traffic investigations department, has been featured as police pin-up of the month ('Sharon's a fair cop') and is among the twenty girls short-listed for the final of the *Herald*'s Swinging Miss competition. (Three of the twenty finalists are black.) So popular is this beauty contest that within two hours of the box-office opening at 6.30 a.m. all 800 seats were sold. The winner will be rewarded by a $(R)500 cash prize, free hair styling for a year, a clothing voucher, the chance of a bursary at a secretarial school and an air trip to Victoria Falls – for two. Naughty Sharon fancies her chances as a model and has already featured in an ad for Partex mini pads 'for light flow days'. Wide, candid eyes: 'No fuss of belts or pins and you can wear what you want.'

The ad agency's photographer, Phil, a former Selous Scout with muscles like mountains and very keen on anthropology, also took a number of pics of Sharon beside the Maddocks pool. One of them got sold for $(R)3 to the *Sunday Mail* and appeared with this caption: 'Nothing to declare . . . but not much concealed either! She's no smuggler but a young lovely, Sharon Maddocks, who wants to learn to swim because she's tired of being thrown into pools at parties.'

Sharon takes Phil to her bedroom and locks the door. At first her mother screamed and took it as a personal insult, in this house of mine! but Sharon looked pityingly at Sheila and asked whether she had never done anything before she got married a hundred years ago and that just about ended the battle.

The only Africans whom the Maddocks women know well are the two domestic servants, cookboy and gardenboy, they employ for $(R)35 and $(R)25 a month respectively. Majority rule doesn't appeal to Sheila Maddocks. 'You won't find me hanging around if the Bishop starts sending his Eyes of Youth to this house!' Besides, as she puts it, 'I want to be able to knock down an African in my car if the idiot runs out in front of me without being lynched on the spot.' Sheila is impossible to parody. For decades novelists have been fascinated by memsahibs, but the memsahibs and their daughters don't seem to read the novels and their performance remains unadulterated by a modicum of self-awareness. For Sheila Maddocks majority rule means pillage and rape, such as occurred in the Congo, or, more likely, the petty humiliations and indignities suffered by a woman friend of hers in Zambia:

'She was taking a bath and her houseboy walked right in. When she shouted at him, he said he was changing the towel!'

Sheila's sister Trish and her husband Jep Botha are frequent visitors. An accountant who specializes in advising farmers how to avoid paying tax, Jep once played rugby for Rhodesia: eight of his farmer clients have been murdered since the war began. Sheila and Trish are rarely together more than five minutes before the conversation turns to servants. Sheila has recently lent money to her gardenboy Joseph to buy a bicycle but (she is convinced) he spent the money on booze. 'Just how many children that Joseph has scattered around the country I'll never know.'

Trish says: 'Give them something and they'll always want more. When Dzingai's hut was burnt down I set him up in new clothes, and his wife and kids too, then he comes to me and asks for more. I told him, "Dzingai! You go to hell." So then he got into our locked cupboard and stole our wedding linen. We never opened that cupboard because we had so much linen. . . .'

Neither Sheila nor Trish has ever ventured into an African township – the riots of the early sixties are not forgotten. Even in the city Sheila tries to avoid the areas and streets where black crowds congregate because she greatly fears knocking someone down or having a puncture and then being surrounded by a crowd of 'coons', hostile or grinning. But she knows what goes on in the townships: extortion, witchcraft, political intimidation. Her sources are (1) her gardenboy, (2) her cookboy.

Jep Botha is strong on the Dutch Reformed Church and has a cousin in the Broederbond. But for liberal-minded missionaries he has no sympathy, particularly the Catholic ones.

'Those missions what did they do? They released a lot of sixth-grade primary-school kids and told them they were ready to run the world. The Russians put them up to it, to undermine what we've built here.'

For years the two sisters have been conducting a dark surreptitious race war in the polished shadows of their suburban homes. According to the Poverty Datum Line figures a man needs $(R)76 a month to support a small family, but wages on that scale are unthinkable, they'd only blow it on booze, their wives and kids would never see it. (The Zimbabwe Federation of Labour wants to abolish the Masters and Servants Act of 1901 which still governs the status of domestic servants and makes it an offence under the law to leave the place of work without permission, to refuse an order, or to get drunk during working hours.)

'Very well,' says Sheila, 'let the nigs cut their own throats, push wages up to impossible levels, and then everyone will be out of a job.'

'Anyway, that's not such a hard life they lead,' says sweet Sharon Maddocks, 'though they know how to grumble. You peep through the hedges on a weekday morning and what do you find? Gardenboys leaning on their spades, nannies drinking tea, and cooks reading the newspaper on the back doorstep . . . I do wish I had their life, I really do. They can lie on their backs under the trees, out there on the roadside, not a care in the world. If I did that, I'd be arrested for vagrancy.'

'People come out here from England and they tell us how badly we treat our servants,' Trish says. 'But believe you me, after six months those same people are treating their munts worse than we would ever dream of doing. Joseph and Ephraim get 3 lb of protein meat, usually chicken, 11 lb of mealie meal, a pound of sugar and as much tea, soap and soap flakes as they need. Now where else in Africa would they get that?'

Sheila nods, distractedly – since girlhood in South Africa both sisters have been madly competitive, it used to be swimming, then boys, a husband, now it's good works. They hurl themselves into the Terrorist Victims' Relief Fund (Sheila), the Women's Voluntary Services (Trish), or helping TV's Jill Baker with Co-ord-A-Nation (Sheila), or looking after pets (Trish) at the SPCA whose fourteen branches are crammed – barking and miaowing and chirping – with pets left behind by whites taking what Trish insists on calling, despite Jep's mild reproaches, 'the yellow route'.

'It could be us next,' he reminds her.

The SPCA has plans to put down all the pets 'in the event of chaos' (majority rule?). Both sisters frenetically work the South African charity circuit; Sheila scored by helping to collect 380 kilos of dried fruits, cherries and nuts from the women of South Africa – 300 huge Christmas cakes will be baked by Rhodesian women for the troopies out in the bush fighting terrorism. 'The South African women were magnificent,' Sheila Maddocks told RBC-TV's 7.45 p.m. news bulletin. Trish gritted and ground her teeth that night.

But she too will be a guest at the Mayoress of Salisbury's annual tea-party where most everyone (as Americans say) wears a broad Ascot hat in the gracious Passing-Out Parade style set by the First Lady, Mrs Wrathall. At the opening of Parliament Mrs Wrathall sits in a long dress, straight-backed in a high chair, pretending to be the Queen.

This year, for the first time, black employees have been invited to the annual staff junket of Alex's import–export company. Sheila is apprehensive:

'I don't want to dance with one, Alex. It's not the black skin I mind but you never know where they have been, do you?'

20. a baby: Natasha Glenny

According to the Farmers' Union's roll of honour, Mr D. R. C. Greef and his wife Mrs M. A. Greef were killed at Plumtree on 15 May. Zapu's periodical, *Zimbabwe Review*, published in Lusaka, claimed that 'our combatants [Zipra] attacked and killed the couple at their home at Lupane' – which is more than 150 kilometres from Plumtree as the vulture flies.

According to the Rhodesian press, small white children and a black nurse standing round a bonfire on the lawn were killed when guerrillas launched a surprise attack on the Shangani recreation club, which stands next to the main Gwelo–Bulawayo road, on 12 July. But Zipra claimed that they killed three policemen 'guarding the place' in the course of their attack. (When I stopped at the club six months later the pretty gardens, with their swimming-pool and children's play area, had still not been walled in.)

During the second week of June guerrillas operating in the Wankie area opened fire on a passing car, killing Petrus du Plessis, 29, his son Karl, 6, and Andries Burger, 46. Two boys, Manie du Plessis, aged 4, and Christopher Swart, were seriously injured.

In the south-east a Ministry of Water Development Engineer, Alastair Wilson, 21, was shot dead when his vehicle was ambushed.

On the morning of 6 August Alan J. Ritson, a farmer and veterinary surgeon from the north of England, was paying out wages at Tsomo Ranch, Filabusi, when armed men in camouflage dress appeared and dragged him protesting into the bush. According to his foreman, Ritson tried to plead but the commander would have none of it: 'This is not the time for talking, it's time for war.' A rifle barked.

When they failed to return home on a day early in August, Stanley Chesworth set out to look for his daughter Kathleen, 19, and her friend Christopher Hales, 20. Mr Chesworth found their car on a road near Bulawayo riddled with bullet holes. Both the young people were dead.

Zipra communiqué: '14 August 1977: Solusi–Bulawayo Road; Lance-Corporal Christopher Allen Hales of Llewellin Barracks and his wife died in an ambush by our commandos. The couple's car was riddled with bullets.'

Mayhem continued up and down the border. Marius Sleigh, a slow-speaking Afrikaner of 50 who farmed 400 hectares of tobacco and maize nineteen kilometres north of Umtali, employed a work-force of thirty, mainly Malawians and Mozambicans who had been with the Sleigh family for twenty years on various farms across the country. At 10 p.m. on 20 August Sleigh and his 16-year-old son heard gunfire from the labour compound, where a Saturday-night beer-party was in progress. On going to investigate they came under fire. The following day the Ministry of Information flew reporters and television crews to the farm, where they inspected fourteen bodies lying on the edge of a tobacco field under a burning midday sun. A pregnant woman in a cheap print dress lay dead, flanked by the bodies of a young boy and girl. The round brick huts of the compound had been gutted by fire.

On 13 September 1977 Charles Ogilvy, 53, and Denzyl William Dunn, 23, were killed during a guerrilla attack on a Shamva farm.

Two murders during September sent shudders of horror and revulsion through white Rhodesia. Both the victims were female, one old and one very young.

Evelyn Rushmore was 70 years old and the daughter of a former Prime Minister of Southern Rhodesia. On the night of Tuesday, 6 September, guerrillas entered Spring Grange Farm, in the Nyamandhlovu area north-west of Bulawayo, and killed the old lady. She was alone at the time. Her husband Edward, a cattle-breeder, had earlier been taken to hospital.

The death of Natasha Glenny provided the Salisbury regime with an ideal propaganda weapon. The smiling, cherubic features of this chubby six-month-old baby appeared on the cover of the Ministry of Information's pamphlet, *Massacre of the Innocents*.

Michael Glenny, 26, was employed in the Chipinga area by the Rhodesian Wattle Company. On 29 September 1977 he and his wife Marinda, 22, were ambushed in their truck, which skidded off the wet dirt road into a culvert. Glenny let off one shot from his pistol. During a nightmare flight through the bush Marinda Glenny fell into a river. Meanwhile a gang of about twenty-five were attacking the Glenny house, where baby Natasha was asleep in her cot. According to her African nursemaid, she snatched up the baby, strapped her to her back and covered her head with a towel. When one of the terrorists pulled back the towel, the nurse (as she reported it) pleaded that the baby was her own, an albino; but the baby was ripped from her back, flung across the veranda, then stabbed in the back with a bayonet.

When Michael and Marinda Glenny arrived home, exhausted and shaken by their own narrow escape, they found their baby lying face down in a pool of blood, her back a mass of lacerations, her flesh white and pulpy.

It turned out that the guerrillas had been living in one of the labour compounds and had not been reported. In February 1978 Elias Nyamadzwayo, a 48-year-old foreman, was sentenced to fifteen years' hard labour for having failed to report three visits by the guerrillas to the farm compound.

21. beware of the dog

Trish's husband Jep Botha has installed a two-metre security fence round his home at Ruwa at a cost of $(R)900. An alarm system and floodlighting set him back by a further $(R)750. Then it seemed wise to invest in a five-barrel anti-ambush shot-gun, which is attached to his mine-proofed Land-Rover. The barrels point upwards until the gun is activated by a spring-loaded pin. As the barrels level out they strike a fixed-firing anvil and blast away at five angles. Cost, $(R)258. Trish Botha has attached certain notices to the security fence, including 'Basopa lo Inja', Beware of the Dog, which is accompanied by a picture of a growling bulldog hot on the heels of a very black Sambo indeed.

Like many ladies Trish carries a light gun, with six locally manufactured semi-automatics to choose from, including the Cobra, the LDP, the Rhogun, the Mamba and the Rhuzi (a Rhodesian version of the famous Israeli Uzi). Jep Botha, increasingly obsessed by guns and gun permits, constantly scans the 'for sale' columns of the *Herald*:

'REVOLVER. ·38 Special, ideal for lady, $150. Plus Winchester shotgun, double barrel, 12B, $150. Phone 43594.

'RIFLE. Brno 6·5 x 57, plus ammo, beautiful model, in perfect cond. $150. To view at Farmers' Co-Op, Salisbury. Phone Norton 74213.

'RIFLE. 7mm Mauser, plus ammo, $230. Phone Headlands 00240 after 6 p.m.'

Norton, Headlands – in such places do Jep Botha's farmer clients live and sometimes die. He lifts the phone and arranges to inspect the Mauser at his office in Robinson House on Baker Avenue. It is Jep's job – more than a job, a vocation – to lead his clients through every conceivable loophole in the tax and Exchange Control regulations. Not that Rhodesian tax is conspicuously onerous: had it been so, there would have been fewer white Rhodesians. Despite the 12·5 per cent tax levy imposed in the budget of July 1977, 'living in clover' is the way Jep privately describes the situation of the Rhodesian taxpayer:

Whereas an Englishman pays £2,400 on the first £6,000 of taxable income, the Rhodesian pays only $(R)1,320 on the first $(R)6,000 of taxable income. Whereas an Englishman in the tax bracket £9,000–£10,000 pays 55 per cent on that portion of his earnings, the Rhodesian pays only 33 per cent on the equivalent slice. An Englishman might pay a total tax bill of £10,840 on an income of £20,000, but the Rhodesian would pay only $(R)6,809.

In England the highest, horrendous rate of tax imposed by the Labour Government is 83 per cent; in Rhodesia the limit is reached at 48·4 per cent.

Jep Botha has a client, a Marandellas farmer called Irwin, who pays $(R)16,489 on a net income slightly in excess of $(R)40,000. When Irwin invited Jep and Trish Botha down for the weekend, Jep took some pleasure in reminding him that in the UK he would have had to fork up the sterling equivalent of $(R)27,660 to the taxman. Farmers, of course, are destitute; it is Jep Botha's job to prove it to the tax inspectors. Yet he knows that if 165 Rhodesian farmers are earning more than $(R)30,000 a year in *declared* income many are earning more in income undeclared.

Indeed, there is prosperity all round: between 1964 and 1975 white salaries rose by 103 per cent while the consumer price index rose by only 49 per cent.

Of a Sunday the Bothas call for a late barbecue lunch, T-bones, at the Maddocks home in Borrowdale. There they encounter an officious French journalist from Le Something who sits at the poolside downing sanctions-breaking imported gins while aggressively firing off questions:

– Why are average white incomes in Rhodesia ten times as high as average black incomes?

– Why does the bottom 40 per cent of the country's working population earn only 8 per cent of national income?

– Why does the state spend fourteen times as much on the education of every white child as on the education of every black child?

– Why does only one African in every 300 have a vote?

Young Rod Maddocks, on temporary R&R from territorial service with RLI Fireforce, is clearly itching to throw the French bum in the pool. Had it been a case of confronting this fellow during a disco dance in the Park Lane Hotel, or wherever, no trouble at all: but a young Rhodesian warrior does not readily assault guests in his own home.

It is his father, Alex Maddocks, whose patience finally runs out. His tone is as sharp as the ABC of hospitality allows: 'The answer to almost all your questions is quite simple: we, the Europeans, are the ones who pay the taxes.

We are the ones who are fighting this war. My son spends half of every year with the RLI in the bush. In my opinion the Afs are always in too much of a hurry. They pay only 0·5 per cent of all personal income tax – ask Jep here, he knows all about that. I say to these black politicians, "OK, so far you go, but no further. I mean, here's the line. I mean, don't give me any paper guarantees you can tear up tomorrow."'

The man from Le Something is not abashed. He expects to meet hostility, even violence, in a white imperialist racist community facing a revolutionary uprising of the impoverished and exploited peasant masses.

For Rod Maddocks and his girl, Saturday night is fever night. At La Bohème Eddie Calvert, the man with the golden trumpet, is playing 'O Mein Papa' and 'Zambezi'. He also offers a few jokes: 'Why did I leave England? Two reasons: One, the wife. Two, Harold Wilson.' Cheers from the police reservists who have taken over several tables and are loudly calling for a belly-dance. Later on they'll head for the Park Lane or the Oasis in search of Afs to beat the shit out of.

Rod would like to go with them. There are times when he regrets the violence within him but it's a habit, almost an addiction, that he can't kick. On New Year's Eve he and four of the lads went to the Kamfinsa multiracial hotel with a chimpanzee they'd hired from a pet-shop. When the chimp drank the beer bought by the Afs standing at the bar, there was the kind of punch-up that Rod Maddocks had a thirst for. On another occasion he and three of his mates got pissed, drove to a friend's house in Highlands, had some more beers, then attacked a car driven by a middle-class coon. When they later offered through their lawyer to pay $(R)300 damages in respect of the munt's car, the kaffir agreed not to press charges for assault and injury to his chest and back.

Rod believes in 'standards' – no objection to having to wear a tie at the Park Lane. When the military police arrive, the redcaps, it doesn't matter whether you're wearing a tie or not, does it? It's every man for himself.

22. freedom fighters come early in the evening

The Catholic diocese of Gwelo is shepherded by Swiss priests whose faces remain pale under the African sun. Bethlehem Fathers are practical men, builders, chemists, linguists, printers, schoolmasters; the Swiss-based Father Superior of the Order, the Reverend J. Amstutz, resembles a provincial primary-school teacher accustomed to clip his trousers and bicycle fifteen kilometres a day to the parish school. In June 1977 he wrote a confidential report describing deteriorating conditions in Gwelo diocese:

'People are disturbed by the diversity of groups: freedom fighters, deserters, groups that have run amok, criminals and finally government troops, the Selous Scouts. But in the long run people are capable of distinguishing between a genuine freedom fighter and an imposter. Freedom fighters come early in the evening, i.e. they do not come at midnight and pull the whole family out of their sleep. They knock gently, do not run down doors, are very courteous and ask for specific help. . . .

'How does the missionary go about his task? He may be prevented from going to some regions. The guerrillas may warn him. Contacts, however, remain alive. . . . Women sit by the roadside, and with a movement of their hand they guide the missionary on his way. . . . This is, for him, an unheard-of experience: suddenly he discovers his complete dependence from [sic: on?] his congregation, where formerly it was the other way round.'

Early in August 1977, on a Sunday, six Zipra guerrillas lined up the staff of Regina Mundi mission in Bulawayo diocese. The gang denounced Germans as supporters of Smith, insisted that missionaries are agents of imperialism, and remonstrated with the black Sisters, calling them 'slaves of the whites'. A building-contractor working at the mission, Rudi Kogler, evidently provoked beyond endurance, shot dead one of the guerrillas with a pistol, and was then himself killed. The mission was closed.

A few days later, at 2.15 p.m. on 10 August, eight Zipra guerrillas arrived at St Paul's mission, Lupane, in northern Matabeleland. Clearly drunk, they rampaged round the maternity ward of the mission hospital, causing some women to flee into the bush with their babies and some without their babies. The guerrillas were berated for their behaviour by two missionaries, Johanna Decker, a German-born doctor who had worked in Rhodesia for twenty-eight years, and Sister Ann Ploner, a 53-year-old South African member of the Order of the Precious Blood who had arrived in Rhodesia six months earlier. Dr Decker handed over the cash box, but they demanded more; on the way to her house both women were shot and lay dead in the dust.

The hospital and school were closed; only three black nuns stayed on, as caretakers. But at the end of February 1978 a gang of youths broke into the mission, set fire to the hospital and church, and chased away the nuns. Nothing further happened at St Paul's, Lupane, for almost two years – until the Cease Fire Monitoring Force moved in to establish a Zipra assembly point.

In mid-September 1977 Joshua Nkomo broadcast from Lusaka over the Voice of Zimbabwe, calling on Zipra to defend the missions against the

Selous Scouts: 'It is a wicked lie to suggest that freedom fighters are molesting or killing missionaries. . . . We greatly need and value the work that you have done and are doing for the African people. . . .'

The situation in the eastern districts was little better. In September the Catholic mission of St Benedict's in Weya TTL, ninety-five kilometres east of Salisbury, was closed after intense guerrilla infiltration of the area brought about an untenable situation.

The first white Protestant missionaries to be murdered by guerrillas were the Reverend Andries Louw Brand and his wife, of Que Que. They were ambushed in their car in the remote Gokwe TTL in October 1977. By early January a trust fund for their six children had reached the sum of $(R)7,375, but it was impossible to prevent the separation of the siblings: the eldest, Coenie, went to live with an uncle and aunt in Verwoerdburg: Marieke with her grandparents in Pretoria; and the four youngest, Este, Ilse, Jaap and Rian, with another uncle and aunt in Pretoria.

23. a man with a vision

'We're not only under physical siege here,' says Hamish Usher as we bump across his 10,000-hectare ranch at Nuanetsi, 'we're also up against a kind of ideological blockade. It's suddenly fashionable to claim that private-enterprise farming is both wicked and inefficient. Haven't you heard that 30 per cent of all farms in south-west Matabeleland are either unoccupied or used only as *pieds-à-terre*? Listen, David. If I want to get myself and my family out of here and put a young farm manager in my place – some fellow with guts and ambition – I'll do so. And it'll still be *my* land.'

Usher weighs sixteen stone, sports a carrot-coloured beard and is a leading light of the Scottish Rhodesia Society. He refers to Britain as 'that bloody country' and owns a fine collection of books about Rhodesia's white Pioneers. Over lunch he celebrates their virtues, with the Agric-Alert occasionally crackling in the background – a contact is taking place only five kilometres away.

'Cecil Rhodes, now there was a man with a vision. Such men are rare. Okay, he had this high, squeaky voice, but he also possessed a second, inner voice, like Joan of Arc, which called to him, beckoned him to build a great country here in a land once abandoned to emptiness after centuries of savagery, sloth and rapine. Rhodes, Huggins, Smith, they have all shared that vision.

'Did you know that Rhodesia was founded without a drop of blood being shed? When the Pioneer Column ran up the flag on 12 September 1890, not a shot had been fired. Those young men rode off to try their fortunes with pick or plough – my great-grandfather was one of them, you see his portrait on the wall there, *that* was a man I can tell you – and they carved a living out of the virgin forest, scattering into small and lonely settlements. The silence of centuries was broken at last by the sounds of civilization, by the ring of axe and hammer and the beat of small steam engines at the little mine workings.

'And the Shona – they welcomed the white man as a protector against Lobengula's marauding Ndebele impis. They entered my great-grandfather's service but of course they didn't understand the notion of regular working hours, or why it's wrong to steal – and they thought we were soft because we put them in prison rather than cut their hands off.

'Then in 1896 you had Dr Jameson's raid into the Transvaal – now *that* was a man – so the Ndebeles took their chance to embark on an orgy of murder, arson and pillage. The farmers had no warning and no means of defence when these hordes bore down on them –'

The Agric-Alert springs to life, Control's voice crackling with a new urgency, and Usher momentarily breaks off to listen. Then he shrugs and resumes – not so much fatalism or indifference to a neighbour's plight as professional pragmatism: anyone who hares about on his own, playing the hero, is a fool.

'The Ndebele also stirred up the Shona to rebel, telling them the white man was on the run. The Shona forgot, as the bantu does forget, the benefits they had received from the white man. Inflamed by witch-doctors and oracles of their dead ancestors, they joined in.

'They were put down, as you know. From 1897 to 1960 – that's a long time, David – no black man was shot in Southern Rhodesia by police or soldiers. I wonder how many readers of your magazine understand that. The pacification of Rhodesia and Nyasaland was an extraordinary achievement. In less than eight years nearly half a million square miles had been cleared of violence and oppression: no more slaving, massacres, stranglings, flayings. For the first time in the history of the bantu the weak could live without fear of the strong. The white man did not carry off their crops, their cattle or their women. The white man taught them justice, David. Above all other qualities, he was even-handed and just. Such was the respect in which they were held, my grandfather and my father, that they could travel anywhere entirely alone without fear.

'Until the Communist powers began to stir things.

'My family has always enjoyed excellent, loyal service from our people. Sometimes your boy will strain the coffee through your socks or use your hairbrush to scrub the saucepans. But neither my mother nor my wife has ever raised her voice to a kaffir; neither my father nor I have ever raised our hand to one. Instead we send them to school. When they're sick we give them medicine. When they die, we pay for their coffins.'

After lunch Usher excuses himself – it is his half-hour for a Churchillian catnap – and puts in my hand a number of tooled leather volumes about the Pioneers. Instead I pick up a pamphlet recently issued by the Rhodesian National Farmers' Union, to whose ranks only whites are admitted. It is a response to the British Government's recent White Paper on Rhodesia. Categorically rejecting any imposed nationalization of farm lands, with or without compensation, it does however, enthusiastically endorse the idea of a trust fund which would 'induce farmers to stay on the land while accumulating a right to remit funds abroad on a sliding scale should they dispose of their properties and emigrate in the normal way during the post-independence era'.

As for citizenship, the RNFU argued that its members should be allowed to remain Rhodesians; or revert to their 'prime nationality'; or assume dual nationality. It seems that Rhodesians are Rhodesians when it suits them, masters of their own destiny like Americans or Australians, but something else, hybrids of tenderly ambiguous identity, when it no longer suits them.

24. suspended sentence

In February 1978 Kenneth David Drummond, aged 23, appeared before Gwanda Magistrates' Court, charged with murdering an African labourer, Josiah Ndlovu. Drummond, who had served in the security forces, had been employed for more than three years as a section manager by Liebig's ranch in the West Nicholson area. On 1 September 1977 he had been transferred from the Lutope section of the ranch to the Sokulele section, where the previous manager had been murdered by guerrillas a few days earlier. Sokulele was heavily infiltrated; Drummond knew his own life to be in constant danger.

To make matters worse, the large labour force had not been paid throughout August and September; a total of about $(R)14,000 was owing in wages. The African wages clerk had been arrested after the murder of the previous manager and Drummond, so he argued in court, had felt unable to pay wages without the help of this clerk since the written records were insufficient. To exacerbate matters further – an insight into the mentality of Liebig's management – it had been decided to issue labourers with orange overalls and to recover the cost from their wages. Not surprisingly, eighty cattle belonging to the ranch were missing on mustering day.

On 5 October a lorry was ambushed and three persons in it murdered. The labour force on the ranch was suspected of involvement. At about 5.30 p.m. on the same day Drummond received a message from ranch headquarters that a number of workers in his section had gathered to complain to the personnel manager about non-payment of their wages. It took him an hour and a half to reach headquarters by Land-Rover; when he arrived, at 7 p.m., it was already dark. The journey itself, at that time of day, was perilous.

Drummond found seventeen complainants at a nearby compound. These men had not received food rations for two days. Drummond gave orders for them to assemble and then, according to three witnesses, grabbed by the collar Josiah Ndlovu, one of two foremen, tripped him, punched him and savagely kicked him on the ground. At his trial Drummond claimed that he was confronted by a menacing mob silhouetted by the headlights of his Land-Rover. 'African music was playing from the darkness and the pungent smell of perspiring Africans and ripe beer filled the air . . .' He claimed that he had to win the 'fight' with Ndlovu to prevent the labourers tearing him apart.

Yet there was no 'fight': the African had not attacked him. But had Ndlovu's behaviour been physically menacing? Three state witnesses denied it. Having beaten Ndlovu unconscious and pulled his alsatian off the African, Drummond had pulled him into the back of the Land-Rover and driven to the clinic where, for reasons which remain obscure, Ndlovu was *not* admitted. Drummond then went off to a neighbour's ranch for dinner, leaving the unconscious Ndlovu with an assistant. Later Drummond did call an ambulance but by the time it arrived the African was dead.

Sentencing Drummond to eighteen months' imprisonment, the Gwanda Magistrate commented that he had shown 'indifference' to Ndlovu's injuries. Drummond was granted bail while appealing the verdict. On 13 May 1978 the guerrillas caught up with him. Ambushed while driving, he suffered severe wounds: all the carpal bones of the left hand were completely destroyed, while a bullet in the right hand resulted in a compound wound of the fifth metacarpal. The African foreman with him died. Drummond was able to keep control of the vehicle only by driving with his arms. His injuries led to a long period in plaster, besides skin and bone grafts. There was a likelihood of permanent partial incapacitation.

When the case came before the Appellate Division of the High Court in Salisbury, judgment was given by Chief Justice Macdonald, with Justices J. P. Lewis and J. A. Davies concurring. Sentence was reduced from eighteen to twelve months and *suspended for five years*, partly on the ground that

Drummond had now suffered enough – a fair point – and partly on the more dubious pretext that since the Gwanda trial new evidence had emerged to suggest that the dead man, Ndlovu, had 'actively assisted the terrorists operating in the area'. The Chief Justice then offered a 'probable' and a 'possible' extenuating circumstance: it seemed 'probable' that the deceased had instigated the complaint about the unpaid wages; and it seemed 'possible' that he had been implicated in the murder of the previous manager. From these tenuous hypotheses, Macdonald concluded, deductively, that Ndlovu must have displayed aggression towards Drummond on the night of his death.

Macdonald's racial partiality is seen in another case of extreme physical violence inflicted by white farmers on a black employee. Wilfred and Darryl Collett, father and son, had taken their foreman Mac Maduma from Mphoengs police station after the African had admitted stealing money but had promised to replace it. Arriving back at Ingwesi Ranch, Plumtree, the Colletts stripped him naked, secured him to a block and tackle by handcuffs, had him hoisted from the ground and given twelve strokes. When the case came to court in February 1978 the magistrate told the two whites that they were guilty of a form of terrorism and fined the 70-year-old father $(R)500 with a three-month prison sentence conditionally suspended; the son got ten months in gaol, of which six months were conditionally suspended. But Chief Justice Hector Macdonald didn't like to see a white man gaoled for beating a black one; in April the Appeal Court set aside Darryl Collett's prison sentence and reduced the verdict from 'assault with intent to do grievous bodily harm' to 'common assault'.

Macdonald had prophesied that capital punishment would be reintroduced in many countries and for a wider range of crimes than previously. 'We are going to be obliged to resort to the most drastic penalties for relatively minor offences.' Obviously he meant: when committed by blacks.

In most cases a white defendant accused of brutality did not need to appeal against his sentence. In March 1977 the press reported the case of a white farmer, Basil Rowlands, who had kicked a 65-year-old labourer to death, and later pleaded that the man was not correctly planting maize pips along a furrow. V. J. Kock, the Magistrate at Salisbury Regional Court, commented that 'although the consequences had been unfortunate he did not consider the assault a serious one'. Rowlands was sentenced to a fine of $(R)300 or two months in jail. (This episode is reported by Denis Hills in his book, *Rebel People*.)

25. born actors, those people

In the course of 1976 the Honde Valley had been thoroughly 'subverted' by landmine explosions and ambushes, by the closing of schools, dip tanks, bus services and corn mills, by lethal attacks on black labourers who ignored warnings and continued to work on the white-owned tea estates. Now, as you drove down from the mountains to the valley 600 metres below, you saw on the upper slopes the abandoned villages, the broken windows, the shops closed. The population had been uprooted to the great 'concentration camps' on the valley floor – what the victims called the 'muwaya', the 'inside-the-wire' or 'cage', where their lives were ruled by men like District Assistant Rufus Chitumba whose grin was very broad and whose khaki hat was trimmed in the red band of Internal Affairs: 'These people here, sir, when we hit them they tell us where the terrorists are . . . I enjoy it too much, sir. I get a lot of money and I like money. These terrorists want to rule the world and Africans can't rule the world.' Rufus readily agreed (another cheerful grin) that the villagers in their hearts supported the terrs: all the young men had fled from the reserve, heading either for the big towns or across the border, to join Zanla.

Appalling sanitary conditions, latrines dug too close to the houses, short-age of water, of wood and fuel, food at exorbitant prices, punishments for this and that (for not obeying Cadet Erica Jones's order to cut the grass outside the fence). At collective punishment time the whole population of the PV may be held within the wire for eighteen hours a day. A priest reported seeing a PV in Chiweshi where a single sanitation pit, serving the whole village, was positioned on a hill sloping down to the source of the water supply.

According to the Justice and Peace Commission, in July 1977 six villages in the Tanda TTL were burnt when their 2,900 people refused to move.

In Manicaland 61,000 people had been herded into thirty-one keeps by August 1977. In the Honde Valley alone 17,500 had been forcibly trans-planted. Internal Affairs, headed by Provincial Commissioner Bob Cunliffe, proclaimed the PVs to be 'growth points' of a more rational future. 'Village of hope rises from the mud,' announced the *Umtali Post*: 'Slowly order and permanence is emerging from the mud at Moyoweshumba, the protected village thrown up hastily after 12 terrorist murders within a month. . . .'

Darryl Plowes, Provincial Agricultural Officer, Manicaland, speaks of the protected villages under his jurisdiction with the pride of an Israeli who has just come in from making the desert bloom. A tall man, very handsome (knows it), dressed today in matching bush jacket and shorts, Plowes wears a scarf at the neck and could well pass for an Ealing Studios Spitfire pilot.

'In the Honde Valley the most suitable sites were selected from aerial photographs, though security factors also intervened. We then mapped out the land in terms of its suitability: arable, grazing, tea . . . Garden areas were allocated as a priority. Of course, you'll appreciate the immense advantages of living in a PV: laid-on water, a school to hand, a shop, a beerhall, all on the spot.'

'Don't people mind walking five or ten kilometres to their fields?'

'Distance doesn't seem to worry them. And time isn't a factor with the African, you see.' (Even when he risks getting shot if he misses the curfew?) 'As for not being allowed to take food out of the keep to the fields, a great many of them customarily work throughout the day without a lunch break.' He smiles. 'So do I.' But Plowes's composure is fragile; bitterness soon surfaces. 'Down in the Sabi Valley, in the Birchenough Bridge area, we offered people in the PVs garden plots next to an irrigation scheme. And they turned it down! Why? Because irrigation is too much work, it involves two crops a year.' It seems that the people of Manicaland like and love Plowes less than they should. Though he tells every story to his own advantage, none accrues:

'Our first PV, since you ask, was at Ruda for Headman Mparutsa's people – like me to spell that for you? When our trucks arrived to carry the people from their old village to the new site, the Headman led them in a flight into the bush. They left their cattle in the huts to die and fled.'

'Had they been warned in advance of your plan to uproot them?'

'Impossible, much too dangerous to move about freely round there. Twelve of my staff have been killed while others have simply disappeared. More than half of my African field staff resigned rather than implement the PV programme: the entire staff at Chipinga, as a matter of fact, and about half of those working in the Honde Valley.' He shrugs coldly: 'What can you do?'

His knee, bare above the top of a long woollen sock, presses into the rim of his desk.

His walls are covered with photographs of soil erosion and dilapidated villages in the reserves. The impact is unnerving: expecting graphs and diagrams depicting spectacular progress – smiling African farmers standing in front of gleaming Ferguson tractors and joyful irrigation jets – the mind hesitates before this morbid and melancholic museum.

The expression surfacing on the Provincial Agricultural Officer's long face is like a smile. 'Europeans from outside don't understand,' he says. 'You have to live here.' I nod and wait. With Plowes no questions are required. 'I have been twenty years with these people and I ought to know.'

The sigh is faintly theatrical. 'Ninety per cent of the TTLs are in a state of deterioration. Oh, you'll say that the Europeans took all the best farming land. Well, they have *some* of the best, and do you know why? Because the Africans were ignorant, they actually preferred the lowlands, the dry terrain with a thick top soil – which is the worst soil. The African is always afraid of change: did you know that? He's superstitious. If an African farmer tries something new all the others warn him not to. Yet they complain – did you know this? – that there are no good tarmac roads in their areas. Now you go and ask them how much a mile of good road costs, most of them will tell you $(R)50 or $(R)100 at most. The true figure is, of course – do you know what it is? – close to $(R)10,000 a mile. They don't understand the realities. They have this population explosion and then they expect us to educate all of them. They have chips on their shoulders, they listen to agitators, to Marxists. Believe me, no one is better at shedding crocodile tears than your African. They are born actors, those people.'

Provincial Agricultural Officer Darryl Plowes seems pleased that I'm taking notes as he talks. He rises and walks round his desk. 'In sociology', he tells me, 'there are two types of society: ours, the open-secular society, and theirs, the traditional-sacred-conformist society. Now that's two different worlds, you see. To understand your African you have to understand that under each chief are separate *dunhu*, or wards, each one under a headman called, in Shona, Sadhunu, each of which is subdivided into kraals . . .' Plowes stops abruptly. The lecture bores him and he has lost his way. Only anger does not wither. 'I utterly despise one man, one vote! It has been a disaster everywhere, including Britain. I favour a system of multiple votes, based on property qualifications.'

From a filing cabinet he extracts several documents. The tutorial picks up again, he is tall, he bestrides the room, it's his room, a corner of Africa they can't take away. 'Of course, *of course*, there are intelligent Africans. The key figures are the teachers. But why are those teachers – can you tell me why? – always, *yes always*, hostile to everything, *yes everything*, that this Department does?' He smiles. 'Still, put a baboon in a cage . . .'

26. Railway Avenue

In July 1976 the Minister of Coordination, Reginald Cowper, had announced that the age limit for military service was to be raised from 30 to 34. Men in the 25–34 bracket would henceforward undergo eighty-four days of continuous initial training instead of two stints of fifty-six and twenty-eight days, But the big shock came in January 1977 when Cowper, now Defence Minister, snapped the handcuffs on all fit men up to the age of fifty. Traditionally fathers make wars and sons fight them. As soon as the middle-aged white males realized that they might have to die to defend the social system they dominated, they raised a predictable outcry about the potential damage to commerce and industry.

In September 1977 it was once more the turn of the young to get it in the neck when Phase 1 National Service was extended from a year to eighteen months. The correspondence columns reverberated with thunder and lightning on behalf of students and potential students: everyone lobbied on behalf of their own kin, some boys were released to study abroad, others were not, and Churchill's children demonstrated that the spirit of 1940 has its limits.

In December the Government tossed out a morsel of consolation by reducing the territorial-reserve commitment from 190 to 120 days a year.

Tuesday evening, 8 o'clock: a large crowd of whites floods out of Salisbury station into Railway Avenue, heading for their cars. The troop train has just departed for Gwelo and Bulawayo carrying away their sons and lovers. Some mothers and grannies are rigid and weeping, but there are also groups of young fellows, brothers or schoolfriends of the new 'intake', who tumble out of the station full of hearty cheer and boisterous horseplay. Only whites suffer conscription; only whites want to fight. They are fighting 'terrorism'.

Jack Maddocks leans out of the window as the train slides down the platform. He waves, smiles. For weeks he has been burning the candle at both ends, frenetic, stormy, out every night, rows with his parents, quarrels about borrowing the car and who can drive it – at one point he told his mother that he was entitled to live his life to the full while he had it. Now, when Sheila gets home, reaches their large Moorish-style residence in Borrowdale, with its watercourse, its pool, its fishpond, there will be peace at last and also a pale pain in her at the sight of his empty room with its poster sellotaped to the wall, showing a group of young white boys, bronzed, fair-haired and smiling confidently, guns at the ready: 'Terrorism Stops Here.'

Tall and muscular like his brother Rod, Jack has excelled on the rugby field and dreamed of joining the Selous Scouts. Now he finds himself with 700 other recruits on the train to Llewelin Barracks at Bulawayo. Of these, 124 will be filtered out for officer training and transferred to the Gwelo School of Infantry. The course at Gwelo will be tough: at the end of twenty-two weeks only fifty-seven will have completed it, forty-one being commissioned as 2nd Lieutenants and sixteen becoming NCOs. Jack can expect three hours' sleep a night at most, but as an officer cadet he will share a black batman whom he will pay $(R)8 a week out of his own initial pay of $(R)45 a month. (After 137 days' service his pay will jump to $(R)105.)

And no drink. The all-night stag party held at the home of Mike Rogers, school cricket captain, two nights ago, when the lads chanted 'Hail, Smithy' up and down Churchill Avenue East, was the last booze for a while.

Jack Maddocks will make it. His proud parents will drive down to Gwelo for the passing-out parade and will hear the Commandant, Lt-Col. J. C. W. Austin, tell the young warriors that they had come through 'perhaps the toughest infantry course in the world' and that their sole aim now is to 'fight Communism'.

Christ, the gooks have got Stalin organs now, what next, Cubans?

Half an hour after the troopies' special left Salisbury station the regular all-night train to Bulawayo left platform 1. Its carriages were divided into four classes. At the back coach after coach was packed with blacks sitting on plain wooden benches.

Jack's father, Alex Maddocks, had fondly believed himself immune, until Defence Minister Reg Cowper did a snatch-and-grab on the 38–50 age group in January 1977. The Association of Rhodesian Industries of course protested strongly, because the move affected some 12,000 men of whom many occupied 'crucial' posts in commerce and industry. Directors even. A firm manufacturing agricultural machinery reported that it had lost $(R)400,000 in one year because 120 of its skilled staff, 60 per cent of the total, had been on reserve duty or police call-up at any one time – a burden increased by the legal requirement on businesses to make up the difference between an employee's military pay and his normal salary. Managing-Directors like Alex Maddocks who spent seventy days of the year stomping the bush were now an expensive proposition.

27. God I hate doing this

Be a Man Among Men urges the Rhodesian recruiting ad. Such a Man is Lt-Col. Robert K. Brown, ex-Special Force 'A' Team leader in Vietnam (maybe), graduate in political science from the University of Colorado (maybe), whose office in Boulder, Colorado carried this sign:

JOIN THE ARMY, TRAVEL TO DISTANT LANDS

MEET INTERESTING PEOPLE

AND KILL THEM.

According to a report by James Howe, Brown's office was decorated with Rhodesian Army posters and a photograph of a village burning while a group of white soldiers nonchalantly smoked cigarettes. Brown had collected piles of Maj. Nick Lamprecht's Rhodesian recruiting material and was now selling it off in packets at five dollars a time, investing the proceeds in the magazine

Soldier of Fortune, which, he claimed, ran to 125,000 copies in its third edition. 'Many Americans would like to fight in Rhodesia to get their revenge on the Communists for defeat in Vietnam,' commented Brown, seated in front of a vast bodyguard with a massive rifle, broad shoulders, mirrored sunglasses and a T-shirt inscribed with a winged skull and the motto: Airborne, Death From Above.

The personal columns of *Soldier of Fortune* were full of inquiries from men who didn't mind what sort of work they did, men who would go anywhere, men who had seen everything, men who were sick of life and keen to lose it. Chewing tobacco and spitting frequently into the ashtray, Brown described his experience of war in Vietnam as 'getting continuous injections of adrenalin'.

The Rhodesians publicly estimated the number of Americans serving in their forces at 400. Although incarnating in its purest form 'external terrorism' (hunting down young Zanla guerrillas born and reared in the Honde Valley, Zimunya, Fort Victoria and Mtoko) these white adventurers, born and reared in Arkansas, Georgia and Indiana, applauded their own crusade against 'external terrorists'. Phil Abbot, serving with an RLI Fireforce in the Shabani area, combats a day's heat with a succession of iced 7-Ups and reflects that after Vietnam and Angola, 'we can't afford to lose any more countries'. Phil had seen an ad in Lt-Col. Brown's *Soldier of Fortune* and, apart from his desire not to lose any more countries, reckoned Rhodesia to be the safest of the three contracts available to him, one in Morocco, one serving with Jonas Savimbi's Unita in southern Angola, the third in what Abbot describes, thrusting a Camel between his lips, as 'a place ah never noo *ex*-isted 'fore ah splashed dahn' – Rhodesia.

On leave in Salisbury, Phil Abbot heads for the home of the rich American novelist Robin Moore, self-styled US Ambassador to Rhodesia, founder of the Crippled Eagles, and author of *The Green Berets* and *The French Connection*. Chatting with the amiable, talkative mercenaries at Moore's poolside, Christopher Hitchens of the *New Statesman* came across Air-Lt Hubert Kirkendall, 'a poor Texan with strong views', who had this to say: 'I should give a damn for those rich guys with their farms and their dough. But I'm fighting for them because they're white, and the white man is running out all over. The blacks think we owe them a living.'

Finally the sub-Spenglerian cliché of the hour: 'If I'm the last man out I'll turn off the lights.'

One frequent visitor to Robin Moore's Crippled Eagles club during 1977 was an Associated Press photographer, J. Ross Baughman. Having cultivated a suitably right-wing image, Baughman met Maj. Mike Williams – the most senior American mercenary serving in Rhodesia – and obtained his permission to accompany a unit of the Grey's Scouts – the mounted infantry unit named after the Scouts founded in the 1890s by the tough, mustachioed Capt. G. Grey – on a counter-insurgency operation in Matabeleland. Associated Press released Baughman's report and photographs on 2 December. One photograph (for which Baughman later won a Pulitzer prize) showed a white soldier squatting on his haunches and pointing a pistol at the heads of five African prisoners whom he was interrogating while forcing them to remain in a 'press-up': their arms stiff, their weight resting on their hands. *The Times* and other newspapers also displayed prominently a Baughman photograph of a young African with a rope noosed round his neck by two mounted soldiers of (presumably) the Grey's Scouts – his expression a study in dignity and resignation.

Baughman claimed that he had accompanied a mounted patrol which looted and burned huts, severely beat a local politician and tortured his wife and daughter. He had also seen two prisoners with nooses round their necks dragged behind horses for several miles.

Because of the problem of verification, the European names given below are fictitious.

On 20 September, according to Baughman, a five-man squad from 3 Troop commanded by Sgt Mick Crombie rounded up ten black youths at an abandoned school near the village of Sipepa, a remote spot eighty kilometres south-west of Lupane. Crombie radioed to Lt Geoff Wallace that they were linked to the UANC. When Wallace reached the school he found a man who turned out to be Moffat Ncube, secretary of the local branch of the UANC, with his hands tied behind his back and his face swollen. Wallace asked him his name, got no answer, then hit him over the head with a bat. According to Baughman, soldiers pulled down the underwear of Ncube's daughter and whipped her; her mother, who got the same treatment, was tied to a bed whose metal springs had been heated over an oven.

Next morning, reported Baughman, Lt Wallace joined another squad led by Sgt Brian Styles at a general store at Kikidoo village, five kilometres from the school. Prisoners from Kikidoo were led into the village yard, asked where weapons were hidden and given the 'water treatment' – a shirt is wrapped round the victim's head before water is poured over the nose and mouth – until they passed out.

Moffat Ncube was stripped and subjected to this form of torture but he resisted, spitting out the water and holding his breath. He was kicked in the ribs. A wire was tied to his genitals and his daughter was forced to pull on it, partially mutilating him. Lt Wallace started yelling at Ncube and fired a shot into the ground five centimetres from his head. 'God I hate doing this,' Wallace said (according to Baughman), walking to his truck. 'This war makes me sick.'

Baughman left Rhodesia on 20 November before the publication of his report and photographs, which dealt the severest of blows to white Rhodesia's image in the west. (Maj. Mike Williams had also departed.) The Government of Rhodesia set up a tribunal of inquiry and invited Baughman to return as a witness, offering him immunity from prosecution, but he declined the offer. Early in December *The Times* quoted a 'high-level' source in the Rhodesian Army to the effect that Baughman's report was 'accurate in substance' but that 75 per cent of the details were either wrong or exaggerated.

On 9 February 1978 the *Herald*'s defence correspondent reported that disciplinary action had been taken against members of a sub-unit of the Selous Scouts following allegations of brutality against tribesmen in the Lupane area the previous September. One officer and several NCOs had been severely fined and reduced in rank – but no names, numbers or details.

I later had it from a pupil of a distinguished Salisbury school that Geoffrey Wallace had been highly regarded while a pupil there; that he had unfairly been made a scapegoat for what had happened; and was now working in a British supermarket.

28. Chimoio

After Nyadzonia, Chimoio – the second great massacre of the war. An interlocking complex of camps situated some eighty kilometres inside Mozambique along the route from Umtali to Beira, Chimoio was a sitting duck when the Rhodesian jets and helicopter-borne troops struck at 7.30 a.m. on Wednesday, 23 November 1977. No trenches had been dug. It was a military camp all right, but the guerrillas liked to have their women and children on hand. And the Rhodesians – notably the Special Air Service – had done their homework, piecing together a remarkably accurate layout of the camp complex from captured guerrillas and aerial photography. The army of Mozambique offered, in the event, no effective resistance. About 1,200 Zimbabweans were killed; the Rhodesians lost one white soldier.

Derek Ingram of the Gemini News Service arrived in the town of Chimoio, nineteen kilometres away, on the morning of the attack. He heard the sound of aircraft, the crunch of bombs; plumes of smoke rose into the sky. The attack lasted for two days. When Ingram finally reached the devastated Zanu camp he saw nearly one hundred children, aged between 11 and 14, buried in a mass grave. Ian Christie reported seeing the bodies of twenty young girls aged between 10 and 14 piled in a single grave; the face of one was marked by the stains of her tears; from the face of another the skin had been entirely burnt off, leaving only the white flesh beneath. Christie counted seventy corpses: 'Some of the bodies I saw were those of guerrillas. But the majority were women and children.' Photographs of the mass graves show bodies heaped layer upon layer in a ghastly indignity, the last embrace of strangers, men and women, half naked; even the dead should not be crushed, suffocated. . . . But they are dead. They experience nothing. They lie still, legs in the air, upside-down in the deep pit. In the hospital yard lie the bodies of eight men beneath a cashew-tree. They have been dragged from Zanu's only mobile clinic and shot in the back of the head.

One of the survivors, Olaria Lucia Chikuhuhu, remembers: 'I was totally confused. I didn't have anywhere to go or hide. No one returned fire.' She took off her bright-coloured clothes and rolled them in mud. 'I started walking out of the radius . . . passing through many sub-bases with a lot of dead bodies of my fellow comrades. . . . I couldn't control my tears. When I looked every direction I saw a Daicotar [Dakota] deploying ground forces. . . . I slept among the dead where blood was flowing like a stream of water. I put my hands in the blood and put it on some parts of my body. When they came at the spot I pretended to be dead and they kicked me and the dead bodies. . . . They lit the dry grass which burnt fiercely towards where I was sleeping. . . .' (Olaria is not alone in using the word 'sleeping' for 'lying still'.)

A woman sits on the ground with her arm curled protectively round her child: both dead. One corpse, that of a man, has (its? his?) hands tied: the leg and foot have been shot off below the knee and lie a few feet away – in their search for senior guerrilla commanders, the Rhodesians did not suffer scruples about torturing their victims. Later, at a press conference, General Walls, whose Comops coordinated the whole operation, regretted that Tongogara and Nhongo had been absent from Chimoio at the time of the attack. 'Although we did not get these two top chaps we got a hell of a lot of their leadership.'

While Parirenyatwa field hospital was set ablaze and its patients gunned down, other Rhodesian units attacked the Chindunduma Primary School just as children aged 8 to 14 began their classes. Napalm first: some were roasted to death. Then came the troops who cracked open their skulls. After Independence the Government lost no time in renaming the Andrew Fleming Hospital, Salisbury, after Parirenyatwa field hospital – a terrible blow to the whites, most of whom found the name impossible to pronounce.

And what of those who survived the onslaught of the redskins with their silky, sun-bleached hair and T-bone stomachs? Five months later, in April, an anonymous correspondent visited Chimoio and came across Matuku, a 14-year-old boy who had seen his parents shot down. Born in a village near Umtali but now a child of the forest, a Mowgli, in filthy camouflaged pants and carrying a rifle almost as big as himself, Matuku's diet was meagre and his hands sticky from fruit picked from nearby trees. Though he slept on the earth under a single blanket his spirit was not broken. 'We must free our people from the yoke of imperialism,' he said; 'we will triumph over the racist oppressors.'

29. the king's thunderbolts are righteous

Perhaps the 1,200 black Zimbabweans who died at Chimoio were a bit short on history – just as the children whom Israeli bombers strike down in Palestinian refugee camps may be lamentably ignorant of what a pogrom involved in nineteenth-century Russia. The victims of Chimoio had probably never heard of 'the spirit of Augsburg', the heroic story of 44 (Rhodesia) Squadron of the Royal Air Force with its motto 'Fulmina Regis Iusta' – the King's Thunderbolts are Righteous. But the 'spirit of Augsburg'? Attacking a U-boat factory at Augsburg under the command of Sqn/Ldr John Nettleton, 44 Squadron's Lancaster bombers had lost five out of six crews, each consisting of seven men.

Thus the RAF was son and heir to the RAF: the word 'Royal' had merely been replaced by the word 'Rhodesian'. Air Chief Marshal Sir Arthur Harris – 'Bomber' Harris, who attempted the systematic extermination of civilian Germany – had once served with the Rhodesia Regiment during the first world war. After the second he came back, in his glory, to sound a symbolic bugle at the Drill Hall, Salisbury; to the Drill Hall also came Wavell, Montgomery, Mountbatten, King George VI himself – in 1943 he had personally presented 44 (Rhodesia) Squadron with its crest. This was the proud creed and cult of which the victims of Chimoio knew little and cared less.

Like Canada, like Scotland, so too Rhodesia had in 1940 welcomed trainee pilots to Thornhill air base at Gwelo. After the war many of them came back to the sunshine and servants. Some went into civilian life, a few others built a new air force, small but beautiful.

At the break-up of the Central African Federation, Britain took a step whose consequences were well known to those who died at Chimoio. The

Federal Air Force was put under the control of the Salisbury Government. Kwame Nkrumah of Ghana tried to block the transfer in the UN, warning prophetically that the planes might one day be used by the white minority regime against neighbouring black states, but Britain ridiculed the suggestion and vetoed the Ghanaian resolution.

According to the International Institute for Strategic Studies, in January 1977 the regime possessed twelve Hawker Hunter F5A-9 fighters, eleven Canberra B-2 bombers, twenty-four Vampire FB-9s and fifty-five Alouette helicopters. In April it was reported that twelve French Mirage fighters and a number of brand-new Alouettes had been obtained. In the Northern Transvaal Rhodesian pilots were completing conversion courses to Mirage jets supplied by South Africa. A French Communist Party spokesman claimed that France was allowing Puma and Alouette helicopters to be built under licence in South Africa, regardless of their destination.

In December it was reported that twenty Cessna counter-insurgency Skymaster aircraft powered by Rolls-Royce engines had reached Rhodesia. They were built in France by Reims Aviation, whose Director was the famous Free French pilot Pierre Closterman, who had served with the RAF during the war and was credited with thirty-three 'kills'. Closterman denied that Reims Aviation had ever sold an aeroplane to Rhodesia, adding: 'But if you want to know my feelings on this, I tell you that if I could have done this legally, I would have done it.' Closterman was moved by reports that Ian Smith, a fellow RAF pilot during the war, had been shot down in the South of France and had fought with the Maquis for a year.

The élite squadron of the Rhodesian Air Force was No. 1 at Thornhill, base of the Hawker Hunter fighters which, acquired second-hand from the Royal Air Force in 1962, had a maximum speed of 1,200 k.p.h., nothing to compare to the MIG 19 or MIG 21 – but the Rhodesians were never challenged to aerial combat from either Zambia or Mozambique. The Squadron Commander of No. 1 was 'Rich' Brand, nephew of Sir Quintin Brand, the first pilot ever to land a plane in Rhodesia (in 1920). 'Rich' became a national legend when he placed a dustbin on the runway at Thornhill, then put five bullets through it from his diving Hunter.

Meanwhile the English Electric Canberra bombers, obsolete and very slow at a maximum speed of 675 k.p.h., but quite good against tribespeople, formed No. 5 Squadron under Sqn/Ldr 'Randy' du Rand. Their motto: 'Find and Destroy.' Most of the gallantry awards, however – Silver Crosses, Bronze Crosses – went to the pilots of Sqn/Ldr Harold Griffiths's No. 7 helicopter squadron, who were more vulnerable to the blowpipes and pangas of the local tribesmen than were the pilots serving under 'Rich' and 'Randy'.

30. Carver

Field Marshal Sir Michael Carver was to be Rhodesia's Resident Commissioner. A soldier of distinction and also the author of standard works on the battles of El Alamein and Tobruk, he had served at El Alamein as a staff officer with the 7th Armoured Division, the legendary Desert Rats. Related to the great Wellington on his mother's side, educated at Winchester and Sandhurst Royal Military Academy, brilliant and precocious, the youngest Brigadier in the British army at the age of 29, winner of the DSO and bar and the MC ('coolness under fire'), Carver was appointed Chief of the General Staff (the top army post) in 1971 and Chief of the Defence Staff two years later. With experience of the Mau Mau rebellion in Kenya and of communal strife in Cyprus, he was also credited with tactful handling of military operations in Northern Ireland. He certainly looked the part – nature does not always endow its warriors with martial visages.

Owen hoped that Carver's credentials would pull the trick with the white Rhodesians. However, Carver himself fully accepted the logic of the Owen plan and dispelled Rhodesian illusions by declaring on television: 'What I am basically committed to is that Rhodesia will become a basically black country run primarily by black Africans for the benefit primarily of black Africans.' Oh ho! The *Rhodesia Herald* complained that the Brit Field Marshal sounded 'even more socialist than his political masters'. On 6 October Carver referred to Smith's 'incredible short-sightedness'. Asked why he had taken part in the suppression of Mau Mau yet had no sympathy for Rhodesia's war of counter-insurgency, Carver offered no plausible answer, while firmly conveying that he did regard the forces of the PF as 'liberation armies'.

Muzorewa met Carver on 4 November 1977 and told him he had been brainwashed if he believed that the PF was an essential element of a cease-fire. Carver remained adamantly brainwashed. He intended to stand down most of the white Rhodesian security forces and make the RAR the core of the new National Army along with guerrillas serving in regular or reserve battalions. Speaking in Umtali, Smith described Carver's visit as a 'lamentable failure' and a 'travelling circus'. Smith now headed for his 'internal settlement' with Muzorewa and Sithole. Early in January Britain warned Smith that any settlement must involve the PF. Muzorewa and the UANC quickly adopted the anti-British rhetoric of the Rhodesian whites, the Bishop disparaging Owen as one who 'wants to sacrifice 200 Zimbabweans a week to win a seat in the British Parliament'.

31. a very dicey situation

A bitter struggle for military control of the Wedza TTL brought havoc to the Franciscan mission of Mount St Mary. Sister Irene Nhandara was arrested, held for thirty days, beaten and released without charge. An Irish Sister working at the mission, Dr Teresa Colby, was deported even though the only qualified physician working in the Buhera and Charter districts. The mission's Superior, Father Pascal Slevin, was also thrown out of the country, as were Father Frank O'Flynn and Slevin's successor, Father Philip Timmons. When Mount St Mary's finally felt itself compelled to close down on 14 February 1978, following an attack by an 'unknown gang', the surrounding countryside was thereby deprived of 350 secondary-school places, 650 primary-school places, a hospital with eighty-five beds and an out-patients' clinic which normally treated 1,000 cases a month.

Father Pascal Slevin is a radical Irish Franciscan of small stature, cheery countenance and a hearty laugh. The mission had been his home for thirteen years when the regime gave him the boot. The guerrillas, who first appeared on the scene early in 1976, came always at night, well armed, to ask for this and that. 'And you gave it to them', Slevin recalls, 'if you believed in holding on to your skin and the like. For some time it was a very dicey situation, to tell you the truth.' By day he managed to maintain good relations with the army. Whenever one side paid a visit, the other wanted to know every detail of what had occurred. Informers abounded.

He sighs a little and smiles broadly. He had survived this double life for about eighteen months. His role, though, had been very far from neutral; the lesson of Ireland's long struggle against colonial oppression was rarely lost on her missionaries to Africa. Not only was Father Slevin in constant contact with the Justice and Peace Commission but he also took the incriminating photographs of acts of brutality by the security forces which illustrated JPC publications in Britain. He knew of rape, beatings and torture; he had officiated at the funeral of a woman shot at close range after being accused of consorting with terrorists. A baby strapped to her back had died of the same bullet. About two weeks before his deportation he had taken pictures of two people badly beaten, one with a fan-belt, the other having suffered boiling beer poured over his head and shoulders. Both photographs appeared in *The Propaganda War*. 'That was the final nail in the coffin, if you like.' Slevin was deported.

In June 1977 a Maryknoll Sister from America, Janice McLaughlin, had come down from Kenya to beef up the work of the Justice and Peace Commission and to help gather evidence of torture, killings and intimidation.

Sister Janice was in fact a swinging revolutionary nun with the awful verve of a college cheerleader – Black Africa was her team. The regime was now poised to strike. In July a banning order was issued against the JPC's *Civil War in Rhodesia*, the police obtained a warrant to search the Commission's offices (a red-brick bungalow on the corner of Selous Avenue and Fourth Street, normally videotaped by Special Branch). Legal actions were set in motion against Father Dieter Scholz, a Jesuit whose unflinching gaze concealed a great tenderness, and Brother Arthur Dupuis, a loyal and courageous servant of the JPC since its beginnings.

On 31 August the police raided the JPC's offices and arrested John Deary, Chairman of the JPC, Scholz, Dupuis and McLaughlin under both the Law and Order (Maintenance) Act and the Official Secrets Act. The three men were remanded on bail of $(R)1,000 – according to Deary, this was the average cost to the JPC of investigating each alleged atrocity – but Sister Janice was driven by the CID to her apartment and later held in Chikurubi prison under the Emergency Powers Act.

Discovered in her apartment were a private diary and notebook soggy with incriminating thoughts and gushing references to 'the boys' – perfect propaganda material for the Ministry of Information. On 22 July the Pittsburgh-born nun, then in her mid-30s, had written: 'I admired the priests who went to join the boys. I hope they will be accepted.' On 1 August (after a trip to Mount St Mary's mission in Wedza TTL, from which Father Pascal Slevin and Dr Teresa Colby were soon to be deported): 'I am sorry that I have just missed the boys. I have romanticised and glorified the boys. It would be useful to meet them.'

Nor had Sister Janice found it in her heart to condemn the terrorist bomb explosions which had killed and wounded innocent blacks in Salisbury. On 8 August: 'The boys say they did the bombing to show urban people they are part of the war. They must be involved. They are too safe and smug in Salisbury.' On 10 August: '[There are] suggestions of my going to Mozambique. I don't want to go to Europe and plead for negotiations that would sacrifice the armed struggle'.

In court she denied ever having made contact with guerrillas and explained that her diary entry about the Salisbury bombings was based on hearsay. Otherwise she ignored the advice of her counsel, Nick McNally, refused to moderate her stance or deny her sympathy for armed struggle, and generally chose the road of Dimitrov. On 22 September, following intercession by American diplomats, Sister Janice was deported. Van der Byl celebrated her enforced departure by describing her as dressed up 'like Gina Lollobrigida on the way to the Cannes film festival'. White society in Salisbury and on the farms had no difficulty at all in labelling the noisy American nun a scarlet woman – the standard strategy for disposing of any woman capable of breaking allegiance.

(*Postscript*: In 1981 Sister Janice McLaughlin returned to Zimbabwe as a field officer for the Zimbabwe Project, an ecumenical scheme for resettling refugees, and was warmly welcomed by President Canaan Banana.)

The Catholic Bishops had rallied with a statement issued on 17 September: 'We believe that the Commission has made a valuable and significant contribution to the cause of true justice and peace in this country.' On 13 November, Dieter Scholz wrote to Mildred Nevile of the CIIR an eloquent but characteristically restrained description of the enmity now confronting the JPC, which Ian Smith had recently denounced in the House of Assembly as 'unscrupulous . . . disreputable . . . biased . . .':

'One has to remind oneself deliberately and consciously that there are friends outside Rhodesia, for the isolation we experience here is painful, albeit but an insignificant way of sharing the suffering of the people. . . . Everyone is gripped by the fear of being picked up in the small hours of the morning.'

In February 1978 I called at the JPC office in Salisbury and met Arthur Dupuis, a small, balding Marist Brother from Canada, known to be an organizational wizard and the only witness to the Special Branch's abduction of Edson Sithole in October 1975. With him were Father Dieter Scholz and John Deary, making up the trinity against whom the state's wrath was directed. We talked of torture: of prisoners hung by their ankles from trees with their heads under water; of prisoners whose heads were trapped in wet towels or plastic bags. 'To gather propaganda', said Scholz softly, 'the Government can go anywhere. But we can't, we have no helicopters.'

These men were not propagandists, they were faithful servants of the truth, sceptical of certain allegations against the security forces, sensibly aware that if they ever argued a case that the Government could puncture by weight of evidence, then the JPC's entire indictment would appear discredited. In February 1976, for example, the London *Daily Mirror* had published a story, 'Slaughter in the Village of No Mercy', in which a certain McCarthy 'confessed' to having taken part in a massacre inside Rhodesia. The JPC had checked the story out and concluded that it was false, concocted for money. 'So far we do not have one thoroughly authenticated confession,' said Scholz, who seemed possessed by gloom at the prospect of Smith cunningly, inexorably, projecting his internal settlement as the last bulwark against Communism.

By now the case against the JPC had been remanded until 28 March and the charges altered from section 49 of the Act, 'causing alarm and despondency', to section 44, 'issuing subversive statements'. The significance of this manoeuvre was that under section 44 truth was not a valid defence, only acting in good faith. But when it became clear that the JPC was determined not to bite the bait and withdraw its plea of truth, the regime beat a retreat, dropping some charges and offering to waive others if Scholz and Dupuis would voluntarily leave Rhodesia. They refused to do so. On 26 April the remaining charges were dropped, ending eight months of intimidatory litigation involving 160 different 'subversive' statements. At the end of June Father Dieter Scholz was deported while Brother Arthur Dupuis left of his own accord, though by no means willingly.

The Rhodesian lay President of the JPC, John Deary, the stubborn thorn in the lean shanks of Ian Smith, soldiered on, courageously exposing the lies and hypocrisy of the regime despite the opprobrium, the smears and the gut accusations of racial treason. Later in the year, when Deary was dogging Smith in the United States and lobbying for non-recognition of the Transitional Government, a stick grenade was thrown through the window of his farmhouse. An Austrian mercenary by the name of Gerrit Pointer was arrested and charged with the attack but 'jumped' bail. In May of the following year he was gaoled by a Viennese court for frauds committed before he left for Rhodesia.

Not all white liberals were unalloyed saints. Their ranks included politicians *manqués* who palpably enjoyed wheeling and dealing not only in the lounge bar of Meikles or the Jameson but also, on occasion, in more far-flung corridors of power – Lusaka, London, Washington. Such men relished the temporary importance bestowed upon them by the Rhodesian crisis; doors which they would normally have never caught sight of now opened before them. Often their faith in African efficiency, tenacity and integrity was minimal. A prominent critic of Smith's 'internal' solution, a liberal who publicly called for an all-party conference embracing the PF, had this to say in private:

'Kaunda and Machel will have to recognize the internal settlement. Vorster has a complete hold on Maputo. As soon as Smith steps down at the end of the year and Africans take over here, the guerrillas will lay down their arms. God knows why Sithole says it will cost $(R)1,000 per guerrilla – surely $(R)250 would be enough. As for the PF, they have been hopelessly outmanoeuvred and their war effort is floundering. Indoctrination at ground level in the rural areas is almost nil. Mugabe has absolutely no chance of coming to power here. He's only a figurehead within Zanu – a gun permanently in his back. Remember how Herbert Chitepo was murdered?'

The white liberal shrugged disparagingly and despairingly. Today he occupies a prominent position in Robert Mugabe's Zimbabwe.

32. St Augustine's: tea and sympathy

Scribbling the priest's name in a notebook, I misspelt it; the Reverend 'Kebbla Prossa', I vaguely imagined, must be black as pitch, and quite possibly a Copt or an Ethiopian. However, on telephoning the Priory of St Augustine's mission at Penhalonga I was greeted by a voice utterly English, a nice blend of Wilfred Hyde White and Margaret Rutherford – as if Ealing Studios had been transplanted to the eastern highlands of Rhodesia. Father Keble Prosser (to give him his real name) turned out to be not so much an Ethiopian as a tall and talkative Englishman of conventional appearance and abundant energy, a person whom one could easily imagine rallying his men at the fall of Singapore, digging out the injured during the Blitz – or, indeed, keeping open a large and famous African secondary school situated only two kilometres from the Mozambique border, a school trapped in a war zone where neither the security forces nor the Zanla guerrillas would allow neutrality.

Father Prosser belongs to the Community of the Resurrection, a 'high' Anglican order whose austere home is at Mirfield in Yorkshire. The Church of England is by tradition patriotic and monarchist, servicing the conscience of a class-bound and imperialist state. At first sight Prosser fits this image quite well; in reality he is an ardent, outspoken member of the Church's Fifth Column and a kaffir-lover. How could the Church truly embrace its African children unless it also embraced their political aspirations to dignity and self-government? And if purblind repression precipitated, finally, a liberation movement dependent on violence, how could the Church step back and wash its hands, embracing the aims but spurning the means? Churchmen of his persuasion – one thinks of Trevor Huddleston, a hero to Prosser and perhaps the most eminent member of the Community of the Resurrection – denounce colonialism because it deflects God's sunshine from His black children; because it is not a loving of thy neighbour nor a doing unto others as one would be done by.

But these are generalities. A school perched on a remote hillside, approachable only by precipitous, rutted dirt tracks, is not a generality; nor are its 500 pupils, the brightest of the nation, periodically whipped to fever pitch by the cruelties of the war, torn between their admiration for the armed struggle and their private dreams of academic advancement, of studying in foreign universities, of becoming doctors (the highest calling), teachers, academics – of leaving behind the poor kraals and wretched protected villages in which they have grown up.

'Brave of you to come,' Prosser would say, 'we don't get so many visitors as we used to.' He takes some pride in his frequent clashes with civil authority; dressed in his long white habit, a grey apron and a dog collar, he stirs in Rhodesian police officers and District Commissioners a deep antipathy offset by a historical respect for the cloth.

Although St Augustine's 1,800-hectare estate is designated European land, Prosser refused to install the standard Agric-Alert alarm system. Local whites drew their own conclusions: not only was the school a nest of subversion but it had no intention of alerting the security forces to a guerrilla presence. When Prosser went to see the Assistant District Commissioner in Umtali, to complain that even blacks born on the estate were unable to obtain passes (situpas), he pointed out that such a situation could only encourage young blacks to cross the Mozambique border and join Zanla. The Assistant DC shrugged contemptuously: 'So what? We'll shoot them when they come back.'

In 1975 no less than eighty-seven pupils disappeared over the border to join Zanla. In 1976, a further forty-four followed; in 1977 the number fell to four. (During the five months from June to October 1976 it was estimated that 700 mission-school pupils crossed the border. In October, eighty out of 300 left St Benedict's north of Rusape.) At the height of this crisis the Rev. Keble Prosser achieved nation-wide notoriety among whites by announcing to the press that it was his brightest and best students who were going across the Mozambique border. An organization, Zanla, which so magnetized young people of such quality, the future leaders of their country, must, he reasoned, have something to be said for it. Bishop Burrough of Mashonaland wasn't the only Anglican who found this hard to swallow. Among others who were incensed by Prosser's attitude was one of his own Brethren, a red-bearded priest and physics teacher who preached a sermon in chapel on the duty to stand by Christianity in the face of intimidation. Prosser – and his was the prevalent view among the Brethren at St Augustine's – held that it was not their duty to draw in the sand the line at which Africans should sacrifice their lives.

The Priory is perched above the school – a celibate Brotherhood meeting at 4.30 for a cup of strong, institutional tea and later for an austere supper in a drab, scrubbed refectory; ageing men long since resigned, perhaps, to knowing all that could be known about themselves and each other. Then it is time for chapel: how like children adults feel when they visit a school whose smells and style of authority offer a negative print of their own adolescence – the chilling summons of that friendly bell. To chapel! Now! Five hundred black boys and girls taking Communion in a vast, high neo-Romanesque chapel whose chilling contours might have been designed to signal to young Africans that this was not a God who welcomed intimacy.

The boys and girls walk up from their dormitories to the chapel, then walk back again. After 6 p.m. a curfew is in force and anyone venturing on foot further than fifty metres from the school buildings can be shot on sight.

In 1975, when the mass exodus of pupils to join Zanla took place, stones were thrown at Prosser out of the darkness as he walked back to the Priory. 'I even considered locking my door at night. Then I realized that the window didn't lock so I left the door open.' At the height of the hysteria he received an unsigned note: 'Clear out by 31 July 1975 or be killed.' Such messages were a commonplace of the war in Rhodesia; it was up to the recipient to assess its authenticity – did it come on the authority of the local Zanla commander? If unsigned, almost certainly it didn't. But such logic induces a thin sleep.

Relentless harassment from Umtali. When the pupils fled over the border under cover of night the police responded by zapping the school and dragging away a number of pupils to Penhalonga police station, in the valley below. Prosser drove down carrying blankets, food, comfort. He secured their release after twenty-four hours: 'I suppose the colour of my skin helped.' Then an irate Provincial Education Officer drove up the twisting dirt track to instruct the Sixth Form about the stupidity, the wickedness, of joining 'terrorists'. The defiant, even downright rude, response of the boys deeply offended him – soldiers duly arrived, scattering propaganda leaflets around the school. On one occasion a visiting white police officer asked Prosser to supply an informer; when the Principal responded that surely the police must already have their own, the officer confessed, 'They're not telling me anything.'

That was one lesson of the mass exodus of pupils in 1975 and 1976. Clearly emissaries of the guerrillas had visited the dormitories at night, but the kids would not talk about this, not even to the African staff. And then they went, burning their Cambridge O-level certificates, filing silently up to the local store under cover of darkness – finally spirited across the mine-infested border by Zanla couriers. An extraordinary act of renunciation, a self-inflicted severance from worldly goods (one boy sent home his surplus pocket money to his father) and worldly ambitions.

While the Ministry of Education was publicly denying that the kids had crossed the border, the distressed parents came to see Father Prosser. Only one, he recalls, blamed him for what had happened. Prosser knows that by the law of averages a proportion of those 135 pupils will now be dead. Now, in

November 1977, he watches the helicopter gunships flying north over the school on their way to the great massacre at Chimoio in Mozambique. His imagination travels with them. Although the security forces cut off the fingers of culled guerrillas and claim they can be identified from their thumbprints, it is Comops policy never to divulge names to parents or head teachers. Prosser has not been allowed to see the lists of the dead. The Geneva Convention has not touched the blue-green mountains of Africa.

So what next, tomorrow? Father Prosser's most pressing fear is that the school will get 'done' at the beginning of term, at the moment 500 pupils arrive clutching their school fees ($(R)125 a year plus $(R)30 for exams and uniforms). Recently the Manama mission in Matabeleland had lost $(R)13,000 in this way.

'Of course,' Prosser reflects cheerfully, 'it could be extremely dangerous to have no money to give. Don't you think?' The imagination flutters briefly in the vacuum of the unknown.

You read of mysterious Africa or, commonly, the mysterious East. This, of course, is a Eurocentric angle of vision; neither Africa nor the East is particularly mysterious to itself. The white Brethren who live together up in the Priory learn some things but not others. The African teaching staff always know far more. The guerrillas' 'Burma Road' runs through their married quarters dotted round the perimeter of the school; it is the black teachers, not the white Brethren, who pay a tenth – a tithe – of their salaries to Zanla.

The bond of Christianity is a fragile one. Since 1890 European missionaries in Rhodesia have baited creed and cult with education and medicine; in the long term, young Africans learned to accept the Cambridge certificates and the inoculations while surreptitiously, perhaps unconsciously, fending off a divinity that had waited nineteen centuries before making itself manifest to them. Prosser knows this, or suspects it – but is it much different in the average British school?

The missionaries serve Christ most effectively when they leave behind the imposing chapel, built in pale-yellow brick, with its two square towers at the west end and its vast, authoritarian nave. Old Father Jacob Wardle takes his life in his hand every alternate Sunday to drive over tortuous dirt tracks in search of the tiny, cowed congregations which, marshalled by their lay catechists, loyally assemble to greet him. Within Zanla there is a growing hostility towards Christianity; nuns are now afraid to wear crucifixes round their necks; Africans are warned, 'We don't want to see you praying.' Father Wardle's shrivelled gatherings of the faithful, mainly elderly people, no longer dare to hold Sunday services in his absence.

At 5 on a Sunday afternoon he arrives back in the Priory common-room, white-haired, gnarled, gentle, for a cup of tea. While two elderly Brethren tune into an ancient radio set for BBC World Service news (on Saturdays they intently absorb the British football results), Father Wardle recounts for my benefit a long list of recent guerrilla atrocities; only later do I learn from Prosser that Wardle has always been wholly in favour of the nationalist movement.

Then evening chapel. The nuns at the back lead the singing in commanding style – there is no organ. Five hundred children are crowded into the pews. It takes half an hour to administer the sacraments. Father Prosser delivers his sermon in English, which is translated, for the benefit of estate workers and their wives, into Shona by a middle-aged African verger in a smart business suit. This is the school tailor, whose brother was killed by guerrillas and his brother-in-law shot dead by soldiers while crossing a river at 2.30 in the afternoon. When Prosser kicked up a fuss, the army blandly replied that the brother-in-law had been breaking the curfew; yet there is no curfew at 2.30 in the afternoon. None of the villagers who witnessed the incident would come forward to testify.

Death in these beautiful blue-green hills. The kids are now singing a hymn in Shona, on a twelve-note register, with drums rolling down from the organ gallery. The Fathers of the Community of the Resurrection flit about the chapel like pale ghosts; Father Wardle is pursuing duties he could execute in his sleep. Behind the immobile, tanned features, topped by white hair still cut in the style of a pre-war English schoolboy, is what the Irish would call a terrible knowledge – the pain of the tribal trust lands. The mission's printer was murdered in his home two years ago, accused of being a 'sell-out', his body dumped in a 'donga' (an earth slit caused by soil erosion) and his relatives forbidden – cruellest and most degrading of punishments – to bury him. Father Wardle had served as a school manager in the Honde Valley. One of his black teachers, outspoken on behalf of law and order, had also been cut down.

The brother-in-law of St Augustine's chief builder had been beaten with an iron bar until his brains spilled out. At first mistaken for his brother-in-law, the builder had only narrowly escaped – and what had he said, what self-degradation had he suffered in that awful moment in order to deflect death from himself to his relative? On this occasion the 'boys' insisted that the victim be buried immediately under the nearest tree.

At Sunday supper the Brethren swallow their anti-malaria pills. Later, as a gesture to the sabbath, they carry their used plates as far as the kitchen. At 9 they will hold a short prayer meeting, depart to their rooms and observe a vow of silence which extends, every night of the week, until the end of breakfast. God's silence over the porridge and tea (a coffee-addict must steer clear of religious communities) nicely eliminates the burden of early-morning intercourse. And there are also the Sisters, mainly parchment white, a few black, both races predominantly elderly: they are regularly 'at home' to the Brothers, and to guests, at 11 on Sunday morning with biscuits and (miracle) coffee. In their charge are the 135 female pupils of St Augustine's; but the Sisters' days are numbered by a massacre now only months away – Elim.

33. never forget the K-factor

The Trojan Nickel Mine at Bindura is owned by the Rhodesian Nickel Corporation, a subsidiary of Harry Oppenheimer's gigantic Anglo-American Corporation, whose sandstone headquarters rise, massive, stately and antique in the city centre of Johannesburg. The General Manager, who has very short hair and intense blue eyes, isn't at all sure whether he should let me go down the mine.

'Our biggest problem, frankly, is the reluctance of Africans with A-levels in science subjects to undergo artisan training. They all want to sit behind a desk.'

The Deputy General Manager, a Fatboy, nods. 'These chappies aren't interested in money, they're not ambitious.'

'We actually prefer to recruit black artisans now,' the General Manager says, 'because the quality of the whites we get has fallen disastrously. I suppose you realize they're using more whites in the Zambian copper mines than before Independence.'

I nod passively at all these contradictory propositions. The Manager's blue eyes twinkle: 'I'm glad you're not taking notes,' he says.

Entering at level 5 we proceed along a tunnel cut horizontally into the hillside. There are puddles everywhere, twin rails for the wagons, untended piles of gelignite, a blackboard on which recent accidents are chalked up. The Assistant Mine Manager, Petrowski, a small, friendly man in high boots, immediately tells me a story about four white ladies who were playing tennis in Zambia when they were robbed at gunpoint. Black mineworkers periodically enter Petrowski's underground office-cave and daub purple-dye thumb-prints on a worksheet in receipt of the small coins (50 cents, 75 cents) that are their reward for not having suffered an accident. Petrowski rebukes one miner (in English) for not having clocked in before starting work; another comes humbly, meekly to whisper his private problem in Shona; after a moment Petrowski, who supervises five white and sixty black miners, just shrugs and turns his back, without a word. The African waits, head down, then walks away. Petrowski proudly shows me the chart of the mine, its levels and vertical hoists, that cover his whitewashed walls.

But what weighs on Petrowski's mind, since I come from London, is the hard time he was recently given at London Airport:

'I have a British passport, see, but one of those issued in Pretoria with "Resident of Rhodesia" stamped in it. They put me in a queue along with a lot of bloody Pakis. They looked up my name in this large book they have and they kept me waiting, too. Then one of them asks me why I live in Rhodesia. I said to him, "Find me a better place and I'll live in it." Then one says to the other, "What shall I do with him?" They ask me how long I stay in England. I tell them, "No longer than I have to, you can be sure of that!" When I come back to England at Dover from the Continent just a couple of weeks later, I go through the whole thing all over again.'

At the top of the pit shaft we climb into a chest-high bucket suspended from a chain. The bucket rotates as it drops; buttresses, girders, flapping air pipes flash past in the semi-darkness. Some 500 metres down the bucket suddenly begins to fall much faster and I am overcome by claustrophobia, the conviction that I am heading for asphyxiation, nearly a kilometre of hillside between me and the open sky. At level 7 three black miners climb up on the rim of the bucket, poise themselves, then take a large, decisive stride across the yawning shaft to safety. A slip would mean certain death. Is Petrowski going to require me to do this at a lower level? The bell rings and we descend into a rising bedlam of drilling until we finally touch down where a team of black miners are preparing to lay gelignite.

Back in his office, he orders tea. Himself a police reservist, he describes terrs as cowards, scum. 'You question the blacks, they say "angazi", a kind of long shrug or sigh meaning "I don't know". But they do know, those kaffirs.' Petrowski taps his heart: 'What do those village kaffirs feel inside here? One villager said to me, "You may kill me if I don't talk, but *they* will kill my children too if I do."' I sip the thick tea: almost every white Rhodesian in uniform tells a variation of this story – what they know of the Shona people they know mainly from each other.

In Chipadze township Bindura's black labour force lives in 1,000 new brick houses at a rent of $(R)10–$(R)20 a month. The Township Manager, a craggy Scot called Cruikshank, is absolute boss here, a religious man in no doubt that he has been Called to supervise the welfare, sanitation and Good Conduct of 9,000 natives. Proudly he shows me the $(R)150,000 Community Centre, equipped with a spacious theatre-cinema, a splendid Council Room in which the largely powerless black bourgeoisie can make dignified speeches and raise points of order, as well as a supernew 'cocktail lounge' for those blacks earning enough of Harry Oppenheimer's money to disdain common beerhalls.

Having delivered a few Presbyterian homilies to his red-helmeted township policemen on duty, Cruikshank drives me to the Coachman Inn, which dates back to the turn of the century when it served as a Rotenberg coach-house. It's now 'multiracial', though you wouldn't guess. Ties have to be worn after 7.30 p.m. Standards. In the luxuriously appointed bar Cruikshank snaps his fingers at the African barman, orders the first round, and introduces a tall beanpole of a man, Whales, who works for the Electrical Supply Commission and shares Cruikshank's deep faith. Whales has had a few, too: his discourse is intermittently slurred.

'You know, David, we've done . . . helluva lot for these munts. Without us there would be nothing, no jobs, no mines, just the bush. These kaffir politicians talk about –'

'Nationalism is a British idea,' Cruikshank cuts in. 'That's where the blacks got it from. Now the British are playing Moscow's game – did you see what Owen said in Moscow, David?'

'David,' says Whales, laying his glass down carefully and giving my shoulder the benefit of his slightly damp hand, 'we're very fair to them . . . here. Very . . . fair. Each man knows he's . . . fair. He has his conscience.'

'You'll regret letting all those blacks into Britain,' says Cruikshank. 'You'll be swamped, you'll sink. It's no good being too compassionate with these people, they'll always take advantage.'

'What people need', says Whales, 'is discipline. Particularly these people. Never forget the K-factor, David. A munt is a munt.' He beckons the barman: 'Three more of the same.' Slowly he appraises me. 'When the soul is pure it goes to a higher place, David. It isn't black and white that counts, it's the soul. I mean . . . I know what I mean by "good" and you know what you mean but we each act according to our conscience, eh? Eh? . . . Eh?'

Cruikshank nods, imbibes: 'The conscience progresses, David. That is the true significance of reincarnation. My own conscience is clear, David. . . . Perhaps no man should ever say that.'

'No . . . man should . . . ever . . . say that,' says Whales. 'No man.'

'They breed like rabbits, you see, David, there's no way to educate them out of it. So I say . . . limit their children to two by law.'

Whales insists on taking me home for dinner. After some delay in finding the key, he climbs unsteadily into his Electrical Supply Commission van. 'Ambushed a year ago today . . . road between here and Shamva . . . tracer bullets, you could see 'em coming . . . one hit this headlamp, one blew out a tyre, one came up through the carpet into my foot if you want to know. One came through the rear side window and ricocheted through my shoulder . . . knew I'd been hit but felt no pain. . . . Well, I'm not afraid of death, not at all. It's either your time or it isn't.'

We pass the troopies' canteen where muscular white and black soldiers now sit side by side, equal before God if not before the paymaster-general. The hills surrounding Bindura are covered with bungalows set down in gorgeous little gardens, each gateway marked by the 'plot' number and each guarded by a dog which barks savagely at Africans, rearing up with hideous jaws behind the wire fence, furious guardian of its paradise of flaming poinsettia, wild fig-trees, canna-lilies, beds of red-hot poker.

Whales and his wife live in a spotless bungalow. The radio is never turned off – a honey-voiced speakerine constantly transmits love and melody from the 'folk on the home front' to 'our lads in the bush'. Mrs Whales has three sons in the bush. Their sporting trophies cover the mantelpiece and the shelves. 'Out here people love sport,' says Whales, who has miraculously sobered up during the short drive from the Coachman Inn. 'It makes you happy, sport, if you like it. What you need in the UK is . . . a strong leader.'

Mrs Whales sits sedately, knees pressed together as if one were trying to see between them, hair permed and dyed. She does regular police reserve duty, mornings. 'We never talk about security matters in front of the servants,' she says. 'If you ask me, it's a shame to have brought them from their own way of life, they were much happier in their kraals.'

'What shall we drink?' Whales asks.

'Well, I'll have a gin,' Mrs Whales says, 'and I'm sure our guest would like something, too.'

Presently the servant appears and announces dinner. The radio is now broadcasting hymns of the revivalist variety.

34. a tale of two cities

Both the white Government and Salisbury's white City Council have washed their hands of the refugees. Yet it is the war waged by whites, the protected villages erected by whites, the displacement of tribal population engineered by whites, that fills the city with starving squatters and creates vast refugee camps in Zambia and Mozambique.

Zengesi is a sprawl of mud huts, rickety shelters made out of plastic garbage sacks, corrugated-iron lean-tos. Here children are dying for lack of food. In the heart of Salisbury's heavy industrial area, by the banks of the Makabusi River, squatters covered in filth and grime scavenge the municipal rubbish dump, scrabbling for a piece of bread, a rotting banana, rank meat. The stink is unbearable. When the new rubbish trucks appear, groaning and grinding slowly over the mud, the squatters swarm up and over them like bluebottles. It turns the stomach. To go and watch is the last word in 'slumming' but it has to be done.

Sister Dymphna Vanwesenbeech is chairperson of Christian Care. She does care. CC helps about 1,000 of Harare's refugees every week, distributing a ration of 5 kg of mealies, 1 kg of beans, a packet of salt. The Red Cross gives $(R)7,000 a month and the Salvation Army also helps. But there are no toilets, no water, no clinics.

Neither the Government nor the City Council gives a penny.

In the evenings makeshift shacks go up at the Harare bus terminus. By morning they are taken down. Recently the municipality of Salisbury embarked on a drive to clear the area, known as Old Bricks, of squatters – 9,800 families were driven away. But there remains a substantial 'invisible' community of squatters. At five in the evening they move on to the area of bare earth near the Terminus, perhaps 4,000 of them. Here among the pools of stagnant water and rubbish heaps crawling with flies each family has its own patch marked by a low wall of raised earth. The shacks are made of plastic draped over a framework of branches tied with string.

In southern Africa the blacks live in 'townships' because they are not allowed to live in towns. Only whites are permitted to live in towns and cities. The blacks pour into the towns during the day, they mill about the great bus stations, they serve and toil, but in the evening they must withdraw to the townships. It is the law. Accommodation in the townships is cramped, crowded and regimented – houses resemble matchboxes set out in neat rows. Nowhere to swing a cat. Soweto is a township, so too is Sharpeville.

In many townships the police station and admin office, surrounded by a high barbed-wire fence or an imposing wall, are sited at the entrance near the main access road. Salisbury's black townships – Highfield, Harare, Kambazuma and Mufukose, etc. – are mainly concentrated to the south-west of the city. It is no coincidence that the main industrial sites extend in a belt round the south-western perimeter, linked by ring roads and radial avenues along which packed buses and heavy trucks pour out ink-black diesel fumes. At the beginning of the day, and again in the evening, relays of buses leave the stations, jam-packed with Karl Marx's surplus value. Invariably the main markets are sited near the bus stations; wares are spread out on stalls, on the ground; Africa walks, squats, waits, watches. Everywhere, in shop windows and factory gates, you see the same sign: Hapana Basa, No Work.

The Khami Road runs due west out of Bulawayo and serves as the access road to a cluster of black townships called Mpopma, Mabutweni and Njube, each of which resembles an army barracks, set out methodically, grimly, with set-square and ruler, to house the worker ants required by the white entrepreneurs. The grid of parallel streets is so finely meshed that there is no room to name them on the Surveyor-General's scale 1:33,333 maps – and are not their inhabitants little more than statistics, units of uprooted labour power, in the imaginations of their rulers?

The township's nerve centre is its police station, a fortress barred, walled and wired against insurrection. To drive into a township is to enter the *univers concentrationnaire*. The dominant presence is that of the police, the hidden eye. A township is a world of informers.

Mike Hove, formerly a Federal MP and High Commissioner in Nigeria, is a black township Superintendent. He is a haggard man, gaunt, handsome once, clearly tense behind an outward show of relaxation. You pronounce his name Hovay. He works in a municipal building protected by a security fence and helmeted guards. 'Of course', he says, 'you can take down everything I say. I don't believe in secrecy, I have always spoken my mind.' He confirms that the townships receive no subsidy at all from the white ratepayers of Bulawayo: housing and other municipal services depend mainly on beer revenues ($(R)8 million a year) and business rents. 'We actually buy our electricity and water from the city of Bulawayo. I'll tell you something else. The industrial areas pay their rates and rents to the City Treasury. It is the black people of the townships who work in those factories, but the revenues are not for us to spend.'

He recalls recently visiting a shanty town of cardboard and grass in the Umguza Valley, a place of terrible squalor; he speaks of successive waves of desperate people, refugees from the war, converging on Bulawayo.

The phone rings. For perhaps two minutes he listens to the caller without saying a word. Then he replaces the receiver. The lines in his face have multiplied, flecks of red appear in his eyes. The police have surrounded a house holding two terrorists, one of whom has been shot while holding a grenade with half the pin out. Hove lays his long brown hands on his bare desk and stares at me.

'You realize you could be arrested for coming here.'

'You're the Superintendent, I had your permission.'

'That wouldn't impress the Special Branch. When you drove here you got lost, you told me, and you got out of your car to ask the way, and you spoke to some Africans who told you the way, right?'

'So?'

'Then *they* know you're here. Supposing *they* pick you up after you leave here and read those notes you've been taking?' He smiles oddly. '*They*'ll tell you all about terrorism. But who is the real terrorist in this country? The Government. You hear about faction-fighting in the townships here but believe me, the security forces systematically provoke them. Listen, I had a phone call recently. A man in a high position who I know well told me to get my wife out of our village because Zanla was due to move in there. This man was no fool – he knows my wife has nothing to fear from Zanla. He was telling me in the only possible way that the Selous Scouts were due to do a job in my area, understand? They like to hit prominent people, to drive a wedge between them and the "boys".' His hands shake and he lights another cigarette. Behind the urban functionary in his brown suit shimmers a remote, dusty village in Matabeleland.

'This is a police state,' Mike Hove says quietly.

The white towns need the black townships because they require cheap and plentiful labour. Salisbury City Council actually increases a man's rent when he loses his job! Drive him out! To keep their houses, unemployed families must pay the unsubsidized or 'economic' rent, which of course they can't afford. (However, only Marxists make a fuss about this, so let's say no more.) By contrast Bulawayo offers sub-economic rents to tenants earning less than $(R)60 a month.

Traditionally the urban councils have been elected by the white residents and all local rates and taxes are ploughed back into the white towns: not a penny of it is spent on the black townships. They must pay their own way, but their Advisory Boards are subordinate to the white urban council. This is southern Africa.

Now the white urban councils must face the wind of change brought on by the impending internal settlement. Their instinctive response is to deflect it. In Salisbury, Councillor Jock Alves, Chairman of the African Affairs Committee, favours the creation of separate, self-governing black and white urban councils. No way would he accept a demand by Harare Advisory Board that Harare should become a ward of the city with direct representation on the City Council. In Gwelo Mayor Sulter puts forward a scheme for self-governing black townships. The Minister, William Irvine, is a diehard. Never in his lifetime would the black majority in the townships flood, overrun, swamp the municipality.

Dr Hugh Ashton does not look his 68 years. Long-haired and deeply tanned, with the air of a distracted professor but a confessed addiction to boating off the South African coast, Ashton has been effective municipal boss of Bulawayo's 200,000 black inhabitants since he came up from Johannesburg in 1949. Born in Basutoland, educated at the universities of London, Oxford and Cape Town, Ashton served as District Commissioner in Bechuanaland and Senior Welfare Officer in Jo'burg before his appointment as Bulawayo's Director of Housing and Community Services. From the Ashton 'stable' in Bulawayo progressive municipal administrators infiltrated the more rigidly conservative cities like Umtali and Salisbury, men who believed in steady – if gradual – evolution towards majority rule and who despised the boneheaded Rhodesian Front's policy of stifling the training and apprenticeship of Africans. Such men were almost invariably opponents of UDI, enlightened paternalists in the mould of the British District Officer.

Throughout Rhodesia African townships are administered by an Advisory Board (mainly composed of blacks), which is always subordinate to the urban council elected by the white ratepayers. In June 1977 Ashton circulated a confidential memorandum urging that the municipal services be reorganized with a view to creating racially integrated councils and administrations. But Salisbury and Umtali refused even to discuss it. Bill Irvine, Scottishborn Minister of Local Government, was in fact pushing in the opposite direction, towards 'separate development', separate black and white urban councils: the white ratepayers would thus not risk being asked to subsidize black housing, nor would they risk being 'swamped' by the much larger electorate of the townships.

Bulawayo City Council recommended to the Minister an end to racially zoned housing, which it was in his power to grant under the 1977 amendment to the Land Tenure Act. Irvine refused to grant it or to allow the central commercial area of any city to be opened up to black business.

Jaap Kitshoff, a heavily built Afrikaner with an open and engaging manner, is Personnel Adviser to the Municipality of Bulawayo. He works in the august and imposing Town Hall, on the corner of Selborne Avenue and Fife Street, where the entrance hall and stairways groan with the portraits of former dignitaries, mayors, town clerks. Kitshoff explains that as from 1 January 1978 all municipal jobs are to be graded according to six criteria, and that all *future* appointments will be made strictly on merit.

'A lot of people here don't like this one bit,' he says. 'It means, you see, that certain unskilled jobs previously reserved for Europeans and pegged to artificially high salary scales will be drastically downgraded. May I give you an example? Your meter readers have always been Europeans. In the future the best man will get the job and he'll be paid only $(R)150 a month instead of $(R)300. Now the man who already has that job won't suffer, but what about his sons?'

Kitshoff is careful to stress that this policy had nothing to do with 'Africanization' (i.e. giving jobs to blacks because they are black) and is indeed largely designed to fend off 'indiscriminate Africanization when we have a majority-rule government in this country'.

This is the stance of white liberalism in southern Africa, even of Dr Hugh Ashton: 'One man, one vote is all very well in the long run, but what we badly need now is an interim franchise with a minority of seats reserved not for whites but for voters of both races possessing certain educational and property qualifications.'

My scepticism is apparent. Ashton's eyes seem to glint more fiercely behind his glasses: 'Don't imagine that either wing of the PF enjoys much support. To call Muzorewa a puppet is to malign him. Rhodesia is now a pawn in an international power game, with the USSR making the running. Why have the Russians put a top KGB agent in Lusaka?'

(In 1981 Nkomo's party swept the board in the municipal elections and took control of Bulawayo's first integrated City Council.)

35. on the shunt

'I'll pick you up from your hotel,' declares the broad northern accent, 'no trouble at all.' Could have been Arthur Scargill, notorious Red leader of the Yorkshire miners, but is in fact Brian Holleran, Acting General Secretary of the Rhodesian Trade Union Congress. We drive to Unity House, headquarters of the élite Railway Workers' Union. A photograph of Ian Smith hangs in the front office. Bulawayo's railway district, its terminal, marshalling yards, warehouses and repair shops resemble a slice of industrial England north of the Humber: the Great Northern Hotel, the Waverley Hotel, Fish and Chips, accents broad and blunt enough to dig an allotment. The Chairman of the Union storms into Holleran's office in a great temper – 'blewdy 'ell this, blewdy 'ell that' – about current negotiations with the Railways. The issue seems to be whether the word 'persons' in a negotiating document is a cunning management trap and whether 'personnel' would be safer. 'Blewdy 'ell, mun, why cun't 't blewdy say what 't blewdy mean?'

There are blacks around the corridors, junior clerks, tea-boys, an old fellow with a mop, all of them keeping their place. The RWU is an élite, white-dominated set-up: only 1,000 out of its 5,000 members are black. Periodically its white members put on the blue uniforms and blue floppy hats of police reservists and stand about with rifles at street corners, legs wide apart, looking firm but fair, as a white man should be. They live with their cotton-frock wives in suburbs called North End and Queen's Park.

Holleran was born in Leeds, served as an NCO in the British army, decided to 'chance my luck' by emigrating to Rhodesia. After some years working on the railways he now has an office of his own and a nice car. As for racial discrimination on the railways, what kind of a Communist had I been listening to?

'The Quenet Commission Report.'

'Ah yes. Well . . .'

The Commission had this to say: 'The [black] engine drivers said that although some of their number had distinguished themselves at their vocational examinations . . . they were . . . constantly superseded by Europeans who were junior to them, some of whom had less satisfactory examination records and far less experience. . . . Because they [the blacks] had not been promoted they were not able to fulfil their ambition of being mainline drivers, they were kept "on the shunt", their salaries were far less than they would otherwise have been. . . .' The Personnel Manager of Rhodesia Railways did not attempt to deny the accuracy of these complaints, he merely reported that no solution had been found – the white drivers had dug in their north British heels.

Holleran denies it all, or most of it, very genially, then gradually admits it all. The intervening process is not unpleasant. We drink tea.

I ask him how he justifies *de facto* segregation of passengers on the railways.

'No way that happens. This isn't South Africa, you know.'

According to the Quenet Report, 'zoning' takes place when the reservation is made, the result being that black and white passengers travelling first class, or second class, find themselves in separate compartments, even if this means squeezing seven blacks into a single compartment while two whites stretch their legs in the one next door.

Holleran's reading material consists mainly of horse-racing mags and crackpot anti-Communist sheets like *Guardian of Liberty*, published by Tibor Kecskesi Tollas of Munich. On the way to the Southern Sun Hotel for a sundowner he expresses deep admiration for Roy Welensky (a former railwayman) and Ian Smith. 'I think,' he says, 'Mr Smith feels very hurt by what is happening now.'

'Hurt?'

'When you meet Mr Smith you'd think he was a very simple man, but he's very shrewd, you know. It's my belief he'll carry us through all this, though don't ask me how. You have to reward people for their skills. That's the trouble with the UK, isn't it, inflation, socialism . . . Mind you I have to admit a lot of people here are prejudiced against trade unions, they think every trade unionist is some kind of Communist. . . .'

I have another appointment. Holleran seems a bit disappointed. His marriage has recently broken up, he has time on his hands. 'I think I'll stay for another lager,' he says. A TV screen has lit up in the corner of the plush lounge-bar. He adjusts the angle of his chair.

On the corner of Lobengula and 13th Avenue is the office of the all-black Railway and Associated Workers' Union (membership 9,800) representing 'Category E' railway workers. The entrance corridor is Third World: any active economic unit operates like a honeypot round which swarm and lethargically buzz friends, relatives, people in from the reserves, people hoping for work, boys anxious to carry messages, vendors of food . . . You push your way through feeling white.

Upstairs the boardroom is spacious and well furnished. P. H. Bohuwa, Assistant General Secretary, young, alert and helpful, wears a purple shirt with a patterned matching tie. He smokes. On either side of him sit two other men, both smoking, both there because I am there and because a day contains long hours and sitting down is comfortable; the table is mirror-polished, there are photographs of union officials on the walls, my pencil is busy but they do nothing with their hands except light cigarettes. Occasionally one of them goes out. I have been in this situation many times before. What game am I playing? Why do I care about Ndebele railway workers today, Iraqi oil workers yesterday, Kuwaiti building workers. . . ? Why do I fill notebooks?

Mr Bohuwa is telling me that yes indeed racial discrimination is a 'most severe' problem: 'Rhodesia Railways do not take on African learner drivers. An African has to work his way up as a stoker, fireman and shunter driver. Only whites can begin at the top as learner drivers. Similarly, white stewards on trains start at Grade 2, whereas blacks must come up through Grade 1.'

I note it down, putting a pencil ring round the word 'similarly'; such felicities do not figure in and among the 'blewdy 'ells' of the white Railway Workers' Union.

I ask Mr Bohuwa why the blacks do not bring about majority rule by means of a general strike. The three men across the table shake their heads vigorously: you might think I had deprived them of a livelihood just by mentioning it.

'Impossible! Three-quarters of our members could be replaced from the ranks of the unemployed. People are flooding into the townships from the TTLs. Besides, the railways are classed as an essential service: the strike leaders could be gaoled.'

'The guerrillas in the bush risk their lives, won't you risk gaol?'

The three men do not accept my logic, which in truth is merely the algebra of the Western scribe passing in the night. For black Zimbabweans the countryside is the place for war, the town is the place for earning wages. There is no war in the town, yet the town sustains the war. The peasant is damned, without hope, therefore revolutionary, but the black worker has something, wants more, will compromise with white power. Yet this neat dichotomy ignores the vast interpretation of town and country, those overloaded buses groaning back and forth, clouds of black diesel belching from their arseholes, the roofs loaded with bundles, boxes, bicycles . . . bombs; medicine for the 'boys', food and money for the 'boys', all by bus and lorry. Hence the long, systematic searches at the police roadblocks.

P. H. Bohuwa and his companions look restless, glance at their watches. 'We don't want Communism here.'

36. Umtali – the Man

The view of Umtali as you descend the spiralling road from Christmas Pass is spectacularly beautiful. The European city gleams on its valley floor, encircled by tier upon tier of blue-green mountains. A white overseer with a huge stomach stands motionless, hands on hips, while a gang of blacks toils to keep the road in good repair – a figure out of Brecht except that this Afrikaner wears a soft bush hat rather than a pith helmet. Army trucks packed with superconfident, bareheaded, Kentucky-fried soldiers descend in triumph to the headquarters of the Rhodesia Regiment on Main Street: their self-conscious image of themselves resembles that of cowboys who have seen too many Westerns.

This is the city where whites of Scottish extraction celebrate Hogmanay singing 'I Belong to Glasgow' to the tune of 'Auld Lang Syne'. A woman in smart white togs takes a moment off from a bowls match on the greens above the city (Scotland versus the Rest) to complain: 'Britain is letting us down badly.' A man who put his house up for sale is in no doubt: 'The gooks have got it, the whole world is supporting the terrs. I'm taking the gap, though I always thought I'd be one of the last out, you know, putting out the lights and burning it all down as we left. I'm going South. You've got more chance where the ratio is only four to one – I could take out four Affies before they took me out.'

Umtali's white population is down from 10,000 to 7,000. There are sporadic guerrilla mortar attacks from the surrounding hills on this valley town. The Forbes Border Post, five miles away, is now sealed off with barbed wire and mines, whereas once the main road had transported holiday-makers to the prawns and other delights of Portuguese Beira, on the Indian Ocean.

Frelimo and Zanla fire off shells and rockets from over the border into the huge pine and eucalyptus plantations, setting the hillsides ablaze and leaving vast scars of scorched earth.

Main Street is thronged by swinging, well-dressed black youths and girls. They look very cheerful. Yet Sakubva township just down the road holds 20,000 war refugees, its population swollen from the authorized 24,000 to 45,000.

Mr Musabaeka is a rich and fat man. Towards dusk he is to be found in a small drab office in a one-storey brick building surrounded by buses. Mr Musabaeka owns fifteen buses. His compound – a grassless, wheel-worn, rutted mud-patch full of puddles from summer rains – stands immediately opposite the entrance to Sakubva township. People hang around the office and from time to time drift in and out – a relative, an employee, someone asking a favour. Musabaeka is 'busy' but quite pleased to see me.

'Now, I ask myself a question. When the Boys' High School hires one of my buses to take a sports team on a round trip to Salisbury, at a cost of $(R)220, they always have enough petrol coupons. But when it's a case of taking a black football team, no coupons are available. I ask myself why. OK, OK, so the whites are now trying to be polite to the blacks, but there are still incidents, believe me . . . incidents. And why can't I own a shop in the city of Umtali? I would like to buy a house for, let us say, $(R)25,000 in Umtali. A nice house, with a garden. Not permitted. I must lease a house over there in Sakubva township with only two bedrooms and no proper kitchen. Did you know that Sakubva has only five-amp electricity? You can run a hotplate off that but not a stove.'

'You feel strongly.'

'I feel strongly, yes!'

Musabaeka believes in the internal settlement: 'Nkomo is played out. In any case, the PF will never accept elections. The whites have skills, we need them, twenty-eight seats for them is reasonable. Many of the guerrillas support Muzorewa, their morale is declining, too much drinking and getting girls pregnant.'

The Superintendent's office is sited just inside the main gate of Sakubva township. My young friend Didymus will have nothing to do with it; if I insist on reporting to the Superintendent, as the regulations stipulate that any visitor to a black township must do, that's my affair. Didymus recently took his A-level certificates to the Umtali Post Office and asked for a job. He noted that every Post Office clerk and every trainee standing at her shoulder was a white girl: the whites needed two wage-earners per family while the blacks had none. Didymus was told there were no vacancies.

Didymus goes off to look for the Man, tense as a cat on a hot tin roof. 'Every tenth house in Sakubva is occupied by a Government informer,' he whispers, then vanishes. Upstairs in the Superintendent's office I find a number of black clerks and a fat, elderly white man in a sky-blue safari suit. His name is Goddard and he holds the rank of Assistant Superintendent.

'I'd like to look round the township.'

'You're not a journalist, are you?'

'I'm in Umtali to visit relatives. Lovely city – you must be proud of it.' It is not my intention to tell Mr Goddard that I have come to Sakubva to ferret out a leading political activist of the UANC.

Goddard evidently needs a white man to talk to. For twenty years he worked in the mines. 'I can remember when the natives went about half naked. The women wore loincloths at the back to cover their big bums, but nothing over their boobs. The men wore the long bit in front to cover their pricks.'

The black clerks are listening, watching: they do not snigger, their expressions are carefully wiped clean of any indicator of feeling. Even so, Goddard abruptly loses his temper, his features blossoming beetroot-red: 'Haven't you got work to do!' When he turns back to me his mood remains irascible.

'So – do our munts look hungry, like the foreign press alleges?'

'Which foreign press?'

'I don't read the foreign press,' Goddard says.

Abruptly he leaves the office, closing the door behind him. Watched by a tinted photograph of former President Clifford Dupont, I flick rapidly through the clipboards hanging on the wall, hoping to uncover some racist infamy but finding only dreary memos about latrines and garbage disposal. After a while I too leave the office, followed by the neutral gaze of the clerks, and start walking through the township in search of Didymus. I find him in the local UANC office, engaged in animated argument with a number of young men; ignorant of the language, I lose patience and haul him away. We drive round Sakubva from one animated argument to another. Is there method in this madness? Didymus seems to think so and his instincts are finally confirmed when the Man and his bodyguard are finally extracted from a small house to which we have been led by two women with babies strapped to their backs.

It is now 4 in the afternoon and the bus station is thick with people. Long columns of workers stream up the Melsetter Road on foot and by bicycle. As we turn out of Sakubva towards Umtali we see three white military policemen halting vehicles at random. In the back seat the Man and his tall bodyguard whisper urgently together in Shona: it crosses my mind that they may be armed and that we might be entering some fairly deep shit. One of the MPs, a giant of a Boshoff, is astride the centre of the road, flagging me down, and I stop thinking altogether as my foot presses on the brake. At the last minute he waves us on; involuntarily my hand lifts from the steering wheel in a gracious white salute, a gesture of complicity.

Didymus knows a place where we can talk – in white Umtali there is no natural, relaxed way the races can converse together except strictly in the context of work, and the sense of a shadow is persistent. We drive to the house of a priest Didymus knows – once again, the Church to the rescue.

The Man is in a terrific state of tension. He is local secretary of the UANC and high on self-dramatization. Three of his sons, he says, have gone over the border to join the 'boys'. He himself has spent the better part of the week in the police station on a charge of being in contact with terrorists. To top it all, 'Selous Scouts' have beaten on the doors of his house in the middle of the night and broken two of his windows. 'But for my neighbours they would have killed me!' I put it to the Man that he, being local branch secretary of the party, might be assaulted by a wide variety of enemies. The Man bangs his fist on the table and insists that 95 per cent of Zimbabweans support the Bishop, including most of the 'boys'.

'They are loyal to the UANC. The boys all have code-names like K2 and F3, all recorded in a central register. When victory comes those who remain alive will parade through the streets and their real names will be announced to the crowds and to the world's press: "K2, step forward, you are the hero Joseph Ndhlovu!"'

The bodyguard nods vigorously and grins. Perhaps he sees himself stepping forward as the hero Joseph Ndhlovu.

37. white man's frontier

Rhodesia's tourist industry took a hammering. From a peak of 339,000 in 1972, the number of tourists plummeted to 140,000 in 1976. The South Africans in particular got cold feet, though you could still find American and German adventure hunters who relished staying at Freddie Pacella's Victoria Falls Motel in the knowledge that it had been 'revved' by 'gooks' on 30 October 1976 and 31 July 1977 – rockets, rifle-fire, B60 grenades. But no one wanted to be in the luxurious Elephant Hills Hotel at Victoria Falls on the night its entire top floor was burnt out by mortar fire from Zambia, nor in the Victoria Falls Hotel at 10.30 in the evening of 17 December 1977 when a rocket struck the tennis-court and ricocheted into the side of the hotel, breaking all the glass in the cocktail bar. Many guests were enjoying a band and a barbecue on the lawn when the lights went out and the bombardment began: they flung themselves to the ground. Half an hour later the bars and the casino were back in operation and the 'spirit was terrific'. Even so, Churchill's children preferred to steer clear of the Falls and Meikles Southern Sun Hotels announced a £2 million loss on their Rhodesian operations.

More than ever the Zambezi became a real man's world, hard drinking, hard gambling, 'booze cruises' up the river, crocodiles, the lot. The white man's frontier: across the broad grey waters hurtling towards the great, two-kilometre-wide Falls Black Africa began. Civilization stops here. On the road from the airport middle-aged reservists smoked away their boredom behind sandbagged emplacements. On the river itself police boats sped upstream and downstream between the islands, Kalunda and Khandahar, and the inevitable Texan tourist extracted enough adrenalin out of this macho performance to repeat the hoary old joke about guerrilla marksmen: 'It's OK, so long as they're aiming at you.'

Even so, the United Touring Company boat hugged the Rhodesian shore.

One patrol-boat crew had explained their mission to the *Sunday Telegraph*'s columnist, Peregrine Worsthorne: 'It's not black rule we're fighting against, it's black misrule. We are not racialists. But how can we be expected to surrender to terrorism, which is evil whatever the colour of its face?'

Worsthorne was deeply moved: '. . . what can one do but take their side? As they chug off in their patrol boat after dinner, I shout "good luck". It is impossible under such circumstances not to feel the pulls of kith and kinship.'

The security forces had established camps and minefields along the hot, sparsely populated Zambezi Valley, so that the parched earth was strewn with the bleached bones of elephants and other wildlife which had detonated mines. Since the days of Frederick Selous this had been a happy hunting-ground for white adventurers and ivory-hunters, and now white game rangers were joined by Selous Scouts following the spoor of Zipra guerrillas, who were ferried across the wide, fearful river in the dug-out canoes of desperately poor Tonga tribesmen.

38. casualty count

As the year ended, Zanla stepped up the level of its attacks on both military and civilian targets. On the night of 17 December an unusually audacious retaliatory assault was launched against Grand Reef air base, near Umtali, by sixty guerrillas who damaged lorries and buildings, killed an African soldier and injured six white servicemen who had been watching a pre-Christmas show on TV. A 75-mm rocket brought down their canteen roof.

When Johannes van Maarseveen, a 40-year-old farmer and father of three, was killed in the Cashel district his death brought the total number of white civilians killed since 1972 to 115. Of these, eighty-two came from farming families.

Black civilian deaths amounted to 2,370.

The security forces claimed to have killed 3,596 'terrorists' inside Rhodesia for the loss of 574 of their own men.

Those slaughtered in cross-border raids (at least 3,000) did not appear in official statistics, even speculatively.

Part Three: 1978

1. a charade

The Salisbury Agreement, known also as the 'internal settlement', was eventually signed by Smith, Muzorewa, Sithole and Chirau on 3 March 1978.

Ian Smith, having pulverized his right-wing rebels in August 1977 and won, yet again, all fifty white seats, was now ready to grant the black nationalists one man, one vote – provided he could sew up a constitution which guaranteed effective white control over the economy, the civil service, the armed forces, the police and the judiciary. The aim was to capitalize on the divisions within the nationalist movement, endow the 'moderates' with the trappings but not the substance of power, isolate the radical guerrilla leadership, and thus obscure the real nature of the war by precipitating a bloody struggle between the black parties. For this strategy Smith had the complete support of the South Africans.

Clearly Muzorewa was the principal 'target'; but to make the Bishop sweat a little, to ensure that in negotiations the tiny Methodist did not become too truculent, Smith had not only brought home the power-hungry Sithole (into whose sticky embrace and shiny Mercedes cars disaffected elements of the UANC promptly hurled themselves), he also held secret talks with Kenneth Kaunda in the hope of detaching Nkomo's Zapu from the Patriotic Front alliance with Mugabe. This manoeuvre, however, failed, despite a second secret meeting at Mfuwe in eastern Zambia on 18 October 1977.

On 24 November Smith announced that he had invited the three 'internal' black leaders, Muzorewa, Sithole and Chirau, to the conference table. It was now that Smith took the historic step of finally and publicly abandoning his adamant opposition to universal adult suffrage. 'Not only do all the black political parties insist,' he explained, 'but the whole of the rest of the world feels the same. And so we are being equally pragmatic.'

To reassure white opinion, a spectacular display of military strength was perhaps inevitable: it took the form of the massacre of some 1,200 Zimbabweans at Chimoio in Mozambique during the last week of November.

Muzorewa went into mourning for a week and Smith began the talks without him.

Sithole and Muzorewa naturally adopted a 'tough' posture, initially bombarding Smith with demands for the immediate release of political detainees, an end to political executions and the removal of banning orders on certain nationalist organizations. This suited Smith perfectly well; he had plenty of time; although there was no prepared script, everyone knew their lines; had the 'internal' leaders appeared too conciliatory at the outset it would have deprived urban Africans of a surrogate drama which they mistook for the real one. 'I must say to you nationalists,' sighed Smith, 'my Government has given in and given in, but got nothing in return from you. It is time you did some giving.'

Sithole's intransigence was a charade; every utterance was for the record (his party headquarters rushed out verbatim transcripts of the bargaining): 'The police force is predominantly white at the top. The prison services are likewise predominantly white at the top. If these were to remain as they are, this will be difficult to talk of genuine independence in Zimbabwe.' But when, four months later, the young Co-Minister of the Civil Service, Byron Hove, made precisely this point, he was promptly dismissed by an Executive Council consisting of Smith, Sithole, Muzorewa and Chirau.

Smith constantly pointed a dire finger north, towards black Africa: 'We want high standards and to keep these offices from political manipulation through nepotic practices . . . I do not have to remind you of stories of sons of PMs and generals who got offices in countries near us and some of them have almost become bankrupt.'

The Rhodesian Front's demands, presented in December 1977, were brutal: (a) whites to elect one-third of the parliamentary seats, with power to block any change in the constitution; (b) white control (though not described as such) of the security forces and the police; (c) absolute career and pensions safeguards for white civil servants; (d) a bill of rights (for which the RF had displayed no enthusiasm while themselves in power); (e) the right to hold dual citizenship (thus perpetuating eighty-eight years of opportunism; (f) an 'independent' judiciary – in essence a bench dominated by the present white High Court judges.

The black parties concentrated their sound and fury on the issue of the franchise. Just why they did so can be explained in terms of what actually occurred when elections were held, a year later, in April 1979. Because the whites held 28 per cent of the seats as of right, Muzorewa, although a clear winner, emerged with only fifty-one seats out of one hundred. When, within weeks, eight of his UANC MPs defected, his absolute majority in the House vanished. Yet had there been no seats reserved for the white majority, Muzorewa would have commanded seventy out of one hundred seats (assuming the same proportion of votes as he actually achieved), putting his supremacy beyond challenge. (With that arithmetic, no one defects.)

There were two issues in contention: how many seats should be reserved for whites; and who should elect them. Smith's position was logical: 'Whites elected by blacks do not represent whites. They become stooges.' But the British and the small white opposition groups inside Rhodesia wanted to weaken the iron grip of the Rhodesian Front by relieving *white voters* of their privileged position. Thus the Anglo-American plan envisaged twenty Specially Elected Members representing the 'minority communities' (i.e. whites, Asians and Coloureds) being chosen by the eighty Normally Elected (black) Members. Muzorewa's initial solution, though similarly motivated, was to give Smith the thirty-three seats he demanded on behalf of the whites, but on condition that they be elected by a single common, multiracial voters' roll. When the UANC abandoned this approach in the face of Smith's intransigence, it attempted to mitigate the concession by reducing its offer of white seats to twenty. On the same day (21 December 1977) the Bishop put in a request for more petrol coupons, 'since we are doing this extra driving which we did not plan for'.

Replied Smith magnanimously: 'A message has been sent to the Petrol Rationing Officer to give your request consideration.' Nor was Smith ever reluctant to remind the Africans sitting opposite him where power lay. 'If you believe that the majority of whites rejoice over what I am doing today you are mistaken. They simply don't understand what I'm doing. They look at the raids into Mozambique and say let's get on with more of them.' On another occasion he snapped: 'The whites tell me that all I have to do is to say I no longer accept majority rule, then we can stop this exflux and start seeing more whites coming here.'

On the face of things Sithole emerged as a far more impressive politician than Muzorewa. The Bishop, who said very little, tended to sulk and quibble and equivocate. Sithole could not obliterate totally his own estimable heritage, the authentic nationalist posture which, in a warped and desperate bid for power, he was now compelled to betray: 'If we have one nation, a sovereign state with a racial blocking group . . . we can't sell such a settlement to ourselves, to the fighters, to the OAU, to the UK, to the USA, and to the UN.' Prophetic words. Yet Sithole spent the remainder of 1978 and the first four months of 1979 as a member of the Transitional Government attempting, in vain, to do precisely that – to sell the unsaleable. Smith duly dropped some small change into Sithole's outstretched palm, notably the right to style his internal party 'Zanu' and thus to present himself as the sole, authentic leader of the 'freedom fighters'.

But the freedom fighters were not convinced.

Under a portrait of Cecil Rhodes the white Prime Minister and three blacks bent on taking the short cut to an ersatz form of power sat down to sign the Salisbury Agreement. It was 3 March 1978 and the Bishop, who wore a brilliant Liberian boubou over his clerical robes, announced that the ceremony marked the end of UDI.

In Salisbury the *National Observer*, which Argus bought in 1978, was euphoric. 'Four smiling faces flashed round the world last week. A wry Prime Minister relaxed and laughed. A nationalist leader at his side proclaimed: "Here it is not *who* is right, but *what* is right, and therefore what is right has to be." Africa, and indeèd the world, might learn from the way black and white Africans in Salisbury are seeking to find a solution to their problems, free from outside pressures.'

The majority of British newspapers hailed the proposed constitution as a major advance. *The Times* called it an 'acceptable compromise' which 'provides no ground for argument that majority rule is prejudiced or unreal, though the Marxist reaction is predictable'.

The *Guardian* was scarcely less enthusiastic: 'As a set of constitutional proposals it is perfectly proper: that Mr Nkomo and Mr Mugabe have not signed it or improved it to their satisfaction is, unhappily, nobody's fault but their own.' The *Guardian* even claimed that the Agreement guaranteed the freedom of the security forces from political interference. The *Daily Telegraph*'s reactions were, as always, conditioned by its unqualified hostility towards the PF.

2. a month of murder

Norton, which takes its name from a family wiped out during the Shona rebellion of 1896, lies to the west of Salisbury, a twenty-minute drive. On 5 January a 'terrorist gang' attacked a Norton beerhall, killing four men, three of them black members of the security forces. A full-scale manhunt in the Lake McIlwaine recreational park yielded no results. Two days after the beerhall attack a local farmer, Bill Cumming, was patrolling the park on Police Reserve duty when he heard shots from the general direction of Camarie Farm, which belonged to his brother George.

Bill and George Cumming are of pioneer stock; their grandfather settled in the area in 1893 and Norton has a road named after the family. Bill Cumming is a Rhodesian patriot with a marked antipathy for Communist-indoctrinated terrorists, the British Labour Party, and journalists. His wife, Sheila, 44, had decided to take her daughters, Sarah, 15, and Victoria, 6, on a Saturday-afternoon visit to George Cumming and his wife at Camarie, a spruce, white-painted farm nestling under a tree-covered hillside. Sarah, a pupil at Queen Elizabeth School in Salisbury, was home for the school holidays but had been promised a trip into town to see *Star Wars*. A year previously she had written a school essay on the theme of 'A Person I Admire', choosing as her idol Ian Smith.

Mrs Cumming and her daughters reached Camarie Farm at about 4.30. A Caltex delivery truck stood in the driveway, its African driver seated in his cabin. What Mrs Cumming did not know was that four terrorists had arrived half an hour earlier and found the house empty except for the gardener, James Kasimu. Two had entered the kitchen looking for food while the others kept a look-out. As soon as Mrs Cumming and her daughters left their car their fate was sealed. They were made to sit on a doorstep at the back with their hands on their heads; the volley of shots that followed, and which Bill Cumming heard in the game park, killed his wife instantly and mortally wounded his daughter Sarah. Little Victoria suffered nine bullet wounds but survived.

The terrified gardener at first denied to the police that he had seen anything – he had been cutting the lawn when he heard shots, that was all. Not until the following day did he confess that he had witnessed the whole sequence of events and had seen the four terrorists bolting in a southerly direction, towards the hills. For this he was duly imprisoned.

Bill Cumming was quoted in the Rhodesian press: 'I'd dearly love to spend a couple of days alone with the terrorists who killed my wife and daughter. . . . It's not just this group that I want to see killed, it's all the terrorist bastards. . . . The only thing that will drive me out of this country is if they behave like this after they take over.'

An hour's drive west of Norton, along the main road to Gwelo and Bulawayo, lies Hartley. Here, two nights after the Cumming murder, a gang of six burst into Rainbow's End Farm and embarked on a holocaust. Shot dead in rapid succession were: Mrs Sheila Brakenridge, 74, who was eating her supper from a bed tray; her son Benjamin, aged 35; her grandson Bruce, aged 15, and a friend of his, Alan Harris, who was visiting from Salisbury during the school holidays. Two other boys, Nigel Brakenridge and Brian Landry, both aged 12, were wounded.

Zipra was blamed for both the Norton and the Hartley attacks. To kill four and wound two *inside* a house, a homestead, was an exceptional event, defying the general pattern of guerrilla attacks on isolated farms. Normally the combination of a security fence and the attacker's caution precluded immediate penetration of the household, encouraging an almost ritualistic overture of small-arms fire, rockets and mortars.

The youngest children of the two families, Victoria Cumming and Nigel Brakenridge, were both taken to the Andrew Fleming Hospital. There Bill Cumming, widower, and Camilla Brakenridge, widow, met; they were married nine months later, in Norton.

On 10 January, when 15-year-old Colin Tilley stepped out of his father's car at Glen Valley Farm, only a few miles from the fashionable Salisbury suburb of Borrowdale, he was gunned down by guerrillas hidden in the boiler-room and on the veranda. His father, Cheriton Tilley, returned fire and the four terrorists fled into the dark, their tracks immediately obliterated by heavy summer rain. Just as the Cumming family's gardener had at first denied any knowledge of the killing, so the Tilleys' 56-year-old Malawian cook, Edward Zulu, only 'confessed' after a nine-hour interrogation by Detective Section Officer Frederick Varkevisser and his colleagues of the CID's Law and Order Section. Zulu's sentence was ten years. Of course, servants caught up in such a situation were guiltless of anything other than a well-founded terror of reprisal.

The year 1978 was not a happy one for Cheriton Tilley and his wife Cynthia. On 3 September their daughter Cheryl, a secretary, died when the Viscount airliner *Hunyani* was shot down by a Zipra rocket while bringing weekenders back to the capital from Kariba. Cheryl had in fact survived the crash and had ripped up her frock to make bandages for the injured when she was shot by guerrillas on the ground.

A peculiar sequel: on 21 April 1980, three days after Zimbabwe celebrated its Independence, Cheriton Tilley heard a truck crash near his home in Glen Forest Road, Borrowdale. He hurried to the scene and found that an army lorry had overturned, injuring or stunning twenty-two former Zanla guerrillas. Mr Tilley dragged them to safety.

Benjamin Vermeulen, 60, was killed during an ambush in the Headlands area on 11 January 1978.

David Watson, a 53-year-old animal-health inspector living in Bulawayo, and born in Dundee, Scotland, was killed in mid-January. It was a traumatic month. For the first four weeks of the new year white civilians were killed at the rate of one per day. Farmers were no longer the sole targets. Any job involving work out of town was now hazardous. Two Portuguese artisans died in quick succession. On 10 January Luis de Carvalho, who worked for the Electrical Supply Commission, was driving back to Salisbury when he was gunned down in the Domboshawa area. He left a widow and an eleven-day-old son. Two weeks later Antonio Gonçalves, 29, died when guerrillas attacked a Roads Department camp.

On the 17th R. S. (Dick) Williams, 52, district estate superintendent for the Rhodesian Wattle Company, was driving in the Nyakapinga Forest Reserve in the eastern Highlands when he noticed a group of Africans near the roadside. Assuming them to be loafing labourers, he got out of his vehicle, realized his mistake too late, shot dead one guerrilla and wounded another with five rounds from his revolver before automatic fire hit him in the legs. Further shots killed him. Married, he left three children and two grandchildren.

A narrow escape: a Mashaba rancher had driven to Fort Victoria where his family were now living. On the way back to his ranch he found the Ngezi River in flood; waiting for it to subside he passed the time shooting at logs floating down the river. Growing impatient after a couple of hours he put his car into the ford, narrowly escaped being swept away by the heavy waters, made the crossing, drove on for about 300 metres and then stopped when he thought he heard a tyre blow out. It was then that he saw six guerrillas beside the road, one carrying an RPD machine-gun and the rest AK rifles. Shoving the gear into third he rammed his foot on the accelerator. At a distance of only five metres the shots rained through the window and past his face, shattering the rear window. The rancher suffered only a cut finger.

Jack and Evelyn Ashworth, both in their sixties, were fatally ambushed when driving on their farm near Umtali on the 18th. Their daughter Ivy, 35, was seriously wounded.

In the Belingwe area 70-year-old Johannes Hofmeyr was farming 730 hectares – mainly Brahman cattle and fruit. In December 1976 his farm had been attacked with rockets and small-arms fire. On 19 January 1978 he was on his way to Shabani when he was ambushed by three groups of guerrillas positioned 130 metres apart. The first lot missed, the second lot got him in the leg, the third in the shoulder. He maintained radio contact with the police and managed to drive on.

A Manicaland farmer had just driven out of his security fence when he found one of his farm labourers standing on the road holding a letter. It said, 'Don't be afraid. We are not going to kill you, you are known to be a good employer.' As he read this message, six or seven men appeared with AK rifles. Their leader engaged him in conversation; apparently his hand shook when the farmer lit his cigarette. The farmer was ordered to take two of the guerrillas to the farmhouse to see his wife. As they approached the house the resourceful farmer put his Land-Rover into second gear and drove it straight into a tree, leaping clear at the last moment. The vehicle turned over with the two guerrillas inside it. The farmer ran a further thirty metres to the house, then emptied a rifle magazine at the unwelcome visitors, who vanished.

Mrs Veryan Addams, widow of Maj. E. C. Addams, killed in 1974, was alone on her Odzi farm when terrorists attacked it, having already ransacked her store. Five of them climbed her security fence. She kept her nerve and drove them off with sustained fire.

On the night of Saturday, 14 January, a group of Zanla guerrillas entered the labour compound on Savillen Forestry Estate, Penhalonga, which belonged to the Umtali Board and Paper Company. They asked the labourers where the white manager was; the labourers replied that he and his wife had gone to Salisbury for the weekend, though aware that they were really in Umtali, only fifteen kilometres away, and were due back that night. Four charge-hands were then hacked to death, plus two further victims in another part of the compound.

3. Leopard Rock

Visitors to the Leopard Rock Hotel frequently remark on its resemblance to a French château: a long façade dotted with windows, ivy-covered turrets, and gardens laid out with regal panache – plus a nine-hole golf-course, a swimming-pool, a tennis-court, towering gum-trees. The hotel shelters under a large rock named after a leopard which had to be put down after savaging sheep and goats; you reach it by driving up into the Vumba mountains from Umtali, then following a winding road, tarred to begin with, then dirt, to a height of 1,370 metres, passing vistas of astonishing beauty, sprawling blue-mist valleys, grey mountain peaks – every S-bend in the slow ascent a perfect ambush point.

The usual all-white New Year's Eve party was held at the Leopard Rock on the last night of 1976: Rhodesian wine, black ties, a six-course dinner served by waiters in scarlet sashes, dancing in the style of the fifties (waltzes, foxtrots, tangos, reels) and then Auld Lang Syne at midnight. Loaded rifles stacked in the corner of the dining-room. The Geneva Conference had just collapsed. The dinner that night was cooked by January Zuze, 65 years of age, who had been chef at the Leopard Rock for forty-five of them; Zuze had cooked for the Queen Mother and Princess Margaret when they visited the hotel in the early fifties. During August and September 1977 guerrillas moved into the hotel's labour compound; apparently Zuze supplied them with food and blankets. Learning of this, the proprietor of the hotel sacked Zuze and the police arrested him: he was found guilty.

What followed was almost certainly an act of retaliation. Early in January 1978 about thirty guerrillas took up positions under cover of darkness on the neatly clipped lawn less than 100 metres from the hotel. It was 3.15 a.m. when they opened up with 3·5 inch rockets and AK47s. One rocket tore through a central turret, exploding in an empty room, another ripped a hole in the roof, rupturing a water main. The few guests staying in the hotel either hurled themselves on to the floor or attempted to return fire into the darkness. Only eight people were asleep in the hotel at the time and, miraculously, no one was hurt. The most embarrassed guest was a married man enjoying a clandestine liaison; the forty bullet holes in his car would be hard to explain to his wife.

In 1972 the hotels in the Vumba had averaged 61 per cent bed occupancy. By 1977 tourism had so collapsed that the figure had fallen to 8 per cent.

Approaching the hotel I hear rifle fire and stop. Two overweight whites, naked from the waist up, the rolls of pale flesh on their beer bellies reddening from the sun, are engaged in target practice. I am the only guest for lunch. The visitors' book since the attack is virtually blank. I buy a bloody mary in the bar and fall into conversation with the proprietor, Mr Geoff Courtney, a man of military bearing. Courtney answers all my questions but balks at my inquiry as to how far away the nearest police camp is. 'I don't think we'll go into that,' he says.

In the dining-room I settle down to the Leopard Rock Good Afternoon Luncheon of minestrone, fried Cape salmon (a poor relation to halibut) with lemon, grilled lamb chop with mint sauce, veg in season, apple turnover with cream, assorted cheese and biscuits, coffee – not bad for $(R)2·25. Mr Courtney clearly knows how to run a hotel, particularly a hotel for white people in a country inhabited mainly by black people. The two overweight mercenaries appear, for lunch, buttoning up their shirts reluctantly to satisfy the proprietor's proprieties. Cockneys: their last job was as security guards at Heathrow Airport. How's London? they ask.

4. a real guerrilla is someone like Ian Smith

The regime traditionally kept the foreign press in line by liberal use of the deportation weapon. By January 1978 more than sixty foreign reporters had been given the boot. Overseas journalists worked on temporary permits renewable every twenty-nine days. Recent casualties had included Brian Barron of the BBC and Max Hastings of the *Evening Standard*. In May 1978

Ken Englade, a freelance reporter, was expelled after publishing an article critical of the numerous hangings taking place in Salisbury gaol.

But often the threat was enough. The Ministry of Information's press officers, Ferris, Brady, Gloster and Costa Pafitis, were adept at blending affability with a hint of displeasure; a cordial message from one would be immediately negated by a severe rebuke from another; a prime weapon in destabilizing a foreign journalist is to pass him from one censor to the next, to erode and obscure his sense of where authority lies, where final decisions are made.

Take the case of 'Simon Bull', the Salisbury correspondent of that prestigious London newspaper, the *Monitor*. He writes an article about the new censorship regulations and takes his copy to Milton Buildings. The military censor passes it. An hour later he receives a telephone call from the Ministry of Information warning him that he would be unwise to dispatch the article. He protests angrily and ten minutes later receives an apology from a different Ministry official: of course he can transmit his copy to London, no problem.

Yet Simon Bull now decides not to send the article, he has seen too many colleagues off at Salisbury Airport in recent months. Simon has his reasons for wanting to stay in Rhodesia. It's currently one of the top stories in the British press and it assures him regular column-inches and prominent bylines (food and drink to a journalist). He has built up a fund of local knowledge, a thick card-index and well-placed contacts, and he doesn't relish starting again in (say) Islamabad or Cairo at a time when things in Rhodesia are permanently on the boil. Besides, the life-style he derides in his reports – swimming-pools, servants, sundowners – does have its charm. . . . So far his non-resident status guarantees him immunity from military service (readers of such papers as *The Times* and the *Financial Times* are no doubt unaware that certain local Salisbury correspondents of those newspapers spend part of their year in uniform on behalf of the illegal regime).

Caution is a habit. Having censored himself once, Simon becomes increasingly inhibited about causing offence – he knows that *they* know he chickened out – and when the Justice and Peace Commission presents him with gold-plated evidence about the impact of martial law on a specific tribal trust land in the eastern region, he doesn't use it. Indeed, when the JPC makes a direct approach to his editor in London, Simon Bull sends a telex advising that publication would be inadvisable because *the evidence is fundamentally suspect.*

Meanwhile the Rhodesian censors dithered about the use of the word 'guerrilla' in dispatches. Normally they insisted on 'terrorist'. 'Frankly,' declared André Holland, the debonair Deputy Minister for Information, 'I'm amazed foreign correspondents persist in using the word "guerrilla" to describe outright terrorists. A real guerrilla is someone like Ian Smith, who fought with the Italian partisans after being shot down.'

From January 1978 foreign correspondents were obliged to submit for censorship all news relating to security matters unless it had been copied down obediently from official communiqués and Parliamentary debates. An agency report submitted on 8 January was purged of its reference to a growing feeling of claustrophobia among whites following the fatal shootings at Norton and the closure of Lake McIlwaine to the public. D-notices rained down. It was permitted neither to print the names of Nkomo and Mugabe, nor to mention the prohibition.

The officials who directed Rhodesia's own propaganda campaign under P. K. van der Byl and André Holland regularly issued a venomous sheet, *Focus on Rhodesia*, specializing in items such as this: 'Samora Machel . . . was a male nurse before he became a terrorist. He has harboured a savage, insane hatred of white people ever since he underwent an operation in Salisbury for an anti-social disease which in order to be successful meant deprivation of his ability to father children.' Nor was the Ministry above concocting fraudulent advertisements like the one that appeared in the *Sunday Mail* on 11 December 1977: 'Who'd swop Borrowdale for Birmingham?' it asked. Accompanying photos left the answer in no doubt. Here we see a pretty, blonde Miss Rhodesia smiling in the lush embrace of a garden suburb; there – grim contrast – we see white and black children standing forlorn in the wasteland slums of a grey, wet, socialist British city.

There was just one snag: the shots of 'Birmingham' had in fact been taken in the Salisbury township of Highfield.

5. Saturday night with the Bishop

A Saturday evening in January 1978. Ink-black summer rainclouds disgorge sheets of water which fall straight and unanswerable: this is African rain. But the Bishop's Mercedes is custom-built for all seasons and the UANC leader arrives on time, with his huge entourage, at the Ridgeview home of the lovely Aisha Kara. It is Aisha's stout brother Ayoub who is tonight splashing a well-calculated fraction of his wealth on a sumptuous party in honour of the Bish. And all his retainers. The tables groan with curries, whisky and sweetmeats.

Aisha was once in the dried-fish business, operating from Beira in Mozambique. When the danger of a Frelimo ambush became acute she switched her freight from road to air: expensive. The final blow was Machel's closure of the border, and the immediate severance of all economic intercourse. Aisha glances over her shoulder; but the Bishop's colleagues, time-servers, yes-men, bodyguards, advisers, chauffeurs, are all safely glued to the tables groaning with curry, whisky and sweetmeats.

'They told the Portuguese they could take all their belongings out of Mozambique. As soon as they were crated, they were confiscated. They can rob your house with impunity, what can you do? Call the police? Then they closed the churches. And couples who are not married are stopped in the street. They can come to your house and say, "Why is your daughter not married?"' Clearly Aisha is not very keen on 'they'.

The Karas are Moslems – Salisbury boasts one mosque. Aisha is quite cynical: freely she admits that her brother Ayoub joined the UANC as an insurance policy. (In fact, as we shall discover later, there was more to it than that: Ayoub Kara is a man of 200 per cent energy and a natural politician, demagogue, power broker.)

The Indian ladies at the feast float across the polished parquet floors in their long, exotic saris, birds of paradise neither inviting nor declining contact with any person, male or female, black or white, not of their own kith and kin. Theirs is a world within a world throughout the world: their inherited culture is to thrive as inconspicuously as possible, to be true to themselves, avoid intermarriage, learn obedience. When a marriage is mooted the parents of the girl will approach the uncle of the boy; later the boy will visit the girl at her home and she will pour tea; between the full cup and the empty one a lifetime must be determined, yes or no – no wonder Indians drink their tea slowly. Rhodesians call them 'Ayshuns'.

Everyone is aware of the flash Bishop. Passing through London he regularly spends a fortune on clothes, on apple-green suits, two-tone shoes, Liberian national costume, the man is a clown. Now he sits regally and tinily in a big white chair while the ambitious edge into his orbit and the diffident stay away. Presently he will tour the room, nodding and smiling, with many a felicitous *bon mot*. A little speech, too: we thank our hosts . . . people of all races . . . Zimbabwe . . . reconciliation. . . . Aiya! Aiya! The retainers, their eyes feverish with alcohol and flickering ambition, lift their arms – none more eagerly than Ayoub Kara – Aiya!

The Bish beams. He is a winner. His enemies are in exile. He is surrounded by bodyguards in poor-quality jackets. Some are said to be ex-guerrillas – that one trained in Moscow, that one with the scar in Peking. . . . When the Bish leaves early, at 10, some of his henchmen linger on, stuffing themselves: their aim is to drink and no one is going to prise the bottle from their hand.

Ayoub Kara is the life and soul of the party. He wears a bright-red shirt open at the neck and talks to me of his business at Que Que. 'Please look me up. I can get you into a TTL without difficulty. We have an arrangement with the local DC at Que Que.' He smiles and winks. 'Smith knows that when we come in he can go back to his farm, whereas the PF would cut his throat.'

Two months later Ayoub (A. M.) Kara was appointed UANC election manager by Bishop Abel Muzorewa.

6. 188 floppies

In the Shabani region an RLI Fireforce is tracking down Zanla guerrillas. Fifty per cent of this killer squad consists of foreign mercenaries on three-year contracts. Richard Lindley and Robin Denselow's brilliant filmed report of this Fireforce operation was screened on BBC TV (*Panorama*) on 17 April 1978.

The scene is a bush camp near Shabani. A hand-held alarm looking like a loud hailer is sounded and soon white commandos with blackened faces are boarding French-built Alouettes, each of which carries a 'stick' of four. It's the old film drama of the scramble, of Spitfire and Hurricane pilots racing for their machines at Biggin Hill – 'bandits' sighted south of Dover, 'gooks' sighted in Belingwe TTL, either way our boys will get to the kill. Sixteen commandos in camouflage-green shirts and shorts will parachute into the contact zone from a Dakota, while ground reinforcements are moved in by Hippos and Rhinos. The operational commander is John Cronin, an American captain with a soft face and a faint, flaxen moustache who had been wounded in 'Nam'. The supporting cast includes a Briton who (he claims) had served in Vietnam and with the French Foreign Legion; a British ex-Marine; and one or two Rhodesians. Between missions they play volleyball.

They are currently tracking Zanla guerrillas who recently blacked out the Shabani asbestos mine. Usually it's a waste of time and money – 'eight lemons in a row,' a pilot remarks. Four Alouettes, two aircraft (a Lynx and a Dakota), three trucks and sixty men have repeatedly hurtled deep into the reserve only to trail home again without blood on their hands. Even so, 3 Commando of the RLI claims that between November 1977 and February 1978 it killed, or culled, 188 terrs (or 'floppies'). 'Killing them is no problem,' drawls baby-face Cronin; 'finding them is the difficulty.' He has even picked up a trimming of Shona: 'We call them magandangas, the defilers, because they move by night. We lost the trail at the river.'

Cronin clearly believes that wars are media spectacles and that he himself has been selected by Central Casting to star in *Apocalypse Now*. His colleague, Lieutenant Fabian Forbes, becomes philosophical: 'Any terrorist war is virtually unwinnable really. You've got to hit the problem at the source of the problem. . . . I feel we should certainly be doing more external operations.' Everyone yearns for the cross-border raids, really fat targets, men, women and children.

Fireforce is on the road before dawn, the summer breeze ruffling the long, straight Caucasian hair of the white troopies in their open truck. Behind them the sun crawls up towards the rim of the African sky, splashing a pink half-light through which the Alouettes will fly provided the horizon is visible. A commando patrol has stumbled across a guerrilla camp; they have one captive, another black with a sack over his head. As they bundle him aboard the truck they shout 'Smile!': all the whites laugh, neat healthy rows of teeth framed in sun-tan. Later that day the cameras are at last rewarded with their lions' feast – eight genuine floppies laid out in a row, their AK rifles resting between their legs, their shirts pulled up to expose their chests. Some carry burn marks from a napalm air strike. The victors report the day's hunting:

'. . . we just swept through the village, and there were contacts, we swept back and forwards and there were contacts just carrying on all the time. There was this gook by a tree. We thought he was dead so two of us went up to him and just as we were about five feet from him he threw a grenade at us.'

The American, Cronin, expresses manly satisfaction: 'At least we've eliminated eleven of them. That's great. That's what Fireforce is all about.'

Evening comes and the men of Fireforce take their ease outside their mess tent; this is the moment for the BBC's reporter to explore their *weltanschauung*. Will the internal settlement under negotiation in Salisbury persuade the guerrillas to give up?

'Well, yeah, I mean, they've got an excuse, like, for coming back in and saying what the hell are we fighting for anyway. They don't know what they were fighting for originally . . . [laughs] . . . they can come back to their kraals, that's all they want, they want to sit outside their little kia and watch their piccaninns grow up and do their grazing and all the rest of it.'

Cronin is a little political wizard, very intense: the internal settlement will have a 'profound impact on the number of terrs now in the bush'. But White Rhodesia is on the skids and Cronin with it: he's rushing about the world shooting at moving targets and trying to adjust his sights to reassure himself that he is at the centre of a pre-Galilean stable universe.

Yet there are some among his comrades who don't buy this messing with 'internal' blacks who were only yesterday rated as gooks. A Rhodesian of 3 RLI puts it this way: 'I don't think anyone in the Rhodesian army is going to work next to the bugger he was fighting two or three years ago. I've thought about it but I won't work for a black government. Because I didn't come into this country to . . . fight in this country and sort of win the war and then end up working for a black government. Next year I'll be out. I'll pack my bags and I'll leave.' He laughs gently. 'Just fight the war from day to day and that's it.'

A troopie with a north-of-England accent says it would be just like taking a battalion of the IRA and sticking them in with the army in Ulster. 'How can you accept something like that?'

7. servant of the nation

The defence budget had rocketed from $(R)64·6 million in 1970 to $(R)400 million in 1979, leaping up from 28 per cent to 47 per cent of the national budget. Simultaneously the budget-account deficit spiralled from $(R)2·3 million in 1975 to $(R)229·3 million in 1978. Rhodesia's war effort depended totally on massive loans and subsidies from South Africa.

A regular army of 6,000 formed the core of the counter-insurgency operation. In the vanguard were 1,000 commandos of the all-white Rhodesian Light Infantry, 1,000 Selous Scouts, 300 mounted infantry in the Grey's Scouts and 200 members of the élite, all-white Special Air Service. The 3,000 black troops of the RAR were regarded essentially as support units.

But the regular forces alone were inadequate to the task, hence Rhodesia's massive dependence on territorials, on a white citizen militia. At any one time 3,250 national-service phase-1 conscripts and 16,500 white territorials were 'under canvas'.

However, the distinction between army and police was less clear-cut than in most countries. Particularly in the countryside the 20,000 Police Reservists, mainly white, were frequently engaged not only in routine patrols and check-points but also in 'hot-pursuit' operations against guerrillas.

The regular police force was 7,000 strong. The Police Anti-Terrorist Unit, which included mounted sections, was virtually indistinguishable from a military arm.

In February the Rhodesian Army put its top brass on display to the black bourgeoisie − backbone of the internal settlement − at a plush Bulawayo hotel. The gathering was organized by the Rhodesian Promotion Council, whose Chairman, C. G. Tracey, boss of a leading tobacco auction house and thus sanctions-buster extraordinary, yet nevertheless able to dine with Lord Carrington etcetera in London, was engaged in a campaign to convert black politicians of all parties to a belief in free enterprise – an economic infrastructure substantially owned and controlled by Europeans.

The message was simple but effective: we need you, you need us. To boost the union, Tracey wheeled in front of his audience a succession of white officers:

– Maj.-Gen. A. N. O. MacIntyre, Chief of Staff (Administration), born in Scotland, served as an officer in the British Army, joined the Central African Federation Army as a sergeant in 1956, attended the Staff College at Camberley in 1965 . . .

– Col. P. J. Hosking, originally commissioned into the British Army, served with the Northern Rhodesia Regiment in Malaya, 1955–6, appointed Director of Military Intelligence, 1974, Commanding Officer of 2 RAR, 1975 . . .

– Lt-Col. J. C. P. McVey, born in Rhodesia, Commando Commander of 1 RLI, 1970, presently CO of 2 RAR . . .

– Maj. W. B. Rooken Smith, born in Kenya, served in the 17/21 Lancers then as an instructor at the Royal Armoured Corps School in Dorset, resigned from the British Army in 1967, joined the Rhodesian Army, presently Acting CO of the Rhodesian Armoured Car Regiment . . .

Star of the show was the plump and palpably vain Army Commander, Lt-Gen. John Hickman. Describing the army as non-political, as the 'servant of the nation', Hickman lost no time in plunging into politics and denouncing as criminal the Owen–Young–Carver plan to base the future army on the so-called liberation forces, 'a cowardly rabble of thugs and murderers' devoid of any communications system or administration. 'Above all, the terrorist is a political animal. He cannot be unbiased and a servant of the nation because he is a politician.'

Addressing a passing-out parade of black officers in March, Hickman once again described the army he led as utterly non-political, dedicated to the service of 'whatever government is elected by the people of Rhodesia'. (But 97 per cent of the 'people of Rhodesia' had no vote.) To point up his own soldierly neutrality, the well-fed General commented that the recently signed Salisbury Agreement of 3 March 1978 between Smith and the 'internal' black leaders almost finalized the country's political evolution.

Hickman's boss, Lt-Gen. Peter Walls, was equally emphatic that the Rhodesian security forces stood above and beyond politics. Addressing some 600 pupils of Gifford High School on 17 February, the Commander, Combined Operations, told his young audience: 'Mugabe comes out with the biggest load of codswallop overseas, and people believe it. We are being conned into giving up our country.' The Portuguese, Walls explained, had been defeated in Mozambique by 'rumours' when militarily they had Frelimo on its knees. Why should the black people of Rhodesia 'be held to ransom by a few thousand thugs out for their own personal gain'?

A family man who lived with his second wife in a leafy suburb of Salisbury and took fishing holidays whenever the burdens of conducting an increasingly destructive war permitted, Walls was making himself the scourge of southern Africa, bringing death from the air and death from the ground to large numbers of black men, women and children. He clearly relished his power, his political influence, his growing prestige among white Rhodesians. He subscribed to the conventional wisdom of counter-insurgency: you must win the 'hearts and minds' of the rural population. 'Any sadistic action is completely counter-productive,' he told foreign journalists, 'and destroys exactly what we are trying to do. If a soldier or a policeman steps over the line then he will get hammered.' (But the Government had rushed through a law granting members of the security forces complete immunity for any action unless it could be shown that they had acted in 'bad faith'. Thus a police reservist, for example, could admit flogging a woman with a rhino hide to gain information, yet be acquitted by the magistrate because he had 'acted as the exigencies of the situation demanded'.)

The son of a Chief of Staff in the Rhodesian Army and of a mother whose parents were members of the Pioneer Column, Peter Walls was commissioned from Sandhurst into a British regiment, the Black Watch, in 1945. When only 28 years old he was sent to Malaya as Commander of C (Rhodesia) Squadron of the SAS – a tough unit for tough men. The lessons of counter-insurgency were not lost on him, nor did he forget Field Marshal Sir Gerald Templer's remark that 'the bandits don't play golf on Sunday and neither will we'.

The first rule of any colonial war is to set native against native, 'askari' against 'rebel' – postage stamps and cigarette cards displaying Indians and Africans in the peacock glory of full regimental dress reflect the Empire's long, slow cunning in dividing those it rules – the gold turban of the Madras Sappers, the red, blue and gold of the 19th KGO Lancers, the black turban with red tassle of the Northern Rhodesia Regiment, the red turban and blue puttees of the King's African Rifles ... ('Wills's Cigarette Picture-Card Album', price one penny.) In the Gold Coast and Nigeria Regiments of the Royal West African Frontier Force the white officers were invariably most attached to the illiterate northern tribesmen, the infantry privates, whose humble loyalty they found most dependable.

But West Africa was highly évolué compared with Rhodesia, its regiments already sporting African captains and majors in the mid-1950s. It was not until June 1977 that the Rhodesians put thirteen old sweats of the RAR through a quick officer-training course as part of the general face-lift.

You can pass through Balla Balla on your way from Shabani to Bulawayo without noticing anything beyond the road sign. But it's to Balla Balla, depot and training-centre of the Rhodesian African Rifles, that potential recruits – famished peasants, desperate refugees from the shanty-towns, and a few genuine Uncle Toms – come in search of $(R)47 a month. The 3,000 men of the RAR are divided into three battalions, one of which is dispersed among racially integrated territorial units of the army: white officers, white conscripts, black regulars of the RAR. Until 1977 all the RAR's officers were white – their hats identical in style to those of the old British West African regiments: a trilby crown and a broad brim extending over the forehead and out to one side. The boss is Maj. Pete Morris, a wiry, British-born major who puts 1,200 recruits at a time through a three-month course: Karangas from Buhera, Bikita and Gutu; Korekore from Mtoko; Ndebeles and Kalangas from Matabeleland – in short the RAR is recruited from precisely the areas which provide Zanla and Zipra with their hardcore of guerrillas.

A white officer saunters along a line of humble, silent, shaven-headed potential recruits waiting beyond a red-and-white barrier.

'You're a bit thin. Where have you come from?'

'Gwelo, sir.'

'No work, eh? Is that why you have no food in your tummy?'

The little African grins sheepishly. He says he is 19 and passed Grade 7 (primary school). 'I want to help Rhodesia,' he says.

'What about helping Zimbabwe?' drawls the officer sadistically. The supplicant doesn't know what to make of this: is it a trap?

'No, sir, no . . . I like to be a soldier. . . .'

Once recruited he will be a marked man, a pariah among his own people, cut off from his roots; his home in the TTLs will be staked out and watched by mujibas. He will not dare to venture home on leave; instead his wife will travel to one of the three 'rest camps' already established near Salisbury, Bulawayo and Fort Victoria to enable 'loyal' troops to have congress with their wives in safety. Meanwhile the officers maintain the standard mumbo-jumbo: 'The day a group of terrorists pass out like that will be the day I'll start to worry,' says Maj. Morris, reviewing one of his own passing-out parades. Col. David Heppenstall, commander of Operation Grapple in the Midlands, solemnly contrasts the RAR's willingness to stand and fight with the hit-and-run tactics of the terrs.

A vast charade: in April 1978 Maj. John Templer leads the 1st Battalion of the RAR with bayonets fixed and a band playing through the streets of

Bulawayo. A posse of white officers marches in front of the black troops; the Lady Mayoress takes the salute, the crowds applaud, it's all going to be all right in multiracial Rhobabwe.

The *Sunday Mail*, 29 January 1978, announces in a centre spread that 'The Black Boots are "Terr Hungry".' The Black Boots turn out to be the BSAP Support Unit, mostly Africans "who crave to kill the gooks who murder and rape their families'. With their terr-chilling slogan of 'Pamberi ne Hondo' (Forward to the War) they are reported to have killed so many gooks in the Thrasher area that finding Zanla grows harder every day. Says base Supt Fred Mason, 'They always run. Sindi Mago was a terr section leader who murdered and bullied the locals. Like the rest of his men he was spineless and gutless, but the locals lived in mortal fear of him. Mago used to tell the tribesmen that he would never die, so when we killed him we had to get the villagers to actually touch him before they'd believe he was dead. . . . All they are is a bunch of bloody gangsters. . . . I'm at a loss to remember when a gook in this area has stopped to fight.'

Everyone in the BSAP Support Unit, white and black, sleeps under the same blanket, eats the same sadza and wild plants, sings the same Shona songs. Says the black constable: 'The white policemen are great. We would follow them anywhere, and none of us know the meaning of discrimination. We are all brothers.'

8. a purely military action

On 22 February a most remarkable three-and-a-half-hour debate took place in the House of Assembly. The sixteen African Members had long been regarded by nationalists as collaborators and stooges, if not sell-outs, yet the war had rapidly radicalized the African Members and their clashes with the Rhodesian Front became increasingly abrasive. On 22 February 1978, two months after his election by chiefs and headmen gathered together in Seki township under the eye of the Provincial Commissioner, Augustine Mabika introduced a Private Member's motion deploring the curfew regulations and the laws requiring people to report the presence of terrorists. Seconding the motion, Elijah Nyandoro pointed out that the Government could provide no protection at all for those tribesmen who did report the presence of terrorists. One African Member after another hurled well-documented instances of police or army brutality at the Minister of Combined Operations, Roger Hawkins. Micah Bhebe raised the temperature in the Chamber even higher by referring to what had happened in Mozambique to former members of the

Portuguese security police, the DGS, after the advent of majority rule. The motion was defeated by 47 white votes to 13 black ones.

The African Members (who had clearly taken trouble to check their facts) described in detail a number of cases of capricious killing or brutality perpetrated by the security forces. Five months later Hawkins answered the allegations by means of a general denial and a number of specific 'refutations'. He also called on the Speaker to consider 'disciplining' the black MPs for having given 'false information to the House'.

Specific cases:

(1) On 28 January 1978, eleven children were killed by helicopter-borne security forces in the Gwazurembaka area of the Charter district. It was three days before their parents were allowed to collect the bodies.

According to Hawkins, however, this was a 'purely military action' in which a Fireforce was called in to deal with a group of thirteen terrorists 'who were being fed'. A subsequent 'sweep of the area revealed dead terrorists, "locals" and a large quantity of terrorist equipment. Security forces had no exact numbers for those killed as police did not go into the area for some time after the contact, but believed parents did remove bodies . . . full blame lies with the terrorists.'

(2) A Mr Mapfumo was teaching at Mount St Mary in Wedza TTL – a Franciscan mission from which several white priests were deported – when African District Assistants came to his house, questioned his wife about the presence of terrorists, fired twelve shots into Mr Mapfumo's car, then beat him when he came running from a neighbour's house. His cut and swollen features were seen by Augustine Mabika, MP for Highveld.

(3) On 28 January, at Mutsaka in Maranke TTL, Phinias Mabeka and his sister Mishiah were crossing from their house to another house 100 metres away, though forbidden to do so under curfew regulations, because they had been told that a child was ill. The man was shot in the leg and his sister cried out, 'Please do not kill us, we are not the magandangas [terrorists].' She was promptly shot through the head and died on the spot.

However, according to Hawkins, the woman's actual name was Mrs Mwashaya Mavisa and she had been the subject of a sudden-death inquiry by Odzi police. An army unit had fired on 'a group of persons at 8.55 p.m. . . . Subsequent investigation showed that they were en route to a meeting with terrorists.' As for the woman having pleaded for the man's life, that, according to Hawkins, was a lie.

(4) A woman, Maria Chidodo, living in the Urungwe area, was pregnant but not expecting to deliver for another two months. When she unexpectedly suffered labour pains and shouted for help (another shout? another lie?)

everybody in the village feared to leave their homes because of the curfew. Next morning they found the new-born baby asleep beside its dead mother.

(5) Majoni Hungwe, Headmaster of Mapnuya School in the Belingwe area, was 'tortured beyond all human endurance . . . by members of the Special Branch' in January and February 1978, forcing him to retire and leave home. The assaults had taken place at Buchwa base camp. Hawkins issued no denial, his statement confining itself to confirmation that Mr Hungwe had left the service of the Department of Education and 'had not been traced, although he was said to have moved to Bulawayo'. Hawkins added that the Belingwe police Member-in-Charge had written to Lot Dewa, MP, requesting further details but had received no reply. Across the floor of the House Lot Dewa angrily denied this.

In many cases it emerged that the police had absolutely no record of their own brutality.

None of this moved the Rhodesian Front. Replying to the debate, Paddy Shields commented: 'I would say that not many governments in Africa would allow so much vilification, so much unsubstantiated attack on the security forces of that country without retribution. . . . I would ask them to thank whatever God they believe in for the fact that they are living in a civilized country.'

Among the boldest of the black MPs was Lot Dewa, a radical who had been detained in 1966, 1967 and 1972 and now represented the vast Matojeni area of south-central Rhodesia. Claiming that threats from the police had made it unsafe for him to remain in his home village of Msase, Dewa bombarded the Minister of Justice, Hilary Squires, with complaints on behalf of his constituents. Squires threatened to sue Dewa for damages if he distributed any further circulars accusing the Minister of dereliction of duty. Born in South Africa, Squires had arrived in Rhodesia in 1956, when 24 years old; an advocate of the High Court of Rhodesia and the Supreme Court of South Africa, he succeeded Hawkins as Minister for Combined Operations. In 1979 he became a judge.

9. Garfield Todd – go well, old man

Hokonui ranch, Shabani: February 1978. A remarkable man lives here with his no less remarkable wife. For thirty years journalists, reporters, camera crews, visiting scholars and biographers have been making the pilgrimage, moths fluttering round a candle. Now he's an old man and a legend; but his life hangs by a fine thread and if he is murdered or ambushed one thing is certain – each side, Government and guerrillas, will accuse the other.

Hokonui: 7,000 hectares of rough, rocky and heavily wooded grassland, plenty of cover and a TTL bordering the ranch to the north – ideal guerrilla terrain. Bouncing slowly along a rutted track I come across a white lady, ankle-deep in mud and surrounded by cattle. An outbreak of ear tick, she explains: the normal dips don't cure it. Grace Todd directs me towards the house, promising to follow shortly for lunch, but I miss a turning and drive for miles over dirt tracks and down through river fords swollen by brown summer floodwaters until it dawns on me that I'm lost.

Here, west of Shabani, north of Belingwe, south of the Runde, Zanla and Zipra forces confront one another in a tense, distrustful stand-off. This is a war zone. Shabani is not only a mining town of importance, it is also the nerve-centre of a ruthlessly conducted counter-insurgency operation involving the Special Branch, the Selous Scouts, Fireforce units of the RLI and – by mid-1978 – black 'auxiliaries' loyal to one or other of the 'internal' nationalist parties. One thing they all have in common, apart from a desire to zap as many gooks as possible, is an intense dislike of Garfield Todd, former Prime Minister of Southern Rhodesia. As a woman put it to me in the Salisbury suburb of Mount Pleasant: 'You know why Nkomo took Todd to the Geneva Conference? You don't? It's because Todd's feeding Nkomo's gooks down at Shabani, that's why.' Her husband, an accountant, agreed; his voice was very soft and tight when he said, 'That's a man Rhodesia could do without.'

Finally, I find the house in time for lunch. Todd laughs at my story. Grace says, 'Gar, will you say grace?' Afterwards we sit on the stoep, gazing down at the slow brown coil of the Ngezi River, its hippos coughing like evening cattle. 'Never get between them and the water,' Garfield Todd advises. 'I once made that mistake down the bank, right there, and I was frightened, I can tell you. A man was found in two pieces on Khandahar Island near Victoria Falls.'

The view from the house is spectacularly beautiful; beyond the carpet of trees which shade and shelter the Todds' 1,200 head of cattle you see the gleaming white buildings of Dadaya mission, five miles away, then the Runde, the blue-green silence of insurgent Africa.

The house at Hokonui has no security fence, no Agric-Alert alarm system, no sign of a weapon. Its sole means of defence resides in the heads of the natives and in the Bible. I float in the blue-blue swimming-pool, washing away the dust of the road, the long fear of the road. The landscape sprawled in afternoon slumber at one's feet offers no warning signals. Yet only a week ago the dog barked in the dead of night and Zanla guerrillas entered the house even as Garfield Todd rose, at the age of 70, from his bed. But the new guest is not informed, for the good reason that consorting with terrorists is a capital offence.

Todd's grandfather, a brickmaker, had emigrated from Scotland to New Zealand in the 1860s and Garfield Todd himself began his working life in the family clay pits which serviced their brickworks and pottery. But in 1931, at the age of 23, he was ordained in the Associated Churches of Christ, an evangelical order; three years later he and Grace dropped anchor in Southern Rhodesia, near Shabani, and took over Dadaya mission, a complex of twelve primary schools and twenty churches. Todd administered the schools and village churches, built the first clinic and delivered hundreds of babies, including, in the course of time, his own daughters.

Grace was the first trained teacher to arrive in the Shabani area. Her *Dadaya Notes of Lessons*, a primer covering the first six years of primary teaching, was constantly reprinted by the Department of African Education and used throughout the country. Her correspondence courses attracted young African students not only from every corner of Rhodesia, but from further afield. Robert Mugabe recalls how, in 1944, when he was 19 years old and teaching at Mapunzure, he frequently visited Grace Todd and how she lent him a book on commercial arithmetic. 'I remember bringing it back to her, with thanks. But I don't think she remembers because she was helping many others.'

It is GT's habit to rise at 4 a.m. every morning. At 70-plus the man's energy is so manifest that it must have been awesome in the middle years when the levers of power were his to exercise from 4 in the morning. In 1946 he entered Parliament as a protégé of the Prime Minister and leader of the United Rhodesia Party, Sir Godfrey Huggins. His first speech on native affairs, delivered in March 1946, opposed any extension of the African electorate, minuscule as it was; in June 1952 he condemned universal suffrage as the key to universal chaos; and when he became Prime Minister of Southern Rhodesia in 1953 his image remained that of a dynamic conservative.

Todd gave up his £400-a-year stipend when elected to Parliament but continued to run Dadaya on an honorary basis until, still in his forties, he became Prime Minister. His entry into the political arena was accompanied by an impressive display of business acumen: the 8,000 hectares of ranchland he bought soon became 20,000.

A paternalist by no means inclined to spoil the child by sparing the rod, in one much-publicized incident he had reacted to a mass boycott by Dadaya's pupils of the food put before them by whacking the lot. 'Dadaya,' he recalls, 'was at that time a primary school. I beat the whole 500, I think, two each on the hands for those who were new, four each on the hands for those who had been at Dadaya for more than two years, and six across the bottom for all who had been more than four years at Dadaya. The stories of bare bottoms, etc. were popular but not true.' One of the teachers at Dadaya, the future nationalist leader Ndabaningi Sithole, organized a protest strike and the case actually came to court.

Todd was Prime Minister of Southern Rhodesia for five years, an immensely assured, dynamic, even charismatic leader. As his popularity grew among Africans (he was often found addressing meetings in the black areas) so an exaggerated alarm possessed the whites. Finally, in 1958, he was brought down by a revolt of his Cabinet colleagues. Yet even now he was no Robespierre. Following the report of the Tredgold Commission, he had merely recommended a common roll based on a compensatory sliding scale between property and educational qualifications: the more a potential voter had of the one, the less he would need of the other in order to qualify.

If Todd's proposal to make ten years of schooling an absolute qualification for the vote had been adopted, the effect would have been to enrol only 6,000 new black voters. Bearing in mind that Ghana had already won its independence on the basis of black majority rule, and that Nigeria, Zambia, Kenya and the French colonies were hurtling towards theirs, the proposal was almost ridiculously modest; yet it was too much for white Rhodesians determined to preserve in pickle (as Lord Blake comments) the fancy franchises and élitist anachronisms of nineteenth-century Britain.

Todd displayed a gift for talking to nationalists which disturbed whites, who duly accused him of putting ideas into the heads of the natives (who never have any of their own). Forced to resign and disowned by his party, GT revived the old United Rhodesia Party and crashed to defeat at the subsequent election, totally repudiated by the white electorate. Todd's party failed to win a single seat. He became, then, something of a legend among blacks. 'Todd is the Moses of our age,' declared *African Weekly*. A Shona song in his honour became a best-selling record:

> 'Todd has left us
> Go well, old man.'

Todd was left only with his innate rectitude, his slow, gentle smile, his stubborn refusal to let go. In 1964 he addressed the Oxford Union to such good effect that the students voted by 580 to 57 to embrace the famous Nibmar formula – No Independence Before Majority Rule. He was on the verge of flying to Scotland to speak at Edinburgh University when the Government of Mr Ian Smith finally lost patience, arrested the former Prime Minister on 18 October 1965, and confined him to his ranch for one year.

But Todd remained a thorn in the side of the Rhodesian Front for the next fifteen years, publicly calling for stiffer economic sanctions and British military intervention, refusing to be cowed by the intense hostility of his fellow whites, by the detention of all the major nationalist leaders, by the apparently effortless suppression of the nascent guerrilla uprising, by the bent necks and lowered eyes of a native population whipped into submission. He knew fear but constantly transcended it; virtually every Rhodesian police officer who was sent to confront him immediately became apologetic, if not obsequious; those who laid unfriendly hands on him knew themselves to be – if only at that moment – Pilate's soldiers.

Lay unfriendly hands on him they did. He was arrested on his ranch, together with his daughter Judith, on 18 January 1972. By the end of the night both had heard prison keys turn behind them, he in Gatooma gaol, she in Marandellas.

From the age of 11 to the time she was 15, Miss Judy Todd had attended Queen Elizabeth's School, Salisbury, and was the daughter of the Prime Minister. Then, abruptly, ejection, humiliation, denigration. Most girls in such circumstances would have hidden from the pain by turning their back on politics and retreating into the bird-brained obscurity of white suburbia. Judy, on the contrary, laid the friendliest of hands on her Dad and became his champion – an extremely beautiful girl with long dark hair and a flair for hurling herself under the wheels of tyranny and causing a temporary derailment.

'We live', she wrote, 'side by side with an "inferior people" who threaten the security of our civilization. Yet we direct the same people to cook our food, wash our clothes, make our beds, tend our children. . . . They perform the most intimate of services for us. . . . They may bath our children, yet they may not wash themselves in our houses . . . if we wish to turn a conveniently blind eye to the Land Apportionment Act, they may inhabit crowded little kias at the end of our gardens, where periodically they will be subject to police raids, ensuring that no "unauthorised" people are living with them. . . .' She was only 22 when she wrote this passage, but she had already graduated as militant, activist and demonstrator from the University of Rhodesia, one of a tiny minority of white students who made common cause with black nationalism. She joined the National Democratic Party and its successor, Nkomo's Zapu. I'm not a liberal, she said, I'm a nationalist.

When Garfield Todd was arrested, a month before Ian Smith declared UDI, his daughter Judith was studying journalism at Columbia University, New York. She flew at once to Britain and displayed a dazzling flair for personalizing an issue without trivializing it; whether calling for military intervention by an all-white Commonwealth force; whether writing to Prime Minister Harold Wilson, swearing loyalty to the Queen or challenging Smith to arrest her as she stepped out of the plane.

Towards the end of 1971 Garfield and Judith Todd joined forces to arouse opinion against the Smith—Home proposals by which the British Foreign Secretary hoped to wash Britain's hands of an intractable problem, by offering to Africans equality and dignity in the never-never land beyond the rainbow. They witnessed, and documented, a ruthless and systematic campaign of intimidation and distortion directed against a black population which, whether literate or not, understood very clearly why the Smith—Home proposals amounted to little more than a shabby legitimation of serfdom. The new African National Council sprang forth out of the townships and tribal trust lands to coordinate resistance and the Todds threw themselves into the fray, loyally supported by Mrs Grace Todd who played, as always, the role of chief mechanic in the pits, servicing husband and daughter as they roared in for fuel and new maps. The Mambo Press ran off a pamphlet, 20,000 copies of which Judy collected and distributed, ignoring prohibitions on unauthorized entry into the reserves. At Mavorovonde she addressed 335 Africans crammed into a tiny church. The Todds wrote twice to the Pearce Commission, which had been appointed by the British Foreign Secretary to visit Rhodesia and test the acceptability of the Smith—Home constitutional proposals, recording the pressure exerted on chiefs and headmen in the Shabani area by the District Commissioner. A few days before his arrest Garfield Todd addressed an ANC rally and called for talks between the regime and the black leaders in detention. None of this suited the Smith regime.

('If you assume they're like us,' Garfield Todd says, climbing back behind the wheel of his pick-up, 'you'll be right more often than wrong.' His smile is tentative and his eyes search out one's reaction; when assent is noted the smile broadens.)

Driving home from Dadaya on 18 January 1972 father and daughter came across four police cars. As soon as she spotted a woman among the nine police officers Judy realized that they wanted her too. The detention order was signed by the Minister of Justice, Desmond Lardner-Burke, a cocky, arrogant, red-faced person with a habit of addressing Parliament with his hands in his pockets: a fairly standard saloon-bar fascist. The police searched the house and packed piles of letters, documents, anything, into plastic bags. Special Branch confiscated the first 30,000 words of Judy's book. She had a last bath, with Policewoman Helen Pronk standing guard outside the half-open door. Supt Tomlinson (who was soon calling Judy 'Miss T.') very decently promised Todd that he wouldn't introduce any incriminating material into his papers; the 65-year-old statesman was shocked by this insight into the custom and practice of the SB. It was now 9 in the evening, so Grace Todd fed them all.

In January 1972 it was safe to drive through the night. The white regime was at the peak of its confidence, sanctions had failed, the economy was booming (though Judy drew a dire portrait in her published reports) and the guerrilla war remained at an easily containable level. They dropped Garfield Todd off at Gatooma prison then drove on, through the centre of Salisbury, to Marandellas, where Judy was deposited soon after dawn. Special Branch officer Nigel Seaward thanked her for her cooperation and she felt close to tears; during the long night on the road a painful intimacy had grown up between captors and captive.

Judy was the only white and the only female in Marandellas gaol; clearly the Director of Prisons, Frank Patch, respected her capacity for subversion. In Gatooma, Garfield Todd, having spontaneously fallen into conversation with African prisoners, was confined to a cell without window glass where the rain (at its annual peak) came through on to his bed. His health deteriorated. He felt, then, too old for this kind of thing. No mention of their arrest was permitted in the Rhodesian press, but the lines between Grace Todd and the British press had not been cut.

Judith Todd was well fed. They allowed her a radio, newspapers, her typewriter, plenty of hot tea. It was always a shock to Judy, how nice, civilized, courteous, the agents of the regime could be – to her; to a white woman. She decided, then, to go on hunger strike and smuggled out a copy of her declaration of intent (even six months later she wouldn't say how she achieved this). The coup worked well and from the first day her hunger strike was prominently reported by Peter Niesewand, correspondent for the BBC and the *Guardian*, and by other foreign newspapers. (A year later it would be Judy's turn to write in *The New York Times* about her friend Niesewand's detention without trial.)

Furious, the Rhodesian prison authorities took away Judy's typewriter, the 40,000 words she had written, and rescinded all such privileges including visits from her mother. A day later she was transferred to Chikurubi prison, nineteen kilometres from Salisbury.

After six days, by which time her stomach was beginning to come to terms with starvation, she was told by a certain Dr Baker Jones that her condition was 'critical' and that he had no option but to force-feed her. The cell filled up rapidly: two wardresses, Miss Wright and Miss Wells, crisp and smart; a large medical orderly called Mr Large whose job was to hold her down; Prison Superintendent van der Merwe, his deputy, a nursing sister. A long tube was thrust down Judy's throat and into her stomach; it hurt. She longed to clutch the large hand of Mr Large spread across the blanket to hold her down. She was advised to breathe through her nose. A thick white fluid was poured down the tube. When the cell turned black and she feared imminent asphyxiation, she desperately yanked the tube up and out. She was given an injection and the operation was repeated. Again she vomited the white fluid up and again she yanked the tube out of her throat. Finally left alone, she staggered to the washroom and collapsed.

The best accounts of what happens to Judy Todd are invariably written by Judy Todd herself. The reader is therefore directed to her book, *The Right to Say No*. Her cruellest weapon is a perfect memory: when arresting her it's best to say nothing at all.

The Todds were released on 22 February 1972 and driven home to Hokonui. Judy completed her book and was allowed to leave the country on 13 July (she didn't return until February 1980), but her father remained under house arrest. Smith had told a press conference that the Todds were responsible for recent violence, intimidation, looting, rioting and stonings; that being the case, it was to be expected that a review tribunal headed by Mr Justice H. E. Davies recommended, on 2 March, continued detention – despite the 'political independence' of the Rhodesian judiciary, its bench had long since achieved an immaculate osmosis with the most vindictive impulses of the Minister of Justice, Mr Desmond Lardner-Burke.

For the first eighteen months, Garfield Todd was confined to within 800 metres of his house; no one could visit him without a police permit, he could neither make nor receive telephone calls, and his mail was intercepted. A police car was often stationed down the drive to ensure he didn't stir up sedition on his own ranch. During the second phase of detention he was allowed to travel anywhere within the ranch so long as he was back in the house by noon. It was a lonely period and the visitors' book at Hokonui shows which friends remained faithful and which ones, by implication, stayed away: GT speaks with particular sadness of a fellow-missionary who kept his distance because, so it transpired, he wanted to buy land from the Government. When Judy got married to Richard Acton in Rome in 1974, only Grace was able to make the journey. In February 1976, following an international campaign for his release, involving US Senators Hubert Humphrey and Edward Kennedy, as well as the Prime Minister of New Zealand, GT was granted three weeks' compassionate leave in England on condition he made no political statement, however oblique. Father and daughter met for the first time in almost four years.

On 5 June 1976, 1,590 days after he and Judy had been arrested, Todd was freed, without conditions. Later that year he attended the Geneva Conference as a member of the Zapu delegation. It was twelve years since he and Nkomo had last met.

And yet the disparity of treatment must have struck them both. Nkomo holed up in the hot hell of Gonakudzingwa (where a young woman called Todd had, of course, visited him); Todd confined but sleeping in his own bed and eating Grace's food. GT himself is the first to make the comparison.

Garfield Todd moves about his ranch dispensing advice, comfort, medicine. He makes money and collects it from his village store, his Post Office, his butchery in Shabani. He pays his wages promptly. The blacks who work at Hokonui are not mere economic units to be hired and fired without compunction, they are people with names and histories he knows intimately. Chances are, he delivered them.

Now, in February 1978, the Todds are living uncomfortably close to contingency. It needs only the arrival of a new, quick-tempered Zanla section commander; or a bad bout of gin; or a clash between Zanla and Zipra; or a rumour that Mr Todd is betraying the 'boys' to JOC, Shabani – anything of this nature, any charged, erratic current of a countryside at war, and it could be curtains.

The pick-up truck bucks through the ruts, cools its tyres in the summer floods. This tall and innately dignified man talks, laughs, tells tales, bends his mind back. His easy-paced, laconic, antipodean narrative style reminds me of Judy's. Well, he's just about out of debt at last, he says, and now he rather regrets having sold off 12,000 hectares some years ago at a mere $(R)2 an acre – a fifth of the current price. But it doesn't weigh on him. He sells about 300 cattle a year at about $(R)150 a head; a further 700 head, specially bought for the purpose, pass through his butchery in Shabani. He recalls an occasion, during a near-riot in the town, when European-owned stores were being looted. Against all prudence he drove straight through the turbulent streets to secure his store; when he came out of it he found men dancing and washing his car.

Yet did not GT suppress urban unrest in the approved manner when Prime Ministerial power was his? Would he willingly yield an acre of his ranchlands to agrarian reform? Is his ardent black nationalism more than sour grapes?

I drive with him to a house on the banks of the Ngezi River, a few miles from his own. Hereby hangs a tale which, briefly, is this.

The Todds' younger daughter Cynthia, more a conventional child of the Rhodesian environment than her sister Judith, had married a policeman, a veteran of the British SAS, and therefore no kaffir-kissing softie. Being son-in-law to GT in no way advanced his career in the police so he became farm manager at Hokonui. His posture remained an embattled one; a friend in his own Police Reserve 'stick' was stoned to death by poachers he had apprehended. ('In the old days', Garfield Todd comments sadly, 'you could arrest poachers single-handed in the remotest spot and they'd wait meekly for the police truck to arrive.') It was here, in this house on the banks of the river, that Cynthia and her husband lived, preparing for a guerrilla attack by building a sandbagged dug-out with gun slits overlooking the river, and by fixing bomb grenades in the surrounding trees to be set off by remote control. But such a posture, of course, inevitably increased the chances of the very attack it was intended to deter – it also put in jeopardy the entire image and life-style of Hokonui. When fresh Police Reserve call-up papers arrived the time came to leave, hurriedly, for Scotland.

The house on the banks of the Ngezi is now occupied by Christine, who manages a store for the Todds. Christine's husband John is not there: for the past two and a half years he has been detained without trial. Garfield Todd dangles their little girl, Christabel, on his knee. Christine is a young woman short of family luck. Not long ago her father, Dube, a farmer in the Gwatemba Purchase Area, was murdered by Zipra guerrillas after ignoring warnings to cease working as a District Assistant. Mr Dube was axed to death in front of his family, who were forbidden to touch the body, which lay in the centre of the village until the following day. Then one of his daughters telephoned the District Commissioner's office: 'He was your man,' she said, 'come and bury him.' And they did. In fact they put on quite a show, a fine coffin, white ladies at the funeral. 'I know my father was a sell-out,' says one of Dube's daughters, 'but my heart is deeply hurt.'

A year later GT and I drove to the house where Christine's father had been murdered – to meet the Zipra guerrillas who had murdered him.

10. priest on a Honda

Father Desmond Donovan had missed the massacre at St Paul's mission, Musami, by a mere three days. According to a Jesuit working at Silveira House, the 50-year-old Yorkshire-born Donovan had not been popular locally – he had a habit, apparently, of shooting stray dogs. A qualified teacher, fluent in Shona, as well as a skilled mechanic, he had been transferred to Makumbe mission. On Sunday, 15 January, he vanished never to be seen again, alive or dead.

According to the version put out by Comops, Donovan had been celebrating Mass in a classroom at Govera mission, thirty kilometres north of

Salisbury, when armed men forced him to leave at gunpoint and led him away into the surrounding hills of the Chinamora TTL. Comops was in no doubt that this was a Zanla gang operating in denim clothing.

No such certainty about the circumstances of Donovan's disappearance prevailed in Jesuit circles. On the following day Father Henry Wardale, head of the Society of Jesus in Rhodesia, reported that he had heard from the CID that the two witnesses who provided the abduction-at-gunpoint story had subsequently reneged on it. But such was the climate of fear prevailing that, even though leading black Catholics, including Archbishop Chakaipa himself, went up to Chinamora to question local people, no one would talk.

It was not until eight days later that Donovan's 175-cc Honda motor cycle, registration number 61-000D, was found in a hole covered with earth some distance from the dirt road between Chinyanga and Govera.

11. the cattle war

The marmalade on the table was made in Rhodesia but the word 'Oxford' appears on the label. (If they can do *that*, they can do anything.) Over breakfast my host, Roger Hyams, scans the farm properties advertised for sale in the *Herald*; his mouth is full of toast, 'Oxford' marmalade and hectares:

'ENKELDOORN: 2,425 hectares. Cattle farm with 28 paddocks, 3 dip tanks, own power plant, 3 stock watering dams and a windmill on the Sebakwe river, 6 reservoirs for stock watering, 7 dams, 7 waterholes. Homestead of brick under iron with 4 bedrooms, lounge, dining room, bathroom, toilet plus 1 bedroom rondavel. Price, $(R)75,000.'

Hyams picks up his gun and strides out on to the stoep. My coffee slops into its saucer as I follow; Zanla guerrillas have been trying to break into my room all night except during occasional snatches of sleep. The countryside is no fun unless you own it.

'I started young out here, without a penny,' Hyams says, pincering two fingers to make sure his small, blond moustache is still in place. 'When I went along to Rhodesia House in the Strand in the early 1950s you needed guts, enterprise and initiative to make a go of it here. Nowadays any riff-raff can come. And they do. Now I own 4,000 hectares and 3,000 beasts of which 1,250 are full cattle units worth $(R)180 a head.'

Soon we are heaving – 7.30 a.m., my stomach cannot accommodate – over the ridges and troughs of his farm tracks in a mine-proofed Land-Rover.

'You'll see the farm is designed on a cartwheel principle, with paddocks radiating out from a central dipping area. Right now I'm training my African stockmen to handle difficult births. It isn't easy. . . .'

'Difficult births aren't easy?'

'Kaffirs aren't easy. It's the famous K-factor.'

The Land-Rover draws to a halt at the perimeter fence where we come across three armed guards, each wearing a woollen balaclava helmet to hamper recognition. Hyams speaks softly to them in Shona; cadences and pauses suggest that he is posing questions but the response is minimal, a few grunts. He climbs back behind the wheel and furiously jabs the stick into first gear: 'I've offered those munts $(R)200 for any cattle rustler they bring in alive or dead. So far, nil return. It's your K-factor again: they're getting $(R)80 a month from me for wearing woollen helmets so why should they push themselves?'

Hyams drives across country to the dip tanks, where each animal is being redaubed with luminous dye to facilitate aerial surveillance and aerial pursuit in the event of the cattle being rustled into the neighbouring TTL.

'If your fencing is good, you can reckon your land is worth $(R)20 an acre round here. Do you know how to tell when you're crossing from European land into the reserve? Trees. There are no trees in the reserve: they burn the wood.'

Yet Hyams burns wood to cure his tobacco. As a young man he had walked into Rhodesia House in the Strand, never glancing up at its infamous Epstein carvings, eager to make good, to mould the raw clay of Africa to his will.

The dip tanks reek of shit and the evil-smelling dip fluid. The beasts rumble and roar as they are herded down into the concrete dips: holding a counter in each hand, Hyams shouts constantly above the bellowing at his black stockmen to ensure that the animals with green paint on their rumps are paddocked separately:

'They're for the cold-storage lorry from Marandellas. You have to book the slaughterhouse six months in advance – can you imagine a kaffir farmer getting a grip of that?'

Hyams is sceptical about the emerging internal settlement. 'It's the thin end of the wedge.' Even so, he still supports Ian Smith. About his Minister of Agriculture, Mark Partridge, whom we are due to meet later in the day, he is less sure:

'We need a 25 per cent rise in the guaranteed price of beef and I'm not kidding you, David. We haven't had a price increase for five years and that's just killing this industry because the price of inputs goes up and up – salt, urea, fencing, droppers, dips, barbed wire. Listen, three years ago one feeder steer was worth twelve rolls of barbed wire; today, barely three rolls.'

It is a Thursday in February 1978. A light aircraft touches down shortly after noon on a grass landing-strip in a 400-hectare safari park near Hyams's farm. From the plane alights a handsome man in a smart business suit and a dark-tinted monocle: Mark Partridge, Minister of Agriculture, Old Boy of St George's, a signatory of the Declaration of Independence in 1965, the RF's most prominent Catholic. Then follows Mrs Partridge, done up for the day; the Minister's secretary, who didn't want to be left behind; a Ministry expert on conservation, a man of curiously twisted aspect; finally a member of the Special Branch who sniffs out my alien presence quickly enough and whose inquiries into my provenance will eventually culminate in the drilling of a fine observation hole through the wall of my Salisbury hotel room.

Allen Ricketts greets them heartily, a big, leathery John Wayne of a man whose grown-up sons and daughters seem designed to adorn travel brochures. There is an equation, somewhere, between the colonial drive to subdue natives and the white man's pride in quelling, conserving, culling, regulating wild animals. The pet lion-cub in the Ricketts's drawing-room is a warning, a demonstration of the white man's audacity and control: let word of that lion run from kraal to kraal. Roger Hyams belongs to a conservation-ist group which periodically talks to local African notables. 'Now we had this chappie, a primary-school headmaster, and we showed him a lion, you see, and this munt said, "What is it?"'

(I had read that a family called Ferguson were currently training a lioness-cub called Zhingeli to guard their Inyanga farm in company with a pack of Ridgeback dogs. 'Africans believe anyone who can tame a lion has supernatural powers,' explained Mr Courtney Ferguson. In the event of an attack the terrs would be put to flight: 'They won't stop short until they've reached Maputo and caught the first flight to Moscow.')

Ricketts lives behind a 2½-metre fence and wire screens shield the windows against grenades. His private zoo houses cheetahs, leopards, a vulture which pecks frenziedly at your finger from the other side of the glass if you tap on the window, and a couple of crocodiles. Seizing two hunks of raw meat, keenly observed by Minister Partridge, his wife, secretary, entourage and a selection of local worthies invited to lunch to meet the Minister, Ricketts scales the wall surrounding the croc pond and takes a few steps towards it. One could call them tentative steps – or the approach of 'a man who knows what he's doing'. The beasts do not cooperate, refuse to show themselves, perhaps they despise the Rhodesian Front as mere plagiarists; in the end he has to toss the meat to the water's edge.

'They don't chew the meat, they just swallow it whole,' Ricketts explains. Mrs Partridge asks him whether the two crocs are 'a boy and a girl'.

Now a dusty black youth appears – straight out of Kipling – followed by two mud-caked baby elephants who rub themselves against a tree. 'They follow him everywhere,' Ricketts tells the Minister's wife. She asks him whether the two elephants are 'a boy and a girl'. He says, 'Yes, but they're still rather young.' Mrs Partridge looks rather disappointed.

We climb into a truck converted for paying guests and, driven by one of Ricketts's model sons, bounce across rough terrain, the local farmers in our party cradling their FN rifles and talking incessantly of recent cattle thefts. We pass a herd of sables – to shoot one of them would cost an American hunter $(R)900 (if American hunters were still around; on the whole they're elsewhere) – then a herd of impala with a single ram, lord and master of his harem.

'There's a lucky boy!' cries the Minister's wife in extreme excitement.

We return to the Ricketts homestead and dismount: nine of the party carry weapons. The buffet lunch is extremely cordon bleu and the lion-cub (now the size of a large dog) gnaws at my ankles. Three local farmers sit on the stoep talking of stock theft. Following spoor by motorbike, pick-up and helicopter, the whites habitually whine like angry hornets across the reserve, raging at the blank, maddeningly agnostic stares of the sightless natives. In the Low Veld farmers have formed horse-mounted Anti-Stock-Theft Units; during 1977 they recovered 628 head of cattle, valued at $(R)78,000, yet 15,000 head had been stolen. The number of cattle stolen from white farms throughout Rhodesia was 26,000 in 1977, 40,000 in 1978 and 92,000 in 1979. 'We're going into the reserves now and taking the first cattle we see. It's the only thing the munts understand,' says Hyams.

We set off for the Country Club. Behind the recently erected protective wall which now shields the club house the whites park their cars – I count some sixty-five people in the hall, women almost as numerous as men, a few kids as well. Some farmers use the gun-racks at the back to offload their weapons, but the majority prefer to keep their guns close to hand, on the floor beside their chairs. It's an odd sight: odder still when you begin to take it for granted, women in flowered dresses carrying sub-machine-guns to the toilet.

The Chairman of the Club introduces Mark Partridge. There is polite applause. Suave, monocled, the Minister removes his jacket (but not his tie) in deference to the summer heat. He is known to stand on the right of the Cabinet and could well have defected with the twelve MPs who formed the Rhodesian Action Party the year before. In the Catholic journal, the *Shield*, Partridge once explained why he had entered politics and joined the RF: 'As I saw it, the trend was to hand over the country to irresponsible people, with the end result that no people of my race would be prepared to stay and therefore everything that I owned was at stake.' In 1896 his grandfather had taken part in the suppression of the Shona rebellion as a member of the Umtali Pioneers.

The Minister refers briefly to the negotiations currently being conducted between Smith, Muzorewa, Sithole and Chirau. 'It will be up to you, in due course, to decide whether or not you accept the outcome of these talks.' He pauses, mops his neck with a silk handkerchief. 'In any case,' Partridge adds almost hopefully, 'the talks may break down.'

An elderly man, tall and stooped, with shaggy white locks about his swollen red ears, rises and announces, with dignity, that he has lost 1,000 head of cattle during the past year. Why does the Government pay only 90 per cent compensation? Why are cattle stolen last September still not compensated for early in February? Why are there on average no less than 750 compensation claims from farmers outstanding? And what about the case of the Mazoe farmer who was waiting for compensation six months after terrs destroyed his store ($(R)11,000), did $(R)400 damage to the farmhouse, gutted the labour compound, killing three employees, wrecked a truck worth $(R)16,000 and so intimidated the work-force that the farmer could not pick his cotton and lost 75 per cent of a crop worth $(R)180,000? 'What does the Minister have to say?'

The Minister rises to reply, aware that he now confronts the heartland of the Rhodesian Front's constituency, the élite, the first and last line of defence against insurgent Africa. He adjusts his monocle.

'Ladies and Gentlemen, let us face facts. One hundred per cent compensation for terrorist action would merely encourage feckless or dishonest farmers – and let's admit it, they do exist – to cut their own fences and quit their farms without loss. . . .'

In fact most farmers use compensation payments to restock their herds or repair damage, but if they don't, the compensation is treated as taxable. The farmers resent this and Mr Partridge is nobody's hero down here: it is, of course, wrong to assume that beleaguered laagers besieged by hollerin' Zulus are thereby purged of internal tensions.

Through the window of the hall a cricket pitch can be seen, tennis-courts, distant cattle drifting under a fleecy blue sky. That all these farmers should regularly gather here, on the same day of every month, is the measure of their contempt for the enemy. Yet there is fear in the room, the kind engendered by epidemics, plagues, by rabies. The discussion inexorably shifts from farm prices to survival. Big Allen Ricketts is up front now, hands on hips, laconic in the unaffected style of the Rhodesian Action Man, a style heavily conditioned by the British commitment to self-effacement. It is said that Ricketts has dug into his own pocket to contribute towards the local defence force's mine-proofed Leopard and a Star Wars Land-Rover equipped by Special Effects: you press a button and blow off the head of every gook south of the Zambezi.

Minister Partridge once again faces a mounting barrage of complaints. It's all spilling out now, each fear triggering the next. Why does the Government impose a 15 per cent sales tax on defence hardware when it's now a matter of life and death? And why are farmers still called out of their own areas on Police Reserve duty? Aren't they more useful defending their families and their neighbours in terrain they own and know? A rumble of support wells up from the gut of the hall.

There are worse areas than this, but already the graveyards are filling up. One farmer was ambushed with his 16-year-old son when driving near his farm with six Africans in the back of the pick-up. The boy was killed outright, the father drove two kilometres before dying with blood spurting from a femoral artery. He left a widow and six children.

Such catastrophes demand resilience. An abandoned farm is a threat to every neighbouring farmer and they recruit furiously to fill the gap:

'EXCITING FARMING OPPORTUNITY for 1 or 2 men with agricultural experience and guts. 150 acres of maize, 50 acres of tobacco, abandoned by farmer due to terrorist activity. Crops are average to good. All facilities other than labour are available. Start immediately. Phone 2240.'

In short, don't expect any black will dare work for you. . . .

Suddenly things are cool. The Chief Engineer of the Electrical Supply Commission has come down from Marandellas to face a barrage of questions: Why don't his men come out at night any more to deal with power failures? Doesn't he realize – a wealthy farmer is on his feet – that during tobacco-curing a whole day's picking can be rotted and ruined if the power fails and isn't rapidly restored?

For the first time I sense positive animosity – something akin to class feeling in England but not quite that; the farmer-warrior class is displaying its contempt for the soft-suburb, for the immigrant artisan whose loyalty to 'Rhodesia' (i.e. to the farmer's tobacco crop) is flimsy. The Chief Engineer in his short-sleeved nylon shirt and his steel-rimmed spectacles retains his dignity under the onslaught:

'I'd like to remind you all that my men drive alone and unprotected into areas which even the security forces steer clear of. It wasn't far from here that my engineer Joe S—— was found chopped into small pieces.'

A groan of sympathy passes through the audience like a fast-moving cloud. They feel a little ashamed now. The Chief Engineer very sensibly pushes his advantage: 'I have an engineer from Glasgow who told me he was getting scared. I reminded him Glasgow is no paradise.' (Laughter.) 'The next night he got three bullets through his windscreen and decided to try Glasgow after all.'

The tables are turned; the admonitions are now travelling in the opposite direction. It is the Chief Engineer who delivers the lecture. Cut down any tree which might fall on a power line and don't forget the tall gum-trees. . . .

Darkness descends. The meeting breaks up. Minister Partridge is rushed under police escort back to his plane. The stalwarts, refusing to flap, make for the bar. Conversation turns to that nearby hotbed of sedition, Mount St Mary's mission, from which Irish Franciscans are now regularly deported. And what about the Justice and Peace Commission, what about that Sister Janice McLaughlin?

'A woman like that', says Roger Hyams, 'needs one thing. It's a damned shame that no big nig was prepared to give it to her.'

Hyams sent me a card for Christmas 1978: 'By far the best man in the Transitional Govt. is Chirau, a selfless chap, dedicated to this country, a man of dignity, but the West tells us he's a puppet and the Kremlin will seal his fate.

'The cattle situation is worse than ever. Three years ago tick-borne diseases like red-water, gallsickness, theieriosis, heartwater, etc. were almost extinct in this country; the tsetse fly had been virtually cleared out and pushed well back into Mozambique. It's reckoned that during 1978 300,000 out of 3 million African-owned cattle have died through either trypanosomiasis (tsetse fly)or tick-borne diseases. Dipping in the reserves has virtually come to a halt. Cheers. Roger.'

12. past call

Cyril Thompson, 60, lived at Louis Trichardt in South Africa but owned a ranch thirty kilometres north of Beitbridge. On 10 February one of his farm managers in Rhodesia, Freddie Wolvaardt, was fatally ambushed. Five days later Thompson drove up across the border in an ambush-protected vehicle accompanied by another farm manager, Petrus Bezuidenhout. Having arrived without incident, Thompson phoned his family to reassure them. The two men then drove along a dirt track to inspect cattle and died when a rocket penetrated their vehicle. Bezuidenhout, 36, left a wife and three children.

Neville Royston, 49, a married man with four children, was fatally ambushed near his farm, Musha Wedu (Our Home) in the Karoi district at 6.15 in the evening of Saturday, 18 February.

Adriaan Hendrikus (Hennie) Stander, 28, died when his vehicle was ambushed on Benjane Ranch, Nuanetsi, during the morning of 22 February. A passenger, Hans van der Merwe, was injured.

13. Andersen

Christian Andersen is MP for Mount Pleasant, head of the Rhodesian Bar, and by repute the brightest lawyer in town. Sandy-haired, cool, logical, he is regarded as a liberal capitulationist by the MPs who broke away to form the RAP in 1977. 'These fellows', he remarks without a hint of feeling, 'either believe blacks are inherently inferior or alternatively they advocate apartheid to curb black capabilities.' And what does Andersen believe, surrounded by leather-bound law books in his handsome seventh-floor office opposite the House of Assembly? And why did he join the RF in any case?

'In 1974 I allowed myself to be persuaded to stand for Mount Pleasant. I was convinced that the RF now believed in advancement on merit, regardless of race. The original RF philosophy was hopeless from the outset, but we now have a broad-based coalition party and the only viable force for change. That's why I decided to join.'

'How can you defend the internal settlement?'

'Very easily.'

'Why will there be no black referendum?'

'Impossible to hold one until the war subsides.'

'The same would apply to a general election, surely?'

'Yes it would.'

'Then you're saying the elections promised in the Salisbury Agreement are really conditional on running down the war?'

'No, I'm not saying that.'

'How else can I construe what you've just said?'

'At the time of Kissinger Smith made just that point and as a result the blacks thought he was in bad faith. So we mustn't give that impression again. It may be implicit in the situation but we're not putting it that way.'

'Does Smith put it that way in the RF Parliamentary caucus?'

'I can't discuss caucus meetings.'

'What do you think about the allegations made by the black MPs against the security forces?'

'Some of their allegations are true. Some are false.'

'Would the guerrillas survive without support from the rural population?'

'They have some support. They also practise intimidation.'

'Will it make any difference if Sithole and Muzorewa join the Government?'

'Yes it will. The war may get worse at first but then we hope it will get better.'

Within the year Andersen was appointed Minister of Justice in the Transitional Government. The war *had* got worse at first; after that it got worse still.

14. RAP

The man is tall, heavy, broad. At 9 on a Saturday morning he marches briskly into the foyer of the Park Lane Hotel and mounts the stairs to the conference room. This is Len Idensohn, sanitary engineer and Klan Wizard of Rhodesian racists. The mood in Salisbury is ugly as the Rhodesian Action Party goes into caucus. Smith is inching towards a settlement with the 'internal' black parties and the wet summer air is heavy with premonitions of betrayal. Hysteria prevails in the correspondence columns.

'We have only two options as white Rhodesians,' writes R. C. Knott of Selukwe. 'We fight or we give in. . . .' According to C. A. L. Meredith of Salisbury, Smith's acceptance of the Kissinger proposals has brought no benefit, only the emigration of thousands of whites. 'John Bull' of Avondale warns: 'Rhodesians are about to become the victims of one of the biggest con-games in history . . . the poor, gullible Rhodesian is completely bewildered and ready to accept any proposal the Prime Minister puts forward. His claims of safeguards are not worth the paper they are about to be written on. I can quote at least 46 valid reasons to back up this statement – namely 46 so-called independent black African states.'

During the first two months of 1978 the RAP tried to thwart Smith's negotiations with a campaign of advertisements and rallies. But the farmers stuck with Smith. In the towns the RAP meetings attracted audiences of up to 500 people, many of them recent immigrants with British accents and a ferocious hatred of socialist Britain. When a BBC TV crew was spotted in the Rhodes Memorial Hall during an RAP rally attended by 450 predominantly middle-aged to elderly whites, there was uproar and demands for the crew's expulsion.

A series of large ads, measuring thirty centimetres by twenty, appeared in the press. They depicted four sturdy soldiers, two white and two black, advancing under the command of a white whose iron will was written into his granite jaw. The caption: 'We are winning the war – Don't lose the peace. Your vote is as important as your FN.' Each ad carried the RAP's symbol, the profiled head of a lion – of iron will and granite jaw.

Ted Sutton Price, a junior Minister in Smith's office throughout 1976, and Colin Barlow, a Salisbury dentist, were two of the twelve RF MPs who had broken away in disgust to form the RAP when Smith amended the Land Tenure Act. Both speak disparagingly of the 'liberal', Chris Andersen.

'Smith claims the South Africans put the screws on him,' Barlow comments. 'That's a lie. The South Africans are open-minded. The fall of Rhodesia would depress white morale in the Republic. The correct strategy is to build up a southern Africa defence unit.'

Sutton Price affably explains the RAP's philosophy over a beer. 'We don't want a multiracial meritocracy. Smith has been working his way towards that ever since the *Tiger* and *Fearless* talks. What we envisage is separate development, the division of this country into racial zones, with a Council of State controlled by whites and responsible for defence, foreign affairs, transport, the media. Lower down, at the second tier of regional government, the Africans could run their own education and health services – and pay for them.'

'The blacks in the reserves are very conservative people,' Barlow says. 'What they want is peace and quiet to carry on their easygoing life. So why does Smith undermine the chiefs by doing business with externally supported terrorists like Muzorewa and Sithole?'

'We must raise the level of this war,' says Sutton Price, jabbing the air with a finger. 'Be ruthless – all means, fair and foul.'

(In 1979 Barlow sold his Avondale home to a black businessman for a reported $(R)55,000 – a transaction which would have been illegal if the RAP's philosophy had prevailed. In November 1979, ten of the twelve MPs who had broken with Smith in 1977 were still living in Rhodesia. According to the *Herald*, Barlow was planning to move to South Africa.)

15. white liberals

The executive of the National Unifying Force also meets behind closed doors in the Park Lane Hotel. The President, Allan Savory, being abroad at the time, his place is taken by Nick McNally, a liberal defence lawyer with a trace of Ireland in his voice and a strong attachment to the Catholic faith. These are nice people and completely powerless.

They loathe Smith but serve in his security forces, as reservists, without a qualm. Many of them believe that guerrilla warfare is the inevitable outcome of racial oppression, yet do not hesitate to join in 'hot pursuit' of 'terrorists'. One or two have even volunteered for PsyAc – the futile exercise of trying to convince tribesmen that the security forces are their friends. When 1,200 blacks were massacred at Chimoio, the NUF protested – but not against the massacre, only against the way it was reported in the media.

This is a white party, there are no blacks round the table. The NUF attracts people who couldn't dabble in politics any other way. The mood is distinctly pro-British and Crown loyalist; never more in their element than when addressing a fringe group of left-leaning wets at a Tory party conference. Their view of recent history almost invariably runs like this:

– The Africans were foolish to throw out the 1961 constitution, they could have had majority rule within fifteen years but they wanted power too quickly. Then we had violence, whites were jostled in the street, pushed down the stairs at the OK Bazaars and thrown into swimming-pools. And you had faction-fighting in the townships. Naturally, Edgar Whitehead had no option but to take emergency powers. A white backlash became inevitable. Smith tried to put the clock back. What a mess we're in! The real problem now, as always, is Smith. But the Patriotic Front is also a problem. We have to talk to them but they want to gain power through the barrel of a gun.

McNally: We feel we know Nkomo and can come to terms with him whereas Mugabe is an unknown quantity. He may be one of several Shonas competing for leadership of Zanu. Zanu frightens us. We want to settle with Nkomo.

Diana Mitchell (a journalist): We should deal with Nkomo but exclude Zanu leaders like Tongogara and Nhongo who are indoctrinating Africans in Marxism.

Muriel Rosen: But Kaunda cannot be allowed to impose Nkomo on us by force. We are determined to resist.

McNally: It's not clear what the PF's programme is. Even Owen has difficulty finding out. And they could easily raise their demands. Certainly they realize they couldn't win an election.

(This meets with unanimous agreement round the table – the PF knows it could never win an election.)

Ewen Greenfield, a Bulawayo lawyer who defends blacks charged with political offences, is extraordinarily hostile to Nkomo in view of the overwhelming support the Zapu leader enjoys throughout Matabeleland.

Greenfield: Nkomo is emptying Ndebeles into Botswana to create a

Palestinian-type refugee situation. He should be allowed on our TV so that he can hang himself out of his own mouth.

(By the end of the year Greenfield had left Rhodesia.)

And what about the core of the Anglo-American plan, the integration of guerrilla units into the security forces? There is an uneasy silence round the table; these whites share the same gut fear – for their wives and daughters – as do those who support Ian Smith. At root it is the fear of black rape.

There are the Women for Peace – how beguiling to spend one's time in their civilized and sympathetic company, sitting on their verandas, consuming their quiches, sipping their sundowners, stroking their large but non-racist dogs, joining their Sunday houseparties, and visiting their friends' unrepresentatively liberal farms. The Women for Peace are a veritable Lorelei upon which the hack could happily wreck his Rhine-barge. As for love, one soon recognizes in oneself the belching, bent-legged sailor, unworthy of any embrace worth embracing.

Most of the peace women are rather well off and live in tastefully inconspicuous luxury, quietly despising the poor white artisans in their bungalows who back Ian Smith. One lady who lives on a beautiful hill beyond the suburbs of Salisbury has recently taken in the children of her maid, after members of the woman's family were killed in crossfire. Another lady illegally shelters the many black children of her servants, shuddering in her knowledge of what life is now like in the TTLs and in the squatters' camps of Salisbury

The women do good things. They lobby the Minister of Justice, Hilary Squires, and demand an end to detention without trial, an end to death sentences, the notification of families after an arrest. They shuttle between the Ministry of Local Government and the City Council in an effort to have greater Salisbury declared a multiracial area. They protest at the exclusion of black children from European schools which have been closed down for lack of pupils – Houghton Park primary school began the term with only forty-eight pupils despite a capacity of 160 and long queues of desperate black kids outside the gate.

The black Women for Peace are often found at the houses of their white sisters, but rarely the other way round. Many of the black women, like Olivia Mutchena and Mrs Winnie Wakatama, are very keen on the Bishop and complain that the PF wants to impose itself through the barrel of a gun. The white ladies partly agree, aren't sure, feel nervous about everything. Many of them have husbands on reserve duty in the bush.

16. Lady Wilson – the view from the border

Jacqueline Wilson is President of the Women for Peace. She stands outside Penhalonga post office, a stocky chain-smoking woman in her 50s with a gruff manner and a Webley pistol given by her father as a wedding present during the Mau Mau rising in Kenya. She has come down the mountain, her mountain, to post thirty large manila envelopes addressed to key figures, white and black, in the Rhodesian political hierarchy. It's the wet season and the track winding up to her hilltop house is not, she warns me, in good shape. 'With front-wheel drive you'll probably make it.'

I follow her station-wagon up the narrow, twisting, rutted track through dense undergrowth and then, on higher ground, through the ominous silence of the forestry estates (her own and Anglo-American's). Lady Wilson's windows and stoep are meshed in anti-grenade wire. She points to the skyline 200 metres away: 'That's the border. The other side – Frelimo. You're looking at a minefield.' She growls back at her neurotic guard dogs. To the west the guerrilla-infested hills of Rhodesia stretch, blue-grey under a cloud-flecked summer sky. By mid-afternoon there will be rain.

A young man pads barefooted through the house carrying an FN rifle, then vanishes: her son Alexander, still too young for military service. Normally she lives up here at Zingesi completely alone; her daughter has a job as secretary at Peterhouse school, Marandellas; her husband is dead.

She lights another cigarette and coughs; she has the classic smoker's hack and it's compounded now by disaster and bitterness. In the good old days, when Mozambique belonged to Portugal, she used to enjoy cordial relations with the customs officials and the Africans who commuted to work across the border. 'They always came to me for medical assistance.' This all ended in March 1976 when Samora Machel 'foolishly' closed the border 'under British pressure'. In August of that year, Rhodesian forces drove up past her house on their way into Mozambique, where they 'killed several hundred Zanla youths training with dummy rifles' (thus she describes the massacre of 1,200 at Nyadzonia). Frelimo sent Lady W. a message threatening retaliation; rockets and small-arms fire raked her house. She sniffs contemptuously: 'Most of it missed.' Later an army patrol was hit and the wounded were brought to Zingesi; things became so hot that two 'bright-lights', Italians from Salisbury, were posted as guards, but by the time of my visit they have been withdrawn. Lady Wilson is alone again.

She was born in Salisbury of British parents – her father a soldier, her mother once a nurse in the East End of London. She worked as a school-teacher (maths) before marrying Ian Wilson who became, in due course, Sir

Ian and Speaker of the House of Assembly of the Federation of Rhodesia and Nyasaland. That was in the 1950s when Lady W. was in her thirties, the best years of her life, the years that a woman widowed at a young age will forever look back to – there were no armed guerrillas and important people used to drive up to Zingesi to spend the weekend with the Wilsons.

When Britain decided to terminate the Federation, to break it up, Jacqueline Wilson assimilated her husband's anger and decided never to forgive Britain. She believes the 1961 constitution was fair and blames Nkomo for reneging on his acceptance of a voters' roll severely restricted by property and educational qualifications. 'After all,' she says, 'it excluded quite a lot of whites.'

She spreads an ordnance map on the dining-room table. Her maid brings tea. The alsatians growl again, she growls back. 'I've always opposed Smith. I've known him since he was a backbencher. He once asked me why all his agreements with black nationalists had fallen through. Ha! I told him why: because Des Frost and his right-wing colleagues invariably denounced every agreement as soon as it was announced.'

Another cigarette. Her hand trembles as she recalls how Zanla closed down her beloved agricultural school. 'Young thugs,' she calls them, and 'Communist bandits'. Founded in 1963 upon the bounty of Lady Courtauld, the school was established to train Africans in animal husbandry and modern agriculture. Lady W. was the first chairman of the trustees. The first superintendent they appointed was good: a white Rhodesian of Dutch origin, a member of the Police Reserve, an honest bloke. When he left they looked for an African of high qualifications to succeed him – misplaced idealism, of course: 'This chap turned out to be a complete crook, didn't look after the cattle, put his hand in the till and consorted with terrorists. Arrogant bastard.'

When the news reached Jacqueline Wilson she lost no time. Terrorists had visited the school, burned the offices, threatened the staff and then shot three black hostages. With four white police reservists, all of them local farmers, Lady W. set out to rescue the cattle, pigs, sheep and turkeys. *En route* they came to a store which the terrs had burnt. Lady Wilson went inside the shell and vomited. The owner of the store, an African woman, had been burnt alive. Three local headmen had also been executed. The attitude of the agricultural-school principal infuriated her. 'He knew nothing, the bastard.' The terrified school staff were now refusing to tend the cows, which were half-starved. 'All they wanted to know was how long they would get paid. I said to them, "Not at all if you don't get those poor beasts into the trucks."' She had no choice but to close the school.

'No, there was no provocation given. The school had no security fence and no Agric-Alert alarm system. When the army wanted to camp there, I said no. It was sheer bloody mindless thuggery.'

Despite her opposition to Ian Smith, she regards the army and the police as the guardians of decency and civilization stretched to the limit in a gallant struggle against the forces of darkness: banditry, drunkenness, chaos. 'Police reservists always came to our house because they were our friends. Later army men came because they were the sons of our friends.' She doesn't agree at all that Ian Smith is any excuse for closing down her agricultural school or firing rockets at Zingesi.

'The blacks round here always trusted me, my husband's servants always consulted him, in the old days you could travel thirty miles on horseback without encountering a single show of animosity. But then your unscrupulous black politicians got into the act and here we are.'

For seven years Jacqueline Wilson ran a circle for the local women, the 'nannies', teaching needlework and domestic crafts. 'Then I told them, I've done my stint, it's time you stood on your own feet.' Almost immediately the circle disintegrated. 'They came running back to me like children.'

The thought of their breeding habits evokes a short sniff and a long sigh. 'The men see their manhood in the number of children they have. One woman asked me what she could give her husband to put him to sleep because he was demanding it five times every night. You see these women all bleary-eyed in the morning. They have no sense of time, no sense of a future. They laugh at you when you suggest they should plant trees for their grandchildren. The Land Apportionment Act reserved half the land for Africans – keep out the Jews. But if the Afs insist on breeding and turning the reserves into dustbowls it's their own fault. I've done my best for these people. When our Government teams come out with sugar-lump vaccine against polio, the black teachers send children home and tell them that the whites are trying to sterilize the Africans. What can you do? I actually like black people, by the way.'

She chuckles, guffaws, disintegrates into a smoker's cough. The dog looks suspicious as if his mistress is suffering an assault.

Three weeks after my visit, on 6 March 1978, Lady W. took her stationwagon down through the forests and the dangerous corners and drove along the good, European tarmac road from Penhalonga to Umtali. It was the anniversary of her husband's death and she had a premonition. Twelve out of fifty white foresters working in the Penhalonga area had been killed or abducted. When she came back the police stopped her in Penhalonga, at the foot of Sir Ian Wilson Drive.

Twenty guerrillas had threaded their way through the border minefield cordon, looted the house, drunk the beer and brandy and asked the cook –

who had been with Lady Wilson for twenty-six years – where her son Alexander was. (He had recently left for England to join the Signal Corps.) The guerrillas then departed, leaving a note warning that they would return.

She closed up the house, moved down to Penhalonga, and began to teach at Umtali Boys' High School. In April she heard Smith address a closed meeting in Umtali in the course of which he assured his all-white audience that the blacks were safely sewn up by the internal settlement. This of course, angered her – not because she opposed the internal settlement, how could she? – but because it was Smith's.

Periodically she drove up to Zingesi under police escort. The shutters had been broken, everything pulled from the walls, the guerrillas had free run of the place now and her beloved market garden was beginning to decay. Finally she could bear the sight of it, the wound of it, the utter humiliation of it, no more. She said goodbye to her cook and her fifteen labourers and set sail from Cape Town taking with her as many worldly goods as Exchange Control allowed. 'Luckily I have some South African shares.'

I found her on a bleak winter day early in 1979, living with her sister on the south coast. She is bitter, loathes David Owen (in whose Parliamentary constituency she now resides), despises the Labour Government's pursuit of sanctions, but offers no answer when asked whether Britain should simply have taken Smith's UDI on the chin. She is against trade unions, strikes and foul weather, but doesn't mind drawing social security while looking for a teaching job.

She chuckles: British military instructors had been impressed by her son's mastery of a rifle. She tells me, now, about a nephew who lost a leg in a car accident then suffered a terrorist attack while on his own, at night, during which he was hit in the stump of his amputated leg yet managed to roll on to the floor as bullets sprayed the bed. For Britain she has nothing good to say. She reminds me that many of the British pilots who went out during the war to train at Thornhill later returned to settle in Rhodesia ... and she has discovered that Prince Philip has an aide of Rhodesian origin, damn funny. . . . 'You'll find young Rhodesians in positions of trust and responsibility throughout the world.'

Later she moved into a cramped, one-room lodging in Hammersmith with her daughter, paying £24 a week for bed and breakfast. She worked half-day, tutoring in maths but not earning much. 'What I'd really enjoy is to be a gardener,' she chuckled, 'but I suppose I'm an unsuitable candidate.' The smoker's cough hadn't got any better. 'If you happen to hear of a cheap flat, do let me know.'

They gave her a job in Hammersmith Town Hall, watering the flowerpots in the various offices. Hating Britain – no one to talk to, one temp job after another, no money to spend at the end of the week – her daughter went home to Peterhouse.

In March 1980 I was staying at St Augustine's and decided to drive up the mountain to take a look at Lady Wilson's house at Zingesi. But the rains had been heavy and I had the wrong car for that rutted, muddy track so I turned back.

17. Provincial Commissioner

'I suppose you realize that the best period of British rule was before universal suffrage was introduced in England. A man should achieve something before he gets the vote.'

The speaker is the top civilian official in Manicaland, an alert, wiry, sandy-haired man with sharp eyes and a compulsive energy. Rhodesia has only eight Provincial Commissioners and Bob Cunliffe is one of them; he and his subordinates in Internal Affairs, the District Commissioners, have supervised the uprooting of thousands of Africans from their kraals and their forced concentration in protected villages. Clearly Cunliffe has achieved enough in his life to deserve the vote.

The Provincial Commissioner is often on the road; the dirt tracks of Manicaland are strewn with mines. 'In this country we have perfected mine-proofing,' he says. 'Vehicles belonging to my department have been blown up thirty times yet we've suffered only one fatality. The terrs aren't very good at laying mines, in fact they're not very good at anything except spouting Marxism and killing babies.'

Mr and Mrs Cunliffe have kindly invited me to dinner. She thinks Britain will pay dearly for having let blacks flood in to their cities.

Cunliffe hopes I realize that the very existence of the tribal trust lands is a mark of 'our generosity to the African'.

'Considering what we've done for them, the way they're behaving now makes me sick,' adds his predecessor as Provincial Commissioner.

'If sanctions were lifted', Cunliffe says, 'we could find a job for every unemployed black in this country. But you people don't want that, you want to keep stirring the pot, as Moscow dictates. Believe me, nationalism is stone-dead now in Rhodesia. Most blacks fear black rule. I work among them every day. They want white rule.'

'If Britain had granted us independence', the older man says, 'we would have made steady progress towards a multiracial society. But R. A. Butler betrayed us. That was hideous. And Winston Field was a fool. So naturally you got a backlash.'

'Britain doesn't give a damn for our blacks or any blacks,' Cunliffe says. 'As for Carter, he's now completely dependent on Andrew Young and the black vote – what we are witnessing, David, is the unfolding of Communism's grand design for world domination.' His eyes flash. 'In my view it would require five years to hold elections here. We can't possibly pacify the country in less.'

Then why, I inquire is Smith talking to Muzorewa and Sithole?

'That's precisely what we're beginning to ask,' snaps Cunliffe's predecessor. 'In any case, who will guarantee our pensions if the blacks come in?'

'Anyone can tear up a constitution,' Cunliffe says.

'This is Africa,' his wife says.

I thank them and leave. The food was excellent, the whisky more than generous, and their hospitality spontaneous in the warm Rhodesian manner.

The following account gives some indication of what was at that time happening in the Manicaland domain of Mr Bob Cunliffe.

As from dawn on 20 January 1978 the Maranke TTL and Mukuni Purchase Area due south of Umtali, centres of intense guerrilla activity, were placed under a draconian curfew lasting from last light until noon. There were now only six hours in every twenty-four when people, cattle, oxen, sheep and goats could move about without risk of being shot. No vehicle or bicycle could be used at any time. All dogs had to be tied up twenty-four hours a day, and juveniles under the age of 16 were not permitted to leave their kraals, on pain of being shot. All schools, stores and grinding-mills were closed.

Ten days after the curfew was imposed security forces raided St Andrew's mission in the southern part of Maranke and arrested Father Alexander Sakaramombe. The police Member-in-Charge, a white, twice struck Father Sakaramombe in the face before giving orders that he, three Sisters, three working-girls and an orphan girl be taken to Mutsago camp to be 'sorted out'. On arrival at this Special Branch camp the priest was put in a cage made of pig wire measuring 2 metres long, 1½ metres wide and 2 metres high. The Sisters and girls were thrown into similar cages, which remained open to the weather day and night.

During the following week (according to Sakaramombe, on whose veracity we here depend) the Sisters and girls were severely assaulted with an iron bar and subjected to electric-shock treatment by the Member-in-Charge and his men. The main assaults on the priest himself took place on 14 and 17

February and were carried out by a black Special Branch officer called Sithole who insisted that he confess to having killed and cooked a sheep for terrorists, having washed their clothes, treated their wounds, and housed them in the mission church. Beaten until he could no longer stand, Father Sakaramombe collapsed and signed a confession implicating the Sisters and the wives of the teachers at the mission. Finally set free on 23 February, he was so weak that it took him three hours to cover the five kilometres to St Andrew's.

Father Desmond Clarke, a Carmelite priest who had been deputizing for Donal Lamont since the Catholic Bishop of Umtali was deported, made strenuous efforts to reach Sakaramombe and the Sisters but Maranke remained under curfew, no one could enter it without permission and the Manicaland authorities detested the Church. The following passages are taken from Father Clarke's letter to Bishop Lamont (then in Ireland), dated 18 April:

'I tried every means possible to get to visit them, but all efforts through the CID, the DC, the Joint Operations Command, and the lawyers were unsuccessful.

'I brought the matter to the new Delegate for the International Committee of the Red Cross, and he tried to get in, but was refused by the DC, the PC [Provincial Commissioner Bob Cunliffe], Head Office of Internal Affairs and also Foreign Affairs. On 21 March (Tuesday in Holy Week) I went to Salisbury and got to see Muzorewa. I put the whole matter before him, pointed out that he was now going to be equally responsible with Ian Smith for what went on in Maranke, and asked him to have the harsh curfew restrictions removed. He said he couldn't promise me the moon, but would do all he could. Then I made an appointment with the Police Commissioner, Peter Allum, for 7 a.m. the following morning. Although I was told I could have ten minutes, I was still there one hour later. I pulled no punches and told him all about the beatings etc. He was (or appeared to be) horrified to hear that a priest and nuns could have been beaten up. I told him that I objected to being refused all contact with the Mission personnel, and I asked that the phone be restored and that I be allowed to visit the Mission. He said that he would get in touch with the Governing Authority for Manicaland, Assistant Commissioner Rich.

'That afternoon I returned to Umtali ... eventually he [Rich] granted permission for me to go into the Maranke despite the curfew etc. I asked that I be allowed to travel in the International Red Cross vehicle. . . . We loaded the Toyota Land Cruiser with two tons of food and medicines and set off early on Thursday morning. There were three of us – André Tieche [the IRC Delegate who was destined to be killed by guerrillas on 18 May while driving the same

Toyota with a Red Cross colleague in the Nyamaropa TTL north of Inyanga], his African Field Assistant and myself. As we turned into Zimunya we strapped ourselves securely in the seat harness. . . . Going through Maranke at 9 a.m. under the special curfew conditions was quite eerie. At what should have been a very busy time of day, there was no sign of life or movement. It might as well have been midnight. The cattle were all in their kraals, and no human dared to move for fear of being shot.

'Yet we knew that we were somehow under observation from the hills and wondered how many pairs of eyes were following our progress. . . . Our eyes were straining to detect any tell tale sign of landmines. All the schools, stores and grinding-mills were closed and shuttered. Some stores had been burnt out. Others even had their window and door spaces bricked up. Talk about a ghost town!

'At last we came within sight of St Andrew's. When we got to the gate of the Mission we could see the Sisters peeping out . . . not knowing who their visitors might be . . . when they heard the truck coming they feared it meant the soldiers again. After all, only the Security Forces had been allowed to use any vehicle in Maranke for more than two months!

'. . . the villagers are suffering because, although it has been a very good year for crops, the curfew regulations do not allow them to supervise the fields except between 12 noon and 6 p.m. As a result, the baboons have just helped themselves and the crops are lost to the people.

'We did a tour of the clinic and the Red Cross man nearly cried when he saw how many beds were unoccupied. Before the curfew the place was overflowing. . . .

'I offered to take all of the Mission personnel out of Maranke . . . but every one of them insisted on staying. They said they wanted to be with the people not just in good times, but in bad also. . . . The one thing they fear is to be beaten up again. If they were to live for 100 years they would never forget their experiences in the Camp.

'My special courier has arrived so I must get this into his hands. We are all well here. Hope you are fit.

'God bless!

'Des.'

18. they didn't seem pleased

The local Salisbury Chairman of Christian Care, Dr Oliver Munyaradzi, was living under constant police surveillance. I finally made contact with him through a medical colleague at Harare Hospital.

When he returned to Rhodesia in October 1971, Munyaradzi was the first black Zimbabwean to have graduated as a Fellow of the Royal College of Surgeons. Within days he was summoned to the large, four-storey, cream-painted building on the corner of Railway Avenue and Inez Terrace (telephone 700171) where four Special Branch officers, of whom three were white, interrogated him, two at a time, waving dossiers under his nose and making it chillingly clear that they could itemize every political meeting he had attended during his student years in London and Glasgow.

'They invited me to turn informer. I refused. They didn't seem pleased.'

Although appointed Senior Registrar, then Consultant, at Harare Hospital, he refused to lead a quiet life and prosper as a member of the rising black bourgeoisie. He angered white medical opinion not only by setting up a part-time private practice in Highfield, but, more seriously, by founding the Zimbabwe Medical Association, a rallying point for black doctors opposed to any form of quasi-military national service.

In July 1976 four CID officers, two of them white, arrived at his home in the African township at about 7 in the evening. Having driven everyone out of the house they carried away his cheque-books, journals, correspondence and – most serious – a manuscript he had been writing about political detainees. 'Unfortunately the book, though fictionalized, culminated in a violent revolutionary climax.' The police also searched his Highfield surgery, accusing him of having bought penicillin in bulk to pass on to terrorists.

'A child from the Mount Darwin area had been brought to me with a badly smashed finger. The boy was a nephew of the UANC Treasurer, the Reverend Kanodereka. He was in my surgery when the police arrived. They wanted to know why he wasn't being treated in hospital and whether he had really hurt his finger in a grinding-mill or as a result of a firearms accident.'

Two days later Munyaradzi was again summoned to Special Branch headquarters on Railway Avenue. On this occasion the interrogators told him their names: one of them was called Thompson or Thomson.

'They asked me why I have received letters from prominent nationalists, and why some of them ended with greetings in the form of slogans. They wanted to know if I was a member of the UANC and they reminded me of my responsibilities as a high-ranking civil servant. Again I was invited to turn informer.'

A month later, on 23 August, 1976, he was about to enter the operating-theatre in Harare Hospital when he was summoned to the office of the Medical Superintendent.

'I went down there in my white operating clothes. Two Special Branch men handed me a detention order and asked me whether I would walk out quietly. The Superintendent went to fetch my street clothes.'

Taken to Chikurubi prison north of Salisbury, he was first put in a cell measuring two metres by three metres with two other prisoners. There were no beds. The latrine bucket was emptied once a day. The diet consisted of sadza and bits of 'African meat', scrag-ends: 'I hardly ate for three days.'

His wife Muriel's first permitted visit, seven days after his arrest, was terminated after ten minutes – they had not been allowed to touch each other. The following day, handcuffed, he was put in a truck under armed guard and driven some 400 kilometres to Buffalo Range prison in the south-east Low Veld. Here his head was shaved and he was dressed in prison fatigues, shorts and a shirt. However, his educational qualifications, job and high salary entitled him to Scale 1 treatment (the formula by which the prison service attempted to disguise the racial basis of its highly discriminatory treatment of prisoners). He was now alone in a cell equipped with a bed, a sheet and blanket, and also a flush toilet with a seat. The food improved and he was granted access to medical textbooks, magazines and novels – but newspapers arrived with their political contents clipped out. When he asked for a radio he was refused. He was allowed to write to his wife once a week.

'But I felt myself to be virtually in solitary confinement. I asked to be transferred to Gatooma and they eventually granted this after I agreed to receive Scale 2 treatment.'

This move, which took place on 22 October 1976, resulted in a stroke of good fortune: Munyaradzi found himself sharing a cell with a veteran nationalist who was one of the founding members of Zanu, Enos Nkala. Three and a half years later Robert Mugabe appointed Nkala Minister of Finance – with Oliver Munyaradzi as his Deputy Minister. Clearly the two prisoners hit it off.

On 21 November he was brought to Salisbury to attend his Review Tribunal. Though, of course, detainees never faced formal charges, they were often presented by the Tribunal with a list of allegations about themselves, and then invited to prove their 'innocence'. Once again he was appalled by the efficiency of the intelligence system operated by Pretoria and Salisbury. There were thirty-two 'accusations'. Why had he agitated for Nkomo to be expelled from the ANC when he began to negotiate with Smith? Why was he reluctant to give medical treatment to members of the security forces, preferring to treat terrorists? Why had he attended a memorial service in Bulawayo for Herbert Chitepo, a leading Zanu activist who had been killed by a bomb in Lusaka in 1975? Why had Munyaradzi invited Ndabaningi Sithole (still classified as a terrorist at this juncture) to his home in Bulawayo?

Why had Munyaradzi been out late on the very night that a grenade was thrown into a Salisbury restaurant?

After four months in gaol he was suddenly released from Gatooma on 22 December 1977. A restriction order obliged him to report to the Special Branch once a week (later mitigated to once a month), to remain within twenty kilometres of the city centre, and not to engage in 'subversive activities'.

'From time to time they lectured me on the futility of armed struggle.'

As soon as he had been arrested Munyaradzi had been summarily dismissed by Harare Hospital. Ten weeks after his release he was granted reinstatement on condition that he closed his private practice.

I asked him which nationalist party he supported. He sat on the veranda of a house in Highlands staring at a large and exotic garden – a house and garden which no African was as yet legally entitled to buy. He smiled faintly:

'Do you know what all the UANC leaders are busy doing? Buying white farms, putting away money: Dumbutshena has one north of Salisbury, Chikerema has one in the Selous–Hartley area, and Mundawarara has bought one at Norton. Meanwhile the freedom fighters are dying in the bush.'

'So you support Mugabe?'

He rose to his feet, offered his hand and drove away.

The new, multiracial Transitional Government began to release detainees in April. By the 29th, 703 had been released but 250, including the Rev. Canaan Banana, remained incarcerated.

In 1982 Oliver Munyaradzi was appointed Minister of Health.

19. all Africans are burglars

Segregated housing tormented the black middle class. Denis Hills records how, at Gwelo Teachers' College (where a racially mixed staff of forty taught 450 black students), there was a shortage of staff accommodation. The surplus white teachers moved into the comfortable residential areas of Gwelo while the black staff were forced to seek places in the African locations of Ascot and Mkoba, rows of matchboxes, overcrowded and far away.

Despite the amendment to the Land Tenure Act, the regime staged a last-ditch defence of segregated housing. In defiance of the law, middle-class blacks began to buy property in the less fashionable districts reserved to whites like Southerton and Houghton Park. In Houghton Park estate agents began selling three- or four-room bungalows in 1,000-square-metre plots to Africans capable of putting down a $(R)1,500 deposit and paying $(R)65 a month towards the price of $(R)15,000. About thirty Africans, mainly doctors, civil servants and lawyers, bought houses, creating a hostile backlash from the poor whites who lived in the area, many of them Portuguese refugees from Angola and Mozambique. The wife of a welder from Angola complained that the blacks upset her dogs, who had been trained to regard all Africans as burglars. One of the 'burglars' who bought a house in Houghton Park was the Rev. Ndabaningi Sithole. On the night of 5 September 1977 police called on thirty-five black families living in this suburb and questioned them about how they came to buy their houses; the estate agents seemed to be the immediate target.

Mrs Florrie Adams, a Coloured woman whose son was serving in the security forces, had illegally bought a house for $(R)13,000 in the white suburb of Prospect. After two years Salisbury Council voted by 18 to 5 to evict her – title-deeds to her property contained a restrictive clause barring its sale to Coloureds, and the Council was legally obliged to enforce the clause. Meanwhile black children who had moved with their parents into Houghton Park and Southerton were refused admission to local white schools even though these schools were more than half empty.

Minister of Housing Irvine ordered a crackdown. Estate agents began to receive letters from Salisbury City Council ordering them to remove illegal tenants. In October the Attorney-General, Brendan Treacy, announced that certain estate agents would be invited to pay deposit fines for having contravened the law. In November Chief Jeremiah Chirau, President of the Council of Chiefs and formerly a Minister in the Smith Government, was refused permission to buy a house in the white suburb of Belvedere.

On 27 January 1978 harassment of the estate agents went a step further when Cyril Weiman of Seltrust Estates and a sub-agent, Algie van del Waal, were brought before Harare Magistrates' Court and accused of having leased a house in Parktown to Hamilton Soko, an African. On 24 March the *Herald* reported that six estate agents had appeared before the Estate Agents' Council, a statutory body with power to fine and to suspend or cancel registration. Admitting having negotiated four illegal deeds of sale in Houghton Park, Leslie Torry pleaded that the practice of leasing to Coloureds who subleased to blacks was already widespread.

Early in April a row blew up when Salisbury City Council voted by 15 to 9 to postpone discussion of segregation zones for another year. On 29 March Irvine went into conclave with the more reactionary councillors and urged them to procrastinate yet again. Said Councillor Charles Antlett: 'We know very sensitive discussions are going on. Any attempt to meddle in these affairs could be mischievous.'

Muzorewa delivered a speech deploring the delays in removing discrimination but displayed a bizarre sense of locale by doing so in Johannesburg. Meanwhile, Air Rhodesia brought in blacks as hostesses and ticket clerks, restructured itself into eight staff grades, and placed all whites in the top two grades. It was not until January 1979 that a parcel of six bills wiped out the Land Tenure Act. The new Public Premises (Prevention of Racial Discrimination) Act outlawed the barring of people from public places because of their colour. All ranks of the police were opened to blacks.

In mid-June 1979 it was reported that, during the three months since the repeal of the Land Tenure Act became effective, an average of six houses a week had been bought by blacks in areas hitherto reserved for white owners.

20. coffee country

Main Street, Chipinga, resembles a mechanized version of a Wild West frontier town. The street is choked with baroque armoured vehicles out of Special Effects; young women stroll into the lounge of the Chipinga Hotel casually bearing Uzi sub-machine-guns under their lovely arms. Soldiers everywhere. Farmers arrive in tractors, deposit loads at the Farmers' Co-Op, pick up sacks of grain from the Afrikaner merchants, lay in household stocks from the Indian stores. Africans are gathered round the Total garage waiting for seats on the morning bus which arrives from Umtali, under armed escort, bringing mail and newspapers.

The local school for white kids is surrounded by a wire fence three metres high; so dangerous are the roads into town from the farming areas that most of the children are now weekly boarders. The great fear among the parents is that one day the terrs will take white children as hostages; the great fear among the kids is that they'll lose one or both parents before the weekend. By December 1978, thirty-four of the 168 children at Chipinga School will have lost at least one parent in the war.

The rolling border country round Chipinga was thinly settled during the early years of the century by Afrikaner cattle men who believed – according to their own legend – that the size of a man's farm should be the distance he could travel on horseback in a single day. Later, during the 1960s, the Government encouraged a new breed of settler by breaking up the 4,000-hectare ranches into coffee plantations. Despite sanctions, the coffee was now earning Rhodesia about $(R)20 million a year in badly needed foreign exchange. Fortunes were being made. A farmer who had brought only £300 when he arrived from England in 1951 reckoned he could now sell his Chipinga farms for the equivalent of £400,000. 'This area will never realize its potential under African management,' said Jim Robinson, Secretary to Chipinga District Council. 'The West is mad to let go. . . .' Robinson threatened to 'destroy every frigging thing' if forced to leave.

The killing season came to Chipinga on 8 June 1976, with an unimaginably horrific landmine explosion. A woman, her two daughters and one of her husband's daughters by a previous marriage were all killed; a 16-year-old girl lost both her legs. More recently, on 29 September 1977, there had been the notorious murder of a white baby, Natasha Glenny, daughter of an employee of the Rhodesian Wattle Company working in the Chipinga area. On the last day of 1977 John Henry was murdered at Ombersley Farm by guerrillas who had twice before visited his compound to ask how much he paid his work-force and whether he was a good man. Henry's foreman was brought to trial, accused of having informed the terrorists about when Henry would next visit his dip tank and how best he could be ambushed. The police set fire to all the huts in the compound and systematically destroyed the labourers' belongings.

The forest estates of the Rhodesian Wattle Company press menacingly on both sides of the Eastern Border Road. Then you break out into European farming land, a pretty patchwork-quilt of greens, of neat tea and coffee plantations banked on their hillsides like the vineyards of the Côte-d'Or in Burgundy, before reaching rougher country with long, straggling coarse grass, good for Brahman cattle and Zanla guerrillas.

Cumberland Farm is surrounded by trees and a security fence. The gates are padlocked. Two large dogs bound across the lawn and rear up, their paws gripping the wire, aggression spurting from their throats, hot of tongue and terrible of jaw. Sasha Randall follows them at a leisurely pace, wearing jeans and chewing gum: 'It's all right,' she says, 'you're white.' I drive in and she locks the gate behind me even though it's mid-morning. Two mine-proofed Land-Rovers and a new (diesel) Mercedes stand in the front drive. Workmen are putting the finishing touches to new stables. New wealth, new everything. Sasha's husband Roy is away, maybe on reserve duty, perhaps abroad, in Kenya, Latin America, somewhere. Sasha is not explicit about it.

A coffee-bush is about a metre and a quarter high, its leaves a dark olive green, its red-brown berries forming in grapelike clusters. Coffee needs heat plus humidity – a high annual rainfall – which is why it thrives in this south-eastern corner of Rhodesia; a demanding mistress, requiring five to seven years of continuous investment from first planting to the first profitable yield, years of mounting debt as $(R)50,000 a year is invested in fertilizer and the insecticide required to keep at bay the deadly fusarium bark disease. But the investment has now paid off; with a crop failure in Brazil skyrocketing the price of coffee on the world market (enraging consumers in New York who threaten to kick the habit altogether), the Randalls are selling coffee beans at $(R)2,400 a tonne.

Of 300 hectares they have planted fifty with coffee. The boom brings an annual profit of close to $(R)500,000. Yet the Randalls' wage bill for 250 workers amounts to only $(R)30,000 a year – less than the outlay on fertilizer. The basic wage is 40 cents a day, with bonuses for additional productivity during the harvest, so a young black afire with fitness and ambition might earn a dollar a day at certain times of the year – but the average is well below that. Of course, if the Randalls paid higher wages it would (a) upset neighbouring white farmers, (b) attract hundreds of applicants for whom there are no jobs, (c) create a precedent, (d) destabilize your kaffir, and (e) lead to drunkenness and loose living.

The Randalls have been advised by their accountant to buy an aeroplane as soon as possible.

Her dogs mean a lot to Sasha and she naturally inoculates them against rabies. They finished off one rabid jackal outside the farm gate; she kicked it into a sack and took it to the vet, who confirmed it. She chews gum a lot and carries around a heavy machine-pistol with a gas-operated bolt. Police Reserve duty takes care of her mornings – voluntary, of course, since Rhodesia, unlike beleaguered Israel, does not conscript women. As she talks about life in the police radio room her hands flutter and tug at her long blonde hair, as if she is trying to pluck an idea – or some final truth – out of her skull. One day they brought in 'a terr, wheels up', one of several Zanla men killed in action on the Eastern Border Road. On his body they found a diary, written in English and dating back three years; reading it, Sasha discovered a man and when she saw his corpse laid out on the slab, shot in the back, she had to leave the room to cope with her tears.

'I'm not at all political,' she says, 'but I don't think the whites had any bloody right to take the Africans' land and impose their own culture and their own God. I used to think of terrs as punk thugs until the truth dawned. That dead terr wasn't so much an eye-opener as the dot at the end of a sentence.'

Recently the Randalls suffered three successive robberies at their store. As a result they installed Adams grenades, triggered by nylon trip-wires, plus claymore bombs in the roof designed to blow to pieces anyone who got that far.

'Actually,' Sasha promises, 'Jack Knight and I are going to rev the store this afternoon. You're welcome to come – you won't like it, but then nor do I.'

Jack Knight is an officer of the Special Branch. He wears suede shoes, long socks, absurdly abbreviated shorts and an FN rifle, which he props against the wall as he sinks into one of Sasha's deep armchairs and drinks the first of three cups of coffee. Jack smokes heavily; in the course of time he will surreptitiously spell out my name on the back of the cigarette-packet. Sasha, a friend of Jack's — 'he's a crack shot' — confesses this to me on the following day, as a sporting gesture, throwing in the information that Jack is presently busy reconditioning captured terrs for the Selous Scouts. Then claps hand to mouth, woman-wise: 'My God, perhaps I'm not supposed to tell you that!' With Sasha the air is always thick with exclamation marks.

Jack's problem is Rhodesia's: too many sacks of mealie meal have been spotted moving towards the Mozambique border ten kilometres away, which means the terrs are getting food. It's Jack's job to stop them 'feeding' (Rhodesians use this demeaning animal term, like the German *fressen*) when he can't interrogate or kill them. The problem is compounded by the high proportion of migrant labour from Mozambique working on Chipinga farms. He accepts another cup of coffee.

It being Saturday afternoon, we set out in convoy, heading for the Randalls' store. I ride in the front vehicle with Jack, who slots his FN into a swivel mount fixed to the windscreen frame, allowing him to drive with one hand and blast the gooks with the other. Born in Rhodesia, he paid his first visit to England two years ago, on holiday. Rhodesian passport no problem at all: between British cops and those of the illegal regime, as between the two military-intelligence outfits, it's kith and kin and straight through Nothing to Declare. Counter-insurgency is an international business: didn't Robert Mugabe express admiration for the IRA?

But what's most immediately on Jack's mind is the five-kilo ration of mealies issued every week to each black family on production of a ration card issued by the European farmer.

'You get storekeepers intimidated into handing out more than the ration. The excess goes to the gooks. But the biggest problem is when families sell their own surplus rations.'

We roar up to the store, the white cop revving his engine like a Hell's Angel, for effect. Unhooking his FN from its swivel mount, he strides into the store and empties it of men, women and children with a slight nod of his blond kopf. Wide-eyed and silent, the Africans slip back and out, into Africa. Born to rule, fat Jack. He fires angry questions at the storeman and Boss Boy but the two blacks remain impenetrable, gesturing innocently, showing the pink palms of their brown hands, knowing nothing. Jack issues warnings then growls away on angry tyres, spurting red dust, into a world he knows well but understands not at all.

21. you are the gazanga

Round the roadside stores and beerhalls of rural Chipinga people stand in Saturday-afternoon clusters, resplendent in their primrose frocks, their best jackets. But they give nothing away beyond the most neutral of stares if one lifts a paw in passing greeting – and why should one expect otherwise, war or no war? Would you drive through a French village blowing kisses?

The turnings off the Eastern Border Road reflect the Afrikaner influence: Randfontein Road, Boosklov Road. . . . Here Fanie Breytenbach is lord and master – though Zanla disputes it – of 2,800 hectares of rough, hilly cattle country criss-crossed by dirt tracks which the vakhomana periodically dig up or mine. One of Breytenbach's cousins had been ambushed on this terrain while driving with his wife and three young children, all of them suffering multiple bullet wounds and only just making it to the safety of Fanie Breytenbach's homestead.

The homestead stands on high ground and is surrounded by a security fence two metres high. The dogs which race snarling and salivating towards the locked perimeter gate almost persuade me back into the car, despite the fence between us. Breytenbach takes his time letting me in, talking his dogs out of their murderous intentions. He looks older than his 41 years. We sit on the stoep. His wife brings tea on a tray, though it's obvious Breytenbach has been on something stronger all morning. She's pale and pretty, with swellings under her eyes suggesting contusions of matrimonial derivation. The two young boys, home for the weekend, are rushing round the grass with wooden guns, playing at 'security forces and terrs'. The previous week they had been travelling with their aunt in the Umtali–Chipinga convoy when it had been ambushed at Hot Springs. At school they undergo regular practice alarms, scrambling for underground shelters as if under mortar attack.

'You'd think they'd no longer see it as a game,' I suggest.

Breytenbach shrugs. 'Kids are kids. But life is no good here any more. They used to roam around this farm and go fishing on their own. That's no longer on.'

Suddenly he is yelling at his most savage dog in guttural Afrikaans, while Mrs Breytenbach, for no discernible reason, is triggered into the same performance towards her sons. Breytenbach fondles the dog's hideous jaws tenderly. 'He won't let any munt into this yard. They beat this poor animal with iron bars when they came here, those terrs.'

'When was that?'

'Two months ago.'

He seems reluctant to pursue the subject, it's too recent, too intimate and painful. I ask him about his family background, the history of the farm. This subject obviously appeals to him.

'My people came up from the Free State several generations back. My grandad arrived in 1902. My father was born near Chipinga in 1910. It was sheep, cattle and wheat in those days, an escape from the overcrowded farm lands in the South. Life wasn't easy; one woman died of black fever soon after arrival.' He speaks slowly, deliberately, courteously; whatever his private opinion of persons such as myself, I am a guest and the code of hospitality is absolute.

Breytenbach owns 900 head of cattle and grows tea. If sanctions were lifted, he says, the price of tea would be much higher – he curses the 'bleddy South African middleman'. And the future? There has to be a settlement, but outsiders should get off Rhodesia's back and stop interfering. As for the breakaway Rhodesian Action Party, you could sympathize with their feelings but he, Breytenbach, remained where he had always been, 100 per cent behind Ian Smith. The main thing was to smash terrorism.

'A lot of it is just banditry, the easy life, robbing the stores. The section leaders are sometimes switched-on types, they keep diaries and their medical kits are impressive. They often carry a large shoulder bag made of real leather, along with their AKs, RPGs and rockets. One terr I killed was wearing green trousers and a light green shirt decorated with dark green patches. Some of them are girls.'

'You killed one yourself?'

He nods, frontier-style. 'I was tipped off that we had eight gooks in my general store.'

'Eight!'

'I went down there, killed one and injured seven. One of the injured gooks got away without his shoes. I nailed those shoes to the door and told my kaffirs this was bad magic and would make that terr hobble. Later I ambushed that same terr at the other end of this farm and killed him.'

The most recent attack on the Breytenbach homestead had taken place while the family was away in Salisbury. The guerrillas had stolen some gramophone records including one by a Rhodesian comedian who specialized in 'taking the mickey out of munts'. But, instead of burning the place down, they had left a note, a sheet of lined paper, folded twice. In the top left-hand corner is a drawing which would disgrace a 6-year-old, portraying two male figures, probably a freedom fighter and Breytenbach. Instead of a date is the curious word 'Ditto'. The letter begins 'Dear Fanny' and is full of mocking 'dear Fanny's' as well as one passage addressed to 'Dear Mrs Fanny'.

A skull and cross-bones appears crudely inked on the middle of the page, which is divided into four boxes of equal size.

The police told Breytenbach that the letter was the work of two hands. The handwriting is legible. Although difficult words like 'characteristic' are spelled correctly, the prose periodically lapses into pidgin: 'Fanny boy, it is not we who are Terrorists, it is you who are Terrorist, you are the Gazanga. It is not your skin we against, boy, it is you and we warn we after you. We are going to Mozambique now but we will be back and then we come and discuss this with you and then it be your time to get dying. You better take our word and get out, Fanny, and leave that stick of you and no more shoes. Mrs Fanny, we don't want hurt you but we kill you and children unless you take our message.'

Here Fanie Breytenbach offers a few scholarly footnotes. 'Stick' in this context means gun. The reference to 'no more shoes' indicates a desire to avenge the nailing of the wounded guerrilla's shoes to the store door.

When I rose to leave neither of the Breytenbachs begged me to stay. Maybe the Saturday-afternoon bottle beckoned Fanie; but no doubt my pseudo-sympathetic mewings sounded as hollow to him as to me.

I learned some months later that the Breytenbachs had abandoned their farm.

In Chipinga the cemetery continued to fill. On 8 March 1978, J. Reyneke; on 17 March, Miss Y. Nicol; on 12 April, G. Swartz.

Grantley Swartz, a married man with four children, employed by the Southdown Tea Estate since 1961, was driving along the Eastern Border Road about three kilometres from the border when he ran into a group of guerrillas. He opened fire with his pistol, they returned fire, no one was hit. But then, according to press reports, he stopped his car further down the road, got out, and received a fatal wound in the stomach.

On 10 June Mrs Catherine Willers, a farmer's wife and mother of two in her mid-40s, was driving along a dirt track from Berry Hill Farm to Chipinga at 7.45 in the morning when her vehicle was hit by a rocket. She was killed. Her husband, Hans Willers, was driving behind her in a second vehicle. Mrs Willers had been a volunteer police reservist who did stints of duty in the Chipinga radio control room.

On 6 July, K. Gifford; on 18 August, M. Cremer; on 29 September, P. H. Fairbanks; on 20 December, W. Bezuidenhout; on 9 January 1979, Miss H. Turner and Miss S. Turner; on 28 January, H. du Plessis . . .

22. shooting from the hip

Despite the Gandhian legacy of Martin Luther King, Andrew Young did not disavow the armed struggle waged by the Patriotic Front. What he did do was to interpret it as a variant of the non-violent campaigns inspired by Gandhi and Martin Luther King. Josiah Tongogara, the Zanla commander, had assured Young that his forces fought only when attacked (well, mainly); most of the time they held meetings, spread the word, sang songs – just like the civil-rights movement in the Deep South!

Young described both Mugabe and Nkomo as gentle fellows, incapable of firing a gun, of killing. The trouble with Mugabe was that he was 'so damned incorruptible. He's inflexible.' Mugabe rejected the compromises that Young and Owen regarded as necessary for a settlement; he wanted everything now. 'The problem is he was educated by Jesuits and when you get the combination of a Jesuit and a Marxist kind of ideology merging in one person, you've got a hell of a guy to deal with,' explained Young.

Rhodesian fury mounted when Owen and Young countered Smith's internal negotiations by meeting the PF in Malta. But the Anglo-American plan had now become hopelessly bogged down. Although the military integration proposals put forward by Carver and the UN's General Prem Chand were acceptable to the PF, the British idea of a Governing Council consisting of Carver, a UN representative, and two members each from Zapu, Zanu, the UANC, ANC (Sithole) and the RF was most definitely not. Indeed Mugabe and Nkomo were infuriated by the British tendency to treat them on a par with Muzorewa and Sithole. Besides, any such scheme would put the PF in a clear minority during the transition. For his part Owen was determined that the Commissioner (Iron-Man Carver) would retain total control over defence and internal security. The PF didn't like it.

Two years later, when Lord Soames became Governor with precisely those powers, the PF's persistent suspicions were confirmed when the Governor unleashed Walls's rednecks and black auxiliaries. More accurately, they unleashed themselves.

The Owen–Young plan enjoyed bipartisan support neither in Britain nor the USA. On 2 February Owen was heckled in the Commons following his return from Malta. John Davies, Opposition spokesman on Foreign Affairs, accused him of pandering to the PF's determination to achieve its ends through the barrel of a gun. Reginald Maudling, referring to the Salisbury talks between Smith, Muzorewa and Sithole, challenged Owen: 'This is the most hopeful thing that has happened in Rhodesia in years. Why in the name of heaven don't you welcome it?' Winston Churchill, Jr, Opposition spokesman on Defence and an ardent Rhodesia lobbyist, remarked of Owen: 'You could forgive the arrogance if he wasn't so wrong-headed about everything. It seems to me he's become Andy Young's poodle.'

It was not so much Tory criticism that led Owen to change his tone after his return from Malta as his desire to bully the PF into a more accommodating posture. In the Commons he called the Salisbury Agreement a 'significant advance'. On TV he said that Smith had now come a long way, though he still had 'quite a long way to go'. Behind the scenes the Foreign Office was praying for a 'Nkomo solution'. Sithole stirred things when he released the minutes of what he claimed the Foreign Secretary had said to him in London in mid-February: 'The further you go down this road without Joshua, the harder it would be for him to come. The noise that he makes does not worry me. His problem is that he cannot be seen to be breaking from Robert Mugabe before he gets a concrete offer. . . . Before he breaks with Robert, he must be assured of success.' After a meeting with Carter, Owen told the Pilgrims' dinner that Britain and the United States were not prepared to condemn out of hand those aspects of the Salisbury Agreement which conformed to the Anglo-American plan.

Meanwhile Andrew Young had his back to the wall. Cyrus Vance was angered by Young's instantaneous denunciation of the internal settlement on 15 February. The President's National Security Adviser, Zbigniew Brzezinski, clearly favoured a solution which would thwart the Communist-backed PF. On 22 February the State Department described the Salisbury Agreement as a 'significant step' – but still preferred the Anglo-American plan. Depressed by the isolationist attitude of the British press and public, and by an undertone of racism in popular attitudes towards Rhodesia, Young resorted to undiplomatic language: 'What are they [the British] going to do – run out and leave us with thirty years of trouble the way they did in 1948?' (The reference was to British withdrawal from Palestine.) Arriving back the following day from his meeting with Carter, Owen said at Heathrow: 'Well, I know and like Andy. And he's made a few statements like this before. I tend to . . . I am very glad he has withdrawn it. But (a laugh) he does sometimes shoot from the hip a bit.' Two months later Young explained: 'My intention in saying what I did was to help strengthen David's position against the pressures he is resisting.'

23. who?

Those who wished they were better informed – to paraphrase the famous *Times* advertisement – turned to the Rhodesian Promotion Council, 'an independent, non-political . . . organisation which aims to promote knowledge of Rhodesia's economic development and potential'. In 1977–9 it spent $(R)68,000 on visitors and 'promotion expenditure'. It brought South African businessmen to Salisbury and it worked hard and effectively to convince the black political parties that when they inherited the political kingdom they would be wise to leave the economic kingdom in the hands of white entrepreneurs.

To this end lavish trips were laid on to visit farms and irrigation schemes in the Low Veld, Dunlop and Supersonic in Bulawayo, United Oil Refineries, Rhodesian Alloys, tobacco farms . . . perpetual flattery. It worked. The internal representatives of Nkomo's party went along with it as willingly as the Bishop's. The moving spirit behind all this was the Chairman of the RPC, C. G. Tracey, also Chairman of a major tobacco auction house.

The RPC offices were located on the fourteenth floor of an office block on Jameson Avenue, Salisbury. David Brewer, a former tobacco dealer wiped out of business by the first impact of sanctions, had served as the RPC's Director for ten years. He now lived out of town and was preoccupied by the problem of obtaining a gun licence for his wife: should he apply to the local police or the DC? But what was Brewer's opinion of the economic philosophies of the various black parties?

'They have no ideas at all,' he snapped. 'What we'll have here is a black Minister and a white Under-Secretary who tells him what to do. Hearing Chinamano talking to Asian businessmen about socialism made me feel sick.'

What made Brewer even sicker was the current behaviour of Owen and Young:

'Tracey wants to explain Rhodesia's position at the UN. But they won't give him a visa to enter the United States. We used to think David Owen was a good chap, we thought we would at least get a square deal out of him. When he was here in April '77 we took twenty-seven black business and professional men to meet him at Marimba House.' Brewer stared at me intently, the easy geniality draining from his face. 'Owen is a double-crossing lying bastard! There isn't a single black politician here who wants to deal with him now – nor with Carver. Those Foreign Office bastards, they're all out of Transport House, aren't they, aren't they?'

It was news to me.

'That bastard Owen should be put up against a wall and shot,' snarled Brewer, his face now wholly given over to the dramatization of hatred.

Late one afternoon, to be precise at 4.15 p.m., Brewer telephoned a distinguished British journalist in his Johannesburg hotel. The distinguished journalist, having met many top people in South Africa – Prime Minister

Botha, Harry Oppenheimer – was planning a four-day visit to Rhodesia: quite long enough for an experienced, case-hardened reporter to sniff the wind. The RPC had undertaken to organize the distinguished reporter's royal itinerary, starting with a day-trip on the Sunday to Victoria Falls and lunch at the Casino Hotel with its owner, Donald Goldin, MP for Wankie and Chairman of the Victoria Falls Chamber of Commerce.

Monday would begin with a visit to the Ministry of Information, where Mr Enoch Gloster would invite the distinguished journalist to sign the standard censorship forms . . .

– I'm afraid it's the new regulations, Brewer explained. Later you'll have a briefing at Comops . . .

– At what?

– Combined Operations Headquarters. We'll also get you to see Mr Bulle . . .

– Who?

– One of the bright stars in the Bishop's party.

– What about Muzorewa himself?

– We'll keep trying on that one. Then there's Chinamano . . .

– Who?

– He's vice-president of Nkomo's party inside the country.

– What about Smith?

– Er . . . we're quite hopeful, though it may be only twenty minutes . . .

In the event the distinguished journalist did see Ian Smith. Returning to Britain, he wrote: 'Rhodesians welcome the internal settlement. The black majority and most of the whites are determined to make it work. The violence now engulfing the tribal trust lands is not liberation but a bloody struggle for power between the black parties.'

24. Nkomo and Mugabe

The PF's supporters were thrown into despondency. The 'internal' blacks were making the running and strutting about the capital like cocks. When Owen called the Salisbury Agreement of 3 March a 'step in the right direction', Nkomo was sufficiently rattled to call the Foreign Secretary a 'racist' who 'cannot trust the Patriotic Front but seems to trust Smith'. Arriving in London in mid-March, Nkomo was rumbling like Mount Etna, a huge man, global in girth, with a small head, small hands, small feet. He deports himself like a king in temporary exile; visitors are ushered into his presence for severely curtailed spans of time; they await their turn in the ante-room until an aide summons them. But this is only a hotel; surely Joshua deserves his presidential palace, Government House in Chancellor Avenue, Salisbury, uniformed flunkeys, a broad-based throne to lay his vast haunches upon. He wants power so badly.

Although his hair is greying now, the brown skin remains baby-smooth, without a wrinkle. He is an emotional man who under the stress of questioning tends to miss the word he is seeking and to take refuge in belligerence. In August 1977 he told the *Telegraph*'s A. J. McIlroy: 'We will defeat Smith, you and the *Daily Telegraph*.' The cut-and-thrust of quick exchanges requires sarcasm but Nkomo, as Conor Cruise O'Brien pointed out, embodied Kipling's dual concept of the bear: a cosy paternal Baloo who might just, in some unfortunate conjuncture, rip half your face off. 'He wobbles cumulatively,' wrote O'Brien, 'as if in physical corroboration of the weight of his argument.'

To gain admission you have to telephone his suite from the lobby of the Britannia Hotel. Despite a firm appointment, his aides may not remember anything about it; or they may. You begin by waiting an hour: they are all 'at the Zambian High Commission' (which sounds logical but may not be the case). Jeremy Thorpe, his career not yet in ruins, sweeps into the hotel breezily, reports at reception, hurries into a lift. Presently he emerges, wearing a politician's smile, and vanishes. By coincidence the Liberal leader is soon followed by a Tory whose days, also, are numbered, though for John Davies fate holds in store not scandal and disgrace but illness and death. The Shadow Foreign Minister and his aide arrive looking severely smart and waste no time in glancing meaningfully at their watches.

'Is Mr Nkomo running behind schedule? I have a division in the Commons in forty minutes.'

For several weeks Davies has been pressing the Foreign Secretary to say that the Salisbury Agreement is a major step forward. One imagines that old Baloo will lose no time in ripping away half of Davies's face when the Tory steps into the bear's bedroom.

Nkomo waddles out: only five minutes to go before his scheduled press conference. He beckons me to a chair beside his. Like other men with huge chests he tends to wheeze. He has heard that Garfield Todd's ranch at Hokonui is overrun by guerrillas – including his own – and he prays that they will continue to leave GT alone. Nkomo says, 'I shall be in Zambia at the end of the month, come out and I'll talk to you.' Brashly I declare a desire to be admitted to Zapu's camps. 'Not the training camps,' he says.

Downstairs, Nkomo enters the press conference on time. Mugabe is due to join him but Mugabe isn't there. Finally Mugabe arrives an hour late and wearing an open-neck shirt. They make an incongruous pair: a whale of a shopkeeper, all flesh and emotion, and the ice-cool professor with his long, solemn face perched on a slender, yoga-supple body. Nkomo must regularly clean out the larder like that other bear, Pooh; you can imagine Mugabe picking uninterestedly at a lettuce leaf and a raw carrot. Nkomo is brown, Mugabe is grey-black: he wears glasses and his voice is calm, precise, metallic, often sardonic. 'David Owen is drifting,' he says. 'We're trying to push him back to his own plan. We're not succeeding.'

A South African reporter suggests that it is sanctions, rather than the war, which has an impact on Rhodesia. Mugabe raises his eyebrows. 'Oh really? How many white farms are now deserted? How many whites left the country last year?' Nkomo nods and adds huskily that every male white now spends half the year in the bush.

When the press conference ends Mugabe and Nkomo separate immediately, engulfed by their own aides. It is Mugabe who magnetizes the young reporters; he is the black Robespierre, pure, uncompromising and author of the terror sweeping eastern Rhodesia. It's not a question of physical presence, still less of charisma, for he has little of either: he is a man who has stripped himself down to essentials, he is a distilled man, a general secretary in the Chinese mould. People gather round him – how many Rhodesian commandos dream of getting this close? – the ones at the back straining to catch the sentences he releases softly.

It is said that his power base is insecure; that he is being used as a front before even harder-liners sweep him aside; that he is too intellectual to retain real power. In fact he has recently arrested and thrown into prison some seventy of his colleagues, including such top Zanu leaders as Gumbo and Hamadzaripi. And every quarterly issue of *Zimbabwe News* is packed with photographs of Comrade President Mugabe. Now he stands in the lobby of the Britannia Hotel on a cold March day, wearing a dark overcoat and a Scotch-tartan scarf, edging towards the car waiting outside.

The whites in Rhodesia cannot be treated as a separate and privileged group, he says. Their economic privileges have got to go. 'They just have to go. We must rewrite history.'

He turns and walks out into the cold March wind. Impossible to imagine him wasting an hour in idle relaxation.

25. Owen and Vance in Africa

Right-wing pressure within the United States Congress began to mount. While the black caucus in the House condemned the Salisbury Agreement,

Senator Clifford Case, ranking Republican on the Senate Foreign Relations Committee, described the internal settlement as a 'fair, moderate political solution' – an alternative to the Administration's policy of 'continuing to side with Russian-armed terrorists'. Case accused Young of ignoring the rights of Rhodesia's white minority. But it was Young who was in step with the UN. On 14 March the Security Council found, by 10 votes to none with 5 abstentions, that the internal settlement was 'illegal and unacceptable'.

Vance now decided to go to Africa himself in search of a solution acceptable to all parties – seventeen months had passed since Kissinger beat the same trail.

Cyrus Vance is a WASP, decent, sane, modest; the lines of his face radiate out from the mouth and chin, narrowing where the small eyes meet tightly at the bridge of the nose. When he smiles he is clearly some kind of children's mascot, not a Muppet but possibly a Womble. The tone of his voice is flat, the delivery uninspired, the prose cautious and insipid; unlike Kissinger he could not play the buccaneer or knock heads together.

In Dar es Salaam he and Owen talked to the PF, with Nyerere attempting to bridge the gap. But the PF would concede to Commissioner-designate Carver complete authority over the army and police inside Rhodesia only if the PF were guaranteed eight out of twelve seats on the Governing Council during the transition period. Angry and disappointed, Vance, Young and Owen flew on to Salisbury in a vain effort to organize an all-party conference. But the black internal leaders were brimming over with confidence – or at least determined so to appear. On their way out to the airport for the return journey, Vance and Young were pelted with eggs, tomatoes and bananas by supporters of Chief Chirau – it had not been a happy trip.

The Tories maintained their offensive. In the House of Lords, Lord Home of the Hirsel (alias Sir Alec Douglas-Home, alias Lord Home) deplored the calculated cynicism of the Russians, who equipped PF terrorists and hoped that Africans blinded by the smoke of colonialism would welcome the Cubans as liberators. In the Commons Sir Frederick Bennett likened the PF to the IRA, while John Page, another Tory MP, complained that Labour vilified the white man in Africa.

Returning from his talks in Dar es Salaam and Salisbury, Owen made a major speech to the Commons in which he pledged that if the Salisbury Agreement proved to be demonstrably acceptable to the people of Rhodesia as a whole, and if the internal elections were seen to be free and fair, then Britain would be bound to grant recognition.

26. the Hove affair – in blood stepped in so far

The Hove affair soon brought the internal settlement face to face with its own cosmetic mask; the mask fell away, exposing the livid features of white power under challenge. Byron Hove (pronounced Hovay) was a bright young lawyer practising as a barrister in the Temple when he was summoned – against expectations – by Muzorewa to fill one of only three portfolios granted to the UANC in the Transitional Government. The first black President of the Students' Union in the early 1960s, and later a nationalist detainee, Hove flew from London, took a room in the Monomatapa, and was sworn in as Co-Minister of Justice, Law and Order. He was 38 years old.

What made Hove's appointment particularly bizarre was the fact that only a year previously he had written a diatribe called *Mankind v Ian Smith and Confederates*, arguing on the Nuremberg precedent that the RF leaders should be tried for war crimes. It's not easy to fathom why he agreed to join the Government; unlike Groucho Marx, he perhaps believed that any club that would admit him couldn't be that bad.

From the moment this tall, willowy barrister, supporter in linear succession of Zapu, Zanu and the UANC, stepped into Vincent Buildings he was determined to show he was no stooge. Hove lost no time in asking Police Commissioner Peter Allum to let him see the file the police had compiled on him; Allum replied, 'Now you are a Minister, sir, the file has been destroyed.' When Garnett, a white civil servant with the title of Secretary for Justice, kept referring to 'terrorists', Hove rebuked him. He refused to accept the white woman assigned to him as private secretary and preferred instead to interview candidates from a prepared list – but they were all white women who had worked for the Government before and who spoke not a word of any native language. He declined them all and it was agreed to place an advertisement. None of this was trivial, but it was his public utterances that provoked a furious white riposte. Recalling his own maltreatment by the police, he demanded a complete overhaul of the BSAP including 'positive discrimination' in favour of blacks. In another speech he pointed out that there was not a single African in the upper echelons of any Ministry and that the judiciary contained not a single African judge.

Hove had – knowingly – walked into a hornet's nest. The fury of the privileged, when threatened, always exceeds the anger of the underprivileged when demanding a measure of equity.

In the entire Rhodesian civil service there were 15,000 whites and 25,000 Africans, but in the higher echelons, in the élite Establishment, years of systematic discrimination yielded 8,222 whites and only 1,700 Africans (plus

3,300 Coloureds and Asians). A survey of Government training programmes showed that there was not a single black enrolled in the programmes run by eleven out of eighteen Departments, including Justice, Local Government and Commerce.

Take the case of the Department of Conservation and Extension (Conex). In 1972 its staff included only seven blacks. When a black graduate in agriculture was promoted to a senior post there was such an outcry that the Minister, David Smith, gave orders that it should not happen again. 'One must be careful', he explained, 'to avoid creating circumstances in which friction can occur.'

When the Quenet Commission asked why in 1976 there was as yet not a single black magistrate or public prosecutor, the Chairman of the Public Services Board replied: 'It is to some extent governed by disabilities to which different races are perhaps subjected and one of the main ones here is this question of undue influence being brought to bear on them.'

Or take Internal Affairs (which had almost forgotten more about the real aspiration of the natives than it had ever known). In 1974 the Ministry, staffed by grim Rhodesian Fronters, advised the University that it could not and would not offer cadetships and bursaries to non-Europeans. By 1976 the Ministry had employed not a single black graduate on a permanent basis. The Secretary of Internal Affairs and the Provincial Commissioners argued that racially discriminatory statutes could only benefit the African:

'The great majority of tribesmen will accept that a European DC is impartial. . . .

'. . . there are vast problems attached to the employment of Africans in senior administrative posts in this Ministry by no means the least of these problems being the tribalistic approach of the Rhodesian African . . . and we doubt that the interests of the African would be best served by large-scale Africanization . . . at the present time.'

On the face of it, Smith secured as good a deal for the white civil servants by his internal settlement as could have been dreamed of. Their pensions were to be paid not out of general (potentially bankrupt) funds but out of the Consolidated Revenue Fund. On top of that all pension rights were to be remittable outside the country to civil servants who chose to leave Rhodesia. A man with twenty years' service and a final salary of $(R)10,000 would be entitled to a pension of just under $(R)5,000 a year.

That was all very well, but once you handed over to blacks, never mind your guaranteed constitution, your bill of rights, your entrenched clauses and so on, you might find yourself in a Zimbabwe resembling the Congo, or Angola, or Mozambique, or Zambia – or anywhere! – and then the whites would scuttle and the blacks would come swinging down from the trees eating constitutions and entrenched clauses like so many bananas.

The Public Servants' Association was therefore determined to persuade guess who – the British Government – to guarantee the pensions of Rhodesian civil servants. Far from presenting themselves as hardline Rhodesian Fronters who had welcomed UDI and the uninhibited suppression of black nationalism, the PSA dug up a more appealing collective portrait – dutiful public servants who had loyally stuck to their posts in 1965 on instructions from Britain's Governor, Sir Humphrey Gibbs, and Britain's Prime Minister, H. Wilson.

Unfortunately, however, on 2 March 1970 the British Foreign Secretary, Michael Stewart, had responded to Smith's declaration that Rhodesia was now a republic quite unequivocally: 'The former Governor's injunction has lapsed and those who serve a regime which asserts illegally that Southern Rhodesia is a republic . . . cannot be regarded as serving the Crown. . . .'

The PSA fell back on 'common sense and decency'; had Mr Stewart really wanted 'to destroy the whole fabric of civilization . . .'?

The big guns of the white power structure were soon booming against young Byron Hove. Walls announced that Hove's statements threatened the immunity of the security forces from 'political interference'. Hove's Co-Minister, Hilary Squires, delivered a speech accusing him of ignoring the Salisbury Agreement. On the morning of 19 April Police Commissioner Allum called on Hove and immediately began: 'Minister, I must convey to you the grave concern of my men.' Hove told Allum that his comments were inappropriate from a civil servant to a Minister. Later the same day Hove received a letter from Allum to the effect that Ian Smith, the Prime Minister, had directed Allum and his officers to have no further contact with Byron Hove until the Co-Minister of Justice had withdrawn his offending remarks. At a meeting of the Council of Ministers David Smith read out a directive from the Executive Council (Smith, Muzorewa, Sithole and Chirau) reprimanding Hove and demanding that he publicly withdraw his remarks. Hove refused to do so. Co-Foreign Minister Elliot Gabellah, at that time attached to Sithole's party and a Moral Rearmament sycophant who was among the first to sign the book of condolences when the President of South Africa died, hastened to shine the shoes of all whites present by apologizing for Hove's ignorance of the Salisbury Agreement.

It was in this critical confrontation that Byron Hove's illusions about Bishop Abel Muzorewa began to peel away. Hove went to UANC headquarters in Charter Road to brief the Bishop. 'I can understand why you said what you did,' Muzorewa remarked, 'because of your own experiences in detention, because of your strong principles, and because you are not aware of the give-and-take spirit of the negotiations.' Hove recalls staring at a notice on the wall as he listened to this stunning rebuke: 'For Evil to Succeed It is Enough for Good Men to Do Nothing.'

Later Muzorewa asked Hove to come and see him at his home. The Executive Council, it emerged, could offer him three alternatives: recantation, resignation, dismissal.

'Are you disowning me?' Hove asked the Bishop.

'No.'

On 9 May the Executive Council confirmed Hove's dismissal, Muzorewa pleading with his own party to put 'the national interest' above all other considerations, and appointed Francis Zindoga to fill Hove's portfolio. The UANC continued to issue radical declarations of principle which its leader ignored or violated in practice. By the end of July Hove had broken his last ties with the Bishop, quoting Macbeth in the process:

> . . . I am in blood
> Stepped in so far, that, should I wade no more,
> Returning were as tedious as go o'er.

27. massacres and deaths

On 5 April John Stanley was killed in his farmhouse near Tengwe. His wife Anne survived the attack. Her sister, Mrs Susan Wallace of Thackley, W. Yorks, wrote a letter to the *Daily Telegraph*, denouncing the Labour Government's conciliation of terrorists.

During a four-day period in April there were attacks on four homesteads in the Shamva area, two of which were set alight. In the course of an attack mounted on 10 April at 6.30 in the morning, guerrillas murdered Eric James Hards, a 66-year-old divorced farmer living alone.

On 18 April a truck was ambushed in the Nuanetsi area. A rocket exploded in the cab killing Frederick Pretorius, 45, of Messina in South Africa, and wounding Rudolph van den Heever, of Mateke Hill Ranch, and four Africans travelling in the back of the truck. Pretorius, who was visiting his former home, left a widow and five children.

In the evening of Saturday, 22 April, John Lyster Roberts, 52, father of three children, was murdered on Sheba Estates, Penhalonga. On the same day Arie Mannix Verbeek, 38, was shot by security forces on Lake Kariba while in his own pleasure boat. Not only was Verbeek white, he was also District Commissioner of Binga, Legion of Merit. Apparently he had not informed the police of his intended movements and gave the impression that he was evading a police boat which pursued him.

One of the casualties of the call-up of middle-aged men was a Glendale farmer, Mike Hattingh, who died of a heart attack while undergoing Police Reserve training. Later, at 7 p.m. on the night of 29 April, guerrillas stormed the Hattingh household at Watchfield Farm, having cut the security fencing, and fired point-blank into the rooms, killing the late Mike Hattingh's 13-year-old son Johan. The attackers were beaten off by his elder brother, Derick; one of them committed suicide with a grenade after the boy had wounded him. On the following day van der Byl took the press to the farm and extolled 16-year-old Derick's heroism while the tall, strongly built lad prowled around with an ammunition belt over his shoulder and a 12-bore automatic shot-gun in his hand. Six months later Ian Smith's wife Janet presented Derick with the Meritorious Conduct Medal at Allan Wilson High School.

On the evening of 8 May guerrillas attacked the Montclair Hotel high in the Inyanga mountains, bursting into the dining-room and spraying the room with automatic fire. Mrs Groenewald, a guest from Salisbury, fell dead, as did Mrs Betty Verran, the hotel accountant, who was dining at the time. Assistant Manager Milos Hales and two further white women were wounded. A few seconds later a rifle-grenade hit a window frame of the dining-room and exploded, after which the guerrillas fired three rockets, two of which struck the side of the hotel.

Mrs Verran was clearly an adventurous woman, having worked as a secretary on the Kariba Dam project, on the Rosario Dam project in the Sudan, as general factotum to Randolph Churchill, and then on the Cabora Bassa Dam scheme. Running out of dams, the 69-year-old lady took a job from Mrs Ann Lount, the 70-year-old widow who owned the Montclair Hotel.

The massacre of an entire village by security forces occurred on 14 May. Responding to a summons by guerrillas, about 150 people had gathered in a compound of huts in the Dewure Purchase Area, Gutu. At about 7 p.m. a report reached the elders of the area that a security-force patrol had been sighted, but the guerrilla leader apparently declined to cancel the meeting. At 9.30 p.m. the Zanla commander was addressing the crowd while his seven or eight comrades, dead-drunk, made dalliance with selected ladies in certain huts: a fair example of a Zanla 'pungwe' during the period when guerrilla discipline sank to its nadir.

At 9.30 a single shot, or a burst of machine-gun fire (accounts differ), was fired at the speaker, who fell dead. The people lay flat on the ground. There was no return of fire. After a short pause heavy and sustained firing was directed by the soldiers at the prostrate villagers from extremely close range. One of the drunken guerrillas apparently fired two or three shots from a distance, then made good his escape with his companions. Finally the soldiers withdrew, returning only at dawn, by which time relatives were searching for their dead. The sight and sound of that scene of carnage and horror, the piled-up bodies, the wailing and screaming of the injured and dying, the whimpering of those who had crawled with their wounds into the bush, cannot be fully imagined.

Government statement: 'In the resulting fire-fight 50 curfew breakers were killed and another 24 wounded.' The JPC announced that it had the names of sixty-one people who had died. Another source put the dead at ninety-four (seventy in the kraal compound, twenty in the surrounding bush). Even Muzorewa and Sithole, both members of the Executive Council, blamed the security forces.

But not themselves.

The Salisbury Agreement and the advent of the Transitional Government changed nothing: the security forces continued their policy of indiscriminate slaughter wherever guerrillas were found in the vicinity of a kraal. On the afternoon of 10 June an air strike was launched against a Zanla position on a hill feature near Domboshawa, in the Chinamora TTL. Five of the guerrillas fled into the bush but the sixth was seen to run towards Mashonganyika, whereupon that village was savagely attacked.

Four helicopters were used. Three of them dropped four-man 'sticks' of white troops on the northern edge of the village while the fourth sprayed the area with cannon fire. A ground force of black troops was ordered to sweep the village.

Twenty-two people were killed, nineteen of whom were women and children. Only one was a guerrilla.

The official communiqué put out by Comops claimed that terrorists (plural) together with civilian accomplices had run to the village. . . . The deaths of nine people inside a hut were attributed to a fire and an ammunition explosion. A Special Correspondent of The Times had a look at this hut: 'Its roof was peppered with holes from cannon fire. Inside the floor was a sea of blood and wreckage. From the position of spent cartridge cases, it appeared that troops had fired through the kitchen door from only five yards away.'

Relatives sat weeping and keening next to the dead. Parents pulled back blankets from dead children to show the gaping wounds in their bodies. In the bars, barracks and suburban homes of Salisbury that night the killers drank beer and watched television.

246

28. what are you dying for now?

From the outset it was clear that the internal settlement cut no ice in the countryside. Carefully stage-managed meetings addressed by white and black Ministers flopped miserably, despite instructions to white police reservists to ensure local displays of enthusiasm. When only seven people turned up at Wankie Colliery to hear three Ministers the meeting had to be cancelled. Bulle and two other black Ministers made a most humiliating trip to the Mtoko area in mid-August. In Mudzonga PV 600 people gave them a rough time and cheered Chief Mtoko when he criticized the behaviour of the Guard Force. Later that month Squires, Bulle and Mgutshini waited for an hour for an audience to materialize in Chiota TTL but they waited in vain. Only a stray cow wandered in front of the empty seats spread round the football field.

Disbelief prevailed. Muzorewa came to Mangwende TTL in a white Mercedes and claimed he intended to abolish the protected villages. The people listened in silence. 'The boys in the bush', he declared petulantly, 'were not born by (sic) the two individuals who shout from the comfortable hotels of foreign capitals and who claim to own the guerrillas.' Credibility was stripped from the Bishop like the feathers of a fowl caught in a barbed-wire fence.

In June Mathias Chitauro, President of Chiweshe Residents' Association, complained of filth, flies, immorality and noise from loudspeakers installed by Internal Affairs, an ear-splitting din all day long. Yet on 9 October the Transitional Government opened nine new protected villages in the Mount Darwin area, making a total of twenty in two months. When Muzorewa, Magaramombe (Zupo) and Kadzviti (Zanu-Sithole) arrived by air to plead that there was no longer any point in the 'boys' continuing the fight, these internal politicians were greeted with vociferous scepticism and open scorn by the inhabitants of the keeps.

That any nationalist aspiring to gain the endorsement of the OAU should deliver his speeches in South Africa passes understanding. It was in Grahamstown that Muzorewa praised the attitude of the British Tories towards the internal settlement; it was in Johannesburg that he refused to comment on the massacre of more than fifty villagers in Gutu by the security forces. 'I am afraid that I could be misquoted and that would not help us.' In the United States he lobbied for an end to sanctions under the auspices of a Senator with a notorious record of hostility to civil-rights legislation, Jesse Helms of North Carolina. Muzorewa, in short, was continually burning his boats.

On 31 July, facing reporters in London, the Bishop was asked about a recent Rhodesian cross-border raid into Mozambique: what details had he known in advance of the raid? 'I don't believe that is of any significance.'

The Bish loves the cameras. Wearing a trilby hat at a rakish angle, he poses for a vastly panoramic photograph at a BSAP passing-out parade. In the front row Muzorewa is flanked and dwarfed by ten white officers, five to his right, five to his left, their imperious gaze worthy of the *Nugget*, 1897, their high brown boots and their Sam Brownes, their brass buckles and their medals all polished by worn black hands.

Today the Bish leaves his Charter Road party headquarters, passes a photograph of a Negro in chains taken from the film *Roots*, and is driven to the RBC TV studios where white girls powder his nose and chin. He stares at the camera and addresses the 'freedom fighters': 'Now is the time to come home. Bring your guns with you. The Zimbabwe you have fought for will become a reality on December 31. What are you dying for now?'

The twenty-first annual congress of the Association of Rhodesian Industries (ARnI) was held at the four-star Casino Hotel at Victoria Falls. More than 200 businessmen paid $(R)135 a head to attend. The main task of the hour was to give Muzorewa, Bulle and Sithole a royal reception and to receive in exchange assurances that nothing would change on the economic front. When ARnI's president, John Hillis, presented Co-Minister of Commerce and Industry Ernest Bulle with a 'memento', both men were wearing identical grey suits with vertical pin stripes. Bulle told the congress what it wanted to hear – there would be no minimum-wage legislation after 'majority rule'.

Off the record, Hillis had earlier briefed foreign reporters in a Salisbury hotel. 'We are engaged in a process of educating the black politicians. We found that most of them had never heard of the Industrial Conciliation Act. We want them to keep it. We are trying to teach a life-style and a culture.'

The UANC's genuinely patriotic elements began to peel away in disgust. Officials of the party's Exchange District at Que Que wrote in some anguish to the National Organizing Secretary: 'All this is far worse than what the executive claim Mr Hove could have caused by his statements. Do you realize you are only catering for the few rich whites in the urban areas yet on the other hand your poor fellowmen are being ruined in the TTLs by your so-called army. . . .' A powerful undercurrent of opposition swelled as it became clear that the guerrillas not only remained unmoved by appeals to lay down their arms, but retained overwhelming support in the countryside. In mid-August Byron Hove was expelled from the UANC together with the Rev. Arthur Kanodereka, former party Treasurer, Z. Muchenje, Secretary for Labour, Max Chigwida and others. On 12 September Hove, Kanodereka and Chigwida signed and circulated a 'Memorandum to the Patriotic Front' in which they virtually put themselves at the PF's disposal. Kanodereka was found murdered in his Alfa-Romeo at the 49·5-kilometre peg on the road to Beatrice. More than sixty bullets had hit the car.

29. what suggestions have you?

June 1978 was a grim month for Rhodesia's mission stations: in the course of it the number of missionaries killed more than doubled, from seventeen to thirty-seven. A desperate post-mortem followed every guerrilla murder, a perhaps futile search for a core of rationality in the choice of target. When Father Donovan was abducted a Jesuit colleague speculated that the victim might have been punished for having called the police and an ambulance when he came upon the casualties of a landmine explosion. 'And he made a habit of shooting stray dogs, too.'

The lethal attacks on Mariannhill missions in Matabeleland which began in June 1978 were interpreted by some liberal Catholics as a response to the innate, even belligerent, conservatism of these German Fathers. The Superior Provincial of the Mariannhill Order, Father Odilo Weeger, had not only refused to read out in church the Bishops' more progressive pastorals, he had also launched an attack in a German publication against progressive Catholics like Father Joseph Amstutz, Superior-General of the Bethlehem Fathers, and Bishop Donal Lamont. A translation of Weeger's article had appeared in the *Bulawayo Chronicle* and the *Sunday Mail*.

Two Mariannhill missions which now came under guerrilla attack, Embakwe and Empandeni, together owned 29,880 hectares of land, three times as much as the next largest Catholic mission in Rhodesia, Triashill. Not only had the Embakwe missionaries moved villagers to make way for the mission's cattle, they had maintained close contact with the security forces and carried weapons wherever they went.

If this was asking for trouble, they got it. In Matabeleland Zipra gangs struck in rapid succession, eradicating almost the entire medical and educational facilities of the south-west within a few weeks. On the night of 2 June a fatal attack was delivered against the Mariannhill mission at Embakwe, close to the Botswana border. Brother Geyermann, 37, a mechanical and electrical engineer, was walking along a veranda when he was shot through the heart from behind. Brother Andrew von Arx, 45, a carpentry teacher, was also shot in the heart at a range of three metres while sitting in his room reading the day's Epistle. Both the dead were German-born. The 62-year-old Principal of the Sacred Heart mission, Father Engelmar Dylon, heard the firing, ran from his study, saw the dead men lying in pools of blood, hurried back and seized a gun. He and Father Anton Jansen returned the fire with automatic weapons.

A bullet hit a brick pillar, rebounded and grazed Father Dylon's forehead, but the gang retreated; indeed Bishop Karlen of Bulawayo believed that this 'swift and courageous' action prevented a massacre. There had been prior warning of an attack and all the primary-school children had already been sent home. Now the secondary school was closed and its 250 pupils departed. The Superior-General of the Mariannhill missionaries flew from Rome for the funeral.

Empandeni mission is located south of Plumtree, not far from the Botswana border, and is reached by a thirty-kilometre drive through dry, desolate scrubland along a dirt track. In April Zipra guerrillas had lined up priests and nuns, threatening to kill them if the mission school was not closed. In July the threat was repeated and the Fathers felt they had no alternative but to inform 600 pupils that the school would not reopen after the holidays. The clinic and the homecraft school were also closed down and the mission's 300 cattle sold. A staff of fifty was reduced to a skeleton crew consisting of 71-year-old Father Andrew Bausenwein, Father Rudolf Anders, Father Pius Ncube, Brother Killian Knore, the Irish overseer of the huge farm, and Brother Horburger, an Austrian administrator. The buildings were bolted and a three-metre-high security fence was erected round the building in which the survivors led a beleaguered existence, their windows covered with wire mesh. Only on Sundays did life stir, when up to 300 people arrived for Mass in the granite church built in 1902.

The fatal raid on the Usher Institute, near Figtree, came on 7 June. A gang of about fifteen sought out the Salvation Army staff and started to march them towards the house of the Principal, Maj. Jean Caldwell, a Londoner. Suddenly the guerrillas scattered into the bush and opened fire indiscriminately, wounding Maj. Gunvor Palsson, from Malmö, Sweden, and Capt. David Cotton from Essex, and killing two young women: Sharon Swindells, 25, from Bangor in Northern Ireland, and Diana Thompson, 28, from London.

This tragedy persuaded the Anglican administration of the Cyrene mission at Figtree to send its 250 pupils home, even though Cyrene itself had not as yet been threatened. The Seventh-Day Adventist College at Figtree also decided that enough was enough: the staff of forty, mainly white Americans, abandoned acres of wheat and a large herd of cattle. At the Anglican mission of St James, some ninety-five kilometres north of Bulawayo, 1,000 pupils were sent home after a threatening message was received. On 13 June the 'boys' arrived at night at the Marist Brothers' College, Dett, and its associated Calvary Novitiate Convent. According to the Principal, Brother Gerald Beaule, they fired shots through the ceiling and threatened to blow the place up if it did not close.

The onslaught extended well beyond the borders of Matabeleland. On 6 June guerrillas ordered teachers and pupils at Daramombe secondary school, Enkeldoorn, to pack their bags and depart. Within a few days local people had stripped the deserted mission bare.

A Baptist from Tennessee, Archie Dunaway, was bayoneted to death at Sanyati mission. When his 58-year-old widow, Margaret, who had run a midwifery course at Sanyati, left Salisbury for America on 19 June she told reporters, her voice breaking with emotion: 'I adore the blacks but don't feel kindly towards the Communists. . . . It's such a loss. Archie and I were together thirty-three years.'

On the afternoon of 27 June two Jesuit missionaries were murdered at St Rupert's mission sixty kilometres north-west of Hartley. Father Gregor Richert, 48, and Brother Bernhard Lisson, 68, had between them served in Rhodesia for nearly sixty years. According to Comops, three Zipra terrorists demanded to see the priest in charge. Both the murdered priests were led into Father Richert's house and the servant told to leave. A single shot was heard, then three shots followed by automatic fire. Although St Rupert's forty-bed hospital was closed, Mgr Helmut Reckter said there were no plans to withdraw the sixteen missions still operating in Sinoia diocese.

Zipra's policy towards rural missions in Wankie diocese was notably harsh, although the Spanish-born Burgos Fathers who administered them were among the most radical and pro-nationalist in Rhodesia. There was strong evidence here, in northern Matabeleland, of outright guerrilla hostility towards Christianity. Tshongokwe, Gomoza and Kaka missions were burnt down. Tshongokwe, situated in the Lupane TTL, had been founded by Father Rubio Díaz, who was later murdered by guerrillas in Gwelo diocese. By August eight missions in Wankie diocese had been evacuated. The Catholic historian Ian Linden describes the situation then prevailing:

'The poorly trained, under-equipped young men that fought in the rural areas from March to July 1978, after several months of being hunted in the bush, were often nervous wrecks, emerging startled into the tranquility of the mission complex, trigger-happy and needing tranquilisers from the dispensary, or drink, before they could begin to relax. Hospital staff began to dread the frequent demand for drugs or drink which made a travesty of the missionaries' hope for genuine liberation. The price of cordial relations might be serious exploitation of the mission, priests commandeered imperiously to drive guerrillas in the mission car, demands for the *best* drink, good meals cooked by frightened girls while the local population went hungry. . . .' (*The Catholic Church and the Struggle for Zimbabwe*, pp. 272–3.)

Alarmed by the rash of murders and mission closures which darkened the middle months of 1978, the Catholic Church urgently sought a meeting at the highest level with the leaders of the PF in exile. The CIIR in London acted as intermediary. On 14 August (ironically the same day that Ian Smith started secret talks with Nkomo and Kaunda in Lusaka) the Rhodesian Catholic delegation, headed by Archbishop Patrick Chapaika, opened its own clandestine discussions with Nkomo in the Zambian capital.

The Church was able to portray itself as an ardent friend of the liberation struggle, as the declared and persecuted enemy of racist legislation, political hangings and atrocities committed in the name of law and order. A direct appeal was made to Nkomo: '. . . the Church is facing the decision of having to withdraw all missionaries from the sensitive areas in order to save their lives. . . . We have come to ask for your guidance in this matter.' Mgr Reckter, the President of the Justice and Peace Commission, and one of two whites in the Catholic delegation, suggested that the guerrillas might concentrate their attacks on the security forces and 'try and avoid contact with the people'. Flanked by George Silundika and two other leading Zapu officials, Nkomo evaded this request and explained that while the PF had always opposed the murder or harassment of missionaries, if the PF *had* ever been guilty of such things, then blame the war, the frustration, a certain amount of ill-discipline and – let's face it – the fact that the Church had in the past supported or seemed to support the system of racial privilege.

The delegation stayed for four days at a seminary in Lusaka while attempts were made to locate Robert Mugabe. When Mugabe finally showed up, accompanied by Tongogara, Muzenda and Tekere, he pointed out that suffering was an inescapable aspect of war. Praising the work of the Church and the JPC, he warned that in free Zimbabwe the Church would have to be guided by the Government in its health and educational services. But he could see no objection to certain schools – St George's was mentioned, a signal for winking among the Old Boys present – being run by Catholics for Catholics.

The Church thus shrewdly registered its claims and goodwill with the future rulers of Zimbabwe. At the same time the Lusaka meeting seems to have resulted in an immediate improvement in the relationship between missionaries and guerrillas – although the causal connection is impossible to prove. In short, the murder of missionaries virtually ceased. When, almost three years later, on 25 April 1981, Father Edmar Sommerreiser, 67, was shot dead by armed men at Regina Mundi mission near Lupane, it was the first murder of a Catholic missionary in Matabeleland since the Lusaka dialogue in August 1978.

The Lusaka meeting, however, did not measurably deflect the guerrillas from their habit of closing down schools as a demonstration of their physical mastery of the countryside. Nor was gentle persuasion the preferred tactic. The Anglican Bishop of Matabeleland quoted from a letter he had received from one of his supplementary clergy, a primary-school teacher:

'On the 26th January our school was closed by guerrillas. We [teachers] were all beaten. First they asked why we opened the school. Then commanded to sleep face down. One of them beat us with a thick stick which they had cut from a nearby tree. After that all school books were burnt. They even burnt my Prayer Book and the Bible.'

In September guerrillas beat Mr Dzoro, Headmaster of Mushunowa School in the Ndanda TTL, so severely that he died in hospital.

In the same month 440 children were sent home after guerrillas closed the Matopos mission of the Brethren of Christ. St Patrick's, an Anglican mission thirty kilometres from Gwelo, was closed down in November when eight guerrillas set light to school books and badly beat the Very Rev. Elliot Dhlula, who had built the school. All 304 pupils were sent home.

Early in December three armed men entered the Catholic mission at Loreto in the Silobela TTL. The Sisters had gathered in their common-room at 7.30 p.m. when the guerrillas, claiming allegiance to Zapu, burst in, stole several hundred dollars from the safe, relieved the staff of their watches, and gave them a day to clear out. Eight hundred children including 173 deaf ones had to be sent home.

At 9 p.m. on 24 January 1979 guerrillas closed down St Mary's mission school near Wankie, giving no reason.

By now 951 primary schools had closed, depriving 230,000 children (one-quarter of the total enrolment) of education and 5,856 teachers of work. In addition thirty-five African secondary schools had closed, depriving 9,000 exceptionally talented teenagers of further education and 455 highly qualified teachers of a job.

30. Elim

The Vumba mountains were cold, shrouded in rain: June is midwinter in Rhodesia. On the night of 23 June 1978 violent death came to the Elim Pentecostal mission when eight Protestant missionaries and four of their children were savagely murdered. Three of the adult victims were men, five were women; a sixth woman, grievously injured, died later, making the final toll thirteen. The scene encapsulated almost every nightmare white people had ever entertained about the barbarities of primitive Africa: rape, the bayoneting of a tiny baby, banana skins scattered about as a sign of apish brute indifference. Only one legendary horror was withheld: the victims had not been eaten.

One European teacher survived. Ian McGarrick, a 39-year-old South African, was in his room marking papers when he heard the normal lights-out whistle at 9 p.m. Three-quarters of an hour later he heard a commotion in the dormitories, went to investigate, and found the pupils milling around in a state of inexplicable ferment. None said anything of significance to him. An hour later he again had to tell them to go to sleep – still he was unable to fathom what was disturbing them. He returned to his own room completely unaware of what had happened. At 6 o'clock next morning – it was a Saturday – he found the pupils clearing books and belongings from their desks. Only now did they explain that guerrillas had arrived to inform them that the school was closing and that they must leave without delay. McGarrick went in search of the Rev. Philip Evans, acting Principal during the absence in the UK of the Rev. Peter Griffiths. The Evans's family flat was empty, its door open . . . then he heard their dog barking. McGarrick walked towards the barking, through a glade of tall acacia trees, crossed a small garden rockery and came to the edge of the dew-drenched games field. It was a very cold morning and Ian McGarrick shivered.

At such moments it is usually the same story. The witness 'sees' an object (a bare leg? a baby's cracked head?) from a distance, misidentifies it or suspends judgement because he lacks a framework of interpretation or because he instinctively associates logs, branches of trees or stones with inert pale matter lying in wet grass. The moment of nausea may be fractionally delayed by puzzlement, disbelief; as the heartbeat races up there is an automatic refusal to comprehend, a kaleidoscope of dreamlike evasions – these are dummies, it's a practical joke. . . .

The Rev. Evans lay with his hands tied, his face hacked open. Beside him lay 55-year-old Miss Catherine Picken, a survivor of the Congo massacres of 1960; her white plastic curlers, soaked in blood, were scattered in the grass. A long-handled axe had been buried in the back of her head. Three children lay in a huddle, next to two women – clusters of bodies around the cricket pavilion, seven kilometres from the Mozambique border. The missionaries and their children had in fact been dragged from their apartments at 8.30 the previous evening, marched to the playing-field, split into groups, beaten with logs, stabbed with bayonets, hatcheted, raped, mutilated in some cases. Two children wore yellow pyjamas, one with a red dressing-gown; the third was in a flowered nightdress.

The youngest victim was only three weeks old. Pamela Lynn was wearing a white smock with large white woolly sock-shoes round her tiny feet. Her eyes were closed. A bayonet had been thrust through the left side of her head and her left arm with its clenched fist remained raised and frozen in death. Her mother Joyce Lynn, 36, lay beside her, her left arm outstretched, her clenched hand across her baby's stomach. Her head had been battered in. A little girl with a smashed skull had the imprint of a boot scarring the side of her face.

One woman, Mary Fisher, 28, had been stabbed, beaten and left for dead. She crawled 300 metres into the bush where she spent a freezing night; later she died in the Andrew Fleming Hospital, Salisbury.

The dead were: the Reverend Peter McCann (32), his wife Sandra (34), their son Philip (5), their daughter Joy (4); the Reverend Philip Evans (29), his wife Susanna (32), their daughter Rebecca (4); the Reverend Roy Lynn (36), his wife Joyce (36), their three-week old baby Pamela. The victims included two unmarried women, Catherine Picken (55) and Elizabeth Wendy Hamilton-White (38).

The police arrived and left the bodies where they lay, for the benefit of the photographers, the reporters. The Ministry of Information flew a batch of journalists in from Salisbury, together with P. K. van der Byl, Lord Privy Seal of Western Civilization.

The funeral took place in the Queen's Hall, Umtali. There were eleven coffins immaculately set out in a soldierly row: baby Lynn had been laid in the same coffin as her mother. The coffins of the three children were small, white, heart-rending to look at. Baby Lynn's brother and sister, Timothy (10) and Rachel (8), pupils of Salisbury boarding-schools and therefore spared the massacre, stood with their grandmother opposite the two coffins which held their parents and baby sister; Rachel carried a small stuffed owl which she had found in her parents' ransacked home up in the Vumba mountains. After the service she placed it on the coffin.

Later, back in England, these orphaned siblings were shown on television: Rachel, a touching and sincere child, said that her parents died for the Lord and had to take little Pamela with them. Did she feel bitterness against the murderers? No, she said – but they should feel ashamed of themselves. She buried her head in her pillow, then, and said her prayers. Timothy believed the murderers were not acting under anyone's orders but did it because they were against Christ.

Nineteen relatives had flown from the UK for the funeral service in Umtali. The lone Foreign Office man in Rhodesia, Fraser Wilson, drove down from Marimba House, Salisbury, to represent the British Government and was relieved to remain unrecognized; anti-British hysteria was now at a peak. Douglas Reed, Mayor of Umtali, delivered an 'eye-for-an-eye' funeral oration, angrily rebutting the plea of the Elim mission's local director, the Rev.

Ronald Chapman, that they should all pray in order that the killers might know grief and repentance. A congregation of 750 gathered for a memorial service in Salisbury's Anglican Cathedral.

The mood during the fifty-five minute debate in the House of Assembly was one of unprecedented ferocity. White MPs expressed their hatred of the killers, these 'vermin, jackals, forces of evil, savages, brutes, dirty sadistic butchers'. Declared Theunis de Klerk: 'The British under their Labour masters have become the prostitutes of the Western world.' When seven black Members tried to speak, to point out that blacks were being killed in larger numbers every day of the year without a concomitant world outcry, they were furiously barracked and heckled. Shouts of rage greeted William Chimpaka's accusation that the 'evil leadership' of the Transitional Government was engaged in slaughtering blacks.

The scenes in the House of Commons were only marginally less emotional. John Davies, official Conservative spokesman, had no hesitation in declaring the PF guilty of the Elim massacre. Right-wing MPs led by Stephen Hastings, Sir John Eden and Maurice Macmillan bombarded David Owen with accusations of supporting the terrorism of the Patriotic Front. Asked to attribute responsibility, the Foreign Secretary replied: 'I do not know. I wish I did know.' (In mid-July Andrew Young suggested that the crime might never be conclusively documented.) On the Labour Left, Andrew Faulds, Robert Hughes and Stan Newens, equally devoted to their own tribalism, suggested that Ian Smith's Selous Scouts might well have perpetrated the massacre.

In fact Robert Mugabe had made precisely the same allegation on the previous day, 25 June: he claimed to have reports from eyewitnesses who had fled from Elim into the bush and contacted bona fide Zanla guerrillas. It had been the same story after the massacre of seven missionaries at St Paul's mission, Musami, in February of the previous year – Mugabe's bush telegraph had immediately brought him convenient proof of the regime's culpability.

The testimony of the black teachers and pupils at the Elim mission was unanimous: the killer gang had identified themselves as Zanla freedom fighters. Elias Chikashana, deputy headmaster, and Andrew Tinonesana, a teacher, giving evidence to the inquest on 21 August, recalled how six guerrillas in balaclavas had arrived at the classrooms at about 8.30 in the evening and marshalled all 250 pupils for an open-air meeting. The school must close, they had said in Shona, 'because the fees go to the Government which uses the money to buy ammunition to kill us'.

Two visiting Tory MPs, John Stokes and Ivor Stanbrook, were taken to Grand Reef base on 11 August to be shown a pair of dead guerrillas. A diary belonging to one of the dead men, named as Luke Madjuimbo, recalled that two Zanla sections had taken part in the Elim massacre and named the respective section leaders. A page in the diary read: 'Friday 23 June is the day near Matondo camp in Zimunya district. Time of operation: from 6.30 to 9 p.m. . . . Total number of comrades who were there, 21.' There followed a list of items 'captured' such as cassettes, screwdrivers, sheets, money. 'We killed 12 whites including four babies, as remembrance of Nyadzonia, Chimoio, Tembwe and in Zimbabwe massacres.'

According to Inspector Bryan Rogers, the same guerrilla sections ambushed a car in the Burma Valley a month after Elim, on 21 July. On 1 August they attacked a Roads Department camp. Ivor Stanbrook, one of the visiting British MPs, declared that after twenty years at the English Criminal Bar he felt entirely satisfied by the evidence presented to him.

Elim triggered off a vein of intensely racial feeling associated with the wilder fringes of Protestant evangelism. The Elim Pentecostal Church had been founded in 1915 by the Rev. George Jefferies and could now claim, according to its Cheltenham headquarters, 400 congregations and 40,000 followers in the UK. A BBC TV programme broadcast on 29 October showed the Rev. David J. Ayling, International Missions Director of the Church and possessed of a fixed corkscrew smile, ranting in the Bible-thumping tradition to students dressed in smart suits and ties. Ayling's aim, it seemed, was to bring to the Lord every human soul before the year 2000 . . . and to forgive the World Council of Churches who had unwittingly aided the Elim killers. . . .

Meanwhile, in America the wealthy evangelical Church of Christian Liberty, Illinois, announced it would send a private force of ex-GIs to the Vumba mountains as an advance guard for over twenty-seven civilian volunteers who would replace the dead missionaries. According to the Rev. Paul Lindstrom, the executive director, it would be quite 'like the days of the Wild West in which all of the mission staff would have a Bible and a gun'.

Lindstrom's advance guard duly appeared in the shape of a baby-faced former Green Beret called Giles Pace, who flew into Rhodesia wearing battledress, combat boots – and a green beret. From his hotel bedroom he outlined his plans to bemused reporters: the 'Emmanuel Volunteer Brigade' would fly the Free Christian flag over the mission, pursue Charlie Tangos into Mozambique, and call in 500 'Free Cubans' if they met any resistance from Castro-type Cubans. Veterans of the Marines, of the Rangers, of the 101st Division and of the First Airborne Cavalry were all lined up to enlist as soldiers of Christ.

Pace then asked the reporters whether they could spare any petrol coupons.

When one contrasts this kind of opportunistic farrago with the grief of Joyce Lynn's orphaned children – with the terrible sadness of Elim, where so much love and idealism reaped such a bitter reward – one is tempted to banish it from the page. To do so, however, would be to forget that the Salisbury newspapers dished up Giles Pace to their readers not merely because here was Captain Vengeance, but because the 'mercenary international' now provided the only external consolation to the beleaguered laager.

31. go, go!

At 10 p.m. on Friday, 20 June, guerrillas attacked the Elephant Walk Hotel, thirty-seven kilometres north of Karoi. Tracer bullets set the thatched roof on fire, causing damage estimated at $(R)20,000. The proprietor, Matt Heany, was a former fencing contractor whose hotel business had picked up when armed convoys were instituted and began to use the Elephant Walk as a staging post. Despite promises from local farmers to repair the hotel free of charge, Heany was forced to abandon the attempt in October because of intimidation of the building workers by guerrillas.

On 17 June a Matopos South farmer, Fred Grobler, 63, was killed with his wife Aletta, 80, in an ambush three kilometres from their farm. Their homestead and trading store were set on fire. A cattle- and citrus-farmer, Grobler had lived in the area for thirty years; his wife had been one of the first teachers in the district when she settled there fifty years ago.

Driving alone was becoming increasingly dangerous. Time and again cars had narrow escapes, driving straight through a hail of bullets and out the other side. But fate was not always so kind. In December 1977 a boy of 9, Ian Johnson, the son of a section manager on an Umvukwes tobacco estate, had died from a single bullet which hit his father's car in the Centenary district.

By the beginning of 1978 the security situation had deteriorated so drastically that armed convoys had been introduced across the board. But a convoy guaranteed no immunity. As early as May 1977 an ambush ten kilometres from Chipinga had killed the 18-year-old front gunner, Patrol Officer Edward Nicholas, and injured four civilians. The thin young policeman who had been riding as tail gunner that day commented that the favourite target was any car straggling behind a convoy's rear support truck. 'But', he added, 'for my money, all convoys are a liability.' In his view the safest tactic was to travel in the company of two or three other fast vehicles 'and then go like hell'.

On 6 February the Umtali–Birchenough convoy was ambushed at Hot Springs. Guerrillas detonated a mine at the roadside then opened fire, bringing the convoy to a halt and forcing the occupants of cars to fling themselves into a ditch.

The most devastating ambush of a convoy occurred near Makuti, in the wild Zambezi wildlife area, on 11 July 1978. Zipra guerrillas opened fire from dense bush, wounding a police reservist in the lead escort vehicle and hitting the black driver of a bus, Samuel Gondo, who was able to drive the bus into a cutting out of the line of fire, although fatally injured. As the bus then keeled over in a ditch, a rocket wooshed over the top, followed by a hail of bullets. Three of the bus passengers were killed, Debra de Bres, 17, and Margaret Turk, both of Salisbury, and 5-year-old Sally Muggleton, of Gwebi.

Jack Dewes, a *Rhodesia Herald* reporter who was travelling in the convoy, reported how drivers pulled off the road and began shooting at a cloud of smoke some sixty metres into the bush. Bullets bit into the rocky hill behind him and gravel stung his ears. A young woman was blazing away with an automatic pistol over the bonnet of her car. Security forces in the escort vehicles yelled at them 'Get going!', 'Put foot!' and 'Go, go!' Some cars then turned back for Makuti while others risked the longer stretch down to Karoi, which was the direction in which the convoy had been travelling. The injured police reservist, Ralph Rea, a farmer when circumstance allowed, was nursed by beautiful Coleen Weedon on the way to the Elephant Walk Hotel (almost entirely destroyed by guerrillas twenty-two days previously), whence he was taken to Sinoia Hospital.

On 18 November four whites and two blacks were injured when guerrillas hit the tail of the Fort Victoria convoy some nineteen kilometres from Bulawayo. The attack came at 11 a.m. One car overturned. The injured whites were taken to Central Hospital, Bulawayo (whites only), the injured blacks to Mpilo Hospital.

In July the famous Troutbeck Inn at Inyanga suffered a mortar attack which destroyed a bedroom wing. Apparently the guerrillas set up their mortars on a golf tee, ranging them with the help of a sign marking the distance to the final green close to the hotel. (Expecting an invasion in 1940, the British had taken down their road signs.) During the weekend of 4 February 1979 Zanla finally closed the Troutbeck by abducting fifteen members of the hotel staff from their compound and ordering the remaining eighty-five to return to their reserves.

Three white farmers were killed in two separate incidents on Sunday 9 July. Leslie Jellicoe was murdered at Karoi; his uncle, of the same name, had been one of the first farmers to be killed when guerrillas attacked his Centenary farm on 4 February 1973. Meanwhile, at Doma, Peter Potgeiter, 48, father of four, and Dassie Riekert, 30, father of one, died in an ambush.

Christian Fanken, 61, was abducted and found murdered on his farm in the Selukwe district on 12 July.

Huntsman Williams, 34, a Turk Mine, Inyati farmer and former Rhodesian cricketer, was killed on 3 August when his vehicle was hit by rockets. Williams was on a police reserve follow-up operation launched after guerrillas burnt down a sawmill. His grandfather had received a grant of land from Cecil Rhodes.

George Bishop, a signal technician, was killed on 8 August by guerrillas at Mepopoma marshalling yards, Bulawayo. An urban attack of this nature was rare.

James Davies was killed on his Alicevale farm in the Vumba on 20 August. The farm had been started by his father sixty years before. Mr Davies left fourteen grandchildren and two great-grandchildren.

32. the deadly triangle

A family was farming 3,240 hectares – cattle and tobacco – at Mayo, 150 kilometres east of Salisbury. In November 1977 guerrillas had warned the labour force to quit the farm, burnt down their huts as a warning, and abducted the foreman or 'boss boy'. Some labourers left, others stayed. In January 1978 the farmer's brother was hit in the chest and leg during an ambush but managed to drive on; his life was saved by open-heart surgery at the Andrew Fleming Hospital. In March the farmer's father-in-law was less lucky: his ambush was fatal. Then, during the last week of June, the farmer's wife had their seven-month-old baby on her lap when the car in which she was driving hit a landmine; the baby was blasted out into the road, the mother suffered a broken leg and a shattered foot. On Friday, 30 June, while her husband was visiting her in hospital, a force of at least twelve guerrillas arrived at the farm soon after dusk and launched an attack with rocket grenades and automatic weapons. Three 'bright-lights' fought off the attack on the farmhouse, whereupon the guerrillas turned their attention to the labour compound. A pregnant woman and five children were burned alive in a grass-roofed hut; next day only two of the bodies were identifiable. Nine male farm workers, recruited to replace others who had fled after previous guerrilla attacks, were marched from their sleeping quarters in a tobacco barn to a bare patch of veld one kilometre away and there made to lie face down. Eight died, one survived; next day security forces recovered more than 190 spent cartridges.

A further family tragedy occurred on 24 May 1978 when a vehicle travelling on a dirt road in the Headlands area hit a mine, killing S. P. Van Blerk, of Inyati Tobacco Estates, his daughter-in-law, Mrs Gerbregt Maria Van Blerk, and her infant daughter Lizelle.

In November 1976 there had been nineteen white families farming in the Mayo area. By January 1980 there were none.

Tim Peech was 30 and a third-generation Rhodesian. His beautiful wife Michaela had been born in Texas, the daughter of a rabbi, and had lived with her husband at Salama Farm, Macheke, for nine years. They had three children. The security problem in this area was so acute that a local defence unit of thirty-five farmers had been formed and granted exemption from normal call-up. Tim Peech held the rank of Captain and was commander of the local defence unit; as such he had struck a kind of deal – or believed he had – with local Zanla section commanders. Provided Zanla avoided attacks on white farms, there would be no search-and-destroy operations against guerrilla positions in the Mangwende TTL. But then – according to Peech's brother Christopher – a new hardline Zanla section moved into the area. Returning to Mrewa on 13 July to report to the JOC, Tim Peech decided to visit a village in the TTL. When a large section of guerrillas surrounded his vehicle he was able to report the fact over his radio: his aim was to talk to them, to renew the mutual stand-off.

Tim Peech was a chubby, short-haired young man, with a reputation among local farmers for being a liberal. In reality he was an 'internal settlement liberal' who staged a Muzorewa rally on his farm, organized a 'friendship drive' among local Africans to convince them that they would get a 'new deal' under the internal settlement, and believed that President Carter, by his refusal to endorse the Salisbury Agreement on 3 March, was 'letting this country go'.

Mrs Peech later recalled: 'I knew something was wrong when he didn't come back that Thursday night. He never let me sweat that long. At 9 p.m. I was frantic. He had been out twenty or more times to seek and discuss instead of seek and destroy, and .each time I wondered if he would ever come back. . . . Until Sunday, my daughter's birthday, I didn't know. . . . It came almost as a relief when they said he was dead.'

A search party had found his burnt-out truck on the Friday, his body near by, robbed of his watch and wedding-ring. There was a hand grenade in his pocket.

Three weeks later, on 8 August, a neighbouring Macheke farmer, David Crombie, 39, was fatally ambushed as he drove out of his farm. When the guerrillas tried to storm the homestead his wife drove them off with a pistol.

A month passed. Shortly after sundown on Friday, 15 September, the van Reenan family were travelling on the Macheke–Virginia road when they ran into a guerrilla ambush. Fifteen-year-old Madelene, a pupil at Marandellas High School, was killed. Later her mother wrote a bitter letter to the press, denouncing Mrs Peech for appeasement:

'Your article and picture of Mrs Tim Peech holding hands with one of her employees nauseated me. It is my contention, and also that of more than half the farmers in that particular area, that it is the labourers that are harbouring the present group of terrorists that are causing so much grief in the area.

'It is our opinion that when an ambush like this has taken place, the whole nearby compound should be "taken out". So what if there MAY be a few innocent people there too? My little girl was innocent, as were many other victims of this war, but those compounds are not innocent. It is time that we took a hard line with this type of thing. Mrs Peech, Alan Savory and his kind we can do without. What good have they done anyway? The war in Macheke, Virginia and Mayo has increased considerably since Mrs Peech held hands with her labourer.' Shelagh van Reenan, Mayo.

At 9 a.m. on 9 March 1978 Jan Nicholas Strydom, a 42-year-old farmer, married with three children, had been shot dead on his farm, Rathcline, in the Rusape area.

The van der Merwes farmed in the Headlands area. Of the twelve neighbouring farmers, three had been killed, one kidnapped, one badly injured, and another had lost his wife, child and father in a single landmine disaster. The van der Merwe family moved house to Rusape, from where Jannie van der Merwe tried to run his farm, spending over $(R)1,200 a month on hiring three security guards. But every time the family took the dirt road leading to the farm the children lapsed into a state of terror, perched on the edge of their seats, waiting for a mine to blow them to pieces. Their 8-year-old daughter would cover her face in sheer misery. Then guerrillas dispersed their labour force: the game was up.

A high proportion of farming families in the Headlands district were Afrikaners. Their morale was further undermined when the highly respected Wickus de Kock, MP for Mtoko, gapped it to South Africa. A third-generation Rhodesian who had captained Rhodesia's rugby team in 1958, de Kock had served as Deputy Minister of Justice before his transfer to the Prime Minister's office in 1974 with responsibility for coordinating counter-insurgency operations. Wickus de Kock was regarded as a pillar of principled resistance to black nationalism. Hotly though he denied in Parliament that he was taking the 'yellow route', de Kock's defection hit the Afrikaner farmers in the gut.

One farmer's wife, Mrs Botha, expressed resentment against both the Salisbury and the Pretoria Governments for making it impossible for the *volk* to trek back south with all their worldly goods intact. 'We surely deserve a better deal from our own people,' she said.

There were now about eighty vacant farms in the Rusape–Headlands area.

33. Currie Cup

Rhodesia is a sporting province of South Africa. The contests against Natal, Transvaal, Eastern Province and the other South African teams are as keen and intimate as those between the English county-cricket teams; as vital and reassuring a landmark on the calendar as the winter rugby matches between England, Ireland, Scotland, Wales and France. In fact that's not a bad parallel: four national teams belonging to a single political entity, plus one outsider. Despite the risk to aircraft and passengers, the South Africans have considered it a matter of honour to persevere with their visits north of the Limpopo.

Every talented schoolboy cricketer aspires to play in the Nuffield inter-provincial schools festival; selection for the South African schools XI awaits the best, the prize being a match against Eastern Province at Port Elizabeth or some comparable senior team. Junior rugby players compete to play in the Craven week (named after Daany Craven, the tsar of Springbok rugby). For young water-polo players there is the Kramer League; for all Rhodesian sportsmen and women the common culture lies to the south.

In May 1978 Rhodesia's women golfers beat the Junior Springboks by six matches to three; black caddies carried the bags. Valerie Walls, daughter of Rhodesia's top soldier, was chosen for the Springbok swimming team after breaking the 200-metres free-style record. When Amanda Martin, at 14 the golden girl of Rhodesian swimming, made off with the 100 metres breast-stroke in the South African championships, she (and her parents) promptly headed for California.

The South African connection lures every sportsman: bowls, combat pistol-shooting, motor-racing, horse trials, hang-gliding, fishing, sailing, golf, squash – Dave Scott was amateur champion of both Rhodesia and South Africa – even a sport called 'underwater hockey', male and female. This gruelling game involves goggles, heavy gloves, snorkels, hockey-sticks and a kind of madness.

Rugby is a symbol of white Rhodesian manhood: the spirit must drive the flesh to surpass itself *pro patria*. During the long war of counter-insurgency soldier-players came in from the bush to prove they were not losing. By Currie Cup standards Rhodesia was not, over the years, one of the strongest teams: ninety wins in 301 matches. Yet the guerrilla war did seem to inspire triumph on the field of play for those who wore the broad green-and-white hoops. In 1977 eight out of eleven matches were won. During the 1978 season seven matches were won, three were lost and one was drawn. The great hero was Ian Robertson, a former pupil of Prince Edward School (how often he was invited to school functions, to appear, neat, modest and alert before the star-struck boys). Something of a fitness fanatic and an ice-cool kicker of drop-goals, Robertson had played at fly-half for the Springboks – the most coveted honour – against New Zealand and France.

All the South African Currie Cup teams were restricted to players of the white race. Proteas, the 'Coloured' team from the Cape, could tour Rhodesia only for 'friendly' games.

Rhodesia's 19–19 draw against a traditionally powerful Transvaal team was a notable triumph. Moments before the final whistle, when all seemed lost, right-wing Danny Delport dashed across the line to score; Ian Robertson coolly converted the try. 'So irrepressible was their spirit and so raw their courage . . .' roared the *Sunday Mail*. There was in fact a raw dimension to many of these encounters: in the thirteenth minute the two packs lashed out at each other after a scrum had collapsed. On another occasion a Rhodesian forward was sent off the field during a match in Johannesburg.

The Rhodes and Founders' weekend early in July is traditionally an occasion for sporting encounters of the most unsparingly competitive kind. As a superb gesture of defiance to the gooks, a gliding competition was held on the Mozambique border, the gliders taking off from Umtali heights and landing at the polocrosse grounds.

Meanwhile, in Salisbury, Founders' Day offers the showpiece encounter against the mighty Northern Transvaal – the first all-ticket rugby match in Rhodesian history. On Monday, 26 June, a queue forms from First Street down Angwa and round the corner into Speke Avenue: people camp out all night, the lucky ones buy eight or ten tickets. Many fans arrive at the Police Ground wearing 'I zap gooks' T-shirts; other chests are emblazoned with the national flag and a rugby-ball. Two thousand schoolboys who have camped outside the ground are admitted provided they arrive smartly dressed in their school uniforms; no scruff here. Ian Smith and the top military commanders take their places among the capacity crowd of 20,000; outside the ground militants of the RAP are handing out leaflets urging white citizens to 'Vote No at the Referendum. Get back to the 1969 Constitution'.

The crowd sing 'Land of Hope and Glory'. Lt-Col. Wood, chaplain of the army, declares, 'This is God's own country.' The mood is one of controlled hysteria and to that extent subtly different from that prevailing among the English rugby enthusiasts who flock to Twickenham. The Rhodesian team is narrowly beaten but is held to have acquitted itself with honour. Afterwards Smith is asked: will our team be called Zimbabwe next year?

'Don't jump to too many conclusions,' he snaps.

34. scandal

Every form of currency evasion flourished. A few examples suffice to show the pattern:

(1) In May 1978 two directors of a Salisbury firm pleaded guilty to the unauthorized purchase of South African currency. In June 1975 they had bought 3,000 rand from a South African resident in Rhodesia, and in September of that year a further 4,000 rand, which was lodged in South African bank accounts.

(2) A Rhodesian had given South Africa's former Trade Commissioner in Salisbury $(R)70,000 on the understanding that he would transfer the money through his own diplomatic account and arrange for it to be exchanged into rand. But in the event the South African spent most of it paying off his Rhodesian debts and the luckless Rhodesian recovered only $(R)30,000 of his 'investment'. The High Court sentenced the South African to fifty-four months in prison for fraud.

(3) A director and major shareholder of a clothing firm appeared on thirty counts of violating Exchange Control regulations, the main charges relating to the channelling of export profits of $(R)300,000 to a South African subsidiary company. To obtain bail the accused had to deposit $(R)50,000, report to Borrowdale police station twice daily, and surrender his travel documents.

(4) Another clothing merchant was charged with having exported twenty-one consignments of clothing between June 1975 and January 1977 to a South African firm of which his brother was the director, and of having failed to remit to Rhodesia the rand accruing from the sales.

(5) Mr X of the X Group of Companies was charged with exporting goods worth $(R)198,000 and not repatriating the payments.

(6) A former game warden and his wife pleaded guilty to having banked the unspent portion of their travel allowance in a South African account opened for them by a friend in Pretoria. They had shown even greater enterprise by paying a total of $(R)803 to tourists visiting a hunting camp near Karoi, in

265

return for which they were rewarded with cash lodged abroad, including an account in Italy.

In July 1978 a major scandal broke. On the 16th two South African newspapers plastered the story over their front pages, naming four prominent Rhodesians as having been charged with misappropriating huge defence funds. Those named by the South African press were Tim Pittard, Chief Customs Security Officer, and a member of Rhodesia's Central Intelligence Organization; Rodney Simmonds, one of the twelve RF MPs who had broken away to form the RAP; Norman Brand, Under-Secretary for Defence; and Eddie Muller, chief executive of Rennies, a firm of customs-clearing and forwarding agents.

The regime immediately slapped a D-notice on the whole story, muzzling the local press; on 17 July police seized all copies of South African newspapers carried by passengers arriving at Salisbury Airport. Smith announced that about $(R)750,000 had been fraudulently extracted from the Defence Fund by the men awaiting trial. The trial was held in camera. On 20 July heavy fines were imposed by the High Court on three unnamed defendants (reporters were forbidden even to look through the windows of the court). Each was found guilty of having foreign currency paid into a personal account abroad. The amounts involved were $(R)64,000, $(R)35,000 and $(R)17,000, the respective fines being $(R)110,000, $(R)65,000 and $(R)35,000. In August Justice Beck acquitted 'B', financial adviser to the Minister of Defence and responsible for the purchase of weapons authorized by the Defence Procurement Board. 'B' had been charged with accepting 'backhanders' outside the country and stealing public funds.

Because of sanctions the opportunities for fraud were rife. Rhodesia was forced to pay US$80 for an FN rifle whose normal market price was US$25. Funds reached French, Italian, and Israeli arms manufacturers through Swiss accounts, where some of the money stuck.

Seething and malignant rumour now reached such a pitch that no one was beyond suspicion. In bars and hotel lounges it was common knowledge that certain leading figures in the RF were breeding Brahman and Santa Gertrudis pedigree cattle for export to South Africa, taking a modest price inside Rhodesia and the balance in rand in the Republic. On 25 August Smith felt constrained to deny publicly that he had bought property in or moved his cattle to South Africa. Lt-Gen. Walls made a similar denial during a speech at the Gwelo School of Infantry.

35. leaving

Ewen Greenfield is descended from New World Scots. He does not wear his heart on his sleeve, but behind the overt quietness of manner there is both conviction and resolve. Working in the Bulawayo law firm of Lazarus & Sarif, he specialized in the defence of Africans charged under the emergency regulations or detained without trial. The son of a judge who had served in the Federal Cabinet, and the grandson of a Presbyterian minister who came out with the Scots Greys during the Boer War, Ewen Greenfield moved within the minority culture of white Rhodesian liberalism – Centre Party, Rhodesia Party, finally the National Unifying Force.

On 2 August 1978 he and his family left Rhodesia for the last time.

As a defence lawyer he had intimate knowledge of the BSAP and Special Branch. The scrutiny, of course, was mutual: his telephone had been tapped and wherever he went there was the likelihood of recognition, of being challenged to justify his defence of 'communist terrorists'. In reality he supported neither the black nationalist movements nor the guerrilla war waged by Zanla and Zipra; and when he was called upon to take the oath of allegiance to 'Rhodesia' he raised no objection. Nevertheless he was publicly critical of RF policies that had led Africans to take up arms.

The security forces engaged in a 'hot pursuit' operation inside Botswana had abducted four Botswanans, who were incarcerated in the notorious 'Fort' outside Bindura, a secret interrogation centre rarely seen by a civilian. Assigned to defend the Botswanans, Greenfield paid his first visit to the Fort, where a buccaneering SB officer called McGuiness was zealously 'turning' ex-guerrillas and setting up pseudo-gangs to stimulate confusion and fear in the surrounding countryside. McGuiness clearly enjoyed discussing politics; he claimed to have sat in on conferences between Smith and Muzorewa. His pockets were well stocked with banknotes almost certainly supplied by the Prime Minister's office, to which SB 2 was directly responsible. At the Fort Greenfield saw prisoners shuffling about in hoods down to their ankles – a practice invariably denied by the police in court. When the defence got the four Botswanans released on the technicality of their illegal arrest, McGuiness, who had prepared a show trial replete with captured weapons, was not pleased.

Time and again the central issue in these political trials was the means used by the Special Branch to obtain confessions. Thousands of men and women were charged with assisting terrorists. The courts veered from draconian life sentences to wholly suspended terms of imprisonment; in which event the defendant would normally be rearrested as he left the court and detained indefinitely in Wha Wha or elsewhere.

Why did the Greenfields decide to leave? It had been Mrs Greenfield's wish for some time. Greenfield himself began to take the idea seriously in 1977. In the general election of that year he fought the Bulawayo Central constituency on behalf of the NUF and emerged badly mauled, despite the high proportion of Asian and Coloured voters living in the area. The outlook seemed hopeless. Soon afterwards he was summoned into the Police Reserve with the 38–50 year-olds and was sent to the Matopos on an induction course. There he discovered that the prevailing spirit among the instructors was 'if it's black, when in doubt, shoot'. (When it's black there's always a doubt.)

Later he patrolled the townships in Land-Rovers, did duty on the main roads and guarded the petrol dumps at Beitbridge as part of the seventy-two-day annual commitment. Things became hairier when he was sent up to the dangerous Gwanda ranching area and assigned to guard a burnt-out farm property, initially without the regulation mine-proofed vehicle. Finding himself on an empty farm owned by an absentee Afrikaner and rented by Kenneth Drummond, who had been badly wounded in an ambush on the same farm only a week earlier (see page 130), Ewen Greenfield let it percolate through to the surrounding countryside that the defence of black political prisoners was his profession. . . .

With the methodical and meticulous approach of a lawyer he now set about clearing a path through a thicket of regulations designed to thwart or discourage emigration. Although possessing only a Rhodesian passport, his father's birthplace entitled him to obtain a South African one, in which a certificate of British patriality could be inserted by the British embassy in Pretoria. The major obstacle was the Exchange Control regulations; fortunately the bank official he dealt with was his secretary's sister and his passage was a relatively smooth one.

'We refer to your application for Emigration Status,' wrote the bank on 18 July, 'and advise the sum of $(R)1,000 may be transferred to you in the United Kingdom after your departure from Rhodesia. You may export household effects, personal belongings and jewellery valued at $(R)7,132 together with a motor car valued at $(R)1,500. Permission is given for payment of up to $(R)5,700 to Glens Removals . . . to meet the cost of [transportation]. . . .

'The balance of your assets deposited with our branch must be blocked and may not be dealt with in any way without the prior approval of the Control.'

The Greenfields had bought enough clothing to last for years (much of it subsequently went out of fashion and was never used), plus linen sheets and a refrigerator. A vital gain was permission to have the insurance on these goods in transit payable in the UK – when a Persian carpet and other items vanished between Pretoria and Durban they in effect converted themselves into the sterling that Greenfield most needed when he first arrived and had not yet found a job. For his house he got a low price but cash on the nail, most of which was absorbed by the costs already mentioned and by the $(R)6,000 he spent on transporting a family of six to Europe.

On 27 July the vital certificate of tax clearance came through and on 2 August the family flew to Johannesburg. As a parting gesture customs at Bulawayo took apart Greenfield's hand baggage. The flight north was by Sabena – cheaper than the orthodox route but slightly unnerving when they touched down in Zaire only a week after the bloody events in Shaba.

In England the family stayed with Mrs Greenfield's sister in Malvern. More fortunate than many refugees, Ewen Greenfield found a job with the Association of County Councils and bought a house in St Albans.

36. Comrade Max and Comrade Mick Jagger

Boss once more of an organization called 'Zanu', by courtesy of Mr Smith, Ndabaningi Sithole launched frenetic claims to be in effective command of Zanla guerrillas operating in the field – at least 3,000 were said to be heeding 'stand off' orders issued by 'the President' himself. Both Muzorewa and Sithole were well aware that both Zanla and Zipra remained relentlessly hostile to the Salisbury Agreement; both knew that they were regarded as quislings and traitors by the vakhomana. Hence the birth of the 'auxiliaries' – paramilitary forces supposedly recruited from defecting guerrillas but in reality dredged up from the shanty-towns and squatters' camps of Salisbury and Bulawayo. There were also reports of military cadres loyal to Muzorewa or Sithole returning from training in Gaddafi's Libya or Idi Amin's Uganda.

It was in August that whites suddenly became alarmed by the rapid burgeoning of the auxiliaries. This followed prominent coverage in the press and on television of Muzorewa holding an AK rifle while visiting auxiliaries in Msana and chatting with their leader 'Comrade Max' who, wearing denims, an animal-skin hat and thumping his rifle butt on the ground, boldly announced, 'I am the new DC in this area.' Shown on TV on 13 August, the film provoked an outcry among RF MPs and their white constituents. (John Meiring, the RBC reporter for the film, lost his accreditation as a defence correspondent, even though he had represented RBC during a recent raid into Mozambique.) Roger Hawkins, Co-Minister of Defence, insisted that auxiliaries were operating under the command of the regular security forces.

Semantic panic ensued: whereas General Walls was prepared to dignify 'on-sides' terrorists as 'guerrillas', Col. George Hartley, Speaker of the House of Assembly, ruled the word 'guerrilla' totally out of order and suggested as an alternative 'auxiliaries'.

Anxious to persevere with the training of auxiliaries while soothing white opinion, District Commissioners began to lay on conducted tours of auxiliary-controlled areas. In November DC David Stephenson arranged a visit by eight reporters to Msana, still the fiefdom of Comrade Max and his 300 to 400 men. Max told his guests that he had left Rhodesia in 1968, trained in Tanzania and Egypt, then spent the years 1972–4 in Moscow and the Ukraine. But Communism and socialism were no good at all for Africans. When Special Branch had made contact with him as an operational Zanla guerrilla commander, offering food, clothes, weapons, he had decided to come on-sides. The letters UANC were now written in or on his heart.

Muzorewa himself was frequently photographed in the company of his loyal Pfumo reVanhu auxiliaries. In November the Bishop visited the 'free zone' in Manyeni TTL, Enkeldoorn, where the auxiliaries were commanded by 'Mick Jagger', a baby-faced character in a baseball hat. Only 21 years old, 'Jagger' had developed a fine reputation for terrorizing local Africans. And then there was 'Comrade Lloyd', boss of Maranda TTL, trained in Idi Amin's Uganda and loyal to Sithole. Greatly instrumental in setting him up in business was a big, bald, white rancher by the name of Bob Gawler who had recently lost 3,000 cattle worth $(R)250,000. (Idi Amin, despite blemishes on his record and a tendency to cut corners, was after all a good anti-Marxist.) The operation had the blessing of Ian Rich, District Commissioner at Nuanetsi.

In November Walls claimed that the corner had been turned and that 2,000 former terrorists had now come over to the Government's side.

The auxiliaries attracted gangsters and created gangsters. Many of them resembled villains in B movies, sporting pendants, hats wrapped in animal skins, fancy shirts, bandoliers of copper-tipped cartridges coiled round their bodies like shark's teeth. Of a contingent of, say, 200 auxiliaries, at most ten or fifteen would be genuine ex-guerrillas. The TTLs they terrorized were officially termed 'free zones'. One of their functions was to herd local people to meetings addressed by Sithole or (more commonly) Muzorewa: free meat and beer were also available, the carrot supplementing the stick.

UANC auxiliaries had, by the end of 1978, established themselves in Msana, Mondoro, Urungwe, Masembura, Chinamora, Chiduku, Maranke, Inyanga and elsewhere, while Sithole's men were known to be operating in Gokwe, Maranda, Copper Queen and parts of the eastern border.

The pattern of complaints from villagers in the reserve was almost universally uniform: intimidation, beatings, demands that the local girls become camp-followers, periodic looting. It was Africans who bore the brunt of the violence employed by the private armies of the internal parties. Evidence of intimidation could not be suppressed. In the Gokwe area Sithole's men were demanding food and forcing villagers to buy Zanu party cards at 50 cents each and to pay dues of 25 cents a week. The African Farmers' Union urgently petitioned the UANC to curb the lawlessness of the auxiliaries.

37. down with lords and ladies

She had a premonition that something was about to happen – a sense of being watched as she took the dog for a walk. Then her maid suddenly acquired acute body odour. Jennifer Plunket suggested she take a bath but the bath did no good. Obviously the maid knew something which brought on a constant sweat. Two days after Lord and Lady Plunket left their Melsetter farm on a trip to Britain the attack took place. Part of the roof was burnt. Chalked on the wall was a slogan: 'Down with lords and ladies.'

The Plunkets felt aggrieved. They were liberals. Their friends had included black nationalists like Herbert Chitepo. Robin Plunket had belonged to the Capricorn Africa Society and its various spiritual successors like the Centre Party and the NUF. The Plunket farmhouse remained without a security fence and an Agric-Alert. But they had given no help to the 'boys'. 'I wasn't prepared to throw in my lot with terrorists,' Lord Plunket recalls, 'any more than I was prepared to collaborate with Smith's security forces to preserve the status quo.'

A valley of fruit and vegetables, Cashel had been a gentle corner of paradise until it became, with Melsetter to the south, one of the most dangerous areas of Rhodesia. Melsetter lies 100 kilometres south of Umtali at the southern end of the great range of mountains which dominate the Mozambique border for 300 kilometres. Huge plantations of pine and wattle (Anglo-American owns large timber estates in this region) provided insurgents with ideal cover. That the whites were finally getting a taste of their own medicine can scarcely be doubted. In 1896 missionaries in the district had complained:

'We hold that the plan of sending native constables through the country collecting the natives by armed force, compelling them to labour here and there . . . whether they are willing or not, their wives being seized as hostages in case they attempt to escape, is unjust and government has no right thus to arrest and impress natives.'

Now, in 1978, it was hazardous in the extreme to drive alone from Umtali to Melsetter. Those who could afford it flew from Tilbury airstrip, a pencil scar in a vista of emerald-green pines, then took a mine-proof, ambush-proof 'Kudu' or whatever – the roaring, straining engine of a heavy vehicle passing through quiet but treacherous countryside was now a familiar sound in rural Rhodesia.

Zanla guerrillas operating out of the Mutambara and other neighbouring reserves waged a highly effective war. During the three years 1976–8 no fewer than 1,053 'terrorist contacts' were recorded in the area. The number of farms in working order crashed dramatically from 105 in 1976 to eight at the end of 1978. In 1978 alone twenty-four homesteads were destroyed. Even though the big timber companies could afford to hire full-time security guards, the number of white families living on the estates slumped from 150 to sixty-two.

The death toll mounted:

1975: Mr C. A. S. Young, 29 April.

1976: Mr P. Valentine and Mr J. E. Hudson-Beck, 12 August; Mr A. C. Newman, 15 October.

1977: Mr D. H. Mackay, 1 January; Mr M. Langeman, 22 January; Mr R. A. Barton, 6 April; Mr C. A. Delaney and Mr B. J. Dean, 20 September; Mr K. D. Viljoen and Mrs E. A. Viljoen, 1 October; Mr H. Holstenberg and Mr R. C. Hunt, 20 October; Mr J. J. F. Van Maarseveen, 4 December; Mr J. F. Coomans, 6 December.

1978: Mr J. L. S. Vorster, 23 January; Mr C. A. Steyn, 4 April; Mr H. Fenzel, 16 April; Mr C. H. Olivey, 15 May; Mr T. H. Elton, 19 May; Mr E. Swanepoel, 22 August; Miss J. Douglass, 22 August; Mr J. K. Syme and Mrs H. A. Syme, 13 September; Mr R. L. Smallman, 16 September; Mr Guy Walton, 4 October; Mr P. Hanson, 20 October; Mr D. A. Galloway, 24 October; Mr F. C. Steyn, 8 December.

Some, like Herbert Fenzel and Robert L. Smallman, died in ambushes. Smallman, 26, senior Superintendent at the Rhodesian Wattle Company Estates, had taken his father-in-law to the 7 a.m. convoy and was passing through the Plunket farm on his way to work when he was fatally ambushed. Others, like the Viljoens, were murdered on their farms. Their foreman (it later emerged) had pleaded with the 'boys' on behalf of the Viljoens, the vakhomana had become threatening, the foreman had closed his mouth.

Jim Syme, 73, and his wife Helen had lived in the Lemon Kop area for almost thirty years, running a mixed farm. Though orthodox 'joiners' – they belonged to the Country Club, the Women's Institute and the Farmers' and

Landowners' Association – they had only recently installed a security fence. On 13 September they were shot dead and their farmhouse set on fire over their bodies.

38. the Viscount *Hunyani*

The safest way to travel around Rhodesia was to fly. Everyone was agreed about that.

The Air Rhodesia four-engined Viscount which took off from Kariba Airport at 5.10 in the afternoon of 3 September was carrying a crew of four and fifty-two passengers, most of whom had been weekending at the lakeside holiday resort, site of the spectacular dam which spans the Zambezi and thus joins Rhodesia to Zambia.

Despite intermittent rocket and mortar attacks from Zambia, Kariba had continued to flourish, with hotel bookings only 11 per cent down on the peak year, 1972. Water-skiing, sailing, fishing and the proximity of abundant game – all this brought tourists and weekenders to the Cutty Sark Hotel or the Arabic-style Caribbea Bay Hotel with its lakeside boathouse and lush bougainvillaea.

Dr Cecil McLaren was returning to Salisbury after a forty-eight-hour spell of duty as visiting dentist to the Central African Generating Authority staff responsible for running the great dam. This stint was a medical man's version of military call-up and his fifty-ninth take-off from Kariba. One of the last to board the plane, he noticed a spare seat at the back next to a woman and her 4-year-old daughter. He took it.

The Viscount *Hunyani* (named after one of Rhodesia's major rivers) gained altitude at the normal rate, crossed the waters of the bright-blue lake, and headed over the remote, sparsely populated bush of the Urungwe TTL. The no-smoking lights went out as McClaren reached for his cigarettes.

At that moment, five minutes out of Kariba, the plane suddenly lurched, there was a loud bang and the inner starboard engine burst into flames. Ground control received a distress call from the *Hunyani*: the two starboard engines had failed. 'I was in no doubt we'd been hit by a heat-seeking missile,' says McLaren, who noted the aircraft's movements during the grim minutes that followed the explosion. It turned ninety degrees from east to due south, then plunged into a rapid descent. Although the air hostesses gallantly made sure that every passenger was strapped in there was what McLaren describes as 'a certain amount of panic'. It was the men who lost their nerve: one man rushed up and down the aisle shouting for a fire extinguisher.

In the flight cabin Capt. Hood managed to keep control of the plane as it fell, aiming its nose for a large clearing in the bush, a cotton-field as it turned out. The passengers received the pilot's last instruction: 'Brace yourselves for impact!' McLaren heard the fuselage and wings scraping against the tops of trees and then the wheels touched down quite smoothly and it seemed they were going to have a fantastic escape. But the centre of the cotton-field was penetrated by a wide irrigation ditch; as the wheels hit it the plane cartwheeled and exploded. When the wreckage finally came to a halt McLaren was upside-down five or six rows from the back and powerful flames were threatening to engulf them from the front of the plane. He tried to open a window but the handle broke in his hands. Even so he managed to release 4-year-old Tracey Cole from her seat-belt and somehow led the child and her mother, Mrs Sharon Cole, out of a hole in the fuselage.

The plane was an inferno. Only eighteen out of fifty-six survived the crash, all of them passengers seated in the rear. Among the other survivors was a friend of McLaren's, Tony Hill; between them they did their best to get the living to a distance of some seventy-five metres from the flaming plane, which they expected to explode any minute. The lucky ones ripped off their clothes to make bandages for the injured; Cynthia Tilley, a young Salisbury bank clerk and sister of 15-year-old Colin Tilley, shot down by guerrillas outside his home in January, shredded her colourful cotton dress and began to tend the wounded.

It was painfully hot: to Cecil McLaren it seemed that the most urgent task was to find water. He led a small party towards the smoke of a nearby village: Mrs Cole and Tracey, as well as Robert and Shannon Hargreaves, a honeymoon couple who were not only stunned and injured but had lost their shoes. (Shannon's hand would remain permanently disfigured, while her husband's twisted back and neck would result in months of pain, medical treatment and bitterness.) McLaren himself was wearing lace-up training shoes.

Although McLaren, born in Rhodesia of Rhodesian-born parents, spoke Shona fluently, the villagers reacted to their presence with suspicion, indeed hostility. When he finally extracted some water McLaren took it back to the survivors at the scene of the crash before returning to the village for more. Like Rider Haggard's Allan Quatermain, beleaguered among hostile natives, McLaren possessed and displayed what Mrs Cole later called 'presence of mind and strength of character'. He is a dark man, Celtic in appearance, shy, courteous and conservative; he speaks in the quiet, clipped Rhodesian manner. As he led his sad little limping party back towards the plane, carrying more water, the light was fading. His mouth and ears were still full of earth – the fuselage had ploughed up the field after the plane turned over – and he failed to pick up new voices at the scene of the crash. Sharon Cole whispered: 'I hear African voices.' Then she heard shouts of 'Buia lapa' followed by 'Come here!' in English.

This was the second act of the nightmare: Zipra.

At that moment the eighteen surviving whites comprised the following: the five in McLaren's group; Tony Hill, who, after searching for a usable weapon in the wreckage, tore off his white shirt and deliberately ran through a grass fire to cover his escape when a dozen Zipra guerrillas showed up; a Mr and Mrs Hansen, who managed to hide themselves in the wreckage, where they covered themselves in dirt and debris and lay still all night; and the remaining ten who were taken captive. At first the guerrillas promised help and water. From a distance McLaren heard an elderly Englishman, the only male among the captives, shout: 'What do you bastards want now?' A guerrilla replied: 'You have taken our land!' A protracted burst of firing followed – all ten fell dead, including Cynthia Tilley and two girls aged 11 and 4.

That brought the death toll to forty-three: for the first time in the war, the blacks were culling the whites. (See also 'slot', 'take-out', 'waste' and 'drill', not to mention 'stonk' – all variations in the white lexicon for killing terrs, gooks and floppies in suitably large numbers.)

McLaren recalls: 'I said to Sharon Cole, "Now we're on our own." ' He was unaware that Tony Hill and the Hansens had survived. In fact Hill spent the night in the same ditch as McLaren's party, though neither was aware of the other's presence. Through much of that long, bitterly cold night they listened to the stomping boots of the killers searching for them. A single high-pitched, hysterical cry of 'Mummy!' from little Tracey could have ended the story, yet she never made a sound and went to sleep, dressed in a cotton dress, on top of McLaren. McLaren again: 'When I heard an owl hoot and a baboon I shuddered. It was the longest and most terrifying night of my life.' Sharon Cole was in great pain from a huge cut in her shoulder.

In the morning, there being no sign of rescue aircraft or helicopters, McLaren decided to head for the main Salisbury–Kariba road. It was here that his coolness in taking note of the Viscount's ninety-degree turn after it was hit paid dividends; the dentist could roughly reckon their present position. It wasn't a happy little party of hikers. The injured Hargreaveses shuffled barefoot behind them, their feet torn and blistered; ever-ingenious, McLaren tried to fashion shoes for them out of bark. Tracey had to be carried. And the villagers along their route remained gloweringly hostile. Towards noon he wondered whether he had made the right decision when they saw paratroopers dropping from Dakotas over the scene of the crash. But when they did finally hit the main road after walking twelve to fifteen kilometres they were almost instantly picked up by a police Land-Rover.

An Alouette helicopter flew them to Karoi. 'Alouettes have no door. I felt terrified. I was clinging to the pilot's safety harness enough to strangle him and hating the low level at which we were flying.' At Karoi the Special Branch debriefed them and warned them not to discuss what had happened. When he got back to Salisbury, and turned on his TV set, he was astounded to hear Capt. Pat Travers, head of Air Rhodesia, describe the crash as an accident. It was self-evident to McLaren that the *Hunyani* had been brought down by a heat-seeking missile.

Not talking to the press presented no problem to a man who harbours the greatest contempt for journalists. One of the sensationalistic Jo'burg papers claimed that the white females had been raped by the terrorists before being murdered, though this was untrue (as was confirmed to me by the doctor who examined the bodies). One local girl reporter told McLaren, 'I'm not here for the truth, I want fiction.' When another reporter, though rebuffed over the phone, showed up on McLaren's doorstep for an interview, the dentist threatened to shoot him if he didn't push off.

Anger and grief turned to insensate fury two days later, on 5 September, when RBC TV relayed the soundtrack of a BBC interview with Joshua Nkomo, in the course of which he not only confirmed that his forces had brought the plane down but chuckled and chortled over his triumph, which he justified on the ground that such planes carry military men. Five days after the disaster the Minister of Transport confirmed that the plane had been shot down by a 9M32 Strela missile, commonly known as a Sam 7. In the House of Assembly, Wing Commander Rob Gaunt called for martial law, the banning of Zapu, and a postponement of the white referendum on the internal settlement. Donald Goddard, the virulent young MP for Matobo, interjected: 'Hang them publicly.' Gaunt warned that Africa was now going to witness the wrath of really angry white men.

For Ian Smith it was a political disaster. Almost simultaneously it was revealed that he had met the murderous Nkomo for secret talks in Lusaka only three weeks earlier. As crowds gathered outside the Anglican Cathedral of St Mary's and All Saints for the funeral service, an irate Rhodesian and father of four, Gideon Tredoux, held up a banner: 'PM Smith – Give Nkomo a message next time you meet him secretly: "Go to hell, you murdering bastard."' When Bishop Paul Burrough pulled down one of the hate posters, he was booed. Two thousand mourners packed into the Cathedral and a further 500 stood outside: the atmosphere was highly charged. At Cynthia Tilley's funeral at the Presbyterian Church on Jameson Avenue, one mourner growled: 'If that is not a satanic act, what is? You don't make a pact with the devil. He should be shot.'

But shooting the devil isn't easy.

39. 'a deafening silence' – the Anglican hierarchy

The funeral service for the victims was the occasion of a remarkable sermon by the Anglican Dean of Salisbury, a fulmination which provoked a long and sour controversy within the churches. The Very Rev. John da Costa is tall, strongly built, bearded, white-robed, flamboyant, with a hale and crunching handshake – and quick-tempered. Trained by the Society of the Sacred Mission, da Costa had worked in West Africa and then among the Coloureds of Cape Town, where he served as adviser on missionary work to the Archbishop.

Gazing down from the cathedral pulpit on 2,000 mourners, da Costa began by dissociating clergymen from politics: 'I will not allow politics to be preached in this Cathedral.' And yet, and yet: 'times come when it is necessary to speak out' against 'murder of the most savage and treacherous sort' which can arouse only 'disbelief . . . revulsion'. Choosing his words carefully, the Dean declared: 'This bestiality, worse than anything in recent history, stinks in the nostrils of heaven.' (The cockney accent is continually surprising.)

Da Costa accused 'the nations which call themselves civilized' of a deafening silence. Neither Dr Owen nor the President of the USA, nor the Pope, nor the Chief Rabbi nor the Archbishop of Canterbury had condemned the deed loudly and clearly. So who was to blame? First, those who fired the guns. And who were they? Men and youths who, as likely as not, had recently attended church schools. Shooting from the hip, the Dean raked not only the TV and cinema screens of the world for glorifying violence, but also the UN and the World Council of Churches who each paraded 'a pseudo-morality which, like all half-truths, is more dangerous than the lie direct'. But really all the churches were to blame for failing to defeat the 'satanic forces' of Communism by means of prayer, praise and religious witness.

Even though the Canon Press sold 38,000 copies of the sermon and a record company sold 25,000 discs (for which the Dean was awarded a golden disc), he describes 'A Deafening Silence' as 'the most disastrous failure of my whole ministry'. Why? Because the brother canons of the Cathedral were angry about it; because nonconformists accused him of violating his own ban on political sermons. Particularly hurtful was the deafening silence with which the Anglican Church in England and overseas greeted 'A Deafening

Silence'. 'I don't see Communists under every bed,' he says, clenching his large fists. 'It's a pity the right-wingers grabbed hold of the sermon: it's a pity Rhodesians missed the point I was making *against them*.'

I ask the Dean – it seems relevant to do so – what he feels about the Rhodesian bombing raids against camps in Mozambique and Zambia, which involved the killing of women and children in far greater numbers than those who perished with the Viscount. Da Costa's response confirms my fears. 'Those women and children', he says, 'are camp-followers of terrorists. Frelimo is teaching them to breed a new generation with no links to the kraals, they're just troops' comforts, those women in the camps, breeding the new breed.' So it's OK to slaughter them? The Dean looks fierce: 'Israel finds pre-emptive raids necessary, so why not Rhodesia?'

No political sermons?

The Dean is angry now – am I trying to make out he is a racist, that he supports the Rhodesian Front? He would like to remind me, as loudly as possible, for God's cause is not always served by meekness, that 'the Bishop and I have gone out and gathered evidence of atrocities committed by the security forces, we reported what we found, the culprits were duly punished'.

I called on the Anglican Bishop of Mashonaland.

Among those typically English faces, begot and distilled out of the National Portrait Gallery in Trafalgar Square, paradigms of the island race, there is an Anglican clerical visage, the long, thin, smooth, upper-class face which English Catholics, too, sometimes can't help having. Bishop Paul Burrough possesses the prototype of this face, the calm, public-school accent, the height and broad shoulders of a former Oxford rowing blue, the medal ribbons which he pins on his surplice with that peculiarly Anglican delight in serving the Crown.

Paul Burrough is Bishop of Mashonaland, one of Rhodesia's two Anglican dioceses. Born in 1916, Burrough was serving as a signals officer in Singapore when taken prisoner by the Japanese and incarcerated for four years. After the war he worked in Korea as a missionary priest, living on £21 per month, without transport, in a room measuring eight feet by eight – 'yet loving people to attend to my needs always surrounded me'. Consecrated Bishop in 1968, by May 1973 he had travelled, at his own reckoning, over 160,000 kilometres through Rhodesia and taken 20,000 confirmations. In Lent 1975 he embarked on a 750-kilometre pilgrimage through his diocese on foot and horseback, setting out from the Hartley hills on Ash Wednesday and working his way through the Sabi Valley and up to Inyanga via Umtali – a splendid tall figure in open-neck shirt, crucifix swinging across his stomach, towering above a clutch of delighted kids as he strode through the long grass.

The record of the Anglican Church in Rhodesia since UDI had been one of equivocation. When Smith made his Unilateral Declaration of Independence, the Archbishop of Canterbury, Michael Ramsey, denounced it. But only three of Britain's twenty-eight Anglican Bishops publicly stepped forward to support the primate's stand. In Rhodesia, the remarkably radical Bishop Kenneth Skelton of Matabeleland sent a telegram of support to Ramsey, but Burrough's predecessor as Bishop of Mashonaland, C. W. Alderson, more accurately reflected white Anglican opinion when he put forward the view that Ramsey was ill-informed; that UDI was 'much less an evil (on all counts) than . . . a rapid transition to unskilled, tribal, racial and nationalist government'.

At the time of the Geneva Conference, in December 1976, Burrough wrote to *The Times* warning that the PF planned to introduce a Marxist state. He also explained that one man, one vote was nothing but an unwanted embarrassment to 'the good African tribesman for it leaves him defenceless against intimidation'. Nor did he forget where an Anglican Bishop's true loyalties should lie. A Marxist state in Rhodesia, he told *The Times*, would bring about 'the consequent loss of the Cape sea routes for Britain by the isolation of South Africa', which in turn 'would cause Britain to be a colony of Russia or a poor satellite of the USA within ten years at the most'. He believed it a serious dereliction of duty that Britain had agreed 'to give independence to a totally unknown government in Rhodesia not later than March 1, 1978'.

That date came and went, without Britain finding itself in a position to give Rhodesia to anybody, but Burrough's obsession with Cape sea routes did not diminish. A letter appeared in *The Times* on 17 March 1978 complaining that Britain was appeasing terrorists. 'Then the puny oil rigs in the North Sea, so tragically vulnerable to a hostile commando force, would do nothing to save Britain from rapid capitulation to an economic blockade.' The Bishop enjoyed writing to *The Times*, which apparently never rejects a letter from an Anglican prelate, and confessed in March 1979 that he was much put down by that famous paper's prolonged non-appearance.

Although he always emphasized his personal opposition to UDI and the RF, his appetite for British military intervention extended to one target only: the Patriotic Front. Following the massacre of nine white missionaries and four children at Elim Pentecostal mission in June 1978, he publicly chided Britain (David Owen) for its failure to react: 'When I was a young man, if this kind of thing happened, two battalions of paratroopers would be sent in to clean up those responsible. But I suppose that kind of thing doesn't happen any more.'

The Bishop frequently used the columns of the Anglican organ, *The Link*, to propagate the virtues of a 'multi-racial, free enterprise society' and, indeed, the virtues of the entrenched clauses engineered by Ian Smith which even Mrs Thatcher ultimately found unacceptable. 'They make it genuinely transitional,' wrote Burrough. 'You can't do everything overnight.' He demanded an immediate end to economic sanctions against Rhodesia; their continuation would merely play into the hands of 'the Communists'.

He points to a wall map. 'I can show you twenty areas where our churches have been forced to go underground as a result of terrorist intimidation. And who finds the $(R)25,000 needed to support the twenty affected priests after funds from the suppressed black congregations have dried up? The whites do.' Burrough leans across his desk and sternly reminds me of the Maoist strategy of breaking up the fabric of established society – schools, cattle dips, churches. Of nine Anglican secondary schools, six had been forcibly closed.

It's true that he has on occasion spoken out against certain policies of the Rhodesian Front: the 1969 constitution, the Land Tenure Act, the notorious Indemnity and Compensation Act of 1975. 'Lardner-Burke threatened me. There are times when you want to kick the RF in the teeth and times when you want to kick the other side.' And he did appear as a defence witness at the trial of Bishop Donal Lamont – refusal to report the presence of terrorists may, he agrees, be the price of a rural priest's survival.

'I do know', he wrote in *The Link*, 'that in answer to the total disregard for life and the obscene cruelty of our enemies, we are in danger of much too high a number of people "killed in crossfire", much too slow a compensation for their relatives (if such compensation ever comes) and shrugging off vindictiveness by the security forces against suspects and terrified tribesmen who do not co-operate with them.'

The Bishop resents any imputation that his stance has been either partisan or unsympathetic to the political aspirations of God's African children.

40. martial law shall prevail

The shooting down of the Viscount *Hunyani*, the massacre of survivors, and Nkomo's gloating interview suited Muzorewa very well. Smith had no option but to discontinue clandestine negotiations with the Bishop's bitter rival and to make the best of his collaboration with the internal black parties, little faith though he now had in their ability to de-escalate the war. To placate incensed white opinion, Smith cracked down on Nkomo's followers within the country, arresting between 150 and 200 officials of the ANC(Z) in dawn raids on 12 September. The whites had been hoping for something more drastic and more dramatic.

On 28 August D-notices were issued again forbidding newspapers to mention Zanu, Zapu or their leaders, editors having discovered that magazines and newspapers carrying profiles of Mugabe sold out instantly in black Salisbury. The closure of the *Zimbabwe Times* on 2 October confirmed the regime's disinclination to countenance freedom of the press. This paper, which had been acquired by 'Tiny' Rowland, boss of the giant firm Lonrho, had given offence by appointing Zapu men like Ciphas Msipa and Willie Musarurwa to its staff, by calling for all-party talks, by publishing a long interview with Robert Mugabe in which he insisted that the Zimbabwean army must be controlled by the guerrillas, and by accusing Muzorewa of packing the UANC's executive with Manyika cronies.

But what happened to one dissident newspaper was of little account compared with the draconian imposition of martial law across the tribal trust lands. As usual the rebel regime copied the solemn legal and parliamentary formulas of the Mother Country, the palaver of Mace and Wig, in an effort to legitimate the same rough-and-ready racial 'justice' inflicted on the natives by the Pioneers – adventurers and rugged frontiersmen – of the 1890s.

'Government Gazette Extraordinary . . . Proclamation by Lieutenant-Colonel the Honourable Henry Breedon Everard, ICD, DSO, TD, Acting President in and over Rhodesia . . . Now do I hereby . . . make known that a state of martial law shall . . . prevail . . .' The new courts martial were restricted neither by the normal concept of a crime, nor by the laws in force – nor by the right of appeal to the civil courts. Kangaroo justice 'by Authority' replaced due process.

It may not have mattered. The security forces already enjoyed a free rein to 'suppress terrorism by all necessary means', a random sample of which can be gleaned from the following cases:

(1) A group of villagers had gathered on 9 August at Nyamaropa for the funeral of a local teacher. Although a red flag was flown to indicate that the gathering was a legitimate funeral, the mourners were nevertheless attacked both from the air and the ground with such ferocity that ten people were killed. The survivors were then ordered to bury the dead immediately, two bodies to a grave. This incident was never officially reported but was verified by the Justice and Peace Commission.

(2) Villagers had gathered in the Makoni TTL for a 'kurovaguva', a Shona rite performed some time after burial, when helicopters swooped from the sky, firing shots and throwing grenades at people as they fled into the surrounding maize-fields. Seven were killed.

(3) In the Dett area south of Wankie security forces killed two guerrillas on 22 September then hung their bodies to rot at two wells where villagers drew their drinking-water. The soldiers checked regularly to make sure that no one had cut the stinking corpses down. The villagers had to abandon the two wells.

According to the Justice and Peace Commission, at least 718 families living in the Catholic dioceses of Salisbury, Gwelo and Umtali had their huts burnt down by security forces during the last four months of 1978. This form of punishment was inflicted on all villages suspected of having harboured guerrillas: on 13 January 1979, 225 families were rendered homeless in the Mangwende TTL when the army set fire to four large kraals. The black MP Lot Dewa reported how all the local kraals were burnt down after an army vehicle detonated a landmine on 8 December on the Shabani–West Nicholson road. Troops from Meyara base camp regularly inflicted forced labour on the tribesmen, who were required to sweep the roads for mines and who were savagely beaten if suspected of failing to report the presence of 'terrorists'.

On extremely rare occasions members of the security forces were punished in the courts. Regional Magistrate D. C. Knight sentenced ten former members of Internal Affairs, all of them African, for multiple rape, violence and stock theft committed on 31 December 1978 in the Nkai area. One man had his skull fractured; an elderly woman's arm was broken while she was defending her head from a rifle-butt blow; a young woman was knocked unconscious and left bleeding from a head wound; two men were held down and beaten with a strap; six women, of whom two were pregnant, were stripped, beaten, raped. According to the prosecution this day's work destroyed the local population's good relationship with the DC's office (just as the gas chambers destroyed Hitler's good relationship with the Jews?). The ten culprits were given sentences ranging up to twelve and a half years.

Yet the odd thing, as the magistrate pointed out, was that the ringleader of the group, the only European involved, David John Price, was not in court; however, Price was eventually sentenced to fourteen years' imprisonment in Bulawayo Regional Court, nine months after terrorizing the local people of Nkai.

41. Ian Smith visits Disneyland

By midsummer the Carter Administration's Rhodesian policy was under heavy fire. On 29 June Senator Jesse Helms, of North Carolina, proposed a resolution to lift sanctions: it was defeated by only 48 votes to 42. Helms's staffer John Carbaugh invited Muzorewa to visit Washington to lobby for the repeal of sanctions. Muzorewa put himself over on Capitol Hill as a black Anwar Sadat – indeed Senators Javits, Case and Moynihan, all of whom criticized the refusal to recognize the internal settlement, were strong supporters of Israel.

On 26 July the Senate passed, by 59 votes to 36, a compromise resolution proposed by Clifford Case and Jacob Javits (Republican, New York), requiring the President to lift sanctions but only after a democratically elected government in Salisbury had committed itself to negotiate with the PF. The Administration's Rhodesia policy could now count on the unqualified support of only fifteen to twenty Senators, including Edward Kennedy. Why was the Administration 'supporting terrorists', why was it turning its back on those Rhodesians who shared our 'Western values', why was it playing the Russians' game for them?

On 14 September twenty-seven out of one hundred United States Senators took the dramatic step of signing a letter inviting Ian Smith and Ndabaningi Sithole to visit Washington. The signatories included not only extremists like Senators Sam Hayakawa, of California, and Jesse Helms, but also moderates who had been persuaded that the regime was now genuinely multiracial. Much of the persuading was performed by Kenneth H. Towsey, head of the Rhodesian Information Office since UDI and possessor of the precious 'green card' for world-wide travel possessed by permanent residents of the USA. Towsey had stage-managed Muzorewa's visit to America in July.

Applying sanctions regulations and heeding strong British objections, the State Department at first refused Smith a visa. The RIO thereupon launched a massive protest and propaganda campaign through right-wing papers and radio stations while Hayakawa and Helms threatened to halt the passage of legislation and Government business during the last two weeks of the Congressional session if visas were not granted to Smith and his entourage. The State Department gave way.

A group of seven British peers and ten MPs seized the opportunity to invite Smith to visit London *en route* to America. The group, which included Lord Salisbury (of 'our kith and kin' fame), Sir John Eden, Maurice Macmillan, Julian Amery and Lord George-Brown, asked the Government to guarantee Smith's immunity from arrest and prosecution. David Owen, recently described by the RF Chairman, Col. Matt Knox, as 'a small man with a big grudge against all Rhodesians, black and white', adamantly refused to do so. There was much spluttering in the pages of the *Daily Telegraph*.

Arriving in Washington on 7 October, Smith and Sithole embarked on a succession of press conferences, interviews, TV panel shows and receptions, at most of which Smith spoke sourly and direly of Communist penetration of southern Africa. He promised elections and agreed to meet the PF at a Camp David-style summit (thus flattering Carter and putting down the British) provided there were no preconditions. In fact Smith was also flattering himself: Israel might be worth a Camp David summit chaired by the President of the United States but Rhodesia wasn't. Carter refused to meet him. Smith was not allowed to lay a wreath in Arlington Cemetery at the tomb of the Unknown Soldier. He spent an hour with Henry Kissinger – and was photographed in Disneyland.

The liberal National Unifying Force dispatched Allan Savory, Nick McNally and Lance Reynolds to counter-lobby in the United States. Savory called for an all-party conference and a neutral administration during the run-up to free elections. This, the NUF leaders told the Americans, was the only way to lick the Communists.

The British, meanwhile, maintained their intelligence links with the rebel regime. Despite the blacklist of key personnel who were barred from entering Britain, Ken Flower, Smith's British-born central intelligence chief, and Derrick Robinson, head of Special Branch 2, regularly entered Britain without hindrance. The Foreign Office clearly hoped that Flower, Robinson, Smith's Cabinet Secretary Jack Gaylard and the Zambians could – with or without the help of 'Tiny' Rowland and Lonrho – persuade Nkomo to throw in his lot with the internal settlement, albeit in a modified form. Lord Carrington, the Tory leader in the House of Lords, also favoured this solution; on 25 September he told the Carlton Club that the internal settlement was unlikely to succeed unless Nkomo was associated with it.

42. motorbike

On 27 September Sister Jennifer Boyd, 34, an Australian-born nurse, and four African District Assistants were killed in the north-east. Sister Boyd survived a landmine explosion but was subsequently shot in the neck.

A Plumtree couple, Marthinus and Esme Meyer, aged 47 and 45, parents of four and South African-born, were killed during an ambush on their ranch on 29 September. Meyer had previously worked for Rhodesian Railways, and subsequently as a land-inspector.

Early in October R. W. G. Puchria, farm manager in the Fort Rixon area about seventy kilometres east of Bulawayo, was ambushed and killed.

Two farmers were killed on Wednesday, 4 October: Peter Gunn in the middle Sabi area, and Guy Walton at Stronchavie Farm, Melsetter.

On 18 October Leslie Osborn, 53, an area manager for a firm of borehole drillers, was killed by a landmine. Born in England, he had settled in Umtali in the 1950s.

Arthur Beamish, a 32-year-old Sipolilo farmer, was killed during an ambush on his farm, together with a Mr Spoon and a Mr Captain. A former Old Hararians rugby player, Beamish had married Gail Murphy, sister of the national rugby coach Brian Murphy.

A motorbike affords the rider no protection except speed, yet Rhodesian farmers frequently used them to tour their farms, perhaps assuming, against all the evidence, that they were inviolate within their own boundaries. Chris Stobart, a Mtoko farmer, had no basis for any such assumption, having suffered two attacks within a year; it was nevertheless by motorbike that he rode down to inspect his tobacco-seed beds on 12 October.

Hearing shots, he opened up his throttle, accelerated, skidded and crashed into a wire fence. He found himself lying in open ground and under fire from eight guerrillas. Having crawled to an anthill fifty metres away, he began to return fire with his FN. Two of the assailants provided covering fire while the rest moved to outflank him. A bullet ripped into his left leg and smashed the femur. During the ensuing twenty minutes he was hit again in the left leg, then below the knee in the right leg. They were now within twenty-five metres of him and bullets were thudding into the anthill next to his face. They also had grenades – shrapnel penetrated his foot.

Finally he had only one bullet left. He put the muzzle of his FN to his head but couldn't pull the trigger. Maybe it was the image of his wife Marjorie and of his four sons that inhibited him. At that moment the Guard Force arrived on the scene and the guerrillas gapped it.

43. like fuckin' ants . . .

The raids of 19 October were by no means the first Rhodesian military incursions into Zambia. More than fifty Zipra guerrillas had been reported killed when Rhodesians crossed Lake Kariba in boats and helicopters in December 1977 and attacked the base at Siampondo. According to a Rhodesian communiqué issued on 7 March 1978, at least thirty-eight Zipra guerrillas and twelve Zambian soldiers were killed during a raid on Luangwa, fifteen kilometres west of the point where the Rhodesian, Zambian and Mozambican borders meet. It was the fifth attack on Zambia since the previous August. In fact the Special Air Service had been operating inside Zambia almost continuously for nine months.

In mid-September commandos parachuted from DC-3s and landed in Alouettes during a four-day operation against twenty-five guerrilla bases inside Mozambique. When Comops launched the first of its new attacks on Zambia on 19 October, the main intention was to extend the principle of mass slaughter – 1,000 at a time – already perpetrated at Nyadzonia and Chimoio in Mozambique, and thus provide white Rhodesians with the cathartic act of revenge demanded by the shooting down of the Viscount airliner.

By the end of the operation the Rhodesians claimed they had killed at least 500 guerrillas in twelve Zambian bases, including FC Camp on Westlands Farm near Lusaka. Nkomo counter-alleged that 1,500 refugees had been killed, not one of them a guerrilla. He also claimed to have shot down nine planes. But journalists were sceptical because they were not allowed to visit the raided camps or inspect the wreckage of the supposedly shot-down planes. Nkomo grew angrier, attacking the Western journalists as racists. 'Who are you?' he bellowed threateningly at a news conference. 'When I listen to your broadcasts I come to the conclusion that we are dealing with journalists plus.'

Mkushi is a remote camp 150 kilometres north-east of Lusaka and its 2,036 Zimbabwean inhabitants perhaps felt themselves to be relatively safe from attack. On 19 October Rhodesian bombs rained down on them and then the paratroopers went in, guns blazing. A big cull, perhaps a couple of hundred, with others injured or dying in the surrounding bush, among the green, gold and orange trees of early summer. It wasn't Lt Angus Neal's first unauthorized visit to Zambia: in June and July he had been operating on foot with an SAS unit in the Gwembe Valley near the southern end of the Lake, 'burning' terrs by laying ambushes and planting mines. As Angus puts it, in his gentle, modest manner, 'Offensive action is the only way, there are so many of them.'

Maybe Mkushi wasn't quite the camp that the Rhodesians thought it was: maybe they were surprised to find that a high proportion of their victims were females. Nkomo said later that most of the 192 dead or missing at Mkushi were girls, training for future police work and the civil service. Even so, it was a camp run on a military basis; when Comops and Special Branch shrewdly flew in selected reporters from Salisbury next day they had no difficulty in displaying piles of rifles, hand-grenades, landmines – and a Soviet-style officer's peak cap lying in the dust. A Rhodesian PR operation is technically a good one. Eddie Adams of Associated Press was reminded of Indo-China – the thatched huts, the tunnels, trenches, foxholes; the sand and heat, the stench of death. It now seems probable that the fifty uniformed bodies left scattered round the camp – 'mainly men but including two young women', wrote Adams – had been deliberately rearranged to conceal the extent to which Mkushi had been a camp for females.

To ram home its victory, the Rhodesian propaganda machine released on RBC the tape of a famously arrogant message from 'Green Leader', a bomber pilot, to Lusaka control tower:

'This is a message for the station commander at Mumbwa [a Zambian air base]. We are attacking the terrorist base at Westlands Farm at this time. This attack is against Rhodesian dissidents and not against Zambia. Rhodesia has no quarrel with Zambia or her security forces. We therefore ask you not to intervene or oppose our attack. However, we are orbiting your airfields at this time and we are under orders to shoot down any Zambian air force aircraft which does not comply with this request and attempts to take off. Did you copy all that?'

Lusaka control tower replied, humbly, 'Roger. Thanks. Cheers,' and asked 'Green Leader' to change radio frequencies 'if it doesn't inconvenience you'.

All terrific, morale-boosting stuff. But it transpires that the Rhodesians set the whole thing up as a propaganda exercise and that 'Green Leader' delivered his 'fuckin' piece of speech', as he called it, on the way out and home. David Martin and Phyllis Johnson acquired the unabridged cockpit recording of the Rhodesian pilot's actual conversation during the attack on Freedom Camp:

'. . . Beautiful, Jesus Christ those fuckin' bombs are beautiful . . . Roger, just let me get onto the fuckin' tower and give them our bloody message here. Where's this fuckin' piece of speech . . . I think it'll be better when we've climbed up. . . . That was mushi, fuckin' hundreds of gooks. . . . There are fuckin' kaffirs everywhere. . . . They're like fuckin' ants running around there, eh?' (*The Struggle for Zimbabwe*, p. 297.)

And so on.

Not surprisingly 'Green Leader' his Hawker Hunters and his Beautiful Bombs brought Zipra to the point of hysteria. On 20 October Nkomo alleged that 226 had been killed during the raid on Chikumbi camp, twelve kilometres north of Lusaka, and 629 hospitalized. For several weeks thereafter guerrillas directed fire at almost any aircraft flying at 500–1,000 metres, fifteen to twenty-five kilometres west of the Lusaka runway. More than one domestic flight was struck by automatic fire as it came in to land.

Those of Zambia's white farmers who farmed in the Botha's Rust area, where the devastated Zapu camps were located, were suddenly subject to a reign of terror. About 500 white farmers, including a number of Afrikaners, remained in Zambia, producing 65 per cent of the country's food and making good money, despite stiff controls on sending funds out of the country and the 1974 law transforming freeholds into ninety-nine-year leases. Miss Muriel Bissell, 67, was found murdered on her farm. Others were warned by their servants not to do anything which might confirm Zipra's conviction that they were spies. Zipra was now convinced that the success of Rhodesia's operations depended on intelligence contacts with whites living in Zambia.

On 2 November another Rhodesian bombing raid further fanned hysteria. Abrie Krige, a farmer who had maintained reasonable terms with the local Zipra camp, was beaten for sixteen hours by guerrillas screaming that he was a spy. Krige was released only after his family and other white farmers had made frantic representations to the Government. An Austrian staying at Yielding Farm, a refugee centre with church connections, was hung by his hands and bayoneted in the feet. His English companion Patricia Taylor had her face battered and ribs broken with AK47s. The *Zambia Daily Mail* called for a rooting out of infiltrators. Papers like *Weekend World* were full of alarm and despondency about white faces and saboteurs. Mobs set upon whites in the streets of Lusaka. Most dangerous was the main thoroughfare, Cairo Road. The town was alive with rumours about new Rhodesian raids of ever greater daring: the press reported that they had parachuted into an industrial area of Lusaka to steal Zambian army uniforms. Half a dozen foreign nationals were held in prison on spying charges and one white farmer, Ian Sutherland, 43, was gaoled for five years for having hidden weapons in oil drums on his farm near Mazabuka. In February 1979 a white Zambian, Karl Bothma, was killed and several members of his family injured when their car was attacked in a farming area outside the capital by three guerrillas.

Angus Neal is proud of his service with the élite Special Air Service – he can free-fall parachute to 250 metres. Now he is spending a weekend at his father's farm, playing an earnest, awkward, scampering game of tennis at the country club, short, muscular and white-skinned in his khaki shorts, a quiet person, self-contained, the sort who can remain sober at a boisterous drink-up without seeming aloof or stand-offish. His mop of hair makes him look like an East End street urchin in a brown-study daguerreotype, *c.* 1860. Plans to study biochemistry at Newcastle University.

If pressed, Angus rates the SAS professional superior to the Selous Scout. Why are there no blacks in the SAS? 'Because even after you make the grade you can be weeded out. Blacks would take umbrage.' Angus's tennis may be clumsy but he is a fitness fanatic: stripped down, he's an anatomy lesson. 'The terrs? In my opinion they're indoctrinated and don't know what they're doing. You kill one and there's always another. Our only hope is offensive action. But we can't survive without outside help. It's about time Europe looked after Europeans – it's the white man who's getting a raw deal throughout the world.'

He spends some of the weekend in a hammock with Peter Armstrong's best-selling *Operation Zambezi*, a fictionalized celebration of what Angus and his fellow-heroes achieved during their super-Aryan Commando raids. The novel revels in the bemused helplessness of the backward foe – one recalls that Israelis cracked jokes about Arab battlefield confusion and panic until the chastening lesson of the Yom Kippur war. The famous insolent message of 'Green Leader' from his bomber to Lusaka control tower, telling the Zambian Air Force to stay on the ground or else – this act of panache, enthusiastically related by novelist Armstrong, brought tears of joy to white Rhodesia and to Angus too.

It's odd – or is it? – that the genuine article, the real SAS commando, should want to soak up a mythological version of his own exploits. Yet we are all amazed by our own photograph, even more by our reincarnation in print; a medal, or a bonus payment, is nothing compared with the miracle of mimesis. Angus is now recharging his batteries, his reserves of belligerence, on Armstrong's depiction of the fictional terrorist Mutandwe who takes fiendish pleasure in watching a mother's face while he dismembers her child limb by limb. This atrocity, of course, provides the required pretext for savage counter-violence: the 'loyal' black, Sgt Nyamadzaya, bereaved and enraged, hangs the terrorist by his heels from a msasa-tree and slowly, s-l-o-w-l-y beats him to death. Finally his boot almost severs the dying man's head from his shoulders. Nice one. Unreal, man.

Angus's hairy legs and arms are curled up, at rest: the hands of a killer hold the paperback gently. Yesterday and perhaps tomorrow his gunship will spin up from the camp, the kraal, the gook lair, and when the dust from its rotor blades settles the vultures will be there, hovering over his day's work.

History repeats itself but Angus Neal does not hear the music. For him black Africa is Congo–Kaunda–Chaos. And Idi Amin. Although the psychiatric ward of the Andrew Fleming Hospital is packed with young warriors whose crisis assumes a form known to pathology, the real crisis is collective and known to philosophy – the flight into false consciousness, the attempt to strip the exploited of their rationality and their humanity.

44. how and why Winston Churchill got the sack

The Tories were now in disarray. At the party's annual conference in October the terminally ill Shadow Foreign Secretary, John Davies, was heckled and jeered for his shilly-shallying failure to advocate an end to economic sanctions against Rhodesia. The Shadow Cabinet shrank from the international consequences of such a course, though backbench Tory opinion, as reflected in the '1922 Committee', strongly favoured outright opposition to the Government's renewal of the annual sanctions order.

Over to the House of Commons. On the Government front bench Foreign Secretary David Owen glances up and around at the galleries – press, visitors – while listening to the debate. Is he really listening? Even his friends accuse the handsome Owen of arrogance. The leader of the Opposition is a smallish woman in a brown suit and matching tan handbag and shoes. Her hair is permed and gleaming and she looks extremely Rhodesian, except that no Rhodesian woman would aspire to run the country, to hire and fire all those dark-suited Tory males sitting beside her and behind her – Thatcher's underlings.

Owen is now on his feet, unrepentant about his refusal to embrace the internal settlement. In America Smith had declared himself ready to attend a conference without preconditions, yet Smith ruled out integration of the rival armies, a UN presence and a neutral, Carver-type chief executive during the transitional phase. And so on: sound stuff. For the Opposition, Francis Pym makes his first speech as Shadow Foreign Secretary, intimating that Owen had committed a 'major blunder' in shunning the internal settlement, which had apparently put an end to the 'struggle of black versus white'. Pym speaks glowingly of Rhodesia's white population: the prosperity of the country depends on them. Then, anti-climax: the Tories don't actually propose immediate recognition of the Salisbury regime or immediate lifting of sanctions because, well, all our friends and allies were rather against it. . . .

No wonder Winston Churchill Jr couldn't stomach this milk-soaked bread pudding; no wonder Rear-Admiral Morgan-Giles (C., Winchester) protested along with Sir John Eden, representing Bournemouth West, haven of genteel retired folk lifting their wrinkled faces up to a tepid Channel sun, and the earthy Mrs Jill Knight, a no-nonsense Birmingham reactionary of solid build. 'Is it the government's policy to rub Mr Smith's nose in the dirt regardless of the consequences?' Morgan-Giles demanded to know. The Rear-Admiral, who had always voted against sanctions, told a hushed (if empty) House that he had once asked Ian Smith whether he would illegally have declared Rhodesia Independent had a British Tory Government been in office at the time: 'Good Lord No,' Smith had replied, 'perish the thought.' An enemy of Treason and Ultra-Loyal to his Sovereign, as a naval officer must be, Morgan-Giles nevertheless managed to be on friendly terms with a rebel who had repudiated the Monarchy and generally earned a place in the darkest dungeon of the Tower.

Eldon Griffiths (C., Bury St Edmunds), Parliamentary spokesman for the Police Federation, was one of several MPs who said, 'I have been in Rhodesia many times. It is a magnificent country' – or words to that effect. Griffiths had told Smith this and he had told Nkomo that Britain should heed its own economic interests and refuse to renew sanctions because (a) they had achieved their objective and (b) had never been effective, as the Bingham Report showed. (Some element of contradiction here, possibly.)

John Farr (C., Harborough) turned out to be a Rhodesian farmer with property near Wankie. British settlers had brought peace and prosperity for one hundred years and now Rhodesia was assailed by 'external enemies, the forces of evil' who were destroying the bonds of affection and trust between whites and tribesmen. The maverick and hugely entertaining Scottish back-bencher Nicholas Fairbairn was speaking of Rhodesia, not Scotland, when he swore that, 'In no other country on earth do we find the excellence of human decency, goodwill and love that we find in that country.'

Reginald Maudling, a former Chancellor of the Exchequer and candidate for the Tory leadership, backed the internal settlement as if he had a 10 per cent stake in it (Maudling's business activities had from time to time sparked controversy) while Julian Amery (C., Brighton Pavilion) who had been to Rhodesia twenty-seven times in twenty-eight years and Sir Frederic Bennett (C., Torbay) – a mere twenty visits – were both hot for an end to sanctions and precipitate recognition of the Salisbury regime.

The loudest voice on the Labour benches was that of the former actor Andrew Faulds who, though barred from Rhodesia since his expulsion in 1966, nevertheless felt qualified to announce that, 'The boys in the bush are now the people who represent the real views of the majority of Africans in Southern Rhodesia.' Nicholas Winterton (C., Macclesfield) was much angered: 'The Hon. Gentleman does what Moscow tells him.' Rear-Admiral Morgan-Giles went even further with a spurious point of order: 'Is it in order for a bit-part television actor to come to this House, disguised as Rasputin, and refer to an international statesman as "Smith"?'

From the Labour side Alex Lyon, a former junior Minister in the Foreign Office (but too ardent an anti-racist to hold office for long), reported that, even in the presence of District Commissioners, Rhodesian kraal heads avowed their support for the 'boys'. Austin Mitchell described the Salisbury regime as 'essentially a white Government which has been blackwashed for the purposes of a public relations exercise'. In his view the internal settlement advanced the interests of only 'the kind of African who wants to use the bars of Meikles Hotel . . .'. Joan Lestor and Robert Hughes, both friends of black Africa, joined in from the Labour benches.

In the event 116 Tory MPs defied the front-bench instruction to abstain in the vote. This act of mutiny cost Winston Churchill his job as Tory spokesman on Defence. Churchill wrote to Mrs Thatcher insisting that lifting sanctions and recognizing the internal settlement offered 'the only hope of preventing the vital mineral wealth of Rhodesia and ultimately of South Africa falling under Soviet control'. Mr Churchill's language was emotive. 'While a British Government is leading the pack in holding down the peoples of Rhodesia so that the surrogates of the Soviets may more speedily slit their throats – unquestionably the most ignominious act of any British Government this century – I cannot in all honesty pretend that I do not know which way to vote.' In a later letter (9 November) Churchill spoke of 'the debt of honour we owe to the countless Rhodesians who came to fight for Britain in her hour of peril'.

Torn between this direct appeal to Grandfather Winston's finest hour and the challenge by the cocky junior colt to her authority, Mrs Thatcher had no hesitation in sending him down – a rustication which was later extended as a result of small scandal. 'For me', wrote Maggie, 'the decision [to fire you] I have had to make brings great personal sadness, as I know it will for Minnie and for your mother.'

In the House of Lords the debate largely followed party lines. Lord Goodman, a lawyer who had played a leading part in negotiating the disastrously ill-judged Smith–Douglas-Home agreement in 1971, now Master of University College, Oxford, declared the internal settlement to be 'a near miracle' and the internal leaders as 'seemingly representative of the great majority of Africans'. (However, he did not favour lifting economic sanctions as yet.) The incredible Lord St Oswald insisted that Smith was no longer *really* Prime Minister. There was also an atavistic intervention by the Earl of Kimberley (whose great-grandfather, a Colonial Secretary, gave his name to the famous diamond town). The Earl of Lytton reminisced about his time in Africa fifty years before: Russia, he declared, is the Enemy.

Viscount Massereene and Ferrard (a real person) said he had always voted against sanctions: Smith had kept the flag of civilization flying in Africa. Lord Hankey, a former Cabinet Secretary, believed that to bring the PF into the settlement on their own terms was to put the Communist cuckoo in the nest: we should not treat 'our own countrymen in Rhodesia so very badly'. Viscount Caldecote, declaring his business interests in Rhodesia, said that Smith had borne his 'heavy burden with courage and fortitude'.

Sanctions were renewed in the Upper House by 166 votes to 65.

45. gone but not forgotten

The war came to Salisbury in spectacular fashion: a vast fire in the city's petrol-storage depot started by guerrillas at 9 p.m. on Monday, 11 December 1978. By Tuesday night a river of flame had flowed down a concrete drainage ditch destroying a section of railway line and creating havoc among the firefighters. Extra supplies of protein foam had to be flown in from South Africa. The lid of one storage tank was blown 200 metres into the night sky. By Friday night a single storage tank was still blazing: twenty-three others were now crumpled in the Shell–BP section of the depot, twisted heaps of charred metal. Never were two rockets more wisely expended: each storage tank was unofficially reckoned to hold 3½ million litres of fuel-petrol, aviation spirit or diesel fuel. Not surprisingly both wings of the Patriotic Front claimed responsibility. The Government refused to disclose how much fuel had been lost or what proportion of the country's total stocks it represented.

It later became known that the attack had been the work of Zanla guerrillas, who had commandeered two taxis in Harare market square. After setting the tanks alight they had forced the taxi-drivers to take them to a spot on the Lomangundi Road. Although the drivers reported this to their superiors the owner of the company decided not to inform the police.

In November a father of six, Fany Wenceslaus, 55, was killed when guerrillas attacked the road gang he was supervising. Wenceslaus lived in Bulawayo.

In the same month David Garley, 65, a retired Latin-teacher, was killed during an attack on his home in the Inyanga district. His wife survived the harrowing ordeal.

On the night of 15 December, Douglas Moorcroft, 69, was killed on his farm at Bindura when a rocket was fired into his bedroom, penetrating two walls on its way. His wife was injured.

On 22 December Gideon Joubert, 73, was killed when guerrillas attacked his farm in the Raffingora area.

On the night of 23 December four people were slaughtered when guerrillas penetrated a Shamva farm at 9.20 in the evening. Killed were John Bennett, 60, his wife Molly, 62, and two boys, Nicholas Nelson, 8, and Thomas Joslin, 7. The bodies of the boys were found in the kitchen, where they had tried to hide.

Six days later an almost identical slaughter took place at Killarney, nine kilometres south of Lalapanzi in the Midlands. Denis Hutchinson, 35, his wife Isobel, 28, and their sons Barry, 6, and Vaughan, 3, were all resting in a bedroom at 3 o'clock in the afternoon when guerrillas entered their farm-house, killed them, and set it on fire.

Gert Muller, 55, father of four, was killed when his Centenary farm was attacked during the night of 25 December. The 'boys' were not interested in Christmas truces.

Two days later Mrs Sylvia Watkins, 21, a rancher's wife from Chiredzi, was ambushed between the ranch and Ngundu Halt while driving with her husband Lyle and her brother. Although about twelve guerrillas were in-volved in the attack, only one bullet found its mark – Sylvia Watkins died two days later.

On the following day guerrillas attacked Unki Farm, Selukwe, which had been left to Mrs Frances Pearson's father by Cecil Rhodes. At the time of the attack her husband was seven kilometres away, dipping cattle. He hurried back to find the workshop and tractors destroyed and his wife dead.

The killing of missionaries was approaching an end now. But on Boxing Day a German Jesuit priest, Father Gerhard Pieper, 38, was found shot, with his hands tied behind his back, at St Francis Xavier mission in the Chesa Purchase Area, Mount Darwin. Apparently some thirty Zanla men, thor-oughly drunk, had dragged him from his bed and accused him in front of the African Sisters of not providing education for the people. According to the *Herald*'s columnist Colin Neilson, Pieper had telephoned him on Christmas Day with the news that things were getting 'a bit hairy' – guerrillas had written to him prophesying a future socialist state in Zimbabwe and the local people now had the Shona spirit-medium Chaminuka on their lips.

A Zanu broadcast from Mozambique promptly blamed the Selous Scouts for Father Pieper's murder and referred to the warm alliance between missionaries and freedom fighters.

Six days later, on New Year's Day 1979, yet another Swiss-born Bethlehem Father was murdered, this time in the Selukwe district. Father Martin Hollenstein, 44, had worked in Rhodesia since 1962.

A war brings dying. Death may be the Great Leveller but the living, the bereaved, fashion ceremonies designed to seal, finally, the corpse with a badge of merit. And a dead man does not cease to belong: indicators such as school or locality signal whether he is ours or not. Thus even if we eliminate the names from the Salisbury newspaper reports we can still tell, at a glance, who was white and who was black:

'Those killed in action were Sgt ——, 25, married from Gutu district; Lance-Cpl ——, single, from Salisbury, a former pupil of Churchill School; Trooper ——, 23, single, from Umtali, formerly a pupil at Prince Edward School Trooper ——, 19, single, from the Buhera district; Trooper ——,

23, divorced, from Salisbury, a former pupil of Cranborne High School.'

There is an unreal orderliness about lists of the dead – the first-class passenger list of a luxury liner looks hollow if the ship has gone down with icy hands clawing at the lifeboats. Death on the field of battle is contingent, violent, anarchic: a list of names is orderly, a way of regrouping in regimental squares after the chaos. This trooper hit a landmine in the Mount Darwin area, that corporal stopped a bullet near Lupane; they rub shoulders for the first time in their lives after their lives have ended. One died in a flash, the other bled slowly, yielding his life through large, ragged wounds. But there is no blood, no sound of dying, on the printed page.

'. . . Cpl David Kruger, 23, of Salisbury; Cpl Royden Orchard, 21, of Salisbury; Rifleman Thomas Shipley, 20, of Bulawayo; Cpl Arthur O'Driscoll, 22, of Salisbury; Rifleman Laurence Shakespeare, of Karoi . . .'

The relatives and close friends of white soldiers killed in action hastened to publish condolences, expressions of grief. There is, of course, a dilemma. Real anguish is private and silent; it cannot broadcast itself without slipping into banality or cliché. Yet silence would be construed as indifference, neglect, even callousness: we are never more slaves of custom and convention than when suffering from profound shock.

The following tributes are taken from the Rhodesian press, with names omitted:

'Since dad's death you have been our big brother and our strength. We love you.'

'My dearest grandson. Gone but not forgotten. I will miss you.'

'My darling brother, you brought laughter and fun to so many. I will always love and remember you. Your heartbroken sister.'

'Everyone's friend. The ultimate sacrifice. Died doing what he believed in. Thanks for being such a wonderful friend. . . . For our country . . . . We'll miss seeing you . . . I'm so sorry . . . Brave young Rhodesian. . . . A great guy. . . . Pamwe chete Selousie.'

(Lt-Col. Ron Reid-Daly customarily printed a tribute to fallen Selous Scouts in both English and Shona.)

Others stayed alive, were cited for heroism.

Lt Andrew Telfer of the RLI was awarded the Silver Cross in January 1980. Under his leadership more than forty guerrillas had been 'eliminated'. In June 1978, while engaged in a Fireforce operation, Telfer came under heavy fire from two guerrillas positioned in a rocky outcrop. After air strikes proved ineffective, he led the assault at great personal risk, killing one and pursuing the other into an open field where, although Telfer again came under heavy fire, he killed the man. In October 1978 he badly hurt his ankle when landing by parachute but led his men during a three-hour operation in the course of which they killed six guerrillas.

Lt Graeme Trass of the RLI was also awarded the Silver Cross. In October 1978 a patrol was pinned down by four guerrillas positioned on a rocky outcrop. Trass led the rescue operation across open ground and skirmished through the guerrilla position, despite heavy fire, killing all four.

Posthumous Silver Cross (June 1979) for Cpl Nicholas van Niekerk of 1 Commando RLI, killed a week before he was due to be discharged. Involved in twenty-five operational parachute drops and more than fifty contacts, he frequently moved in and killed terrorists at close quarters despite great personal risk.

Yet here again the imagination strains at the stock formulas on which citations are built; beyond such words as 'operation', 'eliminated' and 'contact' one can imagine the physical exhaustion, the heavy webbing round the waist (bivouac, food, water), the chest webbing (extra magazines), the weight of the weapon carried, the camouflage jump-suit bathed in sweat, the long elephant grass, nil visibility, the sudden report and the reflex descent to the ground, the bite of the helmet-strap and the horsefly on your hot nose as you strain through the grass to locate the enemy's position . . . the low command from a section leader, the panic as you break cover, the blood, gore and discharged bowels. . . .

Part Four: 1979

1. in responsible hands

On 11 January 1979 Smith began his Yes campaign. The flak he encountered at meetings was deceptive. Addressing 450 whites in Umtali, he was immediately greeted with a cry from the heart which brought warm applause: 'You are betraying your own people – let us fight on!' A woman asked why Rhodesia should succumb to pressure from the so-called Free World even though America and Britain showed themselves powerless in the face of Soviet expansionism. When 700 gathered in the Harry Margolis Hall, Salisbury, about fifty were determined to give the PM a rough ride. 'You have let us down!' shouted a young army reservist. But the result was never in doubt: for more than a year the writing had been on the wall and almost everyone could read it. When the day, 30 January, came, 57,269 whites said yes, 9,805 said no, and 764 ballot papers were spoilt.

In 1969 Smithy had offered them a constitution in which 91,000 whites were entitled to vote but only 7,000 Africans; a constitution in which the House of Assembly was safely dominated by fifty white Members who expected no trouble from the sixteen blacks sitting on the 'cross-benches'. Now the leader of the RF offered a constitution in which every African over the age of 18 would have the vote; blacks would occupy seventy-two out of one hundred seats, and the Prime Minister would be black, likewise the majority of the Ministers.

But Smith had also provided certain 'safeguards'. The new constitution hamstrung the incoming black Prime Minister. He would be required to appoint a proportion of Ministers from political parties other than his own, including the RF, depending on the number of seats they gained in the House. Nor would the Prime Minister be free to Africanize the civil and public service – a matter of immediate, indeed supreme, importance to some 12,000 whites and their families. Appointments would be regulated by a Public Service Commission whose Chairman and members would be – an alternative formula thinly veiled the reality – whites. The forces of 'law and order' would also remain in 'responsible' hands. The police and 'defence forces' were neatly sewn up and the executive powers of the black Prime Minister effectively neutered by means of formulas such as this:

'Each Commander will be appointed by the President, acting on the recommendation of a board appointed for the purpose which will consist of the retiring Commander or, if he is not available, the Chairman of the Defence Forces Service Commission, one of the other Commanders and a third member appointed by the President who is a Secretary of a Ministry in the Public Service.'

The faces of these faceless characters were white.

The right to remit pensions was guaranteed; likewise the sanctity of property. Farmers would keep their farms. Agricultural land could not be appropriated, even with full compensation, unless it had not been used for a continuous period of at least five years. To change any article in the constitution would require 80 out of 100 votes, i.e. every black Member voting in favour plus six white Members. The blacks could of course 'tear up the constitution' once they gained 'power', but then the black Prime Minister would find himself under arrest and generally forced to eat the words he had just torn up. In any case the PM would utterly depend upon the white power structure to fend off the onslaughts of the Patriotic Front.

The Rhodesian Action Party and the tiny splinter groups which had broken away from it in the course of 1978 – each fragment pursuing its own insane formula for salvation or satisfying its own leader's craving to be President of a party, if only a party of one – warned in vain that a Yes vote would spell chaos and disaster. But the new South African Prime Minister, P. W. Botha, explicitly repudiated RAP advertisements implying his support and welcomed the internal settlement as 'a step in the right direction'. When the referendum result came through Colin Barlow, the right-wing dentist, prophesied doom from Save Our Nation HQ, while the RAP's President, Mrs Ina Bursey, hurled anathemas at those whites who had 'sold their souls to the devil and deserve to reap the fruits of the whirlwind', adding on a slightly more practical level: 'We demand our right to depart in peace, together with our hard-earned assets.'

Muzorewa continued to deliver his major 'policy' speeches in Johannesburg and money poured into the Bishop's coffers.

2. uncertainty is gnawing at our guts

The civil servants inhabited a nightmare of their own. Convinced that no black government could be relied upon to guarantee their pensions, they thrashed around for an alternative solution. Only one looked gilt-edged: Britain. Keen supporters of the Rhodesian Front and UDI though most of them were at heart, they now embarked on Operation Grovel, referring to Rhodesia as Southern Rhodesia and projecting themselves as loyal servants of the Crown.

The Public Services Association, in its awful hunger for Africa-proof pensions, cried out for a notional 'return to legality'. When the British Liberal leader David Steel paid a visit to Salisbury in January 1979, the PSA met him behind closed doors and generally begged for the return of Sir Humphrey Gibbs or anyone else as British Governor – anything to persuade Britain to put up £310 million to guarantee the pensions of Rhodesia's white civil servants. The PSA even engaged in the disloyalty of privately denigrating Smith as 'intransigent' and van der Byl as 'leading the people to disaster' – though begging that such blasphemies be neither recorded nor reported.

After all, reasons plump, genial Barry Lennox, President of the PSA and an official of Internal Affairs, why should Rhodesians be less well treated than the civil servants of other British Colonies, Protectorates and Territories? So the plan was for Britain to pay the pensions and send the bill to the Government of Zimbabwe.

But what if Zimbabwe doesn't pay up? The British taxpayer foots the bill?

'Ah, exactly. But we hope it won't happen.'

Educated at Dartford Grammar School, Lennox had left Britain for Rhodesia when only 17 years old: 'I was an imperialist and always have been. If the monarchy went, the UK would go the way of Portugal.'

Does it worry him that his Ministry, Internal Affairs, employs only one black Assistant District Commissioner on the eve of 'majority rule'?

'Well,' he sighs, 'how can you trust these people to be consistent? What this country needs is a *stable* civil service. Do you realize that fifteen out of sixty DCs have quit since January 1978? I tell you, uncertainty is gnawing at our guts here. That can't be good for the country . . . can it?'

After Independence Lennox settled in England.

At the National Archives on the Borrowdale Road, the Director, Mr Turner, brings to bear a wealth of historical eloquence on behalf of the pensions claim. 'We are one of the last remnants of the greatest empire in the history of the world.' Mr Turner recalls Wavell's plea in the House of Lords in July 1949 on behalf of the Indian civil service. Besides: 'We haven't received a cent from Britain since UDI but consider the advances we've made: in the last two years the Archives have taken on ten black honours graduates. We want a bit of British decency. Let bygones be bygones.'

Back in the centre of town John Baty, President of the Posts and Telegraphs (staff) Association, wants 'a fair deal' from Britain. Baty left Britain for Rhodesia in 1948 after seeing an advert. 'I'd been a regional chairman in the Labour Party, you know, but I was frankly fed up with red tape. Besides, I wanted an open-air life.' Baty smiles sadly. 'Quite frankly, you know, these blacks expect us to fight their war for them.'

Ken McGreal, who runs the Local Authorities Pension Fund, agrees. Almost identically phrased: 'After all, we're fighting their war for them.' Having served with the RAF during the war, McGreal arrived in Rhodesia in 1955: 'Things were slow in the UK, you could move more quickly out here. In the UK you're always fetching coke and coal and doing the washing up – here others do it for you. It gives you more spare time. But the skilled men are worried about their future now – their standard of living and an alien culture. Yes, definitely we deserve a fair deal from Britain.'

(*Unhappy postscript*: The Thatcher Government, reluctant to pay its own civil service, declined to assume financial responsibility for Rhodesia's. The clinching, if callous, technical argument was that Rhodesian civil servants had never been employed by the Colonial Office, even before UDI – and that was the end of the matter.)

3. squatters and soldiers

Harare squatters' camp:

This man says he comes from Gutu. There was nothing to eat in Gutu. Now he paints tin cans. His wife and a swarm of kids squat down behind him, the head of the family.

This woman cooking meat came from Mrewa in October '78. When the Transitional Government (not a term she uses) opened her PV they all went back to where their real villages had been, but the war made life impossible. Does she regret having left the PV? No, it was terrible, no hygiene, the Guard Force beat people, they even beat older people for coming in late, after the curfew hour, from the fields. (Among the few words of English she knows are 'beat people'.)

This woman here came from Msana in April '78. The auxiliaries beat us, she says. (The auxiliaries in Msana are commanded by 'Comrade Max' and are loyal to the Bishop. However, this woman doesn't say anything about that.) The other day her brother-in-law was so beaten that he died in Harare Hospital. The auxiliaries, the 'madzajutsaku', had wanted to borrow his bicycle and he had refused. What does she think of the guerrillas? At this she shrugs. Each person thinks differently, she says.

This woman is newly married, followed her husband to Salisbury from Umtali. But he got injured at work and lost his job as a shop assistant. Now he goes to town and collects old newspapers which he resells to shopkeepers. He earns 30–50 cents a day. I lean into this woman's plastic shack and drop a dollar on the floor. She mutters something.

This old man with white hair came originally from Malawi. He worked on a white farm at Shamva until the 'boys' arrived, in September '78, not for the first time, rebuked the workers for ignoring an earlier warning to quit, and set fire to the labour compound. The next day 'the master bought us some clothes'. This greatly angered the 'boys' who came again the following night with a final ultimatum. The farmer, Robert MacManus, moved to a house in Highlands, Salisbury; and this old man became a squatter in Harare.

It was time that the blacks 'did their bit' in the struggle against 'terrorism'. It was time, therefore, that the burden of conscription was extended to young blacks – even though long lines of eager volunteers formed outside the gates of the Rhodesian African Rifles at Balla Balla. In short, the main purpose of black conscription was to placate white opinion.

This became clear when the *Government Gazette* announced on 26 October 1978 that Africans aged 18 to 25 must register for call-up if they had completed three years of secondary education or signed a contract of apprenticeship. Thus the measure was aimed specifically at that section of the black population *from whom the whites feared competition*. The reaction was immediate. Four hundred students at the University of Rhodesia signed a petition of protest. On 24 November police arrested 170 high school students marching with anti-conscription placards in the centre of Salisbury. In Umtali pupils of St Augustine's paraded down Main Street; at St Ignatius Sixth-Formers unanimously expressed contempt for the 'stooges' within the Transitional Government. Sithole's statement that 'the blacks must accept a major role in defending the agreement which confers power upon them' was treated with contempt.

'We will not fight our brothers!'

The struggle extended to skilled workers. World Radio Systems fired seventeen black employees for refusing to fill in conscription forms. Initially 102 out of 107 had resisted, but then the Office of Security Manpower instructed firms to withhold pay.

Intake 163, January 1979, was the first multiracial national-service intake. White and black conscripts were ordered to report for basic training at Llewelin Barracks, Bulawayo, where the commandant, Lt-Col. Bruce Hulley, promised to lick them all into shape. On 17 January the *Herald* obligingly printed a front-page photo of a black instructor bawling out a white recruit, but the grim fact for the regime was that all but 250 out of some 1,800 black conscripts had failed to turn up. According to the Office of Security Manpower, 'hundreds' were subsequently prosecuted and no African freshman was admitted to the University at the start of the academic year in February unless he had begun his military service – in which case he wouldn't be on campus anyway. The University became a place of fury, panic and rumour.

The intimidation seems to have worked. Many students fled abroad. In July the Government claimed that 1,300 out of 1,500 blacks had reported for Intake 165. The basic rationale of the policy – appeasing white fears of competition – was underwritten when the Muzorewa Government, which took office in June, made liable for call-up any African *under the age of 60 who had ever registered as an apprentice.*

In a shrewd move, pay was equalized. As from 1 June all conscripts earned $(R)83·62 per month from the first day of service.

4. stepping over the line

It was one of Lt-Gen. Peter Walls's many proud claims that anyone in his security forces who stepped over the line and was found guilty of needless brutality would be 'dealt with'. Oh yes? Take the rather rare case of 'Archie Owens', a Macheke farmer and police reservist – rare not because of what he did, which was common enough, but because his case came to court.

One of a 'stick' of four mounted police, Owens arrived at Chibanda kraal in Mangwende TTL on 15 January 1979. The 'stick' began to interrogate a woman suspected of having fed terrorists who were known to be operating in the area. The woman was told to explain a number of unwashed plates, etc. Then they made her strip, beat her fore and aft, on bottom, back and legs, until she broke down. None of this was in dispute. But Owens denied *indecent* assault, i.e. whipping her genitals, despite the evidence of scars.

When the case came before Salisbury Regional Court six months later, Magistrate John Redgment acquitted Owens. Extenuating circumstances; terrorism; exigencies of war. . . .

Sgt Sybrand Combrink, 31, was in charge of a Guard Force 'stick' of sixteen men in Mangwende TTL when he forced a woman to strip, made her raise a leg on a chair and told his men to rape her. They refused. Combrink was sentenced to eight months' imprisonment in Marandellas Magistrates' Court, four of them suspended.

In May 1979 a keep Commander, Jose Manuel Martins, 28, pleaded not guilty in the High Court to the murder of Vesi Chibaya on 21 April at

Musarakufa PV, Mtoko. Martins, who came to Rhodesia from Mozambique in 1975, and who spoke little English, admitted administering electric shocks to the victim, who was also beaten with a hosepipe, bound to a tree, ducked in a bucket and tied to the keep's water tower. As usual in such cases, the African Guard Force Corporal pleaded he was acting under the Commander's orders, while the European blamed the indiscipline among his men. Martins was sentenced to eight years' imprisonment for culpable homicide.

5. life and death

James Joliffe, 27, was killed on 2 January when guerrillas attacked his store in the Gatooma district.

On 3 January David Mirams, 39, became the first DC to be killed as a result of guerrilla action, when his Land-Rover hit a mine. District Commissioner for Mrewa, he was born in Rhodesia and spoke fluent Shona. A pupil of Umtali Boys' High School, he was a keen cricket, squash, golf and tennis player.

On 8 January Mrs Rosemarie Hacking, 44, mother of four, was killed when her car hit a landmine near her farm at Wild Park, Odzi.

Early the following day Petrus Blignaut, 54, was killed and his wife June, 47, was wounded when their car was ambushed between Shabani and Selukwe. Their 17-year-old son and his friend returned the fire and beat off the attackers after an exchange lasting several minutes.

The Afrikaners of the Beatrice area were chips off the old block: true trekkers; Boers. (A lonely English-speaking boy had committed suicide as a result of the treatment he received in a Beatrice school on the day England declared war against Hitler in 1939.) Japie Smit, chairman of the Beatrice sports club, had been chairman of the local branch of the RF until he switched allegiance to the breakaway RAP, last bastion of the apartheid principle in Rhodesia. The fatal ambush the guerrillas laid in honour of Japie Smit and his wife Connie extended over 300 metres along the Acton Reynolds Road near the Smit farm, Lisbon. The Smits drove into it on 30 January.

On 1 February guerrillas ambushed and killed Lukas Koen, 34, an animal-health inspector on a farm in the Umvuma area at 9.15 in the morning.

Pieter Steyn, 64, an Odzi farmer, was murdered on 13 February.

A remarkable schoolboy:

Jamie Scott, 15 years old and a pupil of Churchill School, Salisbury, had had a fall, suffered concussion, been in hospital and was now convalescing at home in Beatrice. Riding pillion on his friend Pieter Visser's motor bicycle,

Jamie had the misfortune to run into ten or fifteen guerrillas standing in the road. Hit in the leg and ankle, Pieter Visser, a reduction officer at Joyce Mine, fell from the motorbike. Jamie landed on top of him and played dead in the middle of the road. The 'terrs' swallowed this for a few seconds then started shooting again. Jamie ran to take cover behind the overturned machine, loaded his G3 rifle and returned fire. Hit twice, he was hit again as he dived for roadside cover. Now his rifle jammed, as happens in movies – but this was not a movie. Three 'terrs' were advancing on him. Pulling out the magazine, Jamie found and ejected a bent round, then leapt to his feet and ran straight at the enemy, firing from the hip. At the end of the day Jamie Scott had wounds in his back, thigh, calf and heel – a fifth bullet having grazed his chest. He became only the second recipient of the Conspicuous Gallantry decoration, the highest award for civilians. His mother took him to convalesce at his aunt's home in South Africa.

6. a beautiful sight

Jon Kennerly's story as told by Jon Kennerly:

An apprentice compositor with the *Bulawayo Chronicle*, he had been given four days' leave from his regular night-shift and decided to visit his parents at Beitbridge, where his father worked as a vehicle inspector. He arranged a lift in a Ward's Transport truck. About twelve kilometres from Beitbridge, on the main road, the pantechnicon was waved down by armed guerrillas who relieved the African driver and co-driver of $(R)20 and $(R)10 respectively and abducted Kennerly. Time: 6.30 in the evening of 5 February 1978. His first meal came a day later, at a kraal: sadza, chicken, powdered milk.

They zigzagged across hundreds of miles of wild terrain. On the third day he was handed over to a new group who took his money and bought tins of meat and biscuits from a store. On the fifth day – as he told the story – he was finally left alone while the guerrillas dispersed in twos and threes round a village. When his guard fell asleep, JK ran off. At about 4 in the afternoon, hot and parched, he asked some villagers for water, not knowing there was a river near by. As he was crossing the river he heard a shot; the enraged guerrillas had caught up with him. Now his hands were tied with donkey-hide straps, his feet with a belt. He made another attempt to escape during the night but was too noisy about it: his punishment was a bucket of water thrown over the donkey-hide straps; by morning they had so contracted that his hands were three times their normal size.

After about sixteen days he was taken across the border into Mozambique.

While crossing the Nuanetsi River in a ferry-boat he again tried to escape but was caught, deprived of his shoes for six days and made to walk barefoot through long grass and in water up to his chest.

According to Kennerly, when interrogated he told his captors that he had served in the RLI (he was too young) – 'a whole lot of bilge which they believed'. Taken to Chimoio, he was again interrogated but enjoyed the use of a radio. After five months he was moved to a new camp where he met a more recent abductee, Johannes Maartens, whom JK learned to call 'Oupa', Afrikaans for grandfather. In July this camp was 'revved' by the Rhodesian Air Force: 'I saw the whole thing from behind some rocks 500 metres away. It was a beautiful sight.' To supplement the monotonous diet, JK joined his guards (who clearly became very fond of him) in catching large lizards and tortoises for the pot. 'They were tremendous.'

It was 11 a.m. on 18 May 1978 when Johannes Maartens was kidnapped on his Headlands farm. The 54-year-old farmer, a father of seven, was driving on the farm, unarmed, when he found himself surrounded. For a man with a heart condition the nine-day march into Mozambique was an ordeal, although the guerrillas were sympathetic to his condition, carried his pack, allowed him frequent rests, and assured him they were not racists – they had no wish to chase the whites out of Zimbabwe. When the pious Christian farmer told them they were being manipulated by Communists, they laughed.

Maj. Thomas Wigglesworth, a 61-year-old retired British army and Royal Air Force officer, has published an extremely interesting account of his own captivity, which lasted from 1 August 1978 until the first days of February 1979 (*Perhaps Tomorrow*, Salisbury, Galaxie Press, 1981). Four years earlier, the Major and his wife had tempted providence by moving up from South Africa to the Penhalonga area, where they bought a fruit-and-vegetable farm. Returning home one morning, he found unwelcome guests; the young guerrilla who knocked him down said, 'If you had got out of the car with your gun I would have shot you.' House and farm were rapidly looted: fruit, tomatoes, typewriter, electric sewing machine, the Major's war medals – the lot. 'They were so casual and carefree,' Wigglesworth later recalled, 'as if they had already taken over the country.'

Taken prisoner, Wigglesworth found himself heading west, away from the border; for three days he was held at a camp inside Rhodesia. Then followed a gruelling forced march by night to Vila Manica. Often he fell, his leg, ankle and foot were damaged, he was pushed, pulled, cursed, threatened. Breasting a hill at night, he saw the lights of Umtali only six kilometres to the south.

Not long after his capture the Major was spotted reaching for a hidden revolver, which had remained undetected. For this he paid with a severe beating and the agony of being handcuffed to a guard every night – but what irked him most was the sight of his stolen war medals pinned to the navel of a swaggering goon.

In Mozambique he suffered filthy prison cells, guards who spoke only Portuguese, disgusting latrines and food he could not stomach, particularly sadza. At least Zanla spoke English and it was something of a relief when they moved him by Land-Rover to Chimoio. Whenever his morale slumped they reminded this old soldier, veteran of many distant campaigns, 'you must resist, resist, it's war'. Whenever he asked for a few elementary comforts such as soap, a towel, a razor, he was told: 'That's no problem.' But it was. In the frequent panic marches he underwent – 'Move, move, move!' – TW was less afraid of Rhodesian air strikes than of losing jealously hoarded valuables: tins for boiling water, plastic bottles, tinned fish, blankets.

At Chimoio he met up with Kennerly, Maartens and James Black, a 45-year-old forester who had recently read of Wigglesworth's abduction while on leave in England, and had then returned to Melsetter only to fall into the same trap. All the prisoners were regularly interrogated by a certain Commander Lamec who claimed to have trained in China and who tended to write down the answers to his own questions before they had been voiced. 'What were Hitler's aims in the second world war?' was one that the Major very sensibly declined to wrestle with.

A succession of senior Zanu officials called on the white captives: Tongogara, Nhongo, Tungamirai, Munangagwa, and Mugabe himself. The notables normally arrived accompanied by a guard force fanned out in the shape of a half moon. 'I understand you do not eat sadza,' Mugabe remarked to Wigglesworth. All the whites became obsessed with their bowel movements as one disorder after another hit them. For toilet paper the best substitute was the label off Dutch mackerel tins because it was gummed only at the ends and therefore came away in one piece. In the morning there were house-flies; in the afternoon large tsetse-flies; towards evening irritating mopani-flies; and all night the torture of blood-hungry mosquitoes. On top of that there were leeches, snakes, scorpions, maggots, rats and pinhead-small jigger- (or sand-) fleas which burrowed beneath toenails.

The four whites quarrelled sometimes but Wigglesworth developed a strong respect and affection for Maartens whom he describes as 'a simple, brave, kind and cheerful man' who looked like a Voortrekker in his beard and rancher's hat. He spoke in English but thought – and prayed silently – in Afrikaans.

Largely because of ferocious Rhodesian air attacks, on 10 September the four began a 500-kilometre drive to Tembwe, in the north. On 4 October they were brought south again to a point in the bush near Tete, where they were held for almost three months. On 21 December, believing they were finally being flown to Maputo and freedom, they were horrified to find themselves incarcerated in a filthy prison cell near Nampula, in the north-east, where fat maggots crawled out of the latrine at night and where the four had to sleep on the floor in a space two and a half metres square.

Early in February they were flown to Maputo and handed over to Amnesty International. Mugabe warned them that if they returned to Zimbabwe they might again become casualties of war, but none hesitated. The Rhodesians laid on a showpiece press conference, misjudged the situation entirely, and were angry when Maartens and Black paid tribute to their 'terrorist' captors. Born in Norfolk, Black had arrived in Rhodesia from Kenya in 1969; he was the seventh white to go missing after abduction. He described the Zanla commander, Josiah Tongogara, as a 'humorous and dedicated chap' – not at all the portrait favoured by Salisbury.

Why had these men been taken prisoner rather than killed or simply released? No single explanation is wholly satisfactory and Wigglesworth remained convinced that there had been an element of bungling in it, even after Tongogara himself told him that his crime had been his failure to assist Zanla, unlike many other white farmers. Perhaps his life had been spared because his foreman had pleaded for it and because Wigglesworth had rescued the man's family from a protected village, from 'behind the wire'. Possibly Zanla hoped to barter these white prisoners for Zanu leaders gaoled in Rhodesia; possibly they wanted to prove that they were not just savage terrorists; possibly it was a way of inflicting humiliation.

7. the Viscount *Umniati*

At 6 minutes past 5 in the afternoon of 12 February 1979 a Karoi farmer, John Ashton, looked up, due north, and saw a ball of flame followed by dense smoke falling out of the sky.

Two busloads of white holidaymakers had driven from Kariba to the airport in convoy. On arrival they mingled and chatted round the bar and shop, awaiting the order to board the two Viscounts (painted camouflage grey since the *Hunyani* disaster five months earlier) scheduled to fly them back to Salisbury. Some felt nervous; others believed the *Hunyani* had been a one-off fluke; and some were simply accustomed to take risks.

Prominent among these was Lt-Gen. Peter Walls, Commander of Combined Operations, and his wife.

Those issued with red boarding-cards were called first and boarded the *Umniati*. Passengers carrying green boarding-cards were informed they would leave fifteen minutes later. Walls was among the latter and lodged no complaint, pulled no strings – Rhodesia is an egalitarian society. The *Umniati* took off, heading due east.

As it passed overhead a Zipra section fired a flare to indicate its flight-path. The signal was picked up by a missile crew. At 6 minutes past 5 the Kariba Control Tower heard the plane's 'mayday mayday' distress call and passengers waiting to board the second Viscount noticed four men racing across the tarmac to a light aircraft. This was the moment that the Karoi farmer, John Ashton, looked up and saw a ball of flame falling from the sky.

Six months earlier Captain Hood had managed to bring the *Hunyani* down in a semi-controlled landing, but the *Umniati*, hit in the jet pipe of the inner port engine by a Sam 7, burst into flame and plummeted like a stone into a ravine in the Vuti African Purchase Area, where it burnt for six hours, incinerating almost all of the fifty-four passengers and five crew members beyond recognition. Captain Jan du Plessis, formerly of the South African Air Force and a veteran of the Korean War, stood no chance. (He had recently lost his son Leon in a Rhodesian Air Force flying accident.)

The second Viscount took off in a different direction. It circled tightly over the lake, gaining altitude – the missile ceiling is 3,000 metres – and spiralling out of danger. (Two months later I experienced this corkscrew ascent over Lake Kariba in a military Dakota; one always assumes one is going to be lucky.) The crew of the second Viscount were informed of what had happened but passed on the news to only one passenger, General Walls.

Air Rhodesia had a passenger list for the two flights combined, but the red and green cards had been handed out at random and there was going to be a grim process of checking the survivors before notifying relatives.

Among the victims was an RF Member of the House of Assembly, Donald Goldin. Born in Johannesburg, Goldin had first come to Rhodesia at the time of UDI and had subsequently become Managing Director of the Victoria Falls Casino Hotel and Chairman of the Victoria Falls Town Council.

By a grim coincidence, Dr Cecil McLaren, hero of the *Hunyani*, was a friend of Ian Boyd, who died in the *Umniati*. And a lot worse than that – almost the entire Boyd family was wiped out: Desmond, 53, his wife Gladys, 51, their sons Noel, 26, and Ian, 25, and their daughters Andrea, 16, and Leonie, 14. Ian had arrived in Rhodesia from New Zealand in 1976, worked on a farm, made friends, liked the country, become a patriot, volunteered for military service and become manager of the Old Hararians Club. The other members of his family had arrived for a long visit on 22 December. It fell to

Cecil McLaren to search Ian's flat for the Australian address of the single surviving member of the family, Warren.

After that McLaren flew to Kariba no more.

On the following day, speaking in Addis Ababa, Joshua Nkomo claimed credit for the deed, adding that his men had believed General Walls to be on board. In the House of Assembly Minister of Transport Bill Irvine blamed the British Government as 'really responsible', having supplied arms to Zambia and having admitted that 'vile murderer' Nkomo into Britain. (It was little more than a year after this remark that the same Irvine walked into the same House of Assembly at the side of the same vile murderer: the squeamish do not survive in politics.) Meanwhile Rhodesian security forces, spearheaded by the élite Special Air Service, began a ruthless search-and-destroy operation in the Vuti Purchase Area, designed to drive out of their homes and fields all inhabitants living under the flight paths of aircraft leaving Kariba.

At Warren Hills cemetery a single coffin was cremated to represent all fifty-nine victims. Dean da Costa referred to the symbolic 'Unknown Victim' but carefully avoided any repeat of his disastrous sermon, 'A Deafening Silence'. Ian Smith and his wife attended the ceremony; Smith knew he was stuck with an internal settlement that couldn't work.

Seven out of fifty Air Rhodesia hostesses quit. New heat-deflecting devices were fitted to the engines of Viscounts. South African Airways cancelled its twice-weekly Boeing 747 service between Salisbury and London, as well as its twice-weekly tourist flights from Johannesburg to Victoria Falls. A further nail in the coffin of the tourist industry. Then, ten days after the disaster, Air Rhodesia itself terminated all flights to Wankie and all flights between Kariba and Victoria Falls, although it was still possible to fly to the two resorts from Salisbury.

8. St Augustine's: the guerrillas arrive

St Augustine's had become increasingly embroiled in the war raging along the Mozambique border. In June 1978 helicopters and ground troops had attacked huts on the mission estate, only two miles from the school, leaving twenty-seven people dead. Of these ten were guerrillas, seven were villagers, and ten were girls 'running with' the guerrillas (including three pupils from St Augustine's).

A few weeks later there occurred the chilling slaughter of white missionaries and their children at the Elim Pentecostal mission in the Vumba. What did it signify? Being white, Father Prosser is deaf: only his black Deputy Headmaster can send out soft-footed scouts to interpret the drum-beats, to test the pulse of the Risorgimento's quixotic children. At such moments, meaner motives also surface – one black teacher who advised the white Brethren to leave St Augustine's without delay was later chastised by the guerrillas and made a hasty departure; however, he duly fell on his feet as a member of the new élite after Independence.

Having consulted six black teachers, Father Prosser instructed the white Sisters to slip away from school quietly during morning chapel. He also decided to evacuate all the Brethren from the Priory. Prosser himself commuted to school each day from Umtali but after six weeks of this he grew fed up and the Brethren (but not the Sisters) settled back in the Priory.

The event Keble Prosser dreaded occurred on 2 November 1978. At 9.30 in the evening a Zanla guerrilla carrying an AK rifle walked into his office in the Priory. Prosser offered his hand. It was declined.

'We're not allowed to shake hands,' the guerrilla said. 'Where is your gun?'

'I don't have a gun.'

'All whites have guns.'

The Principal was instructed to summon all the Brethren. This he declined to do, explaining that some of them were getting long in the tooth and 'might not understand'.

The whole school had been assembled in the darkness outside the chapel. Prosser felt at once the mood of adulation verging on hysteria, particularly among the girls. The Zanla commander was a somewhat histrionic character who kept prowling round a bush as if he expected to find General Walls behind it. Presently he intimated to Prosser that his watch was broken: would Prosser care to 'swap' his good watch for the broken one?

'It wasn't exactly a demand,' Prosser recalls. 'I gave him my watch.'

While guerrillas and children together sang Shona freedom songs and celebrated the 'chimurenga', the commander assured Father Prosser that he was most highly regarded and should 'carry on':

'If you have any trouble with your pupils, just come to me.'

Prosser explained that his Fourth-Formers had important exams to take the next day and really ought to get some sleep. Much impressed by this, the Zanla men took their leave, beat an African to death elsewhere on the estate and – still the same night – ambushed a vehicle travelling between Penhalonga and Umtali, setting it ablaze with a rocket and killing 60-year-old Mrs Ethel Ward. Her husband, an electrician working at Old West Mine, was seriously injured.

Father Keble Prosser was keeping mum about the visitation. Two months later he wrote: 'We had a very good and happy third term of the year – despite all the difficulties.' In reality demands for money had become increasingly insistent, although the sums involved were chicken-feed when compared, for example, to the amounts handed over to Zipra and Zanla by Prosser's friend Garfield Todd in the Shabani area. On two occasions St Augustine's paid out $(R)100 to Zanla units who sent their demands from further afield. As for the local vakhomana, the black teachers regularly paid 10 per cent of their salaries, while Prosser forked out a modest $(R)60 a month on behalf of the Priory, disguising these transactions from the Brother Treasurer – 'he wouldn't have approved' – by entering them in the books as a stipend paid to a certain Brother on account of his services as chaplain. The money then reached the guerrillas through the black Deputy Headmaster, on whose good judgement and reputation with the 'boys' the English priest depended.

The local Zanla commander, Hayden (a spruce figure carrying toothbrush and paste in his breast pocket who later disappeared without trace after the cease-fire), instructed Prosser on no account to pay out sums of money to individual guerrillas. But one night a young fellow turned up, wild-eyed and waving a gun, to demand of Prosser 'all the money you have'. The Principal reckoned there was fully $(R)3,000 in the safe next door to his office and he also reckoned this young bandit wasn't getting it. On the other hand an argument might not prove entirely useful.

'I've got about $(R)30, will that do?'

'That'll do.'

'I'll have to get it.'

'OK.'

Instead of following Father Prosser to the next room and shooting him in the back as he opened the safe, the young man remained in the office, accepted what was given him, and vanished into the night.

The security forces did not question Prosser about the guerrilla visit of 2 November – and he certainly did not report it. But a few weeks later the police showed their hand by arresting several pupils without consulting the Principal. He went down to Penhalonga to protest. Later the Special Branch called on him. One young officer sneeringly described all missionaries as Marxists and Communists: 'What have you people ever done for Rhodesia?'

A new Zanla group moved into the area and sent word they wanted girls. A mujiba who fancied himself informed a Sixth-Form girl who was smart enough to tell the Deputy Head. The Deputy Head sent an emissary to the guerrillas. The emissary did not return, so he sent another. When he, too, did not return the Deputy Head went himself. They all spent the night with the 'boys'.

On rock or sand, this school? The fate of the mission lay in the hands of neither Prosser himself nor of the Anglican Bishop of Mashonaland. Although St Augustine's hilly, heavily wooded estate is vested in the Anglican diocese (it was granted in 1891 to Bishop Knight-Bruce by a local chief familiar with the old motto *cuius regio, eius religio*), the power to close the mission resided in the Community's headquarters in Mirfield, Yorkshire.

After the Elim massacre it was decided by the Community that if Prosser himself chose to resume residence at St Augustine's, it should only be until August 1979. But when the Community's Visitor, Bishop Kenneth Skelton, took soundings he came to the conclusion that staff and pupils alike wanted Prosser to continue in office. A former Bishop of Matabeleland, and first head of the Christian Council of Rhodesia, Skelton had in 1965 supported the Archbishop of Canterbury, Michael Ramsey, in calling for police action against the Smith regime's UDI. In 1969 Skelton had protested against the Land Tenure Act in a sermon: 'Are you tamely, passively, going to accept a Land Act based on racial segregation and therefore denying Christ?' Skelton also concluded – as Prosser remarked to me with only the most token resistance to the sin of pride – that St Augustine's survival against all the odds amounted to a considerable victory for the Church. The Bishop's letter so impressed the Community's Superior that Prosser was granted a temporary reprieve – if that word can be used to describe a further season in a war zone.

During the early months of 1979 discipline within Zanla showed a notable deterioration. Local commanders were losing their grip. New units, some trained in Ethiopia, were attempting to discipline and sometimes disarm units which had degenerated into semi-banditry. On 5 August 1979 no less than sixty Zanla guerrillas turned up at St Augustine's. Over-confident and lazy, they failed to post sentries to cover the approaches to the school. No sooner had they assembled the pupils for a political meeting than security forces drove up undetected in lorries and surrounded the hall. Father Prosser did, then, fear a massacre of his own pupils in the forthcoming crossfire. Fortunately the white police officer in charge understood the danger and acted calmly; throwing open the hall doors he read the riot act, precipitating a panic flight of guerrillas and pupils alike (one was later unearthed in Prosser's own bed) through windows and side-doors. One drunk guerrilla got left behind, tried to conceal his weapon, found himself forced to parade before the soldiers along with the senior male pupils, made a dash for freedom in a rondavel, found the door opened the wrong way, and was shot dead. The next day each pupil was made to stare at the corpse, whose guts were spilling out, and asked to identify him. None did. After this fiasco the 'boys' agreed not to come again in term time. Their visits had become too frequent and they tended to stay too late, particularly in the girls' dormitories, causing some disillusionment.

The shoot-out of 5 August was a watershed. For the first time Father Prosser had to submit to police interrogation and 'come clean' (as he put it) about his previous dealings with the guerrillas. He had been committing, indeed, a capital offence; an offence for which his friend Bishop Lamont had been first gaoled then exiled. But by August 1979 the war had bitten so deep that all sides wearily, cynically, understood the rules: the Muzorewa Government lacked the zeal of its predecessors for persecuting white priests.

A letter written by Father Prosser in September 1979 provides an insight into this ultra-English Anglican's revolutionary conservatism, his distaste for the smooth glide into opportunism of those former pupils who contrived to land on their feet a long way from the dying and the misery, thereafter gracing the dinner-tables of the London intelligentsia and expressing their anger at the 'negative tendencies', 'lack of discipline', 'revisionist elements', etc. currently adulterating Zanu's revolutionary purity.

He wrote: 'I have feared all along that when peace comes those who were really idealists and went and did uncomfortable things may find themselves supplanted by those who sat comfortably at home or in London. It makes one sad, not least because so many of our very best went over [the border] and did not take the flesh pots. I am reminded of the prophet Jeremiah and his talking of good and bad figs.' Although he apologized, in virtually the same breath, for being 'too censorious by nature', the edge to his feelings had been rendered rawer by the 'hideous' spectacle on three successive days of planes and helicopters passing over the school, morning and evening, on raids into Mozambique. 'It's hard', he commented, 'to believe that this can help anybody anywhere.'

Yet Prosser's own ambition to keep St Augustine's open, when so many other secondary schools had been closed, was itself a paradox: he himself was leading his sheep to academic pastures available only to a tiny élite of Africans, yet reacting with *Schadenfreude* when they threw it all up, burnt their certificates, and set out on a long night's journey towards an early death.

9. No Go

On 14 March 1979 the UN Security Council resolved, by 10 votes to nil with five abstentions (including the UK and the USA), that any internal election under the auspices of the present Salisbury regime would be illegal. Despite Tory protests, Dr David Owen adamantly refused to send official British observers. In America the Administration resisted intense pressure from within the Senate (which voted $250,000 for the purpose of sending Congressional observers), relying on the blocking power of the fifteen-man black caucus in the House and the anti-Salisbury posture of the House subcommittee on Africa under its new chairman, Stephen Solarz (Democrat, New York).

A statement by Assistant Secretary of State Richard Moose to the Senate Foreign Relations Committee on 7 March highlighted the Administration's dilemma. On the one hand the Case–Javits amendment to the Internal Security Act (1978) legally obligated the President to take account of all information available to him in determining whether the Rhodesian elections were free and fair. On the other hand the reasons offered by Moose for not sending Presidential observers showed that the Administration had made up its mind in advance that the elections would not be free and fair: (1) 85 per cent of the country was under martial law; (2) Zanu and Zapu militants remained in detention, unable to engage in free political activity; (3) blacks had not been asked to endorse the new constitution, which in any case gave disproportionate power to the whites. The non-participation of the Patriotic Front rendered the whole exercise null and void.

Despite hectic, last-minute manoeuvres in both Houses of Congress, it was No Go.

10. one man, one vote

Ayoub Kara strides into his office, big-bellied and blue-chinned, polite, even ingratiating to foreign correspondents who figure in his crude calculations, but curt, brusque, peremptory to the mass of supplicants waiting for him in the corridor. The UANC's Indian election-director unlocks a safe and begins to distribute cash and petrol coupons in prodigious quantities. Forty years old and a Moslem, he neither smokes nor drinks; it was he who coined the slogan 'The Winners' and his heavy jowls and luminous, calculating eyes are oleaginous with impending success.

'Throughout the campaign I have rarely seen my family but I've always found time to pray facing Mecca once a day,' he reveals on the way downstairs to a campaign car. Kara is efficient; he makes things work, happen; he shadows and stage-manages the little Bishop, clapping his hands to orchestrate the ritual cheers – Huruyiadzu! – with noticeable contempt. The Bishop takes comfort from his presence but never seems to acknowledge it by the smallest inflection of the head.

'Living on my father's farm at Msasa,' says Kara, 'I learned to speak Shona with the labourers' children. Nowadays they call me "Chipembere" – the rhino.'

Ayoub Kara drives fast. A second car, packed with bodyguards, shadows us to Hartley.

'You imagine I have an escort wherever I go, David? No way! I travel thousands of miles on dirt roads, hiring buses, organizing rallies, speaking Shona. I travel alone, unguarded.' Disclaiming all personal ambition, he reeks of it; he sells the UANC like a roll of cloth; the people are fodder and when they have cast their miserable votes, heaven help them. Even when the basic drift of his utterances is plausible, every sentence sounds like an opportunistic slogan.

'White power, David, is responsible power. The masses are satisfied with twenty-eight seats for whites, only the university radicals disagree. And how many are they? Look at the misery of quick revolutions in Africa. Smith has carried the torch to bring about majority rule. The man is sincere, David. Did any other Prime Minister ever campaign to bring about the end of his own power?'

From the back seat I ask questions. Though Kara's car and entourage should be an obvious target for guerrillas, I feel completely safe; the man's confidence is contagious. The answers come back, pat, over his shoulder:

– 'The *Zimbabwe Times*? We had no choice but to ban it, David. It went against the state machine.'

– 'The Patriotic Front? Communist bandits, believe me, please.' Kara describes the Bishop as the frame of a bike: everything else can be added or taken away except the frame.

'David, we can call a meeting anywhere in the country within two hours.' He lifts a hand from the steering-wheel and snaps his fingers. 'Just like that. On February 4, in Highfield, we had 500,000 and that's a fact, David. The Bishop is now using a twin-engine plane and addressing four rallies a day. How many rallies does Sithole address? Shall I tell you?'

(By 1982 Ayoub Kara was organizing Zimbabwean Asians in support of Robert Mugabe's 'Communist bandits', who were now the Government. Kara had belatedly spotted the real winner.)

We reach Hartley, a football field on a white farm, a tiny stadium erected out of scaffolding, farm workers sitting waiting in sexually segregated groups, sambo smiles, a woman photographer from a German agency in blue jeans, eventually the Bish's Barnum & Bailey procession, bodyguards out of a B movie and young whites from the Special Branch with straight blond hair, tight brown suits, that blank-neutral-alert expression. The Bishop prances around. His Shona cadences are slow, measured, even faintly episcopal, larded with English phrases such as 'one man, one vote', 'central committee', 'UANC', and even 'Pearce Commission'. The Bishop refers to the various election symbols of his opponents and duly makes fun of them. What about the elephant called Chirau, should we bring him to the city or keep him in the forest? As for Sithole's flaming torch, it resembles an ice-cream cone and what category of the population runs after ice creams?

If the Bishop is offering them a policy, it isn't visible. But, when he addresses white farmers (as at Rusape), what he projects is a particular, reassuring model of black conservatism. Hastings Banda is the incarnation of this 'pragmatism' – a President who does not 'interfere' in Rhodesia or South Africa, the result being that 'today Zambia and Tanzania are buying rice from Malawi'. The theme is clear and effective: 'The OAU will shout at us, but we will be shouting back with full stomachs, and they with empty ones.'

Today, at Hartley, 'the Bish' is wearing a dark blue suit and clerical collar. Pfumo reVanhu thugs in blue jeans and cowboy hats scan the crowd. On the front of their brown T-shirts appears the UANC emblem, the crossed hoe and spear; on the back, the words 'Pamberi Ne Runyararo Muvanhu'. It is 6 in the evening and the sun sets as Muzorewa talks. He talks without histrionics, very few of a preacher's tricks or cadences, sober, reassuring, holding the mike in his left hand and constantly gesturing with the right. Occasionally a specific promise: free health care, free education, free something.

'Sithole is claiming he started the war and he alone can stop it. It's like a divorced woman claiming she's still my wife.' In Meikles Hotel, Muzorewa addresses a different audience: the klieg lights, the flashing cameras, the gins-and-tonic of the international press. 'The whites', he says, 'were born and bred here. They would be as much strangers in England as we blacks would.' What a pity that the American blacks have on the whole adopted so hostile an attitude; they are a 'stumbling-block'; when they tell white Rhodesians to 'go home' they remind him of American racists who tell blacks to go back to Africa.

The reporters are unmoved, likewise their pencils.

The Bishop calls the OAU 'emotional'. Again he praises the outcast Hastings Banda: calm, pragmatic, sober. Attacks the radical front-line states. Answers almost all questions belligerently: 'No, it's not a problem that our army is led by whites – we will not allow any nonsense from cheap journalists.'

Lt-Gen. Walls sits impassively in the front row: grey flannels, green blazer, green regimental tie. He glows. Jack Gaylard, Cabinet Secretary, hit-man for Ian Smith, sits beside him, hollow chest, bulging stomach, blowing smoke out of his nose. Between them they know it all.

'Bishop,' someone calls from the floor, 'can it be right that 4 per cent of the population should get 28 per cent of the seats?'

Muzorewa can't say yes because he said no throughout the Salisbury negotiations a year ago. 'It's a matter of opinion,' he says. Walls and Gaylard look bored.

Now Muzorewa is campaigning in the tribal trust lands north of Salisbury, travelling from one protected village to another encased in a vast armoured vehicle out of Star Wars. Our car, driven by the UANC's Indian Secretary for Finance, Ismail Adam, follows at a discreet distance; the summer rains have ended now and the Bishop's travelling fortress is kicking dust in our faces.

Ismail Adam is an entertaining chauffeur. Like Ayoub Kara he is wealthy and ambitious, but there the resemblance ends. Although born in 1934, Adam has a boyish look – thick glossy black hair falls over his forehead. And though he didn't exactly go to Oxford he almost did: 'David, I'll tell you as one Oxford man to another, our party depends on 25-cent levies from humble villagers.'

'What about the South African slush fund paid out to you by Eschel Roodie?'

'Never! Not a penny. But, David, I will tell you this: a great deal of support would have been forthcoming from the Shah of Iran if the bloody British hadn't intervened. And from the Gulf states, too.'

Clouds of dust obscure the Bishop's armoured vehicle.

'David,' says Ismail, who figures on Zanu's celebrated death list, 'the Bishop's popularity today is comparable to that of Mahatma Gandhi. I tell you, for every twenty guerrillas who come on-sides with us, Sithole can claim only one. David, we are winning this war.'

(After the election Muzorewa appointed Ismail Adam Deputy Minister for Information and Tourism, whereupon the latter immediately embarked on a whistle-stop tour of thirty-five countries none of which, in the event, consented to recognize 'Zimbabwe Rhodesia'. On 10 November, 1981 he was arrested in Lusaka in a police currency trap, then detained in Zimbabwe for three months before being fined $(Z)67,000 for contravening the Exchange Control Act.)

In the PV – Keep 10 – the people are drawn up, waiting passively. Triumphantly the Bishop dismounts from the bowels of his iron horse. The women ululate in greeting. Ayoub Kara strides about, bullish and scowling, orchestrating the chants: 'Heav-ee, heav-ee!' Shadowed by white Special Branch men in very short shorts, Muzorewa begins with a prayer in the name of Jesus.

'Vote for peace,' he says, 'sanctions will be lifted as soon as you vote.' Then he promises free education, from Grade 1 to 7.

'One strong government,' he says, 'one strong leader, one strong nation.' The jaws of the SB bodyguards rotate steadily, mechanically, on their chewing-gum.

'UANC good meat, other parties rotten meat,' says the Bish. 'Sithole's men threaten you,' he says, 'but the people made me their leader in 1972.' What a shit this man is: in 1972 every established nationalist leader was in gaol.

'On voting day, voting is a *must*,' says the Bishop into his microphone. 'No one will be allowed to stay at home.' The 1,000 inhabitants of Keep 10 listen passively, silently, stunned by this panoply of power – a black man so important that all these white men with guns and cameras follow him about. The Bishop waves his ivory stick. 'Kwenge, kwenge,' he says.

At the back of the crowd I approach a knot of young men and start asking questions. A corporal of the Guard Force shows up and offers to 'help'. I ask him to go away. He glowers but obliges. (Obeys?) The young men say they detest the PV but find life inside it safer than outside. Has pressure been put on them to vote, or to vote for Muzorewa?

No, none at all, they say. 'We believe in the election,' one of them volunteers. Several nod, others shrug. I feel faintly disappointed.

On to Gono PV – Keep 12 – at Shamva by helicopter. You can see the shadow of the rotary blades as we pass low across Madziwa TTL. The cloud of red dust and the noise brings the young boys running as we come down. The District Commissioner materializes at this juncture and affably offers to act as guide.

'I'm sure you people have questions to ask, so fire away, we have nothing whatsoever to hide, though we always get the blame for things we haven't done.'

The DC confirms that no food may be taken out of the keep except – he insists – for children on their way to school or the fields.

'All ten PVs in Madziwa were set up at the request of the local chief. As for the auxiliaries, since you ask, they have kept the terrs out of this area. They're simply a local home guard. If they had ever committed atrocities, as one reads in the overseas press, I'd have heard about it.'

One drifts away from the conducted tour. The PV is large enough to get lost in. The DC's story that the local chief personally asked for the PVs to be set up is greeted with universal disbelief and ridicule by the inhabitants. A man who works as a rigger in the Trojan Nickel Mine insists that not even children can take food out of the PV.

'In the fields the mothers find sweet melons for the children,' he explains.

'The DC,' says another man, 'he call meeting, he say to us, "You must vote."'

'*Must* vote?'

'Must vote, yes.'

The Guard Force's keep is sited on a central elevation dominating the PV. Any exchange of fire with vakhomana will pass over the heads of the inhabitants or not pass over their heads: rockets, mortar bombs, grenades constitute that neutral but deadly term, 'crossfire'.

Cpl Rufaru of the Guard Force is 37 and comes from Fort Victoria. It's standard practice to import Karangas into a Zezuru area, and the corporal freely admits that if he went home now the local people would instantly betray him to the vakhomana (whom he calls 'terrorists'). So his wife and children now live at a special camp at Shamva and they have no problems because he earns $(R)120 a month plus $(R)20 food allowance plus free accommodation. That's not bad at all: the skilled rigger at Trojan Nickel Mine gets only $(R)104. The only problem for Cpl Rufaru is the hatred and contempt in which all black members of the Guard Force are held.

A crowd of ragged kids has gathered round the huge South African Puma helicopter. The two crewmen from the Transvaal give them a friendly wave as the rotor-blades begin to turn faster.

11. with Sithole

Sithole's twin-engined, six-seater plane left Charles Prince at 7 a.m. In the front, the SB pilot and a white SB detective; in the middle row, Sithole and his loyal colleague, Co-Minister of Defence Noel Mukono (who wore a revolver in a shoulder-strap under his suit); in the back, a German photographer and myself. We headed east towards the Mozambique border and Noel Mukono just sat there, staring straight ahead of him, never glancing down at the tribal trust lands below, an old soldier with a small bullet head. Beside him, Sithole, impeccable in his pin-striped business suit, fleshy, marble-eyed, stared gloomily at the front-page report detailing the fall and flight of his patron, President Idi Amin.

The pilot puts the plane into a steep descent over the mountains of Nyamaropa. We corkscrew down rapidly over a valley airstrip close to the Mozambique border. This is Zanla territory and Zanla regard Sithole as the ultimate traitor. Something is wrong. Flying low, the pilot circles the airstrip half a dozen times, unwilling to land until the security forces show up. No one in the plane says anything. Sithole looks out of the window. It's Friday the 13th.

Finally the pilot spots a couple of army trucks sheltering beneath a tree. When he gets out of the plane he starts yelling and swearing at the officers in charge. Sithole and Mukono just stand there, on the grass strip, while this loud altercation continues. The pilot is bloody furious: how the fucking hell could he come down if the fucking army hid itself under a fucking tree, on and on.

Sithole has come to address a rally. There will be no rally because there are no people. Two weeks earlier Zanla cleared 10,000 villagers from the fertile valley, leaving fields of maize, cotton and tobacco rotting untended, spoil for the baboons. From the fortified police post you can see the vast confetti of empty kraal huts rimming the abandoned fields. Not the sort of thing you read about in the Rhodesian press. Sithole's auxiliaries had moved in to 'protect' the people – Zanla had therefore moved the people out. There is no rally but Sithole sits under a tree and talks to fifty auxiliaries, holding in his hand a large poster consisting of a portrait of himself and the words 'An Assurance of Leadership'. Hall of mirrors. After that the auxiliaries dance and wave their AK rifles and clap their hands and Sithole smiles while the white SB officers stand in the background, bored.

It's hot and Mukono has taken off his jacket. He has this revolver under his armpit. Once a Zanla commander, he is now Co-Minister of Defence in a Government headed by Ian Smith. I ask him how many of these auxiliaries are genuine guerrillas who have come 'on-sides', where they were retrained, and what their function is. I don't expect to get the truth but I want to hear the lies. After all, this apparently shy man is nominally running Rhodesia's counter-insurgency operation; in theory he could bark 'Walls!' and the noted white Commander of Comops would leap to attention. In theory. Anyway, Mukono has just begun his rather hesitant reply when the white SB officer listening in more or less brushes him aside to 'put me in the picture'. Mukono falls silent. Had it been the other Co-Minister of Defence, Herr Hilary Squires, no SB officer would have brushed him aside.

The police post at Nyamaropa is sandbagged and beleaguered. Its radio room cracks and hums. A young man tells me they'd been revved four times in 1978 and two times in the first three months of 1979. The terrs had sabotaged the irrigation scheme, blown up a canal, mortar attacks from the mountains, stick grenades from close quarters, terrible. When the police went to mend the sabotaged water supply a landmine blew their Land-Rover two metres in the air. The young man smiles:

'They even know each of us here by name. I tell you a bloke can go round the twist in this place. We had one chap here who emptied a grenade of its TNT, I mean no one else knew and then he comes into the mess and takes the pin out. Boy, did we fly out of there.'

Pinned to the mess-room wall are a girlie calendar and a message from Zanla written on carton cardboard, addressed to 'Mabinyas' (Boers). 'Smith is a dog down with dogs' runs the message. 'We want bloodshed to Smiths dogs war not dialogue down with you Smiths dogs. Zanla forces.' The Rev. Sithole takes one glance and leaves the mess despite the offer of a cup of tea. Noel Mukono stays for the tea. Maybe he is reconciled to being one of 'Smiths dogs'.

We fly west to Mangula. This time the police presence is in no doubt: white reservists are guarding the runway at fifty-metre intervals. As we taxi towards the waiting fleet of Zanu party cars the SB detective beside the pilot pulls off his radio earphones and turns to Sithole with a grin of triumph: 'Well, Reverend, last night we took out Joshua Nkomo's headquarters in Lusaka.'

Neither Sithole, member of the Executive Council, nor Mukono, Co-Minister of Defence, had known anything about it. The two blacks sit stunned and silent: Sithole is horrified. His voice is almost a whisper when he asks: 'You mean they killed Nkomo?'

Sithole and Nkomo had been arch-rivals ever since Sithole broke away to form Zanu. Yet only the previous week Sithole, reaching out for Ndebele votes in Matabeleland, had proposed that Zapu's distinguished leader should become figurehead President of the new state of Zimbabwe Rhodesia. Besides, Sithole was well aware that if Nkomo were killed retaliation would be swift.

The Reverend climbs out of the plane and I put my tape recorder under his chin and ask him for an exclusive comment. Splendid orator though this marble-eyed politician is, the words remain locked in his throat. 'Well, well . . . it's very difficult for me to react rationally, so to speak . . . but of course it should be understood that the security forces are under orders to act as quickly as possible . . . there is nothing we can do about it, one accepts it.'

A fleet of cars is waiting at the airport – young hitmen in suits and hard faces. The mood is sour. Three times Sithole's election appearance had been announced locally and three times people had walked to the stadium and stood for hours then gone home. The stadium is nearly empty when we get there – not more than 2,000 supporters. The SB detective who guards Sithole round the clock confides that if the blacks were constitutionally allowed to vote for Ian Smith he would romp home.

Mwenye Zanu! Zanu is the torch! Sithole talks for a while in Chichewa, a language spoken by local mine-workers from Zambia and Malawi, and then, as usual, runs through his standard lecture on the history of the liberation struggle. 'We began the war at Sinoia in 1966 because the RF refused to talk to us. Now they have learned their lesson and they talk to us. Raise your hands if you want a black government.' (Lists African countries which achieved independence through armed struggle.)

Chimurenga!

Sithole's approach is infinitely more intelligent than the Bishop's. He discusses the new constitution and the white referendum. 'Did UANC or Zupo start the war? Then how can they stop it?' He wipes his forehead with a handkerchief. 'When Smith finally signed the settlement I went home and said, "That trouble-maker has agreed!"'

But Sithole is straining. All the time he has to prove his own importance by association – 'I started the war, I did a deal with Smith. Smith is the great and terrible white lion but I am a match for him, he and I have fought for years and now we have decided to settle our differences, he and I.'

Sithole's Mangula rally is a flop. When he launches the chant 'Zanu!' the crowd is notably unresponsive. Immediately he spots this he winds the whole thing up. 'Let's go.' Surely he knows by now that he is going to lose.

We drive in a convoy of cars down into Zwimba TTL, homeland of Chief Chirau, an area overrun by UANC auxiliaries, accompanied now by even more SB officers and more aides. Sithole sits under a tree and talks to about fifty locals, more than half of them children. It just isn't his day. How indefatigable politicians are. Piles of green Zanu posters lie on the grass. There is a table, a bench, and two SB officers take notes when questions are asked. Four years previously one of them had been serving in the British army. Then the romance of police work in sunny climates beckoned him, but it had to be English-speaking sun: 'It was either Hong Kong, Bermuda or Rhodesia. So here I am.'

12. vote, vote, vote

'Your vote means peace', declare the full-page ads placed in all main newspapers by the Transitional Government. 'We are all going to vote'; 'This is what the people want'; 'Your vote will help to open more schools'; 'Your vote will help bring better job opportunities'. The barrage of propaganda is unrelenting: vote, vote, vote.

One thousand employees of the Posts and Telecommunications Corporation assemble at the main Salisbury depot on 11 April to hear Mike Kok of the Department of Information explain the importance of voting. The electoral

Registrar, E. W. Pope Simmonds, announces that he has been a volunteer police reservist since the 1960s. A Women's Voluntary Service canteen churns out hot dogs at King George VI Barracks while white machine-gunners of the 8th Battalion, the Rhodesia Regiment assemble their weapons amidst piles of ammo boxes. 'Bless 'em all, the long, short and the tall' is the rousing caption for a pic of middle-aged police reservists queueing for their kit at the Morris depot.

So comprehensive is the effort that all white males up to the age of 60 are now liable for conscription until 24 April. In Bulawayo a traffic jam builds up outside Brady Barracks as hundreds of white women drop off their husbands and sons, the territorials. In Umtali men of the 4th (Manicaland) Battalion of the Rhodesia Regiment put on dark-green berets with blue-and-white hackles. In Salisbury senior schoolboys of Mount Pleasant School (white shirts, ties, shorts) are pictured raising their right hands and taking the oath as volunteer Police Specials.

'Dear citizen,' wrote Malcolm Thompson, the Ulsterman who chaired the all-white Election Directorate, in a letter circulated to white farmers and employers, 'A high percentage poll is the most effective way of proving to the Western world that we have majority support for the internal settlement. In this way, we have the best opportunity of achieving recognition and lifting sanctions, which must be the aim of all Rhodesians. All white Rhodesians can assist immeasurably by helping their black employees to understand the election procedures . . . and, where possible, actually going to the polls with them.'

Thompson was later appointed by Muzorewa to head the Amnesty Directorate.

Zealously the white housewives tutored their cookboys and their garden-boys, their 119,000 Benjamins and Jacobs, in the mysteries of the secret ballot; helpfully they transported them to special seminars held in schools for domestic servants. On polling day they packed them into the back seat and delivered them, properly tutored, to the voting cubicles. Vote, Benjamin, vote.

Taking no chances, the Election Directorate sent mobile booths not only to remote farms but also to factories and work-places in the towns. Work stopped for a couple of hours while municipal workers in red dungarees lined up to vote in Second Avenue. At W. Dahmer & Co., Msasa, Salisbury, the entire labour force was transported by company trucks to the polling station. Banks closed during working hours so that employees could have no excuse for not voting. The towns, in short, were taken care of.

Likewise the men and women working on white farms, some 600,000 of them, were delivered to the polls like electoral livestock. Grinning humbly, encircled by white territorials for their own protection, they did their thing. 'They're so keen to vote it's unreal.' As for the 500,000 penned in the PVs, no problem. Ninety years ago the white man appeared on the scene with gun and sjambok: he made the rules and killed anyone who seriously disagreed. Nothing has changed. Now his gunships come snarling low over the thatched kraals, his loudspeakers informing the people that they must vote and be free: they obey. At Chipinga, where white farmers are making fortunes from growing coffee, District Commissioner Dirk du Plooy is unrepentant about the uprooting ('uplifting') of 69,000 of 'his' people into PVs. Dressed in a brown suit, flanked by officers of the police and army, du Plooy confidently taps a map of the south-east border region studded with markers. The accent is Afrikaner, the tone administrative-crisp. 'The world thought they were concentration camps, ladies and gentlemen, but we had good results.'

Lord and master of his domain, du Plooy recalls with pride how dip tanks have been reopened, African-owned cattle sold on the market, clinics installed in the PVs, and 10,000 children provided with primary education. He has banned the growing of maize inside the keeps – when it grows to its full height it can be a security hazard: 'They can grow sweet potatoes instead. In my opinion, ladies and gentlemen, the PVs are the future – agricultural planning, drainage, services, a whole basis for development. When this war ends no one will want to leave them.'

As the Dakota lifts off the airstrip the PVs begin to appear, scattered across the brown summer terrain; the shadow of the plane passes over the thatched huts, like a bat.

In Jani village in Mangwende, people were warned that if they didn't vote the village would be bombed. In the Shabani area eight truckloads of soldiers with four heavy guns moved into the Runde, fanning out in search of villagers who were hiding in the bush. At Chebdambuya, in the Makoni district, security forces warned people not to hide in the bush, and duly arrived at 5.30 a.m. to herd the villagers to a polling station three kilometres away. In the Mrewa area buses were stopped at roadblocks: 'Did you vote? Where? When?' In Banket auxiliaries went from door to door warning people to vote 'or just you wait!' In Seke the Pfumo reVanhu herded people to the polls at gunpoint. In Zwimba election meetings were warned that non-voters would be shot.

Bulawayo, polling day. Supt Ian Waters of the Special Branch briefs the press on the subject of terrorist infiltration of Matabeleland: his style of delivery is cool, laconic, English, obsessional; this cucumber is inwardly in a severe twist. Asked whether terrorist leader Nkomo does not in fact command the support of the majority of the Ndebeles, he replies: 'It's academic.'

In the townships the polling stations are surrounded by sandbags and white railway workers disguised as police reservists. At Tshabalala it's mainly expatriate Shonas, kids shouting 'Huruyiadzu!', Sithole men yelling 'Strong leaders!', UANC supporters replying, 'No to the rejected one!' It's all good-natured. These long lines of smiling, chanting enthusiasts want to vote, they believe in this election. But in the Ndebele townships, Iminyela and Pumula, scarcely anyone is voting, the pro-Nkomo boycott is effective despite the recent arrest of 100 Zapu officials allegedly for urging people to spoil their ballot papers if herded to the polls. At the gate of Induba School stand two utterly beautiful girls on behalf of Chief Ndiweni's UNFP, a Ndebele party. They explain softly that they fear cultural subjugation by the Shonas. Asked whether they would vote for a certain unnameable 'external terrorist leader' if given the opportunity, their faces radiate external terrorism.

13. at the Ministry of Justice

'The war may get worse at first,' Christian Andersen had predicted in February 1978, 'but then we hope it will get better.'

A year has passed since Chris Andersen made the prediction. He now occupies the Minister of Justice's handsome office in Vincent Buildings. The war *had* got worse at first and after that it had got worse still.

When Andersen's predecessor, Hilary Squires, was asked by a black MP how many black and how many white Rhodesians had been sentenced to death since UDI, and how many sentences had in fact been carried out, Squires described such questions as 'mischievous and provocative'; he did not deem it in the national interest to reveal such information. I ask Andersen how many have been hanged since he took office.

'We don't disclose that. It's not desirable to state the figures.'

'But surely in all Western democracies which retain the death penalty executions are a matter of public record.'

'You may be right and you may be wrong about that.'

It was in April 1975 that the regime had decreed that executions were to be kept secret and that relatives were not to be informed unless they inquired. Even if they inquired, they would not be given a specific date of execution.

Andersen says: 'I'm not clear that families are not given a specific date. However, you may be right in that regard. In the past advance notice has caused distress to the condemned man and the family. It's more humane to give as little notice as possible.'

'The wife comes with food on her weekly visit and is told: "He's dead." Is that humane?'

According to International Defence and Aid, at least six people were hanged during January 1979 and a further nine were in Chikurubi prison awaiting imminent execution; all were believed to have been sentenced by courts martial under martial law. IDA reckoned that at least twenty-five people had been sentenced to death under the internal settlement, of whom at least eight had been hanged – despite claims from Muzorewa and Sithole that they had put a halt to political executions. IDA estimated that at least 121 people had been sentenced to death from April 1975 to March 1978, but the number of executions was not known.

'How many are detained without trial?'

'We don't provide our enemies with such information. We are at war here, don't forget that,' the Minister says. 'There's no question of detaining people for their opinions, only if they are involved in threats to life and property.'

'Yet after the internal settlement you suddenly released almost all detainees . . . '

'Yes. The March agreement removed the causes of violence so it was logical to release them.'

'And then in September you equally suddenly detained a large number of Zapu militants in retaliation for the shooting down of the Viscount.'

'That is not accurate, if I may correct you. A Review Tribunal reported favourably with regard to certain individuals and they were released.'

'What about Canaan Banana?'

'I cannot discuss individual cases. But speaking in general, there is no restriction on peaceful political activity.'

'Even when D-notices prohibit newspapers from mentioning certain political leaders by name?'

'I personally agree that such restrictions are petty.'

'They come under your own Law and Order portfolio. So does the banning of the *Zimbabwe Times*.'

'That happened before I took office.'

'But the banning order remains. You haven't rescinded it.'

'I can't add to what Squires and Zindoga said at the time. It wasn't a matter of political opinions but a threat to our security. You mustn't take a facile approach, you must read between the lines, understand whether in subtle or devious ways a newspaper is promoting the standing of terrorists. You cannot be namby-pamby in this regard. Would Britain allow Hitler to set up a peaceful PRO office in London?'

'You are boasting about the high proportion of voters taking part in the present election, yet you arrested Zapu militants in Bulawayo for advocating spoiled ballot papers.'

'I deny that. I specifically inquired into those arrests. They were advocating a threat to life and property. There is nothing to prevent the PF from peacefully advocating a boycott of the elections. We banned the internal wings of Zanu and Zapu because they were associated with the external wings. If I may say so I am surprised at the hypocrisy prevalent in your country. You have detention without trial in Northern Ireland.'

'Did. It was a disaster. How do you justify a minimum sentence of nine years for stealing a cow?'

'Stock theft is a rising menace at the present time. It's one way the terrorists hit the economy of the country. But the law is not inflexibly applied. Petitions may be lodged.'

'One of your predecessors in this office was Byron Hove. He didn't last long.'

'I won't comment. It's unfair to ask me about Hove without advance warning. I do recall that Hove said it would be necessary for judges to be removed. The independence of the judiciary is sacred to us.'

'Chief Justice Macdonald never hesitates to express political opinions in summings up. When he and other members of your judiciary upheld the legality of UDI –'

Andersen cuts in. 'It upsets me that you should have a misunderstanding of the independent nature of the judiciary. Don't you know that your own Lord Pearce found, in the House of Lords, that the judges here had acted properly? Outsiders are trying to impose their views on the people of this country.' Andersen rises from his padded white-leather chair. 'Any drastic changes in the public service would undermine white confidence. Farmers and business-men need a sound civil-service infrastructure. Your security forces would wither away. Go and ask our black Ministerial colleagues. Go and ask Zindoga, one of the strongest nationalists at Geneva, go and ask him what happened in Zambia and Mozambique after the whites left.'

(In February 1982 Andersen resigned from the RF. Two months later he accepted a post as Minister of State in Mugabe's Government.)

14. keep your trap shut

Who was Ishmael Kadungure? Why does he claim a place in history? Well, his was the first black face to appear on Rhodesian TV in the highly responsible role of announcer, and it happened on 18 January 1979. Soon there were others, newsreaders even, including a girl whose father was deputy leader of the UANC. The shock to white Rhodesians was reflected in a feeling, widespread if not explicitly stated, that the news is no longer our news if *they* read it out. (Even though 'they' were clearly our 'they' rather than their 'they'.)

Rhodesian television resembled, if you can imagine it, a cut-price commercial station beamed exclusively to the commuter belt of Surrey by persons who had been unable to hold their jobs in the BBC. The same sleekly groomed girls, with names like Jenny Rickard and Trish Johns, their voices clear and resonant, their English accents purged and polished of alien colonial alloy, spoke both the news and the commercials in quick succession. Had this really been Reigate or Esher, rather than Africa, it would have seemed perfectly natural.

– 'You can hire a coach from Express Motorways, cheap and comfortable, with a first-class guide looking after you. Express Motorways!' (*Fractional pause.*) 'Biltong, tasty and nourishing, ideal for the bush, available from Ashdown Park Butchery, visit them tomorrow!' (*Fractional pause.*) 'Lancaster pharmacy for exquisite Easter gifts, French perfume or English lavender . . . Bye!'

Bye! The music then races for a couple of seconds and a strong male voice cuts in: 'Following the main news tonight we shall be screening the first of the Election '79 broadcasts . . .' Now the news tune, very martial: tar-tar-ti-ti-ti-tar. Here it comes. Carter denigrated. Anarchy in Britain. 'Barclays Bank of South Africa reports there has been a remarkable recovery of business confidence in the Republic . . .' Middle East: Sadat the only acceptable Arab. Italy: danger of Communists joining the Government.

Regularly the 7.45 news was followed by a brief 'Keep It to Yourself' ad. Clearly someone had spent the war in Britain. But it wasn't that kind of war. What the guerrillas needed to know they learned in the remote villages of the reserves or in the beerhalls of the townships. Documents classified 'confidential', carried in the brief-cases of white civil servants, were no earthly use to them. But after Trish Johns or Jenny Rickard had poured forth confidence in the future, in our security forces, so-many terrs killed today hooray; after statements of support from far-right American Congressmen, or Mr William Deedes, editor of the *Daily Telegraph*, lisping his lunacies; then came 'Keep It to Yourself,' one for each sex. Followed immediately by the nightly religious spot. The male version of 'Keep It to Yourself' was a manly 'Keep your trap shut'; for the ladies, a severe, middle-aged woman in BSAP uniform appeared holding that document which the evil external terrorists wanted to steal so desperately badly: 'Girls, if it says Confidential, it means Confidential.'

15. staying to make it work

They left the seven bodies face up, on the edge of the kraal; already the kites were wheeling above, high, black and silent. Rod Maddocks had scored the first hit with the 20-mm cannon of the Alouette gunship, blowing the man's leg off as he made for the cover of the kopje which towered over the kraal. The Dakota, which had taken off from Grand Reef air base with men of Fireforce Bravo (code-name of No. 2 Commando of the RLI) fifteen minutes after the helicopters, came in behind and above the choppers, at a height of 550 metres. Moments later the light began flashing above the door and the fourteen commandos jumped over the arid brown wastes of Buhera.

A Zanla force had been spotted at dawn by a Patu patrol, moving north-west towards the Charter district, and a first warning had gone through to Grand Reef. By the time Rod brought the command-post Alouette in over Buhera, with his fellow pilots taking the orbits agreed with the Fireforce Bravo commander, the Zanla force had split and split again, warned by the sound of the chopper's approach, audible six minutes before they arrived overhead. Then radio contact with the Patu patrol led Rod to make a turn thirteen degrees west and almost immediately they saw the seven guerrillas making a break from the kraal. The second one rolled over, tried to rise, collapsed after being hit by high-explosive ammunition; the commandos took out the others, riddling their prostrate bodies for fear of that proverbial grenade, the last laugh of a 'dead' gook.

Seven more freedom fighters would never see the liberation of their country. Yet Buhera was now close to being a semi-liberated zone. In the District Commissioner's office – a spot so remote and bleak you might have been on the moon – Arnold Rudolph, nominal ruler of seven chiefs, twenty-seven headmen and 170,000 people, knew that he was actual ruler of very little. Already fifty-three out of 102 primary schools had been closed; 20,000 people had fled the area, filling the shanty-towns of Umtali and Salisbury. Travelling on the ground was virtually impossible; not only were the dirt tracks strewn with mines but the guerrillas made the local people dig the roads up. No cattle were any longer being dipped, only 'house-dressed' – pulling the ticks off by hand.

All telephone links had been severed for four months. 'That's dreary,' the DC says, 'when you want to talk to your kids in boarding school.' Arnold Rudolph wears, today, powder-blue matching shirt and shorts. On the first day of polling only 355 voters came to the DC's office to vote; on the second day, only one. Arnold Rudolph shrugs: it's all hopeless despite the luminous sticker over his desk – 'I'm staying here to help make it work'; hopeless despite the notices outside his office door offering $(R)5,000 for information leading to the death or capture of a senior terrorist leader, $(R)2,500 for a group leader, etc.; hopeless despite the auxiliaries lounging under the trees. 'We did burn some huts,' he ruminates, 'we try not to turn people against us, you have to be selective.' He sighs. Hopeless. At one stage he closed the grinding-mills, now he is reopening them. He reckons there are 450 'resident' terrs in Buhera, with others passing through towards Charter and Salisbury. They smoke Madisons, drink Bols and order people not to vote. 'Not much we can do about it. On Sunday twelve terrs ambushed seventy troops.'

Zanla control spreads east to the border. The main Umtali–Birchenough Bridge road used to carry sixty to seventy African buses a day, but not one has run since 1 October 1978 when Zanla implemented its warning to keep off the road. That's control: or negative control.

16. keeping out of politics

Lt-Gen. Peter Walls sits under the television lights, a man of modest demeanour, brisk and businesslike, the most coveted guest of honour at school prizegivings. Walls projects a positive image whereas Smith, clearly, is engaged in a retreat. Walls had attended the Shangani Memorial Service at the Allan Wilson High School when the Chaplain-General to the Forces, Lt-Col. the Rev. Norman Wood, dedicated the three new Memorial tennis courts. Walls and Wood share in common a firm belief that soldiers should keep out of politics. Chap.-Gen. Wood then embarked on a tour of the United States:

'I did not try to push either politics or economics . . .' Instead he spoke of the Marxist threat to the churches and the way the Western media distorted Rhodesia's case. He showed American audiences colour photographs of the Elim massacre and told TV viewers, 'Your Government is supporting this kind of thing.' Arriving in Washington, Wood began lobbying Senators to support the motion to send official observers to the internal election.

All this activity, of course, was strictly non-political.

Walls, too, stands beyond politics: 'The black people say thank God for martial law,' he assures the press on 14 April. 'Are you reporters even aware when you enter a martial-law zone? No? So why all the fuss?'

Walls basks under the bright lights. Yesterday's kill rate – ninety dead in forty-eight hours – was the highest of the year. And the attack on Nkomo's command post in Lusaka has been a complete success. Walls permits himself a smile at the thought of fat Nkomo escaping through a toilet window.

'If we had wished to kill him, we would have killed him.'

Asked whether it is true that there are 'liberated zones' in Rhodesia, or 'no-go areas', he answers, crisply:

'None. There's nowhere we can't go – either in this country or in neighbouring countries.'

The reporters laugh sycophantically: 90 per cent of them are white but that's not the point. If in Maputo they'd laugh at Tongogara's jokes too. Of course there's always one trouble-maker, some Swede, a Hollander perhaps or a French Marxist – has Walls read the Justice and Peace Commission's report, *The Man in the Middle*, which documents allegations against the security forces? No, says Walls, but his staff have. But does he accept or reject the evidence contained in the report?

The question bounces off the General.

And is Rhodesia now sponsoring anti-Frelimo guerrillas inside Mozambique? presses the trouble-maker.

If Walls offered a reply to this question not a single journalist present can recall what it was. On the way out he kisses a young woman working for BBC TV.

Postscript: In May 1980 Wood resigned as Chaplain-General, complaining that Zanla political commissars had prevented distribution of the Bible among guerrillas in the assembly points.

17. to be perfectly honest

The glossy photograph shows a young woman, very white and blonde, with pouting lips, mascara'd eyes and healthy breasts; she is holding a Kommando semi-automatic handgun and if *she* can use it so can your wife or daughter so why not spend $(R)150 and maybe save her life?

John Landau, Managing Director of Arms Manufacturing Company (Armscor), is 49, alert, relaxed, friendly, dynamic. He's also Deputy Chief Whip of the Rhodesia Front and very adept at getting promotional material into the *Herald*, not merely blondes with big boobs but also Ministers of the Government, Hilary Squires, van der Byl, Jack Mussett, all firing Armscor's guns. Of the company's five directors, three are MPs: Dennis Divaris, the RF's Chief Whip, Albert Mills, and Landau. Nine MPs are shareholders.

'There's nothing sinister about this,' Landau says.

'Except that you have a financial stake in the war?'

'If the war ended we could diversify. No problem.'

Landau was born in Bulawayo of an Irish father and a South African mother. His uncles settled in Rhodesia in 1890 as the country's first wholesale merchants and he himself read Commerce at the University of Wit-watersrand. In 1965 – he beams with pleasure – he was chosen to run sanctions-busting. 'A special unit was set up under the Ministry of Commerce. I was Rhodesia's answer to James Bond. Unfortunately the women didn't do it.' Grins, ear to ear. 'I have a story to tell. One day!' But it seems that his operations excluded petrol, oil, minerals and foods.

Almost everything he says is salted with two phrases: 'To be perfectly fair . . .' and 'to be perfectly honest with you'. An MP since 1974, he serves as a Major in the territorials seventy-two days a year, a voluntary gesture since MPs are exempt from military service. On the wall behind his desk hangs an ad for the Kommando hand carbine, 'Tested and Proved in Battle'. These words are written in both English and Afrikaans. He sells a lot of these $(R)150 guns in the Republic and shows me the workshop of his Spurn Road factory where sixty black workers are turning out the semi-automatics at a fair pace.

'But to be perfectly honest with you, not fast enough to keep up with demand. Demand is fantastic. Just fantastic.'

In 1978 a new directive had allowed town-dwellers to own semi-automatic weapons provided they obtained permits – extremely convenient legislation in view of the fact that Landau began marketing his LDP in October 1977. Big ads appeared promoting the virtues of a weapon which weighed only three kilos and could fire twenty-five rounds on semi-automatic (which means that only one shot is fired with each pull of the trigger but the bolt automatically blows back and cocks the gun for the next round.)

'Recoil is minimal. You can fire it comfortably with one hand. Ideal for women.'

What about the treatment of black MPs during Parliamentary debates?

'To be fair, you've got to admit they insist on bringing racial overtones to any subject. For example, you propose the police estimates and they complain of no promotion in the police for Africans. But they're fairly treated, to be perfectly honest with you. They're allowed to say their thing and use their clumsy words.' As for their allegations against the security forces, to be fair, some of what they said might be true but a lot was unsubstantiated and you shouldn't debate that. Hawkins's investigation showed it was mostly a pack of lies. 'I'm one of the more liberal chaps, to be perfectly honest with you.' Landau wants to be perfectly fair to everyone involved. 'Your tribesman can't write down his complaint so you get a garbled story transmitted from the headman to the chief to the MP. In war things do happen and heads get knocked together.'

How will Landau feel when the new Assembly convenes and the white MPs find themselves, for the first time, in a minority?

He shrugs easily. 'I always get on well with these chaps. No problem.'

Landau became RF Chief Whip soon afterwards. After Independence he served as Chairman of the House Public Accounts Committee, exposing massive irregularities surrounding the feeding and paying of guerrillas in the APs. He broke with the RF in February 1982, while still Chief Whip (a rump no longer worth whipping?), and two months later accepted a post in Mugabe's Government.

18. killed

Eric Castle was a bit of a maverick. Once a Major in the British army, he arrived in Salisbury from Zambia in 1974, grew his hair long, set himself up as a 'disco king' and involved himself not only in teenagers' drug problems but also in the rehabilitation of wounded servicemen. He organized a Wheelchair Warriors' Ball and quarrelled with the police over his determination to give the proceeds to individuals rather than to the Terrorist Victims' Relief Fund. Early in April 1979 Eric Castle was engaged in patrolling the Beitbridge–Fort Victoria road ahead of a convoy when his vehicle was struck by a rocket. Both Castle and another field reservist were killed.

Basil Kearns, 41, died on 15 April from wounds received three weeks earlier during a terrorist ambush on his farm near Bindura. A crack polo player who at one time had the highest handicap (6) in Rhodesia, Kearns had played the game in Kenya and England, where he got to know the Duke of Edinburgh and received a polo cup from the hands of the Queen. Kearns had captained the Rhodesian team at the 1964 South African games.

Three days later, on 18 April, Gerald Ross, 27-year-old DC for the Nkai area, was killed when a small convoy in which he was travelling was ambushed. The job ran in the family. The son of a former DC, Gerald Ross was also brother-in-law of Ian Rich, DC at Nuanetsi.

19. women and horses

Easter 1979. 'Members of the Rhodesian Horse Society from many parts of the country will be taking part in two important events this holiday weekend – the first being the annual D grade Easter show at the Salisbury showground and the second the Toyota Horse Trials in Johannesburg. . . . Nearly 300 horses and ponies from areas as far apart as Bindura, Umtali, Karoi, Marandellas, Umvukwes and Bulawayo will be competing . . . most of the events will be judged by women. The youngest entrant is 3 years old and there are at least two grandmothers taking part.'

Your correspondent drives to the Royal Agricultural Society Show Ground. The show-jump girls are all white, their hair netted and combed to a sheen, their make-up thick and translucent, their coats and hats of a sexy black velvet. A dustier black are the grooms who tend the horses in the rear enclosure. Picnics, horse-boxes, cars – only those black grooms arrest the overwhelming impression of being in England. And the guns.

Pretty Kathy Conde rode three clear rounds at the Whitsun Horse Show to beat Anne Patterson by 0·3 seconds in the S & T Importers and Exporters A/B Grand Prix. During the show the Marlborough Lions Club staged a fête which raised $(R)4,500 for charity.

Not to be outdone, the Lions Club of Waterfalls organized a Forces Festival in aid of the Terrorist Victims' Relief Fund. Star event was a rugby match between policemen and nurses; according to the rules, the men could score only if carrying both the ball and at least one nurse.

In such a climate female sports stars inevitably contain a proportion of resounding beauties: the queen of softball, for example, tall, lithe Di Laidler, spearhead of Mashonaland A; or the gorgeous blonde diver Antoinette 'Nonnie' Wilken, of Girls' High, who won two golds in the South African championships, took up a diving scholarship at the University of Houston, Texas, finished tenth in the three-metre springboard event when representing Zimbabwe in the Moscow Olympics, and was runner-up a month later in the Jacaranda Queen beauty competition. This earned her a fourteen day Sky-coach holiday sponsored by Durban Publicity Association – leaping for joy across Durban's gleaming, sea-wet sands are Salisbury's Jacaranda Queen Gill Waddacor (centre), with princess Kath Humphrey (right) and Antoinette Wilken (left). Tiny bikinis.

But not a bit less gorgeous is another super-athlete, Lyn Tasker, Zimbabwe's white hope in the Olympic swimming sprints, both free-style and breast-stroke.

20. free and fair

Clearly this was destined to be the only black-majority-rule election in history to win wholehearted support from racists world-wide. Down in the Republic the White Man himself gave it his blessing and sent in Puma helicopters, pilots, Afrikaners in khaki jump-suits; also a number of medium-level observers from Pretoria's Foreign Office who claimed, when asked, that they were really academics, reporters or travel agents.

From Bavaria came hearty cowboys out of the Hofbrauhaus wearing 'ich liebe Zimbabwe Rhodesia' lapel badges; on closer inspection they turned out to be the director-general of the Bavarian Broadcasting Company, etc., friends of Franz Josef Strauss. Four deputies arrived from the French Assembly including the dapper Hervé Lavenir of the Union Démocratique Chrétienne (spelt 'cretin' in the Rhodesian press), an unreconstructed apostle of Algérie française. Like the German cowboys he was most animated and warlike when strapped into a Dakota.

The American extreme right produced its customary crop of bemused ambassadors, men drawling 'free and fair' in plush hotel lobbies. Robin Moore, once patron of Rhodesia's American mercenaries (the Crippled Eagles), best-selling novelist and President of the American Rhodesia Society, turned up with a magisterial token figure called 'Ambassador Lodge'. In a reference to the abhorrently left-wing officials currently influencing State Department policy towards Rhodesia, Moore smirked: 'The Moose drinks out of the Lake.' As for the Patriotic Front, 'It's just a Communist outfit. I ought to know, I've been present when captured terrorists were interrogated.'

Especially prized by Salisbury's Ministry of Information were those few 'distinguished black Americans' who were prepared to give the election a clean bill of health. Clay Claiborne, director of the anti-Communist Black Silent Majority Committee, turned up, claimed that Martin Luther King would have begged the terrorists to lay down their arms, and denigrated King's former aide Andrew Young as a vote-loser among blacks. Another black American with a distinguished record as a civil-rights campaigner, Bayard Rustin, President of the A. Philip Randolph Institute and Chairman of Social Democrats, USA, arrived at the head of a large delegation of observers from Freedom House. During a tour of polling stations in Bulawayo I asked him whether he was struck by indications of a Ndebele boycott of the polls:

'The what?'

'The Ndebeles.'

'Who are they?'

Son of a West Indian, and for ten years political adviser to Martin Luther King, Rustin had fallen into the role of fronting for Cold War liberals. No small delight in occupying the limelight may have been a problem too; when the year 1979 dawned few white Rhodesians had heard of Bayard Rustin yet here he was in Salisbury holding forth at press conferences and being received at the Retreat Ceremony by the President of Rhodesia.

'I have sensed a great exhilaration among Rhodesian blacks this week,' he announced. 'Race relations in Rhodesia are far friendlier than in Detroit or Chicago.' Rustin was now a great old pundit, wise in the world and one of its fools.

The Freedom House final report, though partially objective in its analysis, concluded that the election constituted 'a necessary step toward unfettered majority rule', even though (as the report conceded) opposition leaders were in detention, martial law prevailed, and 'the censored white media are encouraged to present an almost uniformly favourable picture of the internal settlement, the election process, and the country's security and judicial services'.

The British Government refused to send observers, but Mrs Thatcher dispatched a team headed by Lord Boyd, Secretary of State for the Colonies from 1954 to 1959 – a period of reaction during which Britain unsuccessfully attempted to suppress Kenyan nationalism and violent insurrection by force. It was Boyd who kept Jomo Kenyatta 'inside'. Although promoted both by Thatcher and the Rhodesians as an important elder statesman deeply versed in Africa, there was never any doubt where his bias lay. On 12 October 1978 he had published a letter in *The Times* praising an article by Professor John Hutchinson, an English-born Californian who lobbied tirelessly on behalf of Ian Smith.

'The basic problem', wrote Hutchinson in the article endorsed by Lord Boyd, 'is the triple fraudulence of British policy; the commitment to Rhodesian self-determination, but the granting of a veto over its terms to the autocrats of Africa; the continuation of sanctions when majority rule has been conceded . . . and the requirement of free and fair elections while British "neutrality" – by escalating terrorist intimidation – is making these elections increasingly difficult and perhaps impossible to administer.'

Having endorsed this immaculately partial view six months before, Lord Boyd was unlikely to find the 'internal' elections unfree and unfair. This being so, he and his fellow Tory observers were accorded royal treatment on arrival; minions of the Ministry of Information attended to their every wish, their itinerary kept them in regal isolation from other observers and the press, they gave no interviews. A British general election, after all, was imminent; the iron lady, Rhodesia's White Hope, was poised for power.

21. Smith

On 20 April, as the polls finally closed, Ian Smith addressed a large audience of journalists and observers in Meikles Hotel. Confident that the turn-out at the 'internal' elections would by the morrow exceed 60 per cent, he embarked on an uncompromising justification of his own record. More than forty coups in black Africa since the war, so why all this hypocrisy and nit-picking about the election in Rhodesia? Of the five so-called front-line states, two had never had elections (Mozambique, Angola) and two others were one-party states (Tanzania, Zambia). He reminded his audience how, four months previously, Kaunda had effectively banned rival candidates for the Presidency.

Majority rule? 'Our hand was forced' in September 1976. No option but to make the best of it. At Geneva Britain and America reneged on the terms of their agreement. This small, isolated and land-locked country had complied with everything the Free World has asked of it, indeed it had now complied with all of the famous six principles. Its blacks enjoyed a higher standard of living than anywhere else in Africa: 'This is what we have given them.' The West, meanwhile, was simply laying down a red carpet in Africa for the Russians. Look at Angola. 'I am sick and tired of treacherous behaviour.' As for the terrorists, 'We will knock the daylights out of those chaps. They're no match for us.'

22. grave irregularities

According to official statistics, 64 per cent of 2.8 million eligible voters had registered a vote, figures hard to prove since there had been no census of a rapidly expanding population since 1969. In any case the regime proclaimed the whole exercise to have been a triumph of democracy which the world could not ignore.

Ndabaningi Sithole quickly threw a spanner into the works. After twenty years in politics, half of them spent in prison, this supremely ambitious outcast had been humiliatingly rebuffed, gaining only twelve seats (262,928 votes) compared with the UANC's fifty-one. In not a single electoral district had Sithole's Zanu beaten Muzorewa's men into second place.

Sithole immediately cried foul. Reporters and TV crews packed into party headquarters at Century House while Zanu's demoralized staff stood on chairs holding aloft hastily scrawled placards, 'Dr Rhoodie's $1,000,000 has worked.' Sithole finally squeezed into the room as the crews jostled for camera angles and bulbs flashed, then read out a statement complaining of 'grave irregularities', of biased DCs, of UANC auxiliaries intimidating voters . . . Sithole wanted a commission of inquiry. The reporters went away amused, sceptical, cynical. Still, it was a story.

23. a pariah

Allan Savory's pronouncements as President of the National Unifying Force increasingly galled the more timid of his colleagues. 'The Rhodesian Government is losing the war,' he had told the BBC in July 1978, 'in fact it can be said to have lost the war . . . I've often said, and I mean it very much, that had I been a Russian I would willingly have paid Mr Smith and his senior military men salaries over the last few years as they're the greatest agents the Kremlin ever had in Africa.'

Going too far? In March 1979 he issued his last message to the NUF. It was misleading, he said, to argue that the PF was set on gaining power through the barrel of a gun: 'The PF have often stated their willingness to face genuine elections, but their determination to fight rather than have it under Smith's control; they were not invited in until the March 3rd Agreement to suit the RF had been drawn up; they had to give up force of arms while Muzorewa and Sithole were being allowed private armies. They would in fact have been totally under the control of the RF and Security Forces when they had in fact won the war which they fought against RF racialism.'

A few days later Savory was ousted as President of the NUF. Fearing arrest on account of subversive statements he had made abroad, Savory decided to remain temporarily outside the country and telephoned Nick McNally to explain the situation. But the NUF had already issued a statement which amounted in effect to the 18th Brumaire of Louis Bonaparte: Savory had 'resigned' because of business commitments. . . .

The majority of NUF members, meanwhile, girded themselves in khaki or police-blue to defend the elections that Savory had called a sham against the terrorists whom he called guerrillas. McNally took over. Paying tribute to Savory's ability to be right 'time and again', McNally led a stampede to disown everything Savory had stood for: in short, the NUF must make its peace with the internal settlement which would probably be recognized by Mrs Thatcher after she won the British election. 'I am concerned', said McNally, 'at the number of white liberals who are opting out of the NUF because of what they see as its anti-Government and pro-revolutionary stance.' A Catholic lawyer who regarded Zanu's Marxism as a terrible spectre on the horizon, McNally remarked privately: 'The interim Government stands the best chance of winning the war, so we'll have to support it.' The NUF sent a message to President Carter urging him to accept the election as having been as free and fair as circumstances allowed: the result, argued the NUF, gave Muzorewa a mandate to negotiate peace.

The Muzorewa Government later made a determined effort to discredit Allan Savory, to pin the pariah label to his tail. This followed a Rhodesian raid on Zapu headquarters in Lusaka and the discovery of documents recording supposedly conspiratorial conversations between Savory and Zapu officials. Questioned about this, McNally declared that the liberation war was over and that continued armed struggle was no longer justified.

24. beyond endurance

Glendale was the fulcrum of Zanla's spearhead thrust at Salisbury from the north. In April 1979 the security forces – Selous and Grey's Scouts, the RLI – had moved into the Masembura reserve bordering these white farm lands and stonked ninety-five gooks, or so they claimed. Afterwards the troopies toured the white farms soliciting contributions to a $(R)500 all-Rhodesian rave-up.

My hostess, Mrs Milly Jorden, expresses resentment at this levy, even though her own son has done cross-border reconnaissance work inside Mozambique; even though the Selousies had temporarily cleaned the area of Charlie Tangos. Mrs Jorden also complains about the $(R)150 a month required by the Area Defence Coordinating Committee: 'We can't afford it,' she says. 'But we were afraid we wouldn't get protection.' One of her neighbours, a farmer called Herbert Mitchell, the focus of this report, also resents the levy and complained to the Farmers' Union about it. Behind the cohesive façade of white Rhodesia we find mean wrangles, petty squabbles, life and death totted up on ten-cent adding machines.

Milly Jorden is a pert, petite woman, whose frothy consciousness naturally repels beliefs which are mutually consistent. Believing herself to be a liberal – a status she makes manifest by writing letters to the *Herald* and joining Women for Peace – she shares a bed with a husband who pays his labourers only $(R)11 a month and considers this too much, a farmer who complains about the pathetic dependency on him of the Africans' wives, children, relatives; a man who chose to live and farm in Africa but who has long since gone sunstroke-crazy through protracted exposure to the K-factor. Their bedroom is alive with gadgetry designed to sound alarms and turn on the floodlights if the perimeter fence is penetrated. The bedroom window is covered by wire netting with slits for returning fire. She chain-smokes; ash falls on the bedroom carpet.

Light-headed on Rhodesian wine, the liberal Mrs J. offers us all her version of Rhodesian history (different, one must concede, from that of Laurence Vambe). 'Our mistake', she says, 'was to be too bloody paternalistic' (she botches this word at the first two attempts). 'We should have paid the best labourers and told the rest to bugger off and learn capitalism.' She giggles: 'They call me a revolutionary liberal and here I am preaching capitalism.' Her husband shrugs.

Herbert Mitchell shakes his head decisively. 'You're forgetting the Land Apportionment Act,' he says. 'There's no doubt we cheated the blacks out of their land by conquest, by the hut-tax, by bringing in workers from Ethiopia and Nyasaland to depress the wages of the indigenous Shona people.' Elderly, portly, a chain-smoker, Mitchell was born in Rhodesia but resembles an Oxford don (traditional image thereof) in style and accent. During the war he flew in RAF bombers but regards his fellow airman, Ian Smith, as 'a war criminal who should be hanged'. Mitchell's political lineage is familiar (but unusual among farmers): Pat Batsford, the Centre Party, Allan Savory. 'One must talk to the PF,' he says. 'Nothing permanent can be achieved without them.'

Yet he feels only loathing, disgust, for the guerrillas who have relentlessly attacked his property. He talks of 'culling' them. His 1,000-hectare farm borders the Masembura TTL; clearly his admiration for Savory cuts no ice within the African reserve. The first attack came in November 1978 when servants' quarters were burnt and farm workers forced to scatter into the bush. A month later the entire compound was burned down. The third attack took the form of small-arms fire and rifle-grenades. His wife and daughter were not really clued up; they had all talked about shooting practice but had done nothing about it. Now he regretted the oversight. Soon only his own FN was operating. He aimed at the guerrillas' flashes but misjudged the distance; in fact the guerrillas were line abreast fully 100 metres beyond the fence. The attack was called off after thirty minutes, ten minutes before the security forces finally turned up.

Mitchell moved to Salisbury the next day, taking on a white security guard at $(R)300 a month and several black ones at between $(R)65 and $(R)100. (One of the latter was taken away by the police, having used his wages to pay for the favours of local girls.) On 20 March, Mr Baines, the 52-year-old security guard hired by Herbert Mitchell, was shot dead while closing the farm's security gate. The black foreman's sons were abducted, beaten with rocks, thrown in a river – on this occasion the guerrillas actually entered the house, took Mitchell's maps and his Agric-Alert, his guns, sheets and blankets. Thinking about it Herbert Mitchell lights a new cigarette with an unsteady hand. 'I felt the house was soiled and despoiled by their presence.'

The sixth attack came on a Saturday evening in April. Mitchell had gone to bed early, woken up at 11 p.m., and begun to read. At midnight there was the most terrific bang – a rocket. He told a nervous security guard he had with him to fire only one of the 'fire parks', but the fellow managed to detonate all the Adams grenades simultaneously, to no visible effect. The attack continued. Mitchell pressed the Agric-Alert alarm button for four seconds and then spoke into the phone.

The following day the District Commissioner sent him eight men of the black Guard Force. Driving round the farm perimeter on his instructions, they struck a mine of the sort which is detonated by a wheel but explodes under the centre of the vehicle. Crossfire raked the compound. His workforce was down from seventy to forty now and those remaining adamantly refused to spend the night in the compound, preferring to shelter under tarpaulins in the wild.

'The last thing they want you to do is to fence them in for their own protection. They see a fence as a barrier to their escape when trouble starts up.'

What came next was severely disillusioning: the Area Coordinating Committee allocated him four white 'bright-lights', ex-RLI troopies, who proceeded to do more damage than the guerrillas – a hole in the ceiling, a trolley smashed, firing tracer bullets so that they fell in the farm compound. 'No discipline at all.'

Finally the farm was sold at a poor price. 'Of course,' Mitchell reflects, 'the civil war was inevitable. How do you solve land hunger yet preserve free-enterprise farming? A lot of European farmers have behaved with criminal stupidity – they'd go berserk if an African crossed their land by a traditional path even though it might otherwise involve a ten-mile walk. I always laid down footpaths.'

He lights another cigarette.

25. PsyAc

Born in the Cape and conscripted into the South African army, Craig Richards soon rebelled against 'the senseless bullshit, you know' meted out by cropheaded Afrikaner NCOs with long memories. Three years with the

Rhodesian security forces being a legally valid alternative, Craig had signed on. When the Rhodesian recruiters had showed up at Mafeking with their long hair and beards, soft-tongued trackers of the Zambezi escarpment who didn't believe in bullshit or speak Afrikaans, Craig had recognized his destiny.

Craig could ride horses – had modelled cigarette ads riding bareback on the sand flats opposite Table Mountain – and got himself into the Grey's Scouts. It was during the induction course at Inkomo Barracks under Maj. Anthony Stephen that he met blonde Asst-Sgt Cynthia Butler, a South African girl who had qualified as a vet at the Royal College in England and was now happily employed dosing combat horses through nostril tubes. 'I'm completely sold on this country,' Cynthia told Craig. 'I enjoy the work, the team spirit and the open-air life, so why don't you screw me?' Craig did. Cynthia got engaged to a member of Special Branch 2. Craig was posted to the vast open terrain of the Botswana border, hunting down Zipra on cross-bred horses trained to canter away and wait during an exchange of fire.

Then Craig got hit in the leg near Gwai River. They were tracking a terr platoon which had robbed a store and revved the homestead of a white ranch, but these gooks were switched on and doubled right back on their spoor and laid an ambush across their own tracks. The Grey's lost Varelinck, a Belgian hot rod who had served with Major 'Mad Mike' Hoare's outfit in Katanga and later opened a bar in Durban, as well as one black fellow; that night and the day after the Grey's said to anyone who would listen that they mourned the dead black every bit as much as the Belgian.

His damaged knee put Craig out of that scene. For a while he was driving around in an Ojay, a weird ambush- and mine-protected vehicle with a concertina-shaped body of heavy steel surrounded by a shell of thin mild steel – a tumble shield. Manufacturer: Morewear Industries. Craig had been transferred to Intelligence and then on to PsyAc.

Psychological Action.

The job was handing out Department of Information leaflets showing disembowelled labourers, mothers and babies burnt alive in huts, that sort of thing – actually some of the pics had been taken after Hawker Hunters napalmed a kraal in Buhera, just as the Department put out ads displaying the squalor of Birmingham, England by using shots taken just down the road in the African township of Highfield. Craig was also given a glossy pamphlet, *Fighting Forces of Rhodesia*, which he liked: the blend of machismo, comradeship, nostalgia – though none of these words figured in his active vocabulary. There was a picture of a mounted trooper of Pioneer days being shown the direction across country by a half-naked native, with the caption:

'Now as then co-operation is a feature of Rhodesian life. In all Africa, possibly in all the world, there may not be another country where relations between the races are as harmonious as in Rhodesia.'

Craig was amused by this PsyAc thing – touring villages on the eastern border and offering rewards to kids who reported on their parents, brothers, families. Craig's immediate superior, a 36-year-old reservist called Bill Daley, assigned essays on such subjects as 'What I would do if my father fed a terrorist' and got back stuff like this: 'The children were chased by the torist. The torists they always short people. Soldiers not good to because they also shorting people.' The kids (and their nervous, obsequious, hate-harbouring teachers) gave Bill Daley and Craig and PsyAc what they wanted: 'Myself I don't want them to took us children. I want stay at my father eating my mother's food.'

Craig half believed in it, half didn't. Maybe it was all shit. You couldn't trust anything, really – he stood guard, his knee hurting, while Daley gathered the kids under a msasa-tree outside the schoolhouse and Sgt Ndhlovu translated. Daley talked about the importance of keeping the army and police informed. The old rheumy kraalhead observed everything, downright inscrutable, Craig thought lazily, brushing off the flies. Photos of badly mutilated dead guerrillas produced gasps and a few giggles. OK, let's get out of here, the waters will flow back once we've driven half a mile and by nightfall all this junk will be in the hands of the 'boys'.

In September 1978 he was offered a handsome bonus if he would serve until 1982. He signed on. The hope had never quite left him, since the time of Kissinger, that if the Brits temporarily took over again there would be golden handshakes all round. For a while he was on intelligence-interrogation duty, based at Llewelin Barracks, Bulawayo: the Zanla terrs he questioned always said Zipra was the real enemy and that Mugabe would do a deal with the Bishop, and Craig took this at face value, quick to believe what he wanted to hear – a flaw in an intelligence officer but a flaw almost universal in Rhodesian military intelligence.

Now, at the time of the 1979 internal election, Craig's business is the interrogation of captured guerrillas – the ones that don't collaborate are hanged. Craig knows that the Government's 'safe return' policy hasn't worked and that the leaflets dropped from the air have failed to persuade the terrs to give up the struggle. But Zanla, he is convinced, is deeply shaken by the Bishop's election victory.

'Some of those gooks have been telling the people to vote, did you know that? A lot of them are just sitting on the fence waiting to come on-sides. I reckon the Bishop will bring in Mugabe as President, a shrewd move. Mugabe knows his power base is crumbling now – one more push and we've won this war.'

Weekend leave. An all-night rave-up is on at Wedza, somebody's turf, Craig takes a crate of shumbas and his new girl Linda, racing through bad country in a borrowed Datsun, an FN at his side, a semi-automatic across Linda's lap, a Luger nestling between his own tanned legs. It's a fancy-dress affair and the big joke, now that we have 'majority rule', is to come with a blackened face and a golliwog wig, purchased in one of the Indian stores at Marandellas for less than $(R)12, if you're lucky. Or threatening.

A lamb is turning on a spit and disco music throbs through the wide-open windows. Craig says 'Hi' in a soft voice to all the people he knows; to some he says, 'Hi, this is Linda.' His voice is quiet, his vowels clipped, and he fires out his sentences with machine-gun rapidity – maybe Red Indian Braves did that too, when they weren't speaking in English, which kind of slowed them up.

He gazes blankly at Linda's peachsoft beauty. Craig has had a few. 'Sometimes', he says, 'you wonder what you're fighting for and I mean that. They tell you one thing they tell you another, the lads have had it up to here.' He levels his hand with his nose, a habit he picked up after he moved north of the Limpopo. He prowls the room, then leads Linda out to where people are gathered round the spit:

'If Nkomo ever set foot in this country, I'd kill him personally.'

'You would, Craig,' she says, 'if my brother didn't do it first.'

'Listen, these Afs are all the same: that bugger Sithole – I mean once a terr always a terr.'

Craig has heard good reports of a course at Cirencester Agricultural College, in England. He says nothing to Linda. He doesn't know that she's pregnant but he soon will. The camouflaged parenthesis. One day he'll find himself gapping it back to the Cape with a bride and their joint savings secreted round her swollen belly.

26. Garfield Todd – meeting the 'boys'

In December 1978 Garfield Todd had written a letter to the Rhodesian press which it (predictably) declined to publish:

'This is the saddest and most frightening Christmas Rhodesia has ever known. Three-quarters of our country is under martial law. This move is an attempt to combat and defeat the massive resistance of the people to the present Government. . . .

'In this area all the small stores have been closed and all grinding-mills have been dismantled or removed to Shabani . . . children go hungry . . . if a car owner attempts to carry food for his neighbour he will have it confiscated at a road-block. . . .

'I write as a member of the white group which still holds political power in this country and which therefore must accept responsibility for the tragedy which is engulfing the nation. . . .'

On 31 December Senator Chief Mafala and two armed District Assiatants were returning in his Peugeot to his home near old Dadaya. But the Chief never reached his home: his car was waylaid by Zanla guerrillas. Later, after dark, Garfield Todd became aware of women, children and a few men on the road, fleeing from the Mafala area. At 7 the following morning GT found the Chief's burnt-out car: 'At first I thought it had been cleared of all its contents and then I realized that nothing had been touched and that the car had been an inferno . . . there was just a collection of charred bones and whoever had been in the back seat had thrown himself on the floor. . . .'

Although it was illegal to enter a reserve without a permit, Todd drove to Mafala's house. Villages down the valley were burning. The Chief's widow, Barbara, once a maid in Todd's home, was lying in anguish on the floor and her eight children were wailing.

'I sat for half an hour amongst the wailing people. . . . On the wall were the prized photographs of the opening ceremonies of Parliament in which Senator Chief Mafala Matshazi had taken his part. . . . I thought back to the day when Jobe Mafala was about 6 and when the five medicine-men were failing to cure him and his father had sent to get me to come. My clinic helper was a 14-year-old named Ndabaningi Sithole! and we went down. When I saw the little wraith, suffering from wasting dysentery, I left Sithole to guard him. . . . I was hardly back at my house when Sithole came racing to say that the people were cooking stamped mealies for Jobe. I rushed down, strode into the hut in true arrogant fashion and picked the little boy up and took him, despite protests, to the car and up to the house where he was put to bed and Grace provided the chicken soups and milk, etc. which eventually brought him back to health. . . .'

Todd drove to the office of the DC in Shabani, but it was New Year's Day and offices were closed. He then drove six kilometres to the Joint Operations Centre, where he found the commanding officer. Todd urged him to destroy no more homes, and also to ease up on the squeezing of food supplies. But the officer, whom Todd judged to be in his late 30s or early 40s, was a firm believer in the prevailing strategy of counter-insurgency. It had worked so well, he claimed, that it was now virtually impossible for a group of, say, twenty terrs to descend on a kraal and find enough meal to meet their needs.

In Belingwe TTL he had made each village headman responsible for the security of a designated stretch of road. Every day the villagers must sweep the road for mines by tying branches to a couple of oxen. If any family failed to do its duty, the village would be burnt down:

'You see, Mr Todd, we have to convince these people that we mean business . . . we have got to make things so serious that they will cooperate with us. You are not suggesting that out your way there is not a terrorist presence or that the people are not helping the terrorists?'

Mr Todd was not suggesting that. All the people, he told the commanding officer, supported the guerrillas. 'You really cannot win.'

Garfield Todd drove back to the chief's burnt-out car, where he found a white police officer supervising the shovelling of human remains into plastic bags. He continued up the road to the home of the murdered chief: 'Right down the valley for a mile or more the houses were on fire. . . .' The new District Commissioner, Shaw, was there, accompanied by soldiers. The mood was ugly. At one point Shaw turned on Todd and blamed 'you old men' for the mess they were in: 'We were boys at the time and now we have to handle it.' Shaw and his colleagues had learned by two-way radio that Todd had been out to JOC Shabani to protest against the burning of villages. 'We are not burning any more villages,' the DC informed him sullenly.

A uniformed officer approached GT and introduced himself as Det.-Insp. Brown. He wanted to know how Todd had learned so quickly about the Chief's murder. Close liaison with terrorists, Mr Todd?

One day, Mr Todd, one day . . . Thirty-three huts now stood smouldering and roofless to avenge the Chief's death. The people had scattered and their cattle wandered untended. . . . 'After all this is over,' Todd reflected, 'the whites will be saying, as the Germans did, that they really had no knowledge of what was going on around them.'

Grace Todd wrote to her daughter Judy, 24 January 1979: 'Whenever any of our people are picked up they are always asked about Dad's relations with the guerrillas. They want to know why we have no security fence, why we have not lost cattle, who visits us, when do our lights go out.' Recently two employees had been subjected to a two-day interrogation at JOC Shabani, in the course of which they were asked how many terrorist bases existed on the ranch, and why Todd's stores were never burnt down, unlike those of almost every other white farmer in the neighbourhood. They were also asked: 'Why do all the people love Mr Todd?'

Election Supervisory Commission (Professor Dick Christie et alii), *third interim report, 27 May 1979:* Rejected is Mr Garfield Todd's allegation that security forces in the Shabani region had herded people to the polls. Both the

District Commissioner and the officer commanding 2 RAR Support Company have denied it; and they, concludes the Commission, are more likely to know the facts.

When last here at Hokonui, fifteen months ago, I was told that a guerrilla unit had recently arrived at Dadaya mission after dark and insisted on addressing the entire assembled school. What I did not realize was that the Todds themselves had suffered their first 'visitation', in the dead of night, only two weeks earlier. Hearing the dog Honey emit his distinctive danger-alert growl, GT was hardly out of bed when he was confronted by armed men storming the house. He experienced a moment of panic – this is it! – and then compensating relief when he realized that they were friendly, that they wanted food, Cokes and money. He walked for half an hour with them under the stars and they asked him to obtain 180 pairs of leather boots (worth $(R)10 each) for the benefit of a Zanla detachment which had arrived from Mozambique very poorly shod. There was no way that Todd could go to a warehouse and purchase 180 pairs of leather boots. Instead he forked up $(R)1,800 with which they bought the boots, pair by pair, through messengers. The next night Jellina, the cook, came in to the house: 'Your friends are down in the garden to say goodbye.' A dozen men rose from under the orange trees when he walked down into the garden; they had come to thank him and return the Coke bottles.

Grace Todd remarks that the Africans who live and work on the ranch were upset when the 'boys' side-stepped 'proper channels' and approached the Todds directly.

Grace is living on her nerves. Night after night she hears the sounds of war – the vital railway line to South Africa that meanders for fifteen kilometres through the ranch is under constant attack. GT is often away on business, or politicking in Salisbury or London, frequently driving the dangerous roads after dark and trusting to luck. With the guerrillas you never quite know what they'll do next, whereas with the RF there was always a kind of assumption that they'd stop short of assassination. Or so Mrs Todd feels. Painful attacks of arthritis sap her will to stick it out; even so, she won't leave without him.

And he is stubborn. He will not surrender to fear. Not only his worldly goods but his pride is here. He often speaks of his fifty employees and what would become of them if he quit. Nothing good. And no doubt he could hear in his mind's ear the mocking, jubilant laughter of white Rhodesia if he were ever compelled to flee before the very forces he claimed to champion.

He is worried: beneath the certainty of principle he displays to the world at large is a deepening unease. He is well placed to know how precarious is the unity of Zanu and Zapu on the ground; they both send delegations, Zipra

349

complaining that Zanla are encroaching on their territory. So far there have been no armed clashes but he is not sanguine. The strain of feeding so many guerrillas exacerbates his doubts: 'The chickens are finished and the goats are finished and now we're starting on the cattle. . . .'

But his gloom is as short-lived as his night of sleep. 'How', he asks casually, 'would you like to meet the "boys"?'

'Very much.'

'Good. Tomorrow, then.'

A few miles away, at the railway hamlet of Bannockburn, Christine Ndlovu's sister Rosalind, known as Ros, manages the Todd's store. On the way you pass not only the late Chief's burnt-out car but also a waterworks and pumping-station guarded by troops since the guerrilla attack of January 1978, which resulted in damage estimated at $(R)250,000.

'Unreported in the press, like so much else,' GT comments.

Bannockburn's *raison d'être* is to service Rhodesia's vital rail link through Beitbridge to Johannesburg – the only artery to the Republic which does not traverse black Africa. Zanla's operations, designed to hit the local mines and halt the export of chrome, have forced the white railway engineers to move their families from Bannockburn into Shabani. A high security fence surrounds the bungalows but the Todds' store stands outside that fence.

The war here is real. On 20 January a mine planted on a bridge derailed three big diesel locomotives travelling in tandem. Zanla cleared out the black labour force by roughing up the township one night and giving people six hours to leave. On 22 January the slow coal train from Wankie, approaching Bannockburn from Gwelo, was blasted and a white assistant driver killed by small-arms fire. Yet another train was wrecked further along the line at Ngezi, leaving a total of three wrecks blocking the route to South Africa.

A group of Coloured soldiers are lounging on the steps of the store drinking Coke. Ros looks so like her sister Christine, they could be twins. She doesn't spend nights at Bannockburn any longer, too dangerous – it's the soldiers she's afraid of, not the 'boys'. Small, sharp, active, with fine delicate features, she chats for a while then leads the way to a locked office at the back of the store. 'We can talk here,' she says.

A small boy, thin and barefoot, is hovering in the dust outside the store, lurking beneath a tree; he is the last link in a bush telegraph extending to a Zipra section operating twenty kilometres to the west. He brings Ros the green light: it will be OK, tomorrow.

At the time it was not possible to tell the whole truth about that meeting with Zipra guerrillas. The account I published in the *Observer* on 19 August appears, with very few changes, as the Prologue to this book. A degree of camouflage was inevitable since we were all involved in a capital crime and the intelligence services would inevitably scan the report for clues. I set the meeting in Matabeleland whereas it in fact occurred in the Gwatemba Purchase Area on a farm belonging to the family of Christine and Rosalind. Any clue which might point Special Branch's nose in GT's direction had to be removed.

It was in fact he who remarked teasingly in the car that I had left my watch behind – but he had done the same! When we reached the farm we were greeted by young lads acting as scouts. It was quite a long wait, perhaps half an hour, before the 'boys' materialized. 'If something scares them, they don't show up,' GT remarked. Later he handed over what looked like a healthy financial contribution to the war of liberation; his support was genuine, but this was also protection money and I don't believe he was happy about it at all. Although he regarded armed resistance as the inevitable and necessary response to years of white minority rule, these guerrillas were committing acts of violence he could not condone, including the fatal ambush of a fellow farmer, R. D. Kennedy (a post-war England rugby cap) who died on 7 May.

The Zipra 'boys' went back into the hills, to the hard ground and the hard sadza. A couple of hours later, I had emerged from a hot bath to drink a couple of gins and enjoy a three-course dinner served by Grace's smiling black girls. A faint smell of *My Fair Lady*. But for Garfield Todd this was neither the first nor the last of such encounters.

In August 1979 a potentially lethal crisis occurred at Dadaya. The Todds had kept the school open at the cost of thousands of dollars paid out to the 'boys'. In February 1978 Zanla had first assembled staff and students in the school hall, levied a staff contribution, and initiated the practice of setting the girls to prepare them food. The guerrillas brought news of former pupils who had joined the struggle, but made no attempt to recruit. They spoke well of Garfield Todd and warned the Headmaster, Samuel Mutomba, on no account to alert the security forces before 8 a.m. the following day.

When the army turned up next morning they berated Mutomba for his procrastination and generally beat their chests at the thought of a night-time contact with the terrs. A bunch of petrified white reservists then began combing the bush, crawling about on knees and stomach under the sardonic gaze of 67-year-old Mrs Grace Todd, who remained standing upright, in full view of the contending armies, while supervising the dipping of her cattle – a chore that Armageddon would not persuade her to miss.

Special Branch officers summoned the pupils back to the school hall and berated them: the response was icy cold, a sharp contrast to the warm reception accorded to the 'boys'.

The guerrilla visitations became more frequent. On some occasions during term-time Mutomba was forced to accommodate the 'boys' overnight in the dormitories. The Todds prayed, having received distressing reports from the neighbouring reserves of vakhomana forbidding all Christian services on the ground that Christianity is the religion of the white man, the colonizer. But the signboard outside the mission remained in place: Dadaya Mission: Churches of Christ.

Now, in August 1979, Todd held in his hand a note apparently signed by the local Zanla commander, Garikayi, on behalf of the district commander, Mlambo, who on a previous occasion had called on Todd at Hokonui. The note was a directive to close the school and send the pupils home without delay; anyone left at Dadaya by Tuesday would be shot.

But was the note authentic? Accompanied by a young scholar from Dadaya who knew the area, Todd set out for the Mazvihwa TTL. Passing a camp of black troops, he shuddered; to enter any TTL without the DC's permission was illegal. At the first village they reached, a Christian schoolteacher recognized the car from better days when Mrs Todd had driven out to judge the local choirs. This man undertook to act as emissary, and vanished while Todd remained at the village.

At such times men inhabit Africa as animals do.

The local Zanla commander, Garikayi, did not greet GT at all warmly. When Todd told him of the threatening letter, Garikayi asked to see it. Todd replied that he had not brought the letter lest stopped and searched by security forces. Garikayi scowled and asked how he could be sure that Todd had not come as a spy, as an agent for Smith.

Todd recited his political record over forty-five years.

The guerrilla commander replied that he knew all about that but how could he be sure? GT later concluded that what had really irritated Garikayi was Todd's ability to trace his whereabouts – Zanla liked to pay the unexpected calls, not to receive them.

Eventually, however, he thawed and became excessively hospitable, forcing on GT 'only the third brandy of my life'. (The first had been consumed after he delivered his first baby, the second in Paris, a Catholic and sinful place.)

Garikayi took his famous guest on a tour of the local Zanla strongholds. There were festivities, feastings, shooting practice – like Gulliver, Todd found himself swept into another world, a world of people both larger and smaller than himself. When he wanted to leave they bound his hands and feet with hospitality – even so, he was uneasy, sensing that he was being detained with silken cords until after dark, and thus not completely trusted.

Dadaya remained open.

27. iron lady

Britain voted on 3 May. The Conservatives won. The *Herald* described for delighted white Rhodesian readers 'the beaming, confident and controlled smile' of Mrs Margaret Thatcher. In an editorial the *Herald* used the word 'elation' and speculated that the British people might at long last 'experience the smack of firm government' by a Prime Minister capable of restoring Britain's good name. 'Let us hope that the Iron Lady will be able to put some steel into the souls of Western politicians in general and President Carter in particular.' On 6 May the *Sunday Mail* ran a jubilant cartoon by Meintjes showing Thatcher sweeping David Owen and piles of debris down the steps of the Foreign Office. Owen, landing on his arse, with a lock of hair tumbling into his eyes, looked stunned and sour.

In February the Conservatives had issued their election manifesto: 'If the six principles . . . are fully satisfied following the present Rhodesian elections the next Government will have the duty to return Rhodesia to a state of legality, move to lift sanctions, and do its utmost to ensure that the new independent state gains international recognition.' Mrs Thatcher repeated this in a speech on 24 March. 'We will send observers to the election and we will form a balanced judgment on the basis of their report.' What most Rhodesians failed to notice was the note of caution introduced by Shadow Foreign Secretary Francis Pym in the course of speeches delivered on 15 and 23 April: 'It will not be possible to make a snap judgment. . . . The whole issue will require full consideration. . . . It may also be appropriate to have detailed discussions with our European and American Allies and the Commonwealth.'

These last three words sounded the doom of Zimbabwe Rhodesia. When Lord Carrington, destined to become the new Foreign Secretary instead of Pym, spoke on the radio on 25 April he was equally cautious: '. . . if you are going to bring Rhodesia back to legality it will be necessary to get the support and agreement of the international community. . . .' Thus Mrs Thatcher's men did not 'betray' their election pledge after they came to power, they 'betrayed' it before they came to power. Nevertheless it was on 14 May that Carrington, having taken office, left the matter beyond any doubt. The Rhodesian press had to be content with making a meal out of the meaningless visit of a senior Foreign Office wallah, Sir Anthony Duff, to Salisbury. But so precious was the image of Thatcher as White Hope to Rhodesians that they seemed unable to banish hope by facing the awful fact that she, too, was about to betray them – however 'free and fair' Lord Boyd might report the elections to have been.

28. Zimbabwe Rhodesia is born: Rhobabwe

The Acting President and all office-holders in Rhodesia, including Ian Smith, ceased to hold office as of midnight, 31 May. But the 'Rhodesia' in Zimbabwe Rhodesia was alive and kicking; in the Senate the ten RF members plus eight of the Chiefs joined forces to elect as President of the Senate the former Speaker of the House, Col. George Hartley, in preference to the candidate put forward by the UANC.

Muzorewa assumed the key jobs of Combined Operations and Defence in a Cabinet consisting of seventeen members, ten from the UANC, five from the RF, two from Chief Ndiweni's UNFP. Silas Munadawarara became Deputy Prime Minister, Bulle took the Commerce and Industry portfolio, George Nyandoro had Lands, David Smith was given Finance, Muzorewa's acolyte David Mukome got Foreign Affairs, Irvine, a poultry-farmer, got Agriculture, Andersen stayed at Justice, and van der Byl had to accept the relatively unglamorous Transport ministry. But the life of van der Byl was gaining in glamour elsewhere. This ageing bachelor with the pseudo-aristo drawl and the swinish good looks announced in mid-June his engagement to a genuine Habsburg, Princess Charlotte of Liechtenstein, daughter of Archduchess Elizabeth of Austria. 'When the Princess first visited Rhodesia in February, I took her shooting. She bagged two reebok and one blesbok with three shots. Not bad at all.' (Indeed not: but one dead terr would surely have made the day.)

Ian Smith was appointed Minister without Portfolio.

On 1 June the *Herald* offered a banner headline: 'Zimbabwe Rhodesia is Born.' Smith immediately set the right tone by declaring, 'I'm still opposed to black majority rule,' while helpfully suggesting that 'we should get away from race or colour as much as we can'.

The UANC sent its supporters cavorting through the city. The media were flooded by complaints about the thuggery of Ziso reVanhu, the Bishop's newly formed Eyes of the People.

The Bishop commanded fifty-one out of one hundred seats, but not for long. His problem was the furiously discontented Zezuru politicians whom he had tried to dish by downgrading them on the party's electoral lists: First Vice-President James Chikerema, George Nyandoro, Enoch Dumbutshena and Stanlake Samkange. In fact they all got elected; Muzorewa had fumbled it, sticking the knife in but not far enough. Chikerema bounced back, alleging tribalism, nepotism and dictatorship in the party and openly rejoiced that the party had not won more seats.

On 20 June Chikerema finally announced his break with the UANC; he and seven other MPs created the Zimbabwe Democratic Party and demanded a seat in the Cabinet. Since the election had been on the party list system the UANC immediately petitioned the High Court to bar the apostates from taking their seats. On 27 June Justice Beck granted a rule nisi until 11 July barring the eight from taking their seats, but the Appellate Division later ruled that Parliament must regulate its own affairs. The Bishop now commanded only forty-three seats out of one hundred.

29. thanks for the memory

Buy your school uniforms at Barbour's First Street store (girls on the third, boys on the lower ground floor). We stock virtually all uniforms including Allan Wilson Bothashof Churchill Cranborne Ellis Robins Marandellas Marlborough High Mount Pleasant Oriel Peterhouse Plumtree Prince Edward Sinoia High St George's College Vainona High.... The majority are single-sex schools, of course.

Like Edinburgh Scots, Rhodesians are crazy for school uniforms. The senior girls stream out of Queen Elizabeth at lunch-time and parade up Jameson Avenue in blue dresses, blue hats and white socks. Other girls storm the city centre in grey blazers, white blouses with large collars, and straw boaters; and yet others sport blazers of green with mauve stripes.

Chisipite Senior School (200 pupils) celebrates its twenty-fifth anniversary in 1979 with an enchanting display of devotion to the world of Enid Blyton and Angela Brazil. Photos appear of the Headmistress, Mrs Rosaleen Gleeson, and other middle-aged teachers, pillars of rectitude in print dresses, tight hair-dos and severe expressions (which no doubt conceal tender hearts). To celebrate the anniversary 'Chisi's' Musical Director, Mrs Marie Crawford, composes lyrics recalling sporting contests, stage shows and heroines of yore:

> Thanks for the memory;
> For building Chisi School,
> Tennis courts and swimming-pool . . .
> Oh, thank you so much.
>
> Thanks for the memory,
> For coming here to stay . . .
> We're really glad you made it
> And for showing us the way –

What are the sacred areas of racial segregation? They are bed, suburb, school, hospital. Hotels, bars, swimming-pools, Post Offices are relatively peripheral. In any cosmetic reform, they will be the first to take down the prohibitive notices: Right of Admission Reserved.

Now, on the eve of majority rule, a black middle-class invasion of the white suburbs, of Highlands, Avondale and Mount Pleasant, is imminent. How, then, to defend the integrity of state schools strictly reserved for children of Caucasian ancestry? The whites are aware of an appalling pressure, the great cry of the black masses for education. Only 60 per cent of black children of primary-school age are actually attending school; only 34 per cent of the age group complete primary education. Only one child out of five graduating from Grade 7 can find a place in a secondary school (Form 1). Take the situation in Salisbury in December 1978, on the eve of the new school year due to begin in February. Only 5,780 African children have reached Grade 7 – for whom only 1,800 places in secondary schools are available.

There is real alarm now among white parents. After all, the state currently spends $(R)530 a year on each white child in school, compared with only $(R)45·9 on every black pupil. The annual expenditure on the 58,600 white pupils could, if equally distributed, support an additional half million black pupils. This is rarely discussed.

When challenged, whites customarily quoted the expert view of Mrs Kathleen Rea, of the Division of African Education. In 1977 Mrs Rea had assured the Rhodesia Science Congress, with a wealth of statistical projections to support her thesis, that, given the African birth rate, there was· absolutely no prospect of educating all Rhodesia's black children – this side of utopia. No way at all. So let's be practical.

With Muzorewa (or some other black) due to take office on 1 June, the first practical step is to devise a formula which appeases middle-class African aspirations while effectively safeguarding 'standards' (i.e. racial exclusivity) in white state schools.

The soul of privilege is invariably an empty one: K. W. B. Napier, Government Chief Education Officer, sends a confidential circular to all schools instructing them to withdraw any textbooks which have jumped the gun by using the word 'Zimbabwe' in place of Rhodesia. European schools are redesignated 'high fee paying' and restricted to local children of suitable educational standard – thus the white intake would be diluted, or polluted, only by the brighter offspring of Africans wealthy enough to buy homes in the white suburbs.

But even that degree of integration cannot be stomached by the hard core – by our friends the Maddocks family, for example – hence the creation of a brand-new concept, the 'community school'. If parents, of, say, Churchill or

Oriel vote to go 'community', they can buy the school buildings and facilities from the state, having elected a board of governors to administer the school and to pursue whatever policy of intake selection it prefers. The Government, however, will obligingly pay the teachers' salaries.

Some parents, while welcoming the opportunity to evade the dreaded influx of kaffir kids, fear that the fees will escalate beyond their means. In fact the Rhodesian Front has negotiated such advantageous terms that the differential between the future 'high fee paying' schools ($(R)44 per term) and the 'community' schools ($(R)65 a term) is hardly prohibitive, except for the poorest artisans earning $(R)350 per month or so.

There are sharp rows. Schools matter. Passions flare. At Prince Edward the parents vote for 'high fee paying', yet the school council opts for 'community' and calls on the parents to vote a second time. A major row breaks out at Oriel, a handsome, red-brick complex with expansive playing-fields watered against the summer sun by an army of rotating sprinklers. Hilary Squires, MP elect for the enlarged Borrowdale constituency and Co-Minister of Defence, writes to the parents urging them to choose 'community' status. The cutting edge of his appeal, though wrapped round in the soft cloth of cultural cliché, is race and class.

Squires appeals to 'our sense of shared values' and warns that African children could quite easily enter 'high fee paying' schools if their parents owned or leased property in the zone. Raising the awful spectre of an influx from the townships, he sounds the tocsin: 'Ask yourselves what would be the result if Tafara and Mabvuku were added to the zone area serving this school.' Doom. Rabble.

But isn't a school rather an expensive item to buy, even for a cooperative? A black Member of Parliament blows open the dirty little secret by revealing that Borrowdale School has been sold to the parents for only $(R)44,940 – the price of a fair-sized private house.

The first school to function on a 'community' basis is Alexandra Park prep school. Parents are asked if they can help with this and that – 'it's *our* school now, remember' – and their response is of course, 'terrific, super, overwhelming'. Here is Bill Wallis, a self-employed electrician with three kids at the school, servicing the school bus free of charge. Inside the school hall Mr Eric Lightfoot, a company chairman, balances on a step-ladder on the auditorium stage, helping to fix a broken spotlight. By all pulling together the parents keep the fees down to $(R)40 a term.

Two major schools, Churchill (boys) and Roosevelt (girls) go 'community' under a joint board of governors and fix tuition fees at $(R)168 a year. The cost for boarders will be $(R)618.

In Britain, annual fees at a comparable private school in 1979 would be in the region of £1,400 a year for day-pupils and £3,000 for boarders. But, of course, the state does not pay the salaries of teachers at Britain's private schools. One notices that white Rhodesians' contempt for the welfare state, their pride in self-help, rarely inhibits them from emptying the Treasury into their own laps. Only when it's a question of subsidizing the poor, the destitute, is state intervention contemptuously rejected as 'socialism'.

'After all, who pays the tax?'

In the event forty-one white primary schools out of 130 and eight white secondary schools out of thirty-six voted for 'community' status. Within a year it was to become clear that many of these schools were prepared to run down their intake to preserve their racial (or 'cultural') integrity. As white families fled, classrooms and dormitories stood empty.

In time, no doubt, the whites would make common cause with the black bourgeoisie against the people of the townships. Class conflict, normally a prime ingredient of racial stratification, would surface. The Rhodesian Nursery Schools Association clearly signalled the impending adaptation:

'Ours is a very forward-looking and tolerant association. We believe that provided pupils have a similar home and economic background, live in a similar area and come from good business or professional environments, there is no hard and fast line to be drawn between pupils provided standards do not drop.'

30. the fate of a family

At 9 a.m. on 11 May 1979 the convoy to Fort Victoria was hit only three kilometres after leaving Beitbridge. Patrol Officer Needham, a former pupil of Umtali Boys' High School, was killed. Heavy fire raked into a float carrying a racehorse. Chris Dorrington, owner of a horse-transport business, was wounded in the thigh, and the horse had to be put down.

On Saturday, 26 May, Johannes Pietros Du Preez, aged 56, father of two, was killed when ambushed in the Gutu area.

Three days later a 63-year-old businessman, Neville Wilde, and four black civilians with him were killed when they were ambushed near Lynx Mine in the north-east.

Stephanus Johannes (Ben) Stander's Battlefield cattle ranch bordered Gona re Zhou national park, an area rich in game and dense with baobabs and mopani, hilly into the bargain, an ideal retreat for guerrillas. The owner of 900 Brahman cattle, 59-year-old Ben Stander had fought a steady battle against elephant, who menaced his fences, but it was not elephant which decimated his family.

Born on a farm near Rustenberg in the Transvaal, Stander had joined the South African army, been captured at Tobruk, and held POW in Italy. After the war he moved to Kitwe in Northern Rhodesia, where he worked as a miner, but in 1960 he and his brother bought Battlefield Ranch and launched themselves by camping out in the bush with sixty-five cattle bought from the Cold Storage Commission. They worked, they prospered.

The first ambush occurred in April 1976. Ben Stander's wife Gerda was hit by bullets. In September 1977 their nephew Archie Stander lost both legs below the knee while with a Patu patrol in Sengwe TTL. In February 1978 Hennie Stander, another nephew, was killed in the course of an ambush on a neighbouring farm, Benjane. More was to come. In August of that year Ben Stander and his son Adriaan, 28, were driving in separate vehicles 100 metres apart when they were ambushed by a gang of twenty not far from the homestead. Shot in the chest, Adriaan died instantly. His father, having run out of ammunition, grabbed the rifle magazines from his dead son's webbing. Despite severe chest wounds, Ben Stander survived.

After this tragedy Mrs Gerda Stander moved into a rented house with her daughter in Salisbury, but Ben Stander refused to leave Battlefield Ranch and his 900 Brahman. At 8 a.m. on 20 June 1979 he was driving with a friend from Salisbury, Clive Brown, when they were ambushed. Stander and Brown, 25, were both killed.

Seven days later a telephone engineer investigating a line which had been pulled down found Cecil Beale, 64, and his wife Maud lying outside the security fence of their ransacked Ibana farm on the Nala Mine Road about thirty kilometres from Nyamandhlovu village in Matabeleland. Mr Beale, born in Rhodesia, had retired from Rhodesia Railways Road Motor Services eight years earlier. On 2 July he was buried in the Apostolic Faith Mission Church in Bulawayo. His wife Maud died in hospital while the funeral service was in progress and joined her husband in the same grave on the following day. Mrs Beale's father had been a Jameson Raider and her mother had been born during one of the 1890 Pioneer treks into Mashonaland.

31. the African queen

On 7 June Jimmy Carter inspired fury in Salisbury by criticizing the Zimbabwe Rhodesia constitution and its entrenched clauses, which he somewhat inaccurately described as the work of whites alone. On 10 June the *Sunday Mail* lashed him for trying to please the Russians 'and a few tin-pot dictators in black Africa'. The paper demanded 'honesty, decency and fair play'.

Rhodesia's friends in the Senate had not, however, given up. On 13 June the Senate voted an amendment moved by that master of pro-Rhodesia amendments, Senator Harry Byrd, of Virginia, astutely tacked on to the 1980 defence budget and requiring the President to lift sanctions. But the Senate's attitude did not sway the House of Representatives; effective Congressional action required by definition the support of both Houses. On 29 June the House voted massively, by 350 to 37, in favour of a bill sponsored by Rep. Stephen Solarz, Chairman of the House Africa subcommittee, leaving Carter to determine the question of sanctions.

On 11 July Muzorewa was granted an audience with Carter in Washington, yet his cause was hopeless. The resignation of Andrew Young in mid-August brought rejoicing in Salisbury but, as with the case of David Owen's eclipse, the triumph had a sour taste: it wouldn't make any difference. Even so the *Herald* couldn't resist reprinting a Cummings cartoon showing Carter painting the White House black with Andy Young pleading: 'But, Jimmy, I only told a WHITE lie.' In essence Washington was still keeping in step with British initiatives; Carter finally lifted sanctions in December 1979 when British sovereignty in Rhodesia was restored.

For Muzorewa to attack Thatcher or Carrington publicly was futile since no political leverage could be gained by so doing. On 13 July the Bishop met them both in London: he was told that nothing could be resolved before the Lusaka Commonwealth summit. The smiles on the steps of 10 Downing Street were distinctly sheepish. Although Thatcher had said in Australia that she thought sanctions would lapse on 15 November, she was careful not to promise recognition.

British exports to black Africa were now worth £2,000 million a year, of which half went to Nigeria. Carrington and the Foreign Office knew the score – the *Observer* cartoonist Trog brilliantly depicted a dependable Carrington, chest-deep in tropical river water, pulling the boat *African Queen* on which sat a blissfully innocent Thatcher, her arms round her knees. A further reminder of the facts of life was the refusal of the OAU summit in Monrovia to receive a delegation from Muzorewa, and the resolve of even the conservative black states not to break ranks. The summit recognized the PF as the only 'authentic and legitimate representatives of the people of Zimbabwe'. Highly influential in securing this outcome was the Nigerian President, General Obasanjo; to ram home the point, Nigeria seized BP's assets on 1 August, on the eve of the Lusaka summit.

Of what account, against all this, was the endorsement of the April elections by the Boyd Commission?

32. broken hearts and life's earnings

Only the barbarians at the gates held Rome together now. But deep fissures had opened on the Capitol and in the Forum. Eight MPs of the UANC had broken away to form a new party, depriving Muzorewa of his Parliamentary majority. Sithole had refused to take his twelve seats in the Assembly and was petitioning the High Court to declare the entire election null and void. The man who had figured among Rhobabwe's Big Four, protected by police and Special Branch twenty-four hours a day, was now subjected to the old demeaning tactics of harassment – his house and party headquarters constantly searched, his leading officials arrested. On 20 June Muzorewa delivered a lethal blow when he ordered the security forces to 'take out' Sithole's auxiliaries in Gokwe and Nyamaropa: on a single day 183 of them were killed – a demolition far exceeding anything ever inflicted on Zanla or Zipra inside Rhodesia – and a further 1,000 were put behind bars. On the same day the police picked up about 100 of Sithole's men in Salisbury.

Sithole got the message. Zanu took up its seats in the Assembly. Two Zanu Ministers and one Deputy Minister were nominated to join the coalition Government, though the Rev. Ndabaningi himself disdained to serve under the Bishop.

Muzorewa now raised the defence allocation for auxiliary forces to $(ZR)17 million, thus boosting the size of his own private army and cementing its loyalty with pay of $(ZR)84 a month.

But all this internal power play brought the end of the war no nearer; the end of sanctions no nearer; diplomatic recognition no nearer; the end of arduous national service and reserve duty for whites no nearer.

Early in 1978, when negotiating the Salisbury Agreement, both Muzorewa and Sithole had promised a rapid de-escalation of the war as soon as blacks entered the Transitional Government. When nothing of the sort happened both Muzorewa and Sithole explained that the guerrillas did not as yet trust Smith's intentions – only when elections had been held and a majority-rule Government had taken office would the 'boys' heed the call to lay down their arms.

The only place where the vakhomana did lay down their arms after 1 June 1979 was on the front pages of the *Herald* and the *Sunday Mail*. On 20 May the *Mail* reported worn-out, dispirited terrs giving themselves up. 'Their morale is shattered,' remarked a senior police officer who claimed that hundreds more were longing to throw in the towel but feared execution by fanatical cadres 'trained in communist Ethiopia by Cubans'. On 28 May the *Herald* followed up with a bold headline: 'Come home – it's safe: message from ex-terrorists.' Apparently ten former Zanla men were spearheading a Government-sponsored propaganda drive in the Beitbridge area; alas, admitted the *Herald*, farm workers and their families displayed a grim reluctance to get involved. (Fear, of course.) Headline, 11 October: 'Ex-Terrorists tell of low morale, beatings.'

Desperate gimmickry: under 'Operation Disco Scene' planes using loud hailers conducted 'sky shouts': as a result 'scores' of terrorists were said to have given themselves up. The amnesty campaign and its PR was now master-minded by Malcolm Thompson, the Ulsterman who had earlier supervised propaganda – a vote is a vote for peace – during the April election. (With impressive resilience Thompson later emerged as chairman of the Civil Service Commission in Mugabe's Zimbabwe.)

But with 31,000 Zanla and Zipra guerrillas extending across Rhodesia, Mozambique and Zambia remained dead to the 'sky shouts'.

White morale was cracking. Tension generated not only a constant rainfall of bickering but also furious vendettas:

'I write to express my disgust at the latest pronouncement by Mr Young, the Secretary to the Treasury, to the effect that ZR residents cannot be permitted to accumulate nest-eggs outside the country. Europeans have given their lives and health and nerves and blood and toil to try and save civilization in this part of the world. . . .'

Equally symptomatic of a rising hysteria was a letter blaming Britain for trying 'to destroy our identity by dropping our name "Rhodesia"'. If Britain was, however, determined, 'she should pay out those Rhodesians who feel so strongly in this matter and let them leave with their life's earnings and their broken hearts'.

Money and sentiment; property and patriotism.

Morale was low and tempers short among the older generation of conscripts, the daddies in their 40s and 50s. They got no remuneration and had to dig into their own pockets to pay for boots, torch batteries and transport.

Wider discontents were exposed during a stormy meeting held in Gwelo in August. R. R. Price, Director of Security Manpower, and by dint of office the man responsible for ruining everyone's civilian life, assured his sceptical audience that it was current policy to ensure that no man had to close down his business because of conscription. But Ken Winsor, a local industrialist, was not to be mollified:

'In Que Que there are people of 50 who were taken for ten days' training to

Connemara prison before going into the B Reserve. Is this not a waste of money and manpower?'

To this a police spokesman replied: 'We need every man we can get in the Que Que area. To some 58 is old, to others it is young. We go on their medical.'

'Until last year we got a refund of our petrol coupons but we've never been paid nor have we ever been paid mileage.'

Supt Macleod: 'If you use your vehicle on duty you will be paid mileage.'

'But the wardens say no.'

Another malcontent: 'Regular members of the police have no commitment other than their normal duties. You never see Police Commissioners manning road blocks after hours.'

'They're needed for other duties,' replies the Superintendent.

'So are managing directors of businesses!'

Is this the spirit of the Battle of Britain? Are these truly Churchill's children?

Even the Selous Scouts betrayed symptoms of disintegrating morale. In Gwelo a middle-aged couple were fined for allowing their daughter's boy-friend, a Selous Scout, to hide in their home while absent without leave. Meanwhile the Commanding Officer of the Scouts, Lt-Col. Ron Reid-Daly, small, wiry and once an officer in the British version of the SAS, became involved in a blazing row after he unearthed a bugging device in his office on 29 January 1979. Following a bitter, face-to-face altercation in the mess between himself and the Commander of the Army, Lt-Gen. John Hickman (son of a former Rhodesian Commissioner of Police), all Selous Scouts operations were temporarily frozen, amid accusations of gun-running and ivory-poaching. In March Hickman was abruptly relieved of his command; three months later his elder son Richard, 19, died of wounds while serving with the SAS. On 30 May Army HQ announced that Reid-Daly was facing disciplinary charges for insubordination. The court martial took place in June. Reid-Daly was reprimanded but not relieved of his command. However, the extent of the tensions simmering among the top brass became clear at the end of August when Reid-Daly resigned and immediately launched a spectacular civil action, suing the Prime Minister and eight others, including Hickman, Col. J. L. Redfern, Director of Military Intelligence, Maj. Robert Reith, Director of Military Police, and Maj. J. D. Des Fountain, Director of Army Counter-Intelligence. The litigant, who claimed a modest $(ZR)53,000 in damages, complained that the bugging device had been installed in his office, documents removed from his desk and copied, and his movements monitored. Evidently the ace tracker felt that he should be the one to follow the spoor.

Hickman, meanwhile, compounded the farce by engaging in litigation of his own, suing the President and Minister of Defence for wrongful dismissal, even though these personages changed as Rhodesia became Zimbabwe Rhodesia (1 June 1979), then the British colony of Rhodesia (12 December 1979) and finally Zimbabwe (18 April 1980). In effect Hickman ended up by suing wartime enemies for having wrongfully dismissed him while the war was in progress!

To top it all 1979 was a disastrous rugby season, despite the presence in the national side of two three-quarters selected for the Springboks, Ray Mordt and David Smith. It was as if the word 'Zimbabwe' had sapped the Zimbabwe Rhodesia XV's will to win. By mid-July the team had suffered five losses in succession in the Currie Cup. Injuries were one problem, but coach Brian Murphy also complained of a lack of total commitment, of players pulling out because of business obligations: some element of pride was lacking now, and players put less into their training.

In August Zimbabwe Rhodesia went down by 32 points to 18 against Western Province. Defeat at the hands of Transvaal followed: nine games, nine defeats. At the tenth attempt the side scraped a 19–15 win over Natal (regular full-back LeRoy Duberly having been killed earlier in the week when his helicopter was shot down over Mozambique). At the end of each season the bottom team in the 'A' Division plays the top one in the 'B' Division in a make-or-break bid to avoid relegation. On 25 September Zimbabwe Rhodesia saved the day with a 25–12 win over Griqualand West.

By mid-1979 hoteliers and bar owners in Salisbury had hot lines direct to the military police. So endemic was the violence of young servicemen that all Salisbury bars and other liquor outlets were now closed on Saturday afternoons. Calling the civilian police wasn't much use: the psychotic servicemen merely took them on. Periodically white youths crashed into the bars used by blacks and set about any African they could find with any weapon they could lay their hands on. A hotel manager reflected: 'I was in the British army for twenty-two years and I've been all over the world, and I have never seen behaviour like this.' Jimmy Trenchard, manager of Le Coq d'Or, a complex of five bars, groaned helplessly about the vandalism: the toilets ruined, the cisterns destroyed, the pipes ripped from the stalls, the toilet bowls kicked in.

On 18 August three young whites returning from a night-club stopped on Suffolk Road, Strathaven, to urinate. They were Stuart Hodgson and Kevin Tarr, both 22, and a juvenile of 17 whose name was not reported. Was it a coincidence that they did so outside a house recently acquired by Joseph Gopo, a black politician? When Mr Gopo's nephew remonstrated with them they beat him up; when Mr Gopo came to the rescue, he was also attacked.

The culprits were each fined $(ZR)25. (Had a black assaulted a white, particularly at his own home, he would have gone straight to gaol and stayed there.)

On 29 October the *Herald* published a letter from Mr N. Pritchard-Meaker, of Mount Pleasant, complaining about the growing tendency of white youths to assault blacks at random, and describing how he himself had seen a couple of drunks, who had narrowly avoided a serious car accident, beating up an African for no reason at all. He had also witnessed two youths impersonating Police Specials demanding to see situpas then hitting an African in the mouth with a stone. Local police had told him of incidents where carloads of whites stopped black pedestrians to ask for directions as a prelude to smashing them over the head with beer bottles.

33. madam, you are wanted dead or alive

Despite the well-publicized release of four white abductees in Maputo in February 1979, random kidnappings continued. On 14 June Mrs Yvonne Mulligan, of Fairview Farm, Goromonzi, unlocked her security gate at 12.05 p.m. to let out her labourers, who were due their midday meal. Noticing three juveniles outside the gate, she asked them what they wanted. One said they had come to buy cabbages. Another gave a slightly different emphasis to the encounter by pulling out a grenade: 'Madam,' said this mujiba, 'you are wanted dead or alive.' Mrs Mulligan, being plump, cheery, auburn-haired and 28 years old, opted for alive and was marched barefoot into Chikwaka TTL.

From that point on Zanla guerrillas pushed her all the way to Mozambique on a bike and in a wheelbarrow, but they never let her pedal. 'They were very, very good to me,' she later recalled. 'They gave me everything I wanted. Only they would not tell me what was going on.' In Mozambique she was handed over to the women comrades in Zanu camps. Early in September she was released in Maputo and returned to Goromonzi, not very much the wiser.

Denis Hofmeyr had grown up on Craig's Farm, then sold it, and then returned to it five weeks earlier. On 6 July he was driving with his wife at 8.45 in the morning towards the main Gokwe road when eight guerrillas appeared, all on the passenger side of the vehicle. The car was riddled with holes, the throttle jammed wide open and Mr Hofmeyr found himself steering the car at great speed while trying to give his wife Marita mouth-to-mouth resuscitation. But she died when they reached Broomsgrove Farm. Married for fourteen years, the Hofmeyrs were on their way to collect their children from boarding-school.

On 7 July at 8.45 p.m. a gang destroyed a farmhouse near Marandellas. Two bodies were found: those of James Jeffreys, an 81-year-old bachelor, and an African employee.

On the following day death came to Thomas Hartley, 67, who had moved to a 100-hectare Headlands farm a year earlier after his Mtoko farm had been burnt out. A Yorkshireman by birth, Mr Hartley had set up as a builder after he arrived in Rhodesia in 1947.

A tremor ran through the towns whenever a guerrilla attack occurred in a white suburb. After the first attack they suffered, Jack and Betty Weeks, residents of the Weirmouth suburb of Umtali, put up a security fence, grenade screens and protective walls at a cost of $(R)2,000. The Government apparently refused to contribute a cent, on the ground that Weirmouth was not a sensitive area. How sensitive can you get? asked Mr and Mrs Weeks after guerrillas returned in mid-July to put an RPG 7 rocket through their roof while they were watching TV.

The following report is not for the faint-hearted. Abraham Botha, 60, and his wife Susanna, 50, had paid a visit to their daughter in Gwelo and were now returning to their farm with their two small grandchildren, aged 2 and 1. They had driven through the security gate and pulled up at the back door when an African opened fire from a kraal outside the fence. He then moved to open the back gate. When Mrs Botha pointed her LPD at him and told him to drop his gun, he fired at her, hitting her three times. Mr Botha, whose artificial leg was not attached at this moment of crisis, struggled to get out of the car and open the door of the house. The little boy of 2 years old, Albertus Smit, now running back and forth between his grandparents and the guerrilla, was shot twice and died instantly. Without one leg, Abraham Botha managed to crawl into the house carrying the baby, but failed in an attempt to drag in his dying wife as well.

On 2 August, at 11 a.m., a South African forestry worker, Roderick Bowen, aged 28, was reportedly abducted across the Mozambique border from Imbeza estate by four guerrillas.

On 24 August, Henry May, 52, was working on the roof of his house in the Vumba when guerrillas ordered him down. He tried to run for the house, shouting to his wife Marjorie to use the Agric-Alert, but was shot dead. Mrs May locked herself into a bedroom and raised the alarm.

On 26 August, Keith Williams, a 29-year-old electrical engineer working at Pangani Mine, Filabusi, was called out to repair an electrical fault in a shaft near the mine perimeter. Williams, his wife and baby daughter had moved to Pangani only eleven days earlier. Now, working in a corrugated-iron shed above the mine shaft, he found himself being dragged into the bush by five Zanla guerrillas, who joined up with a larger formation of about sixty. When they recognized his belt as that of the South African Defence Force (with whom he had done his national service), Williams was struck with rifle butts and kicked about the body. Then, with his hands tied by wire, he was dragged along by a belt fastened to his wrists on what turned out to be a 650-kilometre nightmare trek to Mozambique. At the border they walked into an ambush. Williams survived it and was later interned at a camp near Chimoio where the main hazard – as other abductees had earlier discovered – was Rhodesian air attacks.

Williams was released after the cease-fire, together with Timothy Peatling, abducted near Inyanga in November. Mugabe told a Salisbury press conference that they were the last abductees held.

John Bradburne was an exceptional man whose death caused exceptional bitterness. A hermit, somewhat resembling in appearance our image of John the Baptist, Bradburne had lived, eaten and prayed with lepers since June 1969. Formerly a teacher, street musician, stoker in a trawler, and Gurkha, he lived in a tin hut with an altar and the pictures he had gathered over the years, close to the Mtemwa leper hospital at Mtoko. On 3 September he was abducted shortly before midnight; two days later security forces found his body, shot dead, twenty kilometres away.

On 6 September, in the Eastern Districts, they murdered a 74-year-old widow, Mrs Molly Hoddinott. The old were easy targets.

Deryck Percy Lamb, 58, a former Battle of Britain pilot, DFC, DSO, had survived the guerrilla war at Driefontein Farm in the perilous, largely abandoned Cashel region until 11 September. On that day he was seized by a gang of over fifty Zanla guerrillas. His family were convinced that he had been carried across the border and the last 'reliable' sighting of him was said to have been at Chimoio on 14 February 1980. By that time the cease-fire was in operation. The family appealed to Lord Soames and Robert Mugabe for intercession.

In vain. In May his remains were found buried only 500 metres from Driefontein Farm. Mr Lamb was identified by his teeth.

The Edridges, father and son, of Mbima Estates, Wedza, were high-quality-tobacco farmers who regularly won prizes for their crop. In 1978 the father was killed in a road accident. On 11 September 1979 his 27-year-old son Simon was killed in an ambush when returning home from police reserve duty.

Dennis Partlett Claircourt, Water Bailiff for Odzani and Old Umtali, had served during the war in RAF Bomber Command, flying from Britain, the Middle East and Burma. After his arrival in Rhodesia in 1948 he had run a garage and repair shop. He was killed on the morning of 13 September when he detonated a booby trap on Leicester Farm.

On 20 September guerrillas ambushed and killed a Rhodesian Front MP in the Nuanetsi area. Theunis de Klerk, 43, was Member for Lundi. The funeral service was held in the Dutch Reformed Church in Jameson Avenue, attended by some 500 people.

Death in action:

Maj. André Dennison, 43, Commander of A Company, 2 RAR, holder of the Bronze Cross, was killed in action early in June while operating in the Victoria Falls area. Dennison had served in the British SAS, seen action in Borneo and Malaya, then served in the Malawi Rifles until 1975, when he moved to Rhodesia. He was buried at Fort Victoria, with all units of the security forces paying their respects. Sarah Barrell, 33-year-old correspondent for *Le Point*, was found dead in her Mazoe Street flat in Salisbury the day after attending the Major's funeral. A revolver lay beside the American-born reporter's body.

Other deaths in action during June included: Cpl Peter Rice, 19, former pupil of Mount Pleasant School; L/Cpl Ewart Nel, 22, from Churchill School; Tpr Christopher Lang, 22; L/Section Officer Vaughan Whitehead-Wilson, 23, from Plumtree School.

Tributes, in memoriam, followed:

'A soldier he was born to be, two years ago he came to this country, to serve it, and to help it be free. But! Someone above said that's enough for thee, and called him to be with his company. God bless you – till our paths cross again – Love Mum and Dad.'

'Lord please make us understand why. I love you so much "Little" brother – Kath.'

'Thanks for all the good times. I will miss you. Sympathy to all in 1 Commando – Lyn.'

'When the gates of Heaven opened, you did not go alone. For part of me went with you. The day God called you home . . .'

To some decimated families the distinction between death in action and death on the home front was academic, if not meaningless. The Rosenfels family, wealthy farmers of Pioneer stock, suffered a terrible blood-letting. Max Rosenfels, chairman of the Bulawayo branch of the RNFU and the owner of several ranches in the south-west, lost two sons and four young relatives. Three were killed on their farms: I. Rosenfels, at Marula, 29 March

1978; D. C. Rosenfels, at Marula, 8 February 1979; and C. Rosenfels, at Kezi, 24 April 1979.

Three others died while serving in the Selous Scouts or RLI. Desmond, son of Mr Ernest Rosenfels, was posthumously awarded the Bronze Cross of Rhodesia for bravery in action with Fireforce, 1 RLI.

Whites killed in action while serving with the security forces: 1977, 123; 1978, 101; 1979, 146.

Guerrillas killed (Salisbury statistics): 1977, 1,682; 1978, 4,041; 1979, 4,542.

34. the great betrayal

What could Muzorewa deliver to the black electorate? What was to be the immediate, tangible yield of his version of 'majority rule'? Very little. The Rhodesian Front leopard had not changed its spots and it was still sitting astride the central branch of the tree. When the UANC parliamentary caucus called for the release of all detainees and political prisoners, the white Minister of Justice, Christian Andersen, politely declined. Was the Justice Ministry's appropriation of $(ZR)14 million accordingly withheld – the time-honoured weapon of legislators thwarted by the executive? It was not.

Although the war was costing $(ZR)402 million a year, income tax remained comfortably low. Muzorewa was reduced to the politics of gesture: a new flag carrying the gold bird of Zimbabwe; the banishment of UDI from the annual calendar; a puerile proposal to charge $(ZR)20,000 as the price of re-entry for citizens who had quit the country; and a plea – furiously rejected by the RF – that the word 'Rhodesia' should be dropped from 'Zimbabwe Rhodesia'.

Muzorewa's energies were committed to gaining international recognition and to winning the war. Although he himself, as titular leader of the ANC, had once been granted a refuge by President Kaunda of Zambia and an office in State House, Lusaka, the Bish now sent the white Rhodesian war machine into action against neighbouring countries. On 26 June the Rhobabweans hit Chikumbi camp, twelve kilometres north of Lusaka, scene of a slaughter the previous October. Helicopter-born assault troops stormed Zapu's intelligence headquarters just a mile from Mulungushi Hall, where the Queen was due to open the Commonwealth Conference. On 1 July commandos took apart JZ camp, twenty-four kilometres west of Lusaka, destroying large quantities of tents, rockets, food, clothes, fuel and canoes.

The war of counter-insurgency could not be won inside Zimbabwe

Rhodesia. It could be won only by inflicting destruction on Zambia and Mozambique on such a scale that Kaunda and Machel either abandoned Nkomo and Mugabe or forced them to accept a humiliating compromise. Walls and Muzorewa were agreed on this tactic. The supreme commander's role was that of outrider for the South Africa-dominated Co-Prosperity sphere. 'We', he told a Johannesburg audience, 'have got less than five years to get it together. With the resources of southern Africa we can be a world power able to take on any foreign threat or ideology.'

His daughter Valerie, a Springbok swimmer and holder of the South African record for the 200-metres free-style, was commissioned into the Rhodesian Women's Service Corps. Walls was there, bemedalled, to give her a kiss: and photographers. Within a year he would be exiled – in South Africa. During the short interim the Conservative British press lionized him, vaguely imagining that he was preferable to Smith.

South Africa was the natural refuge for Rhodesians in flight. Of 48,196 who crossed the Limpopo on the south-bound track between January 1977 and April 1980, 22,225 settled in South Africa. Rhodesia's principal newspapers were owned by a South African company, Argus; on the day that Muzorewa took office the *Herald*'s editor, Roland Fothergill, lauded South Africa for her staunch support in the holy war against the British Labour Party, the front-line states, the OAU and the terrorists (not forgetting their Communist masters).

On 24 July a *Herald* editorial attacked the NUF for demanding an all-party conference. Within three weeks Rhodesians were faced with the shocking decision of the Commonwealth leaders in Lusaka to set up, without delay, precisely that – an all-party conference. The *Sunday Mail* had earlier printed a Meintjes cartoon showing Green Leader grinning smugly in his Hawker Hunter as he gives the Queen permission to land at Lusaka Airport; the Queen leans smiling out of her plane and gives him the thumbs up – the Rhodesian fantasy of racial power, of complicity within the white clan. But now it was thumbs down.

Carrington and the Foreign Office knew well that a settlement which excluded the PF had no hope of international acceptance: not only the OAU and the UN would continue to reject it, so in all probability would Western Europe. Both Carrington and the Australian Prime Minister, Malcolm Fraser, understood that to accord diplomatic recognition to Zimbabwe Rhodesia without bringing the war there to an end would merely be to yield influence in the region to the Communist states, and thus to jeopardize Western strategic and economic interests.

President Julius Nyerere of Tanzania made Thatcher's task easier by the conciliatory tone of his speech at Lusaka: he neither described the PF as the sole, legitimate representative of the Zimbabwean people, nor challenged the notion of seats reserved for the white minority in the Salisbury Parliament. Britain undertook to draw up a new constitution, to convene an all-party conference, to hammer out an agreement, to negotiate a cease-fire and supervise new elections monitored by Commonwealth observers. Thatcher made it clear that Britain did not accept continued white control of the Rhodesian police, army, civil service and judiciary. That was the blow in the gut. On 12 August Britain issued eleven-point constitutional proposals plus invitations to both sides to send delegations of up to twelve members to a conference due to begin in London on 10 September.

The *Mail*'s political columnist Henry Maasdorp was incensed: 'The betrayal of reason by those who are presumed to live by its light is a more frightening thing than the brute onslaughts of its natural enemies.' The *Herald*'s editorials, drained of fire, blew out smoke: 'Mrs Thatcher surely does not believe the Bishop will agree to attend an all-party conference to draw up a new constitution. If she does she is ignoring the new realities of the situation here.' The *Herald* asked whether Mrs Thatcher was 'really a Labour Prime Minister in drag'.

On 14 August Muzorewa agreed to attend an all-party conference.

On 20 August the PF also agreed to attend. The Rhodesian press now had no alternative but to call Mugabe, Nkomo, Zanu and Zapu by their real names.

35. Gokomere – unwelcome visitations

Gokomere mission occupies some 6,000 hectares of land in the European farming area fifteen kilometres north of Fort Victoria. Off the main road a broad dirt track runs up to the mission school, a handsomely endowed complex of red-brick buildings. Bethlehem Fathers are typically middle-aged, solid, short-haired, liable to wear glasses and to walk about in short-sleeved white shirts, grey trousers and sandals. Father Bruno Furer, Principal of Gokomere, is no exception. A chemistry graduate, he had spent twenty years at Gokomere. Five years had elapsed since his last visit to Switzerland.

'What happened here on 12 February last year?' I asked.

'Ah.' He weighed me politely. 'You know about that? Well, it started about 7 in the evening. Our weekly film show had just begun when the vakhomana showed up.'

'How many?'

'About twenty-four of them. Each one was carrying a bottle of gin. They seemed anxious to see the film. The leader was clearly under the influence of drugs. We have an open-air, Roman-style amphitheatre here – you must have driven past it? – but the guerrillas insisted on gathering our pupils in the church. There was a heavy storm all night.'

'How many pupils?'

'We have 600.'

'Were the guerrillas in uniform?'

'They wore denims, blue jeans. There were liberation songs, of course, but the guerrillas were drinking a good deal and the children here got over-excited, particularly the girls. It's all very jolly until you remember that each of these young drunks is carrying an AK rifle. For a while I tried to fend off their demands for girls but in the end it was impossible.' Father Furer smiled. 'There was no lack of volunteers. They lay down together on the portico, on the steps right outside this office. I went away. God will forgive me.'

'Where did the shooting start?'

'It came from within the church. The security forces had arrived. Some say they had had a tip-off, who knows? I hid myself in a storehouse while the shooting lasted so I have no idea who shot whom. Three were killed, ten wounded.'

'You regard the guerrillas as a menace?'

A short, square, solid man, he pondered this carefully.

'Drink,' he said. 'Always drink. That's the problem.'

'Are you afraid they may try to close you down?'

'Of course I'm afraid. Any day it can happen.'

'Is anti-Christian feeling a big factor?'

'With some. One mission was recently closed by a Zanla gang whose commander was a former pupil of the mission, a brilliant fellow, university-educated. But the general pattern, I suspect, is that the ones who close the schools resent their own lack of education.' He shrugged. 'Some of our former pupils are now prominent in the Zanu leadership in Maputo. Does that help Gokomere, does that protect us? – who knows?'

As we talked a line of boys and girls had silently formed on the portico outside his office. He gestured and the first ones shyly approached his desk. Some of the girls chose to kneel before him, others remained on their feet. Each pupil was requesting permission to travel home for the weekend. Father Furer became rather stern now, formidable, as he reached for the fees ledger and checked their names:

'You have not paid your fees. You must bring the money with you when you return. Is that understood? Yes?' Later he said to me: 'They have to pay.

The shrewder parents bring the fees themselves or send them by registered post. We may have a war but we still have registered post!'

'What are the fees?'

'For the first term, $(R)100; thereafter $(R)60. It barely covers the cost of their food.'

Before leading the way to the refectory for lunch he locked his office door. 'I never used to do that. Nowadays nothing is safe. I take the school fees to the bank in Fort Vic every day.' We walked across the pleasant campus, past the Roman-style amphitheatre and the church where the shooting had started, accompanied by a Bethlehem Father who wore shorts and a trilby hat, a building contractor by vocation. He said he thought the internal settlement was worth supporting. I asked Furer whether he was equally impressed.

He laughed. 'I'm not the one they have to impress!'

Six weeks after my visit to Gokomere, on the last day of June 1979, a new band of Zanla guerrillas, twenty-strong, arrived at the mission. To form a cordon sanitaire between themselves and the security forces, they drove the pupils into the surrounding bush. From Father Furer they took all the money they could lay their hands on, plus drink and, for some obscure reason, curtains. Furer was told to close the school – without explanation, though word later reached him that the 'boys' believed soldiers had camped at Gokomere. Furer not only vigorously denies this but doubts whether Zanla really believed it:

'I suspect it was purely a matter of exerting authority.' The area remained bitterly contested, with the army determined to keep the main road to Fort Victoria open.

The pupils were sent home. Furer himself stayed on for a further month, during which time the clinic and workshops continued to operate. Then he left. But the priest's devotion to Gokomere and its pupils was such that he could not bring himself to accept passively so absurd a situation. When he asked the Ministry of Education whether he could rent an empty Coloured school in Fort Victoria, the reply was negative. Nevertheless, such was his driving energy that with the support of parents and the white mayor he cobbled a makeshift school together.

Then Bruno Furer had trouble with his Bishop. Tobias Chiginya, the Catholic Bishop of Gwelo – and thus in overall authority over the Bethlehem Fathers working in the diocese – was so worried about Zanla's possible displeasure at the reopening of the school in Fort Victoria that he himself refused to be the legally required 'responsible authority' and finally took the extreme step of sending Furer back to Switzerland.

Sick at heart, Father Furer busied himself in Switzerland, filling in as parish priest for a colleague while the Lancaster House conference convened in London. Then came a telegram from Bishop Chiginya: the school showed signs of collapse; Father Furer must return to Fort Victoria without delay.

In October he went to London to lobby Zanu leaders, notably his former pupil and fellow chemist, Dzingai Mutumbuka, a member of Zanu's central committee and – as it later turned out – Zimbabwe's first Minister of Education. Furer also told Mugabe about the local situation round Gokomere.

'So what was the immediate outcome of all this?'

'Very little – except that I learned how long and thin is the chain of command from Mozambique to central Rhodesia.'

With the cease-fire, Furer was at last able to reopen the school at the Gokomere mission on 17 January 1980. But there were still armed men at large. Informed by an intermediary that a particular guerrilla was demanding admission as a pupil, Furer checked this out with Dzingai Mutumbuka, then campaigning as No. 2 on Zanu-PF's electoral list in Victoria province. The reply came back: this man is not genuine, he once robbed a store, became a mujiba, but never received guerrilla training.

Then tragedy: on 1 February, five days after Robert Mugabe's triumphant return from Maputo, Father Raymond Machikicho and a lay preacher, both from Gokomere, were cycling to Denje church when they were arrested by the local Zanu-PF chairman in Zimuto TTL and accused of being sell-outs. Subsequently they were confronted by Zanla guerrillas (who should in theory long since have reported to an assembly point) who ordered a group of mujibas to cut sticks and beat the unfortunate priests to death. The party did not, on this occasion, blame the Selous Scouts; Mutumbuka and other leaders attended the funeral in a spirit of profound regret.

On the morning the election result was broadcast jubilant pupils of Gokomere ran to the main road where they stood and cheered and generally displayed harmless jubilation. When the morning's escorted convoy passed by the white drivers and passengers, already traumatized by the news, panicked. The army was called in, shots were fired, one pupil was slightly wounded.

'Nothing serious,' says Father Furer.

36. the last post

Mindful, with Clausewitz, that war is the pursuit of diplomacy by other means, Muzorewa and Walls resumed their cross-border raids as the various parties convened in conference at Lancaster House. During the first week in September a force of 180 men penetrated seventy-five kilometres into Mozambique; encountering intense anti-aircraft fire and a ring of tanks deployed as fixed artillery, the Rhodesians pulled out with the loss of seventeen men, twelve of them killed when an Augusta Bell 205 helicopter was hit by an RPG-7 rocket and burst into a ball of flame.

The shooting down of the helicopter was the worst single military disaster of the war suffered by the Rhodesians. Two of the dead, Tpr Stephen King, 27, and Tpr David Prosser, 26, were Australians; Sgt Michael Jones was from Birmingham, England; and Capt. Johannes du Plooy, 27, was a South African. The remaining eight had all attended Rhodesian or Zambian schools: 2nd Lt Bruce Burns, 26, Jameson High School, Gatooma; Capt. Charles Small, 29, Prince Edward School, Salisbury; Cpl Hugh Fry, of Bulawayo; L/Cpl Peter Fox, 30, Kitwe High School, Zambia; Tpr Jacobus Briel, 20, Que Que High School; and Tpr Brian Eslin, 20, Lord Malvern, Salisbury.

Perhaps the best known of the dead was Corporal LeRoy Duberly, at that time regular full-back for the national rugby team. After a series of severe Currie Cup defeats, the team had travelled to Durban for an honour-saving last game against Natal. The coach, Brian Murphy, had already been advised that Duberly would not be available for the match, and when the news of his death in action came through the team cancelled all social functions. Before the game a lone bugler sounded the last post while the two teams and the crowd stood for two minutes' silence.

Striking at Aldeia de Barragem, 150 kilometres north-west of Maputo, the Rhodesians pressed on with their strategy of destroying Mozambique's transport and communications system. A series of bridges were damaged along the Limpopo Valley, which produces 80 per cent of Mozambique's rice crop. On 27 September Rhodesian forces launched a four-day attack against the new camp of Chimoio (not the scene of the massacre in November 1977), but the defence was now so fierce that the RLI commandos and the Selous Scouts were unable to storm a hilltop concentration of trenches and bomb-proof bunkers manned by Zanla and Frelimo. The fighting cost the Rhodesians a Hawker Hunter and a Canberra bomber.

On 11 October Rhodesian jets bombed three bridges on the Beira–Moatize railway line, cutting Zambia's link with the port of Beira, and followed this up by sending in commandos to blow up a railway bridge in northern Zambia, thus severing the Tanzam railway to Dar es Salaam. In fact Zambia's only outlet now was through Zimbabwe Rhodesia itself. Muzorewa was proving himself a ruthless opponent, not least when on 5 November he ordered that Zambia's desperately needed imports of maize from South Africa should be blocked – 200,000 tonnes were being rushed north with all possible speed to head off starvation.

On 19 November the Rhodesians were back in action against Zambian road bridges and Kaunda vented his frustration on the British, claiming that they were using the Rhodesian attacks as a means of putting pressure on the PF at Lancaster House. Angry demonstrators stormed the British High Commission.

Christopher Ross, 36, a Juliasdale farmer, father of three, was killed in an ambush on 13 October.

Eight days later, at about 7 in the morning, Dennis Bleasdale and his wife Patricia, Penhalonga farmers, were both killed when their vehicle detonated a landmine on their property.

On 29 October two Zipra men broke into the Que Que farm homestead of Mrs Barbara Rich, aged 61, and shot her dead.

The following night Peter Johnson, a 47-year-old employee of Posts and Telecommunications who lived in Umtali, died when guerrillas attacked the camp where he was staying.

Henry Elsworth, Rhodesian Front MP for the Midlands, was a tireless advocate of the commercial farmers' interests in the House of Assembly. At 7 a.m. on 1 November he was rounding up his cattle on one of his farms north-west of Que Que, in expectation of a visit by veterinary staff, when guerrillas who had monitored his movements opened fire from a distance of thirty metres with AK automatic rifles and rifle-grenades. Wounded in the arm, Elsworth fired a device on his roof and made his escape with one tyre shot out until he came across a police patrol eight kilometres away, on the Gokwe road.

Mrs Anne Evans, 25, and two black children were killed at 6 p.m. on 1 November when their vehicle hit a landmine in the Tokwe farming area.

David Briggs, 32, of Beitbridge, father of four, was killed on the night of 2 November when the train of which he was a crew member was attacked by guerrillas in the Beitbridge area.

On the evening of 12 November guerrillas attacked the Hartley farm of Walter Brown, 56, a Supervisor for the Grain Marketing Board. Having just returned from Salisbury with his wife Hazel, Mr Brown had gone into the ration store when he was shot dead by a terrorist standing in the doorway. Mrs Brown and her dog were then killed in the house as she tried to raise the alarm. Hearing shots, 74-year-old John Gilbert, who lived in a cottage on the farm, ran out and he too was shot dead. Two years earlier the Browns' son Ian had been killed in action.

37. Lancaster House and buns with the Queen Mother

Peter Carrington is an aristocrat, a wealthy landowner, an old Etonian. The PF's delegates to Lancaster House, notably Eddison Zvobgo, made no secret of their preference for doing business with 'the British ruling class' rather than with a Labour Government. 'With Carrington we know where we stand. He doesn't have to keep looking over his shoulder.' In fact Carrington's neck had virtually reversed itself so busy was he looking over his shoulder at the Nigerians, the OAU, the EEC nations, the Commonwealth, the UN. The main reason that Owen had been unable to make his plan stick was that the Rhodesians remained convinced they could get a better deal from Thatcher's Tories; once Carrington had removed that last, white hope, the Salisbury regime had no alternative but to eat the cake he offered.

Carrington started with the terms of the future constitution of Zimbabwe; moved on to the transitional arrangements; and concluded with the most sensitive subject, how to achieve a cease-fire. It was a diplomatic exercise without precedent or parallel.

The constitution that Carrington offered removed the *de facto* white blocking mechanism in the Zimbabwe Rhodesia parliament (only seventy-two black seats but 78 votes required to effect a constitutional change) by offering eighty black seats and only 70 votes required for a constitutional change. The new constitution also put military, judicial, police and administrative appointments under the control of the Prime Minister. All this was acceptable to the black parties, both 'internal' and 'external', though the PF would have preferred to see executive power vested in the President rather than the Prime Minister. What stuck in Mugabe's throat was a ten-year guarantee on the inviolability of private property, including white farms, which made nonsense of Zanu's revolutionary programme of agrarian reform. Nor did the PF like Carrington's proposals requiring the future Government of Zimbabwe to guarantee the pensions of Rhodesian civil servants and to guarantee citizenship to all white residents.

Ian Smith set foot on British soil for the first time since UDI, granted immunity from prosecution by the Government. There were some demonstrators, he didn't mind, he had no difficulty in making contact with the genuine Britons. Soon after his arrival he attended the Battle of Britain Association's annual dinner as the personal guest of Sir Douglas Bader. (Bader, speaking at a reception held in his honour by the Mayor of Salisbury, had remarked: 'Rhodesia is not part of Britain and I feel bloody angry about the interference in your affairs by successive British Governments.' He added that he couldn't wait to play on British golf-courses wearing a 'Rhodesia is

Super' T-shirt.) Smith's car was escorted, as usual, by police outriders. Smith saw Harlequins beat Llanelli at Twickenham, sat with top dignitaries in Westminster Abbey during the Battle of Britain service, turned up at soccer matches, was even interviewed on the ITV programme *The Big Match*.

Of the Salisbury delegation, Ian Smith alone voted to reject the British constitutional proposals. David Smith, formerly his Deputy Prime Minister, and now Muzorewa's Minister of Finance, was for acceptance, as were two other RF representatives in London, Cronje and Andersen. On 23 September the RF caucus in Salisbury sent Ian Smith a telegram of support and reaffirmed the importance of the 'safeguards' in the 1979 constitution. William Irvine warned that the 1979 constitution could not be abandoned in London, only by 78 votes in the Salisbury House of Assembly.

On 8 October Smith returned to Salisbury and lashed the British proposals which would give the future Prime Minister 'dictatorial powers' (i.e. powers equivalent to those previously enjoyed by Ian Smith). Again the RF caucus backed his stand. But it was bluff: even Smith admitted they had to wait and see what the whole package contained. Soon he flew back to London.

On 19 October the PF conditionally accepted the constitutional proposals. Carrington moved on to the transitional arrangements and proposed a British Governor vested with both executive and legislative authority, ruling through the Rhodesian civil service and police.

As at Malta in January 1978, the PF produced complicated proposals for the restructuring of the police and army in advance of the election – why should they campaign in alien territory still controlled by their enemies? Carrington said No, the Governor will rule and he will be impartial. No argument.

Mugabe believed that Carrington's intention was to appear accommodating on the surface while driving Zanu so hard on substantive concessions that it walked out of the Lancaster House conference, leaving the British free to negotiate the famous 'second-class solution' with Muzorewa alone. If Nkomo could then be induced to join in, the British would have their beloved 'Option B' and the 'second-class solution' would look first-class – an essentially conservative, pro-capitalist settlement which the world might recognize because of Nkomo's participation.

The rebel general came to London and was accorded VIP treatment. Lt-Gen. Peter Walls and his wife Eunice, a slim, South African-born brunette who had spent over thirty years in Rhodesia, stayed at the Carlton House Towers where the doorman told them that his income had dropped by £500 a month in tips since the Rhodesian guests replaced the normal Arabs. Walls and his wife arrived at the England versus New Zealand rugby match late but,

378

as she recalled, 'The return motorcade was a wonderful experience. We swept through heavy traffic that parted in front of our police escort like the Jordan.' An even more wonderful experience was an invitation to take tea at Clarence House with the Queen Mother. They ate toasted London buns which were quite delicious and made a crunchy noise when you munched them, but the old lady didn't mind. She poured the tea herself out of a silver pot.

Bitter though he pretended to be, Smith was enjoying himself in London. He told the editor of the weekly magazine, the *Spectator*, that Muzorewa was like 'wet putty', that the PF were cleverer than 'our blacks', that Carrington was a 'racialist' who had prevented Smith from talking to Thatcher, that General Walls was Smith's 'creation' and that in any forthcoming election the PF 'would walk it'. This caused an uproar and sent 'the Bish' into a sulk. Then Smith slammed Carrington in the *Sunday Express*, depicting the Foreign Secretary as hell-bent on a course which would lead to a Marxist dictatorship. Why did Carrington keep extending his deadlines and let the PF run circles round him? – precisely the charges that he had levelled at Ivor Richard at the Geneva Conference three years earlier. Smith had a very simple solution: lift sanctions at once and recognize Zimbabwe Rhodesia.

On 9 November Smith gave an interview announcing that no more ground would be gained. 'Accordingly the time has come to tell our people back home that to continue the fight would be sterile, even counter-productive.' Just as he had prepared whites for the internal settlement and the 1979 constitution, now he saw it as his mission to condition them to accept an equally drastic retreat, the return of the PF. 'Many of us went to this conference hoping they would be excluded.' The *Sunday Mail* was in such a panic that on 2 December it actually proposed that the RF contest the twenty white seats under the banner of the UANC to circumvent the new rule forbidding white MPs from forming a coalition government with any minority black party.

Only one RF MP refused to capitulate, to accept the inevitable: Mark Partridge, MP for Highlands and a former Minister of Agriculture. 'I have no doubt that the Communist tiger will eat the UANC mouse that attempts to ride it.' One of the last surviving signatories of UDI still politically active, Partridge found this final submission to Britain unbearable. 'No!' he shouted at the second reading of the bill, a lone voice. On 10 December the Assembly voted by 90 to nil at the third reading to dissolve itself, Mr Partridge having been persuaded not to rock the boat as the waters closed over it.

The cease-fire presented the final hurdle. Muzorewa had agreed on 26 November to the creation of fourteen assembly points (APs) for the PF guerrillas and the withdrawal of the Rhodesian army to barracks once a cease-fire came into operation. By giving assurances about the removal of

South African troops and by doubling the projected Commonwealth Cease Fire Monitoring Force to 1,300 men, Carrington gained the consent of the PF on 5 December.

Maps were now produced and hard bargaining began over the number and location of the APs. The PF claimed to have 31,000 guerrillas operational. The British tended to accept the Rhodesian estimate of 20,000. In the end, by means of brinkmanship, the PF wrested sixteen APs and thirty-nine intermediate rendezvous points out of Carrington, most of them sited around the periphery of the country, at a distance from towns, communications centres and white farms. Both Mugabe and Nkomo greatly feared this corralling of their troops and their consequent vulnerability to attack by Rhodesian or South African forces, which enjoyed complete command of the air. The great strength of guerrilla formations resides in their dispersal across a vast, impenetrable terrain and the protective embrace of the villages from which they sprang.

All this must now be abandoned – on a gamble.

But Mugabe now had little alternative. When he showed signs of digging in his heels on the last furlong President Machel told him bluntly: sign. Between 1976 and 1979 the war had inflicted on Mozambique damage estimated at US$44 million.

On one point, however, Machel did not get his way. His passionate appeal to Zanu to join forces with Zapu and fight the election on a single ticket fell on stony ground.

Part Five: 1980

1. 'God Save the Queen'

His Excellency the Lord Soames, PC, GCMG, GCVO, CBE; or, more simply, His Excellency the Governor, Lord Soames; or, for variety, His Excellency the Rt Hon. Lord Soames; or, to his friends, Christopher. A wit remarked that it was the first time in the history of decolonization that a black President had been displaced by a white Governor. Poor President Gumede, the worthy Ndebele Headmaster and township Superintendent chosen by Muzorewa, vanished into the political obscurity whence he had come.

Rhodesia came under direct British rule for the first time in its history at 2.14 p.m. on 12 December 1979 when His Excellency (who only forty-eight hours earlier asked a journalist whether the Ndebele were blood-drinkers) stepped out of an RAF VC-10 and down to the tarmac where he was greeted by Muzorewa, Police Commissioner Allum and a cross-section of the internal establishment. The guard of honour presented arms, a nice racial mix for the cameras, the band played the short version of 'God Save the Queen', and then Lord and Lady Soames (the latter in a broad white hat) climbed into the Daimler which had been specially flown in from London at the expense of the proverbial British taxpayer.

That night the Governor appeared on television. It was a non-event, as planned. Delighted to be here in Rhodesia . . . daunting task, challenging, must all pull together . . . count on your cooperation . . . fair and orderly manner . . . lift sanctions tonight, thank you. Soames made it clear he wasn't here to change anything. Martial music followed. At such a moment. Poor Soames, dispatched by Carrington with the final words 'Good on you', ahead of a cease-fire, ahead of a final agreement, was in Salisbury to help Carrington put the screws on Mugabe in London. Hence the quick announcement that all parties intending to take part in the election must register by 31 December. Hence the refusal to legalize Zanu and Zapu until they signed the cease-fire – after all, were they not now in armed insurrection against the Crown?

The whites were sour, mainly, although a few liberals and loyalists were jubilant, vindicated, what did we always say. Everyone pointed out to everyone else that it was nonsense to talk about a *return* to British rule since Rhodesia had enjoyed virtual self-government since 1923 (in fact Salisbury had invariably submitted legislation to London for approval). The Governor's bland, moony countenance, his pop eyes and his plummy tones, his smooth advisers who had come to sort out a mess and rescue Rhodesians from their own folly, all this stirred local bellies to fury.

2. the last to die

Despite the third and final act of the Lancaster House conference – or because of it – guerrilla attacks on whites intensified rather than abated during the month. On 1 December Jacobus Odendaal, a 57-year-old Selous farmer, died when ambushed by fifteen Zanla men near his farm. On the 13th Maxwell Stockhill, 38, a farm manager, was killed when his vehicle detonated a landmine in the south-east.

Late in the afternoon of Tuesday, 18 December, only ten days before the cease-fire officially came into effect, Zanla guerrillas killed Donovan Harvey Brown, 66, a retired schoolmaster who was caretaking La Rochelle, a National Trust house in the Imbeza Valley. A second-generation Rhodesian, Don Harvey Brown was widely regarded as an exceptional friend of the African people. Almost simultaneously a second white death occurred in the Imbeza Valley, the victim being Ivor Tapping, 44, who ran a school for black forestry workers. Tapping, who was on his way to a Christmas party at the school, was murdered in front of his pupils.

Two weeks earlier, in the same border area, the elderly Guthrie Hall had been hacked to death in bed.

On Boxing Day they killed a man of 71, Basil Beverley, on his farm at Chiredzi in the south-east Low Veld. Beverley had started out in 1924, at the age of 16, as an assistant on a cattle station. The *Daily Telegraph*'s obituary (4 January 1980) is worth quoting in part:

'In later years he was something of a legend in the Low Veld. It was not thought possible to run cattle or grow crops on the land he eventually worked – arid country of intense heat and little water. But Basil Beverley explored, prospected and hunted over the vast wild areas, and came to know the movement of game, the water courses, and grasses. Despite years of setbacks through drought, disease, cattle sickness and fever, he brought purpose to the land, excavating dams, surveying catchment areas, and laying down irrigation. He built up a strain of cattle resistant to disease, experimented with grasses, trees and crops, so that cotton, wheat and maize flourished. All his profits went back into the land. . . .

'His day started before dawn, always with a gathering at the meeting place by the store. The snuff box would be solemnly handed round, then the talk, a simple joke or two, and great laughter. He understood native law and custom. . . .

'He had no ambitions for himself,' said the *Telegraph*, 'only for the development, prosperity and stability of his ranch, the Low Veld and Rhodesia.'

The young men who worked on his ranch were forced by guerrillas to drive off or maim Basil Beverley's cattle. The cattle foreman, Samson, had been compelled to carry stores into the TTL – before they cut off his arms. Rodgi, the dip supervisor, was killed, as were two old house servants. The banana crop had been hacked down, the winter wheat trampled, the house itself attacked with rockets and machine-gun fire. Then they killed him.

On 29 December, the day after the cease-fire became official, nine members of the van Niekerk family were gathered for Saturday lunch at Mnyame Farm, sixteen kilometres from Gwelo. After lunch the women and children drove into Que Que for the afternoon leaving behind the two adult males, Isaac van Niekerk, 58, the owner-occupant of the farm, and his son John, 35, who lived in Gwelo. Father and son drove to a neighbour's to pick up a milk can. On their return they saw that the security gates stood open. 'My God,' said John van Niekerk, 'it's terrorists.' Indeed it was: about fifty of them, terrorists everywhere, even lying among the cows waiting to be milked. The car was surrounded. Father and son were taken to the bush, threatened with imminent death, and plied with questions. Then back to the ransacked house, where the guerrillas started drinking heavily, killed a ram and ordered the housegirl to cook for them. The second-in-command was all for shooting everybody and drink inflamed his temper.

The women and children duly arrived: Mrs Becker, 65, her daughter Mrs Hester van Niekerk, wife of Isaac, John's pregnant wife, the children. One little girl was made to carry food for the feast, they said how pretty she was and how they would take her to Maputo. Very drunk now, they bestowed African names on all the children including the unborn one. Suddenly the commander, announcing himself to be a doctor, insisted on examining the pregnant Mrs van Niekerk and applied a stethoscope to her chest.

The telephone had long since been ripped out, but now the Agric-Alert sounded, the routine check of farms, that reassuring voice; at gunpoint Mr Isaac van Niekerk reported that all was well. Then they smashed the Agric-Alert.

The white people were led outside and made to sit down with their labour force and sing 'Pamberi ne Mugabe, Pasi Smith'. If Mugabe does not win the election, the war will continue, declared the commander, who boasted of having shot down a plane at Mtoko, and another near Umtali. 'Many whites give us information, we have many friends who are white.'

Presently they went inside to watch the TV news which was largely concerned with reports from the rendezvous and assembly points where these guerrillas were conspicuously not assembling. At 1.30 on Sunday morning the guerrilla commander ordered the family to retire to bed. 'Good night, gogo (granny),' he said to old Mrs Becker. 'You are now our people and belong to Mugabe.' They lay awake, of course, listening. At about 5 in the morning the guerrillas moved away from the farm to a nearby hill, taking with them their extraordinary array of arms, anti-aircraft guns, mortars, rockets. 'You name, they had it,' Mr van Niekerk said later. Then they were gone. It had been a nightmare.

On the same Saturday night, eighteen hours after the cease-fire, a gang of about eighteen guerrillas attacked a farm near Beatrice belonging to a 59-year-old widow, Mrs Anna Hoffman. Mrs Hoffman had lived in the area for thirty-six years and had farmed alone for the twelve years since her husband died. Seeing armed men approaching the homestead, she was able to lock the security gate and alert a neighbour, who came to her assistance. This seemed to frighten the guerrillas off. A reaction stick arrived from Joyce Mine. But an hour later the guerrillas returned, fired a mortar and a rifle-grenade at the house, then moved away into Muda African Purchase Area. No one was hurt. But what gave the experience its crueller dimension was the presence in the house of Mrs Hoffman's daughter, Mrs Magdalena de Wet, confined to a wheelchair since the ambush which killed her husband, Piet de Wet, and wounded her 5-year-old son Wynand. She had been allowed out of St Giles Rehabilitation Centre to visit her mother for Christmas.

Two days after the cease-fire began guerrillas struck again in the Penhalonga area. Edward Wright, 65, was driving in his car when he came across a bus which had been stopped by Zanla and emptied of its passengers. Wright tried to turn around and make a getaway but was shot dead. The guerrillas then fired a rifle-grenade into the bus and recrossed the border into Mozambique.

White civilians killed by guerrillas: in 1977, 68; in 1978, 180; in 1979, 160.

Black civilians allegedly killed by guerrillas: in 1977, 485; in 1978, 1,225; in 1979, 1,041. Total: 2,751.

Black civilians admittedly killed by security forces: in 1977, about 780; in 1978, about 1,080; in 1979, about 1,500. Total: about 3,360.

3. cease-fire – fingers crossed

Radio Mozambique broadcasts Mugabe's cease-fire call every hour but Zanla forces are flooding across the border in defiance of the Lancaster House agreement; Comops claims that 600–700 crossed the frontier on 28 December, the first day of the cease-fire. In an attempt to stem the tide Soames deploys the security forces along the eastern border, but there is no reason why the Rhodesians should succeed now where they have failed for seven years.

Sightseers flood out to Salisbury Airport. First, the blacks from the townships, to welcome home the Zanla and Zipra commanders on Boxing Day; then, in their wake, the whites, to witness the groaning descent of vast aeroplanes, Hercules of the RAF, C141 Starlifters of the United States Air Force, ferrying in 1,200 men of the Cease Fire Monitoring Force and a mass of equipment.

By 28 December about 450 members of the CFMF have scattered into the remote, inhospitable bush, to take up position at mission stations, at abandoned schools and clinics, at wherever the map-makers of Lancaster House designated the sixteen assembly points and thirty-nine interim rendezvous points. Tension runs high as army engineers clear the access roads of mines; at Morgan High School, the CFMF's Salisbury headquarters, Acland and his staff cross their fingers. Nothing like it has ever been attempted before.

Zanla and Zipra have established their headquarters at the Teacher-Training College hostel in Mount Pleasant. Top priority is to ferry the PF's liaison officers to the APs and RPs, by helicopter if necessary, for without them the chances of gaining the confidence of local guerrilla commanders are nil, while the chances of mutual suspicion detonating a shoot-out are high. Thus 'Comrade Mao', 'John' and 'Wonderful Victory', attired in an assortment of Chinese and Soviet-bloc uniforms, spread across the country in the company of British and Australian majors and colonels, some settling under canvas at the APs, others operating as staff officers, billeting in the comfort of hotels and motels in towns such as Bindura and Umtali.

The psychological key to the success of the entire operation resides in the decision to put the CFMF under canvas alongside the guerrillas in the APs. Acland is determined, as far as possible, to avoid the 'man-in-the middle' fate of the UN's blue berets, shot at by both sides in the Lebanon and elsewhere.

By 29 December the Hercules transports which flew Land-Rovers and signal equipment in for the advance guard of the CFMF are flying over remote APs at heights varying between fifty and 400 metres. RAF crewmen from Lyneham in Wiltshire hurl 550-kg packets of tents through the huge rear doors. Soon the RAF will be airlifting 55·8 tonnes of beef a week to the APS from an airport outside Johannesburg, to make up for the shortage in Rhodesia.

Long elephant grass, bushes, scrub, a kopje, a cluster of msasa-trees, a track leading to an old mission station: this is the guerrillas' Zimbabwe. They emerge from cover warily, expecting a trap, an ambush, an air attack; the large white crosses on the CFMF vehicles and tents are reassuring but nothing is taken on trust. On their way in, across mile after mile of tribal trust land, they are persuaded by the PF liaison officer to form three ranks and march their AKs as if it were a great victory; the villagers crowd round dancing, laughing, ululating. The point, now, is to make contact with the PF liaison officers.

A sandy-haired British Captain in the Royal Engineers waits nervously at St Barbara's RP, fifty kilometres north of Umtali. The Rhodesians who guided his party to the right spot offered prophecies of doom – we know these gooks – before departing. Not a single Zanla guerrilla shows up for six days; the whole enterprise becomes shrouded in unreality, heat, dust, flies, an aching thirst. On Thursday, 3 January, 350 guerrillas come out of the bush, line abreast, AKs at the ready. Tense discussions follow; 200 metres from the RP they are persuaded by the PF liaison officer to form three ranks and march in 'for a cup of tea'. But when told they will be transported to Delta AP by bus they become distraught, convinced that they face a trap set by the Rhodesians.

At Bakasa RP the Zanla commander, Shara Perence, edgy and distrustful of a Rhodesian police wireless post on a nearby hill, threatened to take it out and butcher the CFMF into the bargain. Capt. Mark Corbett-Burcher of the 1st Regiment, Royal Horse Artillery, the CFMF officer in charge at Bakasa, had 'only shaved half my face' when Shara Perence began making his threats. When Perence spotted Gordon Farquharson, a reporter for Iana news agency, he accused him of being a spy or a local farmer, insisted on examining his diary, and interpreted references in it to a new Alfa-Romeo as a radio code. Farquharson's official accreditation did not impress him. Hairy.

At an RP twenty-five kilometres from an abandoned school near Mrewa Lt David Hill of the CFMF experienced some 'awfully tense moments' on 29 December – the Zanla men appeared on open ground in battle formation, their rifles levelled at the school. Unarmed, the 20-year-old Hill walked towards them with his sergeant-major, Phil Hall, and said hullo, how do you do, what about a cup of tea?

Three reporters on their way to Foxtrot, in the Sabi TTL, were stopped by hostile Zanla men demanding proof of identity. One of them shouted at

Michael Farr, correspondent of the *Daily Telegraph*, 'British killers . . . kill the British' and opened fire. Perhaps this guerrilla preferred the *Guardian*. Despite a fusillade of bullets, the three managed to drive off unhurt.

Foxtrot, which could be reached only by driving eighty kilometres along dirt tracks, was a focal point for guerrillas operating in the Buhera–Charter districts. Fifty British soldiers, including a contingent of Irish Guards, prepared fall-back emplacements on a high kopje, just in case they should find themselves starring in a remake of the film *Zulu*.

White Rhodesians stared morosely at their newspapers, which for the first time displayed pictures of grinning guerrillas in high morale: normally 'terrorists' were depicted only as corpses, as floppies, with their intestines coiling from their stomachs, or as 'on-sides' renegades who had taken advantage of the amnesty programme. But never this.

After several Rhodesian girls became engaged to British soldiers of the Monitoring Force, a flurry of letters hit the *Herald*. 'Shanie' of Salisbury wrote: 'Let me speak out for our beautiful Rhodesian men. To me, and I speak for many other girls as well, no male from anywhere could take their place, least of all Englishmen. Our Rhodesian men are the greatest. They are strong and at the same time gentle; they are husky, tough, good-looking and sexy and so beautifully tanned! They are men of decision, initiative and resolve and yet remain wonderfully unassuming and quiet. They do not require the airs and arrogance, nor do they need to be supercilious. Yes, they like their shumba, generally. But what is worse, beer by a braai, or an indoor life of bingo and telly-watching?'

The Governor had given the guerrillas a week (28 December to 4 January) to make their way in peace to the APs. By 1 January only 2,100 guerrillas have made contact with the CFMF; by 4.30 p.m. on 2 January the number has doubled but the whole operation looks doomed to failure. At Grand Reef air force base commandos of the RLI Fireforce, reckoned to be responsible for 80 per cent of all guerrilla casualties, remain on standby alert, itching to cull the gooks and 'finish the job'. It is one of Soames's several nightmares that the Rhodesian air force, unbearably tempted by the gathering of terrs into large concentrations, will unleash their Hawker Hunters, turning the APs into Chimoios and Nyadzonias.

In an effort to inspire collaboration the Cease Fire Commission holds its first meeting on 2 January, with Acland occupying the middle ground between Rex Nhongo and Dumiso Dabengwa (the Zipra Commander) and the Rhodesians, represented by Maj.-Gen. H. Bernard and Gp/Capt. H. C. S. Slatter.

The 3rd and 4th of January are days of anxiety at CFMF headquarters, at

Government House, at the Foreign Office in London. When the Friday midnight deadline passes about 12,000 guerrillas have come in, roughly 5,000 short of the number that the CFMF believe to be inside Rhodesia. In principle the Governor refuses to extend the deadline but in practice the RPs are instructed to remain open for business until Sunday the 6th. It's a sensible compromise and it yields handsome dividends: by the second deadline 18,300 guerrillas have reported.

Nhongo and Dabengwa give a press conference in Mount Pleasant, insisting that there are now only two or three thousand more at large and they had better hurry if they want to be counted among the national heroes. Nhongo is at some pains to counter Rhodesian claims that only 5,000 of those in the APs are genuine guerrillas, that the majority of guerrillas have been instructed to remain at large in the countryside, and that mujibas have been sent to the APs to swell the numbers. He denies it all.

Zipra established several assembly points, one of them at St Paul's, Lupane, a mission which Zipra guerrillas had closed by murdering two white nuns in August 1977 and subsequently driving out the remaining black Sisters. When the CFMF arrived they found that the mission and its hospital had been stripped bare; letters from her relatives to the murdered mission doctor, Johanna Decker, still lay scattered about the floor among old medical journals.

Papa AP was located at Rukomechi, an abandoned tsetse-fly research station in a wildlife-reserve, baobab and big-game country – the terrain of Zipra forces operating in the Sipolilo and Urungwe TTLs. After their Rhodesian guides had departed, the seventeen British soldiers sprayed the abandoned buildings with insecticide to combat the deep-biting tsetse flies, set up a signals mast and a Union Jack, and waited. When Zipra forces appeared four days later, dressed in tiger-speckled uniforms and Cuba-style forage caps, the hammer-and-sickle embroidered on their collars, they brought with them a formidable array of weapons and quickly dug in four anti-aircraft guns as well as training mortars on the approach road. Short of meat, they shot an elephant.

Despite the summer heat, Zipra commanders and political commissars registered their rank by proudly wearing fur hats designed to protect Russian soldiers from sub-zero winters. At Lido AP, in the south, Maj. Brian Hewitt of the New Zealand Army commanded twenty-nine members of the CFMF living side by side with the 475 men of a highly disciplined Zipra unit commanded by Lt-Col. Middle Nyathi. Vigilance was maintained through a rigorous daily routine of drill, PT and political discussions. Nyathi and the chief Zipra liaison officer fiercely resented the presence of South African forces at Beitbridge, which they held to be a clear breach of the Lancaster House agreement.

Despite the apparent success of the operation, relations between the British and Zanu PF now deteriorated rapidly. Announcing that 21,284 had reached the APs by 16 January, the Governor's spokesman, Nicholas Fenn, alleged that many of them were non-combatants whose role was to leave the armed guerrillas at liberty to intimidate the local population. Walls demanded a free hand to deploy his security forces and he got it.

4. blowing this whole thing sky high

A District Commissioner got blind drunk and went berserk. Robert Bruce Verdal-Austin had served in the Ministry of Home Affairs for twenty-two years and was now DC for Mudzi. According to the evidence he gave, not only had he been involved in five landmine explosions, four of them in one day, but when he was posted to Mudzi he found administration impossible since Zanla controlled the outlying districts. In the latter half of 1979 the base camp had been subjected to two heavy attacks and morale was undermined not only by the battering from mortars, rockets and small arms, but also by the inadequacy of the Mudzi camp's own weapons.

Urgent requests for additional men and ammunition had been turned down. Inferior practice ammo was sent. As one witness put it, 'All we could do was try to survive.' But the tension took its toll. Everyone drank heavily and fights were frequent. 'I drank spirits from morning until midnight,' said Verdal-Austin. 'We dared not go to sleep earlier because that was the likely time for an attack.' He claimed that the sub-JOC at Mtoko was indifferent to their fate.

Besides Verdal-Austin there was a second defendant in the case – their crime, as we shall see, was a remarkable one. Graeme Bowie Duncan, born in Scotland in 1942, had come to Rhodesia at the age of 10, left the country in 1970, then returned in 1977, working first for the Ministry of Health then Internal Affairs: Duncan had been with Verdal-Austin in Mudzi since early in 1979 and he too drank heavily, mainly in the evenings. It was a grim time: not only had he been assigned to collect the charred bodies of the victims of the first Viscount disaster and to help relatives identify them, but, more recently, his best friend had been killed in Mudzi.

On 28 December 1979 the official cease-fire came into operation and Zanla cadres in the Mtoko area began moving towards their RPs. The bombardments of Mudzi camp stopped but the drinking didn't. On 5 January Duncan drank heavily, went to bed at 2 a.m. and rose at dawn after only a few hours' sleep. Together with Verdal-Austin and a third member of Internal Affairs, Philip von Memerty, he set out for Salisbury. The drinking continued. Before reaching the capital Duncan had consumed more than a third of a 'jack' of pure cane spirit and orange juice. Verdal-Austin and Duncan claimed at their trial that they had passed busloads of Zanla men being ferried by the Cease Fire Monitoring Force to APs; the guerrillas had jeered at the Land-Rover and its three white occupants, who were wearing Rhodesian military uniforms.

Although the journey to Salisbury was more than 150 kilometres, it appears to have been made with no better purpose than a protracted tour of the city's bars; when they set out on the return journey early in the afternoon the three were blind-drunk. Duncan and Verdal-Austin began to fire indiscriminately at motorists and cyclists travelling on the main road; by the time they were brought to a halt at a police roadblock they had killed two men – or so it was alleged – wounded others, and jeopardized the lives of many more.

Both Verdal-Austin, who was driving, and Duncan pleaded that they remembered very little of the return journey, apart from their vehicle breaking down. Duncan professed a hazy recollection of firing at a Daihatsu station-wagon – he kept the finger on the trigger longer than he intended and the barrel of the weapon (he said) lifted with lethal results. Both defendants pleaded that their actions had been politically motivated and designed to sabotage the cease-fire; the country was being sold down the drain, Zanu-PF would 'walk it', and the only way to arrest the slide was 'to blow this whole thing sky high'. Verdal-Austin said that he had advocated 'a full-scale, gloves-off, fight to the finish'.

Prosecutor Pollard was not impressed: in his view they had concocted their defence only when advised that the Governor's Amnesty Ordinance, which was confined to political offences, had been published. Why shoot at civilians on the road? Duncan's answer reflected the desperate mentality of the settler at the hour before midnight: civilians, he said, were legitimate targets because 'they were the backbone of the terrorist forces'.

On 17 April Justice Pittman sentenced them to ten years' hard labour on one count of murder and seven counts of attempted murder. On 27 September the Court of Appeal rejected their appeal, though Justice Goldin, who believed they were entitled to benefit from the Amnesty (General Pardon) Ordinance No. 12 of 1980, dissented.

5. that is no business of any-body

Ayoub Kara inserts a full-page ad in the *Sunday Mail*: 'Victory for the Bishop – as the men who promised to take this country by force accept the ceasefire terms. Bishop Abel Muzorewa. Victorious in all he does. Man of God, Man of Peace, Man of the People. Man of Power.'

The British allowed 'the Bish' to call himself Prime Minister and reside in the grandeur of 'Dzimbabwe', the mansion which Ian Smith used to call Independence when he was the occupant. White police guard the gate at the end of the driveway; black bodyguards at the door put you through an airport-type electronic security frame with your money and your keys screaming. Muzorewa sits at a table beside a glowering Ayoub Kara and complains how Marxism is swarming unhindered across the frontiers intent on collectivizing not only your farm and your business but also your car, your wife, your children, your wrist-watch.

'Wherever I go there is intimidation,' he says and looks really fierce when a couple of reporters laugh. The Bishop answers all questions except the most sycophantic (which are liberally supplied, like flowing mayonnaise, by the local Argus reporters) with the good grace of a pekinese caught by the tail in a door.

'Where do you get your party funds from, Bishop?'

'That is no business of any-body.'

'From South Africa, Bishop?'

'It doesn't matter so long as it's not from Communists.'

Later in the day black members of the BSAP will be entertained here at Dzimbabwe to drink beer and be warned of the fate of all Uncle Toms should the UANC be defeated. The Bishop will shake each by the hand.

6. Mugabe returns

The whites have shielded themselves from reality. Since both Zanu and Zapu were banned, and therefore Africans not permitted to demonstrate in their support, the whites have come to believe in the artificial euphoria surrounding the Bishop. On 24 December came a small shock, news of the first pro-Mugabe demonstration in Seke township. Worse was to follow on Boxing Day when thousands turned out to celebrate the homecoming of eighty-two Zanla and Zipra military commanders at Salisbury Airport. They came by bus, by bicycle and on foot from all the townships, broke down a security fence in their joy, and invaded the domestic terminal, forcing the

BSAP to unleash their dogs. Rex Nhongo and Lookout Masuku, 'demon murderers', were pictured walking together, hand in hand, smiling.

On 30 December Enos Nkala delivered a speech in Highfield in which he announced that Zanu-PF (as it was now called) would contest the poll separately and looked forward to a coalition Government with Zapu. Jongwe, the cock, was not Zanu-PF's original choice of election symbol, but the Election Commission would not allow the crossed AK rifle and hoe. On the other hand Soames did move in Zanu-PF's favour when he issued an edict which in effect froze for the duration of the election Sithole's High Court petition to prevent Zanu-PF from using the title Zanu in any form.

On 15 January Simon Muzenda, Vice-President of Zanu-PF, arrived from Maputo with 108 party officials, including Eddison Zvobgo. On 25 January the first full-page Zanu-PF ad appeared in the *Herald*, urging supporters to greet Mugabe at the Highfield rally scheduled to mark his return. Nkomo had been the first of the two 'external' leaders to return; he flew in from Lusaka bringing with him a Zapu girls' choir. The big man was immediately surrounded by British and Rhodesian security guards to supplement his own. Bearing in mind that every male Rhodesian worth his salt had vowed to kill Nkomo after the Viscount massacre, the police decided to uplift him by Puma helicopter from the airport to the welcoming rally at Zimbabwe grounds in Highfield. The crowd was vast: as usual Zapu had imported busloads of supporters from Bulawayo. The message, predictably, was one of moderation and reconciliation: Josh was not wearing his Soviet marshal's uniform today. His bitterness, now, was directed against Zanu's refusal to run with him on a single ticket. In anger he expropriated the name 'Patriotic Front' for his own party.

Both the British and the Rhodesians hoped that this rift would deepen and that Nkomo would move back into the 'moderate' camp. Ian Smith gave a speech (kiss of death?) recommending Nkomo to white voters as the best bet (not that they could do much about it). The British, unable to state their hopes and preferences publicly, concentrated their overt attacks on Zanla's alleged violations of the Lancaster House agreement. The Governor's spokesman, Nicholas Fenn, charged that Zanla was (1) maintaining 6,000 trained guerrillas on an operational footing inside Rhodesia, (b) packing the APs with mujibas and kids, (c) constantly bringing in reinforcements from Mozambique. As evidence of their displeasure, the British blocked the importation of Zanu-PF vehicles, banned the party's militant campaign literature and, most serious, withheld permission for Mugabe to return. The overt pretext for this was Zanu-PF's failure to release some seventy dissidents, including Gumbo and Hamadzaripi, who had been imprisoned since 1978 in Mozambique.

Zanu-PF produced a manifesto printed on cheap paper and crudely bound with a single staple. The PF, by contrast, relatively well funded (in Gwelo I followed a PF convoy of eight brand-new Toyota cruisers to Monomatapa township), published its manifesto on glossy paper with photographs and linocuts and a message so bland as to defy connection with the Leninist rhetoric issued by Zapu in Lusaka. (When, at the invitation of C. G. Tracey's Zimbabwe Rhodesia Promotion Council, Nkomo trundled into Meikles surrounded by British, Rhodesian and PF security men, to be 'briefed' by white businessmen, he said nothing about socialism and produced a most favourable impression.) The PF manifesto said that 'land belongs to the people', but just how it was to get where it belonged was not explained apart from a solitary reference to cooperatives.

Zanu-PF, on the other hand, promised large state farms and the voluntary collectivization of peasant holdings. The *Sunday Mail* gave Nkomo his due for moderation and warned that under Zanu-PF the state would own everything, the Christian calendar would be abolished, and it would 'not be long before church doors were closed . . .'. White readers naturally assumed that these horrors were promised in the Zanu-PF manifesto.

Mugabe finally left Maputo early in the morning of 27 January and ninety minutes later his plane touched down at Salisbury. After five years of exile, the man the whites most hated and feared had returned. He and Sally Mugabe were roughly handled and crudely insulted by white airport staff – the same people who fawned on them six weeks later. After a short press conference Mugabe proceeded, according to the time-honoured ritual, to the Zimbabwe grounds in Highfield, where probably the largest crowd ever assembled in Rhodesia euphorically hailed a man of whom it had little direct knowledge, since he had spent the past fifteen years either in prison or in exile. The next day whites were faced with a chilling aerial photograph of that vast crowd, that inky smudge of hostility, spread across the front page of the *Herald*. Nevertheless the *Herald* accorded greater emphasis to the return of sixty Zanu-PF dissidents who had been held in detention in Mozambique until the British negotiated their release. 'Mugabe accused of lust for power,' yelled the headline of 30 January. 'Mozambique detainees tell of torture, beatings and life in pits.'

Reluctantly the media had been obliged to jettison the term 'external terrorist alliance'. Since the Zanla and Zipra men gathered in the APs could no longer be described as 'terrorists' they were designated 'elements'; meanwhile radio, television and the press continued to treat communiqués and claims from Comops as gospel truth. Counter-claims were rarely reported.

Mugabe's first meeting with Soames was not a happy one. The air was thick with mutual recriminations. Even Nkomo was complaining how Zanu-PF had killed, abducted and harassed his people. The British cited the confessions of Zanla commanders captured and interrogated since 4 January as evidence of an overall plan to keep armed guerrillas at large in order to cripple the attempts of other parties to reach the people. Mugabe countered bitterly that Soames permitted the security forces and the auxiliaries loyal to the Bishop to move freely about the country while his own men were penned in their APs. Nor did he forgive Soames for having retained the 1,000 (Acland's own figure) South African troops deployed inside Rhodesia.

Soames lost no time (5 February) in showing he meant business by issuing ordinances endowing himself with power to ban parties or individuals from campaigning either nationally or in any of the fifty-six administrative districts. More ominous to Mugabe (as to Nyerere and other African leaders) was the Governor's assumption of the power to disfranchise a whole district if he judged intimidation to have reached such a level that a free election was no longer possible in that area.

On 9 February Mugabe and his Zanla commander, Rex Nhongo, complied with the British request that they broadcast round-the-clock appeals to their men to remain within the APs or, if already at large, to make for the nearest one. The Rhodesians were not impressed, claiming that Zanla cadres had been forewarned to ignore any such instruction. But Mugabe's relationship with the British was deteriorating. On 10 February he threatened to send Zanla back to war if the Governor banned the party locally or nationally. In a speech in Fort Victoria he described Soames as the 'chief violator' of the cease-fire and accused him of planning to tip the scales in favour of other parties. 'Nobody will play the fool with us. It does not matter how painful it may be – if forced to we will return to war.' Soames confined himself to banning further campaigning by the demagogic Enos Nkala and to banning Zanu-PF activity in the Triangle, Hippo Valley area. Mugabe reckoned he could win if only the people were allowed to vote; it would therefore be entirely logical for the British to stop them voting.

Few countries were ready to give Britain the benefit of the doubt; on 2 February the Security Council had voted 14–0 to rebuke the UK for failing to ensure free and fair elections. Even within the Commonwealth there was much suspicion and some anger about the free rein given to the security forces and the auxiliaries, the failure to release all those detained under martial law, the refusal to repeal harsh emergency legislation, the constant harassment of Zanu-PF.

7. the Guv

Soames, like the Pope, had no divisions of his own; and General Walls, like Field Marshal Stalin, knew it. The next best thing is moral authority, but Soames arrived with less of that than almost any Pope. Consequently the Governor's staff set about boosting his personality, in so far as he had any beyond the standard gestures and noises of his social class. A faintly regal mystique was cultivated.

'Up and about by 8 a.m., Lord Soames likes to tackle the new day on a full stomach, a substantial English-style breakfast. Over eggs and bacon he dips into his morning paper.' (Such a man can't be all bad.) At 9 a.m. his staff file in for 'morning prayers', a half-hour briefing session.

The mystique: fine food, fine wines (imported), with journalists and other guests invited in to express their views. Good listener. A portrait of Queen Victoria dominates the dining-room with a mildly reproachful expression. Soames takes a Churchillian catnap of ten minutes after lunch just like his Churchillian father-in-law, Winston Churchill. Informality the keynote. If time allowed he would spend his weekends bagging impala and pursuing deep-sea fish off Beira.

Christopher Soames, tall, moon-faced, bug-eyed, 59 years old, brewing family: he is said to have sold the brewery to Courage for £6 million in 1967. Eton, Sandhurst, Coldstream Guards, 1939–45. Right leg shattered when blown up by mine in Western desert. Later liaison officer with the French in North Africa, took part in the Italian and Normandy campaigns, Croix de Guerre. Served as Churchill's PPS 1952–5, married his daughter Mary, entered the Macmillan Cabinet as Minister of Agriculture in 1960.

Bit of a set-back in 1966: lost his seat. Was therefore amenable when the Wilson Government appointed him Ambassador to France in 1968, his main task being to smooth and soothe de Gaulle and thus open the door to Britain's entry into the EEC. In 1972 Heath sent him to Brussels as Vice-President of the EEC and there he stayed until 1976 when Roy Jenkins, rather than Soames, got the nomination as Britain's first President of the Community.

After a heart bypass operation Soames concluded that his political career was over and he accepted a life peerage plus directorships of Rothschilds, NatWest, etc. The good life continued, wine, gourmet cooking, his own racehorses at Chantilly. It was Thatcher who plucked him from the consolations of clubland and made him Lord Privy Seal, with a place in the Cabinet and special responsibility for the civil service. When Britain needed a Governor to 'achieve the impossible' in Rhodesia, Carrington sensibly avoided a Carver-type military figure and the choice – narrowed to Whitelaw or Soames

– fell upon Churchill's son-in-law. Much quoted is Iain McLeod's comment on Soames that behind the bluff exterior lay a bluff interior.

The Governor imported several aides, including Robert Jackson, a European MP who took a prominent part in the promotional lift-off the British media gave to Soames after his appointment. ('He knows how to be rude when he wants to be. Christopher is the nearest thing in British politics to an African politician. You can quite easily imagine him presiding at an Indaba.') Jackson felt that a Mugabe victory would be highly undesirable: 'One must hope for an anti-Mugabe coalition or a government in which he plays a minor role.'

Relations between the Governor and the Rhodesians remained strained.

Rhodesian Fronters constantly criticized Soames for dithering and for evading his clear duty to curb, ban, disqualify and generally clip the wings of Zanu-PF. Although it had been agreed at Lancaster House that no execution would be carried out during the British interregnum, an outburst of fury greeted Soames's decision to commute the death sentence of eleven murderers. The former Minister of Justice, Chris Andersen, who led the protests, provided the press with dossiers on eight out of the eleven cases; all were indeed brutal crimes, rape, robbery and murder, and in five instances the victims had been white. On 17 January Chief Justice Macdonald expressed the disgust of the Rhodesian judiciary and virtually accused the Governor of trying to abolish capital punishment by massive abuse of the prerogative of mercy. He advised his colleagues to go on passing death sentences in 'the confident belief that their function will not be undermined by unlawful action on the part of the Executive'.

When Walls, Allum and Ken Flower joined forces to persuade the Governor to ban Zanu-PF entirely, he compromised by only forbidding the party to campaign in the Chiredzi area. According to Miles Hudson (*Triumph or Tragedy*, pp. 188–9), at some unspecified date Muzorewa, Smith, Sithole and Ndiweni went to see Soames and demanded that the election be postponed, but on that occasion neither Walls nor Flower concurred 'and the proposal was quickly dropped'.

8. St Augustine's – the white backlash

Father Prosser's dealings with the Zanla 'boys' operating on and around the St Augustine's estate had become increasingly intimate. The priest himself had no choice in the matter. The local Zanla commanders, Hayden, Mike and Marvellous, took pleasure in calling on him. On one occasion Mike complained about the school's failure to accept more than one child from the local primary school in its most recent intake: the Principal promptly found places for three more local children despite their relative lack of academic qualification. He had also begun to issue bogus certificates of residence to the guerrillas, thus enabling them to masquerade, when unarmed and non-operational, as ordinary residents of the estate. These were deep waters in which the Principal had to swim or sink.

His miseries were compounded in December 1979 when two men whom he respected as friends of the African were killed by guerrillas. Guthrie Hall, 85, was murdered in his bed at his Imbeza Valley home. Don Harvey Brown, 66, was killed at La Rochelle the day after Hall's funeral. Ivor Tapping, who ran a forestry school, was the next victim, followed by Ted Wright, 65, who was ambushed on 30 December, two days after the cease-fire nominally came into operation. As a result the whites of Penhalonga were less than ever prepared to tolerate Father Prosser's notorious radicalism – though they little knew how far things had gone.

In that same month Father Prosser paid a visit to the Community at Mirfield in Yorkshire, largely to plead the case for keeping the school open, though two of his predecessors as Prior were advising that the Priory at St Augustine's should be closed by December 1980 at the latest. The Brethren were ageing and their number had shrunk from ten (when Prosser became Principal in 1974) to five. Even so, he once again won a reprieve.

The temperature round St Augustine's simmered as the summer rain-clouds sailed in low, like leisurely spacecraft, dropping their sudden tonnages of water as the black cotton wool split apart on the eastern hilltops. By no means all the Zanla cadres operating near the school had reported to their designated APs by 4 January. The police knew it: Zanu-PF must be defeated.

The local council at Penhalonga and various other authorities refused facilities for a Zanu-PF rally early in February, so Father Prosser obligingly made available the school football pitch, a muddy, waterlogged patch of grass from which champion teams never emerged. Zanla sent word that they should have been consulted. As the rally began the pupils of St Augustine's, succumbing to the security-conscious mania of the hour, decided to search everyone on admission; the police promptly moved in and took over the searching. This alarmed the kids because they knew that Zanla guerrillas would attend the rally and feared that some of them might be carrying concealed weapons.

'You realize what will happen if these people win,' said the Assistant Commissioner of Police to Father Prosser.

At the end of the rally, which passed off peacefully, the Assistant Commissioner lost his temper at the sight of joyous supporters milling round a hired bus, promptly declared the meeting to have become unlawful, and was much moved to collar everyone in sight. Father Prosser's indignation caused the Law to step back a foot in bitter deference to the Cloth. But his pleas could not prevent the police driving round the school campus in a snarling display of force: 'Mugabe or no Mugabe, we're still here!'

Whenever very upset, as now, Prosser had to wrestle with a demonic urge to write a letter to the *Herald*, just as Bishop Burrough of Mashonaland, unable to contain his anger at the threat posed by the Patriotic Front to British North Sea Oil and Civilization as We Know It, would automatically write to *The Times* in London. On this occasion Father Prosser failed to curb his pen and thereby once again crashed the sound barrier of national notoriety:

'Sir – I write in response to the large numbers of letters suggesting that the activities of Mr Mugabe's Zanu-PF are making it impossible to have a free and fair election at the end of this month. I regret this because surely it is really the other way round and it is the present considerable harassment of Zanu-PF that is making a free and fair election difficult.' The writer then detailed four ways by which Europeans were manipulating the outcome.

The letter pages of the *Herald* soon bubbled with heated replies, mainly from residents of Penhalonga. Mrs R. E. Rogers wondered how a man of God could reconcile the principles of Christianity with the avowedly Marxist aims of Zanu-PF. 'The mind', wrote Mrs Rogers, 'simply boggles.' In recent months, she pointed out, terrorists operating in the St Augustine's area had murdered at least seven civilians. As for the recent Zanu-PF meeting at St Augustine's (which Prosser did not mention in his letter), Mrs Rogers had been told that 'speakers displayed in abundant fashion their party's usual racist anti-white attitude and encouraged a hatred . . . towards members of the Police Force, some of whom were obliged to be present in their role of defenders of the peace'. Mrs Rogers concluded, very logically: 'If Mr Prosser is an unwitting tool of Zanla then he is a fool – blindly leading his flock into oppression.' If, however, he condoned the Marxism of Zanu-PF, he should be relieved of his post.

Another resident of Penhalonga, Mrs June F. Reeves, lamented in the *Herald* the extent to which this misguided cleric had been wooed by the ideologies of Marxism. 'The little wood and iron church at Penhalonga, one of the oldest in Rhodesia, used to have a small but regular congregation numbering twelve. This number is now down to nine because three fine, God-loving and God-living men have been butchered by the self-same people whose cause Mr Prosser is championing.'

On the day his letter appeared, Denzil and Peggy Fawcett wrote privately to

Prosser (he gave me his only copy of the letter – 'Keep it, what use is to me?'):

'My husband and I stopped attending Penhalonga Church some years ago because we have felt all along where your sympathies lie. We have continued to say our prayers at home and tried to live Christian lives (in spite of your comment from the pulpit last time we attended St Michael's that ours was not a Christian society). Some 24 of our friends have been killed by Zanu-PF (Zanla) men, and countless others wounded for life in this war. How can you possibly support a political party which has murdered your former Christian communicants at St Michael's and All Angels – Guthrie Hall, Don Harvey Brown, Ivor Tapping, Ted Wright. . . . May God forgive you, because we cannot. "We do not presume to come to this Thy table, O Merciful Lord, trusting in our own righteousness but in Thy manifold and great mercies. We are not fit so much as to gather up the crumbs under Thy table. . . ."'

The Fawcetts strongly urged Father Prosser to repeat this prayer before taking a communion service in any church.

The Provincial Commissioner of Police summoned the rebellious priest in a high rage and demanded evidence to support the allegations made in his letter to the *Herald*. Like his great predecessor, Sir Thomas More, Father Prosser did not cringe before the wrath of the secular power. Meanwhile, in the precincts of Salisbury's Anglican Cathedral, eyebrows were raised. 'Now, why, why,' murmured Dean John da Costa, clutching the edge of his chair with huge hands in a desperate bid for Christian self-control, 'why did Prosser write a letter like that despite those outrageous murders around Penhalonga? After all, he's a sane, calm Oxonian, a Mirfield monk, son of a clergyman. . . .' But da Costa did express the belief that Prosser had never given Zanla active help in the shape of food, clothes or money.

Two months later, after Mugabe's victory, Prosser wrote to me: 'There is a little "European" church in Penhalonga normally looked after by Francis Blake [one of the Brethren of St Augustine's] but I always go at Easter and Christmas as he is busy elsewhere. This time the church warden, who is also chairman of the governors of the school, told Francis that if I went the congregation would stay away. . . . So in the end they had no service, though I know some of them went to St John's, Umtali. But what hope is there for these sort of people accepting reasonable change?'

9. these things can't be done in a hurry

Both of Umtali's white schools had opted for 'community' status. At 7.30 in the morning a succession of cars draws up outside Umtali Girls' High School, dropping off white girls dressed in white socks, beige dresses, dark-brown cardigans and floppy hats in a brilliant primrose yellow. One child steps out of the armadillo shell of an ambush-proof Leopard: I put her age at 8.

The Boys' High School enjoys a dramatically beautiful setting – seventy landscaped hectares surrounded on three sides by tier upon tier of blue-green mountains between which summer clouds, sometimes fluffy white, sometimes ink-black with rain, move like low, slow-cruising spaceships. The Headmaster, Mr Peter Kolbe, points to a line of gum-trees on the hillside: that is the Mozambique border. And there – his arm shoots out again – is Cecil Kop, from which Zanla terrorists rained mortar fire down on the valley city.

Mr Kolbe is inordinately proud of UBHS's running-track, its five tennis-courts, two squash-courts, its fine swimming-pool, its gymnasium, its splendid games pitches. Although I call on him without warning, his response is typical of Rhodesian hospitality.

Generously he examines his enrolment records where – so it turns out – boys are categorized as 'white', 'Greek', 'Portuguese', 'Coloured', 'Asian' and 'black'. Then he becomes aware of my notebook. 'I'm disturbed that you're taking all this down,' he says. 'I'm wondering how much I'm out of order in giving you all this, I'm wondering in actual fact whether these figures are confidential . . .' Mr Kolbe is a chain-smoker.

Too late, it's all mine; out of 450 pupils there are still only forty-two non-whites: nineteen Asians (their parents own stores on downtown Main Street), eleven Coloured, and twelve blacks. Why is Mr Kolbe in a panic about this, bearing in mind that only a year ago no non-white boy had ever set foot in the school? Why?

In the school hall, a photograph of Churchill. Boys clad in white shirts and khaki shorts respectfully remove their green caps as Mr Kolbe passes.

'How much did it cost the parents here to buy this school?'

'Twenty thousand dollars payable over forty years.'

'That's one dollar per year per family!'

Kolbe nods and lights yet another cigarette. My pencil is still busy and he looks unhappy. Maybe I have got hold of the idea that the state virtually gave away public property to these white parents so that they could preserve their racial purity. Maybe he shouldn't have used the word 'influx' when describing what he feared. Anxiously he offers a brochure printed in green ink; it announces that the Governors will admit 'any pupil regardless of his or her colour, race or creed' *provided*, of course, that 'such pupil will readily accept and fit in with the traditions, way of life, discipline, and type of curricula' as have hitherto prevailed in the school.

'What could be fairer than that?' says Mr Kolbe, a born-and-bred Rhodesian of farming stock. 'Otherwise', he adds, 'the parents will simply up and away to South Africa, where education is free. We want to be able to study Shakespeare here, we don't need more black African history or compulsory courses in Shona. That's what people fear. It's a question of preserving your Westernized, Christian concept of education. Besides, we might be forced to play soccer here instead of rugby . . . if we suffered an influx.'

Mr Kolbe plays cricket for Umtali Casuals. Mugabe has just said something about Africans not taking to cricket in Rhodesia. 'Now that disturbs me. Throughout this war we at this school have kept our cricket and rugby fixtures going. Despite the danger of ambushes on the road, we played away matches against Peterhouse, Oriel and St George's. Colonel Soby of 3 Brigade agreed to provide us with an armed escort. Parents drove the cars and I always went along too. We left Umtali at 6 a.m. on a Saturday morning. We never had an incident.'

The school chapel stands on a small hill. His main worry is that the planned war memorial commemorating the forty-seven former pupils killed since 1976 will not be allowed if Mugabe comes to power. He shows me the book honouring the fifty-seven former pupils killed in two world wars, hoping no doubt that an Englishman will extend the validation to the counter-insurgency war against the guerrillas.

Out of 370 white members of the armed forces and 378 white civilians killed, forty-seven had attended UBHS.

And then we stumble across Mr Kolbe's guilty secret, a fine red-brick hostel, set amidst trees and flowering shrubs, empty. Locked up. Silent. UBHS once housed 260 boarders, but today prefers to make do with only 110 rather than allow an 'influx' of black children to fill the vacant places, the vacant beds in that locked-up modern hostel.

'I'd frankly rather you didn't report this,' he says. 'It could easily be misunderstood. I've been honest with you but I don't want you to twist anything I say.'

As it turned out, Mr Kolbe had the last laugh and the last twist. After my report appeared in the *Observer*, an advertisement soliciting pupils for Umtali's Community Schools was published in various Rhodesian newspapers on 31 August 1980:

'"*A paradise of games fields, athletics facilities, tennis and squash courts, set down in 120 landscaped acres*" – UBHS as described by 'The Observer' (London).'

The cutting was sent to me by a certain Rev. Father Keble Prosser, CR, Principal of St Augustine's School at Penhalonga. Prosser had once asked permission to bring ten of his History Sixth-Formers to a seminar on

Bismarck due to be held at UBHS. The request had been turned down flat with the added assurance that the African children would be incapable of understanding the proceedings.

10. dirty tricks (pvt) ltd

When Mugabe moved into his red-roofed bungalow on Quorn Avenue on 1 February, a high protective wall went up overnight. At the gate bodyguards frisked visitors in relays and treated your balls as potential grenades, not at all like having the inside trouser leg measured at Austin Reed's. Even so, grenades were hurled at the house on the night of 7 February (Kumbirai Kangai was hospitalized after a rocket attack on his home the same night) and three days later an expert attempt was made to finish Mugabe off while he was returning from a rally in Fort Victoria to the local airport.

Forty kilos of TNT were detonated electrically by someone concealed in long grass. Although a mine placed in a culvert failed to go off, the whole operation showed considerable expertise. Of course no one knows who was responsible, but it's worth noting that 4 Squadron Engineers were stationed at Fort Vic; their Commanding Officer, Capt. Charles Small, a Beit scholar and graduate of Trinity Hall, Cambridge, had been responsible for blowing up the Barragem road-and-rail bridge in Mozambique in September 1979 shortly before his helicopter crashed, killing all on board.

High-shouldered, beak-nosed, the most hated man in white Rhodesia. Mugabe walks across the lawn, yoga-fit under his smartly pressed suit, and treats the press to a sardonic indictment: 'It was obviously the work of the Rhodesian security forces whom the Governor has chosen to deploy. It is just one of the many strategies which have been worked out by the British, the South Africans and the Rhodesians to prevent my taking part in the elections.' Such was his respect for their capacity to do so that Mugabe attended no more rallies.

Edward Piringondo, one of the first black NCOs to have been commissioned, was a holder of the esteemed Silver Cross of Rhodesia. He was also a Selous Scout. In mid-February he and Cpl Morgan Moyo set out from Inkomo Barracks in a Renault-12 sedan, planted bombs in three Christian churches on a single night (two exploded, causing structural damage), then blew themselves into fragments while preparing to plant a fourth bomb in the Anglican church of St Michael in Harare. (So small were the fragments that the janitor of the church had to use dustpan and brush.) The RF and the press lost no time – as intended – in blaming Marxist atheism, but the culprits' identity was soon known and Comops maintained a sullen silence about the whole episode, causing even Bishop Paul Burrough to express disquiet.

Sunday Mail, 17 February: *Page 1:* 'Family clubbed, buried alive: girl returns from Zanla grave.' *Page 2* (beside a photo of the leggy Radio City Rockettes high-kicking in London): 'Gokwe looks peaceful but terror reigns' — District Commissioner says 411 auxiliaries in the area doing a fine job against Zipra terrorists still at large. *Page 3:* 'Zanla burn two women.' *Page 5:* 'Americans cheer as Smith lashes West.' Meanwhile the *National Observer*, the Argus paper directed mainly at African readers, published an opinion poll showing Muzorewa coming from behind and storming to victory. The paper did not, however, reveal that the poll had been conducted by a South African market-research outfit at the request (and expense) of Rhodesia's very own British South Africa Police.

Saturday, 23 February 1980, Sakubva stadium. Will Mugabe show for Zanu-PF's final rally? During the eleven days since the rather convincing attempt to blow him up on his way from Fort Victoria to the airport, the Zanu-PF leader has not ventured outside Salisbury. South African radio announces that he will not come. At Sakubva stadium stewards say he will. Getting into that stadium is heavy work, relays of stewards conducting body searches, women in this line, men in that. Then the long wait. Finally a fleet of cars arrives in the stadium: Tekere, Zvobgo — but not Mugabe.

Slogans: High Command! Central Committee!

The leaders sit high above the crowd, aloof and distant. Vhoterayi Jongwe! Pamberi ne Zanu-PF!

Dark clouds descend, a huge rain-storm, the crowd stampedes across the grass towards the covered stand, leaping the barriers and pushing up, up; I worry for all the young mothers with babies strapped to their backs, but the stewards hold the line, no one falls, no one is crushed underfoot, no dead babies . . .

I left the rally before the finale and drove to St Augustine's at Penhalonga. The police had put up a roadblock between Christmas Pass and the school to harass pupils returning from the rally. One boy was hauled off the bus for wearing a $(R)3 hat bearing the slogan 'This is Zimbabwe'. By the time Father Keble Prosser reached the scene, a local Afrikaner farmer wearing the blue uniform of the Police Reserve had corralled a knot of resigned teenagers at the roadside while awaiting transport to 'uplift' them to Penhalonga police station.

The rally and the subsequent police harassment sent the Sixth-Formers into a frenzy. They closed so tight round me in their common-room, their fears and accusations raced so fast and furious, that it was hard to believe that these were the same jovial, gurgling Fourth-Formers whom I had addressed two years earlier.

– 'The British are not even-handed!'

– 'Why does Soames use the auxiliaries against the people?'

– 'The British cheated us at Lancaster House! When the cease-fire was signed Umtali was about to fall to Zanla. . . .'

– 'It is we, the people, who suffer!'

The common-room was thick with overlapping voices and raw nerves – their desperate sense of a dream almost within their grasp yet doomed, inevitably, to be vapourized by the white vampire's plots, stratagems, dirty tricks, black propaganda, slush funds; by 'British plans' to surround and incinerate the guerrilla APs, to rig the voting, to bring in 'ten South African divisions if things go wrong'.

And how could I raise a convincing tenor to assure them that all this was fantasy and fabrication?

11. the arrest of Garfield Todd

Shabani Special Branch had been itching to get Garfield Todd for years but had never managed to pin a specific charge on him. Given that his intercourse with Zanla and Zipra guerrillas had become, though not by his own choice, a way of life, his survival entirely depended on the loyalty he inspired among local Africans. When the Lancaster House amnesty neutralized any evidence on file, all danger seemed to have passed.

Todd returned to Rhodesia at the end of January 1980 having been abroad for almost five months. Contrary to expectations, the danger facing him was acute. Virtually a law unto themselves, the Rhodesian security forces had embarked on a final, savage campaign of repression designed to keep Zanu-PF out of power.

The Headmaster of Dadaya, Samuel Mutomba, was in trouble. Early in 1978 a certain Amin Mutensa had taken over as Zanla group commander. Guerrilla demands on the school thereafter became oppressive: the teachers were forced to pay out sums of $(R)50, even $(R)100, at least once and sometimes twice a month, as well as handing over radios, clothes, anything. Amin drank too much; he was reckless. Yet it was only after the cease-fire that Samuel Mutomba set eyes on him for the first time – hitherto he had always dealt with intermediaries and subordinates. While the majority of his guerrillas departed to the designated APs, Amin remained at large and walked around openly, unarmed.

It was at Amin Mutensa's insistence that a long meeting took place at Dadaya throughout most of Sunday, 27 January, during which the staff were made to sing Shona songs, chant Zanu-PF slogans – and hand over more money for 'election expenses'. Mutomba gave $(R)150 out of his own pocket.

Four days later Garfield Todd arrived home. In Bulawayo he received a call from the Postmaster at Dadaya, Ephraim Thebe, to the effect that someone wanted to see him. The call was tapped by the police, whose tails lifted a little in anticipation: this time, maybe. When GT reached Dadaya Post Office (the smallest in the world), Ephraim introduced Todd to three Zanu-PF militants, of whom Amin was one, though Todd did not know his identity as a guerrilla commander. They asked for money to pay the deposit on a car needed for the election campaign. Next day GT met them outside a bank in Shabani and handed over $(R)300 in full view of his employees who were there to collect their wages. It was not the action of a man who thought he had something to hide.

On Tuesday, 5 February, Amin was arrested in the Wedza TTL, given a thorough beating in Shabani Special Branch's torture cell – a squalid, one-storey, corrugated iron shack surrounded by a fence of tattered hessian – and forced to confess. In any case Amin's diary apparently contained the names of those who had paid up, including Mutomba and Todd.

At long last the SB were laughing. Inspector Carl Gibbard drove out to Dadaya and arrested Samuel Mutomba at 1 p.m. on 8 February. Having ransacked the Headmaster's house, the SB found in his bedroom two letters from Amin, further evidence that he had been consorting with terrorists. Mutomba tried to explain to Inspector Gibbard that he had been completely helpless against this highly dangerous man, who posed an acute danger to Dadaya and its entire staff.

'That school of yours could close down now,' Gibbard told him, visibly elated by the prospect. Mutomba spent the night on a concrete floor without even a blanket to cover him. The cell, which contained only one small bucket for pissing and worse, rapidly filled up with new prisoners. Sleep was impossible. White civilization was playing its last card.

As soon as he learned of Mutomba's arrest, Todd, Chairman of the Board of Dadaya, telephoned the police. He was advised to come to the station in Shabani the following morning, a Saturday. He said he wanted to come straight away: 'I intend to set things in motion tonight.'

'You'll regret it if you do.'

The next morning Judy Acton, paying her first visit to Hokonui in eight years, accompanied her father to the police station. On arrival GT was arrested under the Law and Order (Maintenance) Act, that old friend which

Governor Soames had declined to repeal. Now 72 years of age, Todd was charged under two counts: aiding and abetting a person in the commission of acts of terrorism; and failing to report the presence of terrorists.

'Anyway, that's the nitty gritty,' said Det. Sgt Clarke of JOC Shabani.

Todd refused to make a statement. Accompanied by Inspector Carl Gibbard (who had emigrated from Chelmsford, England, only five years before), GT was allowed to return to Hokonui to pack some things and say goodbye to Grace. Once again the satraps of 'law and order' began to whine in the face of the man's vast moral authority. Standing on the stoep, Gibbard fawned:

'If it crosses my desk I have to deal with it. I don't like it.'

Judy took the opportunity to put through emergency calls to one of the Governor's senior British aides in Salisbury, and to Martin Meredith, correspondent of the London *Sunday Times*. History was repeating itself, if not exactly: this time she had no need of a hurried bath with Policewoman Pronk standing guard.

Gibbard led the way back to Shabani in his grey Mazda van. At the Magistrates' Court GT and Judy (who insisted on accompanying him) came across an unshaven figure dressed in a blue safari suit and apparently hastily called in from his Saturday game of golf: this was the Magistrate, Mr S. B. Finch. The Prosecutor, who was wearing a T-shirt at the time, argued that it was essential to lock Todd up without delay lest he repeat the offence, hop the country or intimidate witnesses. Mr Finch took the point. Todd mentioned that he had an appointment to meet the Governor three days later but Mr Finch very properly did not allow himself to be swayed by such irrelevancies.

Judy said goodbye to her Dad at the prison gate. They were both completely stunned and incredulous by the turn of events. Judy soon learned from friends in Government House that the basis of the case against her father was the diary of a captured guerrilla leader.

GT was ignorant of this. 'When I was taken into the prison, I went through the routines. I was given a bar of soap and a roll of toilet paper, told to take my clothes off and put on the prison shirt and trousers. But neither the shirt nor the trousers would fit me, so I had to sit on the bench while they tried to find a pair of trousers that would fit me. When they got them, there were no buttons on them, so I had to sit there while they found a tailor to get the buttons put on. I was still sitting there when a detective inspector came back to say I was going to be released. So I put my own trousers on again.'

The British had interceded. Advised by his Salisbury lawyer to make a statement to Attorney-General Brendan Treacy, Todd did so. When he met Soames as scheduled on the 12th, the Governor said, 'I'm awfully glad you went to see the Attorney-General about it.' Todd also spoke to Mugabe who had, however, other things on his mind, notably the series of attempts on his life. Not until 21 February did the Attorney-General finally drop the charges.

But Samuel Mutomba was neither white nor famous. Three days after his arrest he was taken from the filthy, overcrowded Special Branch cell to prison, via the Magistrates' Court. The atmosphere was ugly, desperate; as the election approached repression intensified. Four black CID officers worked Mutomba over using 'vulgar language and personal insult'.

'You people think you're so clever,' they sneered, 'you think you know everything, you and Mr Todd, but now we've got you, you're foolish not to support a government which gives you a living. The terrs will take away your job and your pension.'

The Dadaya Postmaster, Ephraim Thebe, was also having a rough time. It was he whose phone call to Todd in Bulawayo had been tapped by Special Branch, and it was inevitably the latter who took Thebe along with five Dadaya teachers to the notorious 'radio room' where the confessions were customarily extracted. According to the Postmaster, they were all beaten up by the same white police officer who had acted as Todd's prosecutor in court, and by Inspector Carl Gibbard, in an attempt to get them to 'admit' that Todd had known Amin was a terrorist when he gave him the $(R)300:

'You're trying to protect Todd. But he wouldn't help you. He's up there in the big house, with his wife, drinking tea.'

Ephraim Thebe says he was beaten on the cheek and shoulders with a stick, then made to sit on the floor, shown a sjambok of hippo hide, and ordered to turn his back. It was too much: Ephraim decided to 'confess', to give his tormentors the story they wanted. After his release he signed an affidavit retracting his confession. I sat with him on the stoep outside his tiny Post Office and he finally fell silent out of sheer grief.

When Samuel Mutomba was released on bail on 18 February his troubles were not over. Getting Todd, nailing Todd, remained local priority number one for Inspector Gibbard, whatever he may have mumbled on the stoep about things just crossing his desk. As Mutomba discovered when summoned, the short, stoutish Gibbard sat, together with his black moustache, at a desk under a beaming portrait of Bishop Abel Muzorewa.

'I've got more evidence against you and Todd,' Gibbard warned the Headmaster on the very day that the Attorney-General dropped the charges. 'If you give evidence that Todd knew Amin was a terrorist I'll do everything in my power to lighten your sentence.' Mutomba shook his head. 'Listen,' said Gibbard, 'if Mugabe wins you can always say we beat you up. But if you don't cooperate and Muzorewa wins, you could face the death sentence.'

Mugabe won. Only then were the charges against Mutomba dropped. A vast peace and a great happiness descended on Hokonui, on Dadaya, on Zimbabwe. GT became a Senator. Mrs Grace Todd was appointed one of seven trustees of the Mass Media Trust, which holds 46 per cent of the shares of the main national newspapers. In the fullness of time Robert Mugabe visited Dadaya and reminded its pupils that Garfield Todd was one of relatively few white men who had positively contributed to the liberation of Zimbabwe. The Prime Minister addressed Mr Mutomba as 'Comrade Principal'.

As for Pilate's soldiers, the white terrorists of the SB who had plied their trade behind fences of tattered hessian, some drifted away in disgust, others gritted their teeth and clung to their pension plan. As GT had once predicted in a moment of characteristic prescience, not one of them had done anything to anyone, nor had they known anything about anything.

12. Father Killian Huesser

At 2.30 in the morning of 19 February, Killian Huesser, a Bethlehem Father, was assaulted at the remote mission station of Berenjena. Shot in the leg and bleeding from multiple stab wounds, he died at 9 the following morning in the arms of weeping women whose prayers could not atone for the absence of medical help. Comops, dutifully echoed by the media, blamed Zanla for the murder, but the consensus of opinion among Catholic priests and laymen in Gwelo diocese was that Father Huesser had been the victim of one more dirty trick.

13. brown shirts

The Goromonzi district lies some thirty kilometres east of Salisbury. It's a hot spot, a place of battles and bitterness – after Independence it became the most dangerous area of Zimbabwe for white farmers. But that's another story for another day. Now, in February 1980, Goromonzi is overrun by Pfumo reVanhu auxiliaries in coffee-coloured uniforms. Their commander says he was once a Zanla freedom fighter but 'it was no good' so he came on-sides. Many of his men are recruited from the squatters' camp at Harare and there you have the vicious circle.

The auxiliaries have a camp at Goromonzi heavily fortified, a sea of mud from summer rains. Under the scrutiny of journalists, they resemble the cat who has just killed a rabbit in the garden and now pads politely, decorously, across the carpet to rub his soft fur against your leg, his paws and jowl whistle-clean. But the dark glasses with the mirror lenses are not reassuring, nor their leers and their pathetic aping of white Rhodesian slang ('zapping the gooks').

At the DC's office Inspector Don Joss of the BSAP complains that 'unarmed terrorists' are holding meetings at night and 'politicizing' the people: 'They cache their weapons but people know they have them so it's intimidation.' Questioned about the 185 Pfumo reVanhu under his command, Joss denies stoutly that they carry any political affiliation – their sole passion in life is reopening schools, clinics and dip tanks. The District Commissioner agrees; but he is clearly finding it difficult to accommodate to the new semantic rules and he can't help referring to the 'internal' and 'external' parties.

One cannot exaggerate the rage these men feel at the sight of Zanu-PF campaigning freely. The war is over now, but to prove it isn't they furnish us with a flamboyant armed escort transported in trucks bearing South African registration plates. 'If you get an RPG7 rocket through the vehicle, no one's going to be smiling.' Later the Member-in-Charge halts our convoy as we climb up out of a deep gorge and then discharges round after round of machine-gun fire at the surrounding rocks 'just in case'.

The British Election Supervisor for the area, Maj. Jon Wainright, radiates optimism and geniality: India, Kenya, the Lancers, Ascension Island, 'I've been in Africa before, you know.' In his view the auxiliaries are doing a splendid job, they're under strict discipline and indeed 'they're indispensable'. Does the Major ever move among the people unescorted, to hear their views? Actually, no – too dangerous, one could get lost, so he invariably takes along auxiliaries or black District Assistants who are 'extremely disciplined chaps'. But does this mode of self-presentation not inevitably associate him in the minds of the local people with a detested colonial administration? The Major recoils: 'You can tell from'the way they laugh and chat in a group. Wherever we go people are extremely cheerful and polite.'

It's a breed. These fine old colonial servants with their floppy hats, leathery skins and tins of Three Nuns were chosen on account of their experience of 'Africa'; meeting Rhodesian officials who wear British-style uniforms and call themselves by familiar titles – Superintendent, District Commissioner – the British walnuts imagine they must be witnessing another of those impartial operations which were the glory of the Empire at its sunset. In Seki township I come across a benevolent old figure in baggy shorts and a red skin, Election Supervisor C. Campbell, who spent thirty years as a colonial servant in Kenya and worked as a magistrate there during the Mau Mau uprising.

'The DC and the police run a neutral exercise here,' he says, 'no problem of bias at all. District Assistants? Good blokes, highly respected.'

Yet a few miles down the road, in Dema township, the Zanu-PF chairman has been arrested after a legal rally because some of his supporters were heard chanting 'Pamberi chimurenga' (long live the armed struggle) and 'Pasi Muzorewa' (down with Muzorewa). Right under old Kenya Campbell's nose white reservists of Patu are distributing anti-Marxist leaflets, when not too busy trading their tinned rations for fresh food from the African stores.

The day ends at Goromonzi with a corpse carefully preserved, *in situ*, for display purposes: a young man, 18 or 20 years of age, lying on a rocky hilltop some fifty metres from a small kraal, a neat hole in his head, the waistband of his flower-patterned shirt stained red. This mujiba had allegedly been in the act of throwing a stick-grenade when shot by an eight-man police patrol; everything is on hand, the unexploded grenade, the eight-man patrol. But one bronzed young white in khaki tells me that this bloke had been trying to 'gap it' when they shot him, only later had the grenade been found 'on the ground'.

The corpse has no shoes. On the third finger of his left hand is a broad ring embossed 'Zanu-PF'.

14. early-morning power – Selukwe

Selukwe: here Ian Smith was born, here he still has his farm. The road from Gwelo down to Shabani twists dramatically through densely wooded hills and valleys and for many months it was considered suicidal to travel along it except by armed convoy. Now, soon after 6 a.m., the mists lift, layer upon layer, irradiated by the rising sun, and abruptly the Zanu-PF candidate turns his car off the tarmac road into the tribal trust land. Ten kilometres along the broad dirt road we brake gently: running towards us are some fifty auxiliaries in brown uniforms, the youngest scarcely 12 years old and barely able to carry the weight of their rifles but their expressions alive, delirious, with early-morning power.

Gathered round the Coke store in the tiny business centre of Donga lounge a bunch of cocksure hoodlums from Salisbury – the Bishop's retainers, Mack the Knife's gallant friends. The money, they explain, is good and also the power; besides, do we not realize that Communism takes from you not only your wife but even your fountain-pen? Most of these philosophers are normally unemployed but others command good jobs in Salisbury: evidently employers like the Cold Storage Commission grant leave of absence, pro- vided, of course, it's in the service of the Bishop, the last hope and last ditch of the white man. These city slickers boast how they work hand-in-glove with the auxiliaries here in Selukwe TTL, handing out beer and, as they put it, 'hitting people who open their mouths'.

We say goodbye.

We drive into the mysterious land beyond the shimmering blue horizon where no white man ventured in recent years except when programmed to kill. The Zanu-PF candidate and his comrades decamp on a patch of grass under two msasa-trees, near a village school. There is no one in sight, but the candidate and his comrades don't look at all put out. Soon the people emerge from the countryside, silently except for the faint rustle of grass, many of them in 'Zanu-PF Will Win' white T-shirts.

Snuff is scattered to appease the spirits and then the peace is disturbed by the roar of diesel engines, by armour-plated machines of war which disgorge a dozen police reservists, pink, beefy and faintly contemptuous. They will remain in the background, keeping their distance, leaning on their guns, smoking, while the black scribe they have brought – the official informer – sits under the msasa-trees taking notes in English which will later be sifted for evidence of illegal phrases and banned styles of agitation.

One chap, a Mancunian who emigrated fifteen years ago, suggests that the best election result would be twenty–twenty–twenty (which doesn't add up to eighty seats, but one gets the drift).

'Communism, the Afs don't know what it is, do they?'

Presently a single-engined plane appears overhead, circles, flies in low over the meeting, scattering leaflets, then disappears in a businesslike manner, the large white cross on its fuselage glinting in the sunlight. Everyone laughs: the leaflets remind voters, in the name of the Electoral Supervisory Commission, that the ballot is free and secret. 'To the People of Selukwe. Your Vote is Secret. No One Will Ever Know How You Voted.' The slogans and the songs continue – Pamberi ne Mugabe! – including one or two banned ones – Pasi Muzorewa! – The sky is vast, the singing high, the orator a man whose eloquence emerges from the passage of his people from night into day; their eyes never leave him; the smile on his face is that of pure, sustained pleasure, the smile of cool water bubbling over hot rock. The women ululate, a high wail warbled by a palpitating tongue. . . .

Everyone sings now, 'Motherland Zimbabwe, we've suffered long enough, but we'll be happy. . . .' Then the slogans: 'Pamberi ne Mugabe! Central Committee! High Command! General staff! Masses! Pasi puppets! Voteri Jongwe!'

The local candidate is S. E. Mativenga, tall, hawk-nosed, an accountant from Gwelo who stands sixth on Zanu-PF's electoral list for the Midlands (by no means all the plums and rewards are falling to the returning exiles).

Mativenga is fiery: socialism is good, collective farming is good, under the present system a handful enjoy the profits of the soil and the mines while everyone else is toiling.

'You people here are tilling the poorest land of Selukwe while the white farmers over there [gestures] possess the richest soils. Do you want their land, do you?'

'Yes!'

'Have you been forced to come here?'

'No!' (Cheers, laughter, sidelong glances.)

Mativenga says Carrington sent Soames to help Muzorewa; the candidate then breaks the rules by saying 'Pasi Muzorewa' and the impassive young scribe seated on the ground under the tree notes it down.

The local Zanu-PF District Chairman is a tubby businessman who holds his trousers up with braces because of his stomach. His name is T. Gandire and he is prolific with tales of horror, of midnight raids on his home, of hiding in the bathroom, of piles of human bones in the police camp at Donga. He names two white farmers who burst into his house on the night of 20 February accompanied by Pfumo reVanhu and who on one occasion had threatened to shoot him while he was filling his car at a Selukwe petrol station. He claims that Mr L., president of the local white farmers, not only broke people's arms but forced villagers to attend a UANC rally on 15 February.

I warn Mr Gandire that I must check the story out and he seems delighted. Later I phone Mr L. twice but get no reply. Perhaps he's busy murdering Mr Gandire or fleeing to South Africa with Mr Gandire in hot pursuit.

At 10 the school bell sounds and the children leave the meeting in a single unprompted movement. The candidate and his comrades reckon it's time to drive to the next meeting deeper in the reserve (the white police reservists will follow) and an old man comes forward and claims that earlier that morning auxiliaries had forced people at gunpoint to attend a UANC rally a few miles away. A good story! We drive for ten minutes in the direction indicated by the old man's gnarled finger and there, at the burnt-out stores he mentioned, we encounter fifty Pfumo reVanhu auxiliaries.

The meeting, they vaguely explain, was 'cancelled'. We stay in our car: there is the traditional deference in their expressions but also something else, here and there – the uncowed gangster glare of the Congo, of Amin's Uganda, the moment when the black soldier, like the lion that has once tasted human flesh, loses his respect. A tall fellow in dark glasses and a grin out of Central Casting sidles forward and asks to see our 'papers'. Time to leave, skidding tyres kicking up yellow dust.

15. by hook or by crook

On 19 February Mr Nicholas Fenn, spokesman for the Governor, listed for the benefit of the world's press those tribal trust lands where parties other than Zanu-PF had been able to penetrate only with 'limited success' – intimidation by Zanu-PF being the obstacle.

In Gwelo, and throughout the Midlands, there is a very keen electoral contest between Zanu-PF and Nkomo's PF, for here is a region inhabited by both Shonas and Ndebeles, an area penetrated by both armies of liberation, Zanla and Zipra. But if you go to the PF offices in Gwelo the complaints of intimidation are directed, in the main, not against Zanu-PF but against Muzorewa's auxiliaries. In Gokwe, an area largely loyal to Nkomo, the Pfumo reVanhu moved in immediately Zipra withdrew to the assembly points. When two PF activists, Havaidi and Gakanje, went to put up election posters in the Gwehava and Bopoma areas of Gokwe on 15 February, they were arrested by auxiliaries, detained for two days and then ordered out of the district by an auxiliary commander who signed himself 'District Commissioner Mangwende'.

In Wedza TTL the army and the auxiliaries filled the vacuum left by Zanla after the cease-fire, rounding people up and herding them to a meeting to denounce Mugabe at Mount St Mary's mission. Bringing added sophistication to Dirty Tricks (Pvt) Ltd, PsyAc distributed leaflets in the reserve designed to persuade people to vote for both Nkomo and Mugabe (and thus unwittingly spoil their ballot papers). All this was recounted by Father Pascal Slevin, once Principal of Mount St Mary's, later deported, and now returned.

'Now, I do think that's criminal,' said the Irish Franciscan.

It's true that Lord Soames was not happy about 'his' security forces engaging in blatantly partisan electoral activity, but Comops and Internal Affairs were not deterred. Fenn was ruefully to admit that security forces were distributing political leaflets in PVs right up to the first day of polling, in disregard of the Governor's prohibition. Pamphlets which rained down on villages depicted a happy peasant tilling his land behind two yoked oxen: 'True freedom lets you use your land as you wish, to make your family prosperous.' Juxtaposed was a picture of forced labour under the sneering leers of guards carrying Communist AK rifles: 'Marxism Socialism – your land will be taken and run by the State. Those who are supported by Communist Russia – will rob you of your land.'

South of Salisbury, in the Seki TTL, four white reservists of Patu, two of them accountants, one a town-planner and the other a trainee jeweller, confess how sick and weary they are of serving 140 days a year in the sticks, living off tinned food.

'Yes, we're certainly afraid of the outcome. If Mugabe gets in we don't know what will happen. We've been distributing anti-Marxist leaflets but of course we're not allowed to meddle in politics. These simple people have no idea what Communism is. Mind you, I suppose the TTL system is a form of family-unit Communism. . . .' He shrugs, weary of it all.

'I can tell you,' says another, 'if there's any trouble in Salisbury we'll be out of here and back with our families, orders or no orders.'

The whole objective was to defeat Mugabe – the entire capacity of white Rhodesia was mobilized to achieve this one aim. In Umtali the establishment gathered in the Cecil Hotel periodically to be briefed by Colonel Soby of 3 Brigade. Provincial Commissioners informed closed meetings of Internal Affairs staff that a Marxist government must be prevented; in mid-January Rhodesia's top cop, Peter Allum, delivered the same message to a closed meeting in the Fort Victoria area. 'By hook or by crook' was the phrase used by an Assistant Commissioner addressing BSAP personnel in Salisbury when describing the lengths it was permissible to go to to ensure a victory for the Bishop.

One British Election Supervisor, David Glendening, who was for a time blocked by JOC Thrasher and the Provincial Commissioner of Manicaland, Bob Cunliffe, when he attempted to visit Mutasa South TTL to investigate alleged Zanla intimidation, discovered a supply of anti-Marxist pamphlets in black-and-green covers stacked in the DC's office. He later learned that PsyAc had been responsible for distributing them and that Internal Affairs had ordered the DC not to let Glendening catch sight of them.

Increasingly desperate, the Bishop ran a strident scare campaign. Full-page ads depicted the mutilation of everything precious, prosperous and traditional: 'This is what Communism means. Death. Oppression. Suffering. Poverty. Starvation. Human Misery.' No man would retain his land or his business in Communist Zimbabwe; the state would snatch 'your beloved children' and send them to toil on state farms or be indoctrinated in Marxist schools. All churches would be turned into army barracks, concentration camps and – oddly enough – 'dance halls'.

16. I've been trying to get you for months

Zanu-PF claimed that 10,000 of its officials and activists had been arrested in the course of the campaign. Take, for example, the Midlands region. In

Umvuma the party's District Chairman and Treasurer, Nevy Masendeke and Laxson Dzabula, were among twenty-five arrested. At Lalapanzi, the local Organizing Secretary and Chairman, Messrs Majange and Kufirwa, were locked up in Wha Wha and told they would not be released until they had signed an admission of 'guilt'. The police specialized in admissions of guilt. Zanu-PF supporters returning to Umvuma by bus from a party rally in Bulawayo on Sunday, 17 February, were dragged to the police station and not released until they had signed confessions. Document: 'Admission of Guilt No. 274970. Arrested by Constable Rusere No. 25198. Mary Makere admits guilt under Offences Act, Ch. 68, "Riotous Indecent Conduct".' That these confessions were usually obtained by force cannot be doubted: one of the women who 'confessed' later produced a clinic 'Out-Patient Record Card' No. 421/80, dated 19 February, confirming that she had been kicked in the head by the Special Branch.

At the southern end of the Midlands constituency the SB engaged in a good deal of head kicking, particularly in and around the town of Shabani. It was here that Fred Matanga, officially accredited as Zanu-PF liaison officer with the police, was dragged from his car by UANC men and taken to the SB; it was at Shabani that Zanu-PF activists were arrested for possessing 'illegal' campaign literature; it was at Shabani that Garfield Todd was arrested and a systematic attempt made to present legal campaigning as collusion with terrorists; it was at Shabani that three Parliamentary candidates, Julia Zvobgo, Richard Hove and Zimbarashe Mubengegwe, were arrested at a police roadblock and remanded in custody until 22 February (little guessing that Hove would later assume responsibility for the Zimbabwe Republic Police as Minister of Home Affairs).

At Shabani the JOC and the SB worked in tandem. When Donny Haanei, a Zanla commander operating in the Belingwe area, heard a radio appeal by Mugabe, he led 118 men to Keyara army base camp to link up with the Cease Fire Monitoring Force. But the Rhodesian security forces intervened and 'uplifted' the Zanla men to JOC Shabani where they were beaten up and informed it would be sensible to join the Bishop's auxiliaries. Haanei subsequently made his escape and brought a habeas corpus action in the High Court on behalf of the 118 Zanla guerrillas who had been under his command. In response the Attorney-General's office accounted for only twenty-two of them, all said to be in prison.

More than once the police raided and emptied Zanu-PF's headquarters in Manica Road, Salisbury, on the pretext of a bomb scare, and then embarked on fishing expeditions in the party files. Nathan Shamuyarira, a member of the central committee (and future Minister of Information) was arrested at 2 in the morning on 25 February in the Mushandira Pamwe Hotel, Highfield, on the amazing pretext that a man claimed to have been beaten up on the previous Saturday night by Zanu-PF. Led by Supt Hyam and accompanied by dogs, Southerton police hammered on his door and then held him for nine hours, even though Shamuyarira had demonstrably spent Saturday night in Umtali.

The all-white Gutu coordinating committee, consisting of farmers and officials, sent Soames a telegram urging him to proscribe voting in the whole area on account of Zanla intimidation. 'The secrecy of the ballot is no guarantee for people who believe in witchcraft. People have been herded like cattle to vote for the very ones who murdered their families.'

As the polling days approached the Rhodesians reproduced the scenario of the internal election a year earlier. On 20 February, 3,000 police reservists began their call-up. Once again they were out in their blue floppy hats, erecting roadblocks, waving through cars driven by whites, emptying buses and searching their black passengers at the roadside. On TV one could see heroic volunteers, blacks this time, waving batons and riot shields and charging imaginary mobs – in preparation for what? The message was clear: after the election business would be as usual – except for a final reckoning with the supporters of a certain party.

Despite the church-bombing disaster, one last Dirty Trick was obligatory. The target chosen was the Mambo Press at Gwelo, a publishing-house run by progressive Catholics, Swiss-born Bethlehem Fathers, whose dissident publications had continually provoked the wrath of the RF and the intervention of the censor. Mambo was now once again free to produce the banned paper *Moto*, which vigorously challenged the propaganda emanating from Comops and the Muzorewa camp. On 22 February a fake edition of *Moto* was being given away free on the streets, its front page carrying a venomous attack on Mugabe, insinuating that this ruthless, power-hungry Marxist heathen had, as a result of surgery and of 'experiences endured with other male convicts while in prison' become a homosexual eunuch of vicious, paranoid disposition. The scurrilous motif exactly echoed a Ministry of Information pamphlet hatcheting Samora Machel – one need look no further for the source of the forgery. No sooner had Mambo protested about this counterfeit edition than its presses were blown up at 2 a.m. on Sunday, 24 February. Once again the bombers were unlucky and dismembered themselves.

An inquest was held on 25 April in Gwelo. DSO Duncan Scoular reported having reached the scene of the explosion at 3.30 a.m. Later a leg was found and near it a Tokarev pistol. Covered by rubble was a headless, armless torso which appeared to be African, with a second Tokarev pistol near it. Two other legs were discovered and a Beretta. An African skull lay twenty-five metres from the seat of the blast. Dr Paula Nydam had examined a section of a scalp and concluded that the skin was fair with a thick covering of dark, straight hair of the Caucasian type.

17. the writing on the wall

27 February 1980. By mid-morning the queue outside Harare's main polling-station stretches for a quarter of a mile. In rural areas the first light of dawn reveals long columns of peasant voters extending to two or three kilometres in length. The line in Harare is quiet, sober, in the immediate vicinity of the polling-station; but turn the corner and you are greeted by wave after wave of crowing 'cocks', young men prancing and strutting like roosters. Police reservists withdraw into mute gloom: what they see and hear is a denial, a rebuttal, of everything they have been led to believe.

A truckload of black soldiers of the RAR proceeds up Jameson Avenue crowing deliriously. White shoppers avert their gaze: the writing is on the wall.

In Kambazuma township a circle of young men closes ten-deep round the writer. They speak passionately of land, liberation and land again and they complain bitterly of police harassment, of threats from local gangsters of the Pfumo reVanhu. They specify: over there, outside that shop . . . this morning . . . a big car . . . a certain well-known man . . . A shell-shocked official of the UANC pushes his way through to inform my pen and therefore the world that he is switching allegiance to Mugabe.

Here and there small knots of UANC women keep dancing gallantly, chanting their love of the little Bishop.

18. we've got to forgive these people

In the European farming area of Wedza the farmers bring their labourers and their families to the mobile polling-station on tractor-drawn trailers. The whites gather apart, chat to the officers on duty, take photos of the British bobby sweating under his helmet, and glower at the yellow press card pinned to my shirt – like Southern plantation-owners witnessing the arrival of a Yankee carpet-bagger. Is the Confederacy about to fall? Will the slaves put sentiment before self-interest and desert their masters?

'How do you think they'll vote this time?'

'No idea. They're keeping it to themselves. But we do know that Zanu-PF has been sending people out of the reserve at night to talk to the labour force. What worries me is the prospect of a $(R)100 minimum wage. No ways can I afford that.'

The farmer leans his rifle gently on his boot. 'I believe we've got to forget the past, we've got to look to the future, we can make a great nation here if we all pull together. But if Mugabe stops all the state credit coming into these farms here it's an attack on private enterprise.'

The farmer adjusts his hat; the sun is high and very hot. This man is bursting at the seams.

'We've got to forgive these people for their evils and savageness. I've been in this war for six years, I've seen my friends shot and I'm not prepared to take any nonsense, next time if these external terrorists try anything we won't be so polite about it. We'll sort these gooks out. You've got to keep on top of these guys. I've personally always held that every man should be treated on his merits, regardless of creed and colour. I mean, we have a very special type of black man here in Rhodesia, a very decent bloke, but he wants to be left alone to grow his maize and to sleep and to have his wives – we should never have imposed our Western ideas on him. I mean, it's the same story in Northern Ireland, isn't it? These people have no excuses at all if we continue to look after them, but they think they can just walk into these farms here and take them over.'

In the dusty market square of Wedza township stands a dapper young man of small stature and genial aspect. His name is Sidney Sekeramayi; he is a doctor of medicine whose training has been acquired not only in Sweden and through the British Royal College of Surgeons but in the less clement climate of Chimoio. I ask him about land reform, not suspecting that Mugabe will shortly appoint him to precisely that portfolio. When I express scepticism about his party's genuine commitment to Marxism, he replies, 'Some of us are Marxists and some are not,' adding, to my surprise, that his regular reading of the *New Statesman* had not led him to suspect that I was any kind of Marxist either.

'The big turn in the war', says Sekeramayi, 'occurred when the secondary-school children began coming over the border. There you have the link between the leadership cadres and the peasantry; our leaders will not become aloof from their poor relatives.'

I mention Djilas's book *The New Class*. He knows it. He is full of confidence; victory is assured. He glows with youthful idealism.

Some yards away a group of four heavies in flashy suits are leaning against a big American car scowling at us. A strong smell of Sithole. It was here in the

Wedza TTL that thirty-nine of Sithole's auxiliaries were massacred by Zanla about a year ago. The heavies are giving us the long, slow Chicago look. I approach them. Their spokesman is K. N. Malindi, Sithole's deputy during the Geneva Conference, who had enjoyed a couple of months as Foreign Minister in the Transitional Government. His voice is loud and deep:

'Zanla has herded the people to the polls like sheep. They have their armed men in the TTLs, the Bishop has his armed men in the TTLs, but our auxiliary forces have been eliminated.' From Malindi's barrel chest comes a slow, villainous laugh that would do credit to Captain Hook about to feed little children to the crocodiles. 'But after the elections', he warns, 'we will have our own men in the TTLs. And next week I expect all the foreigners will have gone and probably we will do a little bit of a blood-bath in this country.'

19. Delta

The 270-kilometre drive from Salisbury to Delta assembly point takes one through Mrewa and Mtoko, possibly the most savagely contested of all fighting zones. The blue ribbon of tarmac, maintained in perfect repair by the war machine, winds through wild countryside dotted with huge rock kopjes under the vast, cloud-flecked African sky. Tribespeople walk up the middle of the road, scattering at the last minute like surprised Bushmen. The roadside is littered with burnt-out stores and roofless shells. Brown-shirted Pfumo reVanhu lounge in the shadows.

Towards the Mozambique border the terrain becomes more mountainous and more beautiful; and the premonition is not unlike that felt on approaching a wildlife park from which the beasts of prey are inclined to escape with unpredictable results. A dirt track, turn left . . .

I am looking out for a checkpoint manned by Zanla guerrillas. For five kilometres there is no sign of life, just wheel marks in the yellow dust, and then some kids are coming up the road, or leaving the road, kids in coloured shirts, jeans. Is it a village or what?

It's Zanla. They have left their rifles inside their camp because the law prohibits a man or woman from voting while carrying a weapon. They come down the broad track to the polling tents, in regular phalanxes of sixty, men and women together, moving at the double, mostly in canvas shoes, some bareheaded some not, their chanted war cries interspersed with wolf-pack howls and menacing grunts; here, then, are the men who would have killed one, ambushed one, lurked by the roadside, set fire to the farm buildings, fired rockets through the walls . . . the terrorists. 'Pamberi ne Mugabe! Pamberi ne Mugabe!' Their chanted slogans are larded not only with phrases learned from Frelimo – 'viva', 'imperialismo' – but also with words harvested in distant Swahili territory.

The freedom fighters, these untouchables of the bush, halt in unison, listen attentively to their commissar, then march forward in single file under the orders of a black sergeant of the BSAP – the very Uncle Tom they would gladly have shot down a few weeks ago as a 'sell-out'. This may be less anachronistic than that celebrated exchange of greetings between Tommies and Fritzes on Christmas Day, 1914, but it does stir inconclusive thoughts about the echelons of etiquette by which we pass from war to peace (or vice versa). Dressed in every imaginable garment out of the Portobello Road market, the guerrillas await their turn under the cool, neutral scrutiny of white Rhodesian police officers. The vakhomana stare straight ahead – like soldiers. For ten minutes the guerrilla bows to the world he rose against. But for no longer. The phalanx of sixty re-forms, the harsh, challenging, guttural cries ring out, and the dust stirs as they double in unison up the hill.

For the sake of form the British Election Supervisor has brought along representatives of all the parties to observe the voting. None but Zanu-PF would have dared set foot here otherwise; and none but Zanu-PF is going to pick up a single vote among the 2,700 inhabitants of Delta AP.

Within the bandit camp the tents of the CFMF, mainly beleaguered Aussies with a few Brits, are separated from the vast Zanla encampment by a single, thin rope. Relationships are 'correct' – easier now than when Zanla was on the verge of breaking out of Delta to have a go at encircling Rhodesian units. Greg Pike, a Captain in the Royal Australian Regiment, reckons two-thirds of the men and women in Delta are credible as genuine combatants.

The female guerrillas here number 600 and are by no means to be regarded as camp-followers. The first two women who were officially listed by Comops as dead fighters rather than as 'women running with terrorists' died in November 1976. Throughout 1979 bulletins reported women 'terrorists' killed in combat. Strongly built, with big bottoms and large breasts, the women affirm their military status by greeting visitors to Delta with a fiercer disdain than do the men.

'Very good at carrying heavy loads,' comments the Zanla liaison officer, Takawira, a compact figure in khaki fatigues slashed by vertical streaks of brown.

Capt. Pike pays tribute to Takawira, not only for his skill in handling visiting Rhodesian officers, but also for the influence he exerted in maintaining 'quite remarkable discipline' in the early days when the camp was bereft of food and they were awaiting the first air drop.

Behind the thin sector-rope stands Comrade Chris. He wishes to see our passes; there is no entry to any Zanla camp without written authority from the High Command in Salisbury; obtaining it involves a Third-World tour of the city in search of officials who (inevitably) 'just went out . . . some place . . .'.

A handsome fellow, Comrade Chris describes himself as a freedom fighter who has trained in 'many countries' but declines to specify which, apart from 'Central Europe' and 'Central Africa'. Comrade Chris is 23 and claims the average age at Delta is 20 to 27 – whereas Captain Pike reckons it's 15 to 25. Later, in June, the Mugabe Government announced that 50 per cent of guerrillas in assembly points were aged 19 to 24. Only 15 per cent were aged 18 or under.

Comrade Chris sports a blue T-shirt with the word 'Stockholm' prominently displayed on it, a check buttoned shirt on top, a red beret, khaki trousers and brown boots. Over his shoulder he carries a sub-machine-gun. 'We are political soldiers,' he says at every opportunity (there are many). 'We follow the orders of the party.'

Will white people have a place in Zimbabwe?

'Of course, we are not Russia. We are not tribalistic.'

What does he feel about the 10,000 comrades who have fallen in the war? He shrugs, neither accepting nor refuting the figure. 'War is war,' he says. 'In war you are my enemy. I am your enemy. War is war.'

What about the killing of sell-outs?

Instead of another 'war is war' he guffaws disarmingly: 'We are not Russia.'

Was food a problem in the bush?

'Never a problem. People sent many things from Salisbury.'

Were some phases of the war harder going than others? Did morale ever sink?

He tilts back his beret, smiles: 'Aaaah . . . aaah . . . we were ever victorious. Ever.'

Why had the guerrillas closed schools and dip tanks?

'That is enemy propaganda. We never did this thing. Security forces closed schools. Aaaah . . . they were getting a lot of money from these dip tanks, a lot of money . . .'

'Who was?'

'The Government. But we never close them, we can't let animals die of disease . . .'

Does he fear a Rhodesian air strike against Delta?

'We don't know their motives. We never trust them. Never.'

The crucial question – what will you do if Zanu-PF does not win the election? – is one which no one cares to pose.

20. end of the world

Tuesday, 4 March. During the hour before 9 a.m. the mood in Harare market-place is curiously passive, sullen, fatalistic; no longer cocksure, having been cheated often before, the squatters and market traders expect to be cheated again.

As the Moment approaches a crowd gathers round a radio. When Eric Pope-Simmonds, Registrar and police reservist, begins his solemn, lugubrious declaration, it sounds like white man's mumbo-jumbo and structuralism teaches us to anticipate a white man's result. The people of Harare market-place, whether refugees, squatters or traders, are expert structuralists.

Patriotic Front . . . twenty seats . . . (Nkomo).

United African National Council, three seats . . . (Muzorewa – incredulous whistles).

Zimbabwe African National Union, no seats . . . (Sithole – hoots).

Zimbabwe African National Union Patriotic Front, fifty-seven seats . . . Uproar. Mugabe! Mugabe!

The pattern of voting is crystal clear. The Bishop is smashed, obliterated. Nkomo gets all but five of his twenty seats in Matabeleland. Conversely, Zanu-PF picks up only one seat in Matabeleland. The tribal divide between Shonas and Ndebeles, then, is close to absolute.

Mugabe's percentage (71) of the black seats somewhat flatters his percentage (63) of the popular vote. Zanu-PF's vote logically entitles it to only fifty seats, one short of an overall majority. Instead Mugabe has fifty-seven.

Finally, 2·7 million people have voted compared with 1·8 million in 1979. This reinforces the suspicion widely held in 1979 that the Government statistician Myburgh's projection of a voting population of 2·9 million was too low.

But the crowds swirling through the streets of Harare and Highfield are not consulting their pocket calculators, nor are they preoccupied by abstruse questions of demography. One man waves a dummy AK rifle. The police observe but do not intervene. A special noon edition of the *Herald* sells at street corners like the proverbial hot cakes: 'Massive Win for Mugabe', 'Bishop Shocked and Puzzled', 'Nkomo Accepts the Outcome'.

They dance up Manica Road. Whites recoil. Busloads of cheering youths drive through the centre of town. A white lady says: 'Mugabe will abolish

Christmas and Easter.' Another, drawn by my notebook, doubts whether she can now put her mother into an old people's home, since such places don't exist under Communism. Most whites hurry past, refusing to talk; one or two bitterly blame the calamity on 'people like you'.

'Who will maintain law and order?' a businessman asks. 'Standards will go to pot.' In a gunsmith's shop the young owner snarls, 'No comment.' A schoolgirl in a green dress complains, 'How can they vote for terrorists who burnt down their own schools and houses? This country', she says, 'has gone.'

In the doorway of an insurance office on Manica Road a huddled group of white women employees peep timidly at the victory celebrations as if to step down on to the pavement in full view would be to incur murder rape black africa. Some of them are clearly suffering from clinical shock. One says, 'Why couldn't they have done all this junketing in 1972 and saved us a war?' Another, describing herself as a refugee from Indonesia, announces: 'Communism – I know what it's like.' An old lady on Manica Road takes a long, horrified look at the jubilant crowds of blacks and slowly turns her neck away: 'You see, they're causing trouble already. Power has gone to their heads. One of them put his fist under my face. He said, "I'm the boss now." Soon they'll start pushing you off the pavement. It only requires a spark . . . They're savages at heart – there are some brilliant men among them. South Africa's next on the list.'

Another lady shies away. 'I think I'll keep my opinions to myself.' But she can't. 'I'm originally from South Africa but I've lived in Rhodesia for thirty-five years. I thought Muzorewa would get thirty-five seats. He got . . . how many? Three? Three!' She shakes her head. 'He lost popularity because Africans want everything to happen immediately.' But doesn't she look forward to peace now? She shrugs. 'The war will go on. Mugabe has so many armed men in the field. That man is a strong person, a dictator. Muzorewa was softer but he was a good man.'

Tuesday, 4 March, marks the nadir of white morale. It is the Day of Despair. Many women snatch their children out of school. A woman working in the recently reopened British Airways office in Baker Avenue says she will leave Rhodesia, after twenty-five years. There is panic.

A leading accountant is immediately inundated not only by phone calls but by desperate clients hurling themselves into his office. 'I felt like a doctor.' A woman in her 40s heading a leading nursing agency calls in to describe Mugabe as a Marxist in sheep's clothing – but she will never go to socialist Britain. A wealthy farmer from Marandellas wants to know how he can buy silver bars to smuggle out of the country. 'I can't live under Communism,' he says.

The telephones of estate agents ring continuously while orders pile up on the desks of the removal firms. At Fox & Carney half a dozen houses are put up for sale within forty-five minutes; nothing like it since Angola 'fell'.

The whites wheel out their toys: heavy guns, troop-carriers, armoured vehicles. At street intersections and junctions on the outskirts of Salisbury, the soldiery stages a pantomime display of final resolve. Housewives and secretaries bring cups of tea to the statuesque warriors of the RLI, guardians of our shopping precincts.

'I'm willing to give these people one chance, but only one,' a troopie remarks. 'We built up this country and I'm not prepared to hand it over to a bunch of gooks.'

'I take my hat off to these fellows,' a middle-aged woman says.

At least one-third of white primary-school children stay at home. Security forces ring the schools. The Agricultural Marketing Board is one of numerous organizations which simply close for the day at noon; end of the world. When one of its staff, a member of the Grey's Scouts, arrives home he finds a note from his wife; she has lost no time in driving over the border into South Africa.

The women of a Charismatic Catholic prayer group convene in a state of high emotion. Customarily they thank God for this and praise Him for that, quite pentecostal, slipping in a few supplications at the end. But for what, now, is He to be thanked? The Dutch nun who customarily heads the group is missing, a bad sign. Spontaneous and informal, the prayers begin: 'Thank you, dear God, for teaching us how unsearchable are your ways. You have sent us this trial so that we may endure it. We deserve to suffer.'

A black lady cries out: 'Lord, we have been frightened of this Mugabe!'

An older black woman says in Shona: 'Lord, Mugabe has killed many in my village, please give him a change of heart.' The white ladies cautiously, then eagerly, develop this theme – perhaps Mugabe is the prodigal son who returns to his original Catholic faith. The Bible is scrutinized for confirmation and the emphasis of the meeting shifts; the white ladies now discover that 'We are the elder brother who was the horrible brother and drove out the prodigal son and we ask your forgiveness, Lord'.

Mrs Thatcher is on her feet in the House of Commons: 'The Governor is to be warmly congratulated. So is the Army, the Monitoring Force and the Police.' What Mrs Thatcher does not report to the House is that Lt-Gen. Peter Walls, granted advance intelligence over the weekend of Mugabe's outright victory, has sent a cable urging her to set aside the election result on the ground of massive intimidation.

21. let us join hands

'Operation Quartz' became redundant. The army and police were stunned: their intelligence reports had pointed to a hung result and therefore a coalition led by Nkomo and supported by the Bishop, by Smith, and by the minor black parties – an anti-Mugabe coalition. The plan was for troops to seize key buildings, surround the Zanla assembly points and, if necessary, bomb them. A final reckoning, or merely a prophylactic precaution?

At 8 o'clock on 4 March Mugabe spoke on television. Virtually every white person in Rhodesia over the age of 4 watched in horror as their own dear Jill Baker – the Angela Rippon of Rhodesia – introduced him as 'Comrade Robert G. Mugabe'.

'We will ensure', Mugabe told the nation, 'that there is a place for everyone in this country. We want to ensure a sense of security for both the winners and the losers.' There would be no sweeping nationalization; the pensions and jobs of civil servants were guaranteed; farmers would keep their farms; Zimbabwe would be non-aligned. 'Let us forgive and forget. Let us join hands in a new amity.'

By the morning of 5 March the majority of whites were back at work, their children back at school. Mugabe offered David Smith the Ministry of Commerce and Industry. Smith accepted, even though his party, the RF, remained hostile to the new Government. Denis Norman, President of the Commercial Farmers' Union, accepted the Agriculture portfolio. His desk was piled high with telegrams of congratulation from white farmers, some of them ironic in tone, but all indicative of desperate relief. Fear, hope, suspicion, disbelief, exhaustion – the familiar cycle of those hurled into a state of shock.

At Umtali Boys' High School the Headmaster, Mr Kolbe, confessed himself 'shaken' by the size of Mugabe's victory. 'Me, I was shattered. It looks like a Communist regime.' Mr Kolbe clutched at a straw: 'Mugabe and his wife are both teachers, that means he must be an elitist, I mean he must want to preserve standards. . . .'

Not the least bewildering to the whites was the rapid abandonment of sacred shibboleths and beloved symbols. Exasperated by the new heresy, a 'Proud Relative' wrote to the *Herald* on 12 March in defence of the Selous Scouts: 'They wear their badge with pride. . . . Now their very name is becoming a dirty word. They are reviled, besmirched . . . anything and everything of a filthy nature is attributed to them.'

22. loaves and fishes – St Augustine's

At 11 a.m. on Tuesday, 4 March, two hours after the radio announced that Zanu-PF had won a stunning fifty-seven seats, including a clean sweep here, in Manicaland, three armed vakhomana turned up at St Augustine's to join in the celebrations. Their presence was reported, almost certainly by the children at the primary school who had fathers in the police. Vastly embittered and quite keen to show the Rev. Keble Prosser that power still lay where it always had lain, a combined police–army force from the Grange, Umtali, engulfed St Augustine's on 5 March. Soldiers rifled the dormitories of valuables and tore down Zanu-PF election posters they held to be illegal. A police officer asked the Headmaster of the primary school how he had voted.

That evening a number of police children were set upon in reprisal and beaten, though not seriously. On the following day, Thursday, Police Member-in-Charge Jerryman came storming back to demand whether Prosser could 'guarantee' the safety of the police children in the primary school. The priest replied that he was unable to guarantee anyone's safety, even by means of prayer. Jerryman, who had the air of one who meant to continue in office whatever History's verdict, warned Prosser that the school 'would pay' if anything happened to the police children.

A couple of guerrillas were snatched in huts just up the hill: their stubborn refusal, even now, to move away to their assembly points exasperated Prosser.

'Do you think I should leave this place now, make way for an African? Or would it look as if I were quitting because of majority rule?'

Postscript: About thirty of those who had crossed the border and joined the guerrillas eventually returned to St Augustine's to finish their studies. They did not brag or boast of their experiences: Father Prosser discovered, rather, an almost traumatized reticence, and a desperate desire to resume a normal life.

23. Anglican rage

The events of 1980 left Father Prosser's Bishop, Paul Burrough, somewhat stranded on the beach of history, but he gave no hint of having noticed. In mid-January he was back in *The Times* under the name of '✚Paul Mashonaland': 'Whereas nine months ago there was an election by 64 per cent of the voters which was deemed to be free and fair by the British Government itself, it is now clearly impossible for an election next month to be other than fear-inspired and the victim of venality and force.'

The Bishop was beside himself. On 9 January the *Herald* published a peculiar letter in which he complained that if Zanla and Zipra military activity was officially deemed 'unlawful' from 4 January, this must imply a British view that they were previously lawful. No, he roared, 'the marxist-inspired bands of Zanla and Zipra were and are criminal'.

But was the resounding popular verdict which brought the Mugabe Government to power not enough to quell Burrough's indignation? No: the 'very timid' Shonas, he told *The Times*, had concluded that only through appeasement could peace be restored.

'Suppose that in England 22,000 heavily armed IRA terrorists were encamped at 14 points round the country, moving in and out of the camps and in touch with another 5,000 of their fellows who were living among the civilian population. Would the English people, with not a gun between them, hold out against handing over Northern Ireland? This is a fair analogy of what has just happened here.'

So little had the Bishop of Mashonaland understood his flock.

The National Affairs Association frequently borrowed the Anglican Cathedral church hall to hold its regular lunchtime meetings. But when the Very Rev. J. R. da Costa had learned that leaders of Zanu-PF and the PF would be invited to address the NAA's pre-election meetings, together with leaders of all main parties, the Dean of Salisbury adamantly refused to lend the hall. 'As the mortal remains of many people killed in the war lie within the same precincts, it would hardly be possible for me to welcome those who had publicly stated that they caused such persons' deaths,' declared the author of that famous sermon, 'A Deafening Silence'.

The Dean was not in any way subdued by the election result. Large of hand, foot and mouth, careless of phrase, he wanted to know why the West had allowed the front-line states to decide who should rule here. Like Bishop Burrough, da Costa explained the vote for Mugabe purely as an appeasement, a desperate desire for peace:

'All that political claptrap about the toiling masses; jargon and clichés do their work. And why is the West so weak? I mean take Afghanistan – we should just go to these fellows and say, if you don't cut it out we'll cut off the grants.'

He paraded much gloom. 'They'll keep the church schools closed. Atheistic education's on the way, and I don't mean secular education either. There'll be a war of attrition, an erosion of confidence in the churches. It's all a stepping stone in the plan to bring down South Africa.' Da Costa lauded the white economic infrastructure: 'I've no patience with all that claptrap about colonialism. Most of thē white farmers here are good people, even if they give their workforce an ear bashing from time to time. I knew some real bastard farmers in South Africa but also some good paternalists who take their staff into the familia like the best British aristocrats.'

He was touched that a large number of Cease Fire Monitors and Observers had visited the Cathedral to pursue their devotions. 'General Acland came here early on Ash Wednesday with his Chief of Staff. They came humbly to kneel.'

Nor did he intend to quit. He would stay and he would remain true to his principles – 'Unlike the Catholic Church which waits till the horse is twenty yards from the winning post then puts all its money on it!' A huge snort.

24. don't give me any of that 'comrade' shit

Two young soldiers are drinking Castle lagers in a roadside bar at Rusape, staring in morose silence at a group of Afs across the road who are strutting and crowing and laughing enough to make you want to lift your FN. 'Pamberi ne Jongwe!' The two white soldiers are apprentices in civilian life, both employed by the Shabani Asbestos Mine and both hollow with chagrin and disbelief. We fall into conversation, then their mood changes and they want to beat me up, a shit journalist, so I offer them a lift to Salisbury. The ground rules of Rhodesian chivalry forbid an assault from the moment one enters someone's house or car: 'The army told us a pack of lies they told us Mozorewa would win I reckon the Russians had it all sewn up I mean when we bring in the terrs now we can't even shoot them we just let them go free I've had terrs tell me Mugabe sold out at Lancaster House they're very cocky with all this "comrade" shit I say to them don't give me any of that "comrade" shit not me listen, next time I don't mind what our orders are I'm not going into the bush we're sticking around the towns to look after our families I mean Zanla and Zipra can go into the bush to get these gooks I mean you should live here for three months to see what they're like you give them a finger and they'll take your hand power is all they want they're hungry for power so they can fill their pockets mind you that Mugabe bloke might just be different you can't read the bugger's mind I tell you nobody here trusts him an inch next time it'll be South Africa he had these bases in Mozambique so now he's going to do the same thing against South Africa right? I'm going down there to fight this thing once and for all I mean we've got to stay here and take what comes soon they'll try and take our guns I'm staying here because this is my country but I've got no security so I'll leave but you tell me where I can go I'm not a racialist I'm prepared to work beside a munt or sit in a bar with one or some wog which I can tell you I wasn't prepared to do a few years ago no way but the world was against us and sold us out just because Russia or Communism wanted to get its hands on what we'd built up in this country there's nowhere like Africa I can have a car and go fishing in the dams I can go with my friends and have a drink four times a week and still have money in my pocket you try doing that in a pub in the UK it's very relaxed here I mean I've done two and a half years in the bush and boy I've had it up to here but if you go to South Africa there's this agreement that within three months you'll be called up into the army and you can't get a job unless no qualified South African applies for it I'm an apprentice fitter and turner and my friend here is an electrician we're due to get our papers at the end of the year that means $(R)700 a month instead of $(R)300 and subsidized housing even after tax and deductions you take home $(R)600 but I'm not staying no way I don't give a shit for this country I mean I'm not a racialist but I hate the munt after what he's done to this country I mean it was the munts who suffered in the war you take these black artisans in the mines they get the same pay as we do but they don't need the money your munt has his hut and his mealies and that's it I reckon that Mugabe is really bright that one he won that election with his black box story and his sky satellite story he knows how to put everyone to sleep but you give it sixteen months and you won't find hardly a white person here and I'll tell you why it's because they won't leave us alone sixteen months I don't give a shit what they do except they'll give us this Marxism he's been talking about for the last four years I'll switch off the lights if I'm the last one out.'

Bottle-tops litter the floor of the car. So long as they remain in my debt I am in no danger. A miniature tape recorder – nicknamed Verbatim – turns in my inside pocket. Their aim is to settle into the Park Lane Hotel with several crates of beer and break up the town before it disintegrates.

25. they now belong to your country

At the remote Papa AP, Zipra form a smart guard of honour for their national Commander, Lookout Musuku (who wears a Soviet-bloc, some say East German, peak cap, high and stiff with that distinctive wide circumference at the top) and, more bizarrely, for Brig. John McVey, Commander of Hurricane, their old foe. Also taking part in this vital drama of reconciliation are two top Rhodesian cops, Senior Assistant Commissioner 'Cordy' Hedge and the ranking SB officer for Hurricane, Supt Keith Samler (in whose head, no doubt, reside the intimate secrets of seven years of counter-insurgency). Watched by mild-eyed Britons of the CFMF, a new, national, 'non-political' army is born in hearts and mind. The guard of honour goose-steps away, Soviet-style, tea and biscuits are served, the water supply is now safe.

It's all very odd – the hammer and sickle embroidered on uniform collars, Soviet fur hats, red stars, the lot. Yet the Rhodesians and British realize that these emblems mean nothing; Zipra is not only the more disciplined of the two guerrilla forces, it's also the more conservative force socially and, under Nkomo, the less resistant to rapid integration. Already a Rhodesian Police Support Unit has moved in here, at Papa.

But after Mugabe's election victory Zanla is more amenable. The same Brig. McVey arrives at Rathgar Camp near Mtoko with the Rhodesian Army Chief of Staff, Maj.-Gen. Derry Macintyre, and the British Commander of the CFMF, Maj.-Gen. John Acland. Acland informs the 620 Zanla men, who have been moved from Foxtrot AP, that Mugabe has asked Britain to help train a united national army. Cdr Agnew of the Zanla High Command addresses them in Shona: 'We won the election and we must not become impatient but await developments. Meanwhile, listen to your British and Rhodesian instructors and everything will be all right. And do not fire your guns at aircraft as they now belong to your country.'

To mark the change from guerrilla life to regular army training, the Zanla men at Rathgar are given tents with steel-framed beds and electric lights. They abandon their beloved AK rifles for G3s. And an Irish Guards drill sergeant called Barry Lynas begins bawling at them day and night on a hurriedly bulldozed parade-ground. The guerrillas at Rathgar no longer operate under their own command structure and are suddenly required to obey the following absolutely: eighteen British members of the CFMF; six black instructors from the former RAR; and, most peculiar of all, their new camp commander, Maj. Peter Morris, the zealot who trained RAR recruits at Balla Balla to hunt down 'Communist terrs' (to whom he invariably referred with the utmost contempt).

Meanwhile, Comrade Steve, a Zanla officer, makes an inspection tour of a sub-JOC in the Mount Darwin area, riding pillion on Sgt Alan McCormick's motorbike. At AP Charlie, where Comrade Steve is normally to be found, only 240 out of 1,500 Zanla men will opt for a non-military career.

26. as the referee . . .

When it was all over the Governor allowed himself a little mellow reflection over drinks at Government House and in a lecture delivered at Oxford University. At the gate of Government House on Chancellor Avenue British redcaps continued to take no chances, searching all cars under the bonnet, in the boot, under the chassis, while other impassive sentinels patrolled the immaculate lawns surrounding a bungalow evidently designed for the Indian earthquake zone.

Tall, beaming and pop-eyed, Lord Soames describes Mugabe as a very intelligent fellow who has never served in a government and wants a shoulder to lean on. 'He realizes he has inherited a going concern. He has seen what happened in Mozambique and what happens if you try to do it all too soon.'

Did Soames feel proud of his achievement?

'As the referee, I wanted to see the game played to a finish. But I could not simply turn a blind eye to malpractices going on in some of the scrimmages. Nor on the other side did I want, if I could avoid it, to award so many penalty kicks to one side that the other walked off the pitch – as well it might.'

Happy outcome – but it could have been blown sky-high any time. Meetings with Mugabe had originally been sharp, confrontational, each man flanked by his aides across a table, charges and counter-charges, until Soames decided to talk to him alone on the day before polling began. Soames had chosen not to disfranchise any part of the country – that was the point.

After that everything was jolly good. Mugabe referred to the Governor as 'my good friend' and even said 'let bygones be bygones'.

'My great fear', says Soames – has everybody got a drink? – 'was that Mugabe would get less than an absolute majority, in the middle or late forties, and that after we British pulled out floor-crossing would take place and the new Government would collapse.'

Think about that. It can mean only that if Mugabe had got less than fifty seats, Soames would have put together a coalition *without* him – a coalition which would have crumbled as Members crossed over to Zanu-PF.

No other interpretation is possible.

Above the fireplace in the reception room a portrait of Cecil Rhodes gazes towards the rose garden, impassive, inscrutable, one of the great white knights of the African Round Table.

27. we tried to play it straight down the middle

Both the *Herald* and the *Sunday Mail* turned somersaults to appease and flatter the new masters. Mrs Sally Mugabe's taste in clothes and cooking was suddenly of cardinal importance. In despair, the *Sunday Mail* argued that the election was not what it seemed:

'Before the election we said it was a vote for moderation or Marxism, Christianity or Communism. In truth political ideologies or religious convictions played little part in the outcome.'

Stampeding to join the new era, the Argus papers began frantically to stick knives into that staunchest of allies, South Africa, even though the controlling shareholding in the papers was South African. Unable to compose its own revolutionary prose, the *Mail* turned in despair to the syndication service of the London *Observer*, a liberal newspaper whose correspondents every Rhodesian farmer traditionally longed to shoot or flog: 'The more frustrated Africans grow under a system that denies them political power, the likelier they are to turn to armed struggle and violence. When that happens the leaders are branded as "terrorists". . . .'

Roland Fothergill, editor of the *Herald*, now 58 years of age, had served with the 2nd Parachute Brigade in the Med during the war. Flush-faced, gradually overtaken by the years, he was due to retire the following month. Whatever his paper might *now* be saying about South Africa, that was where he wanted to live – if only he could take out his money and his worldly goods. 'We've always been against apartheid, but I'm not sure South Africa is ready for majority rule yet.' Clearly Mr Fothergill wasn't.

Only nine out of sixty editorial staff working for him were black. Bias during the campaign, not to mention over the years? Not at all. The *Herald* had never supported the Rhodesian Front; 'We were always very unpopular with the white Government.' As for the election, 'We took an independent line, we never said don't vote for Mugabe, we tried to play it straight down the middle.' The enemy without was now the Government within; it was Argus policy always to support the Government of the day.

The editor of the *Umtali Post*, Alistair Syme, had resigned as soon as the election result came through. The *Post* hastily published a letter under the heading 'Mugabe has shown tragic war was futile'. The people of Rhodesia, wrote Mr Arthur Kavanagh, had for eighteen years been 'subjected to the most gigantic confidence trick in modern history . . .'. The *Post*'s prospects looked bleak; only five out of twenty-eight editorial staff were black and circulation was down to 3,744. Mrs J. Maitland-Stewart, abruptly promoted from the news-room to fill in for the vanishing editor, explained gloomily that any 'sudden influx' of black children into the Boys' and Girls' High Schools would drive all the whites out of the country. 'And if the few remaining white doctors leave . . .' The atmosphere was funereal.

Hullo, what's this? Evidently a photograph of a young Zanla guerrilla warmly greeting his parents at an assembly point. Never before had the *Sunday Mail* admitted that guerrillas had families. Only people have families. And why all this praise for the detested Samora Machel? Declared the *Herald* on 30 April: 'Since Zimbabwe is a socialist-oriented state it is only natural that the Government should want to celebrate May Day.' Gosh. But the ultimately doomed attempts of the Argus newspapers in Zimbabwe to stave off nationalization during the remainder of 1980 are another story. . . .

28. Zimbabwe

Prince Charles arrived in an RAF VC10 wearing white naval officer's uniform – a man of many parts – and the blue sash of the Order of the Garter. Greeted at the airport by Soames, Banana and Mugabe, the Prince inspected a guard of honour, received a twenty-one gun salute and asked Enos Nkala, Minister of Finance and the man Soames had banned from campaigning, 'Is there any money in the bank?' Meanwhile 234 remand prisoners broke out of Salisbury gaol and began marching towards the city centre in an orderly fashion.

The Independence ceremony took place on the evening of 17 April in Rufaro Stadium, Harare. It was marred by the police's resort to tear gas because a crowd was getting out of hand outside the stadium. Many people wept. The Prince arrived in a 1953 Rolls-Royce escorted by mounted BSAP whose white solar topees were perhaps meant to remind spectators of Rhodes's Pioneers. Zapu complained they were given only 125 VIP seats. Muzorewa was there. So was Walls. But Smith gave it a miss – a smooth-tongued TV commentator explained that there was no significance in this, he merely had a long-standing speaking engagement in South Africa.

On the dais sat not only the Prince, Carrington, Soames, Banana and Mugabe but also the spectre at the feast, Chief Justice Macdonald. Hector the Hanging Judge (who had announced in November that neither he nor the two other Appellate judges, Lewis and Davies, would stay in office if the PF came to power) now insisted on administering the oath to small, slight, gentle Canaan Banana who, of course, had been detained without trial. The Prince brought a message from the Queen, Carrington brought one from Mrs Thatcher, Soames was beaming. Mugabe stepped austerely out into the arena, accompanied by a smart white officer, to light the eternal flame.

Zanla and Zipra occupied the centre of the stadium flanked by units of the RAR. The cultural mix was interesting: ragged but athletic Shangaan dancers shared the limelight with carefully groomed white teenagers, the boys in dark suits, the girls in white dresses, singing under the urgent coaxing of their choirmistress. White Zimbabweans, all.

A Regimental Sergeant Major of the British Military Police hauled down the Union Jack. The crowd cheered.

Lord Soames flew home in triumph and was greeted at the airport by his boss, the Prime Minister: it had been a jolly good show. Eighteen months later she sacked him.

On 19 April President Banana swore in twenty-one Ministers and thirteen Deputy Ministers. To celebrate Independence, 9,000 prisoners were released from the gaols, including all those who had been convicted of the black man's crime, stock theft. Alas, alas, by mid-May almost 2,000 of them were back behind bars.

The opening of Parliament on 14 May provided a spectacle even more bizarre than the inaugural session of the Zimbabwe Rhodesia Parliament a year before. President Banana arrived in an open Rolls-Royce accompanied by a mounted BSAP escort and a fly-past. On entering the Chamber, the President was preceded by the notorious 'terrorist bandit' Rex Nhongo, wearing open-neck battle fatigues, and by his Zipra counterpart, Lookout Masuku, wearing a general's uniform from somewhere in Eastern Europe. Behind them came the élite of the Rhodesian military establishment, Walls, Mussell, McLean and Police Commissioner Allum. But wait! Next the politicians enter the Chamber, two by two, a Noah's-ark coupling of Mugabe and Smith; of van der Byl and Muzenda; of Irvine and Nkomo. Irvine had been Co-Minister of Transport when Nkomo's Zipra men shot down the two Viscounts; he had referred to Nkomo in the House as 'that vile murderer'. And now...?

29. Moscow gold

Eddison Zvobgo announces that all sporting ties with South Africa will cease. Des van Jaarsveldt, President of the Rugby Union, begs the Government to think again: a whole way of life is at stake. Exactly, that's the point. 'Cricket has not been popular with the Africans here,' comments Mugabe, 'and we'll have to consider whether the game should die.'

And who does he appoint as his first Minister of Sport? A 25-year-old black woman 'terrorist' married to the arch-terrorist, Rex Nhongo. Proudly adhering to her chimurenga name, Teurai Ropa (Spill Blood) Nhongo is herself a veteran guerrilla fighter, political commissar and member of Zanu-PF's Central Committee. She has been in Peking, Albania, Romania and Yugoslavia and she commanded a camp at Chimoio during a devastating air raid, a massacre conducted by the same white sportsmen whose conduct she will now call to order. To the pleas of Mr van Jaarsveldt and of Alwyn Pichanick, President of the Cricket Union, the Cabinet to which she belongs will turn a deaf ear.

The Salisbury Sports Club stretches lavishly along North Avenue, a spreading elysium of pitches, tennis courts, a golf-course, a clubhouse with a famous bar. It is 12.10 p.m., 15 March 1980, and the end of an era: Rhodesia 'B' is playing Eastern Province 'B' in the last Castle Bowl match while the senior Rhodesian side struggles against the South Africans in Bulawayo. Can this really be the death of a tradition stretching back to 1904–5? A group of middle-aged Indians standing inside the gate insist they want Currie and Castle Cup cricket to continue – there is an Asian in the current Rhodesian team. 'After all, apartheid is changing down there,' one says. I raise my eyebrows. 'Slowly, perhaps,' he adds. Young whites drift away from the ground, some still wearing camouflage fatigues.

The Cricket Union saw the light and severed all ties with South Africa on 23 May. As Alwyn Pichanick pointed out, there would be compensations in the form of matches against teams from England, India, Pakistan, Sri Lanka and East Africa.

But for rugby players the loss was irreparable: a vital artery had been severed and morale collapsed. Even though one last season of Currie Cup matches was permitted, playing for 'Zimbabwe' wasn't the same. On 2 August the National side suffered its heaviest-ever defeat, a 60–16 whacking by Northern Transvaal, the 'Blue Bulls', at Lotus Versfeld.

The last game against a South African team – the return match against the Blue Bulls – took place in Salisbury on 13 September. Only 6,000 came to the Police Ground, most of whom defiantly shouted 'Rhodesia!' every time the home side launched an attack. At one point two young men ran on to the field carrying the old green-and-white Rhodesian flag, the flag of UDI. To no avail: 'Zimbabwe' went down by 38–22 and thus suffered their tenth defeat in ten matches.

Curtain.

For the hockey girls it had all looked a bit grim in 1979: the war continued and the South African Women's Hockey Association, in a desperate but unavailing bid to gain admission to the Moscow Olympics – irony! – severed its ties with Rhodesia. One Rhodesian player commented despairingly, 'We are really out in the cold now.' Yet 1980 turned into a fairy story. While the Springboks stayed at home, the white hockey players of Robert Mugabe's Zimbabwe were invited to play in Moscow! Anthea Stewart was the coach, Ann Grant of Old Hararians the Captain and Audrey Palmer would travel as 'chaperone' to a squad whose typically Zimbabwean names deserve a mention: Sarah English, Brenda Phillips, Pat McKillop, Sonia Robertson, Trish Davies, Maureen George, Linda Watson, Sue Huggett, Gill Cowley, Liz Chase, Sandy Chick, Helen Volk, Chrissie Prinsloo, Arlene Boxhall.

On 7 July the girls set off in track suits from New Sarum air base, strapped into Dakotas normally occupied by paratroopers. At Lusaka they transferred for a flight to the black Marxist-terrorist capital, Luanda, whence they flew to Moscow by the Soviet terrorist airline, Aeroflot. Mind-boggling. Would the mums, dads, husbands and children who had waved goodbye at New Sarum ever see them again? In Moscow, the 'Zimbabweans' practised like mad on the artificial astro turf, a contrast to the coarse sharp grass of southern Africa, and began to win their matches.

In this they enjoyed one considerable advantage: because of the American, British and general West European boycott of the Moscow Games, virtually all the major nations originally selected for inclusion by the International Hockey Federation had stayed away. And so it came about that on 1 August the *Herald* was able to announce: 'Pure Gold. Hockey Girls Triumphant in Olympics.' After a final 4–1 win over Austria in the Dynamo Stadium, the team captain, Ann Grant, received the coveted gold medal.

Afterwards the gels swigged champagne and chanted 'Pamberi ne Jongwe!' As they stepped off the plane at Salisbury airport the band of Churchill School struck up while the drum majorettes of Roosevelt marched in their honour, and 500 cheered from the terminal balcony.

It was an odd interlude: Zimbabwe had sent thirty competitors to the Olympics of whom only six were black. It would never happen again.

Postscript

By March 1982 the white population of Zimbabwe was reckoned to have fallen below 170,000. Between Independence and October 1981, 32,000 had departed. The exodus continued at the rate of 1,500 per month. Why? Clearly, material factors played a part: the rapid integration of the schools and health services; a harsh budget; higher minimum wages for all categories of worker, including domestic servants; a freeze on salaries over $(Z)20,000; tighter Exchange Control regulations; long queues outside petrol stations, particularly in Salisbury; a shortage of butter and cheese.

Yet the material standard of living of the whites remained exceptionally high; nor was their style of life substantially threatened. The crucial factors were cultural and psychological. White artisans and engineers departed because they could not stomach a black Government led by 'terrorists' against whom they had fought a bitter, and ultimately humiliating, war. The rapid Africanization of the army, the police and the civil service symbolized the substantive shift in racial power and status which the internal settlement had been designed to stall. A white housewife who arbitrarily dismissed a domestic servant would soon receive a visit, polite but firm, from a Zanu-PF activist. A white farmer who had intercourse with the wife of one of his employees found himself hauled before a jeering village court. Young men with skills soon recognized that they held their jobs on sufferance; scanning an uncertain future, they took the gap.

Whites now suffered a profound sense of alienation. They were constantly accused by the Government and the media of failing to cleanse their minds of colonial attitudes, of clinging to their privileges, of rejecting the great national enterprise of 'reconciliation'. Having been spoon-fed RF propaganda for years, whites now underwent acute traumas every time they opened a newspaper or turned on their television set: as Eddison Zvobgo put it, 'If we watch films of Green Leader over Lusaka we must also be prepared to see freedom fighters in Chimoio.' A world had been overturned; the 'comrades' had come to power; slogans like 'forward with the revolution' penetrated the living rooms of the suburbs. 'Racist South Africa', the dependable White Uncle to whom most Rhodesians had looked for support, was ceaselessly denigrated. Statues of Cecil Rhodes were pulled down and the main avenues of Salisbury renamed in honour of Presidents Machel and Nyerere. 'Salisbury salutes a statesman,' declared the *Herald* in honour of Samora Machel's state visit – whites drove to work trembling with rage.

Early in 1981 the press was nationalized; more precisely, it was put under the control of a new Mass Media Trust whose conscience resided not far from the Ministry of Information. Despite occasional displays of independence, the editors of the *Herald*, the *Chronicle* and the *Sunday Mail* made it plain that their job was to harness the press to the 'aspirations of the masses'; but when striking bus drivers were gaoled and deprived of their jobs, these editors were in no doubt that it was the Government, rather than the strikers, who reflected those aspirations most faithfully.

Early in 1982 the whites suffered new traumas. The majority of gun licences were withdrawn. Every case of armed or violent robbery intensified the mounting sense of insecurity. And then, to mark the second anniversary of Independence, a further cultural revolution was decreed, a wiping of the map: Salisbury became Harare, Umtali was called Mutari, Gwelo re-emerged as Gweru, Shabani as Zvishane, Hartley as Chegutu and Selukwe as Shurugwi. Fort Victoria and Victoria Falls were no more – the cord of history was snapped.

'Reconciliation' was hardly the motto of the twenty Rhodesian Front MPs who gathered in the House of Assembly, determined not only to protect the material interests of their privileged white constituents but also to keep the wounds of the past open and bleeding. Exchanges with the Government benches were abrasive, even vitriolic. Wing Commander Rob Gaunt, a former Rhodesian Air Force pilot, took pleasure in reminding the blacks that the security forces had 'never lost a battle, or even a skirmish'. Donald Goddard, MP for Lundi and formerly a captain in the Selous Scouts, urged Mugabe's Ministers to go back to the bush 'where they belong'. There was uproar when Ian Smith, his reluctant farmer's hands stubbornly gripping the helm of white politics, suggested that the new Government should display proper gratitude and humility towards the fruits of ninety years of white rule.

Yet the politics of parliamentary opposition carried little conviction for white Rhodesians. White or black, this was Africa: the Government rules, suppresses dissent, and punishes tribes of suspect loyalty. Better, surely, to display good will, to recognize Mugabe's victory as irreversible, and to lobby behind the scenes on behalf of white sectional interests. In April 1981 a single RF MP, André Holland, broke ranks, formed the Democratic Party with overt Government encouragement, stood for re-election in his old seat – and was duly thrashed by the RF candidate. A bitter internal debate within the ranks of the RF itself yielded only a cosmetic change of name from Rhodesian Front to Republican Front. The Government responded with a radical budget which accelerated the pace of white emigration.

The tensions within the RF's parliamentary caucus could not be papered over indefinitely, despite the strong tradition of personal loyalty to Ian Smith. In March 1982, nine white MPs broke away, declaring themselves Independents, leaving Smith with an effective rump of nine (one MP was in gaol and another had fled the country).

By far the most capable of the dissidents were Chris Andersen, a former leader of the Rhodesian Bar and Minister of Justice, and John Landau, a successful businessman (and arms manufacturer) who had been the RF's Chief Whip at the time of his defection. White liberals regarded both men as opportunists motivated by ambition; yet both hotly denied to me that they had in any way been motivated by Mugabe's broad hint that he would like to see more whites, untainted by the RF stigma, in his Cabinet.

The knives were out. Bill Irvine, a dire and diehard Rhodesian Fronter since 1965, who had held important portfolios under Smith, dripped malice through cold eyes and a mouth joined to his jaw by lines so bleakly Presbyterian that one would not have been surprised to find a tawse in his Scottish-born hand. 'It's all very well for P.K. van der Byl to abuse the blacks, he's got money down in the Cape. I want to stay in this country.' A prosperous farmer and industrial consultant, Irvine accused the former Rhodesian military leaders of having betrayed the cause by whoring and drinking in Salisbury instead of getting out into the bush. Irvine showed me a carbon copy of a letter he had sent to Smith shortly before his defection; it read less like the message of an old colleague than an invoice from an undertaker to a dead man. 'We never saw our future', Irvine told me, 'in white domination. Not in the long term, anyway.'

The reception room in RF headquarters was still lined with Cabinet photographs from the halcyon days of UDI. While waiting for my appointment with the Chief, a fat, jolly woman who was holding the fort commented that it was 'high time Jesus came down from Heaven and sorted out this mess'.

'What mess?'

'Well, take my cookboy. He's completely fed up with paying a dollar a month to the ruling party. And did you read about that poor Afrikaner foreman at Karoi who got the sack just for doing what he'd always done – calling an idle kaffir an idle kaffir?'

The Old Man drives around alone, now, in a Peugeot estate car, stripped of his official bodyguards, a tall, stooped, hollowed-out figure. Smith had a bad cold. Had his lifelong forebodings about black rule been justified in Zimbabwe? *'It's beginning to go that way,'* he said, citing the exodus of whites *'who make a country run'* and the stuffing of semi-literate black youngsters into white schools. *'You can only teach a class at the pace of the lowest common denominator.'*

What about the nine defectors from the RF? *'I'm disappointed. They're solving a problem by running away from it.'* Did he feel personal resentment towards them? *'Yees. Without me they would never have been elected.'* Should they resign their seats and stand again? *'Yees. They should.'* Would the RF win all nine seats? *'Yees. My party has won every seat in every election since . . . was it 1965? I'm told that's a unique record in the history of the democratic system of government.'*

Had he attempted to collaborate with Mugabe's Government? *'Yees. I always predicted a Patriotic Front victory. They called me an alarmist.'*

Did he support the South African Government's attempts to destabilize Zimbabwe? *'I have no personal contacts, now, with the South African Government. South Africa is behaving in an exemplary manner. But they're concerned, naturally, with the antics of our Government here. It may yet accommodate terrorists here.'* Adroitly agnostic, Smith declined to be drawn by my question about the South African-backed RMA's insurrection in Mozambique or its campaign of sabotage against Zimbabwe's communications with Maputo. *'I don't know about that.'*

Had Vorster let Smith down in 1976, before the meeting with Kissinger? *'Wait for my memoirs.'* Was he working on a book? *'Perhaps that would be exaggerating. I'm short of time . . . I've never had time to read books about myself, or any books for that matter . . . since I became Prime Minister.'*

Did he worry about his own physical safety?

'They say I should be detained, or locked up, or not allowed back into the country. I don't let such things cross my mind.' He wandered out into the fierce heat, coughing and dabbing at his long nose, regretting the passing of the Currie Cup rugby and cricket matches against South African teams – a man bent on defying the known laws of political gravity.

Between Smith and the rebels it was not easy to discern fundamental disagreements about policy; the argument seemed to be about the tone and tactics of white politics. The Western constituency by-election in Matabeleland, which took place one month after the schism, reflected the white electorate's disenchantment; a mere 30 per cent turned out to vote. Of these, almost 70 per cent supported the RF's candidate. André Holland promptly disbanded his Democratic Party. Despite Denis Norman's successful, two-year tenure as Minister of Agriculture, the whites possibly divined that the so-called Independents would dress Mugabe's front window rather than influence events. Although Andersen and Landau had been no less adamant than Smith in condemning the Government's use of Emergency Powers (inherited from the RF) and the continuing detention without trial of an elderly RF MP called Wally Stuttaford, nevertheless, three months after Landau and Andersen accepted Mugabe's invitation to join the Government, Stuttaford remained in prison.

In June Ian Smith collapsed in the House of Assembly. A mild heart attack was reported.

Rhodesia's racially elitist system of education has succumbed to the reforming zeal of the dynamic Minister of Education, Dzingai Mutumbuka. The internal settlement engineered the substitution of class barriers for strictly racial ones; the Group A schools, primary and secondary, were to be restricted to children resident in middle-class suburbs but excluding the offspring of domestic servants. Now these same schools have been invaded by children from the African townships, although the Government offers them no help with their appalling transport problems – one might call it 'bussing-without-buses'.

Mutumbuka has also nipped in the bud the nasty little manoeuvre by which white parents were encouraged to preserve the 'cultural' integrity of their local state schools by 'buying' them from the Government for derisory sums ($(R)40,000 was typical) payable over a hundred years. Despite much wailing, these so-called Community Schools have been deprived of their autonomy and forced to accept genuine racial integration. Mutumbuka's Deputy Minister, Senator Joe Culverwell, the only Coloured member of the Government and something of a firebrand, went down to Umtali and threatened two such schools with instant closure if they didn't stop stalling. They stopped stalling.

Today the Elysian games fields of Mount Pleasant, Oriel, Churchill, Girls' High and Queen Elizabeth are worn by the feet of boys and girls from Highfield, Harare and the other townships which encircle white Salisbury (Harare). White head teachers are powerless to resist what the Head of Oriel Boys', Mr Erasmus, calls 'the floodgates'. By March 1982 240 out of Oriel's 620 boys were black; in Form One only 36 out of 106 pupils were white, a traumatic shock for the white-dominated PTA and a source of acute concern for white boys relegated to the B stream. Such has been the exodus of young white males from Zimbabwe that Oriel's teaching complement of twenty-three included only nine men. In the common-rooms teachers complain incessantly that the majority of new black pupils don't understand a thing.

443

'They'd be better off in the township schools with Shona-speaking teachers,' says Mr Erasmus.

The new black Regional Director for schools, Salisbury, Mr Gapara, sits under a large map of the city dotted with coloured markers. Genial, inclined to laughter, and with a voice as deep as Paul Robeson's, Mr Gapara laments the racism of many white head teachers while freely conceding that a chaotic situation is indeed developing in Forms One and Two. But Senator Culverwell is unrepentant. He showed me a list of complaints brought by parents of black children recently integrated into the Group A schools;

– a teacher had placed seventeen white girls on one side of the classroom and the same number of blacks on the other; both her gaze and her remarks remained consistently directed towards the white girls;

– white girls from Forms Five and Six had been promoted prefect over the heads of nearly a dozen black Sixth Form girls. The Headmistress frequently remarked: 'I've never had to say this before in all my years at the school.'

At Churchill a white boy stood up in class and asked to read a poem. It said, in essence, 'I wish Mugabe were a tree and I were a dog.' When a fight broke out and the white teacher intervened, the white boys accused him of bias: 'If only you knew', they protested, 'what we have to put up with!'

A silent and spontaneous revolution has been taking place in the Zimbabwean countryside: thousands of landless peasants have invaded commercial farms owned by white landlords. The movement is part of the 'crisis of expectations'; it derived its original impetus not only from the dislocation and uprooting of whole populations during the war, but also from Zanu's quasi-revolutionary rhetoric conveyed to the peasantry by Zanla guerrillas and party officials during 'pungwes' and local election rallies. Many white farms stood deserted but absentee landlords were not the only targets; a wave of 'squatting' started in Manicaland soon after Independence and spread to the Headlands area. In Matabeleland fences were cut and the tribesmen drove their emaciated 'mombres' on to the lusher pastures of the great white ranches.

The whites could no longer respond in the traditional manner, by sending armed posses on punitive raids into the tribal trust lands. Although the Lancaster House Agreement protected property rights, the crucial factor in a local equation is not so much the law as the forces of law and order – but the police now served a black Government highly sensitive to the peasants' crisis of expectations. Reluctantly and sullenly, landlords were compelled to bargain, petition and warn of national ruin, while holding their fire. But the squatters kept coming in, emboldened by local headmen, by local party officials, and, not least, by the spirits and graves of their dispossessed ancestors.

In Headlands police station the walls of the Member-in-Charge (a black officer, at last) are covered by large-scale maps depicting squatter concentrations and invasions. The police themselves won't make a move without clear authorization from Salisbury; the landlords may have the law on their side but the squatters enjoy the support of the party's district chairman, Comrade Mauiye. The confrontation is a tense one: nobody involved, be he landlord or peasant, wishes to be publicly identified.

Take the case of 'Mishek Katiwa', who had occupied some seven hectares of 'Folkstone Farm' which is owned, or perhaps leased – Mishek is not sure – by Mr 'Leonard Lyle'. In the company of ten other black families, Mishek's had evacuated the parched, overcrowded Chiduku reserve, hacked down the tall elephant grass in a remote corner of Lyle's estate, and ploughed a plot in which to plant maize. Soon afterwards Mishek found himself imprisoned for three months on a charge of trespass. Lyle and his hired hands took advantage of this interlude to pull down all the squatters' huts, but when Mishek and his comrades were released from gaol their commitment was as strong as ever and they promptly rebuilt their huts. As Lyle came bumping across the dirt tracks, negotiating the anthills in his Peugeot, Mishek stood his ground; he had paid the price exacted by colonial law; now the land was his.

Lyle's logic was of a different order: an eviction notice. '*Munoziiswa kuti murikugara zvisi pamurau mundau inozwi* Folkestone Farm, you are hereby advised that you are trespassing . . . *Ngokudaro munokombirwa*, you are now required, *kurekera kurima pamwe nokuvaka*, to cease cultivation and building immediately.' And Mishek was warned: 'Get off the property by 31 May or face renewed prosecution.'

Now the Government intervened in the energetic personage of Comrade Makoni, a leading trouble-shooter for the Ministry of Lands. Makoni descended on Lyle, castigated him for having pulled down the huts, and warned him that the Minister regarded him as a 'sell-out colonialist and not the kind of farmer we need in Zimbabwe'. Makoni charged Lyle with having brutally ejected the squatter women and children before pulling down the huts; Lyle pleaded that he had done no such thing and that he was confused by the squatters' cunning habit of transferring 'ownership' of their plots from one to another.

'I have my information,' Makoni said. It was a chilling encounter. Lyle hurried to Salisbury to put his case to Makoni's superior. Despite the appointment his secretary had made over the telephone, the official was too busy to see him. Lyle says he banged the desk in sheer frustration: 'I've driven

150 kilometres, you'll see me.' The African shrugged: 'I'll give you five minutes but you're wasting your time. You have the law on your side but this is a political matter.' Lyle now argued that he would indeed come to a *modus vivendi* with the squatters if only they would either dip their cows or sell them to him: but no, these ignorant, stubborn tribesmen insisted on letting their undipped 'mombes' roam at will, thus bringing the danger of anthrax and other tick-borne diseases to Lyle's own herd of 500 beasts – and just at the moment when he hoped to capitalize on the terrible drought in Matabeleland by buying a further 500 head evacuated from the south-west at a bargain price of $(Z)100 each.

The haggling continued. The squatters were persuaded to sign a document, pressing their thumbs in purple dye, promising to vacate Lyle's land by 30 June, after their maize was harvested, and pledging themselves to remove their cattle back to the Chiduku reserve without delay. But they didn't. Lyle prevailed on the police to prosecute. The Member-in-Charge warned him that permission had to be obtained not only from the Ministry of Lands but also from the office of the Prime Minister – Mugabe wants to know every time an eviction order is moved against a squatter. Permission was finally forthcoming. On the appointed day Lyle turned up at Rusape court promptly at 9 a.m. No one was there. Presently the magistrate drifted in; then the prosecutor. Mishek and his comrades had been advised by the local party committee to boycott the proceedings. At 11.30 Lyle was casually informed by the police that the summonses had been withdrawn.

'On whose authority?' he demanded.

He never found out. When I accompanied him on one of his despairing visits to the squatters' lair, Mishek wasn't at home, only a wrinkled old woman surrounded by hens who continued to wipe her plates slowly, calmly, as Lyle displayed his own brand of patience with her. Where was Mishek, eh? She pointed vaguely towards the horizon. And where were the offending cattle? This time her wandering gesture embraced virtually the whole compass of Africa south of the Sahara.

During the war of liberation many whites predicted – and took some pleasure in predicting – that a victory for the combined forces of the Patriotic Front would merely serve as a prelude to factional fighting and tribally based civil war. The whites liked to believe that they alone could reconcile Shonas and Ndebeles within a single nation.

No sooner had the Lancaster House Agreement been signed than Mugabe's Zanu and Nkomo's Zapu fell apart. They contested the election as rival parties. The result demonstrated, as subsequent local elections have done, that Nkomo's hold on Matabeleland remains impregnable but stops there.

Faced with the re-emergence of tribal antipathy, the leaders of Zimbabwe have on the whole displayed a high level of restraint and responsibility, although Mugabe's example has not been imitated by all his Ministers. Despite outbreaks of violence in the guerrilla assembly points; despite a wave of murderous attacks on whites in the Goromonzi area and near anarchy round Mtoko during the first months after Independence; despite serious clashes between Zanla and Zipra in Chitungwiza; despite two appalling outbreaks of armed violence in the Bulawayo township of Entumbane which left many dead; despite localized mutinies within the National Army itself early in 1981; despite these setbacks the gigantic task of integrating some 50,000 Zanla and Zipra guerrillas in 'mixed' battalions has been accomplished with wisdom and energy. Mashonaland, urban and rural, is no longer a dangerous place in which to live or travel.

But the problem of Matabeleland has not yet been solved. In the mind of Zanu-PF, from Mugabe down, this problem is encapsulated in one word: Nkomo. Mugabe wants a one-party state. Joshua Nkomo, with his long and honourable history as a nationalist leader, his international prestige, and his undisguised resentment that the leadership of the nation is not his, remains the thorn, a very broad thorn, in the flesh.

In February 1982 Mugabe, angered by the discovery of vast arms caches on properties associated with Nkomo, fired him from the Government and threatened him with prosecution. Today, five months later, Nkomo remains at liberty. Nevertheless his dismissal so enraged former Zipra combatants that a reported 2,000 decamped from the Army with their weapons. Since that time parts of Matabeleland have suffered acute lawlessness and units of the Army have been called in to suppress the dissidents. Nkomo has condemned the insurgents just as he condemned the attack, late in June, on Mugabe's official residence by soldiers reportedly linked to Zipra.

But Nkomo's future remains uncertain and with it the stability of a united Zimbabwe.

13 July 1982